POPULATION MATTERS

POPULATION MATTERS

People, Resources, Environment, and Immigration

Julian L. Simon

Transaction Publishers
New Brunswick (U.S.A.) and London (U.K.)

Library of Congress Catalog Number: 89-20240
ISBN: 0-88738-300-9
Printed in the United States of America

Library of Congress Cataloging-in-Publication Data

Simon, Julian Lincoln, 1932–
    Population matters : people, resources, environment, and
immigration / Julian L. Simon.
        p.   cm.
    ISBN 0-88738-300-9
    1. United States—Population. 2. Population forecasting—
United States. 3. Natural resources—United States. 4. Natural
resources. 5. United   States—Emigration   and   immigration. 6. Emigration and immigration. 7. Population forecasting. 8. Population. I. Title.
HB3505.S52   1989
304.6'0973—dc20   89-20240
                                                            CIP

To Harold Barnett (he is missed)
Peter T. Bauer
Colin Clark
Alfred Sauvy
Theodore W. Schultz

For their imagination, judgment, and courage.

Contents

Preface

When people hear or read the central message contained in this book and in my other books on the subject, they say that I am an optimist. Though I am indeed optimistic about the long-run future of humanity, I reply with a line swiped from Herman Kahn: I'm not an optimist, I'm a realist.

I am extremely pessimistic, however, about the likelihood that in the shorter run most people in the Western countries will come to have an accurate assessment of the issues discussed in this book and the others. And I foresee great losses of life and wealth as a result of faulty assessments. Twenty years after the first great spasm of environmental concern, the arena is again in the hands of the yahoos, the same people with the same ideas that have been discredited by events and by scientific research since then. The educated public and the journalists seem even more credulous than ever, and there are large numbers of professors on campuses who have been raised in this movement and now teach it as professionals, in comparison to the amateur zealots two decades ago who powered the movement but had no professional stake in carrying on.

It isn't much fun to survey the present scene and to mull on what has been accomplished, by others or by me. Yes, scientific viewpoints on the subject have changed considerably. But there is no more support for "our" views than there was then, in the learned professions and their sources of institutional support. And there is not a single pro-people organizational address in journalists' rolodexes for them to turn to, in contrast to the enormous roster of anti-people organizations described in Selection 51. For this reason among others, in May 1989 as I write, the anti-population-growth message completely dominates the several television network news programs that have been aired on the subject of population growth in the past month, with the interviewees and the words just about identical to those twenty years ago.

In the long run, the inevitable force of progress will roll over these intellectual obstacles. Population will grow, knowledge will increase, economies will develop, liberty will flourish. But in the meantime there will be innumerable avoidable tragedies because the good news goes unreported. How sad that is.

Julian L. Simon

Acknowledgments

The Olin Foundation provided funds that covered many of the expenses of this work, and the Sloan Foundation supported work on my technical study of the economics of immigration. I am grateful for their support. The College of Business and Management of the University of Maryland at College Park, through the good offices of Dean Rudy Lamone, provided an atmosphere of moral support that helped make the work satisfying as well as possible.

Over the years of writing these essays, many many people have made helpful suggestions. The list includes my wife Rita; my children, David, Judith, and Daniel; friends too many to remember all and therefore I shall name none lest I hurt the feelings of those I forget; and editors of magazines and newspapers where these pieces originally appeared, though it is difficult for any writer to accept that there may be merit to an editor's suggestion about how to organize a piece or how to phrase it or (stickiest of all) what to leave out.

Irving Louis Horowitz did what publishers ought to do, but too-seldom actually do: overcome obstacles and get into print ideas that are unconventional and unpopular but which he believes are sound and important.

Same old words again about Helen Demarest: She is the best secretary there is—mind, fingers, nerves, and heart.

Early on as a research assistant, and later as a colleague, Stephen Moore dug up data, struggled with recalcitrant computers, and patched holes in the ideas and the supporting material. He and I have matured together over the course of seven years, a lovely process to experience.

Nancy Young whipped the manuscript (but only prodded the author) into shape for publication, providing both the editorial and the managerial skills that make the difference between a hundred small agonies and an easy passage. It is a pleasure to deal with a skilled professional like her.

I am also grateful to the bottom of my soul to those people who have reached out to me during these decades and said that they agree with and appreciate my efforts, or that they appreciate my efforts even though they do not agree with me. Thank you, and may others be as generous to you when you need help. Thank you, one and all.

Introduction

Raw materials and energy are getting less scarce. The world's food supply is improving. Pollution in the United States has been decreasing. Population growth has long-term benefits, though added people are a burden in the short run. The United States needs more immigrants. . . . These are the messages repeated again and again in this book.

Why not simply laugh off these assertions that run so counter to conventional belief? I hope that the logic of the upcoming arguments eventually persuades you that these assertions are sound. But in the meantime, here is a reason for at least taking them seriously: These messages that "our side" has been struggling since 1970 to have the public hear have stood the test of time. Our predictions have proven sound. None of the well-known doomsayers who espouse the conventional viewpoint can make that statement. (The conventional beliefs have been falsified across the board by events during the last two decades.)

The central theoretical issue addressed by the essays collected here is the effects of the number of people upon the standard of living, with special attention to raw materials (such as metals and grains) and the environment. The most important effects are those that occur in the intermediate and long run, rather than in the very short run before there is an opportunity for society to adjust to the additional people. And on balance the long-run effects are positive, quite in contradiction to the conventional wisdom.

The available data usually refer to countries, and especially the United States. But the relevant intellectual context usually is either the entire more-developed part of the world, or humanity altogether.

Though a particular essay usually discusses either immigration or additional persons being born, the main arguments apply equally well to both these sources of population increase.

1

The main economic mechanism works as follows: Population growth and increase of income expand the demand for raw materials as well as finished products. The resulting actual and expected shortages force up prices of the natural resources. The increased prices trigger the search for new ways to satisfy the demand, and sooner or later new sources and innovative substitutes are found. Eventually these new discoveries lead to natural resources that are cheaper than before this process begins, leaving humanity better off than if the shortages had not appeared. The development of new sources of energy, shifting from wood to coal to oil to nuclear power, exemplifies this process. This is discussed in Selection 5.

The vision that unifies the various selections is that of human beings who create more than they destroy. This vision is set forth in Selection 47.

Readers who have read some of my previous work may wonder how this volume relates to my earlier books on the subject of population. *The Economics of Population Growth* (1977), *The Theory of Population and Economic Growth* (1986), and *The Economic Consequences of Immigration into the U.S.* (1989) are technical analyses intended for scholars. The *Ultimate Resource* (1981) reaches out to a wider audience, but it nevertheless contains a sustained argument that runs through the book in connected fashion, combining both theoretical discussion and empirical data. The *Resourceful Earth* (1983), which Herman Kahn and I edited together, contains detailed studies by leading scholars of various aspects of natural resources and the environment.

In contrast to these earlier books whose sustained arguments can be rather heavy fare, this is a volume of self-contained bite-sized treatments intended for separate consumption. Some of the topics have been covered in the previous volumes; others are discussed for the first time here. The articles, almost all of which have been written since 1981, have two aims: to disseminate to the widest possible audience the broad fundamental ideas developed earlier, by writing in as lively a style as possible and using vivid illustrations, and to introduce some new ideas.

Two themes that were only in the wings in the previous books move onto center stage here:

1. *The social and economic structure of a country* is the central factor in economic development. After this factor is recognized, we are better able to understand the unimportance of population growth and density in the short run, though in the long run the effect of more people is *positive rather than negative*. And in turn, personal freedom—of which economic freedom is an inextricable part—together with the institution of private property, is at the core of social structures which promote economic growth.

By 1989, the relationship of a decentralized market-directed social and political environment to faster economic growth is no longer just a theoretical deduction or an article of faith; it is a statistically demonstrable causal link (this is discussed in Selection 15). When research allows for this factor, there remains much less variation among countries for other influences such as population growth to explain. Hence, recognition of this structural element undercuts the conventional belief that population growth has a negative effect upon economic development.

2. *The relationship of population growth to the overall development of civilization in the very long run,* a matter which was touched on only in passing in my previous works, is explored in these new essays. The growth of population size and density is woven into the warp and woof of institutions, social practices, value systems, and the rise of the market. Our contemporary societies and economies would not be nearly the same as they are today if there had been many fewer people on earth in past centuries, and if there were many fewer of us now. These essays analyze the relationship of civilization to population and argue the importance of the relationship.

Why Is the Popular View So Different?

One inevitably wonders: How is it that, if the views advanced here are scientifically sound, belief in the opposite set of views is so widespread? There are at least five connected elements in the explanation.

A first partial explanation is that there is in all of us a built-in intellectual weakness—understandable, but lamentable—that predisposes us to believe in Malthus-like ideas about population-induced scarcity. We are predisposed in this manner because the negative economic effects of additional people are direct and immediate and local, and therefore obvious. In contrast, the beneficial effects are indirect and global and occur only after the passage of some time; therefore, they are not at all obvious. It is the special genius of economics to discern the indirect and diffuse and delayed effects of social changes, and to enable us to weigh these hard-to-perceive effects together with the obvious ones. Lacking the economic habit of thought, laypeople tend to be susceptible to Malthusian thinking that takes into account only the obvious negative effects of additional persons, and that presents these ideas in the seductively fascinating context of exponential growth and "the law of diminishing returns."

A second cause of continued popular belief in Malthusian views is that several groups have had a parochial self-interest in promoting these doom-saying ideas. This matter is discussed in more detail in Selections 55 and 57 and at length in *The Ultimate Resource.* Suffice it here to say that theses groups include (*a*) the media, for whom impending scarcities make dramatic news; (b) the scientific community, for whom fears about impending scarcities lead to support for research that ostensibly will ease such scarcities; and (c) those political groups that work toward more government intervention in the economy; supposedly worsening scarcities provide an argument in favor of such intervention.

In the face of the irrefutable happy facts about the trends in resource availability and life expectancy, much of the environmentalist and population-control movement tries to convince the public that we face worsening problems, and that the only feasible solution is for the government to "do something" about it. (This is a false conclusion from a demonstrably false premise.) One of their desires is that governments should reduce the number of people so that (they believe) the supply of resources per person would be greater. And they ask for "more equitable distribution" of resources among countries, in the face of the fact that those countries that use a lot of resources are also the countries that create new resources and reduce the costs of resources for all.

A third cause of Malthusian thinking is the propensity of many to view any kind of change as unwelcome. This can be seen in the negative interpretations of changes in the same factor in *both directions*. A few illustrations: (1) Potential warming and potential cooling of the environment have both been billed as disastrous. (2) A stationary population is a common ideal, with both gain and loss in population seen as threats. (3) Not only a rise in oil prices but also a fall in oil prices is regarded with suspicion and fear, amazing as that may seem. In the past decade, declining price has been followed by headines such as "Low Energy Prices Viewed as Threat to Conservation" and "Fall in Oil Prices Causes Problems" (*Washington Post,* March 27, 1988, p. A14). Of course this kind of inconsistency is found in views about other aspects of the economy, too. Both a trade surplus and a trade deficit are labeled as bad when the particular condition holds. And from time to time, people worry about the dollar (or pound or franc or yen) both rising or falling in value relative to other currencies.

Could it be that the desire for no change—a truly "conservative" attitude—tends to be present when people are generally well off and do not feel under great pressure? Exactly the opposite attitude apparently exists among people (such as prisoners) who are in desperate situations; they usually welcome any change, if only to break the boredom, because they feel they have little to lose. This may also be the explanation of the appearance in troubled times of millenarian movements such as that of Sabbatai Zvi among the Eastern European Jews of the seventeenth century.

A fourth cause of continued popular belief in Malthusian ideas are the ideas themselves, together with a closed rather than open vision of the world that we live in. A closed-world vision is associated with a zero-sum-game mentality and other general conceptions. Some aspects of this set of ideas are discussed in selections in Part 7 of this book, while other aspects had been discussed in *The Ultimate Resource* (with some overlap between the discussions.

A fifth reason is the fascination to many people of imagined impending disasters—a sentiment that (perhaps unfairly) seems to me to share the appeal of horror movies. Our current concerns come into perspective when we recognize how they have been present in other times and with respect to other events that plainly were not worth worrying about. Two centuries ago Oliver Goldsmith satirized this tendency (in Goldsmith, Oliver, *The Citizen of the World: Letters Selected and Edited by J. C. Dent M. A.*):

> Of all the arts of distress found out by man for his own torment, perhaps, that of philosophic misery is most truly ridiculous, a passion nowhere carried to so extravagant an excess as in the country where I now reside. It is not enough to engage all the compassion of a philosopher here, that his own globe is harassed with wars, pestilence, or barbarity, he shall grieve for the inhabitants of the moon, if the situation of her imaginary mountains happen to alter; and dread the extinction of the sun, if the spots on his surface happen to increase. . . .

> My landlady some days ago brought me the diary of a philosopher of this desponding sort, who had lodged in the apartment before me. It contains the history of a life which seems to be one continued tissue of sorrow, apprehension, and distress. A single week will serve as a specimen of the whole.

> Monday. In what a transient decaying situation are we placed, and what various reasons does philosophy furnish to make mankind unhappy! A single grain of mustard shall continue to produce its similitude through numberless successions; yet what has been granted to this little seed has been denied to our planetary system; the mustard-seed is still unaltered, but the system is growing old, and must quickly fall to decay. How terrible will it be, when the motions of all the planets have at last become so irregular as to need repairing, when the moon shall fall into frightful paroxysms of alteration, when the earth, deviating from its ancient track, and with every other planet forgetting its circular revolutions, shall become so eccentric, that unconfined by the laws of system, it shall fly off into boundless space, to knock against some distant world, or fall in upon the sun, either extinguishing his light, or burned up by his flames in a moment. Perhaps while I write, this dreadful change is begun. Shield me from universal ruin! Yet idiot man laughs, sings, and rejoices in the very face of the sun, and seems no way touched with his situation.

Goldsmith then takes us through the rest of the "philosopher's" troubled week, to devastating effect. And it is easy to imagine a writer 200 years from now making fun of our current concerns with running out of copper and energy and clean water and PCPs and—yes, perhaps the greenhouse effect and the ozone hole, too—just as Goldsmith did in 1760.

A sixth cause of continued popular belief in conventional Malthusian ideas is the difficulty all of us experience in breaking our attachment to long-held ideas. We all have a propensity to continue thinking as we have been thinking unless we are forced by some compelling circumstance to grapple with the conflicting new evidence. Because this matter is not addressed in any selection in this volume, I shall say some more about it now.

For seventeen years—from 1970 to 1987—my strategy in popular discourse was to state the popular wisdom, piece by piece, confronting each piece of conventional belief with statistical data and with theory. Popular belief after popular belief, I would show that the data utterly contradict that conventional wisdom.

Then I realized that this strategy has mostly been unsuccessful. I have had little or no effect on that vast majority of listeners who believe in the conventional wisdom. Therefore, I began to ponder why this is so.

One reason is that the ideas that have been part of our thinking for many years, and that have been constantly reinforced by similar messages from such media as television and newspapers and school teachers. *do not change readily*. This resistance to change is especially true of what we may call "majority" ideas—that is, ideas that are part of the established wisdom disseminated by our social institutions and large organizations. Conventional ideas about population and resources and environment are very much "majority ideas" nowadays.

I am this way, too. I don't easily give up ideas with which I have lived comfortably for most of my life, even when I am confronted by evidence that casts doubt on these ideas. Very specifically, I know how difficult it is to let go of the idea that population growth is a bad thing. I began to work on the economics of population because I believed population growth to be one of the *two main threats* to humankind—war being the other. And I decided to help the world reduce the rate of growth.

But my reading and research led me into confusion, because the available data did not support the standard theory that asserts that higher population growth causes a lower standard of living. It took me many a month of hard and painful thought before I made the transition from my intellectual starting point to a view that is consistent with the scientific data—that is, to the view that I hold today.

Arthur Koestler, Ignazio Silone, Richard Wright, Andre Gide, Louis Fischer, and Stephen Spender told their stories in *The God that Failed* of how hard it was for them to change their minds about the Communist party in the 1930s, and then to leave it.

In addition to the *specific* ideas that are conventionally held about population and resources, there also is a general set of ideas that adds up to an *entire world view* which makes it difficult to make sense of the data and theories which I offer to you about resources and population. The Malthusian assumption that resources are *finite* implies a *zero-sum-game* view of the economy and society—that is, more consumption by *one* person means *less* consumption by others. This vision is of a closed rather than an open world, one in which the quantity of resources is *fixed* rather than *changeable in response to human efforts*. This closed-world fixity view is consistent with such statements as: The United States has 5 percent of the world's population but uses 40 percent of the world's resources—as if the rest of the world would have more to consume if the United States consumed less.

This fits with a view that when some resources are used, there is less left to be used in the future. If you hold a closed-world vision in which all is fixed in quantity, you are bound to be incredulous when I tell you that *resources are increasing in quantity*. With such a world view, you are not likely to believe me when I say that more people in the United States, using more resources and creating temporary shortages, and then discovering solutions to the shortages, mean that people in other countries will have a *higher rather than a lower* standard of living as a result.

The notion of entropy and the second law of thermodynamics—which fascinates the ecologists—ties in with this view of resources as finite and limited. (See Selections 4 and 5.) All that sort of thinking suggests that one person exploits another, and especially others in generations to come, by using natural resources.

A closed-world, zero-sum vision also points thinking toward *conservation* rather than *creation of resources*. Certainly there is everything to be said for conservation when the economics are currently in its favor. But a closed-world mentality leads people to urge saving newspapers, say, in order to conserve trees, even when it is cheaper for the society to throw away olds newspapers and grow more trees to supply new newspaper. This process of saving becomes a sacred principle because of the fear that our natural resources are fixed and exhaustible. But practicing conservation no matter *what* the cost is not consistent with the view which I urge on you, that all resources—even oil—can be created by human minds and hands. The appropriate question is the *best way to create* resources, and whether it is *cheaper* to create more resources or to prevent use of resources and require saving of waste. It is the tradeoffs that matter.

There is still another mind-set that seems even harder to deal with. I notice that when I speak to anti-abortion audiences, listeners easily accept what I have to say about resources not running out, the world being increasingly better fed than worse fed, the U.S. water and air are becoming cleaner rather than dirtier, and so on. And this is so even though the "right-to-lifers" know that I do *not* share their politics with respect to abortion, though I share many of their sentiments.

There is no special reason for persons who are against abortion to believe these ideas about resources, and for environmentalists to reject them, except that belief in these ideas seems to support the *general* anti-abortion position of favoring a child to be born rather than aborted, while these ideas seem to oppose the environmentalists' *general* position that it is better if a birth is averted rather than occurs. In other words, people seem to be accepting or rejecting these ideas *not on the validity of the data and theories* that are presented, but rather on *whether they believe that the ideas will help or hinder them getting what they want.* The fact that those against abortion happen to be on the side of the scientifically correct view in this case seems almost a matter of coincidence, if my assessment is correct.

If this is true, all the facts and analyses that I might present are unlikely to alter many people's minds. Of course there are always a few people who will not let their preconceptions hold total sway over their learning, and those people are a key bridgehead.

Given this state of affairs, what will help open more minds to the facts? What will crack the wall of hostility that separates me from so many people who believe so strongly in population control, and who think that people like me are some kind of devil trying to pervert the public good for some hidden personal motives?

Much as I dislike taking this tack, the appeal to authority—or at least an appeal in reverse—seems the only possibility. Perhaps if I try to show you how authoritative persons and bodies, who formerly stated and promulgated the very ideas that you now believe, have radically *changed* their views—perhaps then you will be shocked into looking at the evidence with an open mind. And perhaps if you see how the prophecies of doom have systematically failed over the last two decades, perhaps then you may lose some faith in the supposedly authoritative and expert persons and bodies that promulgated these ideas. Indeed, it is the failure of their prophecies that have recently induced such bodies as the World Bank and the National Academy of Sciences to recant their former views.

I have no desire to create doubt in your mind about our public institutions and mainstream authorities. It is essential for any decent society that we have trust and faith in our institutions. We could not function decently otherwise. But like every other virtue, such faith has its accompanying vice, and that vice is the strength of the presumption that what the institutions say always is valid. The line between appropriate faith and appropriate doubt is very delicate, and only wisdom and intellectual courage can help you walk that line successfully.

Now consider some of the huge shifts that have taken place in the views of our most respected organizations:

1. The World Bank for many years was the strongest and shrillest voice calling for reduction in the rate of population growth on the grounds that the world is running out of natural resources. It still is against population growth. But, in its 1984 *World Development Report,* the World Bank did a complete about-face and said that natural resources are not a major reason to be concerned about population growth.

2. From the days of President Lyndon Johnson in the early 1960s, until 1984, it was U.S. policy to urge, and even coerce, developing countries to reduce their population growth rates. (For the Johnson story and its fallout, see Selection 23.) At the World Population Conference in Bucharest in 1974, the United States' voice was the loudest in calling for population control. At the next World Population Conference, in Mexico City in 1984, however, the official U.S. position was *exactly the opposite,* saying that population growth is "neutral" with respect to economic development.

3. The official National Research Council of the National Academy of Sciences was for fifteen years on record that population growth prevents economic growth, following a major report it issued in 1971. But in 1986 the National Academy of Sciences issued another major report that almost totally reversed the 1971 report. For example, it said that "The scarcity of exhaustible resources is at most a minor constraint on economic growth in the near to intermediate term. . . . On balance, then, we find that concern about the impact of rapid population growth on resource exhaustion has *often been exaggerated*" (pp. 16, 17, italics added).

4. The forecasts made by the doomsayers in the 1960s and 1970s have turned out to be laughably wrong. The *Famine 1975!* forecast by the Paddock brothers has been falsified by gluts of food and a farm crisis in the United States. Paul Ehrlich's primal scream about "What will we do when the [gasoline] pumps run dry?" has been answered with cheaper gasoline than we have had since the 1930s. Forecasts of shortages of copper and and other metals have been economic disasters for the mining companies that believed the forecasts, and for the poor countries in which they mines. Even the organizations dedicated to environmentalism and population control dare not now repeat the wild statements that they made in earlier years.

The population-control and environmental organizations now say, "Perhaps we exaggerated. Perhaps the details were wrong. Perhaps we forecast that things would happen earlier than they did. But just wait." Or they move on to new threats—species extinction, the ozone layer, etc., which there has not yet been time to confront or to understand well. But experience suggests that most or all of these newest threats will also prove to be overblown or nonexistent.

It should be noted that the point of view I express with regard to agriculture is not unusual. It is the same view expressed by the mainstream agricultural economists—and it has been so for many years now. Those top agricultural economists, including the one Nobel prize winner, gnash their teeth in outrage and frustration when they find pessimistic views about agriculture being urged by such voices as Lester Brown's World-watch Institute and in the popular press.

The point of view that I express about natural resources is also not original with me. I learned it from the great book by Harold Barnett and Chandler Morse, *Scarcity and Growth,* which appeared in 1963 and pro-vided a wealth of data showing that raw-materials prices had been falling rather than rising since 1870 or so when their data began. This view commands considerable adherence among mineral and energy economists, though not so completely as with respect to agriculture. The view that I express with respect to population growth is still a minority view, but the minority has grown a lot in the past few years.

*   *   *

The book needs some apologies and disclaimers, as follows.

I do not say that all is well everywhere, and I do not predict that all will be rosy in the future. Children are hungry and sick; people live out lives of physical or intellectual poverty, and lack of opportunity; war or some new pollution may finish us. What I am saying is that for most relevant economic matters I have checked, aggregate *trends* are improving rather than deteriorating.

It must be said as loudly and clearly as possible: I believe that a couple's ability to have the family size the couple chooses is one of the greatest goods of human existence. I believe in helping people get the number of children they choose. Personal liberty is my primary value. I am not in principle against a government giving "family planning" assistance to its own citizens or to citizens of another country if they so desire. I especially cheer efforts to strengthen commercial organizations that provide such assistance through market channels. I emphasize all this even though it should not even require saying, because many persons in the population "movement" disingenuously and maliciously assert that people who hold such views as expressed here are against "family planning."

Also, I don't say that a better future happens *automatically* or *without effort*. It will happen because men and women will struggle against difficulties with muscle and mind, and will probably overcome, as people have overcome in the past. The struggle needs to be stressed because there are many people who assume that if the *government* is not doing something about a matter, nothing is being done. If one suggests that the market will provide natural resources in quite satisfactory fashion, many people say: "Oh, you mean to say the situation will take care of itself." Yes and no. If you include the efforts of people struggling with might and main as part of your concept of a market—and that is exactly what constitutes every market—and if you assume that that happens "automatically," then yes, it is reasonable to say that the situation will take care of itself. But we need to remember that it is *people* who are taking care of the situation, and it surely does not seem automatic to them. If, however, you mean by "automatic" that the fine results descend from heaven, then no, it won't occur automatically. The issue is not government action versus benefits descending from heaven, but government action versus private action.

These essays do not suggest that we should desire an economy without rules. Just the opposite. Sound rules are crucial to the working of a free and efficient enterprise society. I agree with Friedrich Hayek when he says that the making of such rules is one of the most difficult activities, and one of the most valuable, that can be performed for society. The best rules are as automatic as possible, with as little arbitrary bureaucratic action as possible, so as to enhance decision-making.

The environment is one of the most difficult and trickiest subjects for rules. Whenever there is a commonly owned good such as the atmosphere and the rivers, the law should structure the costs of using the resource so that they function as a set of signals to use the resource in such manner as best benefits the public. I suggest we not think that the answer to environmental problems is simply more rules like "Thou shalt not use this common property" or "Thou shalt not produce that pollution." Rather, we need rules that will provide maximum freedom for people to try out new and better ways to take advantage of the opportunity to serve the public and make a profit that an environmental constraint imposes.

Making common property private is sometimes another excellent possibility, as we see in the case of streams and lakes in Ireland, and some places in the U.S. West, which are kept in tip-top condition by private owners who sell access for fishing.

More generally, freedom and enterprise are in the background of this tale of progress. New resources and economic advance do not fall like manna from heaven. They are the result of human action in an environment of rules and institutions that protect property and reward initiative. If we want continued progress, we must guard and renew those institutions, and not take them for granted.

This is certainly not a sermon of complacency. In this I agree with the doomsayers—that our world needs the best efforts of all humanity to improve our lot. I part company with the doomsayers in that they expect us to "run out" and to come to a bad end despite the efforts we make, whereas I expect a continuation of successful efforts. And I believe that their message is self-fulfilling, because if you expect your efforts to fail because of inexorable natural limits, you are likely to feel resigned, and therefore to literally resign. But if you recognize the possibility—in fact the probability—of success, you can tap large reservoirs of energy and enthusiasm. Energy and enthusiasm, together with the human mind and spirit, constitute our solid hope for the economic future, just as they have been our salvation in ages past. With these forces at work, we will leave a richer, safer, and more beautiful world to our descendants, just as our ancestors improved the world that they bestowed upon us.

I repeat: adding more people causes problems, but people are also the means to solve these problems. The main fuel to speed the world's progress is our stock of knowledge, and the brake is our lack of imagination. The ultimate resource is people—especially skilled, spirited, and hopeful young people—who will exert their wills and imaginations for their own benefit, and so, inevitably, for the benefit of us all.

*   *   *

The selections are mostly presented here as they were originally written and published. This has the drawback that the data may sometimes seem dated to the reader. But because the trends that are discussed here are so long-term and so slow-moving, one may usually be confident that it does not matter if the series end five or ten years ago. In some cases where it seemed an improvement to the flow of the book, I have moved sections from one essay to another, or added new sections or restored sections that were cut in the process of publication. In no case have I changed a forecast to make it fit more recent events, and in no case would there be motive for doing so because all the forecasts have been validated by the events. (This is also the case with all forecasts I have made in other writings not included here; there has been no choosing among essays for those that turned out well, and again, there would be no motive for so doing because none have turned out badly. Sorry if this seems boastful, but there seems no more attractive way of reassuring you on this all-important point.)

Most of these essays appeared in newspapers and magazines that do not cite the sources of data and quotations. The citations for almost all the immigration material may be found in *The Economic Consequences of Immigration*. The citations for much of the population and resource material may be found in *The Ultimate Resource*. If you should need specific references, however, please write me and I will do my best to supply them.

Writing these essays cost considerable time and energy that would better have gone into research and other writing. That I regret. But writing these essays also was fun, an enjoyable break from the heavier slogging scholar-ship. And there has been a certain pleasure in the battle. Pulling the essays together into this volume was also a pleasure. And I hope that you enjoy reading them.

Also I hope that these essays do not leave the impression that they are my main line of business. Rather, I spend almost all of my time doing the research that is my serious work.

In 1968 or 1970 I asked Simon Kuznets—the greatest economic demog-rapher (among his other achievements) since William Petty simultaneously opened up this field and originated modern economics in the seventeenth century—whether he ever got the urge to reply to the nonsense he read about population economics in the newspapers and heard on television. He replied approximately, "If I were to do that, I could not get my work done." Perhaps Kuznets would have been a good model for me. But my discussion of these issues with nontechnical audiences has often forced me to recognize and confront technical problems that would not have struck me otherwise. So there is benefit as well as cost in this respect.

Another of my great predecessors, Friedrich Hayek, (*The Road to Serfdom*) remarked on a related issue when himself writing a book (*The Road to Serfdom*) intended for a nonprofessional audience:

> For those who, in the current fashion, seek interested motives in every profes-sion of a political opinion, I may, perhaps, be allowed to add that I have every possible reason for not writing or publishing this book. It is certain to offend many people with whom I wish to live on friendly terms; it has forced me to put aside work for which I feel better qualified and to which I attach greater importance in the long run; and, above all, it is certain to prejudice the reception of the results of the more strictly academic work to which all my inclinations lead me.

The selections vary in length and style. I hope that the inelegance resulting from this inconsistency is offset by the invigoration of variation. Also, please forgive some repetition, especially repeated recital of some of the basic facts about trends in resource availability. These essays were originally written to stand alone, and the basic facts were often needed for background. I have removed redundant passages where possible, but some still remain. Since not many of you are likely to read from cover to cover, however, but rather will dip into the book here and there from time to time, the repetition may not trouble you greatly.

Though some of the selections attack viewpoints, groups, and occasion-ally even individuals, I try to avoid discussing individual's motives. Even more so, I attempt to refrain from assaults on people's intellects and characters. This disposition flows from my contempt for the ad hominem attacks which usually indicate intellectual weakness. Furthermore, as John Stuart Mill taught so excellently in *On Liberty* (1859), people with minority views inevitably lose much more than they gain if they resort to the cheap shots that people espousing majority views can get away with.

In this connection, you may wish to examine the rhetoric of two of the most prominent members of the environmentalist camp, Paul Ehrlich and Garret Hardin, in Selections 43 and 44.

Nothing said in this book conflicts with federal, state, and local governments providing as much "safety net" support to the needy as the taxpayers deem necessary and desirable. Here I follow Milton Friedman: If people are poor, give them as much money from the public coffers as the community feels they should get, balancing their need for help and their need for incentive. But the aid should be given in cash, and based on the most automatic sort of needs test with as little bureaucratic intervention as possible.

Hence, I see no reason to charge this writing or me with lacking "compassion" or being biased against the poor. Indeed, I believe that the economic liberty consistent with the analyses contained here will benefit the poor more than any other group, because economic freedom opens opportunities that government controls on business tend to close. And this long-run bias in favor of the poor is one of the main reasons why I espouse the views that I do.

Except in those cases in which the citation is relevant for the authoritativeness of the quotation or the estimate, references are not supplied. This is because most of the selections originally appeared in magazines and newspapers that omit citation, and it would be an insuperable task to insert citations at this time. For consistency, references are also omitted from most of those selections that had references in the original. For those references, you may consult the original source, or feel free to write to me for those or other citations, and I will do my best to supply them.

As I re-read this introduction as well as the articles in the volume, I am distressed that so much seems to be *criticism*—criticism of institutions and their bureaucrats and professors for too-frequent inexcusable ignorance and selfishness and careerism, and criticism of governments and politicians for implementing their own ignorance and selfishness with coercive power. To complete the picture, I'd like to tell you what I praise. I praise men and women as individuals, as families, and as partnerships and teams, who face up to their own problems and struggle with might and main to improve their situations. I praise them when they find opportunity in the economic problems of society at large, look for new ways to grapple with those problems, and promote the new discoveries that they make. I praise them when they succeed, and I praise them when they fail, as Walt Whitman taught, as long as they try. And I believe that if society provides them economic freedom and protection of their property, there will always be many women and men who will advance the welfare of the rest of us by their individual initiatives.

Part 1
GENERAL OVERVIEW

Introduction

This first section contains surveys of the facts and theories discussed in the book. An interchange with critics of one of these pieces—the opening salvos in what has turned out to be a long war—is also included.

Discussions of policy issues, and political considerations are absent from Part 1, but are covered in the final sections of the book.

* * *

A few years ago I was riding in a hotel's van from Newark airport to Spring Lake, New Jersey, along with other conference goers. I mentioned to my seatmate that my talk was about how natural resources have gotten less scarce, and how the U.S. environment has been getting cleaner. He found those thoughts difficult to believe, and he suggested that, in general, life has been getting worse rather than better.

The conversation caused me to look out the van's window and to reflect on our trip from Newark to the New Jersey shore. When I was a child my parents owned two little cottages in the seaside town of Bradley Beach that we rented out for the summer. We usually went to the shore in the spring to fix up and rent them, and in the fall to clean them up and to vacation if the weather was still warm; during the summer we sweltered in the city.

Early one July, however, we had not yet rented one cottage and therefore went to the shore for a weekend during the vacation season. In both directions that trip was literally a nightmare for a child. Each alternative road was bumper-to-bumper most of the 45 miles. When traffic stopped, cars overheated and stalled. Tempers exploded at drivers trying to beat the crowd by driving up the gravel shoulder and then cutting in. Worst of all were the collisions—including head-on collisions in the undivided roads—that caused horrible injuries as people without seatbelts went through windshields whose glass shattered. (That was before shatterproof glass was universal.) The 45-mile trip sometimes took four hours. And waiting until 1 a.m. Friday night or 3 a.m. Monday morning seldom was a worthwhile ploy for the husbands who left their families at the shore during the week so they could escape the sweaty city apartments.

Now here we were breezing down the New Jersey Turnpike in an air-conditioned, reasonably safe van on a safe comfortable highway, at a speed discreetly above the 55 mile-per-hour limit, having a ball. And nowadays, middle-class city residents don't even have to make the trip to escape the heat of summer, because they can switch on the air-conditioners that both they and working-class residents can now afford. Doesn't this comparison make it seem as if U.S. life has gotten better since 1940?

Then last year I was on the Jersey Turnpike at a more northerly point. We passed the impressive Brendan Byrne Arena, in a pleasantly landscaped area. I then remembered that the same area, when I was a boy, was a mosquito-infested marsh. And a trip 5 miles from here past Secaucus on the way to New York was literally a revolting experience. Secaucus was populated with pig farms whose animals were fed with the garbage from New York City across the river—which is why the pig farms were located where they were. When the wind was wrong, the stench across the road was so nauseating that we learned to roll up the car windows before we got there. No more stench now. That isn't progress?

The historical photos and drawings in the book *The Good Old Days— They Were Terrible,* by the famous archivist Otto L. Bettman (1974), make horribly vivid the tragedies of life that were common at the turn of the century—for example, the slum children who slept on the streets; the bums; the loneliness of the isolated prairie farm families who could go nowhere and had no one to talk to, not even over a telephone; as well as other horrors of horse pollution, overcrowded and unsafe tenement housing, crime, financial insecurity, bad food, and much much more. And "between 1870 and 1906 four American cities—Chicago, Boston, Baltimore, and San Francisco burned to the ground" (p. 39)—a world record. Bettman's pictures make this all very real and very believable.

With these memories in mind, I hope you will come to agree that the long-run outlook is for a more abundant material life rather than for increased scarcity and pollution, here in the United States as well as in the world as a whole.

1

Life on Earth Is Getting Better, Not Worse

The title of this selection describes a fundamental fact about our world: The long-term trends have been positive for all economic goods—including life, health, and environmental purity, as well as the standard of living—in the recent past as well as throughout the long sweep of human history. Rising income and life expectancy, declining pollution and disease, plus the unique human talent for creating new resources all point to a brighter future ahead.

How can it be, then, that residents of a rich country such as the United States—even some older people who have personally experienced such changes during their lifetimes—mostly have the contrary impression? How can people who have gone from living in a period in which their children were at substantial risk of dying from childhood diseases such as typhoid fever and infantile paralysis (polio), and lived into a time when their grandchildren are at practically no risk of dying from disease, how can they not understand that the world is a safer place today?

The trend toward a better life can be seen in most of our own families if we look. Personal example: I have mild asthma. Recently I slept in a home where there was a dog, and in the middle of the night I woke with a bad cough and shortness of breath. When I realized that it was caused by the dog dander, I took out my twelve-dollar pocket inhaler, good for 3000 puffs, and took one puff. Within ten minutes my lungs were clear. A small miracle. Forty years ago I would have been sleepless and miserable all night and I would have had to give up the squash playing that I love so much because exercise causes my worst asthma in the absence of an inhaler. Or if your child

Drawn from "Life on Earth Is Getting Better, Not Worse," *The Futurist*, August 1983.

had diabetes a hundred years ago, you had to watch helplessly as the child went blind and died early. Now injections, or even pills, can give the child almost as long and healthy a life as other children. Or centuries ago you had to give up reading when your eyes got dim when you became 40 or 50. Now you can buy glasses at the drugstore for nine dollars. And you can even wear contact lenses and keep your vanity intact. Is there not some condition in your family that in earlier times would have been a lingering misery or a tragedy, but nowadays our increasing knowledge has rendered easily bearable?

New scares have replaced the old threats to life in the journals and on the television screens. Though they may certainly be worth addressing, the new scares are either misplaced or relatively minor. Nevertheless, the cumulative impact of the contemporary scary "news" apparently is so great that people feel that the world is as frightening, or even more frightening, than it was in earlier times. This selection attempts to put these matters into perspective.

If we lift our gaze from the frightening daily headlines and look instead at wide-ranging scientific data as well as the evidence of our senses, we shall see that economic life in the United States and the rest of the world has been getting better rather than worse during recent centuries and decades. There is, moreover, no persuasive reason to believe that these trends will not continue indefinitely.

Longer and Healthier Lives

Life cannot be good unless you are alive. Plentiful resources and a clean environment have little value unless we and others are alive to enjoy them. The fact that your chances of living through any given age now are much better than in earlier times must therefore mean that life has gotten better. In France, for example, female life expectancy at birth rose from under 30 years in the 1740s to 75 years in the 1960s. And this trend has not yet run its course. The increases have been rapid in recent years in the United States: a 2.1-year gain between 1970 and 1976 versus a 0.8-year gain in the entire decade of the 1960s. This pattern is now being repeated in the poorer countries of the world as they improve their economic lot. Life expectancy at birth in low-income countries rose from an average of 35.2 years in 1950 to 49.9 years in 1978, a much bigger jump than the rise from 66.0 to 73.5 years in the industrialized countries.

The threat of our loved ones dying greatly affects our assessment of the quality of our lives. Infant mortality is a reasonable measure of child mortality generally. In Europe in the eighteenth and nineteenth centuries, 200 or more children of each thousand died during their first year. As late as 1900, infant mortality was 200 per 1000 or higher in Spain, Russia, Hungary, and even Germany. Now it is about 15 per 1000 or less in a great many countries.

Health has improved, too. The incidence of both chronic and acute conditions has declined. While a perceived "epidemic" of cancer indicates to some a drop in the quality of life, the data show no increase in cancer except for deaths due to smoking-caused lung cancer. As Philip Handler, president of the National Academy of Sciences, said:

> The United States is not suffering an "epidemic of cancer," it is experiencing an "epidemic of life"—in that an ever greater fraction of the population survives to the advanced ages at which cancer has always been prevalent. The overall, age-corrected incidence of cancer has not been increasing; it has been declining slowly for some years.

Abating Pollution

About pollution now: The main air pollutants—particulates and sulfur dioxide—have declined since 1960 and 1970, respectively, the periods for which there is data in the United States (see Figure 1-1). And the proportion of monitoring sites in the United States having good drinking water has greatly increased since record-keeping began in 1961 (see Figure 1-2).

Pollution in the less-developed countries is a different, though not necesarily discouraging, story. No worldwide pollution data are available. Nevertheless, it is reasonable to assume that pollution of various kinds has increased as poor countries have gotten somewhat less poor. Industrial pollution rises along with new factories. The same is true of consumer pollution—junked cars, plastic wrappers, and such oddments as the hundreds of discarded antibiotics vials I saw on the ground in an isolated Iranian village. Such industrial wastes do not exist in the poorest pre-industrial countries. And in the early stages of development, countries and people are not ready to pay for clean-up operations. But further increases in income almost surely will bring about pollution abatement, just as increases in income in the United States have provided the wherewithal for better garbage collection and cleaner air and water.

The Myth of Finite Resources

Though natural resources are a smaller part of the economy with every succeeding year, they are still important, and their availability causes

Figure 1-1a. Nationwide emissions of particulate matter.

Source: National Air Pollutant Emission Estimates 1940-1987, U.S. Environmental Protection Agency, March 1989.

grave concern to many. Yet, measured by cost or price, the scarcity of all raw materials except lumber and oil has been *decreasing* rather than increasing over the long run. This topic is discussed in greater detail in Selection 4.

More Food for More People

Food is an especially important resource, and the evidence indicates that its supply is increasing despite rising population. The long-run prices of food relative to wages, and even relative to consumer goods are down. Famine deaths have decreased in the past century even in absolute terms, let alone relative to the much larger population, a special boon for poor countries. Per-person food production in the world is up over the last

Figure 1-1b. Nationwide emissions of sulfur oxides.

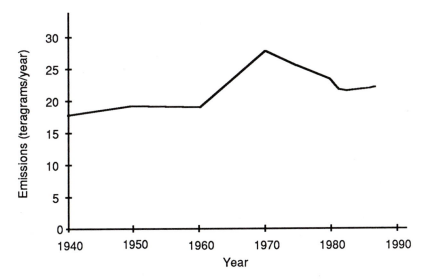

Source: National Air Pollutant Emission Estimates 1940-1987,
U.S. Environmental Protection Agency, March 1989.

thirty years and more. And there are no data showing that the people at
the bottom of the income distribution have fared worse, or have failed to
share in the general improvement, as the average has improved. Africa's
food production per capita is down, but that clearly stems from governmental blunders with price controls, subsidies, farm collectivization, and
other institutional problems.

There is, of course, a food-production problem in the United States
today: too much production. Prices are falling due to high productivity,
falling consumer demand for meat in the United States, and increased
foreign competition in such crops as soybeans. In response to the farmers'
complaints, the government will now foot an unprecedentedly heavy bill
for keeping vast amounts of acreage out of production. See Selections 6
and 7 for more information about food.

Figure 1-1c. Nationwide emissions of reactive volatile organic compounds.

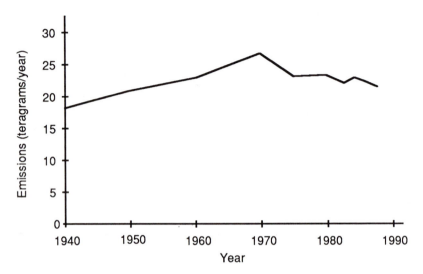

Source: *National Air Pollutant Emission Estimates 1940-1987,*
U.S. Environmental Protection Agency, March 1989.

More Wealth from Less Work

One of the great trends of economic history is the shortening of the workweek coupled with increasing income. A shorter workweek represents an increase in one's freedom to dispose of that most treasured possession—time—as one wishes. In the United States, the decline was from about sixty hours per week in 1870 to less than forty hours at present. This benign trend is true for an array of countries in which the length of the workweek shows an inverse relationship with income.

Another benign trend is the increase in the proportions of students who obtain various levels of education. In 1860, 56.2 percent of persons aged 5–19 were in school in the United States; in 1970, it was 88.3 percent. For "Negroes" (that is, blacks), the figures were 1.8 percent in 1850, 9.9 percent in 1870, 33.8 percent in 1880 (a peculiar jump in the figures occurs between 1870 and 1880), 31.1 percent in 1900, 53.5 percent in 1920, and 85.3 percent in 1970 (*Hist. Stat.*, p. 370).

Figure 1-1d. Nationwide emissions of lead.

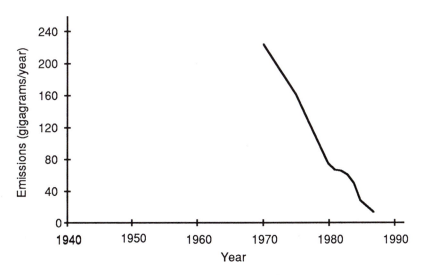

Source: National Air Pollutant Emission Estimates 1940-1987,
U.S. Environmental Protection Agency, March 1989.

In 1940, 79 percent of persons 14–17 were in school in the United States, and 94 percent in 1970; for persons 18–19, the percentage went from 29 percent to 47.7 percent (50.2 in 1969) (*Hist. Stat.*, pp. 370, 372). The percentages of 17-year-olds who were high school graduates in various years were as follows: 1870, 2 percent; 1890, 3.5 percent; 1910, 9 percent; 1920, 16 percent; 1930, 29 percent; 1940, 49 percent; 1970, 76 percent (*Hist. Stat.*, p. 379). For 23-year-olds with BAs or first-professional degrees the percentages were: 1900, 1.9 percent; 1920, 2.6 percent; 1930, 5.7 percent; 1940, 8.1 percent; 1950, 18.2 percent; 1970, 22.3 percent (*Hist. Stat.*, pp. 385–386). (See Figures 1-3*a* and *b*.)

The pupil/teacher ratio in U.S. public secondary education went from 27.8 in 1910 to 14.4 in 1970 (*Hist. Stat.*, p. 368). The average length of school term went from 132 days in 1870 to 157.5 days in 1910 to 175 days in 1940 to 179 days now. The average number of days of school per year per enrolled pupil went from 78 in 1870, to 113 in 1910, to 152 in 1940, to 162 in 1970 (*Hist. Stat.*, pp. 375–6).

Figure 1-1e. Nationwide emissions of nitrogen oxides.

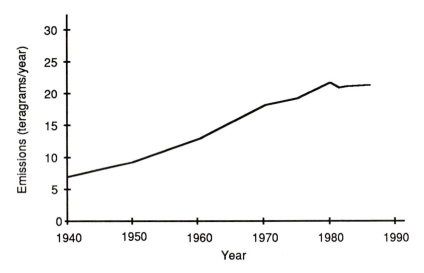

Source: National Air Pollutant Emission Estimates 1940-1987,
U.S. Environmental Protection Agency, March 1989.

The proportion of persons receiving education also has boomed phenomenally in the less-developed countries in recent decades. All this
increased education is an indication of an increase in individuals' occupational and social mobility, and of their increasing opportunities to develop
their talents in a fashion that is personally satisfying as well as socially
useful.

Our housing has been improving, as seen in the data on persons per
room, and on plumbing: In 1940 in the United States, 20.2 percent of
households, but in 1974 only 4.5 percent, had 1.01 or more persons per
room (U.S. Department of Commerce, 1977, p. 90). In 1940, 44.6 percent
of housing units, but in 1974 only 3.2 percent, lacked some or all plumbing
facilities. In 1940, 55.4 percent had all plumbing, whereas in 1974, 96.8
percent had all plumbing (U.S. Department of Commerce, 1977, p. 91).

Paved highways have risen from nothing since the turn of the century in

Figure 1-1f. Nationwide emissions of carbon monoxide.

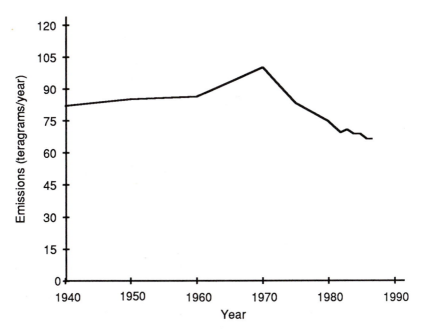

Source: National Air Pollutant Emission Estimates 1940-1987,
U.S. Environmental Protection Agency, March 1989.

the United States. Natural park areas have been rising. And trips to parks
have risen phenomenally. (See Figures 1-4*a* and *b*.)

Life has gotten safer, as shown by the accidental death rates in Figures
1-5 and 1-6.

With respect to progress in income generally, the most straightforward
and meaningful index is the proportion of persons in the labor force
working in agriculture. In 1800, the percentage in the United States was
73.6 percent, whereas in 1980 the proportion was 2.7 percent. That is,
relative to population size, only ½₅ as many persons today are working in
agriculture as in 1800. This suggests that the effort that produced one
bushel of grain or one loaf of bread in 1800 will now produce the bushel of
grain plus what 24 other bushels will buy in other goods, which is
equivalent to an increase in income by a factor of 25.

Measured by earnings, and even more so when measured by earnings

Figure 1-2. Trends in the quality of drinking water in the United States.

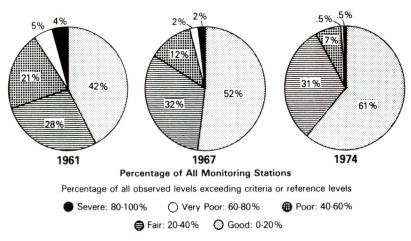

1961   1967   1974

Percentage of All Monitoring Stations

Percentage of all observed levels exceeding criteria or reference levels

● Severe: 80-100%   ○ Very Poor: 60-80%   ⊕ Poor: 40-60%

⊜ Fair: 20-40%   ○ Good: 0-20%

Source: Council on Environmental Quality

plus unearned income from government programs, poverty has declined sharply since World War II. (See Table 1-1.)

When measured in the most important way—the amount of work time necessary to purchase them—goods have declined in price, as Table 1-2 shows for representative items. (Services such as doctors' visits and haircuts are omitted because they necessarily rise with average income.)

Income in less-developed countries has not reached nearly so high a level as in the more-developed countries, by definition. But it would be utterly wrong to think that income in less-developed countries has stagnated rather than risen. In fact, income per person has increased at a proportional rate at least as fast, or faster, in less-developed than in more-developed countries since World War II.

"But in the last few years our income has been falling, not rising," many people in the United States say. If one tries to confront that statement directly, one runs into a bewildering confusion of statistics—family income, personal income, wages, and so on. This is my summary of the U.S. income situation: (1) The gains over the past decade-plus are not overwhelmingly large, but we certainly haven't lost ground. The recent slowdown probably is one of many pauses in the remarkable long-run increase in purchasing power. (2) We only need to reflect on the contents of our homes and public places compared to the contents of homes in 1900 or 1700 or 700 A.D. to realize the enormous sweep of this trend. To focus on five or ten recent years probably is to repeat the worst sort of error in

Figure 1-3a. Percentage of 17-year-olds who are high school graduates.

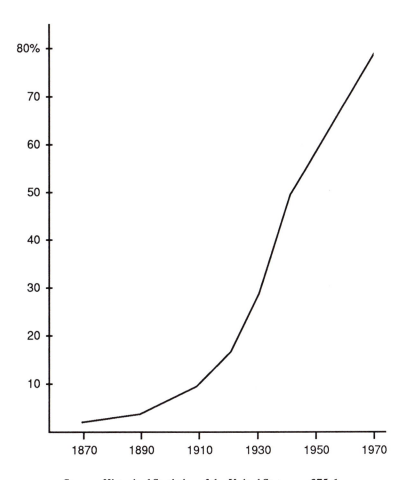

Source: Historical Statistics of the United States, pp.375-6

long-run forecasting, looking at one short recent period. (3) When considering short-run and intermediate-run income statistics, it is crucial to remember that improvement in our material life is understated due to the omission of improvements in product quality, and of new products, from the consumer price indices. A striking example, chosen to bring out this point, is the difference between price and cost trends of tires. "The CPI

Figure 1-3b. Number of 23-year-olds per thousand with BA or first professional degrees.

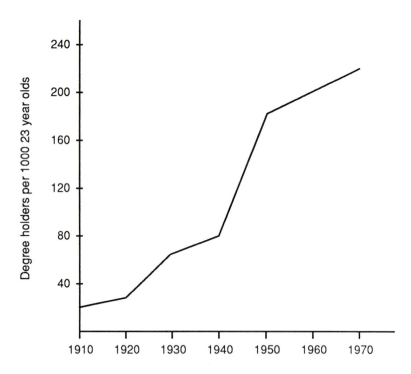

Source: Historical Statistics of the United States

tire index rose 140 percent from 1935 to 1978, an average of 1.9 percent per year. However, had the index been based on cost per tire mile, a far more accurate measure of the product's value to the consumer than price, the index would have reflected a decline of 9 percent in 43 years, or 0.2 percent per year'' (Moore, 1978). The details of the computation are shown in Table 1-3.

What explains the enhancement of our material life in the face of supposed limits to growth? I offer an extended answer in *The Ultimate Resource* (1981) and shorter ones in Parts 3 and 4 of this book.

Figure 1-4a. Total recreation visits—all sites.

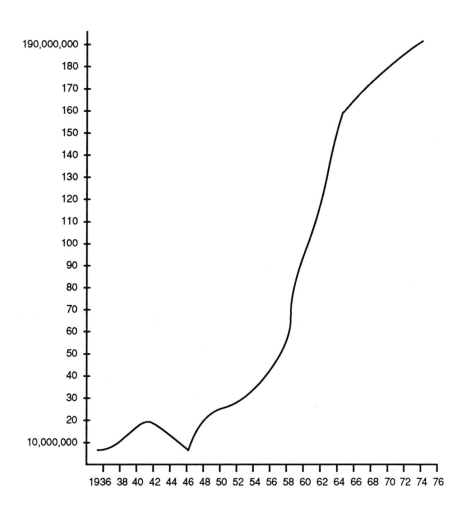

Source: Baden, 1980, p.16.

Figure 1-4b. Visits to principal recreational areas in the United States, 1920–1960.

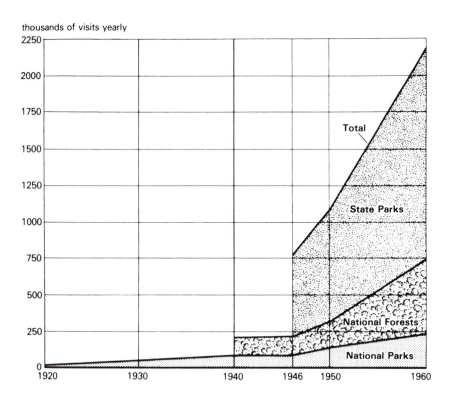

Source: Simon, 1981, Figure 16-5

Figure 1-5. Rates of accidental deaths by cause.

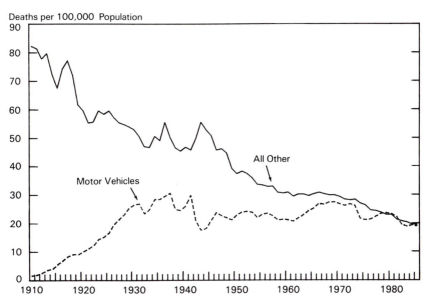

Source: *Economic Report of the President*, 1987, p.180

Figure 1-6. Rates of home and work deaths caused by accidents.

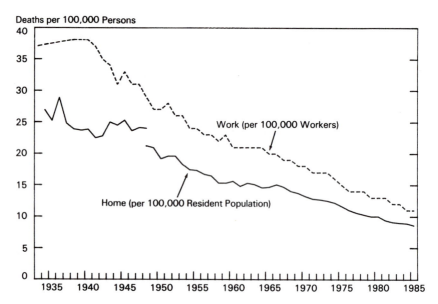

Deaths per 100,000 Persons

Work (per 100,000 Workers)

Home (per 100,000 Resident Population)

Note.—A change in classification resulted in a break in the home accident series in 1948.

Source: Economic Report of the President, 1987, p.181

Table 1-1. Percentage of Persons in Poverty by Income from
Earnings and Total Money Income

Income measure	1939	1949	1959	1969	1979
Earnings	68.1	53.2	35.8	26.9	28.9
Total money income	N.A.	40.5	22.1	14.4	13.1

Source: Ross, Danziger, and Smolensky, *Demography*, 1987, p. 589.
Computations by authors from Public Use Samples of the Decennial
Censuses of 1940-1980.

Table 1-2. What Work Bought in the United States, 1956 and 1986

	1956	1986	Percent Change
Average hourly wage in 1986 dollars (nonfarm workers)	$6.80	$8.80	30
Work time required to buy:			
Kitchen range	125.1 hrs	41.4 hrs	−67
Man's suit	67 hrs	30 hrs	−55
Gallon of paint	3.6 hrs	2.4 hrs	−33
Six-pack of beer	39 min	21 min	−46
Movie ticket	27 min	29 min	7
Chicken (fryer)	15 min	6 min	−64

Source: Fortune, Sept. 14, 1987.

Table 1-3. The Cost of Tires, 1935 and 1978

Tire Price	Tire Cost ($)	
1978 Steel-belted radial: approx. price, $68		
Life: 40,000 miles	0.00170	per mile
Auto wt.: 1.95 tons	0.000872	per ton-mile
Road speed: 50 mph	0.0000174	per ton-mile-mph
1935 4-ply cotton: approx. price, $13		
Life: 7,000 miles	0.00186	per mile
Auto wt.: 1.45 tons	0.00128	per ton-mile
Road speed: 40 mph	0.0000320	per ton-mile-mph
Price per tire rose 423%, but tire life increased 471%	Cost per mile fell 9% Cost per ton-mile fell 32% Cost per ton-mile-mph fell 46%	

Source: Moore, F. Lee Jr. "Index Mischief: Price versus Cost," *Electric Perspectives,* no. 78/5, pp. 8-27

2

Resources, Population, Environment: An Oversupply of False Bad News

This article extracted the most exciting findings from The Ultimate Resource. *In turn, the book was written in order to attract attention to the ideas about population growth which I had published in 1977 in* The Economics of Population Growth. *That book had, as David Hume put it, fallen deadborn from the press.*

Selection 2 was my opening shot in what I thought might be a short intense battle of truth versus false belief. Instead it has turned out to be a prolonged low-level struggle in which scientific truth is like a broomstick being wielded against a rhinoceros. The rhino shakes off most of the blows as irrelevancies and thunders on. Once in a while the stick hits a tender spot, but even that blow seems to be self-healing. As of this moment there may be some accumulating effect, but the accumulation certainly is not a very rapid rate—if it is occurring at all.

Of one point I am sure: If this essay had not appeared, the book from which it was drawn would have had much harder sledding, and perhaps would have had the same silent fate as its technical predecessor. But the Science *piece led to reprints and other articles, then to a very large number of book reviews. That attention in non-technical publications compelled the attention of academics who would otherwise have ignored it. If there ever was a row of dominoes in the sociology of science, this was it, thanks to the herd instinct of journalists.*

In retrospect, the opening reference to Kurt Waldheim is worthy of note. At the time of publication, readers looked askance at the remark because it seemed to be less than respectful of a great and good man. To me, however, he then seemed like just one more phony who

Science, vol. 208, 27 June 1980.

mouthed banalities without checking the facts, in order to enhance his reputation for "compassion."

The wild story of the publication of this article and the exchange that followed may be found in Selection 54.

In September 1977 *Newsweek* reported that "more than 100,000 West Africans perished of hunger" in the Sahel between 1968 and 1973 because of drought. Upon inquiry, the writer of the account, Peter Gwynne, informed me that the estimate came from Kurt Waldheim's message to the United Nations' Desertification Conference. I therefore wrote to Waldheim asking for the source of the estimate.

Three mutually contradictory documents came back from the United Nations' Public Inquiries Unit: (i) Waldheim's message to the conference, saying, "Who can forget the horror of millions of men, women, and children starving, with more than 100,000 dying, because of an ecological calamity that turned grazing land and farms into bleak desert?" (ii) A two-page excerpt from a memo by the U.N. Sahelian Office, dated 8 November 1974, saying, "It is not possible to calculate the present and future impact of this tragedy, on the populations. . . . Although precise figures are not available, indeed unobtainable . . . certainly there has been an extensive and tragic loss of life. . . ." (iii) A one-page memo written for the United Nations by Helen Ware, an Australian expert on African demography, who was a visiting fellow at the University of Ibadan in March 1975 when she wrote it. From calculation of the normal death rate for the area, together with "the highest death rate in any group of nomads" during the drought, she estimated "an absolute, and most improbable, upper limit [of] a hundred thousand. . . . Even as a maximum [this estimate] represents an unreal limit."

Ware's statement, which makes nonsense of Waldheim's well-publicized assesment, was on page one of a document written for the United Nations well before the Desertification Conference. Apparently it was the only calculation the United Nations had, and it was grossly misinterpreted.

More recently, the U.N. press releases have retreated to the more modest assertion that "tens of thousands" died in the Sahelian drought. But even this assertion is undocumented. "The problem with deaths in the Sahel," Ware says, "is precisely that there was so little evidence of them—rather like the photograph of the dead cow which kept turning up in illustration to every newspaper story." A recent summary of the scientific evidence on the drought's effects by John Caldwell, a demographer who was familiar with the area prior to the drought and spent 1973 there, says, "One cannot certainly identify the existence of the drought in the vital statistics . . . nutritional levels, although poor, were similar to those found before the drought in other parts of Africa. The only possible exception was that of very young children.''

This is an example of a common phenomenon: Bad news about population growth, natural resources, and the environment that is based on flimsy evidence or no evidence at all is published widely in the face of contradictory evidence.

Another example comes from the same *Newsweek* piece: "More than one-third of all the land is desert or near-desert. And deserts are spreading inexorably, turning arable land into stony waste or heaps of drifting sand . . . annually destroying twelve million to seventeen million acres." The headline on a front-page story in the *New York Times* said, "14 Million Acres a Year Vanishing as Deserts Spread Around Globe."

Some arable land surely is deteriorating. But these news stories, and the many others originating from the book *Losing Ground,* by Erik Eckholm of Worldwatch Institute, clearly imply a more general proposition: that the world's supply of arable land is decreasing. Yet the truth is exactly the opposite: Joginder Kumar made a country-by-country survey of the changes in arable land from 1950 to 1960. His finding: There was 9 percent more total arable land in 1960 than in 1950 in the 87 countries for which he could find data (constituting 73 percent of the land area of the world)—a gain of almost 1 percent per year (Table 2-1). And the more recent Food and Agriculture Organization data show a rise in "arable and permanent cropland" from 1403 to 1507 million hectares in the world as a whole from 1961–65 to 1974, an annual increase of roughly 0.7 percent. In the developing countries the area increased by 1.1 percent annually over the decade 1960 to 1970.

The increase in the quantity of land that is cultivated rose even faster than 1 percent per year—from 8.9 percent of the total area to 9.9 percent during 1950 to 1960 (Table 2-1). And the increase in effective crop area was greater yet, because of the increase in multiple cropping in Asia and elsewhere. In some places the extension of cultivation has reduced the quality of land, of course, but in other places the process has improved the quality of land.

But does not a larger population necessarily mean "more pressure" on the land, so that ultimately everyone will be scratching out three skimpy meals from 18 hours of work a day on a plot the size of a window box? There has been such a trend in countries that have not yet entered into modernization and industrialization. For example, farm size declined as population increased in Poland from 1787 to 1937 and in China from 1870 to 1930. But the more general trend points in the opposite direction. In all the higher-income industrialized countries in Europe and North America,

Table 2-1. World Land Use, 1950 and 1960

	Arable as % of total		Cultivated as % of arable		Cultivated as % of total		Arable plus pasture as % of total	
	1950	1960	1950	1960	1950	1960	1950	1960
Africa	14.27	15.30	36.21	42.72	5.2	6.5	46.50	49.02
Middle East	12.87	13.91	52.11	57.88	6.7	8.1	13.06	17.34
Asia	19.03	20.78	82.06	86.17	15.6	17.9	46.35	49.60
Frontier countries (North and South America, USSR, Australia, New Zealand)	6.88	7.75	82.85	82.96	5.7	6.4	34.27	38.59
Europe	30.79	30.98	89.02	90.06	27.4	27.9	45.63	46.10
All Regions	10.73	11.73	82.74	83.99	8.9	9.9	37.35	41.07

Source: Simon J., The Ultimate Resource, 1981.

and in Japan, a smaller absolute number of farmers are producing much more food and feeding much larger populations than in the past. An extrapolation of this benign trend, carried to the same absurdity as the nightmare above, would suggest that eventually one person will be farming all the cropland in the United States and feeding everyone. The less-developed countries have not begun this trend, though the relative proportions of their populations that are in agriculture are falling rapidly. We may expect that as they get richer smaller absolute numbers of persons will be doing the farming for larger populations, on ever-larger farm units.

Some Other Myths About Population and Resources

Here are some other examples of publicized, false, bad news and the unpublicized, good-news truth:

Statement: The food situation in less-developed countries is worsening.

"Serious World Food Gap Is Seen Over the Long Run" is a typical *New York Times* headline.

Perhaps most influential in furthering that idea was Paul Ehrlich's best-selling book *The Population Bomb*, which begins, "The battle to feed all of humanity is over. In the 1970s the world will undergo famines—hundreds of millions of people are going to starve to death." Many writers view the situation as so threatening that they call for strong measures to restrict population growth—"compulsion if voluntary methods fail," as Ehrlich put it. Some, such as Paul and William Paddock, authors of the 1967 book *Famine—1975!*, find warrant in these assertions for such policies as "triage—letting the least fit die in order to save the more robust victims of hunger." "My [one of the Paddocks] own opinion as the triage classification of these sample nations is: Haiti, Can't-be-saved; Egypt, Can't-be-saved; The Gambia, Walking Wounded; Tunisia, Should Receive Food; Libya, Walking Wounded; India, Can't-be-saved; Pakistan, Should Receive Food."

Fact: Per capita food production has been increasing at roughly 1 percent yearly—25 percent during the last quarter century (Table 2-2). Even in less-developed countries food production has increased substantially. World food stocks are high now, and even India has large amounts of food in storage. In the United States farmers are worrying about disaster from too much food.

Some countries have done far worse than the average, and have even had declining production, often because of war or political upheaval. And progress in food production has not been steady. But there has been no year, or series of years, so bad as to support a conclusion of long-term retrogression. Some readers might wonder whether my assertions are overly influenced by recent events, but the first draft of this material, for publication in my technical book (1981), was written in 1971 and 1972, when food production was having its worst time in recent decades.

What about the data the other fellows quote to support their worried forecasts? In simple fact there are no other basic data. The data shown in Table 2-2 were published by the United Nations, collected from the individual countries. Of course the data are less reliable than one would like; economic data usually are. But these are the only official data, and data that would show a worsening trend in recent decades simply do not exist.

More details on the food situation may be found in Selection 6.

Statement: The danger of famine is increasing. The U.N. Economic and Social Commission for Asia and the Pacific predicts "500 million starvation deaths in Asia between 1980 and 2025."

Contrary evidence: The course of famines is difficult to measure quanti-

Table 2-2. Per Capita Food Production in the World,
1948 to 1976

Year	Excluding mainland China (1952-56 =100)	Including Mainland China (1961-65 =100)	Combined Index (1948-52 =100)
1948-50	93		100
1952	97		104
1953	100		108
1954	99		106
1955	101		109
1956	103		111
1957	102		110
1958	106		114
1959	106		114
1960	107		115
1961	106		114
1962	108		116
1963	108		116
1964	109	102	118
1965	108	100	116
1966	111	103	119
1967	113	105	121
1968		106	123
1969		105	119
1970		106	123
1971		107	125
1972		104	120
1973		108	126
1974		107	125
1975		108	126
1976		110	128

tatively. But D. Gale Johnson, an agricultural economist who has studied the history of famines intensively, estimates that since World War II there has been a "dramatic decline" in famines. Only a tenth as many people died of famine in the third quarter of the twentieth century as in the last quarter of the ninteenth century, despite the much larger population now. A key cause of the decline in famine deaths has been the improvements in road systems, which allow food to be moved from regions of plenty to regions of shortage. The road-system improvements are themselves a product of increased population density as well as of improvements in technology.

Statement: Higher population growth implies lower per capita economic growth. This has been almost gospel for the World Bank, the State Department's Agency for International Development (AID), and other developmental agencies.

Contrary evidence: Empirical studies find no statistical correlation between countries' population growth and their per capita economic growth, either over the long run or in recent decades. Decadal growth rates of population and output per capita for those countries where long-run data are available are shown in Figure 2-1. No strong relationship appears. Contemporary cross-national comparisons of current rates of population growth and economic growth are another source of evidence. Many such studies have been done by now, and they agree that population growth does not have a negative effect upon economic growth in either more-developed or less-developed countries. These overlapping empirical studies do not show that fast population growth increases per capita income, but they certainly imply that one should not confidently assert that population growth decreases economic growth.

Statement: Sophisticated computer models show that for the next 30 years an increase in population causes a decrease in per capita income.

Phyllis Piotrow documented the decisive impact upon the late 1960s policy of AID and the U.N.'s Fund for Population Activities that was exerted by the first of these models, created in 1958 by Ansley Coale and Edgar Hoover. Largely founded on the Coale-Hoover simulation, the belief that population growth in less-developed countries is bad for the world led the State Department to greatly increase its spending for fertility reduction in poor countries, hand-in-hand with relatively lower spending on mortality reduction and other health programs, as seen in Table 2-3. Along with the hundreds of millions of dollars for fertility reduction, the United States has put pressure on foreign governments to adopt fertility reduction programs.

Response: At the heart of all these models is simply an arithmetical truth: When considering the ratio (total income)/persons and assuming the

Figure 2-1. The nonrelationship between population growth and growth of living standards over half a century (·) and a century (■). A, Australia (1900–04 to 1963–67 and 1861–69 to 1963–67); B, Belgium (1900–04 to 1963–67); C, Canada (1920–24 to 1963–67 and 1870–74 to 1963–67); D, Denmark (1865–69 to 1963–67); F, France (1896 to 1963–66 and 1861–70 to 1963–66); G, Germany (1910–13 to 1963–67 and 1850–59 to 1963–67); GB, Great Britain (1855–64 to 1963–67); I, Italy (1895–99 to 1963–67); J, Japan (1874–79 to 1963–67); N, Netherlands (1900–09 to 1963–67 and 1860–70 to 1963–67); NY, Norway (1865–69 to 1963–67); S, Sweden (1861–69 to 1963–67); SZ, Switzerland (1910 to 1963–67); UK, United Kingdom (1920–24 to 1963–67); US, United States (1910–14 to 1963–67 and 1859 to 1963–67).

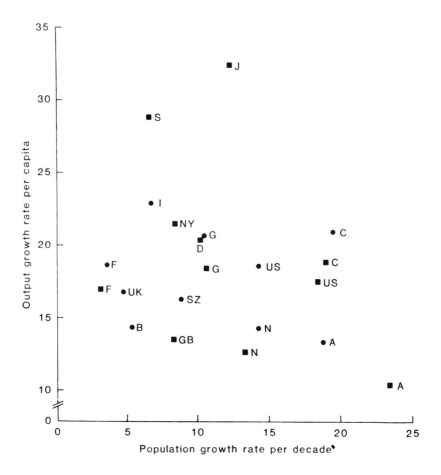

Table 2-3. Monies Obligated (Loans and Disbursements) for
Population and Health Programs by the Agency for International
Development. 1965 to 1977 (in millions of U.S. dollars).

Fiscal Year	Population	Health	Total
1965	1.9	32.4	34.3
1966	3.8	58.7	62.5
1967	4.3	98.1	102.4
1968	34.4	131.3	165.7
1969	43.9	38.3	82.0
1970	73.1	37.1	110.2
1971	94.0	57.7	151.7
1972	120.9	35.4	156.3
1973	121.7	42.9	164.6
1974	100.1	81.5	181.6
1975	100.0	54.5	154.5
1976	103.0	54.4	157.4
1977*	143.4	93.6	237.0

* Estimated

Source: J. Simon, *The Ultimate Resource*, Princeton
University Press, 1981.

numerator (income) to be fixed, an increase in the denominator (persons) implies a decrease in income per capita. That is, an added child with all sharing a given amount of goods means there is less to go around. As Peter Bauer remarked, the instant a calf is born, per capita income and wealth go up, but the instant a child is born, per capita income and wealth go down. This truth was well recognized by Coale and Hoover with respect to their model and findings: "The inauspicious showing of the high-fertility case . . . in levels of living is traceable entirely to the accelerated growth in the number of consumers." The point was crystal-clear to Malthus even without a complex model. He noted that an increase in population "increases the number of people before the means of subsistence are increased. The food therefore which before supported eleven millions, must now be divided among eleven millions and a half."

Once the children grow up, however, and become producers as well as consumers, their impact on per capita income reverses. Eventually the income of other people is higher because of the additional children, as my own technical work has argued. But this takes more than the 25 or 30 years covered by the well-known models.

Another point of view: The main new element in my model for more-developed countries (MDC's) is the contribution of additional people to increasing productivity. This occurs partly through larger markets and economies of scale. But more important are an additional person's contributions to increased knowledge and technical progress. People bring not only mouths and hands into the world but also heads and brains. The source of improvements in productivity is the human mind, and the human mind is seldom found apart from the human body. This is an old idea, going back at least as far as William Petty:

> As for the Arts of Delight and Ornament, they are best promoted by the greatest number of emulators. And it is more likely that one ingenious curious man may rather be found among 4 million than 400 persons. . . . And for the propagation and improvement of useful learning, the same may be said concerning it as above-said concerning . . . the Arts of Delight and Ornaments. . . .

Population growth and productivity increase are not independent forces running a race. Rather, additional persons cause technological advances by inventing, adapting, and diffusing new productive knowledge.

Technical progress, which is the main source of long-run economic growth in MDC's, arises partly from organized scientific R & D and partly from people who are not especially educated and do not work in science—the supermarket manager who finds a method to display more merchandise in a given space, the supermarket clerk who develops a quicker way to stamp the prices on cans, the market researcher who experiments to learn more efficient and cheaper means of advertising the store's prices and sale items, and so on. This is the "learning by doing" phenomenon which has been all-important in raising our standard of living from what it was 20,000 years ago, 200 years ago, 20 years ago, to what it is now. The aggregate economic importance of the technological knowledge factor has clearly emerged in two well-known studies, one by Robert Solow and the other by Edward Denison.

I have added this effect of additional people on productivity to a standard economic model in several variants of Figure 2-2. The result is that additional persons, instead of being a permanent drag, lead to an increase in per worker output starting 30 to 70 years after birth—that is, 10 to 50 years after entry into the labor force. (Economics can therefore

Figure 2-2. Schematic of MDC model.

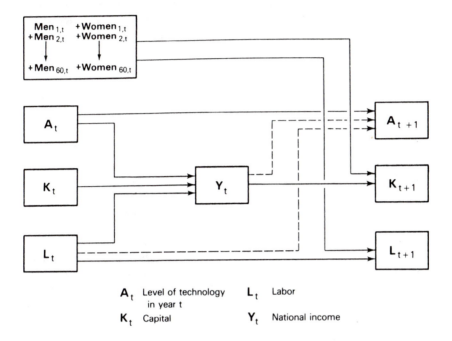

A_t Level of technology
          in year t
K_t Capital

L_t Labor

Y_t National income

be a cheerful science rather than the dismal science Malthus thought it to be.)

Babies do not create knowledge and improve productivity while still in their cradles. And though the family bears most of the cost, society must also unpurse to bring the baby to productive adulthood. This means that if you do not look as far ahead as the next 25 years, the knowledge benefits of someone else's baby born today do not interest you, and that baby therefore appears to be a poor social investment for your taxes. But if you feel some interest in, and obligation for, the longer-run future—perhaps because you yourself are today enjoying the fruits of the investment that someone paid for 25 or 50 or 100 years ago, or because you have children whose future is important to you—then you will view the knowledge produced by today's children as being of great benefit to you.

The mechanism is different in less-developed countries (LDC's). Offsetting the negative capital-dilution force of more people, there are the positive forces of increased work done by parents, extra stimulus to agricultural and industrial investment, increased social infrastructure, and other economies of scale. When all these forces are combined into my

LDC simulation model, an additional child comes to have a positive net effect on the general standard of living after the better part of a century. But this positive net effect is much larger than the negative net effect early on. Once again, most of the cost is borne by the immediate family rather than the rest of society. And the immediate family apparently feels that the benefits from the additional child outweigh the costs in the early years, because they choose to bear the children and the expenses.

In short, economic theory that includes key elements left out of previous models, together with the empirical data, suggests that additional children have positive long-run effects upon the standard of living.

It is true that the long run—30 to 70 years—is far from now, and therefore is of less importance to us than is the short run. But our long run will be someone else's short run, just as our short run was someone else's long run. Some measure of unselfishness should impel us to keep this in mind as we make our decisions about population policy.

Statement: Urban sprawl is paving over the United States, including much "prime agricultural land" and recreational areas.

Fact: All the land used for urban areas plus roadways totals less than 3 percent of the area of the United States. And the increase over the half-century starting in 1920 was only 0.00025 percent of total land annually. The U.S. Department of Agriculture says "we are in no danger of running out of farmland."

Each year 1.25 million acres are converted to efficient cropland by draining swamps and irrigating deserts, while 0.9 million acres are converted to urban and transportation use. The rest of the 2.2 million acres of rural land which goes out of use yearly is abandoned not because of "paving over" but because it has "low soil fertility and a terrain unsuited to efficient use of modern machinery." A million acres yearly goes into additional wilderness recreation areas and wildlife refuges, and another 300,000 acres goes for reservoirs and flood control. The danger to agriculture from "paving over" is another bogeyman.

About wildlife areas, state and national parks: these increased from 8 million acres in 1920 to 73 million acres in 1974 and are still increasing. The number of visits to these recreation areas has risen sharply because of improved transportation and increased income. From 1946 to 1960, for example, visits increased from 780 to 2184 per thousand people yearly.

Statement: We are running out of natural resources and raw materials. "Entering an age of scarcity" is such a commonplace that it is simply assumed and asserted in public discussion by people ranging from B. F. Skinner to Solzhenitzyn.

Response: The only meaningful measure of scarcity in peacetime is the cost of the good in question. The cost trends of almost every natural resource—whether measured in labor time required to produce the energy, in production costs, in the proportion of our incomes spent for energy, or even in the price relative to other consumer goods—have been downward over the course of recorded history.

An hour's work in the United States has bought increasingly more of copper, wheat, and oil (representative and important raw materials) from 1800 to the present. And the same trend has almost surely held throughout human history. Calculations of expenditures for raw materials as a proportion of total family budgets make the same point even more strongly. These trends imply that the raw materials have been getting increasingly available and less scarce relative to the most important and most fundamental element of life, human work time. The prices of raw materials have even been falling relative to consumer goods and the Consumer Price Index. All the items in the Consumer Price Index have been produced with increasing efficiency in terms of labor and capital over the years, but the decrease in cost of raw materials has been even greater than that of other goods, a very strong demonstration of progressively decreasing scarcity and increasing availability of raw materials.

The relative fall in the prices of raw materials understates the positive trend, because as consumers we are interested in the services we get from the raw materials rather than the raw materials themselves. And we have learned to use less of given raw materials for given purposes, as well as to substitute cheaper materials to get the same services. Consider a long-ago copper pot for cooking. The consumer is interested in a container which can be put over heat. After iron and aluminum were discovered, quite satisfactory cooking pots—almost as good as, or perhaps better than, pots of copper—could be made of those materials. The cost that interests us is the cost of providing the cooking service, rather than the cost of copper.

A dramatic example of how the service that copper renders can be supplied much more cheaply by a substitute process: A single communications satellite in space provides intercontinental telephone connections that would otherwise require thousands of tons of copper.

Statement: Energy is getting scarcer.

Response: The facts about the cost of energy are much the same as the facts about other raw materials. The new strength of the OPEC cartel to control oil prices obscures the cost of production. But the production cost of a barrel of oil has not risen, and probably has fallen, in deflated dollars; even after the "oil crisis" of 1973 it was still $0.05 to $0.15 per barrel in the Persian Gulf, which was perhaps a hundredth of the market price. It is reasonable to expect that eventually the price of oil will again return nearer its economic cost of production, and the long-run downward trend in the price of oil will resume its course.

The price of electricity is an interesting measure of the consumer cost of energy, and it is largely unaffected by cartels and politics (though the price of electricity did rise after 1973 because all energy sources, including coal and uranium, jumped in price when the price of oil went up, on account of the improved market power of coal and uranium suppliers). But the long-run cost of electricity clearly has been downward.

In short, the data show that energy has not been getting scarcer in basic economic terms, but rather has been getting more plentiful.

Statement: The supplies of natural resources are finite. This apparently self-evident proposition is the starting point and the all-determining assumption of such models as *The Limits to Growth* and of much popular discussion.

Response: Incredible as it may seem at first, the term "finite" is not only inappropriate but is downright misleading in the context of natural resources, from both the practical and the philosophical points of view. As with so many of the important arguments in this world, this one is "just semantic." Yet the semantics of resource scarcity muddle public discussion and bring about wrongheaded policy decisions.

A definition of resource quantity must be operational to be useful. It must tell us how the quantity of the resource that might be available in the future could be calculated. But the future quantities of a natural resource such as copper cannot be calculated even in principle, because of new lodes, new methods of mining copper, and variations in grades of copper lodes; because copper can be made from other metals; and because of the vagueness of the boundaries within which copper might be found—including the sea and other planets. Even less possible is a reasonable calculation of the amount of future services of the sort we are now accustomed to get from copper, because of recycling and because of the substitution of other materials for copper, as in the case of the communications satellite.

Even the total weight of the earth is not a theoretical limit to the amount of copper that might be available to earthlings in the future. Only the total weight of the universe—if that term has a useful meaning here—would be such a theoretical limit, and I don't think anyone would like to argue the meaningfulness of "finite" in that context.

With respect to energy, it is particularly obvious that the earth does not bound the quantity available to us; our sun (and perhaps other suns) is our basic source of energy in the long run, from vegetation (including fossilized vegetation) as well as from solar energy. As to the practical finiteness and scarcity of resources—that brings us back to cost and price, and by these measures history shows progressively decreasing rather than increasing scarcity.

In summary, because we find new lodes, invent better production methods, and discover new substitutes, the ultimate constraint upon our capacity to enjoy unlimited raw materials at acceptable prices is knowledge. And the source of knowledge is the human mind. Ultimately, then, the key constraint is human imagination and the exercise of educated skills. Hence an increase of human beings constitutes an addition to the crucial stock of resources, along with causing additional consumption of resources.

Statement: The old trends no longer apply. We are at a moment of discontinuity now.

Response: One cannot logically dispute assertions about present or impending discontinuity. And one can find mathematical techniques suggesting discontinuities that will be consistent with any trend data. We can say scientifically, however, that if in the past one had acted on the belief that the long-run price trend was upward rather than downward, one would have lost money on the average.

Statement: The nation's "overall environmental well-being" is declining, according to the Environmental Quality Index (EQI).

Fact: This widely reported index is, according to the National Wildlife Federation, which prepares and disseminates it, "a subjective analysis . . . judgment [which] represents collective thinking of the editors of the National Wildlife Federation Staff." That is, the EQI represents casual observation rather than hard statistical facts. It includes such subjective judgments as that the trend of "living space" is "down . . . vast stretches of America are lost to development yearly." But the objective statistical facts indicate that the environment is getting better. Earlier we saw that "living space" is not declining, and recreational areas are increasing rapdily. The official data of the Council on Environmental Quality concerning major air pollutants show sharp improvements in the last decade (see Figure 1-1). With respect to water, "major improvements in the quality of polluted streams have been documented" (see Figure 1-2). The fish catch in Lake Erie, long ago said to be "dead" by Barry Commoner, has been increasing. The most important indicator of environmental quality is life expectancy; it continues to rise, and at an increasing rate: a gain of 2.1 years from 1970 to 1976, compared with a gain of only 0.8 year in the entire decade of the 1960s.

Statement: "[E]ven if the family size drops gradually—to the two-child average—there will be no year in the next two decades in which the absolute number of births will be less than in 1970," said the President's Commisison on Population Growth, 1972.

Fact: In 1971—the year before this forecast by the President's Commission was transmitted to the President and then published—the absolute number of births (not only the birth rate) was less than in 1970. By 1975, the absolute number of births was barely higher than in 1920, and the number of white births was actually lower than in most years from 1914 to 1924. This scientific fiasco shows how flimsy are the demographic forecasts upon which arguments about growth policy are based. In this case the Commission did not even "backcast" correctly, let alone forecast well.

Another peculiar forecasting episode: Between 1969 and 1978, U.N. and other standard estimates of the world's population in the year 2000 fell from around 7.5 billion to around 5.5 billion. This is a difference of 2 billion people—equal to about half the world's present population—for a date only 30 years or less in the future. There is also grave disagreement even among estimates of current magnitudes. An important example is the population growth rate of China, a fifth of the entire world population: 2.4 percent per year according to the Environmental Fund, 0.8 percent per year according to AID; these estimates correspond to doubling times of about 30 years and about 90 years, respectively, estimates with entirely different implications.

*   *   *

Discussions of why we hear so much wrong news about population, resources, and the environment may be found in Selections 52 and 58.

3

Letters to the Editor of *Science* and Reply

Selection 2 provoked letters to the editor in a number that was most unusual in the experience of Science.

All the letters printed were critical, except for a paragraph of general praise in one of them. However, the Science *staff was good enough to send me the letters that were not used, and a very considerable proportion of them were positive rather than negative. Some of them even praised the article immoderatly.*

The story of how the letters were selected, and of what I was allowed to say in reply, is given in Selection 54.

Only part of one letter is sufficiently provocative to include here, and is accompanied by my reply to it.

Letter to the Editor

. . . Probably the most striking misconceptions in Simon's article are those embedded in its treatment of the scarcity of minerals.

Certainly he is right that delivered services, not supply of raw materials per se, is what well-being is all about. The point he seems to miss is that, historically, availability of many raw materials in cheap abundance led (by economically rational choices) to the delivery of services by materials-intense or energy-intensive means; with equal economic rationality, such means are now being replaced with materials- and energy-frugal ones precisely because of the emerging scarcities that he denies. Such (economic) responses to scarcity make society better off than it would be in the absence of the responses, but not, in general, better off than it would be in the absence of the initial scarcity.[1]

Simon would have us believe that the OPEC (Organization of Petroleum Exporting Countries) price for oil says nothing about oil scarcity, inasmuch as that price is far above OPEC's production cost. The fact is that OPEC is able to maintain its price largely *because* of increasing scarcity of oil (and a lack of immediately available alternatives) in most non-OPEC

Science, Vol. 210, December 19, 1980.

countries. This scarcity precludes meeting demand entirely from sources with production costs below the OPEC price, and ensures that the last units bought are bought on OPEC's terms. Substitution of alternatives— increased efficiency, synfuels from coal and shale—may gradually bring down the quantity of oil demanded at today's OPEC price; but these alternatives are more expensive than oil used to be and they can only ameliorate, not eliminate, the costs of the scarcity of oil.

Simon offers the price of electricity as "an interesting measure of the consumer cost of energy" and, by implication, a measure of energy scarcity. He says the price of electricity rose "after 1973" owing to the "improved market power of coal and uranium suppliers" in the wake of OPEC oil price rises. Then, dismissing this with the statement that "the long-run cost of electricity clearly has been downward," he concludes, "In short, the data show that energy has not been getting scarcer in basic economic terms, but rather has been getting more plentiful." The fact is that real electricity prices bottomed in 1971 and were already up 18 percent from that low point in 1972, before OPEC's actions.[2] The fact is that OPEC's price hikes and the "improved market power" of coal and uranium *both* reflected a new reality based on emerging scarcity of oil and natural gas.[3]

What follows Simon's errors about the economics of scarcity is a discussion of the physical underpinnings of the subject in which he tells us that "the term 'finite' is not only inappropriate but downright misleading in the context of natural resources," because, among other reasons and examples, "copper can be made from other metals." Indeed! Perhaps Simon here has in mind the technique of elemental transformation by bombardment with subatomic particles in accelerators. Producing microgram quantities of copper by this means would be a gargantuan feat. Any implication that production in industrial quantities might be economically or energetically feasible is preposterous, as are his further assertions on this general topic (for instance, "Even the total weight of the earth is not a theoretical limit to the amount of copper that might be available to earthlings in the future. Only the total weight of the universe . . . would be such a theoretical limit. . . .").

With respect to food, Simon is enthusiastic about expanding land under cultivation by, for example, "irrigating deserts." But he does not discuss at all the constraints placed by lack of water on food production from arid and semiarid lands.[4] The withdrawal of water for existing irrigation schemes already has drained some major rivers, such as the Colorado, nearly dry, and rapid depletion of "fossil" water supplies is of enormous concern in areas such as the plains of Texas. Interregional water-transfer schemes are staggeringly expensive and usually beset with political obstacles,[5] not to mention their environmental liabilities. Desalination remains too expensive in energy and in dollars for use on staple crops.[6] And in times of prolonged drought, which are certain to occur in the future as they have in the past, nations relying too heavily on irrigated arid lands for food will be crippled.

On the environmental side, irrigated arid lands are subject to salt-clogging, which reduces and eventually destroys their productivity; this problem plagues arid-land agriculture in the southwestern United States as well as in less-developed countries.[7] Bringing more land under the plow by deforesting hilly terrain in temperate and tropical regions can lead to severe erosion, whereby the extra carrying capacity temporarily gained is literally washed away. On some tropical soils, the benefits of land clearing for agriculture are even shorter lived, as laterization turns the exposed soil to rock. And if deforestation for agriculture proceeds on a large enough scale, the resulting pulse of carbon dioxide may combine with that from increasing fossil-fuel combustion to alter global climate in a way that undermines food production to an unprecedented degree.[8]

Simon proposes that it is not only possible but proper to appropriate all the earth's resources (and more!) for the direct support of human beings. This notion is not unprecedented.[9,10] Perhaps economics cannot deal with concepts as resistant to monetization as the rights of nonhuman species to exist[10] and the aesthetic poverty of a world with no room for unmanaged environments. But even if one were to accept the maximization of the mass of human protoplasm sustainable on earth as a goal superordinate to all others, it would be a monstrous error to think that this goal could be realized without the services derived from largely unmanaged bio-geo-physical processes.

Today such processes regulate climate and the availability of water, screen out harmful radiation from the sun, maintain soil fertility and the chemical quality of air and water, control most potential crop pests and agents and vectors of human disease, and maintain a library of genetic information uniquely useful for the protection of existing food crops and the development of new ones, the development of new drugs and vaccines, the development of new industrial materials, and the understanding of life itself.[11] The intricacy and the immensity of these processes preclude replacing them or their services with technological substitutes on any interesting time scale. . . .

JOHN P. HOLDREN

Energy and Resources Group, University of California, Berkeley 94720

PAUL R. EHRLICH
ANNE H. EHRLICH
*Department of Biological Sciences, Stanford University, Stanford,
California 94305*

JOHN HARTE
*Energy and Environment Division, Lawrence Berkeley Laboratory,
University of California, Berkeley*

References and Notes

1. The general nature of the responses is to substitute, for the increasingly scarce resources, inputs that are less expensive than the scarce resources now are but more expensive than those resources used to be. Thus, installing insulation may save oil at a cost equivalent to paying $10 a barrel for the oil saved; this is a saving compared to buying world-market oil at $30 a barrel, but a net cost (due to oil's increasing scarcity) compared to the cost of keeping warm when oil was $3 a barrel.
2. S. Schurr, J. Darmstadter, H. Perry, W. Ramsay, M. Russell, *Energy in America's Future*, Johns Hopkins Press for Resources for the Future, Baltimore, 1979, p. 93.
3. Interestingly, this turning point was predicted accurately (on basic physical grounds) more than two decades in advance of the event. See, for example, M. K. Hubbert, *Science*, 109, 103 (1949); and President's Materials Policy Commission, *Resources for Freedom*, Government Printing Office, Washington, D.C., 1952.
4. H. E. Dregne, Ed., *Arid Lands in Transition*, American Association for the Advancement of Science, Washington, D.C., 1970.
5. J. Hirshleifer, J. Dehaven, J. Milliman, *Water Supply*, Univ. of Chicago Press, Chicago, 1969.
6. M. Clawson, H. H. Landsberg, L. T. Alexander, *Science*, 164, 1141 (1969). Developments since 1969 have not altered this assessment's conclusion.
7. Council on Environmental Quality, *Environmental Quality—1978*, Government Printing Office, Washington, D.C., 1978, pp. 472–474.
8. Because agriculture is highly adapted to existing climatic patterns, it is far more likely that any major change will reduce food production in the short term than that it will improve it. See, for example, S. H. Schneider and L. Mesirow, *The Genesis Strategy*, Plenum, New York, 1976.
9. See, for example, C. Marchetti, *Energy*, 4, 1107 (1979); H. Kahn, W. Brown, L., Martel, *The Next 200 Years*, Morrow, New York, 1976.
10. Ehrenfeld, D. *The Arrogance of Humanism*, Oxford Univ. Press, New York, 1978.
11. P. Ehrlich, A Ehrlich, J. Holdren, *Ecoscience*, Freeman, San Francisco, 1977.

Reply

On only two points did letters challenge my data's accuracy:
1. In response to my statement that "long-run cost of electricity clearly

has been downward,'' and that prices rose after 1973 due to OPEC pricing, Holdren et al. write: ''The fact is that real electricity prices bottomed in 1971 and were already up 18 percent from that low point in 1972, before OPEC's actions.''

I was taken aback, Holdren and Harte are energy scholars. I checked Figure 3-1 and other sources but could see no sign of their 18 percent. I therefore called the senior author of their reference, and Schurr's assistant read these index numbers: 1967, 100; 1970, 91; 1971, 80.2; 1972, 94.9; 1973, 93.8; 1974, 99.9; 1975, 103.6; 1976, 104.2; 1977, 104.3.

To find out more about the 1971 figure, the basis of the Holdren et al. assertion, Schurr's assistant suggested calling co-author Darmstadter. He, too, was puzzled. Upon investigation, the 1971 number (80.2) proved a typographical error and should have been 93.3. So much for Holdren et al.'s ''fact.''

Central here, however, is not the typo. Even if correct, it would seem

Figure 3-1. Price of electricity relative to consumer price index.

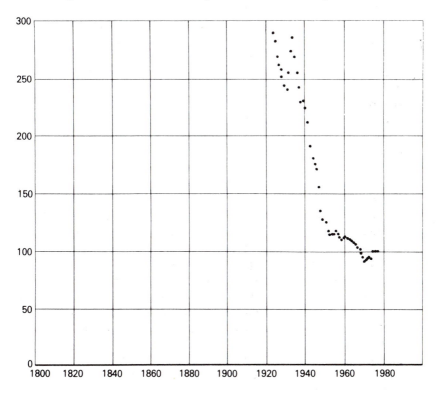

scientifically imprudent to rely for any general conclusion upon a single number against the contrary evidence of a sweep of data three-quarters of a century long (Figure 3-1) that tells a radically different story, especially when widening the inspection slightly would have changed their conclusion entirely.

Upon this one incorrect number, concerning just one among practically all raw materials for which the data show long-run price falls, Holdren et al. build their case that I make "errors about the ecnomics of scarcity." Does not this unfounded bad news reinforce the central point of my article? Perhaps this example and the next will convince some that my arguments are not simply defective scholarship or improper data selection.

2. A letter originally set in galleys, but omitted after I responded, called "incorrect" my statement that there have been "sharp improvements [in environmental quality] in the last decade." As evidence the author reproduced a recent *Scientific American* graph of Likens et al. which he said shows "an overall deterioration in air quality due to sulfur dioxide" from 1974 to 1976. (My graph stopped at 1974.) But Likens et al.'s graph does not refer to air quality, but rather to SO_2 emissions; one is not an index of the other. And the latest Environmental Protection Agency data about SO_2 and air quality show continued improvement in "national trends."

If specialists can believe that the long-run trends in electricity prices and in U.S. air quality are worsening despite easily accessible data, what *will* convince people that things are getting better even when they are? . . . .

Holdren et al. and others had a good laugh about alchemy and making copper from other metals. Even if what I wrote was physically impossible (which it is not), the point would not bear importantly upon the argument, and therefore it is simply a debating device questioning my competence. However, I am not in error in principle, as Holdren et al. note; rather, they claim it is "preposterous" because it is impractical now. But—this is my point—so was electricity considered impractical a century ago. And in perhaps the first full-scale attempt by a great social scientist to evaluate the future energy situation, Jevons concluded in 1865 that oil could never relieve the coal crunch he predicted would strangle Great Britain's economic growth about 1900. (England now exports both coal and oil.). . . .

About "the rights of nonhuman species to exist" in Holdren et al.: Our values differ. In trade-offs between human beings and the rest of nature, my sympathies usually lie with people. But of course I do not hold "the maximization of the mass of human protoplasm . . . as a goal superordinate to all others," if only because human life and welfare are too complex to be jammed into such a simple formula. Nor do I think of people as "human protoplasm," a term which draws attention away from peoples' minds, feelings, personalities, and very humanity. . . .

To summarize: My original assertions about the long-run trends of resource scarcity and of pollution in the United States survive the challenges. My other assertions about trends in land, food, the environment, and the effects of population growth were not challenged statistically. I emphasize aggregate data because one can find special situations that are consistent with any viewpoint one likes. I wonder: What will open people's minds to these facts?

JULIAN L. SIMON

Part 2
NATURAL RESOURCES

Introduction

Part 2 provides basic data and elementary theory concerning availability of the most important natural resources. In each case, the trend shows the resource becoming less scarce and more available, rather than becoming more scarce and less available—just the opposite of popular belief.

Selections 10 and 11 discuss the urbanization of farmland in the United States. Selections 10 and 11 provide the basic data. (Selection 53 describes the politics, including the ignorant and dishonest "research" and the false pronouncements by public officials and private environmental organizations. It also includes the story of how the U.S. Department of Agriculture eventually confessed that it had been wholly in error—but no one paid any attention.)

A comparable net trend with respect to the number of species in existence cannot be tested, because no data are available on the rate at which new species are being created. We can, however, document that the rate at which species are being extinguished is spectacularly less than the rate that is asserted by doomsayers (Selections 12 and 13).

Fascinating examples of how we free ourselves from dependence upon scarce natural resources appear every day in the newspaper. For example, once upon a time, people made cutting tools from flint. Good flint surely became scarce and caused worry at times. But people learned how to make metal cutting tools, which turned out to be better than flint for most purposes. Then later on, diamond became the material of choice to cut the hardest objects. But even industrial diamonds are expensive.

Now we read that thin jets of water under high pressure can do many of the tasks that diamonds can do, as well as many other jobs such as cutting pizzas under factory conditions. (*Wall Street Journal*, May 15, 1987, p. 41.) And water is not about to become scarce soon, if only because it is completely reusable. So with time we have become progressively less dependent upon scarce natural resources for cutting services.

A recent study by the federal Office of Technology Assessment made the obvious official: "The Nation's future has probably never been less constrained by the cost of natural resources." (*Technology and the American Economic Transition*, Washington, 1988, quoted in *Science*, May 20, 1988, p. 977)

4

The Scarcity of Raw Materials

The main theoretical arguments with respect to raw-material scarcity trends are summarized in this selection. A key issue is the appropriate measure of scarcity. Price and cost are the most meaningful indices for economic purposes.

Measured by cost or price, the scarcity of all raw materials except lumber and oil has been decreasing *rather than increasing over the long run. Figure 4-1 shows an enormous decline in the price of copper relative to wages in the United States; this relative price is the most important measure of scarcity because it shows the cost of the material in the most valuable of goods: human time. Figure 4-2 shows that the price of copper has even been declining relative to the consumer price index. This topic is discussed in this selection.*

Another important theoretical question concerns the best method of forecasting future *scarcity. I argue that the economic or "business" approach is preferable to the engineering approach when the former is feasible. (See also Selection 46.) Price trends of raw materials are cited in illustration.*

The proposition that we are entering an age of scarce natural resources is constantly recited, with little more evidence than that "everyone knows" it is true. Behind the proposition is the notion that a reservoir of some necessary material—copper, for example—exists in the earth in lodes that become successively harder to mine and that bear ever lower grades of ore as mining continues. According to this reasoning, the price of copper must rise as copper becomes more difficult, and therefore more expensive, to mine. But here is a peculiar fact: Over the course of history, up to this very moment, copper and other minerals have been becoming

From "The Scarcity of Raw Materials," *The Atlantic Monthly,* June 1981.

Figure 4-1. The scarcity of copper as measured by its price relative to wages.

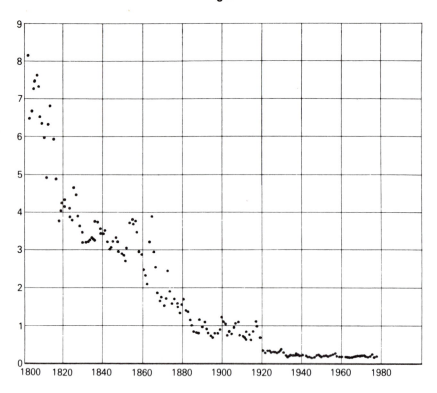

not more scarce but rather more abundant. In this respect, copper follows the same historical trend as radios, undershirts, and other consumer goods, and with even greater force. This fact requires us to ask: What is scarcity? What would be the signs that a raw material is in short supply? Upon reflection, perhaps one would agree that the thing to look for as a sign of scarcity would *not* be a complete absence of the material. Long before the shelf became bare, businesses, operating purely out of their interest in future profits, would begin to hoard supplies for future resale. Of course, the price of the hoarded material would be high, but there would still be some quantities to be found at some price, just as there has always been some small amount of food for sale even in the midst of the very worst famines.

People tend to think that a commodity has gotten scarce when its price has persistently risen. The relationship between price and supply is not

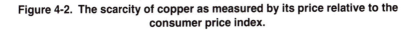

Figure 4-2. The scarcity of copper as measured by its price relative to the consumer price index.

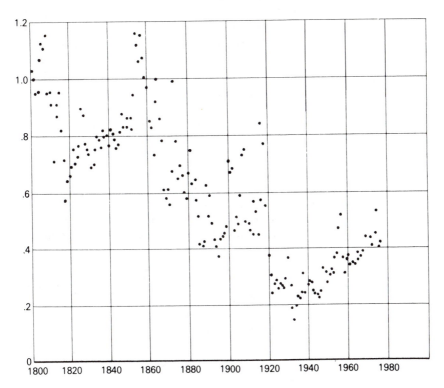

absolute, however. If the price of a raw material is deliberately held down, there may be waiting lines or rationing, and these may also be taken as signs of scarcity. But though lines and rationing can be efficient and fair ways of allocating scarce materials in the short run, in the longer run they are so wasteful that every sort of society tends to prevent them, by letting the price rise above what many buyers will pay. Therefore, we are not likely to see lines and rationing if there is a long-run (as opposed to a temporary) scarcity of a raw material.

In general, then, if a raw material becomes scarce, its price will rise. But the converse need not apply; the price may rise without a true increase in scarcity. For example, a strong cartel may successfully raise prices, as OPEC did in 1973, even though the cost of producing oil had not changed. However, unless we have reason to believe that market prices do not reflect production costs, we should consider market prices as our primary measure of scarcity.

An unsophisticated, but often meaningful, test of scarcity is whether we feel that we can afford to buy the material. That is, the relationship between price and income matters. If the price of food remains constant but income falls sharply, then we perceive that food is getting scarce; and if our wages rise while the price of oil remains constant, our fuller pockets persuade us that there is more oil to buy. A related test of scarcity is the importance of the material in our budgets. We are not likely to say that salt has become scarce even if its price doubles, because relative to the rest of our expenses, salt at any price is cheap.

So price, production cost, and share of income seem to be the appropriate measures of scarcity. It follows that to anticipate how scarce or plentiful a raw material will be, one should try to predict what it will cost.

There are two quite different general methods for forecasting costs of any kind: the engineer's method and the economist's method. Since the engineer's method is the one commonly used in discussions of raw materials, we shall consider it first.

At the root of the technological view of natural resources is the assumption that a certain quantity of a given mineral "exists" in the earth, and that one can, at least in principle, answer a question such as: How much copper is there? But there is no instrument to measure the quantity of copper or iron or oil in the earth. Instead, there are schemes for extrapolating from samples.

Most common technological forecasts are derived from the sum of "known (or proven) reserves"—that is, from the probable yield of lodes and reservoirs that have actually been prospected. This figure is divided by the current rate of use, and the result is called "years of consumption left." The concept of known reserves is useful as a guide to the decisions a business firm must make about whether it is profitable to search for new deposits, just as a running inventory of a retail store tells the manager when to reorder. But known reserves are not a measure of the resources that will be available in the future. The bar graph in Figure 4-3 shows that the known reserves of various raw materials almost all *increased* over the twenty-year period 1950–1970 as demand for them increased, just the way a store inventory often increases as the store's sales volume increases.

There are other measures of physical reserves, also expressed in years of consumption remaining at the current consumption rate. One, the total amount of a material in the earth's crust, is so far beyond the bounds of possibility as to tell us nothing. Another, a more economically reasonable measure, is that of "ultimate recoverable resources," which the U.S. Geological Survey at present sets at one hundredth of one percent of the

Figure 4-3. Known world reserves of selected natural resources, 1950 and 1970.

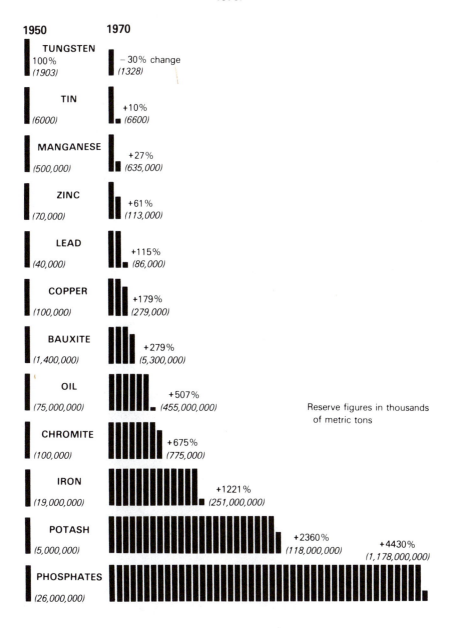

Source: Kahn et al., 1976, p.92.

amount estimated to exist in the top kilometer of the earth's surface. (These figures are given in Table 4–1 to be compared with proven reserves and total abundance in the other figures.) Even this "ultimately recoverable" estimate will surely be enlarged in the future, when mining techniques improve or prices rise.

One problem with all the technological methods is that they confuse abundance in the earth with economic availability. Platinum, gold, and silver are far and away the least abundant minerals. But they have never been plentiful, and so even though it has been progressively harder to find these minerals, few people worry about a "shortage" of them.

A second difficulty with technological forecasts stems from this important property of natural-resource extraction: A small change in the price of a mineral generally makes a very big difference in the potential supplies that are economically available—that is, profitable to extract. As expressed in technical economic terms in an article by Leonard L. Fischman and Hans H. Landsberg (published in the anthology *Population, Resources, and the Environment*): "Mineral supply . . . tends to be highly elastic in terms of price. . . . The addition of currently paramarginal and submarginal resources would increase the 'reserve' category, not by modest amounts, but by multiples of itself." Yet many technological forecasts are limited to supplies of the resource available at current prices with current technology. Given that the most promising lodes will always be mined first, such an approach almost inevitably shows a rapid exhaustion of "reserves," even though this does not portend increasing scarcity.

Third, the technological inventory of the earth's "contents" is at present quite incomplete, for the very good reason that it has never been worthwhile to go to the trouble of making detailed surveys. Why should one count the stones in Montana when there are enough to serve as paperweights right in one's own back yard? This point was made by the World Bank's *Report on the Limits to Growth* (1972):

> We do not know the true extent of the resources that exist in, and can ultimately be recovered from, the earth. Nor will we know in the next two years or ten years. The reason why we do not know the absolute limits of the resources we have is simple and does not even require recourse to elaborate arguments about the wonders of technology. We do not know because no one has as yet found it *necessary* to know and therefore [taken] an accurate inventory.

A fourth difficulty with technological forecasts is that the approaches that do go beyond the known-reserves concept are speculative, necessarily making strong assumptions about discoveries of unknown lodes and about technologies that have yet to be developed. Technological forecasting depends heavily upon how well the forecaster can imagine the methods of

Table 4-1. Number of Years of Consumption Potential for Various Elements

	Known reserves ÷ annual consumption	U.S. Geological Survey's estimates of "ultimate recoverable resources" (=.01% of materials in top kilometer of earth's crust) ÷ annual consumption	Amount estimated in earth's crust ÷ annual consumption
Copper	45	340	242,000,000
Iron	117	2,657	1,815,000,000
Phosphorus	481	1,601	870,000,000
Molybdenum	65	630	422,000,000
Lead	10	162	85,000,000
Zinc	21	618	409,000,000
Sulfur	30	6,897	N.A.
Uranium	50	8,455	1,855,000,000
Aluminum	23	68,066	38,500,000,000
Gold	9	102	57,000,000

Source: William D. Nordhaus in *American Economic Review,* May 1974, p.23

Three different methods are commonly used to estimate the supply of a resource, in years, and their results are compared above for each of ten resources. Each method divides an amount of raw material estimated to exist for "known reserves," in prospected sites; for "ultimate recoverable resources" and for the total in the earth's crust, on the basis of samples - by the rate of consumption for a single recent year. The result is the number of years the estimated supply of a resource will last, if consumption remains the same.

extraction that will be developed in the future. Making the conservative assumption that future technology will be the same as present technology would be like making a forecast of twentieth-century copper production on the basis of eighteenth-century pick-and-shovel technology.

All these difficulties in forecasting resource availability are well known to geologists, even though they are left out of most popular discussions.

Despite these reservations about technological forecasting, I will briefly survey the conclusions of some of the forecasters. My aim is to show that even with relatively conservative guesses about future extraction developments, many qualified forecasters report enormous amounts of resources available—contrary to the glum stories that dominate the daily newspapers. The problem is deciding which expert to believe. One can easily find forecasters who will give pessimistic predictions. For example, the geologist Preston Cloud has written that "food and raw materials place ultimate limits on the size of populations . . . such limits will be reached within the next thirty to one hundred years." *Famine—1975!*, a book by Paul and William Paddock, was a best seller when it was published in 1967. In their book, *The End of Affluence* (1974), Paul and Anne Ehrlich speak of "the dark age to come" as a certainty.

A very different assessment of the raw-materials situation was made in 1976 by Herman Kahn and his associates at the Hudson Institute. Examining the evidence on the twelve principal metals that account for 99.9 percent of world and U.S. metal consumption, they classify the metals in two categories—"clearly inexhaustible" and "probably inexhaustible"—and find *none* that is likely to be exhausted by a date pertinent to contemporary decisions. They conclude that "95 percent of the world demand is for five metals which are not considered exhaustible": iron, aluminum, silicon, magnesium, and titanium.

In a comprehensive survey of natural and technological resources for the next hundred years, published in 1957, Harrison Brown—a respected geochemist, who would not be described as an optimist by anyone who knows his work—looks forward to a time when natural resources will become so plentiful that "mineral resources . . . will cease to play a major role in world economy and politics."

Writing in *Science* magazine in 1978, H. E. Goeller, a chemical engineer, and A. M. Weinberg, a physicist, considered possible substitutions for raw materials that are now essential to civilization and arrived at a "principle of 'infinite' substitutability":

> With three notable exceptions—phosphorus, a few trace elements for agriculture, and energy-producing fossil fuels (CH_x)—society can subsist on inexhaustible or near-inexhaustible minerals with relatively little loss of living standard.

Society would then be based largely on glass, plastics [from carbon in limestone and hydrogen in water], wood, cement, iron, aluminum, and magnesium.

They conclude:

> . . . dwindling mineral resources in the aggregate, with the exception of reduced carbon and hydrogen, are per se unlikely to cause Malthusian catastrophe. But the exception is critically important; man must develop an alternative energy source. Moreover, the incentive to keep the cost of prime energy as low as possible is immense. In the Age of Substitutability energy is the ultimate raw material. The living standard will almost surely depend primarily on the cost of prime energy.

Further, Goeller and Weinberg speculate that with some combination of breeder, fusion, solar, and geothermal power, it will be possible to develop "satisfactory inexhaustible energy sources" at costs that will not disturb society.

Vincent McKelvey, until 1978 the director of the U.S. Geological Survey, said in an official report on United States mineral resources, in 1973, that he was "confident that for millennia to come we can continue to develop the mineral supplies needed to maintain a high level of living for those who now enjoy it and raise it for the impoverished people of our own country and the world."

We have already said that price is the appropriate measure of raw-material scarcity. The economic approach to forecasting assumes that prices will rise or fall in the future according to the patterns they have followed in the past. Considerable data on trends in raw-material prices are available, and they show clearly that costs for extractive materials have fallen over the course of recorded price history. Thus, the economist's first-approximation forecast is that these trends toward less scarcity should continue into the foreseeable future. (For more information about my method of forecasting, and its philosophical foundations, see Selection 46.)

But how can one judge whether a historical trend is a sound basis for a forecast? Specifically, how can we judge whether data showing declines in raw-material costs in the past are a legitimate basis for prediction? A prediction based on past data is likely to be sound if the past and the future can reasonably be assumed to belong to the same statistical universe—that is, if one can expect conditions that held in the past to remain the same in the future. Therefore, we must ask: Have conditions changed so drastically in recent years that data from the past are now meaningless?

The most important elements in raw-material price trends have been the rate of movement from richer to poorer ores and mining locations—the phenomenon of "exhaustion"—and the continuing development of technology. The latter force has dominated the former, as shown by the fall in the costs of natural resources, decade after decade and century after century. This trend should shake us free from the idea that increasing scarcity is the world's fate. It should point us toward recognizing that technological changes are induced by the demand for resources and for the services they provide. Scarcity and technological advance are not two unrelated competitors in a race; rather, each influences the other.

The last major U.S. governmental inquiry into raw materials was made by the President's Materials Policy Commission (Paley Commission), organized in response to fears of raw-material shortages engendered during and just after World War II. In 1952, the commission warned:

> There is no completely satisfactory way to measure the real costs of materials over the long sweep of our history. But clearly the man-hours required per unit of output declined heavily from 1900 to 1940, thanks especially to improvements in production technology and the heavier use of energy and capital equipment per worker. This long term decline in real costs is reflected in the downward drift of prices of various groups of materials in relation to the general level of prices in the economy.
>
> [But since 1940 the trend has been] soaring demands, shrinking resources, the consequent pressure toward rising real costs, the risk of wartime shortages, the strong possibility of an arrest or decline in the standard of living we cherish and hope to share.

Yet for the quarter-century covered by the commission's forecast, production costs and market prices declined rather than rose. The reasons that the Paley Commission's cost predictions were topsy-turvy should help keep us from making the same mistakes. First, the commission reasoned from the notion of finiteness and from a static techological analysis. Second, it put too much emphasis on the trends of costs over the short period from 1940 to 1950, which included World War II and was therefore almost inevitably a period of rising costs, instead of examining the longer period from 1900 to 1940, during which, as the commission said, "the man-hours required per unit of output declined heavily."

My point is that we should look at price trends (and production costs, in cases where they diverge sharply from price, as with oil) for the longest possible period. The OPEC-led price rise in all resources after 1973 is as frightening for us as the temporary 1940–1950 wartime reversal was for the Paley Commission. But the long-run trends make it very clear that both the cost and the scarcity of materials continuously decline with the growth of income and technology. These trends do not mean that a rosy future is guaranteed. There will always be temporary shortages where there are strife, political blundering, and natural calamities—that is, where there are people. But the natural world allows, and the developed world promotes through the marketplace, responses to human needs and shortages such that one backward step leads to 1.001 steps forward, or thereabouts. There is no convincing economic reason that such modest progress should not continue indefinitely.

5

Will We Run Out of Energy?

Many have accepted the idea that energy comes from sources that are both limited and nonrenewable. This selection continues and deepens the discussion that was begun in the previous selection about energy in general, and oil in particular.

The (non) relationship between practical decisions about the use of energy by society, and the concept of entropy (together with its parent Second Law of Thermodynamics) is discussed in Selection 49.

It is reassuring to see how energy "shortages" have been worrying analysts for centuries. In 1864, W. Stanley Jevons, one of the nine-teenth century's truly great social scientists, wrote a careful, compre-hensive book predicting that England's industry would soon grind to a halt with the exhaustion of England's coal. "It will appear that there is no reasonable prospect of any relief from a future want of the main agent of industry," he wrote. "We cannot long continue our present rate of progress. [This] check for our growing prosperity . . . must render our population excessive." Jevons's investigation also proved to him that there was no chance that oil would eventually solve England's problem.

Because of the future need for coal perceived in England and because of the potential profit in meeting that need, prospectors searched out new deposits, inventors discovered better ways to get coal from the earth, and transportation people developed cheaper ways to move the coal. Other countries did the same. In fact, the proven reserves of coal in the United States are enough to supply a level of use far higher than at present for hundreds or thousands of years. In some countries—Germany, for example—the use of coal is subsidized. This suggests that if more coal had been mined in the past, the present generation would be better off, not worse. As for

Dialogue, no. 56-2/1982, pp. 16–20.

England now (according to a report in The Wall Street Journal *in 1979):*

Though Britain may reach energy self-sufficiency late this year or early next, with its huge reserves of North Sea oil and gas lasting well into the next century, the country is moving ahead with an ambitious program to develop its even more plentiful coal reserves.

Energy is an emotional topic. When asked their number one worry in September 1978, seven times as many people said "inflation" as said "energy." By summer 1979, the numbers were roughly equal. In a 1979 Gallup poll of Americans who drive cars, 82 percent said that "the energy situation in the United States" is "very serious" or "fairly serious." Energy is also a topic about which it is extraordinarily difficult to get any agreement among people on different sides of the controversy.

Energy is the master resource because energy enables us to convert one material into another. As natural scientists continue to learn more about the transformation of materials from one form to another with the aid of energy, energy will be even more important. Therefore, if the cost of usable energy is low enough, all other important resources can be made plentiful. For example, low energy costs would enable people to create enormous quantities of useful land. The cost of energy is the prime reason that water desalination is too expensive for general use; reduction in energy cost would make water desalination feasible, and irrigated farming would follow in many areas that are now deserts. And if energy were cheaper, it would be feasible to transport sweet water from areas of surplus to arid areas far away. Another example: if energy costs were low enough, all kinds of raw materials could be mined from the sea.

On the other hand, if there were to be an absolute shortage of energy—that is, if there were no oil in the tanks, no natural gas in the pipelines, no coal to load onto the railroad cars—then our entire economy would come to a halt. Or if energy were available, but only at a very high price, we would produce much smaller amounts of most consumer goods and services.

Because energy plays so central a role, it is most important that we think clearly about the way energy is found and used. An analysis of the supply of mineral resources identifies four factors as being important: (1) the increasing cost of extraction as more of the resource is used, if all other conditions remain the same; (2) the tendency for engineers to develop improved methods of extracting the resource in response to the rising price of the resource; (3) the propensity for scientists and business people to discover substitutes for the resource in response to increasing demand; (4) the increased use of recycled material.

The supply of energy is analogous to the supply of other "extracted" raw materials with the exception of the fourth factor above; minerals such as iron and aluminum can be recycled, whereas coal and oil are "burned up." Of course this distinction is not perfectly clear-cut: quarried marble is cut irreversibly and cannot be recycled by melting, as copper can; yet even cut marble can be used again and again, whereas energy sources cannot.

The practical implication of being "used up" as opposed to being recyclable is that an increased rate of energy use would make the price of energy sources rise sharply, whereas an increased use of iron would not affect iron prices so much because some of the additional iron could be drawn from such previously used stocks as dumps of old autos. All of this may seem to make our energy future look grim. But before we proceed to the analysis itself, it is instructive to see how in the past, energy "shortages" have frightened even the most intelligent of analysts.

There is no reason to believe that the supply of energy is finite, or that the price will not continue its long-run decrease. This statement may sound less preposterous if you consider that for a quantity to be finite it must be measurable. The future supply of oil includes what we usually think of as oil, plus the oil that can be produced from shale, tar sands, and coal. It also includes the oil from plants that we grow, whose key input is sunlight. So the measure of the future oil supply must therefore be at least as large as the sun's seven billion or so years of future life. And it may include other suns whose energy might be exploited in the future—a belief that requires a lot of confidence that the knowledge of the physical world we have developed in the past century will not be superseded in the next seven billion years, plus the belief that the universe is not expanding—this measurement would hardly be relevant for any practical contemporary decision making.

Energy provides a good example of the process by which resources become more abundant and hence cheaper. Seventeenth-century England was full of alarm at an impending energy shortage due to the country's deforestation for firewood. People feared a scarcity of fuel for both heating and the vital iron industry. This impending scarcity led inventors and business people to develop coal.

Then, in the mid-1800s, the English came to worry about an impending coal crisis. But spurred by the impending scarcity of coal (and of whale oil, whose story comes next), ingenious and profit-minded people developed oil into a more desirable fuel than coal ever was. And today England exports both coal and oil.

Another strand in the story: Because of increased demand due to population growth and increased income, the price of whale oil used in lamps jumped in the 1840s. Then the Civil War pushed it even higher, leading to a whale oil "crisis." The resulting high price provided an incentive for imaginative and enterprising people to discover and produce substitutes. First came oil from rapeseed, olives, linseed, and pine trees. Then inventors learned how to get coal oil from coal, which became a flourishing industry. Other ingenious persons produced kerosene from the rock oil that seeped to the surface. Kerosene was so desirable a product that its price rose from 75 cents to $2 a gallon, which stimulated enterprisers to increase its supply. Finally, Edwin L. Drake sunk his famous oil well in Titusville, Pennsylvania. Learning how to refine the oil took a while, but in a few years there were hundreds of small refiners in the United States. Soon the bottom dropped out of the whale oil market; the price fell from $2.50 or more a gallon at its peak around 1866 to well below a dollar.

This story is prototypical of the intertwined history of resources, population, and civilization. The resource problems that arise become opportunities, and turn into the occasions for the advances of knowledge that support and spur economic development. If berries, roots, and rabbits had not become scarce 10,000 years ago, we would probably still be eating wild rabbits and roots, though perhaps with a tastier sauce than they had then. We need more and bigger problems, rather than just having our problems solved, as conventional economics would have it.

And the story spreads out from the energy resources. There is a direct connection between the deforestation crisis in England in the 1600s and the possibility that you can now travel in a train or car, or in an airplane. The development of coal created the new problem of water in coal mines. This problem led to the invention of the first steam engine for the purpose of driving pumps, and afterwards to a series of much improved pumps. Then someone had the bright idea to put wheels under the engine and run it on rails. *Voilá,* the railroad and the steam automobile, and of course factories with central steam power and belts to transmit the power, and steam farm machines to cut back-breaking and expensive labor. Then someone else replaced the idea of steam power in autos with the internal combustion machine, and that meant you could get around without aid of a hayburner or shank's mare or a bicycle, for better or for worse.

This series of ever-extending developments stemming from the original wood energy crisis in England goes on and on, leading to new resources that are cheaper than the old resources as well as being the founts of additional developments. I'll mention just one more new invention that caught my fancy. The search for new sources of raw materials has led to frozen areas in Canada and Alaska, where there are large deposits that in the past could not be exploited because of lack of technical know-how. Now, under the spur of new opportunities because of diminishing deposits elsewhere, we are developing methods for making the frozen ground produce its riches. One specific: Harbors and docks had to be built to handle the ships transporting the materials. But hauling concrete far north is very expensive. So instead, gravel is piled up and then fresh water is poured on top of the gravel. The water quickly hardens into ice, docks are built cheaply, and we are the beneficiaries of technology that we can use elsewhere.

The Long-Run History of Energy Supplies

Running out of oil has long been a nightmare. In 1885, the U.S. Geological Survey saw "little or no chance for oil in California," and in 1891 it prophesied the same for Kansas and Texas. In 1908, the Geological Survey estimated a maximum future supply of oil that has long since been exceeded. And since then, simliar gloomy official prophesies by the Geological Survey, the Bureau of Mines, the Interior Department, and the State Department have regularly been made and subsequently proven false. Of course this does not mean that every gloomy forecast about oil must be wrong. And forecasts can be over-optimistic, too. But it does show that expert forecasts often have been far too pessimistic. We therefore should not simply take them at face value.

A look at the statistical history of energy supplies shows that the trend has been toward plenty rather than toward scarcity. The relevant measures are the production costs of energy (as measured in time and money) and the price to the consumer; and the relevant data are historical. These data for coal, oil, and electricity show an unambiguous trend toward less scarcity and a great availability of energy. (See Figures 5-1 to 5-3.)

The sharp rise of crude-oil prices in the 1970s does not contradict the long-run conclusion that energy will become more available and less costly. The recent rise was clearly caused by the cartel agreements of OPEC. It is the result of political power rather than of rising extraction costs. When consumers are reaching into their pocketbooks, of course, they are concerned about the market price of oil, not about the production costs. But if one is interested in whether there is, or will be, an *economic* shortage of oil, or if one wants to know about the world's capacity for producing oil, the appropriate indicator is the cost of production and transportation—and that cost, since the first OPEC embargo in 1973, has been only a small fraction of the world-market price.

During the years of the "energy crisis," the cost of oil production has

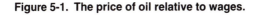

Figure 5-1. The price of oil relative to wages.

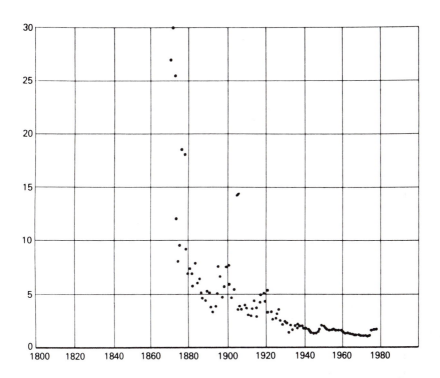

not risen at all. It is far less than 1 percent of the selling price of crude—a cost of perhaps 5 to 20 cents a barrel, in comparison with a selling price of somewhere around $35 a barrel in 1980. For perspective, we should remember that energy prices to the consumer have been falling not only over the very long haul but also in the recent past, since World War II. Before the OPEC cartel went into action, oil prices had been declining relative to those of other commodities. The price of Iranian oil fell from $2.17 a barrel in 1947 to $1.79 in 1959, and the price of oil at Rotterdam was at its lowest point in history in 1969; an adjustment for inflation would

Figure 5-2. The price of oil relative to the consumer price index.

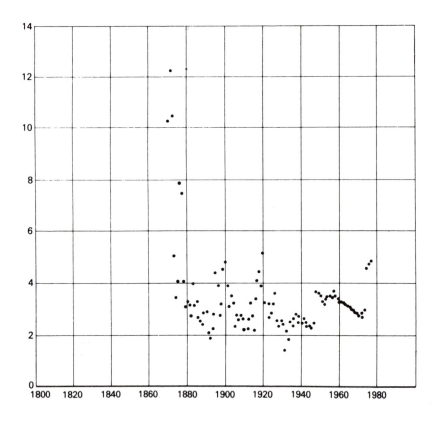

show even more decline. The economist Edward Mitchell has devised an overall index of energy prices, weighted by their dollar values in the economy and deflated by the Consumer Price Index. It shows a steady decline, at an ever-increasing rate, from 1950 to 1973, as follows: 1950, 100; 1955, 96.9; 1960, 93.3; 1965, 87.2; 1970, 79.7; June of 1973 (shortly before OPEC imposed its embargo), 75.3.

Figure 5-3. The price of electricity relative to wages.

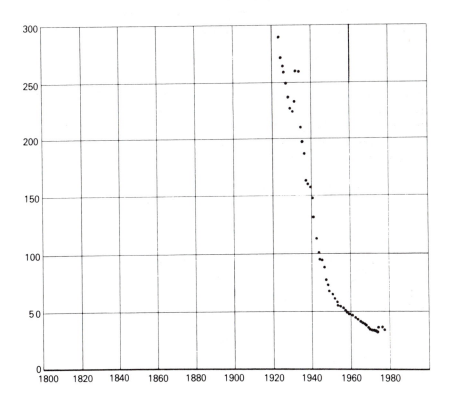

The price history of electricity is particularly revealing because the price of electricity measures the price to the consumer, at home or at work. The ratio of the price of electricity to the average wage in manufacturing shows that the quantity of electricity bought with an hour's wage has steadily increased. Because each year an hour's work has bought more rather than less electricity, this measure suggests that energy has become ever less troublesome in the economy over the recorded period, no matter what the price of energy in current dollars. In short, the trends in energy costs and scarcity have been downward over the entire period for which we have data. And such trends are usually the most reliable bases for forecasts. From these data we may conclude with considerable confidence that energy will be less costly and more available in the future than in the past.

The Theory of Future Energy Supplies

The analysis of the energy future is quite similar to the analysis of natural resources and food, but energy has some special twists of its own that require explanation. First let us dispose of the "law of diminishing returns" with respect to energy. Here is the way environmentalist Barry Commoner uses this idea:

> . . . the law of diminishing returns [is] the major reason why the United States has turned to foreign sources for its oil. . . . Each barrel [of oil] drawn from the earth causes the next one to be more difficult to obtain. . . . The economic consequence is that it causes the cost to increase continuously.

All that need be said here is that this is plain wrong; it costs less today to get oil from the ground in prime sources than it cost 50 years ago to get it from the ground in prime sources.

We must accept that there can be no "true" or "absolute" measure of cost. Rather, different measures of cost give different sorts of information, useful for different purposes. But this we can say with assurance: the average cost of all consumer goods taken together—an index of consumer prices—has fallen over the years in more developed countries, measured in terms of what an unskilled worker can buy, as shown by the long-run increase in the standard of living.

The best way to forecast price trends is to study past price trends, if data are available and if there is no reason to believe that the future will be sharply different from the past.

For energy there are plenty of past price data available, and there is no convincing reason to believe that the future will break completely from the past. Therefore, extrapolation of the trends from available figures is the most reasonable method of forecasting the future of energy supplies and costs, on the assumption that price has been close to cost in the past and will continue to be so in the future. This method of economic forecasting predicts progressively lower energy costs and scarcity.

Geologists and engineers, however, rely on technological rather than price-trend data in their forecasts of energy supplies. Because their forecasts have had so much influence, we must analyze their methods and meanings.

We must first dispose of the preposterous but commonly accepted notion that the energy situation can be forecast with the aid of presently known reserves. This notion is an example of the use of misleading numbers simply because they are the only numbers available.

"Known reserves" are defined as the total amount of oil in areas that have been well prospected. Geologists are quite sure of their existence. Individuals, firms, and governments create known resources by searching for promising drilling areas long in advance of the moment when wells might be drilled—far enough ahead to allow preparation time, but not so far ahead that the investment in prospecting costs will not obtain a satisfactory return. The key idea here is that it costs money to produce information about what are called "known reserves," and therefore people will create only as many known reserves as it is profitable to create at a given moment. The quantity of known reserves at any moment tells us more about the expected profitability of oil wells than it does about the amount of oil in the ground. And the higher the cost of exploration, the lower will be the known reserves that it pays to create. This explains why the quantity of known reserves, as if by coincidence, stays just a step ahead of demand.

Known reserves are much like the food we put into our cupboards at home. We stock enough groceries for a few days or weeks—not so much that we will be carrying a heavy, unneeded inventory that ties up an unnecessary amount of money in groceries, and not so little that we may run out if an unexpected event, such as a blizzard, should descend upon us. The amount of food in our cupboards tells little or nothing about the scarcity of food in our communities, because it does not as a rule reveal how much food is available in the retail stores. Similarly, the oil in the "cupboard"—the quantity of known reserves—tells us nothing about the quantities of oil that can be obtained in the long run at various costs. This explains why the quantity of known reserves, as if by a miracle of coincidence, stays just a step ahead of demand.

A more sophisticated—and even more misleading—approach is to project present growth in demand, assuming the price will remain constant, and then to compare that projection to known reserves, thereby indicating that demand will apparently outstrip supply very soon. Even assuming that the growth in demand at present prices is reasonably estimated—and this would be difficult to do well—all that such a calculation would show is that price must rise in order to lower the demand and raise the supply until demand and supply meet, a basic economic way of looking at supply and demand.

Equally misleading is the assumption that there will be no developments in oil production or in other energy sources that will make future energy costs lower than they would be with the present state of technological knowledge.

Better Technological Forecasting Methods

If one insists on making a technological forecast of the energy supply—even though such a forecast is likely to be inferior to extrapolations of past economic trends—how should it best be done? That is, how might one make a sound technological forecast for oil and energy in the near term—say over the next 10 or 20 years?

During the next decade or two, increases in income and population in the United States and in the world may be assumed to be known, and therefore they can be taken into account as data rather than treated as imponderables. In addition, forecasts of the production of energy in the near-term future utilize two other kinds of information: (1) engineering estimates of the cost of extracting fuel with available technology from such currently unexploited sources as shale oil and wind power, based on calculations of the engineering inputs required for each type of energy source and (2) economic estimates of how many conventional new wells and mines and reactors will be developed at various prices higher and lower than the present energy prices, based on past data about the extent to which firms in the oil, coal, and nuclear industries respond to changes in market prices.

Engineering calculations must play the dominant role in forecasts of the place of nuclear energy, shale oil, solar power, wind power, and other energy sources for which there are considerable uncertainties about technological processes and costs, due to a lack of experience with these sources. But where a source is currently being exploited sufficiently to produce a large body of data about the process of extraction and about producer behavior, as in the case of fossil fuels, empirical economic estimates of supply response to price changes should have the dominant role. The best overall energy forecast, therefore, would be a blend of both the economic and engineering approaches.

There is great variety, however, in the estimates of engineers and scientists about the costs of developing such energy sources as shale oil and nuclear power. Technologists also differ greatly in their guesses about the dangers to life from the various processes. And economists differ considerably in their estimates of the responsiveness of the energy industry to various price levels.

Why do estimates of supply response to price changes differ so widely? There are a host of reasons, including (1) vested interests—for example, the oil companies have a stake in keeping gas prices paid to gas suppliers low so that fewer gas wells will be drilled and more oil will be sold, and hence they want lower estimates of the responsiveness of natural gas supplies to changes in price; in contrast, gas companies have a stake in higher (unregulated) prices, and hence want higher estimates of gas supply responsiveness, (2) basic beliefs about the "finiteness" of potential supplies and about the likelihood of the human imagination to respond to needs with new developments, (3) differences in the scientific imaginations of the engineers and geologists making the estimates, and (4) professional differences among engineers and among economists due to differences in technical approaches.

Let us briefly note which facts all experts agree on, which matters are in dispute, and how the energy situation is tangled with conflicting interests, politics, and ideology.

Agreed-upon facts about oil. (1) Enough oil to supply the world for several decades can be produced in the Middle East at $0.05 to $0.20 per barrel (1978 currency). (2) Transportation from the Middle East to the United States and elsewhere costs $0.50 to $1.50 per barrel. (3) The 1980 world market price for oil was roughly $35.00 per barrel. (4) Apparently, few believe strongly that the price of oil will sharply and continually go up in the future. If anyone really did believe that, it would make sense to buy and stockpile oil for long-term appreciation, even with the cost of storage. (5) Much of the world has not been explored systematically for oil. (6) Estimates of crude-oil reserves are highly sensitive to the definition of crude oil. The U.S. Geological Survey uses a definition that includes only oil that will come to the surface at atmospheric pressure. If one also includes oil that can be forced to the surface under pressure, plus naturally nonliquid oil in shale and tar sands and other sources, the estimate would be considerably greater.

Agreed-upon facts about coal. (1) There are known quantities of coal in the United States and elsewhere that are vast compared with the known quantities of oil. (2) Coal is expensive to transport. (3) In energy yield, coal is clearly cheaper than oil or gas. (4) The use of coal creates pollution that can raise coal's total cost to about that of oil.

Agreed-upon facts about oil substitutes. The market price of oil may affect the market price of other fuels. For example, as soon as OPEC increased the price of oil in 1973, the price of coal and uranium jumped, apparently because the owners of those commodities perceived the greater demand for them. On the other hand, investment in coal and nuclear power is made risky by the possibility that oil prices might fall, which would make investment in coal and nuclear power a financial disaster.

Agreed-upon facts about nuclear power. (1) Electricity can be produced from uranium at perhaps half or two-thirds the current price of oil. This calculation is heavily dependent on the choice of interest rate (more precisely, the cost of capital). (2) In purely physical terms, the supply of nuclear power on this earth alone is awesome and inexhaustible on any human scale. (3) Nuclear fission creates radioactive wastes that raise storage and disposal problems; nuclear fusion is relatively clean, but not yet controllable as an energy source.

The following matters are in dispute:

The future supply of oil. Some technologists tell us that at present prices and rates of consumption, production of oil will peak around the year 1990 and decline thereafter. Other technologists confidently predict that vast new sources of oil will be found as needed. Also in dispute is the amount of oil and other fossil fuels that can be safely burned without creating excessive atmospheric levels of carbon dioxide.

The future supply of natural gas. The American Gas Association says that there is enough gas "to last between 1000 and 2500 years at current consumption." In stark contrast is the estimate quoted by President Carter in 1977. That estimate, made in 1974 by the U.S. Geological Survey, was "6.1 million million cubic meters, 10 years' supply . . . at 1974 technology and 1974 prices." The difference boggles the mind; 10 years' supply versus a 1000 to 2500 years' supply!

The potential effect of oil conservation measures. Some informed persons argue that it is possible to increase greatly the efficiency of oil use, that is, to waste less of it. Other informed persons are doubtful of any great benefits in this respect.

Whether the "alternative" energy sources are practical. Such possible sources as tidal power, ocean thermal power, geothermal power, wind power, fuel cells, conventional solar power, or geopressurized methane and alcohol might be able to compete with oil in the near or not-so-near future if the price of oil were to remain in the long run at the present level. On the other hand, they might not be important even if the price of energy were to double, triple, or quadruple. Tidal power seems the best bet of the lot, especially in Great Britain, where a variety of devices that the sea compresses or bumps to convert its movements into electricity are well into the testing stages. There is less dispute that shale oil, available in vast quantities in the United States and elsewhere, could be profitable at present energy prices.

Also speculative are the possibilities of a variety of new and radical ways to harness solar power, some of which promise energy at remarkably low costs if they are developed.

The danger from nuclear power. The mainline scientific position— expressed in the 1979 report of the National Academy of Sciences Committee on Nuclear and Alternative Energy Systems—concluded that "if one takes all health effects into account (including mining and transportation accidents and the estimated expectations from nuclear accidents), the health effects of coal production and use appear to be a good deal greater than those of the nuclear energy cycle." As to waste disposal, the "risks from the disposal of radioactive waste . . . are less than those of the other parts of the nuclear energy cycle . . . if appropriate action is taken to find suitable long-term disposal sites and method." An article in Scientific American asserts that "the task of disposing of the radioactive waste . . . is not nearly as difficult or as uncertain as many people seem to think it is." And the geoscientist for the American Physical Society's study group on nuclear fuel cycles and waste management says much the same thing: "The problems, including hazards and waste disposal, about which much has been made, are not so serious as commonly pictured." On the other hand, opponents of nuclear energy, such as those associated with the Sierra Club, assert that these assertions about waste-disposal risks are "not true," and are "myths."

The most recent wide-ranging technological survey of long-run energy prospects is that of Herman Kahn and his associates. After surveying the technological, environmental, and cost characteristics of all likely energy sources on the horizon, they concluded, "Energy costs as a whole are very likely to continue the historical downward trend indefinitely. . . ." The basic message is this: "Except for temporary fluctuations caused by bad luck or poor management, the world need not worry about energy shortages or costs in the future."

Conclusions

Extrapolation of long-run cost trends seems to be the most reliable method for estimating future energy availability. Such extrapolation promies continually decreasing scarcity and cost, though this runs counter to popular opinion. At worst, the cost ceiling provided by nuclear power guarantees that the cost of electricity cannot rise far above present energy costs, political obstacles aside.

As to technological forecasts, the best we can do is examine the range of forecasts that are now available and try to learn from the history of such forecasts whether the higher or lower ones are more likely to be correct. In my judgment, Kahn and his associates do their homework best and are on firm technological ground when they say that energy costs are likely to decline indefinitely.

6

The State of World Food Supplies

For decades, fears have been rife that the world is running out of food. This selection responds with data showing that the consumption trend is toward more and better rather than less and worse nutrition, even though the population of the world is growing. The explanation offered in the selection implies that there is no reason to believe that this trend cannot continue forever.

This is being written during the unusually hot summer of 1988. Many people believe that the heat is evidence of the onset of the greenhouse effect. But this is most improbable; the very large variation from year to year around long-term climactic trends makes it quite impossible to conclude anything from the evidence of one or even several years. This is a classic case of leaping to an unsound conclusion because of neglecting statistical variability.

In this summer, too, severe drought is upon the United States. And the drought, with associated fear of food shortages, has occasioned a rash of calls for population control. But the results of the drought actually constitute backhand evidence of the long-run improved condition of the worldwide food situation (aside from the troubles of government surpluses and gluts in rich countries, and of shortages in socialist countries where agriculture is devastated by government control). Though grain production is projected as fully 31 percent below the previous year in the United States, the U.S. Department of Agriculture said "the disaster will have little effect on consumer prices" (Washington Post, *September 13, 1988, p. A4). The shortfall can be buffered by grain in storage, and because food is now readily transported internationally. Compare this with the situation in the seventeenth century, when Gregory King figured that a 30 percent decline in the grain harvest ordinarily led to a rise in food prices of 160 percent (Schumpeter, 1954, pp. 212–213).*

The Atlantic Monthly, July 1981, pp. 72–76.

Starvation deaths in Ethiopia have been cited in the 1980s as evidence of physical constraints upon food supply that require population control. But by 1988 it has become transparently clear that the deaths are the result of actions of the Ethiopian government in reducing food production by forced collectivization as well as forced relocation of some groups for political purposes; even the most zealous anti-populationists no longer claim that population growth is the cause of the tragedy. This appeared in The New York Times *of April 29, 1988 (quoted in* The Freeman, *September, 1988, p. 331):*

> The Government of Ethiopia has so severely restricted emergency relief operations in the country's north, a region ravaged by both drought and war, that as many as two million people are out of reach of any known system of food distribution. . . .

> [H]undreds of thousands of tons of donated food are piling up at ports and may never reach those in need. Agricultural seeds, too, are not being distributed.

The most telling evidence of the trend toward greater food availability and lessened scarcity, despite (and partly as a result of) the growth in the world's population, is the decline in the price of food. This evidence may be seen in Figures 6-1 and 6-2, which show prices relative to wages in the United States, and relative to consumer goods, over the history of the United States, for a representative grain. The meaning of such data is discussed in Selection 40.

The current doomsaying about food and population fulfills the prophecy that I made in The Ultimate Resource. *Following a period of increasing productivity, mounting stocks, and falling prices, Congress enacts restrictions on production—which this year took a record 78.4 million acres out of production—to be compared with the 284 million that are being harvested* (The Wall Street Journal, *September 27, 1988, p. 2). Then a drought occurs, as this year, and the reduced production capacity makes the results more severe than they would otherwise be. That leads to calls for more government intervention, and for population control to prevent impending food shortages. And so it has happened.*

The prediction that food production cannot keep up with population growth has been made repeatedly for more than a decade. For example, in 1968, Paul Ehrlich declared in his best-selling book *The Population Bomb*

Figure 6-1. The price of wheat relative to wages in the United States.

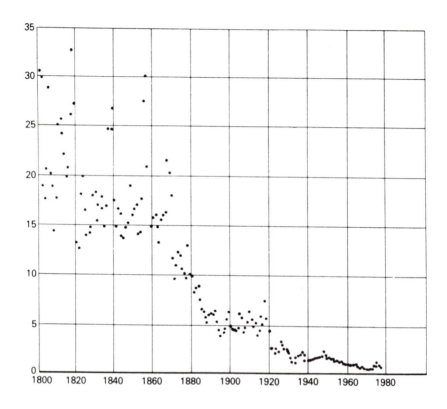

that "the battle to feed all humanity is over. In the 1970s the world will undergo famines—hundreds of millions of people are going to starve to death." In 1975, the United Nations Economic and Social Commission for Asia and the Pacific predicted "500 million starvation deaths in Asia

Figure 6-2. The price of wheat relative to the consumer price index.

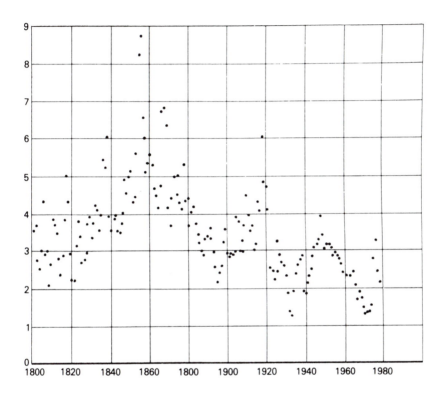

between 1980 and 2025." The following year, the head of the United Nations Food and Agriculture Organization (UNFAO), Edouard Saoma, described the long-term prospects for food production in developing countries as "alarmingly inadequate." In 1975, a full-page advertisement sponsored by the Environmental Fund appeared in leading newspapers. It stated:

> The world as we know it will likely be ruined before the year 2000 and the reason for this will be its inhabitants' failure to comprehend two facts. These facts are:
>
> 1. World food production cannot keep pace with the galloping growth of population.
>
> 2. "Family planning" cannot and will not, in the foreseeable future, check this runaway growth.

The ad was signed by Isaac Asimov, Zbigniew Brzezinski, Malcolm Cowley, Paul Ehrlich, Clifton Fadiman, J. Paul Getty, Henry Luce III, Archibald MacLeish, Albert Szent-Gyorgyi, DeWitt Wallace, and Leonard Woodcock, among others.

Over the past ten years, such pronouncements have multiplied; they seem now to be regarded as facts of life rather than as conjectures. Some people see in these assertions a warrant for triage (see Selection 2 for a discussion of this).

A more severe version of triage is the "lifeboat ethic," proposed by the biologist Garrett Hardin. Hardin argues against giving food to starving people, on the grounds that such aid abets population growth, which will leave future generations worse off.

Despite the popular consensus, buttressed by scientists of various disciplines, that the world is heading toward agricultural ruin, the view of mainstream agricultural economists is quite the contrary. It is an accepted idea among agricultural economists that the trend—as revealed in recent decades by statistics and in the more distant past by historical evidence— has been toward improvement in the food supplies of almost every main population group. For example, in 1973, even before the recent years of bumper harvests, D. Gale Johnson, who teaches agricultural economics at the University of Chicago, told the American Statistical Association that food supply had increased at least enough to match population growth in developing countries for four decades. He discerned a gradual improvement in per capita food consumption for the past two centuries.

The principal evidence for optimism is the record of food production, as represented by data collected by UNFAO from member countries and by the U.S. Department of Agriculture from 104 countries and from American agricultural attachés.

Production of food (as measured by food's adjusted value on the market in a given year, divided by the world population) was either 28 percent or 37 percent higher in 1979 than in the 1948–1952 base period, according to

UNFAO and the USDA, respectively. The difference arises partly from the inclusion of China in the UNFAO figures, and in any case does not qualify the direction of the trend.

Although the two statistical indexes are far less reliable than one would like (economic data usually are), they are all that we have. Numbers that show a worsening trend in recent decades simply do not exist. Nevertheless, people resolutely ignore this silver lining and instead try to find the cloud. Consider, for example, this statement from an article by two demographers in the journal *Population and Development Review*: "During the last 25 years or so the average annual rate of increase of world food production has steadily deteriorated . . . it fell from 3.1 percent in the 1950s to 2.8 percent in the 1960s and 2.2 percent in the first half of the 1970s." I shall leave aside the large question of whether such apparent changes are statistically meaningful. What is interesting for now is the word "deteriorated," which suggests that the world food situation is getting worse. But the data tell us only that the gain—the *improvement*—was greater in the 1950s than it was later; the data *don't* say that food production is not increasing.

Similarly, *Business Week* ran an article on food and illustrated it with a bar graph comparing population with food per capita from 1954 to 1974. It seems at first glance to show population growing faster than food. That would mean a fall in food per capita, which would be a bad sign. But on close inspection we see that food per capita has increased—a good sign. It makes no sense to put a total figure (population) next to a per capita figure (food per capita). Why is it done? People apparently want to believe and to tell others that world food supplies are running out even though—statistically, at least—they are improving.

The incidence of famine is a useful clue to changes in the world's food supply over the years. Famine is hard to define and measure, however, because when nutrition is poor, many people die of diseases and not directly of starvation. Historical studies therefore count as a famine any event that people living in a particular time referred to as such.

According to Johnson, who has surveyed the documentary history of famine and reports the result in his monograph *World Food Problems and Prospects* (1973), "It is highly unlikely that the famine-caused deaths [in the third quarter of the twentieth century] equal a tenth of [those for] the period 75 years earlier." He says that "there has not been a major famine, such as visited China and India in the past, during the past quarter century," and he considers the food supply "far more secure for poor people during the past quarter century than at any other comparable period in the last two or three centuries." Johnson states that many, if not most, of the 12 to 15 million famine deaths that have occurred in this century "were due to deliberate governmental policy, official mismanagement, or war and not to serious crop failure."

Accounts such as this by Johnson are not often mentioned in newspapers or in conversation. Instead, one hears the claim that "a lifetime of malnutrition and actual hunger is the lot of at least two-thirds of mankind," first made by the director of the UNFAO in 1950. Unlike Johnson's assertions, this claim is not based on any data. The UN later reduced its estimate of people in "actual hunger" to between 10 and 15 percent of mankind. Even though the original UNFAO estimate was a guess, a great deal of research into minimum, or satisfactory, dietary needs, and the diets customary in various countries, has now been done, and disproves it. But the statement comes back again and again in popular discussion as evidence that food is not becoming more plentiful.

People say that "the death of a single human being from starvation is an unspeakable human tragedy." This sentiment implies that even if the food supply is improving, the world's population should be reduced so that no person will die from starvation. But, paradoxically, a greater population density seems to diminish the chance of famine. The concentration of population encourages improvements in roads and transportation, and transportation is the key to preventing starvation when crops fail.

The Sahel in Africa is a good example. A reporter for *Newsweek* posted this dispatch in 1972, during the severe drought:

> "Sure, the food is pouring in," observed British Red Cross liaison officer George Bolton, "but how the hell are we going to get it to the people who need it? There isn't a tarred road within a thousand miles of Juba." Bolton wasn't exaggerating. While I was in Juba, I witnessed the arrival of 5000 gallons of cooking oil, which had been diverted from the nearby state of Rwanda. Since the rickety old ferry was not strong enough to carry the oil shipment across the White Nile so it could be distributed to the needy in the interior, the oil was promptly unloaded on the riverbank and stored in Juba.

> And this was not an isolated incident. I saw warehouses in Juba overflowing with millet, dried fish, cooking utensils, agricultural tools, and medical supplies—all useless because nothing could be delivered to the people who needed it.

The Sahel is a case study of food, population, and public relations, as described in Selection 2.

To question the accuracy of the number of dead people in the Sahel may seem heartless, but the number is important: if it exaggerates the magnitude of the problem, we may despair of any solution. Undoubtedly a drought did occur in the Sahel, crops failed, people suffered, and some died. But to suggest that one crop failure was more severe than it was, and that another will be permanent, as the UN has done, is likely to convince us that there is no hope.

Since global data of food production can mask exceptions, let us consider two countries where food has been short: India and Bangladesh.

Net food grain availability—the amount available for human consumption—in kilograms per capita per year has been rising in India since at least 1950–1951. Throughout the 1970s, food production increased at a faster rate than population. Why has India's food supply improved so dramatically? The cause is not an agronomic miracle but an expectable economic event. Most price controls on food were lifted, and price supports were substituted for the controls. Indian farmers had a greater incentive to produce more, so they did. They increased production by planting more crops a year, on more land, and by improving the land they had. They also introduced higher-yield strains and improved fertilizers.

Some people are surprised that Indian farmers could find more land to cultivate. But in fact the total area of Indian cultivated land increased by about 20 percent between 1951 and 1971. In addition, there was a 25 percent increase in irrigated land between 1949–1950 and 1960–1961, and another 39 percent increase between 1961–1965 and 1978.

When Bangladesh became independent, in late 1971, after a devastating war, Henry Kissinger called the country ''an international basket case.'' Since then, the food supply has at times been so low that some writers have advocated ''letting Bangladesh go down the drain,'' whatever that means. Other people organized emergency relief operations. But production began to improve in 1975 and has continued to improve steadily over the years. From 1975 to 1980, Bangladesh's population increased at a rate of 2.7 percent; its food-grain production increased at a rate of 4 percent.

Nevertheless, even though half of the cultivated 22 million acres are suitable for two crops at a time, and some for three, yields per acre remain low. Only 3.4 million acres are irrigated, and there is no strong incentive to increase that amount. Storage capacity in Bangladesh is limited, and about 75 percent of the farms produce for subsistence rather than for the market.

Why would a subsistence farmer grow more than his family can eat? An urban housewife does not buy so many vegetables for the week that they spoil. Malthus spoke of a ''natural want of will on the part of mankind to make efforts for the increase of food beyond what they could possibly consume.'' Food is produced to meet demand, either of subsistence-farming families or of the market. When demand increases, farmers are encouraged to find ways to produce more crops and improve the land.

Food, like other resources, is a market commodity. Wherever it is bought and sold, the most sensible measure of scarcity is price (and the cost of production, which is close to price over the long term). But we must keep in mind that price does not tell us everything about scarcity and social welfare. A product may be readily available, as measured by its low price, and there may still be social damage. For example, a daily ration of vitamin A may be cheap, but if people can't find a store that sells vitamin A, or if they don't believe they need it, then their health is nonetheless jeopardized. On the other hand, caviar may be expensive and scarce, but the lack of caviar has no effect on society's well-being. The price of a week's groceries may be higher now than in a previous year, but there is no harm to society if income also increases. Therefore, though the price of food and the social welfare are often connected, they are not identical.

In this country, the sharp rise in food prices in 1972–1973 was interpreted by many consumers as the harbinger of an increasing scarcity of food. But the trend in food prices over the long term justifies a more cheerful attitude. Because wheat is important in the diets of so many countries, and because its price tends to move in concert with the prices of other grains, it is an important indicator of world food supplies generally. And U.S. export prices for food grains are reasonably representative of world-market prices. Since 1800, the price of wheat relative to wages has fallen sixfold (see Figure 6-1). Relative to an estimated Consumer Price Index over the same period, it has fallen by more than a third (see Figure 6-2). From this point of view, the abrupt price jump that took place in the 1970s is seen to be one of many fluctuations that have occurred in the midst of steady decline.

The decline in wheat prices is hard to believe, especially when one considers the great increase in demand resulting from world population increases and world income increases. But production increased even more—enough to overcome these pressures and keep the price down. There is no reason to assume that the future will not be continuous with the past. Thus, from the historical trend toward cheaper and more plentiful food, it is reasonable to conclude that real prices for food will continue to drop as food becomes more abundant.

Population growth has raised the specter of increased pressure on the land. "More people, less land," the Environmental Fund says.

More people, it is further said, will ruin land, especially in arid areas. *Smithsonian* magazine has editorialized that in the desert, "traditional, more primitive agricultural techniques using natural ecological cycles are all that will work . . . and *that means small populations*." The head of the Population/Food Fund, Charles M. Cargille, M.D., writes that "overpopulation contributes to . . . deforestation and agricultural practices damaging to soil fertility."

Yet the world now eats as well as, or better than, it did in earlier centuries—even in poor countries. This paradox is explained as follows: Reduction in the amount of land available to the farmer causes little hardship if previously he did not need to farm all the land that was available to him. (However, he may have to change his methods so as to cultivate the land more intensively.) Furthermore, when farmers need more land, they make more land. They build land for cultivation by investing their energy, blood, money, and ingenuity in it. The increase in agricultural output as population rises (with or without an accompanying rise in income) has been accomplished, in most countries, largely by increases in the amount of land farmed.

The fact that the amount of arable land in the world is increasing does not forebode diminishing returns in the long run, with successively poorer land being brought into use, because it is also a fact that average yields per acre are increasing. Improvements in yield per acre and total production can be so great that farmers cultivate less land. Such was the case in the United States, for example, until the 1970s.

Although yields have continued to increase in the United States, world demand and changes in government agricultural policies were incentives for farmers to increase their acreage over the last decade. Not only is more pasture and fallow land being cropped now but also new cropland is being created at the rate of 1.25 (or, according to another estimate, 1.7) million acres a year, by irrigation, swamp drainage, and other means. This is a much larger quantity of land than the amount converted to cities and highways each year.

There are places where, for unhappy reasons—usually wars or fights about land tenure—good land that was once cultivated is fallow: Mexico, for example. In the mid-1970s, Mexican peasants, frustrated by the slow pace of agrarian reform, began seizing land. The big estates then cut their investments in fear of more seizures.

The potential for creating new land has increased as knowledge, machinery, and power sources have improved. At one time, most of Europe could not be planted, because the soils were "too heavy." When a plow that could farm the heavy soil was invented, much of Europe suddenly became arable in the eyes of the people who lived there. Most of Ireland and New England were once too hilly and stony for farming, but with effort the stones were removed and the land became "suitable for crops." Now this land is again not worth cropping and has been turned to other uses. In the twentieth century, bulldozers and dynamite have cleared out stumps that kept land from being plowed. And in the future, cheap transportation and desalination may transform what are now deserts into arable lands. The definition of "arable" changes as technology develops and the demand for land rises. Hence any calculation of "arable" land should be seen for what it is—a rough estimate without permanent force.

Experts and laymen alike continue to state the "obvious" (though incorrect) view that there is a limit on the amount of food in the world, and that if some countries consume more, others in need will have less. What I have tried to demonstrate here is that food has no long-run, physical limit. This does not mean that complacency about the food supply is in order. Droughts and famines occur; in some countries, even under orindary circumstances, some people don't have enough to eat. But these conditions are not inevitable; they are rarely permanent. I believe that, with effort and with confidence, they can be reversed.

7

Global Food Prospects: Good News

This selection complements Selection 6 by presenting data on various trends in the food supply—reserve stocks, productivity, arable land, and soil erosion. The article was originally written (with William J. Hudson) as a rebuttal to a writer on food and population whose views are frequently brought to the attention of the public—perhaps as often as all other agricultural economists combined—even though his viewpoint is entirely at odds with the consensus of agricultural economists.

Pessimistic views of the world food picture are rooted in a misreading of historical data. This selection shows that over the long haul, food production per person is rising, prices are falling, and the outlook is for continued improvement.

This piece also offers an opportunity for the reader to assess the quality of the evidence and arguments put forth by a leading doomsayer.

As suggested by the title of his January-February, 1982 article in *Challenge* magazine, "Global Food Prospects: Shadow of Malthus," Lester R. Brown could hardly be more pessimistic about the world's food future. He writes: "The period of global food security is over . . . the worldwide effort to expand food production is losing momentum . . . world food supplies are tightening and the slim margin between food production and population growth continues to narrow."

We think it likely, however, that the events of the future will be exactly the opposite of what Brown predicts. If historical trends continue, the food situation will improve rather than worsen. We so predict because, in our interpretation, the data on past trends show quite a different picture

Challenge, November/December 1982, pp. 40–47 (with William J. Hudson).

from what Brown says they show; his forecasts are based on the wrong empirical premises, we judge. We shall try to present enough data for you to make up your own mind about whose predictions are better founded. And we shall refer back to Brown's earlier forecasts over almost two decades which, we believe, show that his track record has been very poor.

Trends in Total World Grain Production

Brown writes that, "Since 1971, gains in output have barely kept pace with population growth; production per person has fluctuated widely but shown little real increase." Figure 7–1 displays the long-run data for world grain production per capita from 1950, measured in kilograms. These data are similar to those in Brown's basic table except that they cover a longer period, with all the years shown. Why should one compare, as Brown does, the then-peak year 1971 and the "unusually poor harvest" (Brown's words) in 1980? Only such a pick-and-choose comparison is consistent with Brown's gloomy assessment. By almost anyone's statistical or eyeball examination, these data show a continued trend toward more food per person. The improvement in the world food situation is seen to be even more impressive when we look at the data in Figure 7–1 on food production per person, which includes not only grains but also pulses, oilseeds (a very important element in the improvement), vegetables, and fruit (measured by value rather than by weight because of the need to add apples and soybeans). The gain has been at the extraordinary yearly rate of 2.5 percent—and that, remember, is the per person increase, after population growth is allowed for.

The Trend in Food Prices

Brown forecasts that "inevitably real food prices will rise. The question no longer seems to be whether they will rise but how much . . . rising food prices may become a more or less permanent feature of the economic landscape in the years ahead. . . ." But past trends—concerning which Brown shows no data—indicate long-run declines in prices, whether one goes back to 1800 or only to 1900. And it is true whether one measures prices relative to wages in the United States (the most important for U.S. citizens); as a proportion of total income (as with the wage comparison, the fall has been sharper in the now-rich countries, but has also been proceeding in the less developed world); or even relative to the prices of consumer goods, which themselves have been produced ever more cheaply over the years in terms of basic inputs.

Why, then, does Brown think that food prices will rise in the future if

Figure 7-1. World grain and food production per person.

Source: USDA, FAS FG-8-82 (3-15-82); USDA WASDE-133 (5-11-82); Brown, *Building A Sustainable Society* (Norton, 1981), p. 81 (with authors' extrapolation of '81 and '82 population). The Food index includes all food commodities —including grains, pulses, oilseeds, vegetables, and fruit. The index excludes the PRC; the Source: USDA, ERS, Statistical Bulletin No. 669, July 1981. USDA, Personal Communication, Dr. Patrick M. O'Brien (1980, 1981 index).

they have been falling over the long haul? The reason Brown gives is his expectation about energy. He writes about "the new food-fuel competition . . . the shortage of liquid fuel grows. . . . Perhaps more than anything else, the price of food will be influenced by oil price rises." But energy prices, too, have been falling over the long haul, as Figures 5–1 and 5–2 show for oil. (Brown shows no such trend figures for energy to support his forecasts.)

The most recent news about oil prices has told of declines, too, which should reassure those who worry that the long-run trends no longer apply because of structural changes in the world. Though the price of oil jumped enormously in the 1970s, that jump had little or nothing to do with underlying changes in the production costs of oil, but rather reflected the new use of power by OPEC to obtain prices of thirty dollars and more per barrel for Persian Gulf oil that cost thirty cents or less to get out of the ground. We are *not* saying that oil prices will *rapidly* return close to production costs; we only predict that *eventually* they will do so, if all of history and economic knowledge is a guide. And that would bring a trend of lower oil prices rather than the higher prices that Brown forecasts and upon which he builds his forecasts of higher food prices.

Perhaps more than anything else, Brown's forecasts of price rises and other unhappy future trends stem not from dealing carelessly or dishonestly with the data—our impression is that Brown tries hard to be scrupulously honest with the data—but rather arises from his habit of looking at short periods in the past, and choosing to examine those short series at moments when recent fluctuations have been sharply upwards. This short view leads Brown to conclude that there has been a turning point in history, and that the long-run past trends have been reversed. For example, he says, "The long postwar period of food-price stability came to an end with the massive Soviet wheat purchase in 1972. The largest food-import deal in history, it signaled the beginning of a new era." Figure 7–2, reproduced from an earlier book of Brown's, shows how he portrayed the course of then-recent food prices; diagrams like that are enough to lead anyone to forecast doomsday. Examination of Figure 7–3, which shows what happened after the "beginning of a new era," and of the long-run data in Figures 6–1 and 6–2, yields a different impression.

Trends in Soil Quality

Brown sees the United States as exploiting its land for short-run profit, a "sacrifice of the land's long-term productivity . . . mining soils in order to meet the ever growing demand." He writes about "a rate of soil erosion that is draining cropland of its fertility" in the United States and perhaps

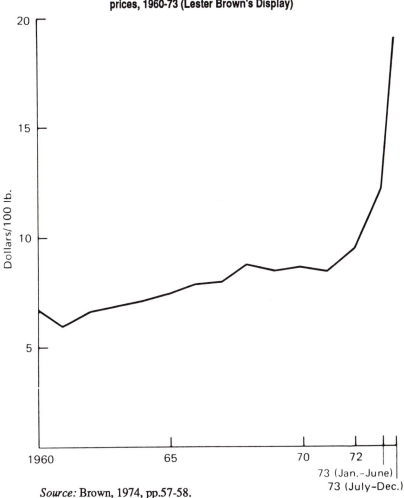

Figure 7-2a. How short-run data can mislead: world rice prices, 1960-73 (Lester Brown's Display)

Source: Brown, 1974, pp.57-58.

elsewhere. And the Worldwatch Institute, which he heads, has raised much public concern about this issue.

Brown does not cite any supporting data. And the aggregate data we know of suggest that the opposite of ruination is happening. Nobel prize-winner Theodore Schultz recently wrote a long article debunking the present scares about soil erosion, following on a discussion by Leo V. Mayer of the U.S. Department of Agriculture (USDA): "There have been two national soil surveys, the first in 1934 and the second in 1977. These surveys provide no support for the many dire pronouncements that soil

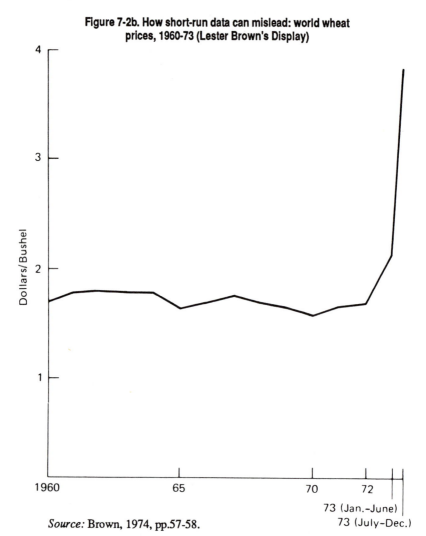

Figure 7-2b. How short-run data can mislead: world wheat prices, 1960-73 (Lester Brown's Display)

Source: Brown, 1974, pp.57-58.

erosion has been going from bad to worse. On the contrary, the proportion of our cropland with only slight erosion increased from 47 percent in 1934 to 77 percent in 1977. To the extent that this evidence is reliable, it is a remarkable achievement. I know of no compelling reasons why this favorable secular trend cannot be continued." Three nationwide survey inventories of land use in 1958, 1967, and 1975 were conducted by the Soil Conservation Service. Their findings were that, "The quality of cropland has been improved by shifts in land use." A larger proportion of the cropland recently has been in the best "capability" classes, and a smaller

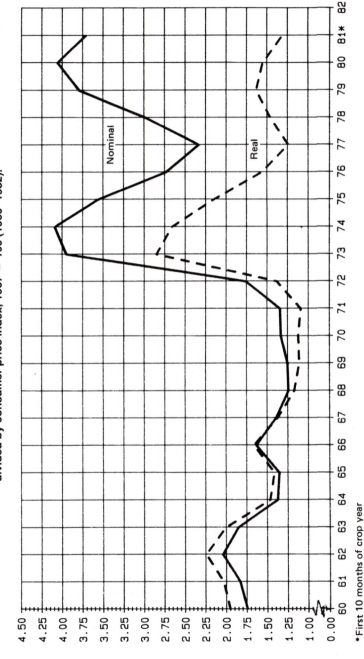

Figure 7-3. Average wheat prices received by U.S. farmers. Real is nominal divided by consumer price index, 1967 = 100 (1960–1982).

*First 10 months of crop year

*First two months of crop year '81-'82.

Source: USDA WAS-23 (10-80); USDA Agricultural Prices, Prl (4-82); 1982 is for first two months of crop year '81-'82.

proportion in the worst capability classes, than in earlier years. Schultz adds: "I am a bit harsh on those who are arguing erosion is catastrophic. It simply isn't true" (letter of March 25, 1982). (See Selection 9.)

Productivity Trends

As of 1978, Brown was writing in the *New York Times* that "per-acre yield of all cereals in the United States peaked in the early '70s." But in his 1982 article in *Challenge,* he shows yields per acre as 1950-1.05; 1960-1.26; 1970-1.62; 1980-1.89. These figures are plotted in Figure 1–2, and show a strong upward trend. Given this evidence that productivity continued to rise, Brown now warns us about a "slower rate of yield increase." But even that is not supported by the data. Earl Swanson shows that yield has continued to rise at the same amount of yield per year. In Figure 7–4 we see his plot of corn yields in the last four decades; the trend is at least linear in absolute gains, and may be faster than linear. Close examination of corn and soybean yields in Illinois, holding weather and other factors constant, confirms the impression given by the figure that, "Both corn and soybean yields in Illinois are still trending upward. Nothing in this study indicates that there is a leveling off, contrary to predictions a few years ago. As long as producers continue to adopt favorable production practices, which stem largely from research efforts, then yields should continue to rise for some time. Only if the research base for developing future management practices declines will there be a leveling off of corn and soybean yields" (1980, p. 9). Overall U.S. agricultural productivity continues to increase at the same absolute rate, too.

Trends in Idle U.S. Cropland

Brown writes that "for the first time in a generation, there is no cropland idled under U.S. farm programs," a key statement of his analysis. But in the months since Brown wrote his article, Secretary of Agriculture John Block was putting strong pressure on farmers to set aside cornland and wheatland. And as of this writing on April 21, 1982, *The Wall Street Journal* reported that "farmers signed up nearly 80% of their eligible cropland for a program that offers them financial benefits on the condition that they plant fewer acres this spring. Corn and grain sorghum farmers signed up 74% of their cropland, and wheat farmers signed up 84%." The result will be food production lower than it would be otherwise. (We wonder whether Brown will consider that a good sign or a bad sign.)

Figure 7-4. Average corn yields in the United States, 1930–1979.

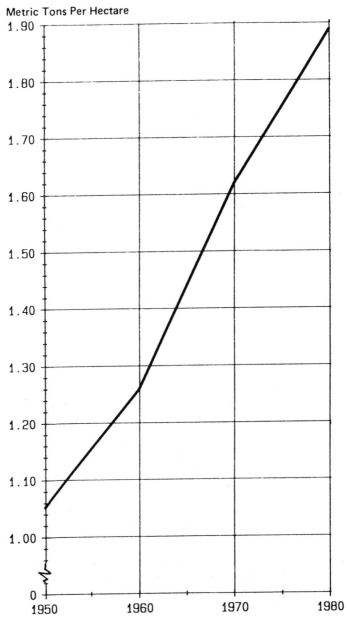

Source: Brown, *Challenge*, January-February 1982, p. 19.

Trends in Food Storage

Brown sees "growing food insecurity" in the trends of world stocks of food reserves. It should be useful to note that he has seen the situation in the same way for quite a while. In 1974 he titled a section of his book, *In The Human Interest*, "Growing Global Food Insecurity." And he presented a graph as shown in Figure 7–5, which purports to show a combination of "global reserve stocks of grain" with the "grain production potential of idle cropland," combined as "world grain reserves."

Just as with his 1982 data, the 1974 figure showed (1) things apparently getting worse, and (2) the data for the first years charted as the best years, and the last years charted as the worst years. Yet despite his 1974 assessment, the food situation has gotten better and more secure, rather than worse and less reliable. Why did Brown go wrong on this, and why do we think he is again headed in the same wrong direction?

We first differ from Brown in that he looks only at an index combining idled farmland and food stocks, whereas we think food stocks alone are the more meaningful measure. But in Figure 7–5 we present both indices for completeness.

Figure 7-5. World grain stock as days of utilization.

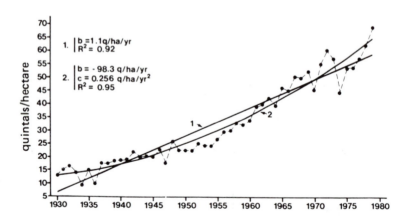

Source: Earl R. Swanson, "Agricultiral Productivity and Technical Progress: Acceleration or Atrophy?" Mimeo working paper, Dept. of Agricultural Economics, University of Illinois. January 1981.

In our view, the best perspective is the longest possible data series, in all detail. We see in Figure 7–5 some long-run trend downward. But in our view this is a good sign, reflecting increased efficiency in worldwide grain storage, just as increased efficiency in industrial inventory control leads to lower inventories and less cost for keeping them.

And the very latest reports? As of this writing on April 17, 1982, the headline on the Associated Press story in our local paper was "U.S. Grain Stockpiles At Record High," and the headline adds "Which May Hurt American Farmers." So—too little grain in storage or too much?

Famine Deaths

In support of his claim that the agricultural situation is worsening, Brown refers to events in India and the Sahel. On the latter he writes: "During the seventies, hunger also took a heavy toll in Africa, where a prolonged drought in the Sahel brought the deteriorating food situation into sharp focus. Senegal, Mauritania, Niger, Upper Volta, Chad, and Mali—all lost lives. No one knows exactly how many died of starvation and hunger-related disease, though Cornell nutritionist Michael Latham testified before the U.S. Congress that the number may have been in excess of 100,000." Earlier one of us dug into this case, and found the astonishing results seen in Selection 2.

Lumber

Lumber has been cited as an exception to the general story of falling agriculture costs. For decades in the United States, farmers clearing land disposed of trees as a nuisance. As lumber came to be more a commercial crop and a good for builders and railroad men, its price rose. For some time, resource economists expected the price to hit a plateau and then follow the course of other raw materials as the transition to a commercial crop would be completed. There was evidence consistent with this view in the increase, rather than the popularly supposed decrease, in the tree stock in the United States, yet for some time the price did not fall. But now that expectation seems finally to have been realized as prices of lumber have fallen to a fourth of their peak in the late 1970s. Selection 4 goes into more details about natural resources.

Whom Should You Believe?

At this point, the reader naturally wonders: Whom should I believe? You can rest assured that the data we offer here are the only data that exist, stemming from the United Nations and the USDA; there is no discrepancy between our data and Brown's, because Brown does not offer trend data pertaining to most of the issues in dispute. But Brown and the

Worldwatch Institute are surely the most quoted sources on agricultural matters in the U.S. press, and they are the source of many of the current scary stories on soil erosion, urbanization of land, and world desertification. Is it even possible that they might be completely wrong?

It should be illuminating to know that Brown has changed his mind completely on these matters, and not just once but twice. When he began his public career he argued that the food situation was frightening. Beginning in 1964, he worked with Secretary of Agriculture Orville L. Freeman as advisor on foreign agricultural policy and as Administrator of the International Development Service, the technical assistance arm of the Department. His point of view is captured in the opening line of a statement he prepared for the Secretary of Agriculture in 1965: "The less developed world is losing the capacity to feed itself."

Then came the "new, high-yielding cereals and the men who developed them . . . I am fortunate to have had a front-row seat in this historic drama," he wrote. Brown was so impressed that his 1970 book, *Seeds of Change*, "tells the story of the turnaround on the food front." He became so optimistic that his main worry became whether the poor countries would be able to export all the food they would grow. "The pivotal question is whether the rich countries . . . are prepared to open their internal markets to cereal exports from the poor countries."

Then his view changed again—despite the fact that there had been no basic change in the food-supply trends of the previous two decades and more—and he again became exceedingly pessimistic, as we have seen. This was not the double-flip-flop of an amateur or casual observer. Brown has been deeply involved in food and agriculture as a professional since 1964.

All honor to a person who can change his or her mind, and all admiration for a person who has the courage to reverse his or her public stand. But as Arthur Schlesinger wrote in another context: "How many times does an expert have to be wrong before he loses his reputation for expertise?"

8

Worldwide, Land for Agriculture Is Increasing

In the 1970s, the world's food future was widely believed to be
jeopardized by a decline in arable land caused by "desertification"
and urbanization. This short piece documents that the fear of desert-
ification is (forgive me) groundless. Urbanization will be addressed in
selections to come.

When looking down from an airliner window and seeing how much
of the land below is devoid of any signs of human life—I once read
that 95 percent of the world's population lives within a short distance
of the ocean or a river—I find myself wondering how people can worry
about humanity running out of land to live on. And this is how Tom
Wolfe in The Right Stuff *summarized Antoine de Saint-Exupery's*
experience: "As he gazed down upon the world . . . from up there
. . . during transcontinental flights, the good Saint-Ex saw civilization
as a series of tiny fragile patches clinging to the otherwise barren
rock of Earth. He felt like a lonely sentinel, a protector of those
vulnerable little oases . . ." (Bantam, 1979, p. 32).

The amount of agricultural land in the world is continuing to rise, just as
in the past centuries, despite popular belief that it is fixed in quantity. The
United States' food supply is not endangered by the conversion of United
States farmland to other uses.

Despite reports about waterlogging and salting up of land, and advancing
deserts, the overall world trend shows increasing rather than decreasing
cropland.

A demographer, Joginder Kumar, found in a study at the University of
California at Berkeley that there was 9 percent more total arable land in

The New York Times, October 7, 1980, p. 23.

1960 than in 1950 in 87 countries for which data were available and which constituted 73 percent of the world's total land area. And United Nations data show a 6 percent rise in the world's arable, permanent cropland from around 1963 to 1977 (the last date for which data are available).

More people imply smaller farms per farmer, everything else being equal, and hence a harder struggle to produce enough to eat. A larger population seems to mean more "pressure" on the land, until each of us is nightmarishly scratching out three skimpy meals from 18 hours of work a day on a plot the size of a windowbox. But the data tell a different story: In America, England, and other developed countries, the absolute number of farm workers is going down and the absolute amount of land per farm worker is going up, despite the fact that the total population is growing. That is, the absolute number of acres per farmer is increasing, despite increases in population and income.

The total amount of cultivated land is going down in some countries such as the United States. But this decline is by no means a bad sign. Total agricultural output and yield per acre in America have been going up so sharply that "overproduction" is a problem. This high output is obtained in large part with huge farm machines requiring flat land for efficiency. The combination of increased productivity per acre of good land, and increased use of equipment adapted to flat land, has made it unprofitable to farm some land that once was cultivated.

Does population growth produce "urban sprawl," and do highways "pave over" and take away "prime farm land" from agricultural and recreational uses? There are a total of 2.3 billion acres in the United States. Urban areas plus highways, nonagricultural roads, railroads, and airports total only 61 million acres—just 2.7 percent of the total. Clearly, there is little competition between agriculture and cities and roads.

How about the trends? From 1920 to 1974 (the most recent accounting, in the 1974 census of agriculture), land in urban and transportation uses rose from 29 million acres to 61 million acres—a change of 32 million acres (1.42 percent) out of the total of 2266 million acres in America. (Data from the 1978 census of agriculture are not yet available.) During those 54 years, population increased from 106 million to 211 million people.

Even if this trend were to continue—and population growth clearly is slower than before—there would be no significant impact on agriculture. Furthermore, between 1.25 million and 1.7 million acres of cropland are being created yearly with irrigation, swamp drainage, and other reclamation techniques. This is a much larger quantity of new farmland than the amount that is converted to cities and highways each year. Compare this with the nightmarish view that land is fixed in quantity and that agricultural land capacity is being "lost" to cities and highways.

A larger number of people and increasing use of land for cities and agriculture apparently implies less recreational land and the disappearance of wilderness. But the facts are otherwise. Land dedicated to wildlife areas and state and recreational parks has risen from 8 million acres in 1920 to more than 61 million acres now. Even more important than the number of acres of land for recreation is the availability to the potential user of recreational land and wilderness. The average American now has far greater access to recreational land and wilderness than did people at any earlier time—greater than did a king 200 or 100 years ago—because of fast, safe transportation.

I am not suggesting that we cease worrying about the supply of land, worldwide or nationally. Just as each homeowner must take care of his lawn lest it go to ruin, and just as every farmer must continually protect and renew his acres, so must every country take care that its stock of good land is increased and improved. What I am suggesting is that there is no ground for the panic into which anecdotal accounts can throw us. And there is no basis in the data examined here for opposition to economic or population growth.

9

Are We Losing Our Farmland?

In 1989 it seems hard to believe that urbanization of farmland could
have been whipped up into a big enough issue to warrant cover
articles in news magazines and feature stories on television. The
whole scare was cooked up at the end of the 1970s from a single
misanalyzed tiny survey, together with the desire of affluent home-
owners that rural land near their homes not become new housing.

This selection, together with Selections 10 and 11, presents the
underlying facts. Selection 53 discusses the journalism and politics of
the matter.

The scare stories in the newspapers and on television about the loss of
cropland to urbanization in the United States are statistically unsound, yet
the misinformation contained in them has already had destructive effects
on individuals and upon the economy. Bernard J. Frieden, in the Spring
1979 issue of *The Public Interest,* discussed the impact on people who
want to build and buy new homes. But there are also ill effects on industrial
development, on farm planning, and on the incentive to farm—all the
outcomes of restrictions on economic mobility in the name of "saving
prime farmland."

The source of many or most of these news stories was the National
Agricultural Lands Study (NALS), whose booklet—distributed across the
country and given away in lots of 5000 and 10,000 to a variety of organizations—was titled, "Where Have the Farmlands Gone?"

The issue is clearcut: Should we be concerned about the amount of U.S.
farmland, and of cropland in particular, that is currently being converted
for urban uses? I emphasize that this is the all-important question, because

The Public Interest, No. 67, Spring, 1982, pp. 49–62.

it is easy to forget just what it is we *are* interested in amid all the confusing arguments, counter-arguments, and numbers.

The answer to the central question must depend on *how much* of our cropland, present and potential, is currently being transformed for urban uses. I suggest that the likely amount is only about *one-third* of the amount claimed by NALS in its national campaign to arouse concern about the issue, a rate probably no greater but rather less than in the past, and certainly not three times the rate of the recent past as claimed by NALS. This true rate is not likely to worry those knowledgeable about agriculture.

What *Is* Farmland?

To avoid grave confusion, some terms must be defined. "Farmland" or "agricultural land" usually includes cropland, pastureland, forest land, and land in other agricultural uses. "Cropland" means land on which field crops such as corn and wheat are usually grown. The statistical and economic differences between "farmland" and "cropland" are enormous, and have led to gross confusion. For example, a recent estimate of conversions of pastureland and forestland to other uses (including "wetlands") has been almost 3 million acres, even though absolutely no one seriously claims that the amount of cropland being converted annually is greater than two-thirds of a million acres. "Harvested cropland" for a given year excludes cropland left fallow for that year. "Prime farmland," as the term is used by the Soil Conservation Service (SCS), is most peculiar: It includes some land that is now covered with water and some that has never been used for agriculture, and it also refers to potential cropland as well as land currently used for crops. (This is quite different from common usage, and would make most farmers laugh. For example, in the farm advertising section of *The Wall Street Journal,* "prime" invariably refers to land that is now highly productive of crops.)

Another important likely source of confusion lies in the NALS's extraordinary definition of "agricultural land." It includes all nonfederal land not in "nonagricultural" uses such as rural transportation rights-of-way and water impoundments. That is, their definition of agricultural land includes all waste land, such as deserts, swamps, and mountain ranges. The possible mixups caused by this definition need not be spelled out.

Our Ultimate Concerns

The farmland-preservation campaigners suggest that we are riding negative trends, that bad things have happened and are happening to us because of the conversion of land to built-up uses. For example, Cecil D.

Andrus, former Secretary of the Interior and now a speaker for the American Farmland Trust, said in a talk called "Pave now, pay later": "The federal government itself has been one of the worst land-abusers in the nation; every mile of interstate highway, for example, consumed 48 acres of land. . . ." But consider this: The number of acres of land covered by rural highways actually *went down* from 1969 to 1977—according to NALS data! This apparent absurdity is the result of a small amount of roadway changing from the rural to urban category, and should be ignored, but it does make clear that there is no substantial *increase* in rural highways. And if we look at the more inclusive category of *all* roads and streets, rural and municipal, the U.S. totals for 1950, 1960, 1970, and 1978 were 3313; 3546; 3730; and 3885 thousand miles respectively. In light of those data, there is no conceivable way that anyone can find a credible threat to farmland due to road building.

Now let us go to broader issues. We must first examine a few long-term trends to see if we really have been moving in a negative direction, focusing on what *ultimately* concerns us—quantities and prices of food, trees, housing, and so on. We must remember that farmland by itself is only an instrument to provide food and fiber rather than being of intrinsic value, except to those who love it for its own sake.

The Quantity of Food

U.S. food production has been going up by leaps and bounds. To avoid trying to add apples and oranges, which can only be done by summing their money value, let us look at one representative and very important crop—corn. Figure 9–1 shows that total corn production has been rising rapidly in recent decades. This means more to be consumed by Americans as vegetable and meat, and more to sell abroad. No grounds for concern there.

The Price of Food

We are said by prominent worriers to be on a rising price trend. With each successive year less and less work has been required to buy a bushel of wheat. This means that a smaller proportion of our income has been needed to buy farm output with each passing year. And even compared to other products, as measured by the consumer price index, the price of food has not been going up and probably has gone downward. Those trends look cheering rather than distressing.

Figure 9-1. U.S. acreage, yield, and production of corn, 1870–1960.

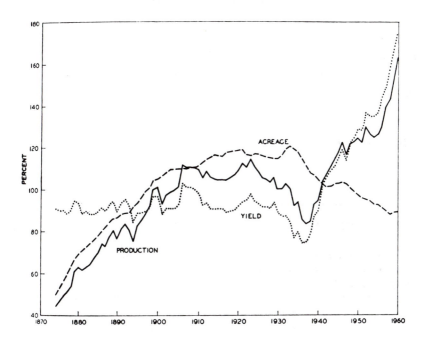

Source: James O. Bray and Patricia Watkins, "Corn Production
in the United States, 1870-1960," *Journal of Farm Economics,*
1964, p.753.

Trees

We must consider whether increased food production is at the expense
of other important goods and services. Trees are a possible competitor,
both for recreation and for wood. Table 9–1 shows that the amount of
wood being grown has been on the rise rather than on the decline in recent
years; the forest acreage has about stabilized. Lumber prices have risen as
we have made the transition to commercial tree-growing from cutting wood
for farmland; this upward trend therefore need not continue in the long-
run future.

Recreation Land

Land devoted to recreational uses has been increasing and visits to
recreation areas have been growing by leaps and bounds.

Table 9-1. Net Annual Growth of Sawtimber and Growing Stock on Commercial Timberland, by Region

Region	1952	1962	1970
North	4.1	4.9	5.5
South	6.3	7.5	8.6
Rocky Mountain	1.2	1.3	1.4
Pacific Coast	2.3	2.7	3.1
Total	13.9	16.4	18.6

Source: Perspectives on Prime Lands, U.S. Department of Agriculture, Background papers for Seminar on the Retention of Prime Lands July 16-17, 1975, sponsored by the USDA Committee on Land Use, p.21. Originally from U.S. Department of Agriculture, Forest Service 1973, *The Outlook for Timber in the United States,* For Res. Rpt. No. 20. Data for 1952 and 1962 differ from data published in earlier reports because of adjustments based on newer information from remeasured forest survey plots. Data for all years are "trend level" estimates. Data may not add to totals because of rounding.

Wetlands

Perhaps most amazing is that even the amount of "wetlands"—what used to be called swamp and marsh—is increasing even though environmentalists have been lamenting its decline. That is, new wetlands are being created faster than the old ones are being drained. About 7 million new acres of wetlands were created between 1967 and 1975. And the Soil Conservation Service says that "there is strong evidence that the total acreage of water and associated wetlands will increase rather than decrease in the future."

Cropland and Farm Productivity

Cropland

Now the astonishing trend in cropland: For some crops such as corn, the trend has been somewhat downward, as seen in Figure 9–1. By now this trend may be understood as not worrisome, but largely a response to increased yield and to the demand for other valuable crops, rather than "encroachment" by cities. Land in field crops taken altogether clearly has been increasing rather than decreasing. One source of data is the Censuses of Agriculture for 1969, 1974, and 1978. Harvested cropland rose from 1969 to 1974, and then from 1974 to 1978. An even more reliable source of such data is the Crop Reporting Board. After a drop, harvested cropland rose from just over 290 million acres between the mid 1960s and the early-1970s, to around 340 million acres near the end of the 1970s, according to the CRB.

These data show, as conclusively as such data can ever show anything, that the Soil Conservation Service's claims about decreases in cropland are unfounded. Based only on their 1967 and 1975 surveys—the main source of data for all the recent stories in the media—they say that between 1967 and 1975, "Cropland declined from 431 million to 400 million acres." And if the SCS and the NALS are so wrong about this key number, there is reason to be sceptical of their other assertions.

It may well be true that we would have even more trees and parks and wetlands if farmland did not compete with them. But to say so is simply to recognize that now, as always, we live in a world of scarcities, which is not news. What *is* news is that, with respect to all these farmland-related goods and services, our situation has been getting better rather than worse, less scarcity rather than more. This set of trends may well seem paradoxical. We often think of ours as a zero-sum world: It seems to us that having more of one thing must mean less of others. Instead, we have been getting more of *all* the good things.

The mechanism enabling all these good things to happen at once—together with the increase in cropland, which we shall consider next—is increased farm productivity. We can see the startling recent productivity gains in Figure 9–1. Please note that this increased productivity is relatively recent, starting in the late 1930s.

One may wonder whether some sort of subtle exploitation of our existing capital is going on, enabling us to have all these good things at once. One candidate might be agricultural land quality. Are we doing all this at the expense of destroying prime land and lowering the quality of agricultural land? In fact, the quality of the cropland in use has been going up year by year. To quote the Soil Conservation Service:

> The quality of cropland has been improved by shifts in land use. In 1975, 86 percent (344 million acres) of America's cropland (400 million acres) was in capability classes I–III, compared with 83 percent in 1967 and 1958. In 1975 only 10 percent of the cropland was in capability class IV, compared with 11 percent in 1967 and 1958. Cropland in capability classes V–VIII also declined— in 1975 it was 4 percent, compared with 5 percent in 1967 and 6 percent in 1958.

And on the subject of cropland quality the SCS surveys are well-fitted to provide a reliable assessment.

Why the Numbers Do Not Add Up

A reasonable reader will surely ask at this point: What is the basis of the widely publicized claims by the National Agricultural Lands Study, the Soil Conservation Service, the Department of Agriculture, the Council on Environmental Quality, and other organizations, that we are "losing" farmland at a rate which they say is dangerous to future nutrition and the economy? The NALS and SCS people do not deny that the trends described above are correctly represented. They say, however, that there has recently been a major break with the past in the rate of urbanization of farmland, that recent history is fundamentally different from earlier history. More specifically, they say that the rate of conversion of farmland jumped around 1967 from less than 1 million acres a year to around 3 million acres a year. We must examine closely the SCS survey evidence that they offer for that claim, and we will find the evidence is flawed.

Before discussing the methods used in the SCS surveys, please consider for yourself whether a "loss" of 3 million acres a year is at all plausible in light of other contradictory data, and of the following general considerations.

1. One of the troublesome aspects of dealing with the statistical statements being publicized by NALS is that many different versions are given for the same magnitude, even by the same organization. For example, on the first page of the "Executive Summary" of the NALS "Final Report" we find:

> The United States has been converting agricultural land to nonagricultural uses at the rate of about three million acres per year—of which about one million acres is from the cropland base. This land has been paved over, built on, or permanently flooded, i.e., converted to nonagricultural uses. For practical purposes, the loss of this resource to U.S. agriculture is irreversible.

The quote says that this estimate includes conversions to water. Elsewhere in NALS literature, however, we come across an estimate of 3 million acres yearly that does *not* include conversions to water. And in the NALS literature we sometimes find a figure of 2 million acres a year for urban land, and other times we find a larger figure for urban and water. And we also frequently read that the Potential Cropland Study data indicate that 675,000 acres of cropland became urban or water, which is quite at odds with the "one million acres" in the quote just above for which no documentation is shown anywhere (which is not to say that 675,000 acres is nearly correct, either).

Another example: A November, 1979 SCS memo (revised February 1980) called "Basic Statistics: 1977 National Resources Inventory" gives 89,956 million acres for "urban and built-up land." In the Agricultural Land Data Sheet prepared by NALS (presumably from the same 1977 NRI) 68,789 is given for "urban and built-up" in 1977 and 25,408 for "rural transportation," a total of 94,197 million acres. These discrepancies do not seem explicable as typographical errors, and they make it very difficult for the outsider to come to grips with this body of data and the NALS presentation of it. (These are only the *internal* inconsistencies in the SCS-NALS material; we have yet to consider *external* inconsistencies. Still within the USDA, the Economic Research Service's estimate for "urban and built-up" is 61 million acres whereas the NRI estimate is 90 or 94 million.)

2. NALS and everyone else agrees that the *total* urban-and-built-up area in the United States (excluding transportation) was around 31–35 million acres as of 1967.[1] There is also agreement that the *rate* of urbanization had been constant or slowing, a lower rate in 1960–1970 than in 1950–1960. Yet NALS says that over only ten years, from 1967 to 1977, there was a 29 million acre *increase* in urban-and-built-up land. That is, over the course of more than two centuries, in the process of reaching a population of about 200 million people, the U.S. built towns on between 31 and 35 million acres. Then (NALS says) suddenly in the course of another 10 years, and with a population increase of only 18 million people, the urban-and-built-up acres increased by 29 million acres (almost none of it due to transportation), a near-doubling. Does that make sense?

To put it differently, the long-run trend in the decades up to 1970 was about one million acres of *total* land urbanized per year. SCS asserts that the rate then jumped to between 2 and 3 million acres yearly from 1967 to 1976 or 1977, depending on which version you read. Even stronger, if the 1 million acre yearly trend held until 1970, then SCS would necessarily be estimating an even *higher* rate for the shorter period from 1970 to 1975, up to 5 million acres a year. Can you remember any basic changes taking place in our society that would be consistent with a shift of that magnitude—from 1 million to 3 or 5 million acres yearly?

The South and the Swamps

3. SCS shows (Table 9–2) the biggest "loss" of agricultural land in general, and of cropland in particular, in the South—12.0 out of 23.2 million total acres, and 2.5 out of 5.4 million cropland acres, respectively.

Table 9-2. Agricultural Land Converted to Urban, Built-up, Transportation, and Water Uses by Selected Census Regions, 1967 to 1975

Region	Cropland	Pastureland and Rangeland	Forestland	Other Agricultural Uses	Total
West	0.7	1.3	0.5	0.5	3.0
North Central	1.6	0.8	0.7	2.1	5.2
South	2.5	2.1	3.9	3.5	12.0
Northeast	0.6	0.1	1.4	0.9	3.0
Total	5.4	4.3	6.5	7.0	23.2

Source: Potential Cropland Study, USDA-SCS, 1977. In its text NALS talks about 24 million acres—17 million connected to urban and 7 to water—and therefore I have adopted their usage in the text, despite the 23.2-million-acre total in this table.

But it is amply clear that the land story of the South in recent decades has been the massive abandonment of cropland to forest and to scrubland simply because it is no longer economical to farm cotton and similar crops.

That there is something wrong with the SCS land-conversion data may be seen in an analysis of purported conversion of agricultural land to urban and water in the Southeast. If we look at the Southeast states alone—Florida, Georgia, North Carolina, and South Carolina—we see in Table 9-2 that they account for 5.9 million acres, fully 25 percent of the 23.2 million total U.S. acres said to be converted to urban uses. These states contain about 7.7 percent of total U.S. population. This seems implausible. Nor have those states accounted for a huge preponderance of recent population increase.

Part of the reason for these numbers is conversion to water—3.3 million acres of the total 5.9 million acres converted in the Southeast—and this does not seem to signal an agricultural problem of any sort.[2] This is probably mostly *swamp,* because this quantity is much larger than the 2.6 million acres they estimate as having shifted into urban uses in the Southeast; it clearly does not represent reservoirs or other bodies of water for urban purposes. (Chances are that much of the 3.3 million acre shift is simply due to reclassification of the Everglades.) Furthermore, the 2.6

milion acres said to be urbanized in the Southeast is about 15 percent of the U.S. total of 17 million acres. This suggests that some land that simply went out of cropland use probably became recorded as urban, because we know that much of the South has done just that—either become forest or gone out of use entirely.

In short, worry about the loss of "prime farmland" (or *any* farmland) to urbanized areas in the South seems groundless. And these "conversions" in the South are a very substantial chunk of NALS's all-U.S. figures; removing them would lower the "loss" figures by about half. The same is true of the Northeast. In New Hampshire the tillable area was 2,367,000 acres in 1860, but by 1974 it had declined to 172,000 acres, though New Hampshire now has lots of forest. Would it make sense to worry about loss of farmland in places like New Hampshire? The land went out of cultivation because it was stony and hilly, and because crops grow cheaper in the Midwest, not because of "encroaching" cities.

4. At last estimate, between 1.3 and 1.7 million acres a year of new cropland are being created by drainage of swamps, irrigation, and so on. That is more than the million or so acres a year of cropland that were being urbanized up through 1970—and probably up until now, too.

5. NALS points to migration within the United States as being largely responsible for an increased rate of conversion of "prime farmland" since 1967. But recent migration has been largely toward the Sunbelt rather than toward the Midwest, that is, away from rather than toward "prime farmland" areas. The point is even more salient if one is concerned with *export* crops, rather than the table vegetables grown in Southern California.

6. For the period 1900–1950, the number of persons per acre remained relatively constant in cities of given size. Given the observed population growth rate in recent years, unless people were moving out of bigger cities into smaller cities at a rate much faster than anyone has estimated, the SCS estimate of newly urbanized land would imply a sharp break in historical experience with respect to urban densities. Is it reasonable to think that there has been such a major break with history in this respect?

7. There is disagreement whether the rate at which total land was being converted to "urbanized and built up" rose significantly in the 1970s. But there is no disagreement that even if there was a rise, it certainly was not in the "urban" category, but rather would have been in "open country and hamlets," and to a lesser degree in nonmetropolitan incorporated places. Apparently much of this possible growth would have been in developments sufficiently far from cities that the homes are without sewers, homes which tend to have relatively large lots. (But please note that such lots are mostly not paved, or built on, which should allay some

worry about "paving over" America.) So what we see is *not* "urban sprawl," but rather shifts in population to rural and small-town settings.

The Problems of Estimation

8. The best method for studying the rate of urbanization is a series of aerial photographs. No nationwide study has yet been done for the U.S. as a whole, but Zeimetz, et al., studied photographs of the 53 counties that grew fastest between 1960 and 1970, and Fischel re-analyzed their findings. These counties accounted for fully 20 percent of the total population increase for the U.S. between those years, but required only 85,560 additional acres for urbanization. And this increase of 85,560 acres represented only a 23 percent increase in urbanized areas in these fastest-growing counties. One would reasonably expect that the rate of increase in *less* rapidly growing counties would therefore be less than 23 percent. Yet the NALS figures imply a much higher rate for the U.S. as a whole, an increase of *47 percent* for the country as a whole between 1967 and 1977. It seems most implausible that the U.S. as a whole should have a much higher rate of urbanization than the fastest growing counties.

To put it differently, if the rest of the U.S. were to require additional land at the same ratio of land per person as the fastest-growing counties, the nationwide increase would have been 427,800 acres converted yearly to urban uses, according to Fischel. Compare this with the 2 million acres figure from the 1967–1975 PCS estimate, or the 2.9 million (or 3.3 million) acres estimate from the 1967–1977 NRI comparisons. And to repeat, aerial photography is by far the most accurate method of measuring this phenomenon.

The estimation methods used by NALS and SCS would be grounds for suspicion even if their results did not conflict with those of more reputable studies—as we have just seen they do.

The U.S. Geological Survey, noting these discrepancies, compared its own careful aerial-photography method with SCS's somewhat hit-or-miss method in selected counties within four states in which they had both done work. USGS found very large SCS errors in three of the four states, including a discrepancy of over 2 million acres in Florida. These mistakes amount to 28 percent of *total* urbanized land as estimated by SCS, a huge amount by any criterion.

NALS based its case for the conversion of farmland into urban areas entirely on the 1975 Potential Cropland Study (PCS), even though they had rejected other SCS data comparisons as wildly inaccurate for this particular purpose. From all the information I have been able to obtain, the amount of data collected in that PCS study is far too little to support the estimates of urbanization NALS uses it to make. I figure roughly as follows: Nine 160-acre plots were selected from each of the 506 counties in their sample. Within each of these plots there were nine observations, but they contain little more information than a single observation for this purpose. We can therefore assume that there were about 4554 observations. From the PCS tables, I calculate that about $\frac{1}{240}$ of the U.S. is land converted to urban areas from "prime" categories between 1967 and 1975. Multiplying this by 4554 suggests that about 19 plots changed from "prime" to "urban." Obviously 19 observations would be thoroughly inadequate information for the individual regions, let alone for the U.S. as a whole.

There are also important likely sources of measurement error and bias in the SCS survey procedures. Perhaps the most serious problem is that there was a progressive narrowing in the agricultural land sampling frame which necessarily biases the estimates in the direction of showing more conversions than actually occurred. That is, as soon as a plot is designated "urban," it is removed from the sampling frame and cannot subsequently be classified as "agricultural" even if the original designation was in error. And there is no possibility in the procedure for counterbalancing errors of previously classified urban land being classified as agricultural, because urban land was never reexamined after it was taken out of the agricultural inventory.

Bad News Travels Fast

The episode of the very misleading assertions about conversion of farmland to urbanized uses is interesting—and frightening—in several ways. First, it illustrates how public officials and agencies can be astonishingly casual about important numbers. NALS blithely publicized a figure of 3 million acres yearly even though this is *three times* the historical rate, and they did so in the face of a formidable array of other (sound) research suggesting that the 1-million acre historical rate had not changed. Second, it shows how, with a governmental budget for printing plus the "official" imprimatur, a quite inaccurate piece of information can be disseminated so widely that it becomes common knowledge. Third, it illustrates how shaky the structure of social-science research knowledge is. One badly done survey of very inadequate size—a survey carried out orginally for very different purposes—was able to serve as the basis for wrong and misleading statements without the matter being a case of obvious scientific fraud. Fourth, the NALS publications are shot through with glaring internal inconsistencies, but the press—which has given much attention to the matter—never noticed. The media seem to have looked no further than the publicity handouts and "executive summaries," and certainly never investigated far enough to learn that the research staff of NALS, which was bitterly at odds with the "politicos" who directed the study, renounced the publicized figures that supposedly came from it.

I did not take up the fascinating issues of why the misleading scare stories were so readily—even eagerly—accepted by a wide public, or who the parties are who have a special interest in instituting public policies to restrict the conversion of farmland. That will make good story to tell on another occasion.

Notes

1. (a) Census of Population figures are 25 million and 34 million acres for 1960 and 1970 for "urban area"—say 31 million for 1967—plus 25 and 26 million acres for transportation in 1960 and 1970 (ESS estimates). (b) SCS's estimate is 64 million acres for 1977 for urban (1977 NRI, 1980) with an increase of 29 million (including transportation, but that shows little change) since 1967, which implies 35 million acres in 1967.

2. Conversion to water hardly seems worrisome from a farm production point of view. No owner will voluntarily convert farmland to water unless the farmland is of little value. And the indicated water conversions in the Southeast are all of land class 3g and below, that is, poor land. Also, the conversions are all within 4 of the 15 land classes, with zeros in the other classes, suggesting a few big shifts rather than a broadly based pattern.

10

The Phantom Farmland in Illinois

Selections 9 and 11 on the urbanization of farmland refer to the United States as a whole. It should be of interest to see in the first short piece (10a) how the issue was argued in the context of a single county in Illinois, which was surely typical of the situation—both with respect to the farmland itself and with respect to the foofaraw in the local newspapers.

The second short piece (10b) on urbanization of farmland in one state complements the previous piece on a single county. Both articles show how much research is necessary to refute assertions that can be made casually and then are widely believed.

10a. The Phantom 330,000 Acres of Lost Farmland in Champaign County

Incorrect numbers for the amount of cropland being "lost" to urbanization in Champaign County, in the State of Illinois, and in the U.S. have recently been stated in *The News-Gazette*. The yearly conversion rate in Champaign County probably is about 320 acres a year instead of the average of 1667 acres—30,000 acres from 1960–1978—that has been quoted repeatedly.

Cropland in Illinois as a whole has been increasing rather than decreasing. And the rate of urbanization in the U.S. is about 1 million acres per year rather than the figures of 2.1 million acres and 3 million acres that have been publicized widely.

Let's consider Champaign County. On March 3, 1981, Kenneth Kessler, chairman of the Champaign County Soil and Water Conservation District,

---

The Champaign-Urbana News-Gazette, May 17, 1981(a), and June 9, 1981(b).

was quoted in *The News-Gazette* as saying that "Between 1960–78, 29,990 acres of Champaign County cropland was converted to irreversible, non-agricultural use." On March 8, an editorial said that "30,000 acres of Champaign County—the equivalent of 75 average-sized farms—was transferred from farmland to development." On March 12, Jon Linfield, state director of the federal Farmer's Home Administration, went further by describing the quality as well as the quantity of the "lost" land: "Between 1960 and 1978, 29,990 acres of Champaign County cropland—virtually all of it prime—was irrevocably converted," a statement which was repeated in large type.

Compare "30,000 acres" to these other numbers: (1) The total—not change, but total—amount of urban area in Champaign County was 35,000 acres in 1975, according to Ron Lowery of the Champaign County Soil Conservation Service. That figure comes from aerial photography, which is at least as accurate as any other method of estimation. All of Champaign-Urbana plus Savoy only accounted for 18,695 acres in 1975, according to Lowery.

(2) Based on aerial photography done in 1966 and 1975, Lowery estimates that the increase in urbanized areas is about 320 acres a year, a far cry from the 1667 acres a year implicit in the 30,000 lost acres figure from 1960–1978.

(3) Champaign County contains only 640,000 acres in total. Thirty thousand acres would represent an increase in the urban area of almost 5 percent of the total acreage in 18 years.

If the total urbanized land in 1960 was about as large as the claimed increase from 1960 to 1978—which it was—this would mean that in 1978 almost 10 percent of Champaign County was urbanized. Casual traveling through the county makes this seem most unlikely.

(4) For the years between 1958 and 1967, the Soil Conservation Service showed an increase of 4841 acres in urban and built up acreage—from 30,600 to 35,441 acres over nine years, or 538 acres a year. This is far below an increase of 30,000 acres over 18 years, or 1667 acres per year. The SCS figures are by no means gospel, but SCS has never been known for systematically understating the amount of farmland converted to urban uses.

(5) Bill McNamara of the University of Illinois Agriculture Extension Office quoted figures from the 1978 Census of Agriculture showing that, of the 640,000 total acres in the county, 615,680 were in farms, 588,578 acres were in cropland, with 570,862 acres harvested and the rest fallow that year. This suggests a maximum of 25,420 acres urbanized and built up in 1978.

(6) According to the Census of Agriculture, in 1974 the land in farms in

Champaign County was 592,571 acres, total cropland acres 554,536, and harvested acres 538,463, indicating a very large increase between 1974 and 1978. No plausible change in census methods can explain away this large increase. For a longer perspective, and because, about the 1974 Census of Agriculture, an official in the Bureau of the Census says: "We're not too proud of the numbers," here are comparable data for 1969: total land in farms, 605,282; total cropland, 574,035; harvested cropland, 484,662. No matter how you slice it, you cannot find a recent loss of prime farmland in those numbers.

(7) Historically, the ratio of persons to built-up land has remained quite constant. Therefore, an increase of 100 percent in the urbanized area from 1960 to 1978 would hardly square with the increase in population of Champaign County shown by the censuses—from 132,436 in 1960 to 163,281 in 1970, and then only slight growth since.

In short, the figure of 30,000 acres "lost" between 1960 and 1978 seems quite inconsistent with the other fairly authoritative figures. It is vastly higher than the other figures suggest the real increase could be.

In an attempt to understand the discrepancy, associates and I asked the persons mentioned in *The News-Gazette* where they got the 30,000-acre figure. Mr. Kessler was at first away from his office, so we started with Mr. Linfield. He said he didn't know where the number have come from, but thought it may have come from the Champaign County Regional Planning Commission. We followed the lead backward through RPC, the Champaign County Development Council, the county zoning office, and finally back to Mr. Kessler. His office said that the figure came from the October 1980 *Newsletter* of the Illinois Department of Agriculture, Division of Natural Resources, which inquiry proved it did.

The state's source of the data in the DNR Newsletter was the Illinois Agricultural Statistics Assessors Annual Farm Census, which shows 586,061 acres of farmland for 1960 and 556,071 acres for 1978. These data come from tax assessments, whose definitions and practices change from time to time and differ from place to place, as most property owners know. The effects of these variations can be seen in the extraordinary 47 percent decline in farmland shown for Perry County—from 215,637 acres to 114,314 acres—and the 49.6 percent decline—from 184,964 acres to 93,401 acres—for Union County.

Glance at your map and ask yourself whether you think that much farmland in those counties could have been "lost" to urbanization during that period. And the DNR's Champaign County figure of 556,071 acres of farmland in 1978 does not at all square with the 1978 Census of Agriculture figures cited above for Champaign County. Nor does the claimed all-Illinois decline between 1960 and 1978 from 30.48 million acres to 26.78

million acres of farmland—a 12.2 percent drop—square with the accurate Federal Crop Reporting Bureau data showing an increase in cropland acres harvested in Illinois from 20.11 million to 23.54 million acres between 1970 and 1979 (though of course "farmland" includes more than "cropland" or "acres harvested").

Ron Darden of DNR acknowledged that the *Newsletter* figures are "grossly inaccurate," and said that DNR had not used them after October 1980. Since then, DNR has shifted to Census of Agriculture figures following receipt of a recent letter from the Bureau of Census concerning adjustments in the reported data. DNR believes that letter enables DNR to continue saying that Illinois farmland has been decreasing rather than increasing.

Furthermore—and this is crucial—even if the Champaign County 30,000-acres-of-lost-farmland figure were correct, it would reveal nothing about land "lost" to urbanization. To assume that a decrease in either farmland or cropland implies an increase in urbanized or built-up area is very far from the mark. Land goes out of farm and crop use for a variety of reasons, of which conversion to building use is not one of the more important nationwide. So there is no basis in any farmland data for statements about urbanization.

10b. Cropland Increasing Rather Than Decreasing

Joe Barkley of the Champaign County Soil and Water Conservation District wrote in *The News-Gazette* on May 26 that "We are obviously losing too much of our food producing land to erosion and irreversible non-farm uses," apparently referring to the state of Illinois.

But cropland and farmland have been increasing in Illinois (and in the U.S.) in the 1970s, contrary to much publicity.

In 1979 the Illinois Farmers Home Administration of the USDA publicized the "loss of 100,000 agricultural acres every year" in Illinois, and Gov. James Thompson on July 22, 1980, issued an Executive Order for Preservation of Illinois Farmland citing this 100,000 acres figure.

Then late last year data from the 1978 Census of Agriculture came out, which showed substantial cropland increases rather than decreases for Illinois and for the U.S. as a whole since 1974. Just whose hollering the Illinois Department of Agriculture's Department of Natural Resources heard I don't know; Dale McLaren of the Greater Wabash Regional Planning Commission wrote about the cropland increase in the Mt. Carmel newspapers and brought it to my attention, and as a result we wrote about it in the Illinois Business Review and *The Wall Street Journal*.

But in any case, the DNR contacted the U.S. Bureau of the Census'

Agriculture Division for help. The National Agricultural Lands Study in Washington—the source of the current scare figures of 3 million acres being "lost" to urbanization nationwide—also got into the act somehow. Those organizations then produced preliminary "adjusted" figures apparently based on a definition change between the 1969 and 1978 censuses, plus an allowance (derived from a special sample) for farms not included on the mailing list of farms that were brought into the 1978 census.

Here the story begins to be even more technical (and, regrettably, boring to the lay reader). The preliminary adjusted figures sent to DNR by the Agriculture Division of the Bureau of the Census—showing a decline from 30,209,337 farmland acres in 1974 to 29,733,904 in 1978, instead of an increase from 29,094,794 acres—have been offered by DNR as evidence that cropland really went down rather than up in Illinois between 1974 and 1978.

But these adjusted figures are themselves not sound. The main element in them is the estimate that in 1974, 3.7 percent of the farmland was not counted, whereas a special additional sample to remedy the under-count was included in the 1978 figure. The published 1974 figure was therefore multiplied by 1.037 to get an adjusted 1974 figure. There are two things wrong with this adjustment, however.

First, the 1978 coverage was not complete, either, so 3.7 percent is too big an adjustment. Probably more important, the adjustment refers to all farms, including animal farms, tree farms, pastures, and the like. And the special Census Bureau sample shows that the adjustment applies much less than proportionally to fieldcrop farms than to other sorts of farms, and hence the all-farmland adjustment does not at all show that cropland has decreased, contrary to the claim.

Happily, the Census for Agriculture has now published detailed data on the appropriate adjustment (Illinois Preliminary Report, AC78-P-17-000). For land in farms, 253,284 acres should be subtracted from the published total of 29,733,904—that is, an adjusted total of 29,480,620 acres—to be compared with the 29,094,794 acres for 1974; so land in farms indeed increased from 1974 to 1978. And for cropland the story is the same but more so; the adjustment leaves 1978 cropland at (25,366,407 − 196,400) equals 25,170,007 acres, to be compared with 24,399,558 acres for 1974.

Corroborating evidence comes from the excellent yearly data from the Crop Reporting Board, where no such adjustments are involved. Those data show substantial increases in Illinois cropland in recent years, from 20,118,000 to 23,546,000 harvested acres between 1970 and 1979.

In short, cropland has been increasing recently in the state (and nationally) contrary to what seems "obvious." And the average quality of crop acres has been increasing, too, according to SCS. In light of these facts that we are increasing our farmland and cropland, it does not seem at all obvious that we are "losing too much of our good producing land."

11

The Farmer and the Mall: Are American Farmlands Disappearing?

The saga of the farmland-urbanization scam continues in this selection. It contains an account of the politics involved in creating the farmland scare, and then in defending the scare against irrefutable evidence. The denouement comes in Selection 53, which describes how the USDA perpetrators of the scam finally 'fessed up.

• Robert Lam, a schoolteacher in Springville, Iowa, owns and operates an 80-acre farm. He wants to give a one-acre lot to each of his four children "to help me farm evenings and weekends and to have a lifestyle we have all worked for." But Linn County is considering enacting a law that would require Lam to pay a $50 fee and receive county permission to give the lots to his children to build on. "It goes against my grain to have to say 'Please may I do this with the land,' " he says.

• State Representative Richard Mugalian was delighted to chair the zoning committee of the Illinois House of Representatives. He had always been interested in urban zoning issues, and he thought this would be a chance to put some of his ideas to work. But he soon found the committee's preoccupation with preventing farmland conversion made it difficult to get the committee to attend to any urban zoning issues at all.

• The Reifsteck family owns as good a piece of potential heavy-industry development land as exists in Champaign County, Illinois. It abuts on a railroad siding, is very close to the intersection of two interstate highways, is next to an area already being used for heavy industry, and is even located so that the prevailing winds would blow any odors away from town. The proposed development was opposed in hearing before the zoning commission and the city council by people who claim that the development would mean a loss of prime farmland vital to the nation and

The American Spectator, August 1982, pp. 18–20 and 40–41.

the world. Some spoke of possible starvation in the future. Others simply said it is not right to take some of the most fertile land in the world and pave it over, even if this would increase the value and output of that land.

• Victor and Margot Sturm of Princeton Township, Illinois, who raise Arabian horses, requested a zoning change from agricultural to rural estate for a 2.5-acre homesite. There was agreement that the land is wet and hence hardly prime for farming. And the Sturms even offered to put in a special septic system. A letter with eleven signatures, however, objecting to the conversion of "prime farmland," caused the request to be tabled by the County Zoning Board despite being approved by the County Planning Commission, the County Zoning Board of Appeals, and the County Board's zoning committee.

• And then there are these headlines from a sampling of recent newspaper and magazine stories: "Vanishing Farmlands: Selling Out the Soil" (*Saturday Review*); "Farmland Losses Could End U.S. Food Exports" (*Chicago Tribune*); "As World Needs Food, U.S. Keeps Losing Soil to Land Developers" (*The Wall Street Journal*); "The Peril of Vanishing Farmlands" (*The New York Times*); not to mention the many other stories from the *Christian Science Monitor,* Gannett News Service, and the Associated Press, typically reprinted with alarmist headlines in the smaller newspapers across the country.

One of the main agents in whipping up this scare about "vanishing" farmland has been the National Agricultural Lands Study (NALS), a creature of the Carter Administration. And the scare has not departed with the arrival of Ronald Reagan. Secretary of Agriculture John Block is on record as agreeing with this product of the Carter years, referring to the loss of agricultural land as "a crisis in the making," similar to the energy situation ten years ago. NALS "has built a strong case for protecting good agricultural land," he says.

The heart of the NALS case is that farmland—and particularly cropland, as distinct from pasture, forest, and other farmland—is being urbanized at an unprecedented rate. This claim is being fueled by false statistical assertions. The likely rate is only about *a third* of the amount claimed by the National Agricultural Lands Study, a rate probably no greater but rather less than in the past, and certainly not three times the rate in the recent past as claimed by NALS. Selection 9 discusses related trends in land use that should dispel some of the false perceptions currently obscuring the issue.

NALS's claim that three million acres a year are being converted from farmland is a political scam. Its only apparent support is a faulty Soil Conservation Service re-survey in 1975 of a small portion of the observation points used in a 1967 survey, a sampling which proved much too small to be reliable: Only about 55 of the re-survey points represented agricultural land that had become urbanized and less than 20 of these were cropland. Together with Seymour Sudman in the *International Regional Science Review*, I have analyzed some of the major procedural problems with the re-survey, most stemming from the fact that the re-survey was intended to throw light not on farmland losses but on conservation practices.

The three-million-acre figure, moreover, is contradicted by all other available evidence. A U.S. Geological Survey that compared its aerial photography data on land conversion with the Soil Conservation Service materials in four test states revealed major errors in the SCS findings stemming from misclassification and simple blunders. The three-million-acre claim is as preposterous as any "official" statistic ever rushed into print. The true figure, as we shall see, is one-third or less of that figure— about one million acres per year, which is at or below the average for the decades since 1950. This represents only a microscopic proportion of U.S. land; *total* urbanized land in the United States is less than 3 percent. Furthermore, only a portion of the one million acres converted annually is cropland, the rest being pasture, wasteland, and so on.

Now NALS asserts that the amount of cropland—especially "prime" cropland—constitutes the ultimate public interest in the discussion. Thus, when the Census of Agriculture figures published late in 1980 showed that cropland had been rising from 1974 to 1978, NALS quickly arranged for, and widely publicized, an adjustment purporting to show that this increase in cropland was in fact the result of underreporting in earlier years, an adjustment very large relative to the other magnitudes involved. As soon as NALS began to publish its claims of increases in the rate of land urbanization, critics inside and outside NALS asserted that such claims were unfounded. NALS management responded by applying personal pressure on insiders, and employed various bureaucratic tactics to confute outsiders: I shall describe one of these moves, one which I know firsthand.

In 1979 the Illinois Farmers Home Administration of the USDA publicized a "loss of 100,000 agricultural acres every year" in Illinois, and on July 22, 1980, Governor James Thompson issued an Executive Order for Preservation of Illinois Farmlands, citing this 100,000-acre figure. Then along came data from a 1978 Census of Agriculture, which showed substantial cropland increases rather than decreases for Illinois (and the U.S. as a whole) since 1974. Dale McLaren of the Greater Wabash Regional Planning Commission wrote about the increase in the Mt. Carmel Newspapers and brought it to my attention, and as a result we wrote about it in *The Wall Street Journal*. Here is how the *Journal of Soil and Water Conservation* describes what happened next:

Ironically, the new information came out of a feud between the Illinois Department of Agriculture and Julian Simon, a University of Illinois economics professor. Simon has argued in a number of popular articles that environmentalists have produced "an oversupply of false bad news" about the state of the planet. Citing figures from the Census of Agriculture that showed an increase in the amount of land in farms [author's note: McLaren and I wrote about cropland, not farmland] in Illinois, Simon dismissed farmland preservation as "scaremongering."

"We were also confronted at the national level by experts in the field who contended the 1974 and 1978 census showed about an 8-million-acre increase in the land in farms [nationally]," sad [NALS officials] Gray and Benbrook. "On this basis, they questioned what all the fuss over conversion was about."

Simon's assertions did not sit so well with Illinois agriculture officials. They decided to contact the Bureau of Census in Washington because they could not believe that land in farms had increased. The Bureau responded that the 1969 and 1974 censuses had underenumerated land in farms. Revised figures showed that between 1974 and 1978 Illinois's land in farms had declined by 425,000 acres. The earlier figures had shown a 639,000 acre increase.

"When we became aware of the underenumeration problem in Illinois, we made our own inquiries and were told that similar adjustments were needed nationwide," said Gray and Benbrook.

The result: The latest data show a national decline of 88 million acres in land in farms between 1969 and 1978—an annual rate of 9.8 million acres. . . .

In other words, the Census Agriculture Division and NALS produced "adjusted" figures apparently based on a definition change between the 1969 and 1978 censuses, plus an allowance for farms not included in the 1978 census. But upon inspection, the adjustment could be seen to be as full of holes as Swiss cheese. And eventually the Census of Agriculture revealed detailed data on the appropriate adjustment showing that land in Illinois farms and in cropland indeed increased from 1974 to 1978.

Corroborating evidence came from the yearly data from the Crop Reporting Board, where no such adjustments are involved, showing substantial increases in Illinois cropland in recent years. After the episode was over, Arnold Bollenbacher, Chief of the Agriculture Division of the Bureau of the Census, summed up in a letter, "Even with some decrease in total land in farms, cropland increased in Illinois and in the United States."

This episode seems to show a determined urge on the part of NALS to disseminate data showing loss of cropland irrespective of the facts.

The preoccupation with the loss of "prime land" seems to involve a fundamental misunderstanding of economic principles. Take the example of a new shopping mall, called Market Place, near Champaign-Urbana, Illinois. Wonderful though this Illinois land is for growing corn and soybeans, it has greater value to the economy as a shopping center, which is why the mall investors could pay the farmer enough to make it worthwhile for him to sell.

Suppose that the corn-and-soybeans farmer who owned the land sold it instead to the producer of an exotic new crop called, say "whornseat," a hybrid of corn and wheat. The land would be more productive growing whornseat than corn, as shown by the higher profits the whornseat farmer would make as compared with the corn and soybeans farmer, and as shown also by the higher price the whornseat farmer is willing to pay for the land. Under these conditions, no one would ever argue that the land should be required to remain in the production of corn and soybeans.

A shopping mall is similar to a whornseat farm. It *seems* different, however, because the mall does not use the land for agriculture. Yet economically there is no real difference between the mall and whornseat farming.

One may say: "Why not put the shopping mall on inferior wasteland that cannot be used for corn and soybeans?" The mall owners would be delighted to find and buy such land—so long as it were equally convenient for shoppers. But there is no such wasteland close to town. And "wasteland" far away from Champaign-Urbana is like land that is not fertile for whornseat—the former will not produce whornseat and the latter will not produce shoppers.

Some may argue that we should "keep our options open," because "paving is irreversible," In fact, it is not. But more important, however, is that keeping options open costs us real resources. Stockpiling food in your basement in case of possible calamity may be wise, but you lose the use of the money tied up in the food inventory. So it is with farmland: If it is kept from other uses, no other benefits are derived in the meantime. These benefits must be greater than we can get from farmland in agriculture, or investors would not be willing to convert the land from farmland to other uses.

Muddled economics aside, what has led so many people to worry about the conversion of farmland? For many, farmland preservation is a front for other concerns, as Pierre Crosson has pointed out: "Some who argue for preservation of agricultural land to protect productive capacity do so to cloak purely private interests, e.g., some farmers in metropolitan areas who seek to have their land taxed at its value in agriculture rather than at its value in urban uses." This group has had particular success in achieving favorable zoning laws in such Eastern states as New York, where farmers have obtained lower tax rates for land used for farming at the same time that they have retained the right to sell the land for other uses.

But more important, Crosson notes, "Some of those ostensibly concerned with the adequacy of land as a factor of agricultural production are really concerned about it as a source of amenity values." It is no accident that much of the push for farmland "preservation" has arisen in such states as Connecticut which are not exactly the nation's granary. It is natural enough for gentry to want to view bucolic fields rather than tacky housing developments from their front windows. But the rest of us should not have to pay the price.

Finally, Crosson explains why the amenity issue is never discussed openly:

> . . . If much of the concern about the adequacy of agricultural land is really concern with preservation of amenity values rather than of production capacity, why is the discussion typically cast in terms of [productive] capacity? Why are the amenity [esthetic] issues and the capacity issues not treated separately, as they should be? One cannot be sure, but two reasons come to mind. One is muddled thinking, a simple failure to recognize that agricultural land provides both commodity values and amenity values, but not in fixed proportions. The other reason is that maintenance of capacity is more likely to enlist political support for preservation of agricultural land than maintenance of amenity values. This reason is likely to be particularly compelling if the objective is to shape national policies for agricultural land preservation. Threats to our ability to feed ourselves and meet our felt obligations to a hungry world are more likely to mobilize a political response to pressure agricultural land than threats to the pleasures of a Sunday afternoon drive through the countryside.

The concern for farmland preservation is not a new phenomenon. Years ago, various individuals and organizations began to campaign for zoning changes and other farmland preservation laws. But once Washington politicos jumped onto the issue with both feet, the scale of these activities increased dramatically.

In 1979, the Carter Administration established the National Agricultural Lands Study, a joint effort of the Council on Environmental Quality and the Department of Agriculture with the participation of a flock of other government agencies, including eight Departments, the Environmental Protection Agency, and the Water Resource Council. (The more government agencies that back a project, the more confidence the electorate is supposed to have in the project.) Appointed to head up NALS was Robert Gray, former aide to Congressman James Jeffords of Vermont, who had once sponsored an unsuccessful farmland preservation bill. NALS proceeded to publicize the three-million-acre figure, as well as many other dubious claims—even though members of NALS's own research staff made it very clear to Gray that their studies did not substantiate such claims.

Information on internal criticism of NALS comes from Michael Brewer, head of the research staff, and is corroborated by another member of that staff. According to the staff member, "The politicos didn't give a damn what the data said. The reports cast doubt on the scarcity of farmland, but that didn't find its way into the Final Report, which was 180 degrees away from the research input in many cases." Brewer seems to have just about disavowed the NALS findings: "Efforts to determine the 'nature, rate, extent and causes of reduction in the land base' led NALS into a morass of inconsistent and conflicting numbers that left issues possibly more confused than previously."

In the final days of the Carter Administration there arose an organization called the American Farmland Trust, which began to solicit funds to preserve farmland, but without saying how the money would be used.[1] After the defeat of the Carter Administration, the names of Robert Gray and Carter Secretary of the Interior Cecil Andrus appeared as prominent functionaries of American Farmland Trust.

Lest the reader think my views unusual or out of the mainstream, I wish to conclude by citing some of the nation's leading agricultural economists. Marion Clawson of Resources for the Future says straight out: "We're not very worried around here about the loss of prime farmland."[2] Clifton B. Luttrell of the St. Louis Federal Reserve Bank finds "there is no evidence that the quantity of cropland is shrinking or that shortages of food are imminent. Furthermore, even if the alleged problem did exist, there is no evidence that it could be solved more efficiently by social planning than by market participants."

Philip Raup, of the University of Minnesota, sees the issue not as one of cropland versus built-up land, but rather of cropland versus forest, and adds, "The short-term prospect is for a substantial reduction in the pressure of urban demand on rural lands." Pierre Crosson described the consensus reached at a recent Resources for the Future Conference as follows: "While one should not be complacent about the agricultural land issue neither is it a matter of pressing current national concern."

Toward the end of his discussion of "Urban Encroachment on Rural Areas," geographer John Fraser Hart asks: "If urban encroachment on rural land is not a serious problem in the United States, then why has so much arrant nonsense been written and spoken on the subject?" His own answer is a fitting way to end this discussion: "It is all too easy for the layman to generalize New York to the entirety of urban America or to believe that the unique agricultural situation in parts of California is typical of the entire nation. Some people seem to want to believe that the world is going to hell in a handbasket, and some simply do not know any better than to repeat what they have read or what someone has told them."

Notes

1. Readers might be interested in a letter from American Farmland Trust to Robert J. Kelly, who had inquired about the claims made by the Trust in a direct mail package. I am grateful to Mr. Kelly for bringing this to my attention.

   Rather than refute the logic of Professor Simon that you brought to our attention, I would encourage you to consider carefully the findings of the National Agricultural Lands Study that will be presented to President Carter shortly after January 1, 1981. My reasoning on this is quite simple. Julian Simon represents the thinking of himself only—we do not know his personal objectives for furthering his position. On the other hand, the work of NALS represents the collective analysis of some of the most knowledgeable people in this country on the issue of agricultural land use. These analysts have access to the best and latest data on the topic, and have been charged with painting the most realistic picture possible of present farmland conditions for the president.

   The American Farmland Trust does not want you, or anyone else, to simply take our word that the loss of American farmland is a real and growing threat to our national well-being. Please listen to and study the words of national experts. Write to:

   National Agriculture Lands Study
   Room 5020
   New Executive Office Building
   Washington, D.C. 20006

2. A more complete statement of Clawson's point of view: "Preservation of prime agricultural land is important, but so is the preservation of land prime for other uses. Agricultural land use must be viewed in a wider context than agricultural alone. Prime land is important, but so are all the other inputs in the agricultural production equation. Agricultural research in particular must be fostered and protected."

12

Truth Almost Extinct in Tales of Imperiled Species

Consider the opening paragraphs from a fund-raising letter of the World Wildlife Fund-U.S., signed by Russell E. Train, President (received by me July 23, 1983):

> *Dear Friend,*
>
> Suddenly everyone in the hearing room knew what the Endangered Species Act was all about.
>
> A small bottle in the hand of a prominent biologist was their clue.
>
> The bottle, explained Dr. Thomas Eisner, contained tiny invertebrate marine animals called *bryozoa.* Unfamiliar even to most biologists, these minute creatures are typical of life forms that could slip into extinction through mankind's carelessness.
>
> *Yet some of these obscure invertebrates have been found to produce an anti-cancer substance of extraordinary potency.*
>
> Some scientists believe that up to one million species of life will become extinct by the end of this century. How many cures for cancer or other diseases will be lost before they are discovered?
>
> Members of Congress were so impressed with the testimony of Dr. Eisner and other scientists mobilized by World Wildlife Fund that they re-authorized the Endangered Species Act and rejected strong lobbying efforts to limit its effectiveness.
>
> That victory capped a year in which World Wildlife fund gave top priority to re-authorization of the Endangered Species Act.

The letter asserts calamitous effects of the purported loss of a million species.

Big money—$8 billion is a number bandied about—would be in-

The Washington Times, September 19, 1984.

volved in "protecting imperiled species" throughout the world. The
State Department's AID already makes a big issue of species conser-
vation in its programs abroad. But the facts are almost unbelievably
far from the claims. (I say "almost" because the gap between facts
and claims is a reality, and therefore must *be believed.) This short*
piece introduces the topic, which will be explored at greater length in
the next selection.

Front page story, *The Washington Post,* Jan. 1, 1984: "A potential
biological transformation of the planet unequaled perhaps since the disappearance of the dinosaur," says Thomas Lovejoy of the World Wildlife
Fund. "The folly our descendants are least likely to forgive us," says
Edward O. Wilson of Harvard.

These statements typify the scary rhetoric the public hears about potential species extinction, usually a prediction that a million or more existing
species could be lost to mankind in the next two decades if remedial action
isn't taken at once. (To be fair, the *Post*'s story was much less overheated
than is usually the case with this issue.)

Yet—there is absolutely no solid evidence supporting the prediction that
a million or more existing species will be lost to mankind in the next two
decades if radical remedial steps are not taken by the governments of the
world. A fair reading of the available data suggests a prediction perhaps
one-thousandth that great. But the conservationists are beating the big
drum for money and action based on their frightening claims.

A recent fund-raising pitch from the World Wildlife Fund-U.S., signed
by its president, Russell E. Train, describes in detail how the organization
rallied support for reauthorization of the Endangered Species Act, which
Mr. Train asserts was itself endangered. They did so by informing Congress that "some scientists believe that up to 1 million species of life will
become extinct by the end of this century" unless governments "do
something" about it.

"When we talk about the loss of 1 million species," Train says in his
letter, "we are talking about a global loss with consequences that science
can scarcely begin to predict.

"The future of the world could be altered drastically if we allow a million
species to disappear by the year 2000."

I couldn't agree more; the sudden disappearance of a million life forms
would have major ecological effects. However, the WWF prediction completely lacks factual basis.

WWF backs the million-species claim only with the statement "some
scientists believe." This is no scientific evidence at all. You can find "some

scientists'' who will say they believe almost any proposition you like, even if the established scientific facts are quite the opposite. In the advertising trade (a usually honorable trade that I practiced in my youth), such a statement is known as weasel-wording. Such weasel-wording would draw the ire of the Federal Trade Commission if made on behalf of a deodorant.

The available evidence on species suggests an astonishingly different picture, however.

The proximate source for WWF's forecast is the 1979 book, *The Sinking Ark*, by Norman Myers. Mr. Myers gives these two statistics: the estimated extinction rate of known species between the years 1600 and 1900 was about one every four years. And the estimated rate from 1900 to the present was about one a year. Mr. Myers gives no sources for these two estimates, but let us assume they are valid.

The extinction-rate data presented refer only to animals. But there are no data for other species, to my knowledge.

Mr. Myers then departs spectacularly from that modest evidence. He goes on to say that some scientists have ''hazarded a guess'' that the extinction rate ''could now have reached'' 100 species per year.

Next, this pure conjecture about upper limit of present species extinction is increased and used by Mr. Myers and WWF scientist Thomas Lovejoy as the basis for the ''projections'' quoted in the fundraising letter and elsewhere. Mr. Lovejoy—by converting what was an estimated upper limit into a present best-estimate—says that government inaction is ''likely to lead'' to the extinction of between 14 and 20 percent of all species before the year 2000. This comes to about 40,000 species lost per year, or about one million from 1980 to 2000.

In brief, this extinction rate is nothing but pure guesswork. The forecast is a thousand times greater than the present—yet it has been published in newspapers and understood as a scientific statement.

Thomas Lovejoy and Norman Myers were at a meeting when I first presented this critique. They found no statistical flaw in it, although they did attack my interpretation, motives, and credentials to discuss biological data.

Simply demonstrating that other peoples' data do not support their conclusion may not be as convincing as presenting independent contradictory data. But apparently there are no other data to be found. The statistical analysis above certainly demonstrates that the WWF warning of an extraordinary rate of species extinction does not follow from the known facts, even the facts presented by WWF itself.

Should this not be enough to discredit their assertion?

Three additional observations are worth keeping in mind. First, there is currently much support for putting samples of endangered species into "banks" which can preserve their genetic possibilities for future generations. Second, genetic recombination techniques now enable biologists to create new variations of species. Finally, it is not easy to extinguish an important species even when we try, as the experience of fighting smallpox and the medfly revealed.

The facts cast the phenomenon of species extinction in a much less frightening light than the WWF picture of fragile valuable species dying off forever with no possibility of replacing or substituting for them.

13

Disappearing Species, Deforestation, and Data

This selection documents at greater length the statistical fraud being perpetrated by environmental organizations and biologists in order to promote U.S. and other governmental programs to "conserve" species. The piece also provides some data on the related "deforestation" scam. The proponents of these frauds are so secure in the support they enjoy among journalists, as well as with various governmental and nonprofit agencies, that they do not even deign to reply to the charges made here, apparently (and apparently correctly) confident that they can safely ignore them.

This article draws upon and updates an article by Simon and Aaron Wildavsky in The Resourceful Earth *(1984).*

The issue of species loss is heating up. In 1983, the United States Congress set up a task force to develop a strategy for the conservation of biological diversity, and the task force produced a report in 1985. The Congressional Office of Technology Assessment (OTA) commissioned 50 papers and drafted a study document, *Technologies to Maintain Biological Diversity*, which culminates in a discussion of "policy issues and options for Congressional action." People are clearly worrying about the implications of extinction, but I believe that they are calling for action before they know what action is required.

The OTA's study grows out of the 1980 *Global 2000 Report* to the President, which expressed concern over the possible loss of species between now and the year 2000. The "major findings and conclusions" section said: "Extinctions of plant and animal species will increase dramatically. Hundreds of thousands of species—perhaps as many as 20 percent of all species on Earth—will be irretrievably lost as their habitats

New Scientist, May 15, 1986.

vanish, especially in tropical forests." *Global 2000* also expressed concern about deforestation, especially in the tropics, and its effect upon species loss. "The projections indicate that by 2000 some 40 percent of the remaining forest cover in LDCs (less developed countries) will be gone."

Concern is now widespread. An article dealing with *Global 2000* in *Science* ends like this: "We cannot afford the extinction of '15 to 20 percent of all species on Earth' by the year 2000, as predicted in *Global 2000*." And the U.S. Agency for International Development, citing the relationship of species to forests, says that "destruction of humid tropical forests is one of the most important environmental issues for the remainder of this century." Both are typical responses.

The available facts, however, are not consistent with the level of concern. I do not suggest that our society, and humanity at large, should not attend to possible dangers to species. Species constitute a valuable endowment, and we should guard their survival just as we guard our other physical and social assets. But we should strive for a clear and unbiased view of this set of assets in order to make the best possible judgments about how much time and money to spend in guarding them.

Because the OTA's document is still under embargo, I will take *Global 2000* as my text. It said: "Efforts to meet basic human needs and rising expectations are likely to lead to the extinction of between one-fifth and one-seventh of all species over the next two decades." That projection is based on a statement by Thomas Lovejoy of the World Wildlife Fund that "of the 3–10 million species now present on the Earth, at least 500,000–600,000 will be extinguished during the next two decades." This estimate is just guesswork, as I shall show. And it is at variance with the existing evidence.

The basis of any useful projection for the future must be a body of experience collected in situations that encompass the expected conditions, or that can reasonably be extrapolated to the expected conditions. However, none of Lovejoy's references contains any scientifically impressive body of experience. The only published source given for his key table is Norman Myer's book *The Sinking Ark,* written under the auspices of a committee of which Lovejoy was one of three members. The writings of Myers and Lovejoy, which are not independent, appear to be the basic source of all the widely discussed forecasts of species extinction.

Myers sums up the argument like this:

> At least 90 percent of all species that have existed have disappeared. But almost all of them have gone under by virtue of natural processes. Only in the recent past, perhaps from around 50,000 years ago, has man exerted much influence . . . from the year AD 1600, he became able, through advancing technology, to

over-hunt animals to extinction in just a few years, and to disrupt extensive environments just as rapidly. Between the years 1600 and 1900, man eliminated around 75 known species, almost all of them mammals and birds. . . . Since 1900 man has eliminated around another 75 known species—again, almost all of them mammals and birds, with hardly anything known about how many other creatures have faded from the scene. . . .

Since 1960, however, when growth in human numbers and human aspirations began to exert greater impact on natural environments, vast territories in several major regions of the world have become so modified as to be cleared of much of their main wildlife. The result is that the extinction rate has certainly soared, though details mostly remain undocumented. In 1974 a gathering of scientists concerned with the problem hazarded a guess that the overall extinction rate among all species, whether known to science or not, could now have reached 100 species per year. [Here Myers refers to *Science* 1974, pp. 646–647.] [See Table 13–1 and Figure 13–1.]

This, at any rate, is a source. But it is only a consensus "guess" among scientists of an upper limit to the rate of extinction. And it refers to all species, not just birds or mammals. Myers goes on:

A single ecological zone, the tropical moist forests, is believed to contain between two and five million species. If present patterns of exploitations persist in tropical moist forests, much virgin forest is likely to have disappeared by the end of the century, and much of the remainder will have been severely degraded. This will cause huge numbers of species to be wiped out. . . .

Let us suppose that . . . the final one-quarter of this century witnesses the elimination of one million species—a far from unlikely prospect. This would work out . . . at an average extinction rate of . . . over 100 species per day . . . Already the disruptive processes are well under way, and it is not unrealistic to suppose that, right now, at least one species is disappearing each day. By the late 1980s we could be facing a situation where one species becomes extinct each hour.

Table 13-1. Rates of extinction

Records of	⎰ 1600-1900	One per four years
birds and mammals	⎱ 1900-1980	One per year
Guess	1980	100 per year
Extrapolated from guess	1980-2000	40,000 per year

Estimates of the rate at which species go extinct are on shaky ground when we extrapolate into the future

Figure 13-1. Myers-Lovejoy estimates of species extinction and their extrapolations to the year 2000.

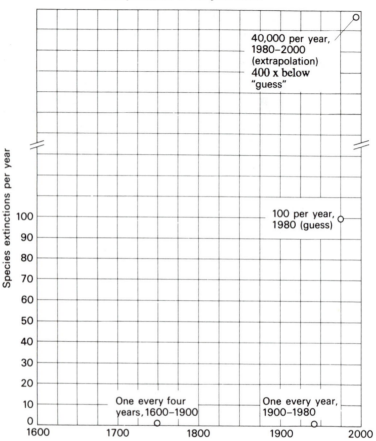

I will restate the key points from the above quotation:

(1) The estimated extinction rate was one known species every four years between the years from 1600 to 1900.

(2) The estimated rate is about one species a year from 1900 to the present. (No sources are given for these two estimates, either on the page from which the quote is taken or on the pages of Myers's book where these estimates are discussed.)

(3) Some scientists have (in Myers's words) "hazarded a guess" that the extinction rate "could now have reached" 100 species per year. That is, the estimate is simply·conjecture and is not even a point estimate but rather an upper bound. The source given by Myers for the "some scien-

tists'' statement is a report written by a member of the staff of a news magazine. Note also that the subject of this guess is different from the subject of the estimates in (1) and (2); the former includes mainly or exclusively birds or mammals whereas the latter includes all species. While this difference implies that (1) and (2) may constitute too low a basis for estimating the present extinction rate of all species, it also implies that there is even less statistical basis than there might otherwise seem for estimating the extinction rate for species other than birds and mammals.

(4) The guessed upper limit in (3) is then increased and used by Myers, and then by Lovejoy, as the basis for the ''projections'' quoted above. In *Global 2000* ''could now have reached'' has become ''are likely to lead'' to the extinction of between 14 and 20 percent of all species before the year 2000. That is, an upper limit for the present—which is pure guess-work—has become the basis of a forecast for the future. That forecast has in turn been published in newspapers to be read by tens or hundreds of millions of people, and is presumably understood by them as a scientific statement.

Given the two historical rates provided by Myers—the OTA's documents of 1986 and other recent statements cite no additional evidence on the matter—one could extrapolate almost any rate for the year 2000. Lovejoy's extrapolation has no better claim to belief than a rate, say, one-hundredth as large. Considering the two historical points alone, many forecasters would project a rate much closer to the past rate than to Lovejoy's. The common wisdom is that in the absence of additional information, the best first approximation for a variable tomorrow is its value today, and the best second approximation is that the variable will change at the same rate in the future that it has in the past. Lovejoy uses an accelerating rate of change to project from two points.

Underlying the huge jump from the observed rates of the past to the projected rates of the future is an assumed relationship between deforestation and species loss, together with an estimate of future change in forested area. I will, therefore, now examine both of these elements.

To connect an assumed rate of deforestation to a rate of species loss we need systematic evidence on the relationship. But no such empirical evidence is given by Lovejoy, Myers, *Global 2000*, the OTA, or any other reference I have checked. Nor does the 1986 OTA draft document refer to any empirical evidence on the matter. Rather, *Global 2000* relied entirely upon a hypothetical graph drawn by Lovejoy connecting the zero points for proportions of deforestation and of species lost, with the 100 percent points for both variables, in a slightly bowed curve. Other students of the subject see the matter differently, denying that (say) 10 percent deforesta-tion would result in almost 10 percent loss in species, as Lovejoy's diagram would have it. So this supposed relationship is a frail logical link for an argument about loss of species in the future.

It might well be reasonable without further ado to adjudge as quite unproven the case that large numbers of species are in danger of being lost as a result of deforestation in the next two decades. Nevertheless, let us give every benefit of the doubt to those who warn of rapid species loss, and move on to deforestation itself. *Global 2000* says "Significant losses of world forests will continue over the next 20 years. . . ." But *Global 2000* presents no time-series data on such losses.

Only a historical series of comparable observations can establish the existence of a trend scientifically and statistically. Observation at one moment can convey only impressions about a trend. The impressions may be sound if they are made on the basis of first-hand contact, previous wide experience, and wise judgment. But such impressions provide a very different basis for policy decisions than well-grounded statistical estimates of trends.

The Food and Agricultural Organisation (FAO) of the United Nations has published estimates of total world forest area since the late 1940s, and these show two things. First, the data are too crude and irregular to show any trend reliably. Secondly, there is no obvious recent downward trend in world forests—no obvious "losses" at all, and certainly no "near catastrophic" loss. Surveys by *World Wood* since 1965 of the countries with the largest forests show much the same. At Resources for the Future, a long-established research institution, Roger Sedjo and Marion Clawson have also studied deforestation. Clawson has been the pre-eminent student of forest economics for half a century, and Sedjo and Clawson conclude that "there is certainly nothing in the data to suggest that the world is experiencing significant net deforestation."

Global 2000, Lovejoy, Myers, and others focus on *tropical* forests (rather than total world forests) as particularly liable to deforestation. *Global Future*, a supplement to *Global 2000*, opens its section on tropical forests with "The world's tropical forests are disappearing at alarming rates . . . tropical deforestation is an urgent problem. . . ."

Lovejoy estimated species loss with two assumed deforestation rates for tropical forests. The "low" projection assumed a 50 percent deforestation rate between 1980 and 2000 for Latin America, a 20 percent rate for Africa (Africa is the least important in terms of total species), and 60 percent for South and Southeast Asia. The "high" projection assumed 67 percent deforestation for all regions between 1980 and 2000. Lovejoy cites Chapter 8 of *Global 2000* as his source for the alternative assumptions. But no trend data are given there to support any such estimate. The main sources in that section of *Global 2000* are studies by Reidar Persson and by R. H. Whittaker and G. E. Likens. The former provides one-time inventory of world forests as a whole. The latter contains no original survey data. Neither supports Lovejoy's assumptions about tropical deforestation.

Sedjo and Clawson dug into the available evidence and compared it with the estimates found in *Global 2000*. They write: "Information about the tropical moist forests is relatively scant. What information we do have comes more from anecdotal evidence—provided by isolated investigations at single times and places—than from systematic studies conducted over large areas and lengths of time. . . . A hard look at the available data supports the view that some regions are experiencing rapid deforestation. However, the view that this is a pervasive phenomenon on a global level is questionable.

Working with Sedjo and Clawson at Resources for the Future, Julia Allen and Douglas Barnes compared, country by country, the estimates for recent deforestation from three studies. They used the FAO's report of 1979, Myers's report in 1980 to the National Academy of Sciences, and an FAO-UN Environmental Program study by J. P. Lanly published in 1982. Lanly is Forestry Coordinator for the UNEP/FAO Tropical Resources Assessment Project, and Sedjo and Clawson consider the Lanly report "the most thorough." That study "estimated the rate of deforestation of the closed tropical broadleaf forests at 7.1 million hectares per annum (0.60 percent) for 1976–80 or 30–50 percent of Myers' estimates of 20–24 million hectares per annum." Lovejoy's assumptions about deforestation rates are too high.

Sedjo and Clawson make another key point: "Importantly and somewhat surprisingly, the [UN-Lanly] study indicates that the undisturbed or 'virgin' broadleaved closed forests have a far lower rate of deforestation than the total, being only 0.27 percent annually as compared with 2.06 percent annually for logged over secondary forest. This figure indicates that deforestation pressure on the more pristine and generally more genetically diverse tropical forests is quite low." Sedjo and Clawson note that "these findings are in sharp contrast to the conventional view that the tropical forests 'are disappearing at alarming rates,' and suggest that concerns over the imminent loss of some of the most important residences of the world's diverse genetic base, based on rates of tropical deforestation, are probably grossly exaggerated." Early on, Sandra Brown, professor of forestry at the University of Illinois, and Ariel Lugo, project leader at the U.S. Forest Service's Institute of Tropical Forestry, also studied the available data. Brown and Lugo concluded that "dangerous" misinterpretation and exaggeration of the rate of deforestation has become common.

Brazil and its Amazon region attract special concern. But the materials used by *Global 2000* to support its assertions that Brazil is being rapidly deforested seem quite incompetent to support such evidence. The main source for Lovejoy's report was a single set of satellite photographs taken in 1978 and reported in the *Washington Post* to show that "as much as one-tenth of the Brazilian Amazon forest has been razed." Robert Buschbacher is an ecologist currently working as a Fulbright scholar in Brazil. According to a more recent description of that Landsat study that he relates, it "concluded that 1.55 percent of the Brazilian portion of the Amazon has been deforested." On the basis of this and other evidence, Buschbacher says: "Because of a relatively low percentage of forest clearing and the remarkable capacity of the forest to recover its structure . . . the threat of turning the Amazon into a wasteland is exaggerated." Even more importantly, at best such photographs constitute a single observation which provides no trend data.

Another of the sources frequently referred to is Adrian Sommer. He predicts future deforestation in the Amazon region of Brazil by simply comparing the road networks built in the 1960s and 1970s and planned for the future, and then assuming that the forests will be cleared around the roads. This is a flimsy basis for any prediction.

Nor is there need to rely on such evidence. The two UN studies and even Myers agree closely in their estimates of the Brazilian deforestation rate—between 0.0025 and 0.004 percent per year. At such a rate, it would be a great many years before many species are threatened, it would seem. If this rate were to continue unchanged, even Lovejoy's "low" assumption would be perhaps 10 times too high.

Each year *World Wood* publishes an assessment of the commercial forest situation for Brazil (and for each other country). Those assessments differ from accounts such as those of Lovejoy and Myers. For example, M. K. Muthoo, leader of a FAO/UNDP/IBDF Project Team, wrote in 1978: "Brazil has abundant natural forest. It holds the world's biggest tropical forest reserve, in the Amazon, which can be continuously used and improved at the same time, but has hardly been tapped."

The famous Jari project of Daniel Ludwig had planted only 100,000 hectares and planned another 300,000 before it folded, an insignificant area by any measure. Furthermore, the Brazilians are acutely aware of the importance of their forests, and the government has established incentive programs to encourage sensible forest plantations.

Why is there such a large difference in perceptions of Brazil's and the Amazon's forests? Perhaps different people look at different aspects of the matter. The environmentalists may have in mind specific areas of the Amazon, perhaps those about which Muthoo writes: "Since over-ex-

ploited forests in the Atlantic coastal belt and the Parana area in the south
and elsewhere have been eroded phenomenally, they cannot sustain supplies to suffice local requirements, much less to meet growing national and
international raw material requirements.'' The environmentalists may also
be influenced by the impressive and even frightening visages of the huge
machines that now can cut down and saw up trees like a lawnmower goes
through grass. The commercial foresters focus instead on the large un-
touched areas of forests, on the smallness of Brazilian, and world demand
for wood relative to the potential supply, on the lack of Brazilian demand
for new agricultural lands relative to the area available, and on the
possibilities for improved yields of food and tree crops.

Overexploitation of local areas near transportation networks may or
may not be ugly, painful, and a serious problem in Brazil or other
countries. But such local exploitation would not seem to the threaten
species just as long as there are isolated similar habitats nearby. There
may be some species that can live in only one small area. But such species
are likely to be less important to humankind and the rest of nature for that
very reason.

Biologists with whom I have discussed this material agree that the
numbers in question are most uncertain. But they say the numbers do not
matter scientifically. The conclusion would be the same, they say, if the
numbers were different even by several orders of magnitude. If that is so,
why mention any numbers at all? The answer, quite clearly, is that these
numbers do matter in one important way: they have the power to frighten
in a fashion that numbers much smaller would not. The OTA 1986 document says: ''Conveying the importance of biological diversity will require
a formulation of the issue in terms that are easily understandable and
convincing.'' These frightening numbers meet that test. I can find no
scientific justification for such use of numbers.

Some have said that Rachel Carson's *Silent Spring* was an important
force for good, even though it exaggerated. Maybe so, but the account is
not yet closed on the indirect and long-run consequences of ill-founded
concerns about environmental dangers. It seems to me that, without some
very special justification, there should be a presumption in favour of
statements that lead to the facts as best we know them, especially in a
scientific context.

Still, the question remains: How should decisions be made, and sound
policies formulated, with respect to the danger of species extinction? I do
not offer a full answer. It does seem clear that we cannot simply propose
saving all species at any cost, any more than we can responsibly propose
a policy of saving all human lives at any cost. Certainly we must try to
establish some informed estimates about the social value, present and

future, of species that might be lost. In the same way we find that we must estimate the value of human life in order to make rational policies about public health care services such as hospitals and surgery, and about indemnities to survivors of accidents. Just as with human life, valuing species relative to other social assets will not be easy, especially because we must value some species that we do not know about, but the job must be done somehow.

We must also try to get more reliable information about the number of species that might be lost with various changes in the forests. This is a tough task too, and one that might exercise the best faculties of many a statistician and designer of experiments.

Lastly, any policy analysis concerning species loss must explicitly evaluate the total cost of the safeguarding activity, for example, cessation of foresting in an area. Such an estimate of total cost must include the long-run indirect costs of reduction of economic growth to a community's education and general advancement, as well as the short-run costs of foregone wood or agricultural sales. To ignore such indirect costs because they are hard to estimate would be no more reasonable, and in fact probably considerably less so, than to ignore the loss of species that we have not as yet identified.

To summarize: There is now no prima-facie case for any expensive policy of safeguarding species without more extensive analysis than has so far been done. But the warnings that have been sounded should persuade us of the need for deeper thought, and more careful and wide ranging analysis, than has been done until now.

Part 3
POPULATION GROWTH

Introduction

Population growth is at the heart of the topics discussed in Section 3, just as it is at the heart of my interest. The other substantive topics discussed in this book—natural resources and the environment—followed from this interest in population economics because pollution and raw-material scarcity have commonly been thought to result from additional people.

These essays are inevitably somewhat superficial. In a newspaper or popular magazine article one cannot hope to discuss a complex economic issue in full theoretical depth or in satisfactory comprehensiveness, nor present empirical evidence that is sufficient to make a conclusive scientific case. Thoroughly covering even a portion of the field to my own satisfaction has required the 500-plus pages of theory and empirical results in *The Economics of Population Growth* (1977), my painfully-abstract 1986 book, *The Theory of Population and Economic Growth,* and dozens of abstruse articles guaranteed to cause headache in all persons except specialists. Nor does *The Ultimate Resource* (1981) do the job comprehensively and in sufficient depth, though it is at least a continuous and integrated treatment.

A reader who believes that he or she understands the economics of population after reading only these essays will be under a regrettable misapprehension. But I trust that the essays at least present sufficient argument and information to demonstrate that the common Malthusian wisdom about population growth is worse than useless. Nevertheless, that literature continues to be published widely and acted upon by the governments of billions of people. The policies built upon that literature are without foundation, and are counter-productive. I hope the sketchy treatment in these essays at least whets your interest and your desire for a deeper knowledge of the subject.

14

World Population Growth: Facts and Consequences

This essay presents some broad facts and general theories about the history of population growth. It also introduces some of the main ideas about the effects of population growth, ideas to be developed in subsequent selections. But again, a satisfactory treatment of these ideas requires a lengthy and detailed treatment found in the technical 1977 and 1987 books, and in The Ultimate Resource *(1981) from which this selection is drawn.*

Every schoolchild seems to "know" that the natural environment is deteriorating and that food is in increasingly short supply. The children's books leave no doubt that population size and growth are the villains. In the *Golden Stamp Book of Earth and Ecology* we read: "If the population continues to explode, many people will starve. About half of the world's population is underfed now, with many approaching starvation. . . . All of the major environmental problems can be traced to people—more specifically, to too many people." But these facts, which are reported to children with so much assurance, are either unproven or wrong.

The demographic facts, to the extent that they are known, are indeed frightening, at first glance. The human population appears to be expanding with self-generated natural force at an exponential rate, restrained only by starvation and disease. It seems that, without some drastic intervention to check this geometric growth, there will soon be "standing room only."

Worry about population growth is not new. Euripides, Polybius, Plato, and Tertullian are on record as citizens who feared that population growth would cause food shortages and environmental degradation. Malthus did "standing room only" arithmetic. In 1802, a Dutch colonial official wrote

The Atlantic Monthly, August 1981.

that Java, which had a population of 4 million, was "overcrowded with unemployed." Now most of Indonesia's 125 million people live in Java, and again the country is said to be overcrowded.

The common view of population growth—especially of population growth in poor countries—is that people breed "naturally." That is, poor people are assumed to have sexual intercourse without concern for the possible consequences. In the words of the environmentalist William Vogt, whose book *Road to Survival* (1948) sold millions of copies, population growth in Asia is the result of "untrammeled copulation" by Moslems, Sikhs, Hindus, and the rest of "the backward billion." A. J. Carlson, a physician, wrote in a 1955 issue of the *Journal of the American Medical Association,* "If we breed like rabbits, in the long run we have to live and die like rabbits." This idea goes hand in hand with the view that population growth will increase geometrically until starvation or disease halts it.

The idea of "natural breeding," "natural fertility," or "untrammeled copulation" has been buttressed by experiments in animal ecology, which some biologists say can serve as models of human population growth. The analogies that have been proposed include John B. Calhoun's famous observations of Norwegian rats in a pen, the putative behavior of flies in a bottle or of germs in a bucket, and the proclivities of meadow mice and cotton rats—creatures that keep multiplying until they die for lack of sustenance. But as Malthus himself acknowledged in the revised edition of his *Essay on Population,* human beings are very different from flies or rats. When faced with a bottle-like situation, people are capable of foresight and may abstain from having children for "fear of misery." That is, people can choose a level of fertility to fit the resources that will be available. Malthus wrote, "Impelled to the increase of his species by an equally powerful instinct, reason interrupts his career, and asks him whether he may not bring beings into the world, for whom he cannot provide the means of support."

Demographic history offers evidence that people can also alter the limit—expand the bottle. That is, they can increase resources when they need to. Population growth seems not to have been at all constant or steady over the long sweep of time. The broadest picture of the past million years shows three momentous and sudden changes, according to the paleo-ecologist Edward Deevey. The first such change, a rapid increase in population around 1 million B.C., followed the innovations of tool-using and tool-making. Deevey speculates that the aid of various tools "gave the food gatherer and hunter access to the widest range of environments." But when the new power from the use of primitive tools had been exploited, the rate of population growth fell and population size became almost stable.

The next rapid jump in population started perhaps 10,000 years ago, when people began to keep herds and to plow and plant the earth, rather than simply foraging for the plants and game that grew naturally. Once again, the rate of population growth abated after the initial productivity gains from the new technology had been exploited, and again population size became nearly stable in comparison with the rapid growth previously experienced.

These two episodes of a sharp rise and a subsequent fall in the rate of population growth suggest that the present rapid growth—which began in the West between 250 and 350 years ago—may also slow down when, or if, the new industrial and agricultural knowledge that followed the Industrial Revolution begins to yield fewer innovations. Of course, the current knowledge revolution may continue without foreseeable end. Either way, over the long term, population size can be seen to adjust to productive conditions, contrary to the popular belief in constant geometric growth. In this view, population growth represents economic success and human triumph, rather than social failure.

Deevey's account of population history still leaves us with the impression that population growth has an irresistible, self-reinforcing logic of its own. That perspective is so broad, however, that it can be misleading. For example, the demographers Colin Clark and Margaret Haswell have shown in their book *The Economics of Subsistence Agriculture* that even in as large an area as Europe, where local ups and downs might be expected to cancel each other out, population from 14 A.D. to 1800 did not grow at a constant rate, nor did it always grow. Instead, there were advances and reverses, provoked by a variety of forces; famine and epidemic were not the only checks.

Income has a decisive effect on population. Along with a temporary jump in fertility as income rises in poor countries comes a fall in child mortality, because of better nutrition, better sanitation, and better health care (though in the twentieth century mortality has declined in some poor countries without a rise in income). As people see that fewer births are necessary to achieve a given family size, they adjust fertility downward. Increased income also brings education and contraception within reach of more people, makes children more expensive to raise, and perhaps influences the desire to have children. It usually initiates a trend toward city living; in the city, children cost more and produce less income for the family than they do in the country.

The process by which these effects of economic development reduce fertility in the long run is called the "demographic transition." We see clearly in the excellent historical data for Sweden that the deathrate began to fall *before* the birthrate fell. We can see the same relationship between income and birthrate in many other countries. At present, the birthrate is far below replacement—that is, below zero population growth—for a number of the largest countries in Europe. Fertility has been falling in many developing countries as well. For example, the birthrate per thousand people declined in Cuba and Singapore from 1965 to 1975 by 40 percent; in Hong Kong by 36 percent; in South Korea by 32 percent; in Costa Rica by 29 percent; in Taiwan by 20 percent; in China by 24 percent; in India by 16 percent. I think we can be reasonably sure that the European pattern of demographic transition is being repeated now in other parts of the world as mortality falls and income rises.

When looking at the demographic facts with an eye to judging what ought to be done about population, we want to know what the future holds, how great the "pressures" of population size and growth will be. However, the history of demographic predictions gives us reason to be humble about turning forecasts into policy. In the 1930s, most Western countries expected and feared a decline in their populations. The most extensive investigation of the matter was undertaken in Sweden, in 1935, by some of the world's best social scientists. All four of their projections predicted that the number of Swedes would decline by as much as 2 million by 1985. But all of their hypotheses about the future—intended to bracket all of the conceivable possibilities—turned out to be far below the actual course of population, which has instead grown by about 2 million. That is, the future turned out far better, from the point of view of those scientists, than any of them guessed it might. If the Swedes had introduced fertility-increasing programs, as the demographers advised, the results would have been contrary to what they *now* want.

The Swedes were not alone in making inaccurate, pessimistic forecasts. A research committee of eminent scientists appointed by Herbert Hoover in 1933 reported that "we shall probably attain a population between 145 and 150 million during the present century." None of a variety of forecasts made in the 1930s and 1940s by America's greatest demographic experts predicted a population as large as 200 million people even for the year 2000, but the U.S. reached a population of 200 million sometime around the year 1969, and is far beyond that now. A good many of the forecasters actually predicted a decline in population before the year 2000, which at the present time we know is impossible unless there is a holocaust.

There is no reason to believe that contemporary forecasting methods are better than older ones. We have seen great variety in forecasts of world population through the 1970s. For example, in 1976, "the best demographic estimates" of world population for the year 2000 set it at "nearly 7 billion," according to the executive director of the United Nations Fund for Population Activities (UNFPA), Raphael Salas. By 1979, Mr. Salas spoke of nearly 6 billion people by 2000. Thus, in three years, Mr. Salas's figures declined by almost a billion people, or nearly one-seventh.

In the U.S., as recently as 1972, the President's Commission on Population Growth forecast that "even if the family size drops gradually—to the two-child average—there will be no year in the next two decades in which the absolute number of births will be less than in 1970." How did it turn out? In 1971—the year *before* this forecast was transmitted to the President and then published—the absolute number of births (not the birthrate) was already less than in 1970. By 1975, the absolute number of births was barely higher than in 1920, and the number of white births was actually lower than in most years between 1914 and 1924. In this case, the commission did not even backcast correctly, let alone forecast well. Embarrassing mistakes like this ought to make us think twice before we take demographic predictions to heart.

Making forecasts of population size requires making assumptions about people's choices; such assumptions have proven wrong in the past, as we have seen. We can expect that income will continue to rise, but how much of it will people expect a child to cost them? What other activities will compete with child-rearing for parents' interest and time? Such hard-to-predict judgments are likely to be the main determinants of population growth. We can at least say confidently, however, that the growth of population during the past few centuries is no proof that population will continue to grow straight upward toward infinity and doom.

Although no one knows what population size or rate of growth the future holds in store, one often hears that zero population growth, or ZPG, is the only tolerable state. Classical economic theory bolsters this conviction. It purports to show that population growth inevitably reduces the standard of living. The heart of all economic theory of population, from Malthus to *The Limits to Growth,* can be stated in a single sentence: The more people using a stock of resources, the lower the income per person, if all else remains equal. This proposition derives from the so-called law of diminishing returns. Two men cannot use the same tool, or farm the same piece of land, without producing less than they would if they did not have to share. A related idea is that two people cannot nourish themselves as well as one person can from a given stock of food. The age distribution that results from a high birthrate reinforces this effect: the number of children in proportion to workers will be larger. Also, the more children women have, the less chance they have to work outside the home, so the work force is diminished further.

According to this reasoning, both sheer numbers of people and the age distribution that occurs in the process of getting to the higher numbers ought to have the effect of a smaller per capita product. But the evidence does not confirm the conventional theory. It suggests that population growth almost certainly does not hinder, and perhaps even helps, economic growth.

One piece of historical evidence is the concurrent explosion of population and economic development in Europe from 1650 onward. Further evidence comes from a comparison of the rates of population growth and output per capita in those developed countries for which data are available for the past century. No strong relationship between the two variables appears. For example, population has grown six times faster in the United States than in France, but the rate of increase in output per capita has been about the same. The populations of Great Britain and Norway grew at the same pace for the past century, but the rate of Norway's output per capita was about a third faster. Australia, on the other hand, had a very fast rate of population growth, but its rate of increase in output per capita was quite slow.

Studies of recent rates of population growth and economic growth are another source of evidence. In less-developed countries, per capita income has been growing as fast as or faster than in the developed countries, according to a World Bank survey for the years 1950 to 1975, despite the fact that population has grown faster in developing countries than in developed countries.

Such evidence does not show that fast population growth in developed countries *increases* per capita income. But it does contradict the belief that population growth inevitably *decreases* economic growth. The lack of a cause-and-effect relationship between population and economic growth has a number of explanations, as follows:

• People make special efforts when they perceive a special need. For example, American fathers work extra, the equivalent of two to five weeks a year, for each additional child. In the long run, this yearly 4 to 10 percent increase in work may fully (or more than fully) balance the temporary loss of labor by the mother. (The other side of this coin is that people may slack off when population growth slows and demands lessen.)

• The larger proportion of young people in the labor force which results from population growth has advantages. Young workers produce more in relation to what they consume than older workers, largely because the older workers receive increases in pay with seniority, regardless of productivity. And because each generation enters the labor force with more education than the previous generation, the average worker becomes more and more knowledgeable.

• Population growth creates business opportunities and facilitates change. It makes expansion investment and new ventures more attractive, by reducing risk and by increasing total demand. For example, if housing is overbuilt or excess capacity is created in an industry, a growing population can take up the slack and remedy the error.

• More job opportunities and more young people working mean that there will be more mobility within the labor force. And mobility greatly enhances the efficient allocation of resources: the best matching of people to jobs.

• Population growth promotes "economies of scale": the greater efficiency of larger-scale production. Through this mechanism, the more people, the larger the market, and therefore the greater the need for bigger and more efficient machinery, division of labor, and improved transportation and communication. Hollis B. Chenery, an economist, compared manufacturing in less-developed countries and found that, all else being equal, if one country is twice as populous as another, output per worker is 20 percent larger. It is an established economic truth that the faster an industry grows, the faster its efficiency improves. One study, which compared the output of selected industries in the U.S. with the output of those same industries in the United Kingdom and Canada, showed that if you quadruple the size of an industry, you may expect to double the output per worker and per unit of capital employed. This should hold true for the developed world in general.

A larger population also provides economies of scale for many expensive social investments that would not be profitable otherwise—for example, railroads, irrigation systems, and ports. And public services, such as fire protection, can also be provided at lower cost per person when the population is larger.

All of the explanations just summarized have economic force, but the most important benefit that population growth confers on an economy is that people increase the stock of useful knowledge. It is your mind that matters economically, as much as or more than your mouth or hands. In the long run, the contributions people make to knowledge are great enough to overcome all the costs of population growth. This is a strong statement, but the evidence for it seems strong as well.

The importance of technological knowledge has clearly emerged in two famous studies, by Robert Solow in 1957 and by Edward Denison in 1962. Using different methods, both calculated the extent to which the growth of physical capital and of the labor force could account for economic growth in the U.S. Denison made the same calculations for Europe. They found that even after capital and labor are allowed for, much of the economic growth cannot be explained by any factor other than improvement in technological practice (including improved organization). Economies of scale as a result of larger factories do not appear to be very important from this point of view, though technology improves more rapidly in large, fast-growing industries than in small, slow-growing ones. This improvement in productivity doesn't come for free; much of it is bought with investments in research and development. But that does not alter its importance.

What is the connection between innovation and population size and growth? Since ideas come from people, it seems reasonable that the number of improvements depends on the number of people using their heads. This is not a new idea. William Petty wrote in 1683 that "it is more likely that one ingenious curious man may rather be found out among 4 millions than 400 persons." Hans Bethe, who won the Nobel Prize for physics in 1967, has said that the prospects for nuclear fusion would be rosier if the population of scientists were larger. Bethe said, "Money is not the limiting factor. . . . Progress is limited rather by the availability of highly trained workers."

Even a casual consideration of history shows that as population has grown in the last century, there have been many more discoveries and a faster rate of growth in productivity than in previous centuries. In prehistoric times, progress was agonizingly slow. For example, whereas routinely we develop new materials—say, plastics and metals—millennia passed between the invention of copper metallurgy and of iron metallurgy. If the population had been larger, technological discoveries would surely have come along faster. Ancient Greece and Rome have often been suggested as examples contrary to this line of reasoning. Therefore, I plotted the numbers of great discoveries, as recorded by historians of science who have made such lists, against Greek and Roman populations in various centuries. This comparison showed that an increase in population or its rate of growth (or both) was associated with an increase in scientific activity, and population decline with a decrease.

In modern times, there is some fairly strong evidence to confirm the positive effect of population growth on science and technology: in countries at the same level of income, scientific output is proportional to population size. For example, the standard of living in the U.S. and in Sweden is roughly the same, but the U.S. is much larger than Sweden and it produces much more scientific knowledge. A consideration of the references used in Swedish and U.S. scientific papers and of the number of patented processes that Sweden licenses from the U.S. bears this out.

Why isn't populous India a prosperous and advanced country? I have not argued that a large population will by itself overcome all the other variables in a society—its climate, culture, history, political structure. I have said only that there is no evidence to prove that a large population *creates* poverty and underdevelopment. India is poor and underdeveloped for many reasons, and it might be even more so if it had a smaller population. The proper comparison is not India and the United States but India and other poor countries, and the fact is that India has one of the largest scientific establishments in the Third World—perhaps in part because of its large population.

It cannot be emphasized too strongly that "techonological and scientific advance" does not mean only sophisticated research, and geniuses are not the only source of knowledge. Much technological advance comes from people who are neither well-educated nor well-paid: the dispatcher who develops a slightly better way of deploying the taxis in his ten-taxi fleet, the shipper who discovers that garbage cans make excellent cheap containers.

Population growth spurs the adoption of existing technology as well as the invention of new technology. This has been well-documented in agriculture, where people turn to successively more "advanced" but more laborious methods of getting food as population density increases—methods that may have been known but were ignored because they weren't needed. For example, hunting and gathering—which require very few hours of work a week to provide a full diet—give way to migratory slash-and-burn agriculture, which yields to settled, long-fallow agriculture, and that to short-fallow agriculture. Eventually fertilizer, irrigation, and multiple cropping are adopted. Though each stage initially requires more labor than the one before, the end point is a more efficient and productive system.

This phenomenon also explains why the advance of civilization is not a race between technology and population, each progressing independently of the other. Contrary to the Malthusian view, there is no direct link between each food-increasing invention and increased production of food. Some inventions, such as a better calendar for planting, may be adopted as soon as they prove successful, because they will increase production with no more labor. Others, such as settled agriculture or irrigated multi-cropping, require more labor, and thus will not be adopted until there is demand.

The fact that people learn by doing is a key to the improvement of productivity in particular industries, and in the economies of nations. The idea is simple: the bigger the population, the more of everything that is produced. With a greater volume come more chances for people to improve their skills and to devise better methods. Industrial engineers have understood this process for many decades, but economists first grasped its importance when they examined the production of airplanes during World War II. They discovered that when twice as many airplanes were produced, the labor required per plane is reduced by 20 percent. That is, if the first airplane requires 1000 units of labor, the second will require 800 units, and so on, though after some time the gains from increased efficiency level off. Similar "progress ratios" describe the production of lathes, machine tools, textiles machines, and ships. The effect of learning by doing can also be seen in the progressive reduction in price of new consumer devices in the years following their introduction to the market—room air-conditioners and color television sets, for example.

We have seen that population size and growth have a variety of economic effects. Economists must take account of the size and importance of all these effects, and of their influences. They do so by constructing a model that integrates the important elements of an economy and using it to compare the per capita incomes that result at various rates of population growth.

Whether mathematical or verbal, simple or complex, computerized or not, conventional models of the effect of additional people on the standard of living have first-edition Malthus as a common root. If, however, we add to the Malthusian model another fundamental fact of economic growth— the increase in productivity that results from people's creative powers— we arrive at a very different result. Such a model does not treat human beings simply as human capital, a commodity that is essentially plastic and inert like physical capital. Rather, it treats people as people, who respond to their economic needs with physical and mental efforts up to and including the creative spark. Imagination and creativity are not concepts commonly included in economic models, but let us recognize their importance without embarrassment, and give them their due.

I studied the economic effects of different rates of population growth— zero growth, one-percent growth a year, and two-percent growth a year, among others—on the developed world, using a model designed to take account of the contributions of additional people to technological advance. Under every set of conditions, the hypothetical economies subjected to faster population growth come to have higher per-worker income than is yielded by economies subjected to slower population growth, in eighty years at most. Under some conditions, the higher fertility rates overtake the one-percent growth rate in output per worker after only thirty years— that is, only about ten years after the first additional child enters the work force. Furthermore, economic effects of the various rates of population growth do not differ much, by any absolute measure, in the short run. It is the long-run differences that are large.

It is true that thirty to eighty years is a long way off. But we ought to remember that our future will be someone else's present, just as our present was someone else's future. Some measure of unselfishness should compel us to remember this as we make decisions about population policy. For example, readers might check the conclusions drawn from this model with their intuitions about whether the U.S, would be better off today if the population in 1830 had been reduced by half. To me it seems reasonably plain that our ancestors bestowed upon us the benefits of knowledge and economies of scale, and if we did not have as many ancestors our legacy would have been smaller.

For developing countries, the conventional economic models are even more baleful about population growth than they are for developed countries. A model by Ansley J. Coale and Edgar M. Hoover has had decisive effect on demographic thinking and on government policy for more than twenty years. "The Coale-Hoover thesis eventually provided the justification for birth control as a part of U.S. foreign aid policy," according to Phyllis Piotrow, in her book *World Population Crisis: The United States' Response.* Coale and Hoover simply assumed that the total national product in a developing country will not be increased by population growth for the thirty-year period of their model, either by a larger labor force or by additional productive efforts. Therefore, their arithmetic boils down to the ratio of output divided by consumers; an increase in the number of consumers decreases the per-capita consumption, no matter what.

There are other influences to be accounted for, however: the positive effect of increased demand on business and agricultural investment; the propensity of people to devote more hours to work when family size increases; the shift in labor from agriculture to industry; economies of scale in public works; and the larger number of workers. When these elements are included, and when reasonable assumptions are made about the likely behavior of the economies of developing countries, the results are nothing like the dark predictions we've grown accustomed to hearing. According to my model, a population that grows slowly or not at all has slightly higher output per capita than more rapidly growing populations for about the first sixty years. But thereafter (120 to 180 years), moderate population growth produces considerably better economic performance. A declining population does very badly in the long run.

Therefore, for developing countries, as for developed countries, our judgment of population growth depends on how we value the present as compared with the future. If we pay attention only to the present, then additional children are a burden on the economies of developing countries. But if we can be as concerned about the welfare of future generations as we are about our own, then we will consider additional children a benefit. Given the economic analysis outlined here, anyone who takes a long-range view of the world should prefer a growing population to one that is stationary or declining.

In the short run, all resources are limited: the pulpwood that went into making this book, the pages the publisher will allow me, and the attention you, the reader, will devote to what I say. The longer run, however, is a different story. The standard of living has risen along with the size of the world's population since the beginning of recorded time. There is no convincing economic reason why these trends toward a better life should not continue indefinitely. Adding more people causes problems, but people are also the means to solve these problems. The main fuel to speed the world's progress is our stock of knowledge, and the brake is our lack of imagination. The ultimate resource is people—skilled, spirited, and hopeful people—who will exert their wills and imaginations for their own benefit, and so, inevitably, for the benefit of us all.

15

Why Do We Still Think Babies Cause Poverty?

This selection surveys the effects of population growth in less-developed countries. Together with Selections 2 and 14, as well as Part 2, it draws upon and summarizes the main arguments of The Ultimate Resource. *Selection 15, however, emphasizes the importance of property rights, economic freedom, and a decentralized economy in economic development. Once these factors are accounted for, it becomes understandable that population growth does not have a negative effect upon economic growth.*

Why do we still believe that population growth slows economic development?

For 25 years our institutions have misanalyzed such world development problems as starving children, illiteracy, pollution, supplies of natural resources and slow growth. The World Bank, the State Department's Aid to International Development (AID), The United Nations Fund for Population Activities (UNFPA), and the environmental organizations have asserted that the cause is population growth—the population "explosion" or "bomb" or "plague."

But for almost as long, there has been a body of statistical evidence that contradicts this conventional wisdom about the effects of population policy toward less-developed countries.

This error has cost dearly. It has directed our attention away from the factor that we now know is central in a country's economic development, its economic and political system.

Furthermore, misplaced belief that population growth slows economic development has been the basis for inhumane programs of coercion and

The Washington Post, October 13, 1985.

the denial of personal liberty in one of the most valued choices a family can make—the number of children that it wishes to bear and raise.

One of the reasons this idea stays in currency is that in an ideologically divided world, the population bogey has been the rare sweet issue everyone could agree upon. I ran into this perverted amity at a discussion of population economics in India last winter attended by many employes of international agencies. In four days, there was not a single mention of the role of the economic system, whether market-directed or state-controlled. And when I suggested that the subject should at least be aired, I was met by silence in the formal meeting, and I was told informally that the issue simply is outside the scope of attention. "It's like talking religion," one said.

Nevertheless, by 1985 we know that unlike religion—which is a matter of personal preference and not of science—there is objective evidence that a free enterprise system works better than does a planned economy.

As we shall see, among comparable populations, such as those of North and South Korea, East and West Germany, or China and Taiwan (or China and Hong Kong or Singapore), the part with the enterprise system has obviously produced greater economic well-being.

Moreover, population growth under an enterprise system poses less of a problem in the short run, and brings many more benefits in the long run, than under conditions of government planning of the economy.

There are about a dozen competent statistical studies opposing the population-explosion theorists. They began in 1967 with an analysis by Nobel laureate economist Simon Kuznets covering the few countries for which data are available over the past century, and analyses by Kuznets and Richard Easterlin of the data covering many countries since World War II.

The basic method is to gather data on each country's rate of population growth and its rate of economic growth, and then to examine whether—looking at all the data in the sample together—the countries with high population growth rates have economic growth rates lower than average, and countries with low population growth rates have economic growth rates higher than average.

The studies agree that faster population growth is not associated with slower economic growth. On average, countries whose populations grew faster did not grow slower economically.

Of course, as countries develop economically, the fertility rate tends to fall. But it is the economic level that influences the rate of population growth, not the reverse. Costs and benefits of having children change with the shift from rural to urban living along with increases in education and shifts in attitudes—this being the famous "demographic transition."

The examples of Taiwan, South Korea, Singapore, and Hong Kong have already been cited. Countries with high population growth and high economic growth include Thailand, Malaysia, Ecuador, Jordan, Brazil, Mexico, Syria, Panama, Taiwan, South Korea, Singapore, and Hong Kong.

Typically, Thailand's population more than doubled from 20 million to 43 million between 1950 and 1977, around 3 percent growth yearly. And its rate of growth of income per person was around 4 percent over the same years. Of course there are counterbalancing examples of high population growth and low economic growth, such as many countries in Africa, where the political-economic system dominates the economic outcome just as it does in the countries with high economic growth.

In a review commissioned by the International Union for the Scientific Study of Population, Ronald D. Lee summarized: "Dozens of studies, starting with Kuznets', have found no association between the population growth rate and the per-capita income growth rate."

Yet not a single one of these studies is cited by the extensive World Bank Report, which has been so widely publicized, or in such literature as the Worldwatch Institute's new book by Lester Brown.

The research-wise reader may wonder whether population density is more important than population growth. But the data show that higher density is associated with better rather than poorer economic results.

Check for yourself: fly over Hong Kong—just a few decades ago a place seemingly without prospects because of insoluble resource problems—and you will marvel at the astounding collection of modern high-rise apartments and office buildings. Take a ride on its excellent smooth-flowing highways for an hour, and you will realize that a very dense concentration of human beings—40 times the density of China—does not prevent comfortable existence and exciting economic expansion, as long as the economic system gives individuals the freedom to exercise their talents and to take advantage of opportunities.

The experience of Singapore demonstrates that Hong Kong is not unique. Its population density and its soaring per-person income—over $5000 by 1982—are like Hong Kong's. Two such examples do not prove the case, of course. But these dramatic illustrations are backed by the evidence from the aggregate sample of countries.

Hong Kong is a special thrill for me because I first saw it in 1955 when I went ashore from a U.S. Navy destroyer. At the time I pitied the thousands who slept every night on the sidewalks or on small boats. It then seemed clear to me, as it must have to all, that it would be impossible for Hong Kong to surmount its problems—huge masses of impoverished people without jobs, total lack of exploitable natural resources, more refugees pouring across the border each day. But upon returning in 1983, I saw bustling crowds of healthy, vital people full of hope and energy. No cause for pity now.

And there is growing agreement with the viewpoint expressed here. Mine is certainly not a lone voice.

For example, P. T. Bauer—made a lord for his services as economic adviser to Prime Minister Margaret Thatcher and nowadays perhaps the most influential theorist on economic development—says that rapid population growth "has not inhibited economic progress in either the West or in the contemporary Third World." And a book length review of the subject by the national Academy of Sciences to be released soon reaches a much less negative conclusion about population growth's effects than did its previous report in 1971.

The layman inevitably wonders: How can the persuasive common sense embodied in the Malthusian theory be wrong? To be sure, in the short run an additional person—baby or immigrant—inevitably means a lower standard of living for everyone; every parent knows that. More consumers mean less of the fixed available stock of goods to be divided among more people. And more workers laboring with the same fixed current stock of capital means that there will be less output per worker. The latter effect, known as "the law of diminshing returns," is the essence of Malthus's theory.

But if the resources with which people work are not fixed over the period being analyzed, then the Malthusian logic of diminishing returns does not apply. And the plain fact is that, given some time to adjust to shortages, the resource base does not remain fixed. People create more resources of all kinds. When horse-powered transportation became insufficient to meet needs, the railroad and the motor car were developed. When schoolhouses become crowded, we build new schools—more modern and better than the old ones.

As with man-made production capital, so it is with natural resources. When a shortage of elephant tusks for ivory billiard bills threatened in the last century, and a prize was offered for a substitute, celluloid was invented, followed by the rest of our plastics. The English learned to use coal in industry when trees became scarce in the 16th century. Satellites and fiber-optics derived from sand replace now-expensive copper for telephone transmission. And the new resources wind up cheaper than the old ones were. Such has been the entire course of civilization.

Extraordinary as it seems, natural-resource scarcity—that is, the cost of raw materials, which is the relevant economic measure of scarcity—has tended to decrease rather than to increase over the entire sweep of history. The prices of all natural resources, measured in the wages necessary to pay for given quantities of them, have been falling as far back as data exist. A pound of copper now costs an American only a twentieth of what it cost in hourly wages two centuries ago, and perhaps a thousandth of what it cost 3000 years ago.

The most extraordinary part of the resource-creation process is that temporary or expected shortages, whether due to population growth income growth or other causes, tend to leave us even better off than if the shortages had never arisen, because of the continuing benefit of the intellectual and physical capital created to meet the shortage.

For all practical purposes there are no resources until we find them, identify their possible uses, and develop ways to obtain and process them. We perform these tasks with increasing skill as technology develops. Hence, scarcity diminishes.

Besides, the general trend is toward natural resources becoming less and less important with economic development. Extractive industries are only a very small part of a modern economy, say a twentieth or less, whereas they constitute the lion's share of poor economies. Japan and Hong King prosper despite the lack of natural resources, whereas such independence was impossible in earlier centuries.

And though agriculture is thought to be a very important part of the American economy, if all of our agricultural land passed out of our ownership tomorrow, our loss of wealth would only equal about a ninth of one year's gross national product.

There is, however, one crucial natural resource that is becoming more scarce—human beings. Yes, there are more people on earth now than in the past. But if we measure the scarcity of people the same way we measure the scarcity of economic goods—by the market price—then people are indeed becoming more scarce, because the price of labor time has been rising almost everywhere in the world.

Just a few years after Egypt was said to have a labor surplus, agricultural wages in Egypt have soared, for example, and people complain of a labor shortage, because of the demand for workers in the Persian Gulf.

Even the World Bank, for years the leading worrier about population and natural resources, has muted its alarms. "The difficulties caused by rapid population growth are not primarily due to finite natural resources," its 1984 Report states. But no sooner is one fear about population growth scotched, then another takes its place.

The latest bugaboo is the effect of population growth upon education. The World Bank now worries that even if a higher birthrate does not imply fewer natural resources, it does imply less education per person. Once more, it just ain't so.

Studies have shown that societies with relatively high proportions of youths somehow find the resources to educate their children almost or equally as well as do countries at similar income levels with lower birth rates. Outstanding examples of high rates of education in the face of relatively large numbers of children include the Philippines, Costa Rica, Peru, Jordan, and Thailand.

Now we come to the matter that the international development institutions consider poor form to mention when discussing economic development: economic and social systems.

Compare China with Singapore. China's coercive population policy, including forced abortions, is often called "pragmatic" because its economic development supposedly requires population control.

Singapore, despite its very high population density, now suffers from a labor shortage, and imports workers. It is even considering incentives for middle-class families to have more children, in contrast to its previous across-the-board antinatality policy. This raises the question whether there are economic grounds for China to even ask, much less compel, people to have only one child.

It is said, however: Hong Kong and Singapore are different because they are city-states. But what does that mean—that if large hinterlands were attached to those "city-states," they would then be caused to be as poor as China?

Compare countries that have the same culture and history, and had much the same standard of living when they split apart after World War II. Tables 15–1 through 15–5 show centrally planned communist countries that had and still have less population per square mile than the market-directed noncommunist countries. The communist and noncommunist countries in each pair also started with much the same birthrates and population growth rates.

The tables make clear, despite the frequent absence of data for the centrally-planned countries, that the market-directed economies have performed much better economically, no matter how you measure economic progress. Income per person is higher. Wages have grown faster.

Further, indexes such as telephones per person show a much higher level of development. And indicators of individual wealth and personal consumption, such as autos and newsprint, show enormous advantages for the market-directed enterprise economies compared to the centrally planned, centrally controlled economies.

Table 15–6 shows recent data for the two Germanies wherein the advantage of West Germany is seen to have grown quite large. And if one were to include quality differences among such items as autos, the differences would be even larger. But housing costs might show to the advantage of East Germany.

The health-care system has also suffered from the relative poverty in

Table 15-1. Population Density and Growth, Selected Countries, 1950-83

	East Germany	West Germany	North Korea	South Korea	China	Taiwan	Hong Kong	Singapore	U.S.S.R.	U.S.A.	India	Japan
Population per sq km, 1950	171	201	76	212	57	212	2236	1759	8	16	110	224
% change in pop., 1950	1.2	1.1	-7.8	0.1	1.9	3.3	-10.4	4.4	1.7	1.7	1.7	1.6
% change in pop., 1955	-1.3	1.2	3.5	2.2	2.4	3.5	4.9	4.9	1.8	1.8	1.9	1.0
% change in pop., 1960	-0.7	1.3	3.0	3.3	1.8	3.1	3.0	3.3	1.8	1.7	2.0	0.9
% change in pop., 1970	-0.1	1.0	3.0	2.4	2.4	2.2	2.2	1.7	1.0	1.1	2.2	1.3
% change in pop., 1983	-0.3	-0.2	2.1-2.6	1.4-1.6	1.3-1.6	1.8	1.5	1.2	0.7-0.9	0.9	2.1-2.2	0.6

Sources: Population per square kilometer: United Nations Educational, Scientific, and Cultural Organization, *UNESCO Yearbook* (1963, pp. 12-21). Percentage change in population: U.S. Department of Commerce, *World Population* (1978); United Nations, Report on *World Population* (1984).

Table 15-2. Real Income per Capita, Selected Countries, 1950-82

	East Germany	West Germany	North Korea	South Korea	China	Taiwan	Hong Kong	Singapore	U.S.S.R.	U.S.A.	India	Japan
Real GDP per capita, 1950 [a]	1480	1888	N.A.	N.A.	300	508	N.A.	N.A.	1373	4550	333	810
Real GDP per capita, 1960	3006	3711	N.A.	631	505	733	919	1054	2084	5195	428	1674
Real GDP per capita, 1970	4100	5356	N.A.	1112	711	1298	2005	2012	3142	6629	450	4215
Real GDP per capita, 1980	5532 [c]	6967 [c]	N.A.	2007	1135	2522	3973	3948	3943	8089	498	5996
Real GNP per capita, 1950 [b]	Same as W. Germ.	2943	Same as S. Korea	193	N.A.	417	1053	N.A.	N.A.	7447	217	649
Real GNP per capita, 1960	N.A.	3959	N.A.	473	N.A.	429	979	1330	N.A.	8573	220	1403
Real GNP per capita, 1970	6584	6839	556	615	556	868	1807	2065	4670	10769	219	4380
Real GNP per capita, 1982	9914 [c]	11032 [c]	817	1611	630	2579	5064	5600	5991	12482	235	9774

a   Figures for real gross domestic product (GDP) per capita are based on 1975 international prices.
b   Figures for real gross national product (GNP) per capita are based on 1981 constant U.S. dollars.
c   See Table 15-6.

Sources: Real GDP per capita: Summers and Heston (1984). Real GNP per capita: International Bank for Reconstruction and Development (IBRD), *World Tables* (1980). GNP deflator: Council of Economic Advisers (1986, Table B-3).

Table 15-3. Life Expectancy and Infant Mortality, Selected Countries, 1960-82

	East Germany	West Germany	North Korea	South Korea	China	Taiwan	Hong Kong	Singapore	U.S.S.R.	U.S.A.	India	Japan
Life expectancy at birth, 1960	68	69	54	54	53	65	65	64	68	70	43	68
Life expectancy at birth, 1982	73	74	65	68	67	73	76	73	69	75	55	77
Infant Mortality, 1960	39	34	78	78	165	32	37	35	33	26	165	30
Infant Mortality, 1982	12 [a]	12 [a]	32	32	67	18	10	11	28	11	94	7

a In 1987, infant mortality had risen to be 32 percent higher in East Germany *(Wall Street Journal,* September 4, 1987, p.10).

Source: IBRD, *World Development Report* (1985, pp. 260-61).

Table 15-4. Industrialization and Urbanization, Selected Countries, 1960-82

	East Germany	West Germany	North Korea	South Korea	China	Taiwan	Hong Kong	Singapore	U.S.S.R.	U.S.A.	India	Japan
% Labor force in agric., 1960	18	14	62	66	N.A.	N.A.	8	8	42	7	74	33
% Labor force in agric., 1980	10	4	49	34	69	37 (1978)	3	2	14	2	71	12
% Urbanized 1960	72	77	40	28	18	58	89	100	49	70	18	63
% Urbanized 1982	77	85	63	61	21	70 (1978)	91	100	63	78	24	78

Sources: Labor force in agriculture: IBRD *World Development Report* (1985, pp. 258-59). Urban population: IBRD, *World Development Report* (1985, pp. 260-61).

Table 15-5. Education and Consumption, Selected Countries, Various Years

	East Germany	West Germany	North Korea	South Korea	China	Taiwan	Hong Kong	Singapore	U.S.S.R.	U.S.A.	India	Japan
Higher education enrollment, 1960	16	6	N.A.	5	N.A.	N.A.	4	6	11	32	3	10
Higher education enrollment, 1982	30	30	N.A.	22	1	N.A.	12	10	21	56	9	31
Newsprint per person, 1950-54	3.5	5.1	N.A.	0.6	N.A.	0.9	4.3	N.A.	1.2	35.0	0.2	3.3
Newsprint per person, 1982	9.6	21.5	0.1	5.8	1.2	N.A.	16.4	32.1	4.5	44.1	0.4	24.0
Telephones per 100 pop., 1983	20.6	57.1	N.A.	14.9	0.5	25.8	38.2	36.7	9.8	76.0	0.5	52.0
Autos per 100 pop., 1960	0.9	8.2	N.A.	0.1	0.005	0.1	1.0	4.2	0.3	34.4	0.1	0.5
Autos per 100 pop., 1970	6.7	24.1	N.A.	0.2	0.018	N.A.	2.8	7.2	0.7	43.9	0.1	8.5
Autos per 100 pop., 1984	18.9	41.3	N.A.	1.1	0.010	3.1	4.6	9.3	3.9	55.5	0.2	22.8

Sources: Higher education: IBRD *World Development Report* (1985, pp. 266-67). Newsprint: *UNESCO Yearbook* (1963, pp. 400-409). Telephones: U.S. Department of Commerce, *Statistical Abstract* (1986, p. 845). Automobiles: Motor Vehicle Manufacturers Association of the U.S. Inc., *World Motor Vehicle Data* (various years).

Table 15-6. Living Standards in West and East Germany as of 1987

	West Germany	East Germany
Population (in millions)	61.3	16.7
Area (in sq. miles)	95,975	41,768
Gross national product in 1980	1,265.5*	234.0*
Working hours needed to buy		
Car	607	3,807
Refrigerator	40	293
Man's suit	13	67
Housing facilities, percent that have		
Central heating	70	36
Indoor toilet	95	60
Bath/shower	92	68

* In billions of West German and East German marks, respectively. The official exchange rate of the West German and East German marks is one to one, but one West German mark buys five or six East German marks on the black market. One West German mark is the equivalent of about 58 U.S. cents.

Source: Wall Street Journal, September 4, 1987, p.1. Originally from "A Report on the National Situation in a Divided Germany," West German Ministry for Inter-German Relations, 1987.

East Germany. "Today, the infant mortality rate is 32 percent higher in the East" (*The Wall Street Journal,* September 4, 1987, p. 10).

Table 15–7 shows similar data for the town of Cesky Krumlov in Czechoslovakia and Freistadt in Austria just 40 miles distant across the border. The results are similar to those for East and West Germany.

Also, birth rates fell at least as early and as fast in the market-directed countries as in the centrally planned countries.

China's problem is not too many children, but rather a defective political-economic system. With free markets China might soon experience the same sort of labor shortage as Singapore—which is vastly more densely settled, and has zero natural resources. (And this does not mean a "free" system such as China is talking about now; it is quite unlikely that a truly free market can coexist with a totalitarian political system, because a free economy is too great a political threat.)

Even the most skilled persons require a social and economic framework that rewards hard work and risks, enabling their talents to flower. The key elements of such a framework are economic liberty, respect for property, fair and sensible rules of the market that are enforced equally for all, and

Table 15-7. Living Standards, Austria and Czechoslovakia

	Cesky Krumlov, Czechoslovakia	Freistadt, Austria
One-pound steak	2.5 hours	1 hour
Shoes	22 hours	11 hours
One month's rent	25 hours	41 hours
Color television	565 hours	109 hours
Compact car	4,130 hours	2,054 hours
Three-bedroom house	43,487 hours	20,547 hours

Note: For all products except steak, quality is considerably higher in Freistadt than in Cesky Krumlov.

Source: Washington Post, Sept. 18, 1988.

the personal freedom that is particularly compatible with economic freedom.

What should we do about population policy? These are the key issues: First, should we encourage and aid countries to implement coercive population policies, as we have in the past with China, India, Indonesia, and many other places? The answer depends upon one's values, of course. But we should recognize that the scientific evidence about the long-run economic consequences offers no support for such policies.

And what should our vision be? Should we heed the message of the doomsayers of the population control movement? This is a message of limits, decreasing resources, a zero-sum game where one gains wealth at the expense of others, conservation, deterioration, fear, conflict, and calling for more governmental intervention in markets and family affairs.

Or should our vision be that of those who look optimistically upon people as a resource rather than as a burden? This is a message of receding limits, increasing resources and possibilities, a process in which wealth is created, consistent with the belief that persons and firms, acting spontaneously in search of their individual welfare, regulated only by rules of a fair game, will produce enough to maintain and increase economic progress and promote liberty.

16

Population Growth and Scientific Evidence

Many of the selections mention the large and competent body of econometric studies that inquire into the empirical relationship between nations' rates of population growth and their rates of economic growth. It was the first of those studies that completely turned around my thinking about population economics. But until recently almost no one interested in demography has embraced those studies and their conclusions, and even in 1988 few have done so even after several well-respected reviews of the literature and "official" reports have noted their importance. This selection attempts to refute some of the unsound criticisms that have been made of that body of literature.

A dilemma of modern society: We must decide about issues that hinge on scientific questions. But the science seems too complex for newspapers to publish and readers to comprehend. As a result, simple but wrong arguments dictate many policy decisions.

The effect of nations' population growth rates on their rates of economic development illustrates the point. More than a few sentences are needed to interpret the statistical studies properly. Critics (for example, Robert Repetto of the World Resources Institute, in *The Washington Post,* November 2, 1985, p. A21), therefore have been able to dismiss this solid body of scientific work with catchy nonsense such as "correlation does not prove causation."

Determining the connection between population growth and economic development is a casebook example of the use and abuse of scientific method. The problem before us is to decide whether additional children being born cause a nation's material progress to be slowed, or whether there is instead no effect or even a positive effect. We wish to reach a conclusion that is warranted by the empirical evidence rather than resting on prejudice or intuition or metaphysical speculation or casual observation.

It is instructive to compare how scientists tackle the analogous problem of deciding whether smoking cigarettes causes lung cancer. The question first arose when some physicians noticed that a high proportion of patients afflicted with lung cancer were smokers. And pathologists observed dark, tarry material in the lungs of corpses of persons who had died of that disease.

Medical researchers therefore investigated samples of smokers and nonsmokers, and found a higher proportion of lung-cancer sufferers among smokers. They recognized that the conclusion might later be found invalid. Nevertheless, they concluded that this evidence by itself, with or without various hypotheses that might explain such a connection, was sufficiently meaningful to advise patients not to smoke.

Similarly, various social scientists thought that countries with high birth rates tended to have low rates of economic advance. Malthusian reasoning supported that observation. Therefore, Simon Kuznets—a Nobel prize-winner, and perhaps the greatest statistical economic historian of modern times—examined the records of the few countries that have century-long data series. And he and Richard Easterlin separately examined the records of the large number of countries for which data are available since World War II.

Unlike the results with smoking and cancer, however, the studies did *not* reveal a correlation between the rates of population growth and economic growth. Many similar studies since then have corroborated this result. And there are a variety of reasonable explanations why this could be so. Therefore, it is appropriate to conclude that faster population growth does not cause slower economic development.

The smoking researchers pushed on to check the possibility of third-factor causation. They examined whether such variables as income, geography, and race could be the "real" cause of the observed correlation. When they found that the other reasonable possibilities could be ruled out, they expressed even stronger belief that smoking causes lung cancer.

The likelihood is greater that some "third factor" would be responsible for an observed positive correlation (as in smoking and cancer) than for an observed noncorrelation (as in population and development). Hence, this conclusion is more solid than is the smoking-causes-cancer conclusion based on the same sort of simple correlational evidence. For a third factor to somehow offset a "real" influence in a way that would cause a zero correlation would require a causal network of extraordinary complexity. The possibility of third-factor causation therefore can safely be ignored unless someone finds empirical evidence that such a mechanism really does operate.

Nevertheless, population economists widened their analysis to include such variables as geography, income level, form of economic system, and amount of investment. When they still found no relationship between population growth and economic development, the conclusion was strengthened that the former does not hinder the latter.

The direction of the influence between the two correlated variables also must be checked. Causal directionality is easier to establish when there is experimental evidence than when—as in the smoking-and-cancer and the population-and-development sample surveys—the evidence is not experimental. If an experimental increase in fertilizer correlates with an increase in plant growth, we can immediately rule out the possibility that the rate of plant growth causes the rate of fertilizer addition. But to rule out the possibility that a genetic propensity to cancer causes one to smoke, or that faster economic development causes higher fertility, needs further study before it should be ruled out.

Animal experiments are auxiliary supporting evidence that smoking causes cancer rather than the reverse. But of course animals are not people, and hence those experiments are not ironclad proof.

The fact that a correlation is not observed between the rate of economic development and the rate of population growth makes almost moot the issue of the direction of causality. Nevertheless, it is logically possible that a positive influence running from the former to the latter might counterbalance a negative effect running in the other direction. The *level* of people's income affects their fertility. But there is no persuasive reason to think that the *rate of change* of income should influence fertility. This auxiliary logical support helps rule out the possibility that the rate of economic development influences the rate of population growth.

The endpoint of this interlocking body of evidence, theory, and logic is a rather solid conclusion that population growth does not slow a nation's economic development. The conclusion may not be quite as solid as the conclusion that smoking causes cancer. But that is not surprising given that many many times more researchers and money have been focused on the effect of smoking than on the effect of population growth. And the scientific and journalistic communities have been much less hostile to the idea that smoking is harmful than that population growth is not harmful.

Is it not time for journalists to attempt to rectify the unfounded negative judgment about the effects of additional human beings that has been promulgated so widely during the last two decades? Is it not time that they take seriously the body of statistical studies contradicting this conclusion?

17

A Parable of Raquetball, Squash, and Population Growth at U. of I.

Over the course of years the difficulty I experienced in making a persuasive argument about the positive long-run efects of population growth led me to try a variety of rhetorical devices. The tactic adopted in this piece is to describe a scenario which could seem real to the reader of this piece in the college newspaper, in hopes that the immediacy of the situation would make it easier for the reader to imagine the long-run indirect effects which usually are less compelling than the immediate effects of congestion before adjustments can be made.

There are twenty-three wonderful handball-racquetball courts on the Urbana campus of the University of Illinois, and seven excellent squash courts, in addition to a batch of old courts. The new racquetball courts are frequently crowded nowadays, though not so badly that people complain a lot. From time to time, however, players worry about the future growth of the university, saying that it is going to be tough to get a racquetball court. And I have heard people argue against increasing the number of students for that reason.

The racquetball court situtation exemplifies the country's situation with respect to population growth and the supply of capital. If there come to be more people there will immediately be an increased demand for the courts. It will also be harder to find parking space, and perhaps a job. That is, the immediate effect of an increase in population is an increase in congestion. The individual suffers because of the greater competition for the good things that are available and because of the greater out-of-pocket costs of providing more of these good things to take care of the added population. This increase in costs is inevitable and undeniable.

From *The Ultimate Resource*, 1981.

But now let us take a slightly longer view. Why are we so lucky as to have twenty-three wonderful racquetball courts and seven squash courts at the University of Illinois? Years ago there were sixteen dingy, wrong-sized courts to be used for both sports together. But then came a rapid population growth at the university. Our superb new facilities were built in response to that population growth—though at a considerable cost to the taxpayers and the students at that time.

So we are now reaping the benefits of the rapid population growth in the past and at the same time talking against further population growth so that we do not have to share this stock of capital—the benefits of past population growth—with more people, and so that we do not have to cough up the investment necessary for additional population growth. There is nothing illogical about this point of view. As the sage Hillel put it, "If I am not for myself, who will be for me?" But if we see ourselves as part of a longer historical process than this instant of our own consciousness, and if we take into account the welfare of ourselves and our children in the years to come—as people before us took *our* welfare into account—then we will see that we ought to cooperate and put back as well as take from the pot. As Hillel added, "But if I am for myself alone, what am I?"

Our children may well have more racquetball courts in the future—and better ones—if more children are born year after year than if fewer are born. That is, if the population does grow at the university, more courts and better courts will be built, whereas if the population stabilizes at its present size, no more facilities will be built.

More generally, if farmers had not come to Illinois and developed the land and built up the state so that it could support a university, there would certainly be no racquetball courts at all for us to enjoy now. Central Illinois, with its remarkably productive cornfields, would still be a malarial and unproductive swamp.

Let's consider the squash courts too. I can get into a squash court at any time of the day, except very occasionally at 5:00 in the afternoon, when there are one or two courts too few for all those who would like to play. Most of the day the squash courts are used hardly at all. From one point of view, this is paradise for squash players like me. On the other hand, there are often too few people to play with. Furthermore, there is a slightly depressing air about the squash courts. It seems a bit like a home for the aged, because most of the players are thirty-five and up except for those who have come from England or South Africa. Few young students or faculty members have taken up the game, which is why there is no problem in getting a court. In contrast, there is a vitality around the racquetball courts. There are always people watching and giving advice and jostling a bit and checking out the challenge court to see the newest rising star. The racquetball courts have produced some national-level competitors in a short time. Around the squash courts it is all very dignified and peaceful. But as I said, it is also a bit depressing.

What about the future? If the population of the university grows, there is a good chance that we shall still have plenty of squash courts fifteen years from now—except that the players will be doddering incompetents. And by that time the squash courts will be in rundown condition, whereas chances are that there will be a whole new battery of racquetball courts. The run-down squash courts (and players) will be the cost of having no growth in the population of squash players.

So which do you want? Will you choose the genteel, run-down, peaceful, and slightly depressing no-growth policy, as with the squash courts? Or do you prefer the less-peaceful, slightly jostling population growth that costs you capital for awhile, as with the racquetball courts?

18

The Impending Shortage of People

The population of the world is much greater now than it has been in the past. This observation usually evokes the knee-jerk reaction that "we" are therefore facing increased social problems. One hears that "we" have more people than "we" have "need" of, though "we" inevitably goes undefined. What amazing arrogance and self-centeredness!

This selection shows that though there has been an increase in absolute numbers of humans on earth, the "need" for people has grown even faster. This makes sense when we measure the trend in the need for people the same way we measure the need for all economic goods—that is, by price. The increasing price of the services of people indicates that, along with the growth in total population, people have indeed been becoming more scarce. This theme will be repeated with the other kinds of data in the coming selections on immigration.

Irving (Duke) Johnson, 66, has polished shoes on U Street in Washington, D. C. for 27 years. He "remembers when more than 25 'bootblacks' were working along the street." Now Johnson is the only one, according to the newspaper story.

The decline in the number of shoe polishers could in theory be due to a decline in either the demands for shoe polishing or in the supply of workers. But Booker T. Carrington, the "dean of the shoe-shine professionals" who has "more than half a century of experience," asserts that the explanation is a decline in the labor supply. The young boys "all are looking for the big money," he says. In other words, the pay necessary to attract shoe polishers has increased over the years.

So there has been an increasing shortage of shoe polishers in the nation's capital. By the same reasoning, there has been an decreasing supply of all labor in the United States and in the world. This is shown by the higher price that one must pay to obtain almost any type of help, from journalists in Washington to drivers in Delhi. And one can just as well say that there has been a growing shortage of people in the world.

Though paradoxical, this sounds quite unlike the conventional doomsday warnings, which point to the world's growing population. It is economic fact: We have been experiencing an increasing shortage of people even though there are more people on earth with each passing year. And we ought to start planning to make the necessary adjustments. Ben Wattenberg laments the "birth dearth" in the United States mainly for other reasons, but his call for more Americans complements the argument here.

To compound the paradox, the past centuries also reveal an amazing increase in natural resources. Yes, you read correctly. And this needs explaining. How can it be that we use some of our stock of a raw material, and yet we have even more available to us than we started with?

First we must be clear about the economic meaning of scarcity. As consumers, we complain that a good has become more scarce when we have to pay more for the services than we want from the resource. Conversely, we say a good has become less scarce when the price goes down. Current and future prices are all that matter economically with respect to resources. Discussion about how much of a good "really exists" is quite beside the point for economic purposes.

By now, "pure" economists and "practical" marketers agree that all raw material prices have been trending downward as far back as the data go. The most important price to consumers is the amount of labor time that one must trade to get a pound of, say, copper or iron. The U.S. prices of these and all other metals, relative to wages, have fallen by an astonishing factor of perhaps twenty since the founding of the country. And in U.S. terms, they have fallen by a factor of perhaps a thousand over the last few millenia. The prices of raw materials relative to consumer goods—the "terms of trade"—have also been falling over the years.

The doomsayers somehow remain unaware or unconvinced of this astonishing trend toward greater availability of natural resources relative to manufactured goods and services. The basis of their unbelief can only be theological or mystical or emotional, because there is no doubt about the statistical evidence.

The explanation lies in the increasing stock of knowledge about resources. A resource does not really exist until we understand what it will do for us, discover where to find it, and learn how to make it ready for our use. Finding new lodes of old resources, figuring out how to mine and refine them more efficiently, and discovering how to substitute new resources for the old ones all push the price down. The process usually begins with an expected or actual shortage caused by increased population or income. And the process usually ends with us having more resources and being better off than if the shortage had not threatened.

Now about people. World population has been growing rapidly. But does this imply "overpopulation"? Too many people? People becoming less scarce? The proper answer to all is "no."

Using normal economic procedure, let us compare the present state of scarcity to past scarcity by examining changes in the price of obtaining the services of people. The two appropriate price measures—wages and income—both clearly show that the average price of people has recently been going up everywhere in the world, except in a few exceptional situations. The logic is inescapable: Despite the rising numbers of people, human beings have been getting more scarce.

Determining the long-run price of labor is trickier. The most meaningful index is the proportion of the labor force occupied in producing basic foodstuffs—that is, grain. To make arithmetic easy, let's assume a starting point of everyone working in subsistence agriculture, although even in the least-developed society perhaps 5 or 10 percent of the working population occupy themselves being priests or chiefs. (The actual figures both for China in 1949, and for the United States in 1800, were about 80 percent working in agriculture.) And let each working man stand for an entire household, neglecting the fact that in many places women do most of the farming work.

Think of a society that progresses from the entire labor force working in agriculture to only half working in agriculture. This shift means that each working person can support his own family plus that of another working person. And the other working person can now spend all his time producing other goods to trade for half of the agricultural output. Now both the agricultural and the nonagricultural workers have an income composed of as much food as in the original state, plus other goods that are of equal value, if both workers are of equal efficiency. Hence, each worker has an income equal to twice what it was in the original state.

Now compare the situation of the United States today, where each farmer provides food for about fifty other working persons. This implies that the farmer's production provides him about fifty times as much income as it did in the original state of subsistence agriculture. This squares with the fact that income per worker might be about $400 in the poorest country in the world and perhaps $20,000 in the United States.

We can dramatize this history by projecting it into the future. Another such multiplication of U.S. income would imply an average worker earning today's equivalent of $1,000,000 every year instead of, say, $20,000. And it is not beyond possibility that there should be another forty-fold increase in fewer years than passed between 1800 and now, given the speedup in the rate of productivity increase over the years.

Another dramatization: Poor countries now embarking on economic development may reach a level of income comparable to that of the United States now in perhaps half a century, or considerably less than a century.

The implication of this historical shift for a person's lifetime welfare is even more amazing. In addition to wages per hour and income per year rising, the number of years that a person lives to produce and enjoy this material welfare have increased greatly. The wage alone tells us how much it costs to purchase another person's services for an hour. But lifetime income tells us how much an entire human life is worth. (This was the way the market valued a slave, but that does not disqualify the concept. It is the appropriate concept when one thinks about the value of one's own human capital created with education.). This increase in length of life implies yet another doubling or tripling of a person's lifetime income, compared to the original state of subsistence agriculture.

The economic changes that lead to an increased shortage of people, and to increased economic value of life, have a variety of practical implications. The most obvious implication for business activity is that the poor countries will become much like today's rich countries in their purchasing and consumption patterns, as well as in their production patterns. Businesses in today's poor countries, and those that deal with countries that are now poor, will have to alter both what they produce and how they produce.

Production will have to adjust by giving up the idea that "life is cheap." This implies providing better protection against safety hazards. More costly will be the shift to technologies that use physical capital more intensively, along with less unskilled labor. This continues trends that began more than a century ago in such places as Great Britain and the United States.

The most important implication of the increased value of people is that it may reverse the trend toward a declining birth rate—if parents can find a way to recover their "investment" in their children. At present, parents in rich countries do not expect to be repaid for sending their children to expensive universities where the children acquire skills that will produce a high income return on the investment. Therefore, the high cost of education to the parents currently works to reduce the birth rate in rich countries.

If new mechanisms develop whereby the children repay their parents' investment in them, either privately or through some government mechanism, there will arise an increased incentive to have more children. Any such mechanism is complex, however, and we do not know which would be best. To work that out is a task for the future. And in the meantime in the United States, we would do well to stop the gap with the talented foreigners who wish to come here as immigrants, with great gain to all (See Part 5).

19

China and Trashy Western Population Ideas

China implemented Malthusian ideas with speed and efficiency and rigor far exceeding any other country. This selection applies the general ideas discussed in Selection 15 to China's population-control program. Selection 24 discusses the "voluntariness" of the Chinese program.

Once again China is falling prey to trashy Western ideas. This time the false idea is the need for population control. The resulting loss of human life may dwarf the death toll of the Great Leap Forward famine in 1958–60 and the breaking of the dikes on the Yangtze River to flood the Japanese invaders. But these lives never lived are accorded no value in Chinese government planning.

Perhaps Western population-control proponents are not the entire cause. Perhaps the Marxism that is willing to sacrifice lives for putative economic gains, and to construe creating new lives as "human production" on the same footing as goods production, also is an important intellectual influence. But Marxism and Western environmental views clearly are fellow travelers on this matter.

Fifteen years ago, the Club of Rome's *Limit to Growth* was damned as foolishness or fraud by every reputable economist who reviewed it. Just four years after that book appeared and sold more than a million copies, the Club of Rome itself repudiated the book as fundamentally misguided. Yet on a recent stay in Beijing I heard that its translation is selling wildly in China and causing a great stir.

In the 1960s and 1970s, a clutch of talented American physical scientists applied their mathematical skills to population and economic development. Most of them quickly learned that demographic economics is not an

The Asian Wall Street Journal, November 24, 1987.

amateur's game. Valid research requires that one know a body of facts and economic theory. But like a re-run of a bad old movie, the "intellectuals" behind China's current population policy are rocket engineers and control-theory mathematicians, repeating all the arrogant foolishness that natural scientists foisted off on the U.S. public in the late '60s and '70s.

Fully two decades ago, Nobel-prizewinner Simon Kuznets and Richard Easterlin separately made statistical studies of the relationship of population growth to economic growth, and concluded that there is no observable connection between the rates of growth of population and of economic development. But twenty years later the Chinese are paying no official heed to that body of scientific work.

Admittedly, Western demographers also were not quick to grasp the implication of this body of research. Nor until 1984 did policymakers in the United States notice the accumulating body of other economic-demographic research that illuminates the mechanisms underlying the bare aggregate statistical relationship that Kuznets and others found. But in the last few years there has been a tidal change in the West, marked most sharply by a 1986 report from the National Academy of Sciences that turned almost completely from its earlier stand that population growth has an important negative effect upon economic development. But this turnabout is unknown in China, so far as I could tell on a recent visit.

Club-of-Rome-type ideas are appealing because they link up with primitive but persuasive "common sense" reasoning. For example, in China people point to jam-packed buses and say that stopping population growth is the way to relieve the problem. This echoes Planned Parenthood in the United States in the early 1970s urging reduction of population growth to relieve shortages of parking places.

This intellectually-vulgar thinking arises from gross confusion between the standard of living and economic development, mistaking the consumption level of a society for the production capacities of an economy.

For a quarter century, American foreign policy toward population growth in developing countries was built upon exactly this confusion, as put forth in a famous 1958 book by Ansley Coale and Edgar Hoover, *Population Growth and Economic Development in Low Income Countries*. That book used consumption and the standard of living as its central concept. Hence it did not deal at all with economic development, even though that was the subject of its title. The ensuing confusion has been foisted off on developing countries around the world. For example, Coale-Hoover thinking in India underlayed Indira Ghandi's program of forced sterilizations. The protest then toppled her first government.

"But China is different from other developing countries," the Chinese experts say, "because she has a billion people and so little land." One billion is an impressive number. In itself it has no meaning, however. China's situation would be the same if the borders were drawn to make China ten countries with 100 million population each. Population density rather than total population is the key issue. And China's population density is not exceptionally high. Its density is much lower than that of Japan, say, or Korea or Taiwan.

China is fairly sparsely populated, aside from the coastal and river regions. (All over the world, most people live next to rivers and oceans for reasons of transportation.) The matter is put in perspective when we consider Tiananmen Square in Beijing, on which a million people can stand. Only a thousand such squares, just a portion of the area of Beijing, would be enough for the entire population of China to stand upon.

It is now clear that China's food production capacity is huge. The new "responsibility system," which since 1979 has made a farm household's income depend upon its production, was able to raise production an amazing 60 percent in less than ten years. Under this free-enterprise system, farmers continue to increase productivity in a variety of ways. This system also frees up much labor for industrial use by giving farmers an incentive to invest their new wealth in labor-saving equipment that allows them to farm bigger areas. More than half of Chinese food is still eaten by the producing households, mainly due to lack of roads to bring produce to market. When more farm-to-market roads are built, agricultural production will expand much more.

China is indeed different from noncommunist countries in one crucial way: People get more of such goods as housing and transportation free, rather than paying the full cost. This constitutes what are known to economists as "negative externalities." Or to put it in Chinese terms, people eat from the communal pot.

From the last decade's experience in farming with the "responsibility system" China has learned the indelible lesson that breaking the communal pot leads to rapid agricultural development as well as to better lives. If China also breaks the communal pot in the cities with respect to such goods as housing, transportation, and education, rapid economic growth also can take place in the urban sector. Interestingly, people will then have a rational reason to want fewer children than they now want because the cost of children will be greater.

Ironically, the ideas of Marx and Engels clearly oppose China's coercive one-child family policy, which causes parental distress now and loss of economic growth in the future. Though China's "intellectuals" exert great ingenuity in arguing otherwise, Engels and Marx considered Malthusian thinking foolish and contemptible. They were greatly impressed with the nineteenth-century invention of artificial fertilizer by chemist Johan Liebig. From that discovery they learned that the services we desire from natural resources can be expanded greatly when we need them.

Marx and Engels were absolutely correct in this respect, and the main line of classical western economics was wrong—with such honorable exceptions as the nineteenth-century Austrian, Karl Menger. What a twist that the Chinese should swear total fealty to Marxism-Leninism and yet reject completely its one element that is thoroughly sound! It is even more ironic that the Chinese argued the Marxist position on population with extraordinary passion at the World Population Conference in Bucharest in 1974.

Help yourself, China, by throwing away the West's intellectual trash about population control.

Part 4
POPULATION POLICIES, PROGRAMS, AND BELIEFS

Introduction

Though the United States does not have an enunciated, integrated population policy, many federal activities bear upon domestic and foreign demographic matters. Abroad, for example, the United States gives money to the United Nations Fund for Population Activities, which works to reduce population growth rates in the world as a whole and in individual countries. And the State Department's Agency for International Development has a long and sordid history of promoting population control abroad, undertaking some of the activities directly and supporting others through the UNFPA and other "multilateral" organizations. Part 4 examines some aspects of these activities, which are discussed more systematically in my 1981 *The Ultimate Resource,* and by Jacqueline Kasun in her 1988 *The War on Population.* Selection 24 discusses the current policy of China.

One might expect that theology and tradition would lead religious leaders, more than laypeople, to emphasize the value of human life. And in earlier times and other places, most religious leaders have indeed looked with favor upon raising many children if the family can afford to do so.

In 1982, Allen Kelley asked a group of clergy about the relationship of population and development. He found that "To the person they all felt population growth was bad" in both more-developed and less-developed countries. "Moreover, some even felt that nonvoluntary birth control was an appropriate policy for the LDC's" (letter of October 7, 1982). (I'll bet that few indeed of these clergy would not consider an increase in the size of their congregations to be a good thing, though.) Kelley's findings are testimony to the power of newspapers and television to mold thought even when the media's point of view runs against the traditions from which the religious leaders emerge. This issue is discussed for Judaism and Roman Catholicism in Selections 25 and 26, respectively.

An interesting aspect of religion and environmentalism is that many devout Christians and Jews espouse views that those religions consider to be paganism, expecially the idea that animals and plants are on the same footing as humans with respect to their "rights" to existence—views held and expressed with quasi-religious passion. This is quite in contradiction to Genesis, which bids us to "have dominion over the fish of the sea, and over the fowl of the air, and over every living thing that creepeth upon the earth . . . every herb yielding seed, which is upon the face of the earth, and every tree, which is the fruit of a tree yielding seed—to you it shall be for food".

Regulating the flow of immigrants involves an important set of domestic population policies. Various selections in Part 5 discuss some of those activities.

20

The Role of Foreign Aid for Population Assistance

The wisdom of U.S. funding of foreign population activites is examined in this Selection. It is an unexamined assumption that foreign aid of all kinds is a benefit to the recipients. But just as with assistance given to children or to the poor, compassionate acts sometimes have counterproductive or destructive consequences. The value of assisting should be considered coolly, just as should the implications of not assisting, which then forces the potential recipient to proceed with the recipient's own resources alone.

The Role of Foreign Aid for "Family Planning"

I believe that a couple's ability to have the family size the couple chooses is one of the great goods of human existence. And I am not in principle against a government's giving "family planning" assistance to its own citizens or to citizens of another country if they so desire. I especially cheer efforts to strengthen commercial organizations that provide such assistance through market channels. But it does *not* follow from being in favor of informed, responsible parenthood that the United States should automatically give foreign aid to organizations that request funds in the name of "family planning," on the grounds that *some* good will be done by the funds even if they are largely wasted or used perversely.

If you ask the population "establishment" why we should and do give such "aid," the answer almost invariably is a masterpiece of doubletalk, arguments made out of both sides of the mouth. On the one hand, the United Nations Fund for Population Activities (UNFPA) and such congressional population-control enthusiasts as James Scheuer and Sander Levin say that their aim simply is to supply "family planning" in order to help

Drawn from "Population Growth, Economic Growth, and Foreign Aid," *Cato Journal,* vol. 7, Spring/Summer 1987, pp. 159–186.

people achieve the family size that they wish. Everyone that I know of—including the Vatican, as I understand it—agrees with the aim that families should have the number of children that they wish and believe they can raise well. If family planning were all there is to the matter, we could all easily agree on a one-page statement of goals and means (putting aside the troublesome but obfuscating issue of abortion), and we would not need multi-million dollar conferences and reams of documents and bushels of expensive research reports and fancy organizational publications financed directly and indirectly by the Ameriican taxpayer. We could simply say that as an act of plain helpful generosity, we recommend that governments do what they can to provide contraceptive information and devices through private and public channels, and we will do what we can to help.

The arguments of the population organizations are another matter, however. They wring their hands over population growth rates, economic development, natural resource availability, unemployment, social conflict, and the like. A typical example is from a January 1986 cover letter to the annual report from Bradman Weerakoon, the secretary general of the International Planned Parenthood Federation (IPPF): "IPPF believes that knowledge of family planning is a fundamental human right and that a balance between the population of the world and its natural resources and productivity is a necessary condition of human happiness, prosperity and peace." It is clear, especially in the UNFPA statements, that their aim is not simply to help individuals achieve the family size that the individual couples would otherwise like. Rather, these organizations aim at population growth-rate goals—more specifically, at zero population growth—that the leaders of these organizations have decided are desirable for the world.

Furthermore, even the most "moderate" group, the recent NAS Committee on Population, is prepared to go beyond simple provision of information and devices: "When a couple's childbearing decision imposes external costs on other families—in overexploitation of common resources, congestion of public services, or contribution to a socially undesirable distribution of income—a case may be made for policies that go 'beyond family planning' " (NAS 1986, p. 93). The policies discussed include persuasive campaigns to change family size norms as well as combinations of incentives and taxes related to family size.

Those who call for aid to family planning have usually assumed that poor couples in poor countries do not have their fertility rates under reasonable control as a result of sensible decision making, and need guidance from Western population-planning experts. But couples tend to recognize that in the short run an additional person—whether a baby or an immigrant—inevitably means a lower standard of living for everyone. And the parents who carry almost all the burden, as well as the communities that also carry a small part of the burden, at some point say "enough," even while recognizing that more children would be good to have in the longer run.

Criteria for Giving Foreign Aid

What are reasonable grounds for giving foreign aid, or charity in general? Economics does not supply the criteria. "There is *no generally accepted economic rationale for foreign aid,*" wrote Theodore Schultz (1981, p. 124). And, in an essay labeled "a systematic reexamination of aid and its role in development," Anne Krueger (1986, p. 58) referred only to "the rationale for aid, 'aid effectiveness'—that is the degree to which different types of aid are conducive to accelerating development." Nor have I found a set of criteria in the literatures of other disciplines. Therefore, I hazard the following test: Charity is appropriate when the following conditions are present: First, *the recipient person or nation "needs" the help.* (The caveat here is that the presence of need is not always clearcut. The "need" of a bleeding child for medical assistance is not arguable, but the "need" of an unconverted person for religious salvation depends on the values and worldview of the potential giver.) Second, *the recipient wants the help.* Third, *the gift will not have bad effects* in the long run on the recipient or others. Fourth, *the charity will be used more-or-less efficiently* rather than largely wastefully or simply to obtain more money in a pyramid scheme. Fifth, *the charity will not produce hate toward the giver.* Let us test foreign aid to family planning against these criteria.

Do LDCs "Need" Family Planning Assistance?

In ordinary welfare programs, the criterion of need usually involves a means test. A person who owns a yacht is thought not to be an appropriate recipient for welfare, and a similar test might be applied to countries. In this spirit let us look at Table 20-1, which contains data on public expenditures for education, defense, and family planning in various countries, as well as public expenditures on family planning that include foreign donations, for those countries for which I could find data. In no case is the public expenditure for family planning, with or without foreign funds, more than a tiny fraction of spending for education. The implication is that if family planning is a high priority item, it is within the discretion of governments to redirect needed funding from other educational expenditures. Lest one worry about the social loss involved in shifting funds from other educational uses, in almost every case the large size of the "defense"

Table 20-1. Defense, Education, and Family Planning Expenditures for 25 Countries

Country	Defense $/person	Education $/person	Family planning Domestic $/person	Family planning Foreign $/person	
	(range 1978–81)		(most recent estimate)		
Bangladesh	1–2	2	0.06	0.12	(1976)
Bolivia	27–34	29–35	0.00	0.02	(1977)
Brazil	14–17	61–64	0.00	0.05	(1985)
Colombia	9–16	21–34	0.13	0.13	(1983)
Dominican Rep.	17–23	19–26	0.18	0.20	(1977)
Egypt	61–78	25 (1977)	0.06	0.25	(1983)
El Salvador	16–28	23–30	1.25	0.38	(1980)
Ghana	13–26	33	0.13	0.02	(1977)
Hong Kong	N.A.	83–140	0.10	0.20	(1983)
India	6–7	7	0.46	0.06	(1983)
Indonesia	16–19	7–12	0.34	0.12	(1983)
Iran	202–456	75–198	0.92	0.00	(1977)
Kenya	10–16	21–24	0.15	0.39	(1978)
Korea, South	87–103	32–61	0.42	0.04	(1980)
Malaysia	54–102	108–117	0.60	0.19	(1980)
Mauritius	1–6	72–77	0.66	0.25	(1982)
Pakistan	16–17	5–6	0.12	0.10	(1979)
Philippines	14–16	12–13	0.25	0.18	(1983)
Rwanda	3–4	4–6	N.A.	N.A.	
Singapore	234–304	84–207	0.76	0.00	(1983)
Taiwan	N.A.	N.A.	0.33	0.00	(1983)
Tanzania	7–27	N.A.	0.00	0.03	(1976)
Thailand	24–28	17–28	0.18	0.09	(1983)
Tunisia	7–16	49–73	0.10	0.26	(1980)
Zimbabwe	16–57	28	0.25	0.00	(1978)

Sources: Defense per person: U.S. Arms Control and Disarmament Agency (1985, Table 1). Educational expenditure: United Nations Statistical Office, *Statistical Yearbook* (various years); United Nations Educational, Scientific, and Cultural Organization, *UNESCO Yearbook* (various years). Population: Nortman (editions 9-12). Family Planning Expenditures: Nortman (editions 9-12).

budgets relative to the education budgets make clear that there is a pool of public expenditures into which countries could dip without causing social loss by reducing education expenditures. It would seem that the potential recipients own gunboats if not yachts, and therefore flunk the means test for charity.

Another standard criterion of need is that the good or service being provided will be something that is thought by the giver to be of a nature that will improve the life of the recipient. Agricultural know-how has this nature. Birth-control capacity might be another. One might then wonder whether or not *individual* women and couples need assistance and have no way to pay for it, even if their governments could afford to provide it. Perhaps there are some such cases. But the actual cost of contraceptive information and devices is exceedingly small (which is, incidentally, a major problem in commercial distribution). The funds devoted to "family planning" programs overwhelmingly are spent for things other than "hardware" and straightforward services. What is called "information" and "education," but which is to a considerable degree persuasion, accounts for a large proportion of the expenditures that actually reach the field. Often, it is forced upon societies by U.S. efforts; there is plenty of documentation of this in the recent book by Jacqueline Kasun (1988).

When reminded of such events, officials at AID routinely admit that they occurred in the past, but assert that the "present" policy would not allow them. However, that assertion has been made over and over again, each one implicitly giving the lie to the past ones. It is this propaganda that many proponents of family planning activities believe that people "need" (compare the quotation from the NAS report above). I consider this to be at best arguable rather than obvious. But I do not believe that to be against propaganda implies that one is against true family-planning assistance.

Still, if a true family-planning program were to provide information and devices to some couples to whom they would not otherwise be available, this might be seen as filling a true social need. And the program might be viewed as passing this test.

Do the Potential Recipients Want the Assistance?

One test of whether people "want" something is whether they allocate their resources to that good. Table 20–1 does not indicate any massive allocation of countries' own funds to family planning.

But do not foreign politicians, and persons involved in family-planning activities abroad, often express the desire for these funds? Of course they do. We must ask what these expressions mean, however. To a politician, any foreign dollar coming into the country is another dollar to allocate to one constituency or another, or even to be turned to personal use. (Does anyone doubt that some foreign aid dollars went to buy shoes for Imelda Marcos?) Therefore, more such dollars are always welcome. And for those who work for family-planning organizations, cutting aid funds breaks their rice bowl, and removes such perks as trips to Mexico City for a UNFPA conference.[1]

Does the Assistance Do Harm?

Economic thought contains few apparent contradictions. One such contradiction, however, is between the fundamental assumption (actually a definition) that an increase in assets ("endowment") increases welfare,[2] and the common-sense observation that giving gifts sometimes harms recipients in the long run by changing their attitudes and habits.[3]

Resolving the apparent contradiction requires the recognition that a person's propensity to exert effort is a function of that person's wealth (as well as of the opportunities facing him or her).[4] General foreign aid programs may have this ill effect on recipients by reducing their propensity to exert effort (for example, the compensation to the natives of Bikini and the payments to certain Native American tribes), but the funds for family-planning assistance surely are too small to have this sort of ill effect.[5]

Another ill effect that may flow from foreign aid is damage to a key industry. The dumped food aid of P. L. #480 apparently damaged the agricultures of India, Egypt, and South American nations by lowering prices and reducing incentives for farmers to produce crops (Schultz, 1981 and citations therein). But again this sort of harm is not relevant to family-planning assistance.

Foreign aid programs can also do damage by directing policymakers' attention away from the fundamental mechanism of economic growth, and away from the obstacles to growth that may exist in a society. This is the gravamen of Bauer's charge (1984, ch. 5) that the Pope and the proponents of a New International Economic Order caused people to dwell on envy and redistribution rather than on personal hard work together with societal changes that would promote liberty and enterprise. And here I think that concern about population growth, and for family-planning programs that are intended to reduce population growth, have caused great damage.

Another ill effect of foreign aid for population control is suggested by Alan Rufus Waters (1985, p.3): "Foreign aid used for population activities gives enormous resources and control apparatus to the local administrative elite and thus sustains the authoritarian attitudes corrosive to the development process." This sort of effect is difficult to demonstrate statistically, but Waters's vantage point as former Chief Economist for the U.S. Agency for International Developement (USAID) gives him credentials as an expert witness on the subject.[6]

I have my own candidate for the title of worst harm from foreign aid: the advice that goes along with it. The root of the damage lies in the idea that artful manipulation by clever economists is the way to produce economic development. International organizations such as the World Bank have finally realized that prices matter in influencing economic activity. And they have proceeded from this realization to the proposition that countries should "get the prices right." But for them this does not mean that markets should be allowed to set prices, but rather that governments should set the prices with the help of the World Bank and its expert economists. Warren Baum and Stokes Tolbert (1985, p. 51) provide the following summary of the Bank's attitude toward intervention:

> As to the appropriate level of prices, the basic principle, dictated by the need to make the most efficient use of the economy's resources, is that the price of any product should equal the marginal cost of producing the last unit sold. A free competitive market would achieve the desired result of bringing prices into line with marginal costs, thereby allocating resources efficiently. In the real world, however, market conditions nearly always diverge from the competitive ideal. Even where there is a high degree of competition, the results produced by the market are efficient only for a given distribution of income. They may, therefore, not be consonant with other objectives, such as greater equity or social justice. Governments can intervene to improve the distribution of income by such means as imposing taxes or providing subsidies. The price system, if it is functioning properly, will then help to establish an allocation of resources which again is broadly efficient, but with a greater degree of social justice. In general, the best results will be obtained when producers face prices based on efficiency criteria, with indirect taxes and subsidies applied to consumer prices to achieve social objectives.

Under the stewardship of Robert MacNamara and A. W. Clausen, the World Bank—along with USAID—has been the strongest force pushing population-control programs.[7] In the name of "getting the prices right," persons who work for the World Bank advise governments—backed by the threat that recipient countries could lose Bank funds—about the appropriate set of prices to stimulate production and generate economic growth. The "experts" at the Bank, in other words, substitute their judgments for the free market's most important function: automatically producing the prices that give the correct signals to producers. That is, the advisers at the Bank believe they know better than a freely operating market what the "right" prices should be. The implicit grounds for this belief, I would guess, are faith in their own cleverness and the assumption that markets will fail to do the job correctly.

This phenomen particularly horrifies me because in the name of economics, these persons deny the birthright of Western economists since Mandeville, Hume, and Smith, of whom the present-day prophets are Hayek, Bauer, and Friedman—the vision of the hidden hand that spontaneously produces benign results which central planning cannot accomplish. And the continuation of this practice of advising countries about appropriate prices seems inexorable as long as organizations such as the World Bank exist and (inevitably) employ economists who must find something to do. Giving the advice that governments should stop interfering with markets does not require time-consuming and expensive research, with "missions" from Washington to the capitals of benighted poor countries. But advice to free up markets would render unnecessary many jobs, and therefore it has no chance of coming about as long as the World Bank exists.

What Kinds of Foreign Assistance Are Most Beneficial?

Lest the reader think that I am against any foreign aid in principle, a few unoriginal words seem in order about programs than can make economic sense. Agricultural research, including the organization and development of foreign agricultural research, has the great advantage that it puts no fungible funds or goods into the hands of bureaucrats, and causes no distortions in prices or other disruptions in markets. And the benefit/cost ratios have been calculated to be high. The provision of education in the United States to talented foreigners, especially if they are chosen by objective test, has many of the same advantages, as well as the advantage of making bright students familiar with the United States, and leaving them with impressions and ideas that they can take home with them. This also provides the opportunity for the United States to recruit valuable young persons of skill, energy, and imagination as temporary or permanent immigrants.

Conclusion

If we apply Hazlitt's central lesson on economics to the nexus of population growth and economic development, and take account of the indirect and lagged effects of economic freedom as well as the most obvious Malthusian effects that occur in the very short run, we can see that on net balance, additional persons being born are not a drag on progress in the long run. And foreign aid given for "family-planning" programs may have more ill effects than good effects, and should not simply be viewed as a charitable act that improves the situation of poor people in poor countries.

Notes

1. Allegations about motives are difficult to substantiate and are often odious, and hence I seldom make them. But in this case, see Selection 56.
2. An example in the context of foreign aid: "Clearly, a recipient's potential welfare could always be increased by a grant" (Kruger 1986, p. 63).
3. The famous mathematician Mark Kac wrote in his autobiography (1985, pp. 7–8): "My great-grandfather . . . amassed what in those days must have been a sizable fortune and at his death, sometime early in the century, he left every one of his eighty grandchildren enough money to relieve them of any need to work for a living. All of them, with the exception of my father, chose a life of idle leisure until the First World War, when their inheritance was wiped out."
4. This is the subject of my book, *Effort, Opportunity, and Wealth* (Simon 1987).
5. Doug Bandow (1985) made a similar point in his introduction to *U.S. Aid to the Developing World*, which contains much interesting discussion on the general subject of foreign aid.
6. It is of some interest that other persons who have been involved in USAID activities have also come out strongly against programs of "family-planning" aid. These include Peter Huessey, author of a Heritage Backgrounder, and Nicholas Demerath, who wrote *Birth Control and Foreign Policy* (1976).
7. Baum and Tolbert (1985, pp. 213, 217) provide the following up-to-date statement of the World Bank's policy position: "Rapid population growth slows development. . . . For population, the principal objective of most developing countries should be to slow the rate of growth."

21

Policy Issues at the 1984 World Population Conference

*The position of the United States at the World Population Conference
in 1984 was quite the opposite of its position at the Bucharest
conference in 1974, when it lectured all the countries of the world on
the need for them to reduce their birth rates. Ironicallly, China
switched its position in the other direction. It was as if the United
States and China had exchanged their old position papers.*

*This selection urges the position that the United States ultimately
adopted.*

The U. N.'s World Population Conference is to be held in Mexico City
next week. But the ferocious battle over the U.S. platform continues right
up to the last minute. The U.S. delegation was not chosen until two weeks
ago, and congressional hearings on the White House's policy statement
were still being held last week, in hopes of influencing the U.S. delegation's
activities.

All attention has focused on just two sentences in the early White House
statement that concern a cutoff of funds to population programs promoting
abortion. This is unfortunate since the underlying crucial issue has been
little discussed.

The key question has been whether the U.S. delegation would be
composed only of those in favor of population control, no holds barred, as
the population lobby and the State Department wished and as was the case
at the previous World Population Conference in Bucharest in 1974. Alter-
natively, the views offered could manifest the diversity of U.S. opinion on
the question. The population lobby and its friends in Congress are furious
that ex-Sen. James Buckley was finally chosen to head the delegation, and

The Wall Street Journal, August 3, 1984.

that the policy structure that they have carefully built over the past 15 years is now being challenged.

It would seem fair for the nation's diversity of views to be shown. Furthermore, such a broad-minded view could win back friends lost because of coercive U.S.-backed population-control programs in nations such as India and Indonesia.

Concerns of Opposing Sides

On one side of this fight, anti-abortion groups that emphasize personal freedom and worry about interference by governments in family life, backed by those who see state birth-control efforts as an interference by governments in family life, are joined by a few who judge Malthusian thinking to be unfounded and wrong. President Reagan apparently shares these views. On the other side is the population lobby composed of environmental and zero-growth organizations that worry about the effect of more people upon resources and the environment, plus the State Department and the Agency for International Development, which have long maintained that more people mean reduced economic growth and increased political instability. Most of Congress and some administration officials share this view, which has been buttressed by the World Bank's recent world-development report, which agonizes over the size of the human population.

The State Department has floated a pro-population-control policy draft opposing the White House statement. The reasons it gives for reducing population growth are as follows: "Population growth . . . is contributing to unusual economic, social, and resource pressures that threaten to undermine U.S. initiatives for peace, economic progress, and human dignity and freedom in many areas throught the world. . . ."

These frightening assertions are not supported by the facts.

It is untrue that population growth is politically unsettling. The State Department refers to "Fast-growing youth populations . . . growing faster than most developing countries can absorb them . . . creating growing political and social tensions in Africa, the Near East, Asia, and Central and South America." It asserts, "The combination of overcrowding, unmet expectations, and different ethnic, religious, and social groups makes a politically volatile mix. Violent demonstrations and mass riots over food or sectarian causes in the recent past . . . are manifestations of these growing pressures."

The body of scientific literature on the political aspects of the subject is thin. To the extent that there is systematic analysis—notably the great body of work on war through the ages by Quincy Wright, then of the

University of Chicago, and the work on recent wars by Nazli Choucri of the Massachusetts Institute of Technology—I read the conclusion as being one of no connection between population growth and war or other political instability due to the struggle for economic resources. The purported connection is another of those notions that everyone "knows" is true, and that seems perfectly logical, but has no basis in the factual evidence.

Turning to economics, about which much more is known, the population-control line is straight Mathusianism, such as is found in The Limits to Growth project of the Club of Rome and in *The Global 2000* "Report to the President" of 1980. Many "intellectuals" in the poorer countries share this point of view. But many leaders and much public opinion in those countries reject it, correctly viewing it as scientifically mistaken and regarding it as U.S. imperialistic interference.

The purported negative effect of additional people upon natural resources also was stated prominently in the State Department draft: "The current situation of many developing countries . . . differs in certain ways from conditions in 19th-century Europe and the U.S. The rates and dimensions of population growth are much higher now, the pressures of land, water, and resources are greater. . . ." If the phrase "pressures . . . are greater" is to have any meaning, it must be that these resources are scarcer now than earlier.

But this assertion has been completely refuted by data showing that the prices of food, metals, and other raw materials have been declining by every measure since the beginning of the 19th century and as far back as we know. That is, raw materials have been getting less scarce rather than more scarce throughout history, despite the common sense that if one begins with an inventory of a resource and uses some up, there will be less left. More generally, the life expectancies and the incomes of the people of the world have been rising along with rising population, despite the increasing use of resources.

Benefits of Population Growth

Population increase—immigration is a particularly potent form—tends to create business opportunities and facilitate change. More people generally make it more attractive to invest in expansion and new ventures, by reducing risk and increasing demand. Thus there are more job opportunities, more young people working, and greater mobility within the labor force. Such mobility enhances the efficient allocation of resources and produces the best match of people to jobs. But the most important benefit of population growth is the increase it brings to our stock of useful knowledge. Minds matter economically as much as, or more than, hands or mouths.

The main fuel to speed the world's progress is our stock of human knowledge. Our ultimate resource is skilled, spirited, and hopeful people exerting their wills and imaginations to provide for themselves and for their families, and thereby inevitably providing for the benefit of us all. Let us not tell the world otherwise. And even more important, let us not coerce them to follow unsound counsel about the most fundamental of human affairs.

22

The War on People

This selection complements Selection 21. It focuses on the role of the U.S. population "establishment" in this event, and on its rhetoric and organization.

Time still screams "The Population Curse" on its cover. The World Bank still says "the situation is grave. . . . Failure to act now to slow growth is likely to mean a lower quality of life for millions of people." Polite talk for fifteen years has not increased fidelity to the facts. So the time has come to tell it plain and simple: population growth, which was the focus of last year's World Population Conference in Mexico City and which exercises our State Department and much of Congress, is a phony issue in three important ways.

First, as the American delegation asserted, population growth does not reduce economic growth, despite the apparently inescapable Malthusian logic. Since 1967, many empirical studies of the relationship of the population growth rate to the economic growth rate per person have shown that there is no observable connection. It is these data that converted me from an activist for population control to a believer in the long-run benefits of population growth. Yet the United Nations Fund for Population Activities (UNFPA), organizer of the Mexico City conference, and the World Bank in its *World Development Report* published in 1984, proceed as if those data did not exist. They find ingenious ways to imply that reducing the population growth rate will indeed have a positive effect upon the economic growth rate, and that countries have a responsibility to the world to produce fewer people, while adding enough disclaimers to protect them from the charge of advocating coercion.

Of course more children are a burden in the short run; every parent

Challenge, March–April 1985.

trend is upward. In addition to the improving prospects for food and natural resources, the most important facts concern life and death: after inching up, from the twenties to the thirties, over the course of millennia, life expectancy in the last two centuries has risen from the thirties to the seventies in the rich countries. In the poor countries, it has jumped perhaps thirteen years in the last three decades. Life expectancy in China has risen fully twenty years, to the high sixties, since the 1950s.

One may view the large numbers of human beings who are alive now, and will be alive in the future, as a triumph rather than as a problem. Of course values matter here. But if one believes that human life is good, it seems logical to think that more human life is good, assuming that no tragic cost need be paid thereby—and it need not, as shown by the better health and increased length of life all over the globe.

Despite the irrefutable happy facts about resource availability and life expectancy, the population lobby continues to forecast that our situation is getting worse, and that we therefore must have fewer people so as to enable the supply of resources to go around. They ask for more "equitable" distribution of resources among countries, in the face of the fact that those countries that use a good deal of resources are also the countries that reduce the costs of resources for all. And they ask for government intervention in the supply of resources on the grounds that the trends are toward greater resource scarcity. This is a false conclusion from a demonstrably false premise. By now the population lobby cannot be unaware of these facts, and therefore its argument deserves to be called phony.

Who Opposes Family Planning?

The third phony element is complex. On the one hand, the UNFPA and such congressional population "leaders" as James Scheuer and Sander Levin say that their aim is simply to supply "family planning" in order to help people get the family size that they wish. With the aim that families should have the number of children that they wish and believe that they can raise well, everyone that I know of agrees—including the Vatican, as I understand it. Statements that people who hold such views as mine are against "family planning" are disingenuous at best. If family planning were all there is to the matter, we could all easily agree on a one-page statement of goals and means (putting aside the troublesome but obfuscating issue of abortion), and we would not need multimillion-dollar conferences and reams of documents and bushels of expensive research reports and fancy organizational publications financed directly and indirectly by the American taxpayer. We could simply say that as an act of plain helpful generosity, we recommend that governments do what they can to provide contraceptive information and devices through private and public channels; we will do what we can to help. End of statement.

The arguments of the population organizations are another matter, however. They wring their hands about population growth rates, economic development, unemployment, social conflict, availability of natural resources, and the like. It is clear that their aim is not simply to help individual couples achieve the family size that they would otherwise like; rather, they aim at growth-rate goals that the leaders of these organizations have decided are desirable for the world.

Cynical observers have suggested that talk about growth rates is just eyewash to obtain more support for the laudable goal of effective family planning. There are two things wrong with this argument. First, if one thinks that way, how do we know that instead it is not the family-planning appeal that is being manipulated to obtain the goal of population reduction? Second and more important, is false rhetoric to be justified if the end is thought to be good? What about the terribly costly ill effects of resource gloom and doom over the past two decades?

Should we consider such spirit-destroying rhetoric as acceptable because it leads to the reduction some wish in the number of brown, black, yellow, and—yes—white human beings on the face of the earth, justified by the false belief that this reduction has, on balance, positive economic effects? And should we assume no cost to the effect of false propaganda upon public credibility and belief in the political process?

How come we hear that things are getting worse when they are really getting better? The answers are too many and complex to address here. One element worth mentioning, however, is that many make a leap from the fact that things are not good in some places to the belief that things are getting worse. This is coupled with a lack of historical perspective—for example, not knowing how much worse shape Mexico City and its people were in twenty or fifty years ago.

The key issues are these: first, should we aid and even encourage countries to adopt coercive population policies as we have with respect to China, India, Indonesia, and many other places? The answer depends upon one's values, of course, but we can say scientifically that the long-run economic consequences offer no support for such policies. And second, should we cry for sadness or for joy at the state of the world? The population restrictionists say we should be sad and worry. I and many others believe that the trends suggest joy and celebration at our newfound capacity to support human life, healthily and with fast-increasing access to education and opportunity all over the world. Wringing our hands has the bad effect of causing despair and resignation, when we need hopeful expectation that energetic efforts will prevail.

23

Why Is the United States Trying to Reduce Black Births?

The U.S. State Department's Agency for International Development (AID), and the leaders of the U.S. population "establishment," give the impression that the motives for official U.S. population activities abroad are purely humanitarian and benevolent. Though humanitarianism and benevolence are not absent, the evidence is irrefutable that these are not the only *operative motives, as this selection shows.*

When AID population policies are criticized, its officials concede that there have been unacceptable practices in the past, but things are different now. Without in any way suggesting that the United States is like the Soviet Union, it is interesting to notice that the same bureaucratic dodges are used everywhere, this one among them. Natan Sharansky ("As I see Gorbachev," Commentary, *March 1988, p. 29) writes about the KGB's new face as of 1988. "They acknowledge almost every problem in the distant past, but they really won't confront problems that are still going on now."*

Population control has ugly as well as humanitarian causes. The link between racism and population control is less in evidence nowadays than in earlier times because it is no longer acceptable to publicly voice racist sentiments. But it would be foolish to doubt the existence of this link, given the evidence from those earlier times. For example, "Subjects to do with breeding and race seem . . . to have held a certain fascination for" President Franklin D. Roosevelt, who talked, perhaps jokingly, about using (in Roosevelt's words) "the methods which Hitler used effectively" to reduce Puerto Rico's birth rate, methods which, he assumed, were "all very simple and painless—you have people pass through a narrow passage and then there is a brrrr of an electric apparatus. They stay there for twenty seconds and from then on they are sterile." (Quoted by Mike W. Perry, "The Sound of the Machine," The Freeman, July, 1988, p. 259, from "Annex to memo. of March 15, 199445, Taussig Papers, Box 52." In Christopher Thorne, Allies of a Kind: The United States, Britain and the War Against Japan, 1941-1945 *[New York: Oxford University Press, 1978], pp. 158-159.)*

Population control not only has some ugly causes, it also has some ugly effects. For example, it has been a justification for abortion policy, even in the United States. "As [Supreme Court Justice Potter] Stewart saw it, abortion was becoming one reasonable solution to population control," and hence he decided to join other justices in the 1973 pro-abortion Supreme Court decision. (Newsweek, *September 14, 1987, p. 33, quoting Bob Woodward and Scott Armstrong in* The Brethren*). Without entering here into the question of good reasons to be in favor of abortion freedom, this clearly is not one of them.*

Why is the United States applying pressure upon African governments to reduce the number of black children that are brought into the world? And why the push to have fewer yellow and brown births?

A racial discourtesy in a retail store, or a cross-burning by juvenile delinquents, gets headlines. But suppression of the world's black population gets nary a public word. No civil rights organization pickets the State Department's Agency for International Development to protest this policy. Nor have deceptive and forcible sterilizations of poor black women in the United States by the thousands caused an outcry.

We're not discussing real "family planning" services. Helping people have the family size they desire is a great human work. Many truly voluntary U.S. programs are valuable and respectworthy. But coercing couples to reduce fertility with force, bribery, or group pressure and government propaganda is something else.

Until the 1950s, the United States would have nothing to do with population control abroad. Then we got rolling with a vengeance. Joseph Califano tells us that President Lyndon Johnson "repeatedly rejected the unanimous pleas of his advisors from Secretary of State Dean Rusk to National Security Advisor Walt Rostow to ship wheat to the starving Indians during their 1966 famine. He demanded that the Indian government first agree to mount a massive birth control program. The Indians finally moved and Johnson released the wheat over a sufficiently extended period to make certain the birth control program was off the ground." And L. K. Jha, the ex-ambassador of India to the United States remembers in 1988 how Johnson's policies "had been adding to her [Indira Ghandi's] political difficulties. . . . He . . . kept India on tenterhooks in regard to PL-480 shipments of wheat which were desperately needed because of repeated droughts in the mid'60s. In consequence, Indira Ghandi resolved to put an end to PL-480 imports by making the country self-sufficient in food-grains." So Johnson's insistence that India adopt a birth-control campaign damaged the foreign relations of the United States.

Planning by U.S. advisers led to forced sterilization programs in India in the 1970s. For example, the government of India "motivated" employees to undergo sterilization after three children by threatening loss of subsidized housing, travel allowances, and free hospital treatment. Public outrage led to the downfall of Indira Ghandi.

Indonesia, whose "family planning program is considered a model of government-sponsored fertility control in a developing country," was recently analysed by Harvard professor Donald P. Warwick. "Heavy-handed social and administrative pressure had been applied" in the representative village that was studied. "In the presence of civilian, military, and police leaders, women were taken to a house in which IUD's were being inserted. They were asked to go in one door and put under very strong pressure to accept an IUD before they could leave by another door. Whether this was coercion or heavy persuasion, it denied voluntary choice to acceptors. . . . Today that approach is no longer followed, partly because of public resentment against its earlier use."

The Indonesian Department of Home Affairs puts pressure upon regional officials to meet family-planning "targets," the regional officials put pressure upon village heads and religious leaders, and they in turn bring the full weight of the community upon individuals. The village officials' "positions gave them authority to call people together." Lectures and contraceptives are distributed at the meetings. Then, if an individual is "unresponsive to persuasion or accepted but later dropped out of the program, the village head, other administrators, their wives, or members of acceptors' groups were likely to stop by to talk about family planning."

The Indonesian program runs against people's wishes all along the line. "If regional officials were freed from pressure . . . the family planning program would be the first to be dropped," according to Warwick.

The United States is directly implicated in Indonesian interference in the private lives of individuals, aiding and abetting the strong-arm government program. One can imagine the uproar if the subjects were our own citizens rather than the colored citizens of some other country.

Section 104(f) of the Foreign Assistance Act forbids "any financial incentive to any person to undergo sterilization." But U.S. AID gives money to Bangladesh for population activities, and Bangladesh has made millions of dollars in payments to men who agree to be sterilized, according to William M. O'Reilly. O'Reilly has worked for AID, and spent three months in Bangladesh which included visits to U.S.-funded clinics.

The illegal payments to Bangladesh are disguised in two ways. First, the term "incentive" is replaced in official communications with "compensation." Second, with the aid of dishonest accounting the funds for the incentives are labeled as coming from the UNFPA and the World Bank, leaving the United States to pay for nonprohibited family-planning activities. But this is mere slight-of-hand, since all the money goes into and comes out of the same pool of funds. Of the $68 million budget for Bangladesh's population control program in 1984, $27 million came directly from AID, $25 million came from the World Bank, and $6 million from UNFPA. Furthermore, both the World Bank and the UNFPA are heavily supported by the United States, so their activities must be seen as extensions of U.S. actions. Clearly, the U.S. policy is to reduce Bangladeshi births by hook or crook.

Anthropologist Stephen Mosher and a series in *The Washington Post* document that after a single child, China has forcibly aborted women even seven months pregnant. Funds and doctrine from the United States by way of the United Nations Fund for Population Activities propelled the Chinese program. UNFPA asks us to believe that the dollars it gets from the United States are not the same dollars that the UNFPA gives to Chinese programs. Nonsense. Money is fungible. To say otherwise is rhetorical slight-of-hand.

Now the main target is Africa. For example, with respect to the Ivory Coast: AID informed the comptroller general that it planned to assign a full-time "population officer" to Abidjan in order to "help create awareness of the impact of population growth and foster greater private and government involvement in supplying family planning services." Translated from bureaucratese, AID intends to tell the Africans that they had better get cracking or else. And in many countries we have made our other development assistance contingent on their efforts to reduce population growth, by requiring a "development project population impact statement" before funding. In other words, if you want our help, you've got to have fewer children. A key instrument of AID policy in the 1980s is a project called RAPID. In an AID consultant's words, "At the bottom line, RAPID seeks to influence public policy in countries where the U.S. provides significant assistance."

RAPID provides to African countries computers and a computer program that purports to prove that fewer children being born will benefit African economies. In the words of the AID report, RAPID is "designed to create a sensitivity to the adverse consequences of rapid population growth among political leaders responsible for setting national agendas and creating public policies.''

AID officials recognize that population control is a sensitive issue in Africa, and sentiment for large families is very strong. Therefore, AID has been very careful not to repeat past public-relations blunders made in other countries. Despite AID's careful language chosen to avoid arousing hostility, ''Some wonder whether you are just trying to get them worried,'' according to one African involved in the project. He says that RAPID ''clashes with traditional African norms of large family, even among educated and affluent classes.'' But African university professors and government officials are induced to accept and promote RAPID with the promise of free computers and software.

Why is the United States promoting population control abroad? There are three main reasons: (1) humanitarian concern, (2) racism, and (3) belief that lower birth rates in other countries are in the economic and political self-interest of the United States. It is difficult to determine which motive is operating in any particular instance, partly because racism is taboo nowadays and must operate in other guises. As the Commission on the Organization of the Government for the Conduct of Foreign Policy, established by Public Law 92-352, said in 1975 about the motives of the ''constituency supporting American [population] activities:'' ''this view [that ''nonwhite populations . . . represent a threat . . . and . . . ''are less desirable''], for obvious reasons, is never publicly expressed, and this is difficult to capture empirically.''

Evidence abounds that self-interest fuels the population program. The just-mentioned Commission opened its section on population with ''Excessive rates of population growth in underdeveloped countries aggravate conditions that frustrate the achievement of American foreign policy objectives.'' Later on it said, ''the persistence of high population growth rates in underdeveloped countries represents an adverse condition for American foreign policy interests.''

Reimert T. Ravenholt, the first and long-time director of AID's population activities, justified population control as ''needed to maintain the normal operation of U.S. commercial interests around the world,'' according to a newspaper interview. ''The self-interest thing is a compelling element,'' he said. Ravenholt is a physician, not an economist, and his statement is arrant economic nonsense. But it does reveal an underlying element of official thinking. United States policy clearly is not wholly selfless.

Though the racist motivation is difficult to discern, the same Commission made clear that it is there, describing it this way: ''Rapid population growth occurs in nonwhite societies, and its continuation represents a threat to values inherent in western civilization as we know it. Nonwhite populations are less desirable because they are less capable and less productive. . . ." It attributed this motive to "key members of the Congress responsible for foreign aid authorizations and appropriations, and some of the private citizens who have been associated with activities to curb rapid population growth."

We can also learn about mixed motives from domestic experience with birth-control programs. The date of opening state-supported birth-control clinics was closely related to the concentrations of poor black people in various states. As of 1965, 79 percent of the state-supported clinics in the United States were in the ten states of Alabama, Arkansas, Florida, Georgia, Kentucky, Mississippi, North Carolina, South Carolina, Tennessee, and Virginia, which have only 19 percent of the country's population. Analysis that allows for per capita income shows that the proportion of blacks in a local population is closely related to the density of family-planning clinics.

Can one be surprised that many white people in the United States want there to be fewer black people in the world? In sad truth, it is no more surprising than Hindus in India and Christians in Lebanon fearing a high Moslem birthrate, blacks in Uganda tossing out Indians, and so on throughout the world. But in this age when prejudice is not publicly acceptable, racist acts are justified on the basis of supposed economic, political, sociological, and environmental considerations.

South Africa campaigns for its blacks to reduce their fertility because— yes, they really say it—South Africa is so short of water that it cannot support additional people. If you suggest that there may be a smidgin of racism in that policy, South African officials seem as offended as do AID officials if you suggest that racism may be involved in U.S. population policies.

Writing about the politics of population control, Thomas Littlewood sagely noted that "humanitarian and bigot can find room under the same tent." But even "humanitarian" population-control efforts are misplaced because they are based on a faulty assumption. The population establishment justifies its activities with the proposition that slower population growth leads to faster economic growth. But since 1967 there has been solid statistical evidence of the absence of such a connection. A large body of concurring studies, the earliest by Simon Kuznets, who won a Nobel prize and was the greatest-ever statistician of economic-demographic history, has been entirely ignored by the population controllers. The situation reminds one of the tobacco industry pretending for so long that there was no evidence on the health effects of smoking.

Just last year, the National Research Council and the National Academy of Sciences issued a report on *Population Growth and Economic Development* that almost completely reversed a 1971 report on the same subject from the same institution. On the specific issue of raw materials that has been the subject of so much alarm, NRC-NAS concluded: "The scarcity of exhaustible resources is at most a minor constraint on economic growth . . . the concern about the impact of rapid population growth on resource exhaustion has often been exaggerated." But AID has trimmed its population-control sails as slightly as possible, finding ingenious new ways to say the same old thing.

Only the three monkeys could continue to be unaware that color and intended self-interest are part of the "family-planning" story, along with misplaced humanitarian impulses. No one should be surprised if U.S. zeal comes back to haunt us in the future, just as the sterilization issue brought down Indira Ghandi's government.

24

China's "Voluntary" Population Policy—and Ours

Because the U.S. population establishment favors China reducing its birthrate, its members have tried to whitewash the Chinese program as "voluntary." This selection presents evidence from official Chinese publications that this is quite untrue, given the ordinary definition of "voluntary."

Up-to-the-minute evidence that the situation has not changed appears in a letter to Science *from Zhao Zhipei of the State Family Planning Commission in Beijing (November 20, 1987, p. 1026). He says that "China has carried out public education in various forms to encourage the practice of the one-child family norm, but has not used coercion to force it upon the people." He also writes that "Chinese regulations do stipulate . . . that . . . couples, if having a second child, will have to pay certain fees to the public welfare fund. . . ."*

This is part of the birth-control regulations put into effect on January 1, 1987, in the Dongpu precinct in Canton: "Any pregnant woman who is not married should be ordered to have an abortion. . . . Any woman who does not have an intrauterine device inserted within four months after giving birth shall be fined 20 yuan per month until she accepts the device. . . . If a woman who has had one child fails at birth control, the pregnancy must be terminated and the woman sterilized. . . . If any unauthorized baby dies within three months of birth, the penalty will be only 300 yuan." (Quoted from China Spring *by Bradford Trebach in* The Wall Street Journal *letter, March 10, 1988, p. 25.) This obviously invites infanticide.*

Earlier, Steven Mosher has provided documentary evidence in Broken Earth *that abortions are often forced upon women in China.*

And he published the story of a Chinese couple studying in the United States *who came under enormous pressure from the Chinese authorities at home to have an abortion here, or else—as a last resort—they literally ordered the woman to return to China to have an abortion there. The letter from the Population Control Office at the Walfantia Bearing Factory in Dalian, Manchuria, where she worked ended:*

> *The punishment for this kind of violation [having a second child] is very severe, and we strongly advise you not to risk it.*
>
> *If you cannot have this abortion done abroad, then the factory director orders you to return to China immediately. Any further delays, and you will be punished according to the law.*
>
> *There is nothing ambiguous about our order! Make up your mind immediately.* (The Washington Post *April 10, 1988, p. B1)*

John Aird, who was the chief of the China desk at the Bureau of the Census, is blunt about the matter: "Attempts by Chinese officials and by foreign apologists to represent recent changes in China's family planning policies as a major relaxation of program requirements do not accord with the facts. . . . The Chinese program remains highly coercive." (Quoted by Steven W. Mosher in National Right to Life News, *December 3, 1987, p. 9.)*

Let's give China the benefit of the doubt, and assume that any forced abortions are against policy. We could even agree that the one-child population-control program is their own business. Still there is excellent reason for the United States not to assist that program through the United Nations Fund for Population Activities.

Instead, the United States could devote the funds pulled from that activity—and more—to a related but better purpose, the education in the United States of more Chinese students of demography.

Planned Parenthood and the rest of the population establishment apparently think that the Chinese program is voluntary, as that word is understood by Americans. They should think again. To the Chinese, the word "voluntary" includes pressuring someone until she or he agrees to contracept or abort. In the United States we refer to the same facts as out-and-out coercion.

The official *China: An Introduction* says: "The government has adopted many effective measures of population planning, including explaining to the masses the need for population control, giving technical guidance, giving awards to those who do well in family planning and adopting economic sanctions against those who violate government policies in this respect."

Importantly, this quote is from an official source. Particular events such as coerced seventh-month abortions can be—and are—repudiated by Chinese authorities as unrepresentative excesses. But the presence of government coercion in Chinese family affairs cannot be denied.

Consider the "Eight Steps" that constitute the family planning program in Hengdong County, Hunan Province, described in an article in an English-language Peking University professional journal:

The "eight visits" are paid to constantly and regularly. . . .

1. The visit is paid to youths at marriageable age for heart-to-heart talks persuading them of late marriage. . . . Consequently, all the youths, except those couples who were approved for marriage because of actual difficulties, postponed marriage of their own accord. . . .

2. The visit is paid to newlyweds who are greeted with congratulations and who are mobilized for late childbearing . . . visited by cadres . . . to know their life after marriage, to introduce the knowledge about contraception, to examine their contraceptive measures and to persuade their practice of late childbearing. . . .

3. The visit is made to single child families to mobilize the couples to get single child certificates. There is a specialized processor called Yand Renjun who was reluctant to pledge to have a single child after having a daughter and thus his wife had an unplanned pregnancy in 1984. Yand's case was talked about among the local people. Learning the story, deputy township party secretary Guo Shangchi paid a visit to Yand and made heart-to-heart talks with him. Like Yand, Guo had also an only daughter, but he not only pledged to have a single child, but also underwent sterilization. Immediately after the talks, Yand Renjun said, "Though I become well-off now, I should do what the Party calls for. I am ready to get the single child certificate." Moreover, he accompanied his wife, in the very afternoon, to the hospital for the surgical operation. . . .

4. The visit is made to married women of childbearing age to persuade them, by thorough and painstaking ideological work, of practicing birth control. By doing so, seven people in a village changed their minds of having second births.

Visits 5 and 6 are made after sterilization, to visiting one-child families.

Visit 7 "is paid to the employees who are on home leave for family reunion, and they are reminded of contraception." And visit 8 is to "old folks to show care-taking for them. . . ."

The report of the activities as of 1981 in another county, Rongcheng in Shandong, is best read with a conceptual mirror:

A few years ago, we were rather prone to launch several crash drives in doing family planning work each year, encouraging induced abortion at every rip-tide.

Although some successes were achieved . . . the neglect of day-to-day work had . . . disadvantages. . . . As the tasks came crashing down in all haste, slackness in ideological work might lead to harsh penalties and coercion, causing unnecessary reluctance on the part of the masses.

The new policies were then described:

In our county there are 171 family planning center leaders, more than 1100 full-time cadres working in the production brigades and 3838 family planning leaders in the production teams. . . .

Each team leader for family planning work is responsible for a certain number of households. They are required to make *frequent* home calls, publicize policies and report the matter to their superiors. . . . Full-time cadres in the production brigades are to *persist in making inspections* on a monthly and quarterly basis. . . .

The communes and production brigades each keep files of the newly-weds, births, couples who pledge to have one child, birth control measures taken by couples of childbearing age and distribution of contraceptives. They are kept in separate dossiers for handy information and better management. . . .

The communes make *x-ray checks* once every three months of the women using contraceptive devices. . . .

The striking results of the program are then stated proudly:

1. We have improved the work and met the targets set in the plan. . . . A total of 5472 new borns were registered in the first half of this year, of whom 5233 are first births, 38 and 200 second births conforming to and outside of plan respectively and only one, third birth. The first-birth rate is 95.63%, and it exceeds 96% in 14 communes and towns of this county.

2. The rate of induced abortion has dropped—thanks to contraceptive measures. All the *110,000 married* women of childbearing age in the county have come to know the significance of birth control and the contraceptive measures, resulting in a higher rate of contraception. In the first half of 1982, the abortion rate [fell] compared with the same period of 1981. *Late-stage abortions* in 1981 compared with 1980 recorded a drop of 8.9%, and it further dropped by 10.3% in the first half of 1982.

3. The idea of having one child has struck a deeper root and *less people are punished* for violating the birth control plan. 38,635 or 99.52% of the 38,822 couples having one child in the county have applied for the one-child certificate. In 1981, 3.7% of the new babies were born outside the plan and the parents were duly punished.

The case of "self-managed laborers" should dispel any lingering doubt that many families do not voluntarily choose to have only one child. As of 1987, "circulars and regulations are being drafted to . . . strengthen birth control among traveling self-managed laborers, because they have been having more than one child—some more than four." They have done so because "supervision of the size of their families has been rather weak because of their mobility . . . ," said the official English-language newspaper. This implies that other couples do not go beyond one child simply because the government effectively prevents doing so.

The difference between American and Chinese notions of voluntariness stems from our different views of government telling people how to live their lives. The Chinese family-planning theorists make much of the comments of Marx concerning the "production" of human beings. A member of China's Family Planning Commission interprets Marx as follows:

> [S]ocial production is composed *of material production and human reproduction.* . . . The socialist system in China [emphasizes both] material production and human reproduction, and [must] *regulate population growth in a planned way, as we regulate material production following plans.*

The Chinese view of human rights and reproductive freedom clearly is far different from the West's.

The Chinese have complained about U.S. value judgments about their program. Xu Dixin, the chairman of the China Population Society, wrote:

> Recently *some Americans* advertised that since population would automatically decrease with the development of free economy, there was no need to "limit births." . . . They have proposed undisguisedly that China's population problem can be settled only by changing her social system and practicing "free economy." Such arguments made by some Americans are *presumptuous* to interfere politically in China's internal affairs and to sabotage her socialist system.

But refraining from comment on "internal affairs" does not imply that we should help. Certainly the Chinese agree that a country has no obligation to assist activities of which it does not approve. And if the United States gives money to the United Nations Fund for Population Activities, which then gives money to the Chinese population program, as it does at present, the United States is aiding activities of which it does not approve.

We need not do anything that even the most touchy Chinese could interpret as internal interference. We can simply stop giving money to the U.N.'s Fund for Population Activities, then directly support population activities we can believe in—say, training more Chinese (and other countries') demographers in the United States, a program with many immediate and indirect benefits to all. What could be simpler, purer of heart, and more productive of desirable results?

25

Re-thinking the Jewish View of the "Population Explosion"

As with so many other groups, many Jews favor there being more babies being born to Jews and less babies being born to other people. Just how much the latter preference is due to ignorance of population economics, and how much to demographic competition, it is not possible to tell. This article, originally published in a little avant-garde periodical for Jews, attacks the peculiar logic of the Jewish religious position on this matter.

The article was first sent to the periodical about 1975, at which time it was rejected on the ground that all "reasonable" people and all the "experts" agreed that population growth's effects are destructive. Some six years later, after the publication and wide review of The Ultimate Resource *had brought my viewpoint within the realm of consideration (if still not to be believed), the piece appeared in the periodical.*

It is a *mitzvah* (a good deed) to have additional children, other considerations aside. But it is also a *mitzvah* to balance the principle of *peru urevu* (be fruitful and multiply) with the well-being of the family, especially with the considerations of health and *shalom bayit* (the peacefulness of the home). This is the traditional Jewish viewpoint as summarized in the penultimate paragraph of Rabbi David Feldman's well known and interesting book, *Marital Relations, Birth Control, and Abortion in Jewish Law.*

But then in the very last paragraph of the book, Feldman introduces for the very first time a set of radically different and non-Talmudic considerations, which he offers as qualifications to the book's Talmudic conclusions. These non-Talmudic considerations may be summarized as follows: (1)

Sh'ma, Nov. 13, 1981.

There is a "population explosion" which is a "world problem." This implies that the human race must restrain its fertility; "it would be just as recklessly self-indulgent to overbreed as to refrain from procreation." That is, *peru urevu* is not the simple *mitzvah* stated in Jewish Law. (2) But in contrast to the population "problem of the world at large," the Jewish community need not restrain its fertility, because the Jewish community must "replenish its depleted ranks" after the Holocaust.

These non-Talmudic qualifications are, respectively, factually and morally inappropriate, in my view. If so, it follows—given the basic Jewish value judgments—that the Talmudic view is appropriate for both Jews and non-Jews, without qualifications deriving from present world population conditions. I'll take up these matters in the opposite order than listed above.

The argument is a bit confusing, because it seems to change direction. I'll first argue that the Jews have no special claim to have as many children as they wish. But then I will seem to reverse direction when I argue that no special claim is needed.

Actually there is no contradiction in these two arguments and the matter of special claim might simply be ignored. But it runs the risk of reaching the right conclusion for the wrong reason, which is not helpful, especially when there are excellent reasons for reaching that conclusion.

Jews Have No Special Claims

If world conditions really do imply "scientifically" and "objectively" that population growth ought to cease or be lower than it is, why should the Jews be less subject to this requirement than any other group? Feldman's answer is that Jews have suffered grave losses in numbers, (a) by exile and other social forces, and (b) by murder. But if reduction in numbers by social forces gives a group a special warrant to reproduce, then why do the Jews have a better warrant than the Assyrians, the Aztecs, and goodness knows how many other groups? And if being murdered gives a group such a warrant, then what about the Armenians, American Indians, Russians, and others? With the aid of a good lawyer, *any* group could work up an impressive argument that it has a special right to reproduce.

Feldman's brief for the Jews finds response in my heart because I'm a Jew and I wish that there be many Jews now and forever. But the basis for his brief really is only special pleading.

The matter of a special Jewish claim to reproduction rights is irrelevant, however, because there is no purely "objective" or "scientific" case for reducing or stopping U.S. population growth. Hence no one, neither Jew or non-Jew, needs to justify to others his desire for more children. (A brief summary of scientific knowledge of the subject is here in the original, along with a reference to my *The Economics of Population Growth*.)

Special Jewish Value

So whether an additional child is good or bad from the viewpoint of society (other than the child's parents) depends upon (1) how you weigh the short-run small negative economic effects versus the long-run large positive economic effects and (2) how you weigh the human value of there being more rather than less children and life. Hence even if—contrary to the spirit of Judaism—one placed no special value on more people and more life, it would be strictly a matter of taste and values about how to weigh small economic costs in the short-run versus the big economic gains in the long-run.

But Judaism does have a special value about life and people—*peru urevu*. So Jews as Jews may, and ought to, desire and give life to more children—subject, of course, to such constraints as health and *shalom bayit* discussed so well by Rabbi Feldman up until just before the very last paragraph of his book.

26

The Church's Responsibility to Teach the Value of Life: A Surprising Dialogue between Catholic and Jew

At a time when it seemed that public opinion was unanimous that having more human beings—or even just having the human beings who already had been born—was a great evil, it was important comfort to me that Jim Carey, my closest friend at the University of Illinois, saw eye to eye with me on these matters, including not only theoretical issues but also such practical matters as the desirability of the Catholic Church and others engaging in a political struggle against abortion; we both regarded that as a sinkhole of effort, a distraction from the central issue of the value of life, a fount of partisan feeling and strife, and an impossible cause.

After reading Jim's part of this selection (which I find beautiful and moving), you will understand some of the reasons—his religious values, and his sense of history—why he thought as he did. Perhaps our talks had something to do with it, too; I hope so.

In his role as chairman of the speaker's committee of the YMCA's luncheon lecture series in 1970, Jim had the temerity to invite me to speak in place of a speaker who fortuitously canceled his appearance. (There was therefore no need to consult with his full board; such are the opportunities that life sometimes presents.) The reactions to this event had to be observed to be believed, including a spate of letters to the editor of the local newspaper by people who had not been at the talk yet not only criticized my views but also protested that I had been given the opportunity to speak.

The cessation of the Planned Parenthood television campaign that we discuss in the selection (that story is one of the main reasons for

By James W. Carey and Julian L. Simon, written about 1974.

including this selection even though it is so much Jim's writing) amazed us, as we were also amazed that we were the only ones to have ever protested against it. We knew that public opinion on the subject was monolithic, but we believed that there surely would be at least some Catholics in or out of the television and advertising businesses who would have expressed a "conservative" religious opinion.

My section is somewhat redundant, but seems necessary for the integrity of the selection. It also shows what I had been saying since 1970.

James W. Carey

To summarize what we want to argue with you this evening: Planned Parenthood, the Zero Population Growth movement, and other groups have mounted a campaign of population control to constrain the size of the population of the United States and of other countries. That campaign has had a strong impact on Americans generally and also on American Catholics. In presenting the case against population growth these groups rely upon some exceedingly shaky scientific evidence. But more to the point, they call into question the notion that life itself is a value, a value superordinate to other values that animate social life. This value—the value of life itself, unmodified and uncompromised—has been at the center of Catholic experience, Catholic belief, and Catholic liturgy. The church, as a community of people, can perform, we believe, a spiritual as well as a social service in these times by preaching to Catholics and non-Catholics the value of life as the central value in human affairs.

But has the church done so? Let's take an extended example. You may have seen an advertising campaign staged by Planned Parenthood that ran on radio, television, and in many national magazines. There were a number of specific ads in the campaign including one that was headlined "How Many Children Should You Have? Three? Two? One?"; another that adduced "Ten Reasons for Not Having Children"; and, finally, the most offensive one was called the "Family Game": the game was staged on a great monopoly board and every time the dice of life were thrown and a child was born—rather like going to jail without passing "go"—the background audio announced the disasters that came in the wake of children— "there goes the vacation" or "there goes the family room." We watched these ads with increasing annoyance and finally wrote the following letter to the Advertising Council, which had sponsored the campaign on behalf of Planned Parenthood:

The Advertising Council has undertaken to aid people in controlling the size and spacing of their families by cooperating in a family planning campaign with the Planned Parenthood Council.

We agree that intelligent family planning is a valid personal and social goal and one that is supported by a majority of the American people. The actual Planned Parenthood campaign, to which the Advertising Council has lent its endorsement and assistance, goes considerably beyond family planning however. Implicitly and explicitly the campaign aims at population control, that is, the reduction of family size even among those people who know quite well how to plan their families. The campaign aims to change the values and attitudes of Americans toward family size and fertility behavior.

We believe that a substantial group of Americans do not support this goal of the advertising campaign. Persuasion to reduce the family size in the United States violates the values of the undersigned, for example, and undoubtedly those of many others, too. Furthermore, population control does not have conclusive or even solid scientific support—a surprising but incontestable fact. Finally, it is a questionable practice for the Advertising Council to support population control by implication and innuendo in a campaign ostensibly aimed at encouraging family planning. Let us expand on each of these points.

1. To prevent any possible misunderstanding, let us state that we are completely in favor of anything that will aid individual families in achieving the size of family they wish, to have the children they want and not to have others. We support as strongly as we can each person's freedom to choose in these matters. We also recognize that people's wants are complex, that they change in response to persuasion and other pressures, and in the course of a pregnancy itself.

2. On the scientific situation: Instead of detailing the scientific arguments here, we shall even point out that there is far from scientific consensus on population control, and that authorities of the highest repute do not believe that slower population growth in the United States is scientifically warranted.

3. On the evils of confusing the issues: There is nothing wrong in the Advertising Council campaigning for family planning *or* for population control. A voluntary organization in a democracy has the moral right to advocate almost anything it wishes. However, we do not think it is appropriate to sell one idea (population control) covertly by joining it to a more accepted notion (family planning).

With that background out of the way let us get to the central point. There is a proverb from another country that a "child brings a cake under each arm." The point of the proverb is not that children are unalloyed gifts but that life itself is a gift, a gift to be compared to a feast. As with any feast there must be planning, and too many diners can spoil the meal. But those obvious reservations should not obscure the central value, and that human life—its growth, development, and enhancement—should be the object of public policy. If more children should mean that in the short run other members of families will have a smaller share of the family's income and wealth, this does not by itself imply that families ought to have fewer children. In fact, and in general, the opposite conclusion is, by our values, warranted: the major advantage of increased wealth is that we can support more life and offer all the complicated opportunities of life to more people. By our values it is often good to share people for a while. (And the scientific evidence convinces us that in the *long run* more people do not necessarily mean smaller shares of wealth on the average, at least in a developed country like the United States.)

One of the most disturbing things about the Planned Parenthood campaign is its determined appeal to that which is worst in us. Each new life is weighted against a vacation, an addition to the house, another car, more savings. We do not doubt the need to calculate the costs of a child against the advantages it might bring. But is the calculus solely one of material possessions? Is life itself to be solely defined by possessions? For us, as in the proverb, children bring something to life in themselves, and the decision to make this gift available cannot be exhaustively determined by the perusal of bank statements. Security, vacations, automobiles are desirable objects. But to make them, as the ads implicitly do, the spiritual end of life is to massively confuse our purposes and to indulge in that often mentioned American materialism that intelligent people regularly condemn and then regularly cultivate whenever it serves their purpose.

But there is more. One of the ads enjoins young people to "enjoy your freedom" before, by having children, you let some of that freedom go. Such a theme—and it is not uncommon in American rhetoric—continues the view that the contribution children make to persons and to society is a purely negative one. In this view children are a loss: they take space, constrict freedom, use income that can be invested in vacations, family rooms, and automobiles. We find no consideration here of how children enhance freedom, and of how the advantages of freedom itself are realized when shared rather than prizes as a purely personal possession. Finally, one of the ads encapsulates the spirit of the entire campaign: "How many children should a couple have? Three? Two? One? None?" Such an ad belies the claim that the advertising avoids the designation of any specific number of children as 'preferred.' Why not twelve? eleven? ten? or six? five? four? In the same ad, in order to lead audience thinking, it is noted that the decision to have children "could depend on their concern for the effect population growth can have on society." The direction of the effect on society is implied, but nowhere is the effect analyzed, or even clearly stated.

In summary, the ads not only teach family planning but recommend population control. Moreover, they do this by defining the range of acceptable family size as between zero and three, by placing children as negative objects alongside the positive goods supplied by industry, by equating the bringing up of children with merely equipping them with these same goods, by viewing children as an essential constriction of human freedom, and by suppressing a view of life and children that might lead people to think that having more children is a positive and rewarding act. There are values, not just techniques embodied in those ads, but they are not the most heroic or ennobling of values. Certainly they are not the values of the undersigned.

To our surprise, we heard from the Advertising Council. They were "stunned" by the letter. It was, Robert Keim the president said, the first complaint about the campaign they had received. They found the ideas in the letter rather strange, particularly as they were held by "educated people," and they talked at some length to see if we were serious about knows that. And the parents who carry almost all the burden of the children, as well as the communities that carry a small part of the burden, at some point say "enough" even while recognizing that more children would be nice to have in the longer run. Furthermore, parents and countries may even overshoot—having more children than they would if they knew that infant mortality rate had fallen as fast as it has, and that education was accessible but also expensive. If there were a superbeing who knew the present and future, and who understood perfectly the preferences and feelings of each set of parents, perhaps it could choose an "optimum" level of childbearing for each couple and country better than they will achieve by themselves.

But such a superbeing does not exist. And to think that a United Nations Population World Plan of Action is such a superbeing, and that its "recommendations"—well circumscribed with pious statements about "voluntarism," "sovereignty," "individual human rights," and the like, but clearly intended to influence the practices of parents and countries—will be closer to such an "optimum" than will decisions arrived at independently by individual couples and countries is both arrogant and ridiculous.

A second phony element: population reductionists justify population control on the grounds that the world's natural-resource and environmental situation is getting worse, and that life is becoming more "precarious." With respect to resources, all signs—going back in history as far as any evidence exists—show that resources have been getting more abundant and less scarce even as population has grown. In fact, resources have become more abundant—lower in cost—*because* of population and income growth, rather than despite them. Again and again, temporary scarcities induced by the growth of population and income have induced the search for solutions which, when found, left us better off than if the scarcities had never arisen.

The Facts of Life

With respect to the state of the environment and its most important consequence, health, the facts cannot be called anything but miraculous, rather than dismaying. If Mexico City had standing in court, it would sue *Time* for libel; the delegates joked about the rats they were supposed to be seeing on the streets and the face masks against pollution that had been pictured. And the rest of humanity would properly sue the newspapers, Walter Cronkite, and the population lobby for defamation of character and some as-yet-unnamed crime of assault upon the survival of the race, for publishing that the human enterprise is in bad shape and getting worse. It is in fact in better shape materially than ever before in history—and the

the whole business. They assured us the Council had been thoughtfully concerned about people's reaction to the campaign, that it even had been supervised by a Catholic, and that they had received no complaints from Catholics, lay or clerical, until our letter came along. The Advertising Council itself was not hostile to life, Keim averred, and they had based the campaign on what they took to be the best scientific evidence.

The fact there had been no Catholic reaction to the campaign puzzled us in the light of what we took the Catholic position on life to be. The campaign was implicitly hostile to Catholic values as I understand them. Julian Simon came to that conclusion as well, viewing the matter from without the church. Why, then, was there acceptance, or at least apathy toward the campaign, by Catholics, attitudes that extend to the entire zero population growth movement? There were three possible explanations: First, that the abortion issue had sapped the energy and narrowed the horizons of the Catholic community; there was nothing left over to fight skirmishes about such an advertising campaign. Second, that Catholics in significant numbers had accepted the views of Planned Parenthood and ZPG toward the value of life. And finally that Catholics had also accepted the view, popularized in works such as Paul Ehrlich's book *The Population Bomb,* that population growth in the United States would have disastrous consequences.

Our disquiet was reinforced by the response to a lecture we had jointly given on population to a class of Catholic students in a course on Christian ethics. The students discussed population, and many related problems, in a strictly secular vocabulary without recourse to any religious language or imagination; the students used the language of conditioning, reinforcement, and scientific determinism. Not much room for ethics there. We realized, of course, that Catholic students were not unique in this. Had we lectured in any of the other religious foundations we probably would have found similar secular vision of these ethical questions. The students shared, in other words, the fashionable ideas alive in the culture about the population question. And while this is understandable, it is not fertile ground for the Holy Spirit.

We would like in the remainder of this lecture to take up the three explanations for the indifference of Catholics to the Planned Parenthood campaign. Let us begin with the scientific evidence concerning the consequences of population growth, evidence which speaks, we think, in rather direct contradiction to the position Paul Ehrlich has popularized.

Julian L. Simon

In the past decade popular journalism, and even some of the scientific press, has presented only a single set of views of the effects of population growth on economic growth, and this view has therefore become accepted as simple truth. This set of views is that (1) in less-developed countries (LDC's) lower population growth means faster economic development, (2) in more-developed countries (MDC's) lower population growth means higher per-worker output and income, and (3) continued population growth means worldwide disaster, as described in the Club of Rome's *Limits to Growth*.

But these conclusions and analyses are *not* necessarily correct—though they *may* be, of course. Therefore, my key message is that to push ahead with antinatalist policies on the assumption that these views *are* correct *might* be a tragic mistake—economically as well as humanly.

One fundamental reason why it is not an open-and-shut case that population growth is a bad thing is that whether population is now too large, or is growing too fast, cannot be decided on scientific grounds alone. This judgment depends upon one's values, a matter about which science must be silent. The judgment about which policies are good or bad, and which policies should be chosen, rests squarely upon one's values. Whether you think that it is better for a country to have a population of, say, 50 million human beings at $4000 per year per-capita income, or 100 million human beings at $3000, is strictly a matter of what you consider important. Therefore, a judgment that population growth is too fast or too slow is not a scientific judgment, but rather a value judgment. This proposition is as true for less-developed as for more-developed countries: The judgment about whether population is growing too fast depends on values, and cannot be found in science alone.

I'll come back later to the matter of values. Now let's talk about the *economic* effects of population growth in less-developed and more-developed countries, remembering that our main subject tonight is our own society, which is an MDC. (A section is omitted here. See Selections 14, 15, and 16 for the arguments.)

So in brief summary: In the long run the effect of faster population growth may well be *positive,* though in the short run it is negative. If this is so, a choice must be made between, *on the one hand a higher economic level in the long run for people living in the future,* and on the other hand, a somewhat higher per-capita income *now.* And when considering just the level of per-capita income *now,* values come into play in deciding about the trade-off between more people in the short run and higher average income in the short run.

About values now—this is really the key issue in judgments about population growth. Let us be absolutely clear on this: All judgments about population size hinge on value judgments. Economists, for example, have long used the concept of "optimum population" for a given country, and this sounds very scientific. But these discussions about optimum population sizes or growth rates must have some criterion of better and worse, and this criterion is usually *per-capita income* of the present population, including "quality of life" considerations.

No one, however, is prepared to take the per-capita income criterion to its logical conclusions. Two implications of this criterion are: (1) Do away with all lower-income people. Removing the lower half of the income distribution in any country will raise the average income of the country as a whole by a purely arithmetic process. And logically one should then carry this to the point at which one leaves only one person—the richest person to start with. Of course this is absurd, but this is the kind of absurdity that the average-income quality-of-life criterion leads to. Such absurdities should make the criterion suspect. (2) Another implication of an average-income criterion is that the birthrate should be driven down to ridiculously low levels, and perhaps to zero births—the particular level depending upon the weight one gives to the future relative to the present. For example, if the future is discounted at perhaps 10 percent per year, the present value of per-person income into the infinite future would be maximized *if we stop having babies completely*. This is because it will be a long time before the babies begin to produce anything, though they will be consuming immediately. Hence a baby born today lowers the income of everyone else, on the average. Having no babies at all next year would be good for per-capita income next year. But no one wants to go so far with this implication of an average-income criterion.

An alternative value criterion—the one that I wish to use as a criterion for decisions about population growth is one that I think a great many other people subscribe to also—as they will find if they inspect their beliefs closely. This is the value about people and life that is held by sources as disparate as the Bible, which is the foundation for much of our Western morality, and the Utilitarian philosophers, whose thinking underlies so much of our legal and social and economic philosophy. In Biblical terms it is "Be fruitful and multiply." In Utilitarian terms it is "The greatest good for the greatest number." That is, my judgment about the welfare of a community depends *both* on the average income *and* on the number of people who partake of that standard of living.

Other things being equal, a greater number of people is a good thing, according to this value criterion. Furthermore, this criterion suggests that a society may even be better off with a *lower* average income if more people are partaking of it—though *how much* lower is a tricky matter, of course. One must decide on which basis one wishes to trade people for material welfare. Should 10 percent fewer people be traded for 5 percent more income per person? Or should the trade-off be 10 percent fewer people for 1 percent, or for 20 percent, more income per person? This is an ethical choice, of course, but one that must be made either explicitly or implicitly when setting a population policy about the amount of pressure that will be put upon people to have small families. The important point here is that I reject average income by itself as a criterion for judgements about population size. Under some conditions I accept that it is better to have more people and lower per-capita income. And I think a lot of other people share this value.

This criterion seems to me to be consistent with our other values—our abhorrence of killing, and our desire to prevent disease and early mortality.

I had always assumed that Judaism espoused the value of "Be fruitful and multiply," of believing that it is virtuous to have more rather than less children consistent with bringing them up well, of course. I was distressed to find that though many Orthodox Jews do in fact believe that this is the Jewish view, Jewish religious thinkers generally do not espouse it any more—even religious theological writings. (A recent tract on birth control ends with an ecological statement about the dangers of the population explosion. See Selection 25.) This change is possible because there is considerable flexibility in Judaism for religious thinkers to interpret the law as seems appropriate to current conditions.

Clearly Protestantism does not today urge "Be fruitful and multiply." And I was saddened that Judaism does not either. As a non-Catholic, however, I was sure that at least the Roman Catholic is still committed to this belief, and I hoped that the Catholic Church would take the lead in promulgating the message about what I consider to be a fundamental tenet of our common religious heritage—that life is good.

James W. Carey

But is life the central value in Catholic thought? I always presumed it was; that the admonition to "Be fruitful and multiply" was part of the shared heritage of Judaism and Christianity and that it was more than an incitement to copulation or domination. Life was, I thought, the greatest gift of God to man. The ability to create life was God's noblest bestowal upon us and, in turn, the creation of life was the greatest gift we could return to God. It was, I thought, the central belief of Catholicism that not only did the Word become flesh but in return the flesh became word. Life, however mean or dispirited in a material sense, remained the source of awe, mystery, and joy.

And it is precisely this sense of life that the population control movement attempts to undercut. By playing on a modern reversal of meanings, such movements find that life is awful rather than awe-ful. In the literature of this movement there is a frequent metaphor in which life consists of "worms in a bucket." People in groups and crowds are described as "massed" and "teeming"; they are depicted as consuming the earth: eating, fornicating, defecating, and despoiling. Such people are rarely seen as spiritual creatures, creatures capable of love, nobility, and friendship, capable of contributing to a shared life. This image and this metaphor have taken over the discussion of population: an image of massed humanity, and a metaphor of animality. Its implicit commitment is to the belief that life is only really lived in American communities at a particular standard of living; others, living at "lower" standards of living are less alive, less spiritual, less human. This image and metaphor and the beliefs that they harbor are contrary to Catholic experience and value.

We are certainly not the people to discuss church doctrine on these matters. But we have looked at John Noonan's histories of Catholic attitudes toward contraception and abortion and what we have to say seems consistent at least with a major stream of Catholic thought.

Church discussions of contraception, abortion, and infanticide arose within a Catholic community living amidst the Roman Empire where these were widespread practices. "By these signs they shall know us." Christians distinguished themselves from the Roman community by the reverence they expressed for life. The ordinary practices of Roman life were opposed because they were not only morally repugnant in themselves but because they sinned against a larger conception of human nature and human value. It should be remembered that the central iconography of the early church was not the crucifixion. (Though it should also be remembered that an emphasis on death does not preclude, indeed it often discloses, an intense interest in life, as it is said, metaphorically, through death into life.) Not until the tenth century does the crucifixion move from a marginal to a central place in Christian iconography. Early Christian art is concerned with healing, miracles, the hopeful aspects of faith like the Ascension and Resurrection. Indeed, church art and liturgy was a direct expression of the force of life itself: growth, healing, exfoliation. To many modern minds, including some Catholic minds, this belief seems now naive and parochial.

The early church, the doctrinal church, was drawn to an interest in contraception and abortion because these practices pointed beyond themselves toward a value at the root of the Christian community: the value of life itself and the supreme position relative to those other clamorous values with which it has always struggled: wealth, power, success, domination. But to discover the value of life in Catholic experience and belief one needs to look beyond the doctrinal church to the living community. In an exchange of letters between John Henry Cardinal Newman and Sir James

Stephens, Stephens implores Newman to take up the attack against the Utilitarians, "the most subtle enemy which Christianity has ever had." Newman replies something to the effect that Stephens had it wrong: the Utilitarians attacked the doctrines of the Church but the Church was not principally doctrines. It is a church of sacraments and tradition. It is in the Church of sacraments and tradition, the church as community, that one encounters the value of life. No one, let us remember, ever joined the Church, and only few left it, because of a conflict over abstract doctrine. One joins and stays with the Church because of what one encounters sacramentally; the actual physical exchange through taste, touch, and ear with the Godhead, that sacramental realization and promise that one will come to know life and brotherhood. These central sacramental symbols are precisely about life itself. To put it this way—the only way possible in discursive prose—is to immediately distort the matter. The "idea of life" is never experienced as an "idea" about anything. The Church is not about ideas. Life is experienced through touch, taste, and sight as an immediately apprehensible truth and reality. It is not a doctrine to be debated or a truth to be realized by the methods of formal philosophy.

There are two ways of losing sight of the central place that life holds as a value in the church. The first is to become preoccupied by the connection to death of the central symbols of ritual, on Passion Sunday, on Ash Wednesday, on Good Friday one is again directly reminded of the power of death. However, one cannot be interested in life without also being interested in death. (It is the attempt to deny both that is so troubling in modern culture.) One is merely the reverse of the other. Those who find life the ultimate value will also be, in general at least, intensely interested in death: in the special meanings and possibilities that the shadow of death casts back upon life.

The second way to miss the point of the living church is to assume that life is a central value only insofar as it is spiritual life we are discussing, to assume that spiritual life has no direct, intrinsic connection and linkage to human, corporeal life. Yet, the most attractive figure in the modern church, St. Francis, contradicts such a view and his immense influence stems from his capacity to blend the spiritual and natural. His joyful prayers and canticles celebrate the world he so happily abjured.

Whenever life is presented in the liturgy of the Catholic community, spiritual life and human life are happily interfused. One does not live spiritually by casting up a world of forms independent of the concretely human. And, therefore, in the liturgy there is a constant, reiterated presentation of the spiritual and natural fused, but not transcended, in metaphor: "it will become for us the bread of life," "by rising from the dead he destroyed death and restored life," "the resurrection of the death and the life of the world to come," "the lord and the giver of life."

The same emphasis is found in the liturgical calendar, which fixes the beginning of the year in Advent: the beginning of life, in pregnancy. Life is seen as human and divine at Christmastide, and as if to punctuate the relation of humanity and divinity, the Annunciation is placed nine months before the birth of Christ. The entire liturgical year pivots about this central event of birth.

That this emphasis has not always been present in Christianity we all know, but we know it as a measure of loss. Christmas did not become a holiday in Protestant countries until late in the nineteenth century. Indeed, Christmas constituted part of the battleground of the Reformation. Against the severe spirituality of Protestant life the Catholic tradition emphasized the Christ Mass, the central symbol of which was the presence of the child, while the regeneration of life itself was the central historical and spiritual event in Christian life. That emphasis was maintained at cost and pain, for Christmas was forbidden as a holy day in Scotland in the sixteenth century and in England in the seventeenth. But against bans, strictures and commercials the essential Catholic meaning of Christmas keeps cracking through: it is the creation and manifestation of life, and through life the possibility of soul, that is the essential mystery and source of joyful satisfaction within existence.

This meaning was, of course, central to many pagan peoples. The Church in its early years attempted to vivify pagan celebrations of life by deepening and widening their spiritual significance. The ancient practices of bounding seeds off the buttocks of a woman or throwing the same seeds at the womb of a bride testifies eloquently to the longstanding reverence for life and the capacity for so-called primitive peoples to see life in the widest context. Contemporary man is often so divorced from this structure of feeling that he can see in the central symbols of primitive art—the representation of female genitals—only eroticism (though that should not be forbidden) or nascent pornography. But if one is part of a people who revere life, who find it the central, mysterious problem of existence, who see it in the regenerative and creative process of nature, the linkage between man and his world, then how better to represent this awe and belief in potent and dramatic form than in the sexual organ. The breast engorged with milk is the gift of nature that sustains the gift of life.

Catholic tradition infused these pagan practices with the personage of Christ and Mary: Mother as creator and child as the gift of life. And from the personage derives the central core of Catholic belief: that it is good to increase life, to share it with as many as can partake of its banquet. While the value is not arbitrary, it recognizes after all the existence of a prudential world of limitation and complication. Yet within that recognition is a commitment to the vocation of life.

In closing I would like to read to you a brief passage from a book at once intensely Catholic and deeply agnostic, and, in addition, one of the greatest books written in English in the last decade, William Gibson's *A Mass for the Dead*. Gibson wrote this "mass" as a necessary substitute for offering one, and the sections of the book bear titles such as *"Sanctus," "Pater Noster," "Confiteor," "Dies Iraw," "Ite, Missa Est."* In a section entitled *"Kyrie"* he writes of his dead uncle and of the relationship of his uncle to his own children:

> It is my uncle's shadow that falls upon my boys. The sense of mortality irks them at odd moments, and sleepless at bedtime one boy invites me to "figure out a way" he need not die, and I think how the animal wants to live; sitting at his hip I say he will be immortal in his son as I am in mine, which satisfied neither of us. . . .

> But when he is asleep, and I am out on the hill for my nightly count of stars, I think is this townful of roofs not a miracle? I can tell my son how we have dug for the forgotten hands and surmised a million centuries that crept by the beast living isolate in caves; only yesterday he perceived that in bands he might overcome the mammoth and changed wilderness into cities; and he did not change himself? It was outgrow or die, and he outgrew. He forbade himself rape, homicide, plunder, incest, cannibalism; he laid down another imperative, it was the tool he invented chief of all tools, and it moved the earth. He called it conscience, a knowing together, and I can tell my boy it is our warranty of human life, which houses us under the hope of these roofs.

> Tonight the wind is contaminated; on other roofs in each country men are measuring the fall of the shadow, strontium, carbon, cesium, across the loins of every child. . . . Murder enough is around me on this hill, mole, snake, owl, and I make this eleison to the stars. . . . Now, as before it is outgrow or die. . . . And faint in the roar of the foundries I hear again the feet of my father walking the streets of the city that year, with his brother dead, when . . . he marked on the calendar for the wife and kids his vow to outgrow, and taught me the animal wants to live.

> It is his eleison I make. Have mercy upon my increase. And thus saith God himself that formed the earth and made it; he hath established it, he created it not in vain, he formed it to be inhabited.

Not in vain, but to be inhabited, to be filled with life; this is the essence of Catholic life as I understand it. An essence consistent, as Julian has argued, with the laws of economics, but more to the point, consistent with the essence of the Christian admonition: "I have come to give you life and give it more abundantly."

As a Catholic I am worried that this essence is draining out of the Catholic community, partly because it has been under savage assault from those who find life an affront to nature and mechanics and, paradoxically enough, from those as well who center Catholic thought and action on the problem of abortion and the Right to Life movement. We are the ultimate heirs, the contemporary proprietors, of a grand and noble vision of the value of life and that is what we must keep firmly in mind. Life is the issue, social, moral, and theological; not the selling of condoms in Connecticut or the performance of abortion in New York. Abortion is only a concern in terms of the larger theological commitment to what is behind and transcendent to it: life itself in all its enigma and complexity. Abortion may, I fear, stand in the same relationship to Catholic history as did the temperance movement to Protestant history: an episode in which a people win a battle but lose a culture. Protestants, too, tried to reform a community not by witness and humility but by assertiveness and constitutional amendment. In struggling so hard with the dragon they become dragons themselves. Catholics may have to so redefine their entire culture in order to secure legislative and congressional acceptance, that they forget the historical meaning and experience that animates their concern and win a merely pyrrhic victory. Catholics must largely accept the secular definitions of life in order to politically struggle for the "right to life." But the right to life is not a constitutional right, not a legal right, not even a natural right in the western political sense. Life, its growth and development, and enhancement, as a gift from and for God is the Catholic value and no court, only a community of faith and belief, will protect it.

The great contribution the Catholic community has to make to contemporary life is not to struggle in the courts and legislature about technical definitions of whether or not the fetus is protected by the first ten amendments, though in simple justice I think it should be. Its real contribution comes from the commitment, as witnessed presentation, that life is the central value in human experience. Catholics are the only group (the Latter Day Saints excepted), in which this value—this sense—is a known remnant of historical experience and living theological concern. The nurture of this sense is the contribution of Catholics to themselves and to the wider community in which they live.

Julian L. Simon

The Catholic church seems the only U.S. institution that is committed to the message that more life is good, and to encouraging people to have as many children as they can bring up well.

As an economist I can tell you that this message does not fly in the face of economics or resource matters, in the short run and the long run.

As a non-Catholic I hope the Roman Catholic church can be *really* catholic and can bring this message to the rest of the United States. I hope the church will not be inward-looking and self-preoccupied, or bashful. I hope it will try to persuade others of this truth that the church, Jim, and I all believe is so fundamentally nonsectarian.

27

People Are Not the Problem

Ever since Robert MacNamara imposed his zeal for population con-trol (perhaps "mania" would be a better word) on the World Bank, that institution has been the most vocal institution on this subject. By the time of its 1984 World Development Report, *however, it had backed away from its former line about the impending exhaustion of resources, and instead found new purported reasons to espouse reduction of the population growth rate. This selection criticizes that 1984 report.*

The World Bank's World Development Report that came out last month left a frightening impression. In his foreword, bank president A. W. Clausen wrote, "The situation is grave. . . . Failure to act now to slow growth is likely to mean a lower quality of life for millions of people." And newspaper headlines said "World Bank warns population will be 10 billion by 2050 without controls." But the data contained in the report do not lend support to a grim assessment. And a special set of values underlies the bank's interpretation of the situation.

There is no question that the raw data contained in the report are correct. And the body of the text, prepared by an honest and diligent staff, includes much sound and useful analysis. But whether one views recent population developments as good news or bad news depends heavily on one's values about human life.

The standard interpretation—of which the report is typical—is that the United States should urge other nations to reduce population growth rates. The argument runs as follows: Population is growing at a faster rate than in earlier times. The upcoming number of human beings will be large by comparison with the past and even the present. Based upon observed

The Washington Times, August 6, 1984, p. 61.

production of food and existing supplies of land and other resources, there is no obvious prospect that consumption must not fall. Therefore, it makes sense to reduce the population growth rate. But one may interpret the facts quite differently. One may view the large numbers of human beings who are alive now, and will be alive in the future if all goes well, as a triumph rather than as a problem. Additional children certainly are a burden for their parents, and to a much smaller extent, for the community. But the world's present capacity to support our present billions of people, and at continually increasing standards of living, is the greatest economic and scientific success story in the history of humankind.

Of course values matter here. But if one believes that human life is good, it seems logical to think that more human life is good, assuming that no tragic cost need be paid thereby—and it need not, as is seen in increased length of life and better health all over the globe.

The cause of the population increase is increase in life expectancy. In the rich countries in just the past two centuries, life expectancy has risen from less than 35 years at birth to more than 70 years. In the poor countries, life expectancy has jumped perhaps 13 years in just the past three decades. Are these not the most important facts about the state of our environment and supplies of natural resources?

The report simply assumes—without offering any evidence—that additional births slow economic development. As Mr. Clausen puts it in his foreword, "a vicious circle: the slow pace at which development reaches the poor contributes to rapid population growth, making the elimination of poverty increasingly difficult." But the statistical relationship between population growth and economic growth clearly tells another story: There is no observable relationship between the rates of population growth and economic growth per person. It is these data that converted me from an activist for population control to a believer in the long-run benefits of population growth.

The report properly notes that population growth does not seem to have the negative effect upon savings, which was a source of worry to many for a long time. But the report puts heavy stress upon "schooling requirements and (human) capital widening." Like so many ideas about population economics that seem obvious and commonsensical, however this one is contradicted by studies showing that there is little effect of population growth upon years of education or amount of expenditure per child.

A set of philosophical ideas underlying the report may seem innocuous but represent a specific value orientation. For example, the report talks of a "social contract to lower fertility" which "provides the basis for public subsidies to family planning." The bank may espouse such a point of view, and it may seem ridiculous to many in and around government that one might think otherwise. But neither individuals nor the administration are obliged by logic to think this way. Similarly, the bank asserts that "there is a balance between the private right of procreation and social responsibility." This obviously is the kind of notion that could justify any kind of community intervention that one might wish. Again, the United States need not adopt such a concept, and especially not without careful thought about just what the concept would mean in practice.

The report asserts that there is a "gap between the private and social gains from having many children." The implication is that the difference is negative, a social cost; no notice is taken of the fact—demonstrated by the increase of material welfare over the course of civilization—that on balance the difference must be a benefit to society rather than a cost, in the sense that we are all beneficiaries of the fruits of people born in the past, whose parents paid for their upbringing.

The report suggests that more children inflict damage, for example, that "a large number of children in the family has a negative effect on classroom performance and test scores." This does not accord with my reading of the literature on the subject, which is more a battlefield than a settled field. The report also says that "even when parents seem to gain from large families, children may lose." This remark is particularly egregious; aside from the fact that there is obviously less family income per person with more children, ill effects have not been shown. Even worse, there is no recognition that children who might not be born have something to lose—the chance at life. It seems to me that such assertions reveal prejudice more than anything else.

In short, the body of the report is mostly straightforward statistical material. But that content does not support the conclusions put forth in Mr. Clausen's foreword. The text does not show, as the foreword asserts, "that slowing the pace of population growth can make a difference—and that the ingredients for doing so are also those that will increase economic growth." The foreword simply does not square with the data, and the report is devoid of scientific support for government intervention to cause families to have fewer children than they would otherwise choose. Yet the foreword has been the source of a raft of prominent, frightening new stories, which heavily influence the public's views about U.S. and international population policies.

It is time, and simple decency, that the World Bank stop its longtime practice of issuing statements of personal prejudice about population matters as if they are statements of scientific fact.

28

New Cure for the Jobs Shortage

This piece tackles an important and dangerous misconception—that the number of jobs is fixed, and therefore that more people necessarily imply more unemployment. This misconception is a classic case of taking into account only what Bastiat calls "the seen" and not taking account of the "unseen"—that is, the process of creation of new jobs.

The notion that labor-saving technology causes unemployment is of the same intellectual stripe. And if economic logic alone were not enough to refute this notion, the history of the human enterprise should demonstrate conclusively that new technology on average creates more jobs than it eliminates. This process promises a future of ever-increasing demand for human labor, in an ever-increasing diversity of economic roles.

Uncharacteristically, Peter Drucker recently began a recent article with one of the grossest and most destructive misconceptions in economics. In China, he says, "huge numbers of people are grossly underemployed. They may nominally be on a payroll, but there is no work for them." (*The Wall Street Journal,* November 19, 1987.) Mr. Drucker went on to accuse "overpopulation," which he says "has been the curse of China for 200 years," as being the cause of "millions of underemployed peasants" having "neither jobs nor housing . . . in the overcrowded, desperately job-short cities."

Just the opposite is true. There is more work to be done in China than anyplace else in the world. A fifth of the world's population needs the work that will build better housing, better transportation, better infrastructure, better education, and better everything—all the way from the remark-

Asian Wall Street Journal, May 27–28, 1988, p. 8.

ably low income level at present to the highest level attainable under present technology as seen in the rich countries.

This whole world is not short of work to be done. Roads need building, furniture needs repairing, rooms need repainting, and yards needs yard-work. If you are not convinced, come over to my house with your old clothes on.

Yet unions agonize about new jobs for people who lose their old ones to automation and foreign competition. And jobs shortage is a standard argument for population control and against immigration in the United States as well as other countries.

Something seems out of whack. Why don't people who are looking for jobs get together with the work that needs to be done? What is lacking is not work, but rather a mechanism that will translate the work into jobs. The mechanism is lying inert—like a coiled spring—but is kept from operating by government constraint. The mechanism is economic freedom, and the free markets that will almost instantly develop when people regain their freedom and believe that they will continue to have it in the future. First I'll explain the economics. Then I'll offer a new partial remedy for the United States that would cost the public nothing.

There are many reasons why people remain unemployed for months and years despite all the undone work. Many lack information about the labor market, about which more later. Some refuse to work at the price they can get in the market for their labor because they prefer to do without the money rather than accept that wage. Others prefer a combination of leisure plus government benefits to the market wage. Still others feel that the work offered is below their dignity.

Often a potential employer and a potential worker do not get together because the government keeps them apart. The barriers to employment that governments erect vary from country to country. In the United States, the minimum wage law is a notorious enemy of employment to young people and others who could be profitably employed but are not worth the minimum wage. Instead of having an opportunity to improve their market value by learning on the job, they remain without jobs. In China, bans on private enterprise in the cities, and restriction of people to the areas in which they presently live, keep many from finding gainful work. European countries forbid employers from closing factories, and hence increase the risk of opening them.

Hong Kong illustrates what happens when government does not hinder employers and workers from making a wage bargain. Hong Kong's popu-lation grew from 700,000 in 1945 to 5.6 million people in 1987, faster labor force-growth than any other country. Yet Hong Kong has never suffered from the kind of long-run unemployment problem many countries have today. There is some cyclic fluctuating unemployment, but not the sort of semi-permanent unemployment we're addressing here. Earnings have risen at unprecedented rates, and it is unlikely they would have risen even faster if population had grown more slowly. This happy situation has resulted because—except for basic regulations about worker safety—the Hong Kong government has interfered little in the labor market.

Hong Kong provides an excellent answer to the frequently asked question, "How will the government create enough jobs?" Its government does not create *any jobs at all*. It is sufficient that government not gum up the private job-creating process for there to be enough jobs.

Unfortunately, too many people do not understand the basic mechanism whereby private individuals create markets and jobs. Too many citizens and politicians labor under the destructive belief that if government does not do something, it will not get done. Just the opposite with jobs. If government tries to create jobs, jobs will eventually become scarce.

And there are many—politicians and citizens in the United States and elsewhere—who so hate the motivation of profit that they would rather not have its benefits, including plentiful jobs, rather than let the market operate. This anti-private-enterprise attitude is another cause of the misery associated with unemployment.

Consider the job "creation" by Wing Ho (not his real name), an ex-teacher in a village outside Chengde, China. All his life Wing has been interested in raising grapes. Less than a decade ago he noticed a dry riverbed outside the village, which was worthless for ordinary farming because the soil is too sandy but which would produce grapes well, he figured. Under the new Chinese free-enterprise "responsibility system" in rural areas, he arranged with the village to use the land, and then started operations in a small way. Today he employs forty people on the land he rents. That is, he has "created" forty jobs.

Several of Wing's employees have gone off to agricultural school with an eye to starting vineyards of their own. Wing also publishes a newsletter about grapes that is circulated all over China, free of charge. And he has plans afoot for a joint venture with a person in the next province who has located land. Wing's contribution will be his knowledge and the grape varieties he has found will grow well in his area.

Not understanding the process by which jobs increase when a new worker spends his or her income, many conclude that the number of jobs is limited by the nature of availability of capital. The only real limit on jobs is the constraint on the freedom of enterprisers like Wing to venture into business, for his own sake and inevitably for the benefit of others.

An opposite example: A new government steel mill in any country usually is an expensive and worthless attempt to provide jobs. Such mills are inefficient. They distort economies. And worse, they hinder the initiatives of efficient private producers. Additionally, they induce inflation.

There is still another important reason why jobseekers and available work do not find each other. Jobseekers sometimes lack information about where there is work to be done. And on the other side, people with work needing to be done sometimes lack information about where there are people who would like to do the work at the going price of labor for that job. Various mechanisms bridge this information gap—employment agencies, newspaper advertisements, government labor exchanges, and informal contacts. But sometimes these mechanisms are not enough.

Consider Dan, a student who painted our house excellently. When he finished, he walked around the neighborhood and propositioned owners of houses that looked shabby, but he found no takers. He was discouraged, and about to quit.

He told me the situation sitting in my university office. So I stepped out the door and started down the corridor knocking at the doors of my colleagues. By telling them that Dan was an excellent painter who would work at a cheap rate, within ten minutes I found him two houses to paint. Clearly there was painting to be done. But the information gap blocked the meeting of work and worker.

Unskilled people especially lack knowledge of markets, which partly accounts for the greater unemployment among them than among skilled people. Labor contractors profit by filling this information gap, bringing together unskilled people and people who have work to be done. But American society makes it difficult for labor contractors to perform this valuable service.

Labor contracting can reduce unemployment. But labor contractors are harassed by the law and by newspapers. They are pictured as parasites. Therefore, there is much less labor contracting than would take place if it were encouraged rather than discouraged. And people who would otherwise have jobs remain unemployed.

A lurid recent expose in *The Washington Post* described unscrupulous exploitation of poor Washington blacks by contractors who shanghai them south for agricultural work. The stories made the situation sound like slavery. And perhaps there were grave abuses. But the writer made it seem as if the root of the problem is the institution of labor contracting, and implied it should be abolished. The abuses stem from individual wrongdoing, however. And sensible laws and rules can prevent such abuses without reducing the amount of labor-contracting activity.

We may not like the conditions under which poor people work for a labor contractor. But we can trust people not to continue if the work is worse than the other alternatives. If a labor contractor really abuses people, word gets around. You can take advantage of someone once, but not day after day if there are better opportunities.

Labor contractors create jobs for people who need them at no cost to the government, and with benefit to the public. We need more such contractors. So let's glorify them as entrepreneurial heroes instead of castigating them as exploiters. This might be the easiest quick fix for the unemployment problem.

Part 5
IMMIGRATION

Introduction

Immigration, and especially illegal immigration, has been much in the news in the last few years. After the Simpson-Mazzoli bill was enacted into law in 1986, attention shifted to legal immigration. This is good, because legal immigration is by far the more important phenomenon for the American economy and society.

The selections in this section present statistics about the size of immigrations flows, and analyses of the economic effects of immigrants—all quite the opposite of popular belief. Curiously, the rise of the welfare role of the state makes immigrants even *more* valuable to natives than in earlier times; this is not commonly understood even by economists who generally favor immigration. The explanation is that immigrants contribute more taxes that pay for welfare services than they use of such services, and hence the net positive balance for natives is larger when welfare costs are higher.

A full understanding of the economics of immigration requires close technical analysis and a wide range of data. Both may be found in my *The Economic Consequences of Immigration* (Basil Blackwell). The short discussions in this section cannot in themselves be considered satisfactory foundation for policy decisions pertaining to immigration, but I hope they at least dispel some misunderstandings.

29

Don't Close Our Borders

This first selection on immigration presents some of the key data necessary for understanding the situation in the United States.

Many Americans think of immigrants as tired and poor. And too many believe that they live on welfare or that they displace natives from scarce jobs by accepting low wages. These complaints and others will be heard as Congress tries to secure this country's borders by way of the Simpson-Mazzoli bill. The proposed law includes amnesty for longtime illegal immigrants, sanctions against those who hire them, and a national identity card, but its main impact would be to reduce the total number of illegal and legal immigrants into the United States.

Opponents of immigration believe they are guarding their own economic interests when they argue that immigrants damage our pocketbooks and our environment. But recent research shows that many of their beliefs are dead wrong and are based on myth.

Myth 1. The United States Is Being Flooded by Mexican Illegals.

Leonard Chapman, then the commissioner of the Immigration and Naturalization Service, first scared us in the 1970s with an estimate that up to 12 million people were illegally in this country. It was just a guess, but now ingenious statisticians using a variety of methods report that the total number of illegals is almost certainly below 6 million, and may be only 3.5 to 5 million. Furthermore, the number of illegals in the country overstates the number of Mexicans who intend to remain permanently, leaving perhaps 1.3 million Mexican illegals—certainly not a large number

Newsweek, February 27, 1984.

by any economic test, and far less than the scare figures promulgated earlier.

By September 1985 the numbers were even smaller. Based on all the evidence available up to 1980, a crack team of demographers at the Census Bureau estimated that net illegal immigration is only 200,000 to 250,000 per year—much less than the 500,000 to 1 million that the Immigration and Naturalization Service still tells us are entering each year. And the following also could be said: This June, a National Research Council study lowered the estimate to zero—yes, zero. That is, on the basis of the most recent and best evidence, no net illegal immigration has occurred since 1977. The council says there are 2 million to 4 million illegal aliens, a far cry from INS's inflammatory estimates of 12 million or more.

Myth 2. Illegal and Legal Immigrants Abuse Welfare and Government Services.

Study after study shows that small proportions of illegals use government services: free medical, 5 percent; unemployment insurance, 4; food stamps, 1; welfare payments, 1; child schooling, 4. Illegals are afraid of being caught if they apply for welfare. Practically none receive social security, the costliest service of all, but 77 percent pay social security taxes, and 73 percent have federal taxes withheld.

In an analysis of Census Bureau data I conducted for the Select Commission on Immigration and Refugee Policy, I found that, aside from social security and Medicare, immigrant families average about the same level of welfare services as do citizens. When programs for the elderly are included, immigrant families use far *less* public funds than do natives. During the first five years in the United States, the average immigrant family receives $1404 (in 1975 dollars) in welfare compared with $2279 received by a native family. The receipts become equal in later years, but when immigrants retire, their own children contribute to their support and so they place no new or delayed burdens upon the tax system.

Immigrants also pay more than their share of taxes. Within three to five years, immigrant-family earnings reach and pass those of the average American family. The tax and welfare data together indicate that, on balance, immigrants contribute to the public coffers an average of $1300 or more each year that family is in the United States.

Myth 3. Immigration Is High.

An article in the prestigious journal Foreign Affairs states that "immigration and refugee flows to the United States in the late 1970s were at or near the highest levels ever experienced." This is just wrong even in absolute terms. There were 800,000 immigrants in 1980—the most recent high—yet near the turn of the century and for six years, immigration topped the million mark. The burden of absorbing it was, in fact, greater then. Between 1901 and 1910, immigrants constituted 9.6 percent of the population: between 1961 and 1970, they were only 1.6 percent. Or consider this. In 1910, 14.6 percent of the population was foreign-born. In 1970 only 4.7 percent had been born abroad, or less than 1 person in 20, including those who had come many years ago. Amazingly, this "country of immigrants," as the politicians often put it, has a smaller share of foreign-borns than more "homogeneous" countries like Great Britain, Sweden, Switzerland, France, Australia and Canada.

Myth 4. Immigrants Are "Huddled Masses"—Uneducated and Unskilled.

The central economic fact now—as it has been throughout U.S. history—is that, in contrast to the rapidly aging U.S. population, immigrants tend to arrive in their 20s and 30s, when they are physically and mentally vigorous and in the prime of their work life. On average, they have about as much education as do natives, and did so even at the turn of the century. Immigrants also tend to be unusually self-reliant and innovative: they have the courage and the belief in themselves that is necessary for the awesome challenge of changing one's culture and language.

Myth 5. Immigrants Cause Native Unemployment.

This has always been the major fear. If the number of jobs is fixed and immigrants occupy some jobs, then there are fewer jobs for natives. This overlooks the dynamic that immigrants create jobs as well as take them. Their purchases increase the demand for labor, leading to new hires. They frequently open small businesses that are a main source of new jobs.

Experiments conducted by INS show little, if any, damage to citizens even in the few areas where immigrants—legal and illegal—concentrate: in the restaurant and hotel industries. Most Americans, having better alternatives (including welfare programs), do not accept these jobs on the conditions offered.

On balance, immigrants are far from a drag on the economy. As workers, consumers, entrepreneurs and taxpayers, they invigorate it and contribute healthy economic benefits. By increasing the work force, they also help solve our social-security problem. Immigrants tend to come at the start of their work lives but when they retire and collect social security, they typically have raised children who are then contributing taxes to the system.

This country needs more, not fewer, immigrants. The U.S. birthrate is low and our future work force is shrinking. By opening our doors we will not only do good but the evidence indicates we will also do well.

30

Immigrants Are Paying Customers

This selection offers more key statistics, most of them pertaining to the personal characteristics of immigrants. This piece was written on the occasion of the hundredth birthday of the Statue of Liberty. I aimed to remind people that immigrants are not charity cases, but I hoped to do so in a fashion that would not seem sour or take pleasure away from the lovely occasion.

The United States can sharply increase its rate of advance in technology and industrial productivity by adding top talent from all over the world, at no cost and with substantial benefit to U.S. citizens. We need simply relax our barriers against skilled immigrants.

As matters now stand, the United States admits only about 50,000 people—about 10 percent of total admittances—on the basis of their possessing job skills in short supply here. Many more highly talented people seek to come.

While immigration presents for the United States a safe, sure and costless opportunity to forge ahead, the Soviet Union struggles to prevent its top scientists and engineers from leaving. In fact, Mikhail Gorbachev complained of this problem on U.S. television. Yet we insist on kicking away this golden opportunity, barring the door to many of the most economically productive workers in the world.

Forgive me for saying it on wonderful Miss Liberty's birthday: Emma Lazarus' poem at the base of the Statue is baloney, and an injustice to immigrants.

Immigrants are not tired, poor, huddled masses, not "wretched refuse." Rather, they are usually young and vigorous adults, well-educated and

Scripps-Howard newspapers, June 28, 1968.

highly skilled, with excellent earnings potential. It was much the same in the past.

The "refuse" nonsense makes us think we are sacrificing to give alms. Sure, our hearts have been in the right place. But rather than being charity cases, immigrants bestow upon us an increased standard of living and a lower welfare burden.

The United States has much to be proud of in our treatment of immigrants. But pitying them, in connection with patting ourselves on the back, helps justify wrong-headed and mean-hearted immigration policies such as the immigration bill now before the Congress.

Age is a key economic characteristic. Immigrants now, as throughout U.S. history, are mostly just entering the prime of their work lives, the best time for them to make a maximum contribution.

They are concentrated in their 20s and 30s, the time of greatest physical and mental vigor, when they are flexible about job location, and therefore help the economy adjust to changing conditions.

Whereas 32.5 percent of the U.S. population is in the 20–39 age bracket, 46.3 percent of the immigrant cohort is in that prime bracket. And among immigrants who are admitted on the basis of their occupations rather than their family connections, a whopping 61.6 percent are in that age bracket.

The U.S. population is rapidly aging. Whereas 11.3 percent of the total U.S. population is in the 65-and-older category, who tend to be economically dependent because they consume rather than produce, only 2.9 percent of immigrants are that old. Among those who are admitted based on occupations rather than family ties, almost none is above 50.

In addition to being young and vigorous, the immigrants possess extensive educations, and professional capabilities in greater proportions than the native labor force. Hence immigrants are not poor in the important sense of having high earning potential.

The facts run contrary to common belief. In 1980, 16 percent of employed natives were professional and technical workers. The corresponding figure for recent immigrants was 26 percent.

Even when Miss Lazarus wrote her heartwarming poem a century ago, immigrants compared favorably with the native population in occupational skill, according to P.J. Hill.

Bernard Bailyn's research on the colonial-period Registry of Emigrants from Great Britain reveals that immigrants had excellent economic characteristics, being mainly young "useful artisans" and farmers.

This makes sense. Those with little education and skill understand that without saleable human capital, life is particularly tough in a new environment, and therefore it is wiser to stay at home where one knows how to cope. On the other hand, it is sensible for a person with a goodly amount of saleable human capital to take the chance and immigrate from a poor country to a rich one.

Along with youth and skill, immigrants tend to bring an unusually high degree of self-reliance, initiative, and innovative flair. Whose experience does not agree that it is such pioneer types who have the courage and the belief in themselves necessary to undertake the awesome journey of leaving home and starting a new life in a foreign country?

Yes, immigrants (and especially refugees) often are bewildered, exhausted, and scared when they arrive—as affluent Americans often are when they arrive abroad for an extended stay. But given a little time to settle down, find a job, and make friends, an astonishing transformation takes place from bedraggled confusion to buoyant confidence.

Don't let your thinking be transfixed by those television shots of refugees with their noses and fingers through chain-linked fences. Check on those folks a few months later, and you'll find well-employed women and men hustling to save for a house in the suburbs.

In these days of frightening news stories about our being overwhelmed by floods of illegal aliens, the reader is likely to cast a doubting eye on these data. But despite the impression left by these scare stories, the overwhelming bulk of immigrants are legal. According to a recent study released by the National Academy of Science, net illegal immigration may even be zero now. Hence there is no reason to doubt that the picture I have drawn is representative.

The favorable age and occupation characteristics of immigrants also explain why the popular belief that immigrants are welfare abusers is astonishingly wrong. My research, based on a nationwide survey of natives and immigrants done by the Census Bureau, shows that immigrant families pay more in taxes than do native families, on average, and use less in welfare services.

On July 4, we would do well to remember that the Declaration of Independence gave as one reason for the Revolution: "The present King of Great Britain . . . has endeavored to prevent the population of these States; for that purpose obstructing the laws of naturalization of foreigners; refusing to pass others to encourage their migration hither."

The immigration that our Founding Fathers considered economically good for them is even better for us. Let us cheer the creative newcomers as we celebrate the open spirit that welcomes them.

31

Adding Up the Costs of Our New Immigrants

These data, which show that immigrants are even more beneficial for natives in an era of the welfare state than before there was a welfare state, are very compelling scientifically. Immigrants benefit natives through the public coffers since they use less than their share of services and pay more than their share of taxes. Nevertheless, because the results run so much against the common wisdom, politicians and anti-immigration organizations that have been made aware of these data brazenly still say that immigrants are a drag on natives because of their use of welfare programs—and they get away with this disinformation.

Shocking recent news stories and photographs of newly arrived refugee Cubans, Haitians and Vietnamese have worried many Americans about the effect on our economy. Evidence about the effect of immigrants on the standard of living of native Americans, therefore, is crucial—and surprising in what it reveals.

In 1976 the Census Bureau surveyed 156,000 households (including about 15,000 mostly legal immigrant families) to learn about 1975 family income and welfare services. From this sample I constructed a picture of lifetime economic behavior by assuming that the information on immigrants who had been here, say, two years as of 1975 describes the representative immigrant family after two years, those here 10 years in 1975 stand for the tenth year in the U.S. of a representative family, and so on.

The services that most often catch the public eye are welfare and supplemental security, unemployment compensation, aid to dependent children and food stamps. The average native-born U.S. family received

The Wall Street Journal, February 26, 1981.

$498 from these programs in 1975 (calculations include families getting no assistance). The average for immigrant families that arrived between 1950 and 1974 was $548. Not much difference.

Retirement programs bulk larger. Native U.S. families received on average $735 for Social Security, $167 for Medicare and $20 for Medicaid, a total of $922. Immigrant families received a total of $92 during the first five years in the U.S., $227 the second five years, $435 the third five years and $520 the fourth and fifth five-year periods. The difference in favor of natives is large. The reason immigrants get less Social Security and Medicare is simply because of their age. Coming to the U.S., they tend to be young and strong, as always with immigrants.

Cost of Schooling

Providing school for immigrant children during a family's first five years costs slightly less than the $859 for the average native family, because immigrants come before family completion. After that, expenditures on immigrants are higher, rising from $1068 to $1237 during the next 15 years. (The difference is not because immigrants have many children, but because the average native family is older, with many children no longer in school.)

By summing the figures we find that the average immigrant family receives $1404 in welfare services in years 1–5, $1941 in years 6–10, $2247 in years 11–15, and $2279 in years 16–25. Natives average $2279, considerably more than the immigrants get during their early years in the U.S. These early years are more relevant because rational policy decisions weigh the distant future less heavily than the near future.

But what about Social Security when immigrants age? The answer depends not on entitlements or legal obligations, but on the flow of real resources from workers to retirees. The children of retired immigrants support them with their taxes, just as with natives.

If immigrants paid relatively little in taxes they might still burden natives, even with less welfare services for immigrants than for natives. We lack direct information on taxes paid, but from data on family earnings we can estimate tolerably.

Within three to five years after entry, immigrant family earnings reach and pass those of the average native family, due to the age compositions of native and immigrant families. The average native family paid $3008 in taxes in 1975. In comparison, immigrant families here 10 years paid $3359, those here 11 to 15 years paid $3564, and those here 16 to 25 years paid $3592, substantial differences benefiting natives.

Assuming 20 percent of taxes finance activities that are little affected by population size (for example, maintaining the armed forces and Statue of

Liberty), consolidating the data on services used and taxes paid shows substantial differences in favor of natives: an average of $1354 yearly for the years 1–5, and $1329, $1535 and $1353 for years 6–10, 11–15 and 16–25 respectively. These are the amounts that each year natives are enriched through the public coffers for each additional immigrant family. Evaluating the future stream of differences as one would a dam or harbor, the present value of an immigrant family discounted at 3 percent (inflation adjusted) was $20,600 in 1975 dollars, and almost two years' average earnings for a native family; at 6 percent the present value is $15,800 and $12,400 at 9 percent.

Immigrants affect the standard of living of natives through other channels too, and not all immigrant groups are alike. For example, the federal government pays $1000 per person to resettlement organizations to cover overhead and start-up money for Vietnamese, Russian and other refugees. This plus such costs as special refugee schooling should be deducted from the above present-value calculation for the average immigrant family. But it isn't likely that these deductions would make the calculation negative.

For illegals such as the Mexicans who cross into the U.S., the adjustment goes the other way, because illegals get little in welfare services due to their status. (See Selection 29 for more on this.)

Immigrants can harm natives through capital dilution, that is, Malthusian diminishing returns caused by the presence of more workers but the same capital. If the private sector were like the government sector—where workers' pay is assumed equal to the full value of what they produce, with nothing left for the owner of the capital—then capital dilution would indeed lower average native income. But in the private sector additional workers imply higher earnings by owners about equal to the loss of earnings by other workers, a trade-off leaving native per-capita income unchanged.

Yet "workers" suffer as "capitalists" gain. That is, to the extent that the classes are separate, there is a transfer from workers' pockets to owners' pockets. But in fact much of our private capital is owned indirectly by "workers" through pension funds, and by way of the taxes paid on interest and dividends. Hence the loss to the "worker" class is unclear.

As to special groups of workers, especially low-income earners, the negative effect is probably less than commonly thought and may be nonexistent. Nowadays *legal* immigrants arrive with considerable education and skills, and they enter a wide variety of occupations, hurting no occupation or income level much, even in the short run. (In the longer run, occupations on average benefit from additional jobs created by the purchases made by immigrants to about the same extent that immigrants take existing jobs within the occupations. In short, immigrants make jobs as well as take jobs.)

Regarding the public capital used by immigrants: We must worry only about the additional capital outlays needed to equip immigrants—the extra schoolrooms, hospital beds, firehouses and the like. Not relevant is the use of public goods not affecting natives' use or pocketbooks—looking at the Washington Monument, or riding on a lightly used interstate highway. Luckily we are spared difficult conceptual problems of valuing existing capital because we are nearly on a pay-as-you-go basis with respect to capital expenditures; the debt service on past public borrowings roughly equals outlays on new capital. So through taxes, immigrants pay enough "rent" on public facilities so that natives feel no extra burden.

Productivity Increases

Lastly, and what is likely the most important long-run effect of immigrants: The impact on productivity of these additional workers and consumers is likely to dwarf all else after a few years in the country. Some productivity increase arises from immigrants working in industries and laboratories here that are at the forefront of world technique. We benefit along with others from the contribution to world productivity in, say, genetic engineering and so forth that immigrants would not be able to make in their home countries.

Other increases in productivity—about which we have more solid evidence—come from increased production in particular industries through learning-by-doing and other gains from larger industry scale. I built these productivity benefits into a macro-model along with the other factors mentioned above, and the calculations indicate very large increments to natives' incomes.

In sum, immigrants benefit natives through the public coffers by using less than their share of services and paying more than their share of taxes. They cover the additional public capital needed on their account through the debt service on past investments. In the long run, lower-paid workers will not suffer from the new immigrants because immigrants' occupations and educations cover the income spectrum. But some native workers do suffer from short-run dislocation, just as imports of goods cause temporary dislocation to some native workers; the same general-welfare argument applies as for free trade, but it is cold comfort to the dislocated persons. Other than this inequity, immigrants viewed in economic terms seem an excellent bargain.

32

Immigration Does Not Displace Natives from Jobs

The fear that immigrants cause unemployment arises in every country and in every period of immigration. This piece attempts—undoubtedly with little success—to dispel this fear with economic reasoning and data. Since this article was written in 1984, a considerable body of empirical economic research has appeared that substantiates the key idea. References to that literature, and to the Simon-Moore article mentioned in this selection, may be found in my The Economic Consequences of Immigration *(Chapter 12).*

That immigrants increase unemployment by displacing natives from jobs is the most emotional and influential fear about immigration. A headline in a Florida newspaper reads: "Haitian Refugees Take Away Jobs." In Texas, the winner of a Senate primary asserts that "Sixty-five Americans lose their jobs for every 100 undocumented workers who are here." In Colorado, Gov. Richard D. Lamm says that importing more labor would be "demographic and economic insanity." And early on, the A.F.L.-C.I.O., went on record that it would fight the "hiring of foreigners as temporary workers."

The complaint is ancient. John Toland wrote in 1714: "The vulgar, I confess, are seldom pleas'd in a country with the coming in of Foreners. . . . from their grudging at more persons sharing the same trades or business with them." The complaint also seems to make sense: If jobs are limited and immigrants occupy some, there must be fewer jobs for natives. Some displacements and some reduction in wages must occur when potential workers are added to an occupation, whether laboring or doctoring.

The New York Times, August 2, 1984.

There are, however, two opposing forces at work—expansion in aggregate demand and creation of new businesses by immigrants. The income immigrants earn increases the demand for goods and for workers to produce them, which in turn produces more income and more new jobs. This continues until the economy approaches a new equilibrium, with the same rate of unemployment as before. Toland understood this process well: "We deny not that there will thus be more taylors and shoomakers; but there will also be more suits and shoos made than before."

Immigrants also start new businesses. A Canadian sample found that 5 percent of adult immigrants started businesses within their first three years.

The direct evidence about displacement is of two kinds—within specific industries and within the economy as a whole. A reliable study of the effects of the Bracero guest-worker program in the Southwest from 1942 to 1964 showed that one native agricultural worker was displaced for each four Mexican guest workers. But this greatly overstates total displacement because some or most displaced workers find jobs elsewhere, and some would be displaced by machines if not by Mexicans.

The Immigration and Naturalization Service conducted two mass, forcible removals of illegal immigrants from jobs in California. Later checks on the illegals' jobs showed a low rate of substitution of natives for the illegals. And, in another study, Thomas Muller of the Urban Institute found no evidence of increased unemployment in California due to Mexicans, though he did find evidence of lowered wages.

With Stephen Moore, I examined how the rates of immigration into a large number of cities in the United States from 1960 to 1976 related to changes in unemployment rates. We found that no matter how we looked at it, the effect was either very small or nonexistent. While our study has not been examined in detail by colleagues, we believe it contains much more solid evidence on the matter than provided by previous studies that have been cited in the newspapers but also have not been available for scrutiny.

In sum, workers in a particular industry may be injured. But in the economy as a whole, immigrants not only take jobs, they make jobs. Their income adds to total demand, creating new jobs, and they open businesses that employ natives as well as other immigrants and themselves. Job displacement is mainly a false fear, and rational Americans should not let this fear influence immigration legislation.

33

A Parable Illustrating the Effects of Immigration

Economists often tell simple stories in order to illuminate the opera-
tion of complex economic relationships—in this case, the effects of
immigration. The "parable" typically strips away a great deal of the
realistic detail of an actual economy that obscures the main line of
the analysis. I hope that nothing crucial is lost in this process of
abstraction, but analysts can and do differ in their judgments about
the soundness of such abstraction.

Consider an idealized farming "nation" composed of a hundred identical
farmers, each with the same amount and quality of farmland, each working
the same hours and producing the same output. Along comes a foreigner
who offers himself as a hired laborer to the first farmer he meets. (For now
this is entirely a male community, with no other family members.) The
"rational" farmer is willing to hire the foreigner as long as the wage will
be even a bit less than the value of the increase in output that the foreigner
produces. A shrewd bargainer, however, the farmer offers the foreigner a
wage considerably less than the amount the foreigner asks. Not less
shrewd, the foreigner proceeds to offer his labor to all hundred farmers,
going back and forth until he can strike the best deal. He eventually settles
for just a tiny bit less than the value of the additional output if the
"market" works well. This is his "market wage."

Let us assess the economic impact of the entry of this immigrant into
the community. The farmer who employs the immigrant increases his own
income by just a tiny bit, but that tiny bit is preferable to no increase at
all. The "nation's" citizens as a whole are better off, because 99 farmers
have their incomes unchanged whereas one has his income increased

slightly, and hence the average income goes up just a tiny bit. If we include the immigrant "laborer" in the calculation, computed mean income goes down, however, because the immigrant laborer's income is lower than the average farmer's; in the very short run, and assuming the number of hours worked per person stays the same, the incremental output of the second person working on the farm is not as great as that of the first worker—the famous "law" of diminishing returns. But that decline in the average masks the fact that *each person's* income is unchanged or has gone up— including the immigrant's, because we assume he would not immigrate here unless his income is higher than in the country that he left.

A word about the impact during the first moments that the immigrant is in the hypothetical society: Any simpleton can—and a great many do— show conclusively that a new immigrant or a new baby has an immediate negative effect upon the country's standard of living. Before the new person begins to work, he or she reduces per person income purely by arithmetic. [To paraphrase Peter Bauer, when a new calf arrives, per person income automatically increases, but when a new person (baby or immigrant) arrives, per person income automatically decreases.] Of course the changed statistical measure does not necessarily hurt the rest of us, but it surely sounds bad. And if the new entrant gets any help from the society before he or she goes to work, then there is a real negative effect upon the rest of us, as well as the apparent effect.

Now let us change the story by moving ahead to a moment after considerable immigration has occurred, when there is one immigrant laborer working for wages on *each* farm, a hundred in all. The wage of each will be just about the same as the market wage that the first immigrant got. And let's say that each immigrant now has been made a new citizen. But the new citizens have not yet had time to buy any land, so the old citizens still have higher incomes than the new citizens.

Now along comes still another foreigner looking for a job. He goes back and forth until he strikes the best deal, which will be for a wage just a tiny bit below the value of the increase in output his employer will obtain from the *third* person working on his farm. And then another 99 more foreigners follow, so on each farm we now have one native-citizen owner (who also does farm work), one naturalized-citizen laborer, and one new-immigrant laborer.

But now something else happens, too: The wage of the naturalized laborers falls to the level of the new-immigrant laborers. The reason is that all 200 of the landless laborers are now competing for the same jobs, and no owner needs to pay more than the incremental output of a *second* laborer on the farm in order to hire two laborers, because the amount of work done by all the laborers is the same. And the farm owners are now making a bigger profit than before, because they only have to pay the first laborer the value of the second laborer's output; the fact that some laborers are citizens while others are not does not affect their wages.

The overall results of the second wave of immigration may now be seen as follows: The native owners are better off than before. The new-immigrant laborers are better off than in the country from which they came. The naturalized-citizen laborers are better off than in the old country, but worse off than before the second wave of new-immigrant laborers came. And therefore, the naturalized-citizen laborers will (in advance of the event) surely make a political protest against letting the second wave enter the country, although some of them will, for sentimental reasons, wish to have more of their compatriots enter the country even though the wage does fall.

Let us again change the facts. Assume that the one hundred naturalized-citizen laborers have been in the country long enough to buy half-ownership in each farm from the native-citizen original owners. The total yearly proceeds from each farm are now split between the native citizen and the naturalized citizen. Along come the hundred new-immigrant laborers. Assume that all three workers on each farm receive as *wages* only the value of the incremental output of the third worker. The native-citizen and naturalized-citizen owners are no worse off, however, because the drop in their ''wages'' is equal to their gain in ''returns to capital.'' If this is so, the naturalized citizens are not injured by the entry of the second wave of immigrant laborers.

It seems, then, that whether the existing stock of workers is or is not injured by the new wave of immigrants depends upon who gets the returns to the capital with which the workers work. And here we may refer back to the realistic world of the United States in 1989. The ''workers''—that is, people who earn wages and salaries—own a very sizable portion of the productive capital of the country, to a considerable extent through pension funds. This means that the situation is not simply one in which ''labor'' loses and ''owners'' gain by immigration. The extent to which a working person gains or loses by immigration depends upon the actual facts about the extent to which that working person has an ownership stake in the capital of the country.

Now let us complicate the situation just one bit more before we leave this analysis of the effect of immigrants through the labor market. There is also some additional benefit to natives from immigrants because the immigrants do not arrive in such neat one-to-a-farm waves as assumed above. If a given farm successively employs two new immigrant laborers at a wage equal to the incremental output of the ''last'' of the two (the ''marginal'' worker), then the citizen owner(s) of the land will obtain the difference between the wage of the next-to-last immigrant—which now equals the incremental output of the last immigrant—and the incremental output of the next-to-last immigrant. But this quantity is not of much practical importance and therefore can be disregarded, though it is very neat theoretically.

The main conclusion to be drawn from the model so far is that in the short run, additional immigrant workers do not damage the welfare of citizens taken altogether by diluting the capital stock, but may damage "workers" if as a class the workers do not get most of the returns to capital. This effect is transitory, however, and in the long run it is likely to be dominated by many other dynamic effects—especially the effect of immigration upon productivity, and the effect through welfare transfer from and to, and tax transfers to, the public coffers—even for classes of people who might be hit hard by this particular effect.

This model (as is the propensity of such models) has operated frictionlessly and instantly. But real markets do not operate so perfectly, and this leads us to the question of unemployment. Instead of assuming all the original hundred citizens to be farmers producing the same output, let us assume that they constitute a self-contained community producing a variety of goods and services that they then consume—grain, laundry service, transportation, religious services, meat, and the like. Each business is composed of one citizen owner and one citizen laborer.

Along comes an immigrant looking for a job. But there are no laborer's jobs open. So the immigrant goes to one of the farmers whose barn obviously needs painting, and says "I'll paint your barn for a cheap price, and do a good job." The farmer thinks about it for a few minutes, and decides that at the price the immigrant has set, the farmer's own time is more valuable—either for other work or for recreation—than that amount, and he therefore tells the immigrant to go ahead. So unemployment is not increased by the immigrant's arrival.

The immigrant spends her resulting income for goods and services in the community, while the farmer spends an equal amount less because he has that much less to spend. So total income to businesses remains the same, though some businesses will lose as others gain if the immigrant buys different goods than would the farmer. If the farmer uses the time to paint a picture instead of the barn, *average* income of the community (including the new immigrant who is now included in the calculation) goes down because *total* income remains the same, and now is divided among more persons. But everyone is better off, or at least no worse off, than before the immigrant came. (The reader will note that the pictures the farmer paints are not counted as income even though the farmer is getting benefit from them.) If instead of painting the barn the farmer uses the time to paint pictures that he sells to others, total income goes up, and average income might either go down or go up.

But perhaps one of the citizen laborers is out sick, or meditating in the woods on unpaid leave, at the moment the immigrant arrives. The immigrant latches onto that citizen's job. When the previous occupant of the job gets back, he cannot immediately find another job and classifies himself as unemployed. Another possibility: The immigrant arrives, goes to the nearest business, and says: "I'll work harder and cheaper than the laborer you now employ." And the owner promptly fires the citizen and hires the immigrant. These are the cases that the labor unions worry about most, and which constitute the strongest political objection to immigration now and always. And it undoubtedly does happen this way sometimes.

Another possibility: After she finishes the farmer's barn, the immigrant goes around to all the other farmers, points to the fine job that she did, and makes deals to paint four other buildings. She realizes that she cannot do all the work by herself, so she hires three footloose citizens, and brings over her cousin from the old country as well. Presto, a new business, and *increased* total employment; unemployment might then be either less or more than before.

As noted above, some "displacement" of particular natives from jobs by immigrants takes place, just as some new creation of jobs by immigrants and on account of immigrants, surely takes place. But the job-creating forces must typically operate at least as strongly as displacement, because on balance immigrants do not cause much if any native unemployment. The newest immigrants themselves do at first suffer from relatively high unemployment when times are bad, but that suffering by immigrants provides something of a buffer for natives.

Now let us add to the original farmer model that each farmer has a wife, two aged retired parents, and two dependent children. Each farm family pays (say) 20 percent of its income in taxes to provide stipends for the aged and schooling for the children, along with standard family welfare services. The immigrant laborers come without aged parents, though wives, single women, and some children do come with them. The immigrants also pay 20 percent of their income as taxes at first. But it is soon found that there is a surplus in the public coffers because most of the taxes go to support aged people, the cohort of which remained the same while tax collections rose as the immigrants arrived. So the tax rate to natives (and to immigrants) would thereby be reduced below 20 percent. Hence the tax-and-transfer mechanism results in benefits to natives because, as the data show (and contrary to popular belief) immigrants use less rather than more of the standard family welfare services than do native families. (See Selection 31.)

34

In Favor of Immigration

The various issues treated separately in the previous three short selections are combined here with additional aspects of the economics of immigration. Selection 34 concludes that immigration bestows benefits not only on immigrants but also on natives.

Contrary to popular opinion, legal immigrants to the United States bestow important economic benefits upon natives. These include a reduced burden of social security taxes without a reduction in benefits, increased productivity, an entrepreneurial shot in the arm to business, and new vitality and cultural diversity.

Opponents of immigration seek to persuade us that new immigrants damage society economically, politically, and culturally. Immigration restrictions are intended to "protect us" in the same way as tariffs and trade quotas. But like trade barriers, immigration restrictions largely protect us from benefits. This is not to say that immigration brings no adjustment costs. But historical and current evidence shows that the costs are exaggerated and the benefits vastly underappreciated.

Immigration at first seems to be an issue with two ideological faces. One face: The freedom to move across national boundaries is a human right that ought to be recognized. As F. A. Hayek reminds us, "A person's legal duties are to be the same toward all, including the stranger and even the foreigner." Hayek damns those groups such as unions that call for "social justice" yet "reject such claims raised on behalf of foreigners." The other face: The right to the fruits of one's labor is at times construed as the basis for excluding foreigners from our shores. In this apparent quandary, the facts about the economic impacts of immigration are relevant.

"The Case for Immigration," *Inquiry*, May 1983.

Let us first look at some of the bum raps that have been leveled at immigration.

The most powerful political argument against admitting immigrants has always been that they take jobs held by natives. The speculative basis of the fear is simple: If the number of jobs is fixed, and immigrants take some jobs, there will be fewer available jobs for natives.

In the immediate present, the demand for any particular sort of worker is indeed inflexible. Thus immigrants who start working in a given occupation must in theory have some negative impact on wages or employment among people in that occupation. For example, the large recent influx of foreign physicians means additional competition and lower incomes for American physicians, whose high earnings now reflect the advantage of an artificially limited supply of physicians. Such negative effects on particular occupations could only be avoided if immigrants were to come into all occupations in proportion to the size of those occupations. Citizens whose occupations immigrants will enter disproportionately can be expected to complain, though consumers are not likely to.

Economic theory tells us that there must be *some* unemployment caused in *some* industries. But it does not tell us whether the effect will be huge or trivial; for that we need empirical research. No research has shown noticeable unemployment caused by immigrants, either in the United States as a whole or in particular areas of high immigration. One reason is that potential immigrants have considerable awareness of labor-market conditions here and tend not to come if their skills are in small demand. Also, immigrants tend to have a variety of skills and do not affect only a few industries. At the same time, immigrants increase the demand for labor across the range of occupations; they consume goods and services as well as produce them. In the long run, they create as many jobs with their spending as they themselves occupy.

Even in the few industries where immigrants concentrate, such as the restaurant and hotel industries, they do little harm to native workers. According to various studies, few natives want those jobs, because the work is hard and the pay is low.

The impact of immigration on wages can be expected to be greater than the impact on unemployment rates because potential immigrants with skills in low demand choose not to migrate and those with salable skills gravitate to industries where there are jobs. Immigrant physicians, for example, are more likely to reduce a native physician's income than to throw him or her out of work. But a study by Barton Smith and Robert Newman found that adjusted wages are just 8 percent lower in Texas border cities, where the proportion of Mexicans is relatively high, than elsewhere in the United States—a considerably smaller difference than they had expected. Much of the apparent difference is accounted for by the lower cost of living in the border cities.

The heart of the Malthusian objection to immigration is the fear of "capital dilution," that is, the belief that the law of diminishing returns will cause output per worker to fall as workers are added to same capital equipment. It has great seductive power because it is so marvelously simple, direct, and common-sensical. It is grist for any family newspaper. In contrast, the arguments that demonstrate the inapplicability of Malthusian capital dilution to immigration are complex and indirect.

Nowadays, what is most important is human capital—the education and skills that people own and carry with them—rather than the capitalist's machines and tools. Still, there is *some* harm to natives caused by the addition of workers. In the private sector, additional workers (and lower wages) imply higher earnings by owners about equal to the earnings lost by workers. This trade-off leaves overall native per-capita income roughly unchanged.

Nevertheless, workers suffer as capitalists gain, to the extent that these categories are separate. But, in fact, much of our private capital is owned indirectly by workers through pension funds. Hence it is unclear how much workers actually lose.

As to special groups of workers, especially low-income earners, the negative effect is probably less than commonly thought, and may be nonexistent. As I've said, legal immigrants arrive with considerable education and skills and enter a wide variety of occupations, hurting no occupation or income level much, even in the short run.

Immigrants not only create new jobs indirectly with their spending, they do so directly with the new businesses that they are more likely than natives to start. A Canadian government survey, which should also describe U.S. experience, found that almost 5 percent—ninety-one of the 1746 males and 291 single females—had started their own businesses within their first three years in Canada. Not only did they employ themselves, they employed others too, "creating" a total of 606 jobs. Thus roughly 30 percent as many new jobs were created as were held by immigrants. Furthermore, these numbers surely were rising rapidly after the three-year study period; within one year 71 self-employed immigrants had created 264 jobs, compared with the 91 and 606 respectively after three years.

The significance is that, even if one native Canadian was pushed out of a preexisting job by every five immigrants—an improbably high number—it was more than made up for by the new jobs created by the immigrants' businesses and occupied by natives. The businesses immigrants start are small at first, of course, but small businesses are the major source of new jobs.

Historically, migrants have tended to come in good times and leave in bad, buffering unemployment for citizens. I am not arguing that immigration cannot have drawbacks. Imagine a billion Asians, Africans, and South Africans without education or skills suddenly arriving in the United States tomorrow. Everyone would be in terrible shape. The immigrants would lack jobs at first, and the economy would be unable to respond quickly. To know whether a given flow of immigrants is large enough to produce such a short-run squeeze, we should consider historical situations where the flow was large relative to resident population: the United States throughout its early history, but especially at the turn of the century; West Germany and Japan after World War II, absorbing many ethnic Germans and Japanese from areas no longer held by those governments; Israel in the 1950s, with massive immigration from Arab countries. Those periods of large infusions of people were difficult, but all were successful economically according to almost every study.

These experiences could mean that the theoretical bad effects are not really present or that they operate to an insignificant degree. It might also be that the relative size of those immigrations, massive as they were, still was not enough for negative forces to come into play strongly. Either way, history should give us pause before relying on those theoretical arguments to shut off immigration.

Moreover, the period during which the immigrants' inferior informally learned skills—related to language and lack of experience with communications technology—detract from productivity appears fairly short. In perhaps two to five years, immigrants pick up the informal learning and then forge ahead of natives. The average immigrant worker comes to have higher earnings than the average American worker after a few years, due in large part to his or her youth and high level of education.

A second charge against immigration is that immigrants become public charges, draining welfare money from American taxpayers. Solid evidence gives the lie to this charge. (See Selection 31.)

Still another bum rap is that immigrants cause a natural-resource squeeze for natives. For example, Zero Population Growth's honorary president, Paul R. Ehrlich, asks us to think about the effect of additional people on the "perilously shrinking water supply in this country. And to our food supply. Think of the competition they'll cause for housing and jobs."

Much of that charge is demonstrable buncombe. U.S. water and food supplies have been improving in past decades by every reasonable measure of quantity and purity, though this is too-little known. The air, too, has been getting less polluted, according to the official Pollutant Standard Index prepared by the U.S. Environmental Protection Agency. And over the long run, natural resources have been getting less scarce rather than more scarce, as indicated by the fundamental economic measure of cost.

But not all such propositions about the effects of immigrants on resources are so easily rebutted. Consider, for example, this statement by the Environmental Fund in an article called "Immigration and the American Conscience": "Had the United States stabilized its population in 1970, we could have the same level of energy consumption and standard of living as we do today [1981] *without* any Iranian oil or a single nuclear power plant." The statement probably is true. But it is terribly misleading.

One important flaw in the statement is that the eleven-year period it encompasses is much too short for the most important effects of population change to occur. Babies take a quarter century to mature into producers of goods and ideas; even immigrants may require several years to reach their full productivity.

It takes even longer for the following historically crucial cycle to take place: (a) An immigrant-swelled population leads to greater use of natural resources than otherwise. (b) Prices of raw materials then rise. (c) The price rise and the resultant fear about scarcity impel individuals to seek more raw materials, new production technologies, and new substitutes for the resource. (d) Eventually the price of the service of the resource in question falls lower than it was before the temporary scarcity began. All of this takes a while and is quite indirect. Yet this process has been the mainspring of economic advance for 5000 years.

A stationary population would in the long run have a lower economic level than a growing population. Test this for yourself by imagining the results after 100 or 500 years later, or now, of stabilizing world population in 1000 B.C., 1 A.D., 1000 A.D., 1750 A.D., or 1900 A.D.

A key characteristic of a high level of economic civilization is that it contains the capacity to resolve newly arising problems more quickly than did lower economic civilizations. For example, the incidence of famine has declined sharply in the past century because of modern roads and transportation systems. Food scarcity as a result of rapid population growth took much longer to remedy in 1300 A.D. than now, because we have systematic ways of finding and applying new knowledge that will meliorate the scarcity. There are no natural or physical "limits" that are an increasing constraint on our powers. The improvement that has occurred in the world's resource availability would not have taken place if population density had remained at the lower levels of the past.

We have seen that immigration generally does not harm the current citizenry. Now let us look at the actual benefits. Though hard to nail down, the long-run benefits on productivity of these additional workers and consumers are likely to dwarf all other effects. Some of the productivity increase comes from immigrants working in industries and laboratories that are at the forefront of world technique. We benefit along with others from the contribution to world productivity in, say, genetic engineering that immigrants would not be able to make in their home countries. More immigrants mean more working persons to think up productivity-enhancing ideas. As Soichiro Honda (of motorcycle and auto fame) said: "Where 100 people think, there are 100 powers; if 1000 people think, there are 1000 powers." Moreover, immigrants' facility with languages other than English is valuable for industry in, for instance, export projects.

Other increases in productivity—about which we have more solid evidence—come from increased production in particular industries through learning-by-doing and other gains from larger industry scale. Also, increasing the number of customers and workers increases investment, which brings more new technology into use. Perhaps the greatest contribution of immigrants is the push they give to this country's vitality and growth. They contribute to the vitality of our institutions because they tend to be more intellectually vigorous as well as harder-working than natives. How much of this vigor is due to being "hungry" rather than settled and affluent, how much due to their being self-selected for vigor among the populations they come from, and how much due to the stimulating effects of living in the tension of two cultures are open questions, but not crucial in this policy context.

One of the nice things heard about immigration is that it increases cultural variety. Chinese and French restaurants are common examples. But the benefits of variety go beyond consumer and esthetic pleasures. Variety is a key ingredient of invention. Immigrants also stimulate natives to produce more and be more innovative as the natives attempt to keep up with the new competition. And we should not forget that just as the movement of people in earlier times was crucial in transmitting ideas, it is important today.

One of the most attractive aspects of admitting immigrants is that we can do good in a humanitarian sense as we do well for ourselves economically. But not everyone believes this. Restrictions are sometimes proposed to protect potential immigrants. Occasionally one hears the argument (though mostly with respect to illegals) that we ought not to let immigrants in because they will be exploited with low wages. At the base of this argument is the notion that the speaker knows better what is good for the potential immigrant, that even if the potential immigrant prefers to work in the United States for low wages, it would be better to stay home and earn even less. This is nothing but arrogance parading as ideology and idealism.

Garrett Hardin and the Environmental Fund offer the ingenious argument that it is really idealistic of us to shut immigrants out, because it allows us to keep ourselves strong and able to help the rest of the world. If we were economically weak, Hardin says, the rest of the world would not have the benefits of our technological contributions. But as long as we recognize that admitting immigrants makes us stronger rather than weaker, scientifically as well as economically, this argument goes up in smoke.

Hardin perhaps sees his argument as a way out of an ethical dilemma. But let me emphasize that there is no such dilemma. We do not need to balance the gains to others against the sacrifice to ourselves. We do not need to consider the ethical basis of drawing a boundary around our nation and saying that those lucky enough to be born within are entitled to opportunities that we deny to others. Immigration is good for ourselves at the same time that it is good for the immigrants.

We sometimes seem frightened at the number of persons who want to come to the United States; we act as if we are under siege. I suggest that we should be glad that our society is sufficiently attractive to have such a problem. The Soviet Union apparently has no difficulty of this sort.

In 1981 a *Wall Street Journal* article was titled, "Romania Acts to Keep People from Emigrating." The Berlin Wall, with the memorials to people who were killed trying to leave East Germany, makes every Western viewer shiver. What a sad commentary on a society that people want to leave so much that they are willing to risk their lives. This should remind us how wonderful it is that people want to come here.

35

Auction the Right to Be an Immigrant

This is the first of several selections that offer ideas for U.S. policy with respect to immigration.

The current method of allocating immigration visas is wholly inconsistent with the basic egalitarian values of our society. Obtaining a visa depends mostly upon your connections—*that is, whether you have relatives who are citizens—rather than upon one's personal* merit. *The current system also is far less beneficial for the United States economically than would be a system based on a person's potential productivity.*

Selecting immigrants by auction at first seems radical and distasteful. This selection argues that, upon closer examination, such a system may be seen to be the best one available.

Selling the right to immigrate to the United States would be fairer, as well as more beneficial economically to citizens of the United States and the poorer countries, than the present system. Admission presently depends mostly upon having the proper relatives. In contrast, selling admission would allocate the visas impartially. Those persons who have the most to gain economically will offer the highest prices. And, inevitably, these are the people who have the most to contribute economically to the rest of us.

Other economists—Gary Becker and Barry Chiswick—have also suggested similar versions of the plan suggested here. And the prominent economists whom we have consulted about the scheme, including Milton Friedman and Melvin Reder, agree on its desirable features. But noneconomists tend to get hung up on the notion that a market solution means trafficking in human flesh, and on its present political infeasibility.

The New York Times, January 28, 1986.

An auction system would begin with a worldwide quota for the number of persons admitted to the United States in a given year. For political convenience, the quota might at first be the same size as at present. The United States would benefit from admitting many more immigrants than it does at present, and far more than are conceivable under present political arrangements. However, we start with a quota in order to focus on the auction system rather than on arguments about a more open policy.

The most straightforward method would be as follows: (1) Ask for written bids from all comers, anyplace in the world, perhaps twice a year. (2) Rank the bids from high to low. (3) Notify enough high bidders to fill the quota, plus enough more to make up the shortfall due to some high bidders changing their minds, just the way a college notifies students of acceptance. (Under one variant, each person would pay the amount he or she bids. Under another variant, each would pay the amount bid by the lowest winning bidder.)

The plan's advantage to U.S. natives derives from the auction's ability to identify the persons who have an especially large capacity to produce goods of high economic value while working in the United States. Charging a fee for admission would also accentuate the propensity of immigrants to move when they are young and strong, because admission has higher (discounted) future lifetime value for young persons than for older persons, other things equal.

Would an auction system mean that only the wealthiest persons abroad could get in? One way to prevent this is to allow "buyers" to pay from income later, as with the income tax. To enforce payment, the United States would have the strong sanction of deportation. Furthermore, there is little reason to believe that the very wealthy would desire to move here. Tax havens such as the Caribbean countries and Monaco are financially more attractive for those with large assets. And wealthy persons can always come to the United States as tourists if they simply like life here. It is ambitious persons, for whom the United States represents a large and rich market in which to make a lot of money, who will especially want to immigrate. To such persons, a large payment to purchase a ticket of immigration would represent an investment, which would often be accompanied by further investment in business assets. This additional investment would be an added benefit to natives. And an immigrant who makes a lot of money for herself or himself will benefit the community by providing jobs and contributing taxes.

The present policy is discriminatory because it does not offer all potential immigrants the same opportunity to be admitted to the United States. Present practice is not even fair in the sense of giving the same opportunity to all persons with the same qualifications. Persons in some countries (say,

Canada or Great Britain) have a much better chance of admission than do similar persons in other countries (say, Malaysia or India). But the most serious departure from fairness is that the relatives of persons in the United States have a vastly greater chance of being admitted than do similar persons without relatives; this is allocation by "connections" on the grandest scale imaginable, and the lack of fairness is not mitigated by the social reasons for such a policy.

Instead of discriminating by connections, an auction discriminates according to the standard of a market-oriented society—ability and willingness to pay. An auction would be fair in the sense that it would allow any person in any part of the world to have the same opportunity to purchase a visa. Hence the auction scheme could be seen as a gain in fairness.

Some will worry about the effect on people too poor to pay for admission who are now admitted. But it should be remembered that for each person the United States now admits by means of our complex system of family ties plus allocation by length of time in the queue, another person is implicitly denied admission. If we are especially concerned about the least-favored persons, we could simply provide direct support to them abroad out of admission-fee proceeds, with a consequent increase in total "fairness" and benevolence, no matter how one would wish to define those terms. Because of the greater productivity in the United States of those who are willing to pay more for the opportunity to immigrate than for those who will not bid as high, the United States could surely improve the lot of a larger number of poor persons in the countries of origin than at present by treating the fees as a charity fund for those poor persons, even if only part were sent back.

A specific plan to combine selling admission with aid to poor people in poor countries: Use some (or even all) of the sales proceeds to finance scholarships for poor and talented children and young adults to study in schools and colleges in the United States. Such a plan has multiple benefits. It provides magnificent opportunities for deserving poor young people. Those young people will learn skills that can contribute greatly to the development of their countries. They will also learn for themselves the goods and bads of the American system, society, and values; if we believe that our society is a better one to live in than others, we should believe that to experience it is to appreciate it and then proselitize for it. And the beneficiaries of these scholarships can be chosen on the "fair" basis of their talent rather than on the arbitrary basis of their family connections in the United States. Some of these people will remain in the United States as permanent immigrants. This will bestow additional benefits of various kinds upon the United States and upon the countries of origin as well.

What about the loss to sending countries of some of their most productive people? Clearly the residents of those countries who will submit winning bids and emigrate are made better off if they earn more in the United States than at home. But others might be injured—by the loss of the services of physicians, for example. If the United States is concerned with not inflicting such losses upon the sending countries, it can easily compensate the sending countries for the harm with only a small portion of the fees collected in the auction, because it is most unlikely that the damages to the countries of origin are anywhere near the size of the fees that would be paid by the successful bidders.

Because an admission-fee plan would result in high-skill people immigrating legally, the United States would become even more inviting than at present for low-skill persons to enter illegally, with the attendant problems of "lawlessness." But a guestworker program *in tandem with* an admission-by-fee plan would be a businesslike overall policy, and would avoid the lawlessness problem almost completely. Such a policy would, however, require greater sanctions against any illegals that did come anyway—perhaps most of them high-skill persons—because allowing them to remain illegally would be quite unfair to those who pay high admission fees, and also would spoil the market. If immigration policy were to be put on such a businesslike basis, it would then be less painful than at present to enforce laws on the books that require deportation if the immigrant becomes a welfare burden.

In brief, the key to the efficiency of an auction system is that individuals are able to assess their own economic capacities better than can any other system. Those persons who will stake their own money that they are right about their productive capacities are *ipso facto* the best possible bets to be economic stars in the United States. The fees from the auction would put additional purchasing power into the hands of natives, and provide a kitty for such foreign aid or scholarships in the United States for deserving foreign students. And an auction is less arbitrary, and thus fairer, than the existing policy as well as most alternative policies.

We can make our immigration policy more equitable, more productive economically for U.S. citizens, and more beneficial to people in the poorer countries, if we will accept a market solution to this social issue. Under the present practice, admission depends mostly upon family connections, a rotten system for all—natives and foreigners—except those who have the proper relatives. In contrast, selling immigration rights would allocate the visas impartially, and could funnel more economic welfare to the poor abroad than happens now.

Ask: Who are the most desirable immigrants for us to admit? Obviously, those who will be the most productive economically. Ask next: How can we identify such people? The clear-cut answer is that those persons who, by moving to the United States, will produce the largest economic profit for themselves—and inevitably for natives as well—will pay the most for the right to immigrate. That is, those persons who will offer the highest bid in an auction for immigration visas will be those who have the most to gain economically by receiving the visa. The genius of the auction system is that it automatically selects those who have most to gain by winning bids. And those auction winners are the people who have the most to contribute economically to the rest of us.

The payments from the winning bidders will then transfer a considerable part of the "profit" from the pocket of the immigrants to the pockets of natives. Whether or not it is moral for natives to extract this "profit" from immigrants is an interesting question, but it certainly seems no less moral than the central features of the current immigration system.

A point system based on education and occupation would also discriminate among potential immigrants by their economic worth to natives. But a system of rationing by auction has all the best features of a point system and more, because it *self-selects* persons who have the best chance to make an economic success. High bidders can and will take into account not only their occupations and the demand for them, but also their personal talents in their occupations and their willingness to work hard for success, characteristics that cannot be easily established objectively for a point system.

There are also other interesting managerial issues, such as whether the price should be different for persons of different ages, but these issues are secondary to the overall auction policy, and therefore should not delay us here. But this should be agreed on: Once a person purchases admission, no relatives could be brought in without them paying the auction price, too; the bidder would therefore take this eventually into account when submitting a bid. Only thus can the system remain free of the family-connections chain migration that dominates immigration at present. Most persons who are willing to pay a lot to enter the country will do so because they believe that the opportunity to do so will be profitable to them.

Reluctance to ration admission to the United States by ability and willingness to pay for it would seem to stem from the same psychological root as does our reluctance to use the market to ration such other "merit goods" as food and gasoline in times of shortage, in contrast to our everyday policy of allocating according to readiness to pay. But the aim of an equal-ration policy is to ensure that everyone in a well-defined population gets the same amount so that none suffers irreparable injury. The auction plan is closer to rationing health care on the battlefield, where the aim is to try to provide care to those who need it most. But to apply any sort of merit-good principle to immigration is to intermix two objectives—

our own self-interest, and charity to others—at the expense of both (though perhaps with the very purpose of confusing the issue so as to make it easier to attain a hidden objective—fewer immigrants of any kind).

36

Raise Immigration Quotas, Not Taxes

A larger immigration quota would reduce the burden of social security and other programs for the aged, in addition to bestowing the other benefits of immigration upon both natives and immigrants.

After the demands of programs for the elderly and defense, there is precious little remaining for other worthy federal programs. Privatizing social security may reduce the squeeze in the long run, but not in the short run. And with the current low birthrate, there is no hope that a larger number of working-age people will eventually enter the labor force to distribute the cost of supporting the elderly more widely.

Other than raising taxes, only a larger legal immigration quota can immediately help the federal budget. Immigration mainly increases the number of young skilled working people who pay high taxes and use few government services.

The average immigrant begins working—and contributing to the public coffers—quite soon after arriving in this country. The immigrant's own eventual receipt of social security benefits, decades down the pike, does not offset these immediate benefits to others.

Those benefits stem in large part from the difference in age composition between the native population and that of each immigrant group. Immigrants tend to move when they are near the start of their work lives. For example, perhaps 4 percent of immigrants are aged 60 or over, while about 15 percent of the United States population is 60 or over. And while perhaps 26 percent of the U.S. population is in the early prime labor force ages of 20 to 39, perhaps 46 percent of immigrants is in that age bracket. Moreover, even the small number of immigrants who are elderly are not eligible for social security. Therefore, each group of new immigrants, in proportion to

The Christian Science Monitor, July 29, 1987.

its numbers, contributes substantially to reducing the social security burden of natives in the new country.

Anti-immigration lobby groups pooh-pooh this benefit from immigrants by saying that the total dependency burden of the U.S. population is not now increasing, owing to the decreasing number of dependent children. Over the next generation, the reasoning goes, each member of the labor force will support fewer nonworkers, even with less immigration than at present. There will be more older nonworkers to support, but fewer young ones.

Dependent children, however, affect the taxpayer differently than do the elderly. Parents pay most of the cost of raising their own children in this country. Also, yearly living costs of a child are far less than the living costs of an aged adult. This is obvious when one reflects on the comparative costs of housing, medical care, and transportation. Children's public school expenses do not much alter the overall picture.

Must U.S. natives pay the piper for this benefit from immigrants when the immigrants get older and themselves receive social security? The answer is "no," for two reasons. First, the impact of this year's immigrants on social security perhaps 30 years from now properly has little weight in the overall economic assessment, because a dollar to be received or paid out in 30 years is worth little now when discounted at even a modest rate. Second and more important: By the time new immigrants retire, they typically have raised children who are then contributing to social security, balancing out the parents' receipts, just as with native families. Hence there is a one-time benefit to natives because the immigrants arrive without a generation of elderly parents who receive social security.

Immigration is not a complete cure for the social security problem, because the number that might be admitted under any likely U.S. policy is limited. But the extent to which immigrants can be at least a partial remedy is easily underestimated.

One reason that social security taxes per worker are now high is that—contrary to the impression suggested by the anti-immigration lobby—in recent decades this country has admitted far fewer immigrants as a proportion of the population than it did around the turn of the century.

As a result, only about 6 percent of the present U.S. population—a bit more than one person in 20—is foreign born. That includes the aged immigrants who came many years ago, as well as those who came as children and grew up as American as apple pie. Not exactly a nation of raw immigrants. If instead, say, a quarter of our labor force were now immigrants, the social security tax would be almost a quarter lower than it now is. That ain't chicken feed.

37

Let Some "Illegals" Come Temporarily to the U.S.

A guestworker program would eliminate the problems associated with illegal immigration, and would contribute to the U.S. economy. It would also aid the Mexican economy, and would improve relations between the U.S. and Mexico, argues this selection (written before the passage of the Simpson-Rodino bill in 1987).

Sen. Alan K. Simpson (R) of Wyoming has reintroduced his immigration reform bill, which aims in part to control illegal immigration. The core of the bill is sanctions against employers who hire illegal workers. In the House of Representatives, Peter W. Rodino Jr. (D) of New Jersey has come forward to sponsor a similar proposal.

A legal guest-worker program is a better way of achieving the same goals. It is a more humane approach than focusing on employers and foreign-looking applicants. It fits better with the spirit of the United States. And it would be more effective.

Although illegal immigration captures the attention of the Congress and the public, it is far less important in the long run than legal immigration. More legal immigration is good for the U.S. economically, no matter how you look at it. But legal immigration gets lost in the hue and cry about the illegal flow. The risk exists that people who are against *any* immigration for their own reasons will be able to choke the flow of legal immigrants, a threat to the long-run vitality of the United States.

Assertions by those opposed to immigration that more migrants are coming now than ever before are untrue. The number of immigrants in the recent peak year of 1980 was far below the number around the turn of the century. More important is that in proportion to the size of the native

The Christian Science Monitor, August 22, 1985.

population, the immigration rate now is only about a sixth of what it was then.

Nowhere near as many illegal immigrants are in the country now, even on a temporary basis, as the Immigration and Naturalization Service and others claim there are. Last month the National Research Council put the number at between 2 million and 4 million, in contrast to the 12 million figure so often cited. And Jeffrey Passell, in charge of studying the subject for the Census Bureau, estimates that the annual net inflow of illegals is 200,000 people, or at most 250,000. (A net yearly inflow of 100,000 to 300,000 illegal immigrants is the estimate as of 1987.)

Study after reliable study shows that illegal workers, far from being a drain on the U.S. Treasury, actually contribute between 3 and 10 times as much to Uncle Sam through taxes and social security payments as the cost of the government services they use.

An instant way to get rid of illegal entry is to make the same act legal, at least for some entrants. By far the largest portion of the illegals are temporary, especially the Mexicans who are the cause of so much concern; a program that would legalize their temporary entry could eliminate illegal immigration by filling the available jobs with legal workers.

An orderly legal guest-worker program not only gets rid of lawlessness, but it is fair to all comers and does not benefit those who take the law into their own hands. Administering a legal program is cheaper and more humane than having the border patrol chase illegals. There are objections to a guest-worker program, but the difficulties can be surmounted. If we worry that the illegals will not go home—an unnecessary worry in most cases—we can require that a portion of their pay be deducted and held in escrow, as with income taxes, to be returned to them when they leave. Guaranteeing decent working conditions is not more difficult in principle than it is for native workers, as long as the immigrants are legal. The biggest objection is political: Unions don't want guest workers, legal or illegal. But they are going to get competition from the workers one way or another, and it might just as well be legally.

Another way to reduce the scope of the problem would be to ask the Mexican government to allow U.S. companies to operate freely within Mexico without having to meet troublesome restrictions—such as taking on Mexican controlling partners. Then many companies could undertake the same business activities within Mexico that they now conduct in this country with illegal workers. Mexicans could then work legally without leaving home, and fewer illegals would seek to enter the U.S. With the bulk of illegal immigrants now being employed in industry, instead of agriculture as formerly, this potential solution to the problem becomes even more feasible.

Unions worry that illegals or guest workers would displace poor Americans from jobs. But research suggests that the effect on unemployment would not be large, although there would be some wage depression. And much of the job displacement for citizens is mitigated because they find other jobs. Just as permanent immigrants do, temporary workers create new jobs elsewhere in the economy; hence eventually there is no job loss.

38

Do Aliens Make Us Scofflaws?

More about illegal immigration, its supposed evils, and their prevention.

The alleged "flood" of illegal immigrants from Mexico into the United States, it is said, has not only created economic problems for native Americans in the Southwest, it has also helped "breed" lawlessness and the "flouting" of society's rules. In order to keep a bad situation from getting worse, heavy pressure has been put on Congress to enact strong sanctions to prevent Mexicans from coming to the United States and working here illegally.

The lawlessness issue makes an appealing argument, and I myself agreed with it until recently. But, on reflection, I now think it's a smokescreen, a convenient way of avoiding having to deal with the prejudices many Americans harbor toward our poor, brown-skinned, Spanish-speaking neighbors to the South.

What about the charge that ignoring illegal immigration causes general disregard for the law? The final report of the Select Commission on Immigration and Refugee Policy put it bluntly, "Illegality breeds illegality. . . . As long as undocumented migration flouts U.S. immigration law, its most devastating impact may be the disregard it breeds for other U.S. laws."

Disregard of the law certainly is bad and destructive. But any fair-minded person would have to agree that the 55 mile-per-hour speed limit and especially the present structure of income tax laws, breed incomparably more lawlessness than does illegal immigration. Perhaps one can argue for keeping the 55 mile-per-hour limit on the grounds that it may deter at least some speeders and thereby save at least some lives. But that argu-

The Washington Times, August 14, 1984.

ment does not hold with respect to the present income taxes. There are many substitute devices for filling the government coffers that are also superior to consistency and efficiency, and whose only drawback is their political opposition. The income tax laws induce a very large proportion of Americans to venture perilously close to the law if not actually beyond it, unlike illegal immigration, which touches very few Americans in this way.

So if one is serious about eliminating breeding grounds for lawlessness, one should be in the vanguard of the fight for a simpler tax system, and perhaps for abolition of laws against gambling, rather than just taking up the cudgels against immigrants.

One cannot make the argument that preventing illegal immigration reduces moral corruption, as one might with anti-prostitution or anti-pornography laws, or that it saves people from injuring themselves, as is the case with laws against suicide.

Let us agree nevertheless that, all else equal, it is not good for people to break the law knowingly. Well, then, if illegality is bad, why not let them in legally?

Ask this question and you will be told that unless there are barriers to immigration, vast numbers of Mexicans and others will flood into the United States. Letters to the newspapers say such things as "We cannot make it easy for the millions of potential immigrants to come to this country."

But there is much reason to doubt that enormous numbers of Mexicans would come to the United States as permanent residents even if there were no barriers at all. Fears of an "onslaught" still seem to derive from the now-discredited estimates, disseminated by the Immigration and Naturalization Service in the 1970s, of up to 12 million illegals in the United States, most of them Mexicans. In the latter 1970s and early 1980s, demographers applied a variety of ingenious methods to the problem, and finally settled on estimates of 2–4 million illegal residents, many of them only temporary. And the demographers estimated that the net inflow per year might be somewhere between 250,000 and zero persons per year. The results of the amnesty program in 1987 and 1988—about 1.5 million persons registering—square with the earlier estimates. And perhaps only half are Mexicans.

Figure 38-1 contains even more impressive evidence, showing that a program of admitting legal temporary workers—the Bracero program that operated from 1942 to 1964—reduced the demand for illegal workers so sharply that the flow of illegal apprehensions fell almost to zero. Certainly the overall demand for labor has risen greatly since then. Nevertheless, those data suggest that a positive net flow of illegals is not inexorable, but

Figure 38–1. Mexican migration to the United States, 1943–1978.

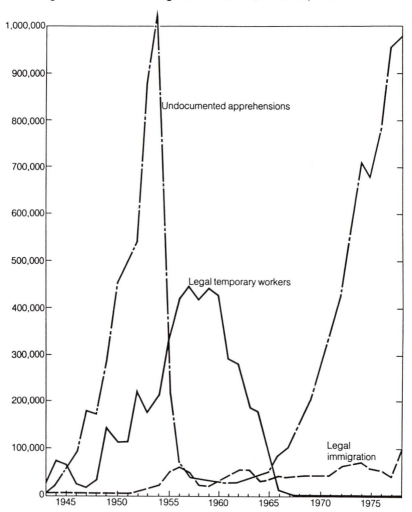

Source: Select Commission on Immigration and Refugee Policy, *Staff Report*, 1981, p.471.

rather may be almost eliminated with a manageable temporary-worker program.

These findings imply that we could do away with the lawlessness in the present situation without increasing the number of Mexicans in the United States very much, if we would allow them to come in legally. That is, we could legalize temporary stays for the purpose of working in the United States.

Such a program has both pros and cons. The main objection comes from the labor unions who believe—without reasonable evidence—that the program would take additional jobs from native workers. Unfortunately, a Bracero program has not been adequately discussed as part of current immigration reform efforts.

Should not the possibility of a temporary-worker program at least be the subject of national debate before the nation undertakes a far-reaching new immigration policy? It is certainly a more honest way of dealing with undocumented immigration from Mexico than simply condemning it as "lawless."

Part 6
Failed Prophecies and the Doomsaying Establishment

Introduction

During the past two decades, the United States and the world have suffered a large number of egregiously wrong prophecies about resources, the environment, and the effects of population growth. The record of these forecasts would be funny if it had not been so costly.

Apologists for the doomsayers have tried to reassure us that though the forecasts were wrong, they nevertheless were useful in alerting us to dangers. Indeed, the doomsayers argue, the very fact that the dangers did not come to pass is a tribute to these forecasts.

But there is no evidence that the dangers were averted by the forecasts. And the forecasts have not been harmless. Rather, the false forecasts of resource gloom-and-doom over the past two decades terribly damaged the economy as well as the morale of the United States and of other countries.

For example, airlines, airplane manufacturers, and automobile industries have lost tens of billions of dollars in design and manufacturing expenses because they relied upon—or were forced by government regulation to rely upon—forecasts that the price of gasoline would soon be $3 a gallon. The banks that lent money to oil ventures now find they are eating tens of billions of dollars in bad loans made on the basis of those forecasts of increasing scarcity. The U.S. agriculture industry, and therefore Congress and the taxpayers, are now suffering greatly because farmers believed that population growth would push up prices for food and increase demand and prices of farmland. Many U.S. paper manufacturers came crying to the federal government for relief from contracts they entered into on the assumption that wood prices would rise, as the U.S. Department of Agriculture had foretold to them—on grounds that the government is responsible because of its faulty forecasts. And so on.

The spirit-destroying rhetoric of impending scarcity apparently has led to a general pessimism, the sort found in these casually clipped newspaper-story headlines: "B.F. Skinner Now Sees Little Hope for the World Salvation" (*The New York Times*, September 15, 1981); "Teenagers Today Have No Great Expectations, a Discussion with a Dozen in New Jersey Finds" (*The Wall Street Journal*, June 16, 1982, p. 48); "The New Pessimism" (*Newsweek*, June 14, 1982, p. 20).

Even the pope gets caught up in this trendy sort of talk, though it is wholly inconsistent with the general viewpoint of the Roman Catholic Church, as I understand it, as well as inconsistent with the facts. John Paul II's *Encyclical on Social Concerns: Sollicitudo Rei Socialis* of March 3, 1988, says that "one cannot deny that the present situation of the world, from the point of development, offers a rather negative impression" (p. 645). It goes on to say that "production and distribution of foodstuffs, hygiene, health and housing, availability of drinking water . . . life expectancy . . . the general picture is a disappointing one" (p. 646). And it charges that "Responsibility for this deterioration is due to various causes," among them the "high rate of population growth" in "the developing countries" (p. 647). "One cannot deny the existence, especially in the Southern Hemisphere, of a demographic problem which creates difficulties for development" (p. 649). And it cites "limits of available resources and of the need to respect the integrity and the cycles of nature . . . ecological concern" (p. 650). This sounds as if it were taken direct from a press release of the Audubon Society or Zero Population Growth.

Many of the young people in the Western world—I saw this most recently in a survey of high school students in Australia, of all places— have been thrown into despair by the belief that the world is running out of resources and must inevitably get poorer, a course of events supposedly exacerbated by selfish consumption in the rich countries in which they live. Teachers observed this despair when discussing "major global problems" at the University of North Carolina: "What remedies, such as hands-on experience, can we offer to counter the depression many students experience when they learn about major global problems?" (North Carolina Academy of Science, "Public Affairs and Policy Statement," by Charles E. Jenner and Martha G. Jenner, April 10, 1980.)

Various fears seem to have reinforced each other in such fashion that, whereas people had a general mind-set about progress in earlier years, we now have a general mind-set about retrogression. For example, Muth carefully analyzed housing costs since 1965, and found—somewhat to his surprise—that costs have fallen rather than risen, despite population increase. He then ended with "a question for which I have not found a satisfactory answer: 'Why do we believe in a housing crisis when the evidence so strongly suggests the contrary?' " (1982, p. 319). Perhaps part of the answer to his question is that once you begin viewing a series of matters as getting worse, you generalize that—in the absence of strong evidence to the contrary—most everything *must* be getting worse. These feelings of powerlessness and guilt over resource use and exhaustion may sap our will to move ahead economically and politically.

In World War II the slogan of the Seabees (U.S. Navy Construction Battalions) was "The difficult we do immediately; the impossible takes a little longer." To have a can-do motto and spirit like the Seabees requires that you believe that difficult feats are *possible*. The notion of limits to growth denies that possibility, and therefore renders less likely a can-do mentality.

Does a limits mentality portend the decline of the United States as an economic and political power, in the manner of Rome, Spain, and England? Does such a view, as Gimpel (1976) argues, reinforce other psychological forces—such as the slackening of the aspiration to achieve that comes with affluence? No one can know now. But it would be wise to remember that in the 1930s a reasonable observer would not have put high odds on the United States' likelihood of achieving the heights it reached during and after World War II.

       *   *   *

Along with the forecasts, the selections in this section briefly review the forecasters who have been most prominent among the doomsayers. Astonishingly, all of them continue today as actively as before, making the same gloomy forecasts with no hint of embarrassment. If challenged on their records, they either say that their forecasts were self-negating and therefore valuable, or they assert that they simply chose too early a date for the grim events to eventuate. The public continues to accept these failed prophets as prophets, without loss of adulation or reduction in lecture fees.

Why do reporters not find and quote the agricultural forecasters who were right in the 1970s? Why did our Department of Defense and our airlines believe the conventional oil forecasts of $3 per gallon gasoline, at enormous cost to the United States public in many ways? And why does most of the public still believe the forecasts about natural resources, food, and energy by the folks who were absolutely dead wrong on Earth Day in 1970 and are saying exactly the same thing today?

Our human credulity is often amazing. We are willing to believe the most outlandish ideas if they are said or written by someone who claims to be an expert and behaves with the proper gravity and a bit of impressive mystery. Credibility is enhanced if the source is "official." We assume that authorities know what they are doing.

The organizations that disseminated these failed forecasts have not been stilled by the events that have falsified them. More, they also have sustained or even intensified their efforts to bend the federal government's powers and budgets to their desires. The later selections in this section describe some of the activities of these organizations, the composite of which is regarded by many as among the most powerful and effective lobbies in Washington.

The question of *why* the public has heard so much false bad news about population and resources is addressed in Part 7.

39

Anti-Growth Prophets Use Cracked Crystal Balls

This selection is a brief introduction to the failed prophecies that have scared people in previous decades.

The anti-population-growth doomsters have been flat wrong on every one of their forecasts since the late 1960s.

The price of grains has fallen, rather than rising as they predicted. Their forecast of $3 per gallon for gasoline has become a happy joke. The world's copper and tin mines are faced with disastrous glut and low prices, not the shortage crises the population-environment movement said would face us now.

The latest falsification of the doom prophets is a historical updating of world fish catches, prepared by biologist John Wise. A centerpiece of the influential *Global 2000* report to the president prepared by the State Department for Jimmy Carter in 1980—over a million copies sold, with translations around the world—was that the total fish catch of the world had peaked. *Global 2000* forecast a plateau at the 1975 level, which would have meant less and less fish per person as population grew larger.

Even before the report had hit Carter's desk, the catch had jumped from 65.7 million tons in 1975 to 69.2 million tons in 1976. Now the latest 1984 figures show a huge leap to 82.8 million tons. So the catch not only has not stagnated as *Global 2000* forecast, but actually has risen even faster proportionally than has population since World War II.

The prophets who have been wrong at every turn—the likes of Paul Ehrlich, Lester Brown, and Daniel Yergin—have lost none of their appeal

Scripps-Howard newspapers, December 29, 1986.

and still command vast audiences and huge fees from business people who continue to consider them "experts."

No one seems to notice as they jump from one inexcusable scientific error to the next, forecasting that population growth will be a disaster for our natural resources.

In reality additional people cause us to have more resources rather than less.

Let us first be clear that throughout the long sweep of history, a larger world population has been accompanied by greater availability rather than greater scarcity. There are a lot more people on earth nowadays than there were 100 years ago, and we have more of the services that we desire from copper, iron, oil, and all the other resources than we did then. The same is true of 1000 years ago, and 10,000 years ago.

In the Western world, population grew at hitherto-unknown rates during the Industrial Revolution, and so did resource availability and the standard of living. The many statistical analyses of population-growth rates and rates of growth of income indicate no negative relationship, either over the last century for the few countries which have data, or among the many countries for which data are available since World War II.

True, in the short run, before the economy has a chance to adjust, additional people cause increased pressure and shortages. But the pressure of additional people—and also pressure from increasing income levels—tends eventually to leave us better off than if the shortages had never arisen.

Given some time to adjust to shortages with already-known methods as well as with new inventions and creative substitutions, in the presence of economic freedom, people create additional resources. The result of the process is greater resource availability than ever.

This is the story of human civilization. If roots and rabbits had not become scarce a few millenia ago, we would still dig roots and chase rabbits for lunch, instead of reaping the fruits of agriculture at the local supermarket.

Why have so many people, for so long, believed so many wrong ideas about population's effects? Part of the answer lies in people's short-run self-interest. If the public fears environmental and resource problems, there will be more government funds to fight the "problems." But the main cause of misunderstanding about population growth is, as Frederic Bastiat put it a century ago, the difference between what is seen and what is not seen.

All the immediately obvious effects of population growth are negative—

greater pressure on existing resources; need to make new adjustments; reduction in the existing output available for each person.

In contrast, all the positive effects are diffuse, long-term, and require imagination to comprehend: responses by inventors and entrepreneurs to the new opportunities for profit caused by temporary scarcities, which leads to more productive knowledge than we had before; new transportation and communication infrastructure developed to deal with the congestion, providing more modern facilities than we began with; new social arrangements that cause us to be better organized than before population pressure was added.

So bring on the resource problems! The progressive future needs them.

40

Should We Heed the Prophets of Doom?

The foremost among the failed prophets of doom are introduced in this selection.

Are you against feeding phony bad news to the public, even if that news is intended for the good of the environment? Do you believe that factual accuracy and truthful evaluations will serve mankind best in the long run? Do you think we should not place our confidence in prophets with poor forecasting performances? If so, you might like to know something about the outcome of past fuel and food crises, and about the track records of some of the best-known forecasters of environmental and resource doom during the past 15 years—Lester Brown, Paul Ehrlich, Garrett Hardin, and the Limits to Growth group and their large claque.

Global 2000 Report to the President and Lester Brown's book *Building a Sustainable Society* are among the latest gloomy forecasts. The persuasive logic that underlies these forecasts is Malthusian. Combined with this idea are various biological and physical principles that assume fixed resources and no technological change in response to environmental problems. As long as you accept these premises, there is no way to argue successfully that the world's situation will not get worse as population increases. Nor can one demonstrate with logic alone that these premises are not reasonable—though of course it is also not possible for logic alone to demonstrate that these premises *are* in fact reasonable.

If one checks back, however, and finds that the same sorts of predictions made earlier by others—or in Brown's case, the very same predictions made by himself—have fallen flat on their faces time after time, then a prudent person will look beyond such doomsday forecasts to find a more reliable basis for prediction and policy decisions. We can gain perspective

Science Digest, October 1982.

by remembering the repeated doomsday predictions about food and fuel shortages, triggered either by some foreboding change in the situation or simply by depletion logic. (See Selection 5 for the multi-century history of the wood and coal energy fears in Great Britain.)

Did the doomsayers learn from this history? In our own time we have Paul Ehrlich talking about the day "when the pumps run dry." The panic that followed the 1973 oil embargo rivaled any past panic in intensity. Even governments and big businesses signed multi-billion-dollar contracts based on these predictions that energy prices would continue to rise out of sight. But they have since rued these contracts, what with the newspapers talking of an oil glut and falling prices.

The history of frightening prophecies about impending shortages of food is a long one. Yet the world's food situation has continued to improve over the years, whether you measure it in quantities eaten per person, absolute number of people dying of famine from decade to decade, the quality of food or food prices. (Yes, food prices. The trend over the entire history of the United States, for example, is *falling* prices for wheat and other foodstuffs. See Selections 6 and 7 for data on the world food-shortage scare of the 1960s and 1980s.)

Yet in 1967 we had the widely read book by William and Paul Paddock, *Famine 1975*, which told their whole story in the title. We had Paul Ehrlich opening his 1968 tract, *The Population Bomb*, by writing, "The battle to feed all of humanity is over." And the camp followers of Ehrlich and the Paddocks then competed with one another to find the most frightening titles for their own doomsday books. Many of these writers called for coercion to force people to have fewer children. This outcry led to the disastrous forced-sterilization campaigns in India that brought riots and forced Prime Minister Indira Gandhi out of office. The same set of writers also called for governments to take over agriculture. Such government programs led to the near ruination of agriculture in too many countries.

Now in the 1980s we have already had the gloomy *Global 2000 Report to the President*, the Willy Brandt report, and most recently Lester Brown's *Building a Sustainable Society*. *Global 2000* has had a marked effect on public opinion and public policy in the United States and abroad, but the book is fatally flawed by lack of historical perspective. It shows no awareness that humankind's history has been a sequence of worrisome scarcities and resulting solutions *that left us better off than before the scarcity arose*. And it does not present the long-run data covering many decades that showed beyond doubt that the resource situation has improved and energy prices have fallen. *Global 2000* does not show the data that prove that pollution has *lessened* in the United States over the past decade and more.

Brown's *Sustainable Society* is full of gloomy forecasts about all aspects of our environment and resources. But let's concentrate on Brown's assertions about his main subject—food, which was introduced in Selection 6. It is important to pay close attention to the manner in which he treats this question, because he presents much recent data that appear to support his assertions, but in fact do not.

Brown now writes, for example, "Since 1971, gains in output have barely kept pace with population growth; production per person has fluctuated widely but shown little real increase." If, however, one looks at UN data on world grain production since 1950 (the same data Brown uses), almost anyone's statistical or eyeball examination shows a trend *toward more food per person*. Why should we compare, as Brown does, the then-peak year 1971 and the "unusually poor harvest" (Brown's words) in 1980? Only such a pick-and-choose comparison is consistent with Brown's gloomy assessment. This is typical of how the doomsayers find in the data the basis for the gloomy projections.

The flipflops and reversals in Brown's record of forecasts ought to give one pause. When Brown began his public career in 1964, he thought that the food situation was frightening. Here is the opening line of a statement he prepared for the Secretary of Agriculture in 1965: "The less developed world is losing the capacity to feed itself." But then came, in his words, the "new high-yielding cereals and the men who developed them. I am fortunate to have had a front row seat in this historic drama." His 1970 book, *Seeds of Change,* "tells the story of the turn-around on the food front." He became so optimistic that his main worry was whether the poor countries would be able to export all the food they would grow: "The pivotal question is whether the rich countries . . . are prepared to open their internal markets to cereal exports from the poor countries."

Then Brown's view changed again—though there had been no basic change in the food-supply trends of the previous two decades and more—and he again became exceedingly pessimistic, as his latest book makes clear.

Paul Ehrlich is another example. He now says he can "predict with extreme accuracy the end result of continuing our assaults on Earth's systems: the collapse of civilization as we know it." His predictions are examined at length in Selection 25.

When you point out that their past forecasts have failed, the doomsayers typically say, "But *this* time it will be different." And of course this time they *may* be right. But for sound planning, we want to know the *probability* that a dire forecast will come about, just as weather forecasters give us probabilities of rain or snow so that we can base our decisions on that probability. Unfortunately, Brown, Ehrlich and company do not express their forecasts in terms of such probabilities. Furthermore, their miserable track record suggests that they would not be a valuable source of such estimates.

Another response the doomsayers frequently give is that "the earlier forecasts were correct, but the dates were off." That's like a weather forecaster predicting rain for a day that turns out clear, and then justifying the forecast by saying that only the date of the predicted rain was incorrect. To repeat Arthur Schlesinger's remarks: "How many times does an expert have to be wrong before he loses his reputation for expertise?"

41

Global Confusion, 1980: A Hard Look at the Global 2000 Report

The Global 2000 Report *to President Jimmy Carter (GTS hereafter) was the most momentous event in the doomsaying movement since the publication of the Club of Rome's* The Limits to Growth *in 1972. Almost every economist, agricultural economist, and statistician who has examined that report—as well as some environmentalists such as Rene Dubos—considers it to be fatally flawed in method, lacking in historical foundation, and misleading in its conclusions about the global "trends" it purports to describe (e.g., Dubos, 1981; Kahn and Schneider, 1981; Clawson, 1981; Simon 1981; see Selection 43 for references). Nevertheless, GTS has served as the focal point for the Global Tomorrow Coalition. And it has been the model of similar studies in several other countries.*

The Global Tomorrow Coalition is the key player in the so-called Global 2000 Movement, which grew out of GTS. The Global Tomorrow Coalition, made up of 49 organizations that use GTS as their so-called bible, have a large number of staff members in Washington who lobby Congress and the executive branch. Altogether, there are now over 80 registered environmental lobbyists on Capitol Hill, compared to two or three in the late 1960s. And there are five environmental political action committees, one of which—The League of Conservative Voters—had a budget of almost $900,000 to back about 70 candidates in the 1982 elections.

The Global 2000 movement has deeply affected the national policies of the United States and other nations. A number of bills and resolutions before Congress show the influence of Global 2000. For

The Public Interest, Winter, 1981.

instance, a letter from Sen. Mark Hatfield, R-Ore., to Sen. William Roth, R-Del., regarding S.1771, the Global Resources, Environment, and Population Act, calls for creation of a Council on Global Resources to unify government planning in the areas of natural resources, environment, and population policy. The main impetus for this legislation, Hatfield wrote, "was the publication of the 'Global 2000 Report to the President.' "

In short, those members of Congress have fallen victim to a special interest movement that seeks only to enlarge its own coffers by justifying its existence with frightening and fallicious research.

This movement already has caused misallocation of natural resources in the United States, deterioration in public morale, and a loss of confidence (with consequent reduction in risk investment) in the business community.

The real danger lies in the fact that there are no organizations or communications media dedicated to setting the record straight or to opposing the Global 2000 initiatives.

This selection discuss some of the assertions of GTS *in light of the known facts.*

More than one million copies of the original Global 2000 Report to the President of the United States *have been distributed. It has been translated into five major languages. Other countries such as West Germany, Japan, and China have commissioned studies imitating* Global 2000.

Global 2000 *also underlies important U.S. policy pronouncements. For example, the following paragraphs, and the rest of the full speech at the Alpbach European Forum in 1980, which was an official "American perspective on the world economy in the 1980s," were founded squarely on* Global 2000:

> *Defying the generally buoyant mood, Richard Cooper, U.S. under secretary of state for economic affairs, delivered a grim message. If present trends continue, he said, the world population will swell to five billion by 1990 from four billion at present, leading to "open conflict, greater terrorism and possibly localized anarchy," as well as "congestion, famine, deforestation."*
>
> *The decade's population growth would equal "nearly half the total world population when I was born," he said. Even then, he added ominously, "some political leaders were calling for more lebensraum" (or living space).* (The Wall Street Journal, *September 15, 1980, p. 32*)

Before Global 2000 *was even completed, President Carter had discussed its conclusions with other world leaders at an economic summit held in Italy. Immediately upon receiving the report, the*

President established a task force to ensure that Global 2000 *received priority attention. The task force included the Secretary of State, the director of the Office of Management and Budget, the President's Assistant for Domestic Affairs, and the director of the Office of Science and Technology Policy. Secretary of State Edmund Muskie used* Global 2000 *as the centerpiece for an address to the UN General Assembly. The Joint Economic Committee of Congress launched a series of hearings on the report. The President instructed the State Department to arrange an international meeting of environmental and economic experts to discuss population, natural resources, environment, and economic development, the subjects of* Global 2000. *Finally, in his farewell address to the nation, President Carter referred to the subject of* Global 2000 *as one of the three most important problems facing the American people (the other two being arms control and human rights). And* Global 2000's *effect did not disappear with the change of administration. It continues to be cited as support for a wide variety of forecasts by governmental agencies.*

The press received Global 2000 *with great respect and enormous attention.* Time *and* Newsweek *ran full-page stories, and* Global 2000 *made front-page newspaper headlines across the country as an "official" government study forecasting global disaster. Though the report included some qualifications, it was interpreted by all as a prediction of gloom and doom. For example,* Science's *story title was: "Global 2000 Report: Vision of a Gloomy World."* Time's *title was "Toward a Troubled 21st Century: a presidential panel finds the global outlook extremely bleak."* Newsweek's *title was "A Grim Year 2000." The typical local paper in central Illinois had this banner across the top of the front page: "U.S. Report Says World Faces Ecological Disaster." And its story began:*

> *Mass poverty, malnutrition and deterioration of the planet's water and atmosphere resources—that's a bleak government prediction that says civilization has perhaps 20 years to act to head off such a world-wide disaster.*

A full-page advertisement for the volume in The New York Review of Books *was headed: Government Report as follows: Poisoned seas, acid rain, water running out, atmosphere dying.*

However—and seldom can there have been a bigger "however" in the history of such reports—the original Global 2000 *is totally wrong in its specific assertions and its general conclusion. It is replete with major factual errors, not just minor blemishes. Its language is vague at key points, and features many loaded terms. Many of its arguments are illogical or misleading. It paints an overall picture of global trends that is fundamentally wrong, partly because it relies on non-facts and partly because it misinterprets the facts it does present. (In partial defense of the writers who prepared the* Global 2000 *work, the summary Volume I—which was the main basis for the news stories— egregiously misstated, for reasons that we can only surmise, many analyses and conclusions in the working-paper Volume II, thereby turning optimistic projections into pessimistic ones.)*

Now the Global 2000 Study makes it official that the world is going to hell in a handbasket. As *Time* says, "The U.S. government has added its full voice to the chorus of environmental Cassandras . . . a presidential panel warns that time is fast running out for averting a global calamity." President Carter requested the Global 2000 Study, it was chaired by the Council on Environmental Quality and the Department of State, and eleven agencies "cooperated," including the Departments of Agriculture, Energy, and Interior, the Agency for International Development, the CIA, the Environmental Protection Agency, the National Aeronautics and Space Administration, the National Science Foundation, and three other agencies with names slightly less well-known. That's pretty official.

This is the report's own thumbnail summary of the Global 2000 findings:

> If present trends continue, the world in 2000 will be more crowded, more polluted, less stable ecologically, and more vulnerable to disruption than the world we live in now. Serious stresses involving population, resources, and environment are clearly visible ahead. Despite greater material output, the world's people will be poorer in many ways than they are today.

> For hundreds of millions of the desperately poor, the outlook for food and other necessities of life will be no better. For many it will be worse. Barring revolutionary advances in technology, life for most people on earth will be more precarious in 2000 than it is now.

Fortunately, these assertions about resources and the environment are baseless. The authors of the Global 2000 Study (GTS hereafter) offer no persuasive evidence for their "scenario." The facts, as I read them, point in quite the opposite direction on every single important aspect of their prediction for which I could find any data at all.

Six Limits to Accuracy

A newspaperman wondered: How can the report be as wrong as I say it is if GTS worked on it for three years, and spent a big bundle of government money? It *is* hard to take, I agree, but being so wrong is not implausible when we notice some of the features of the work process.

First, when the study's director, Gerald Barney, began work, he was told he had six months to deliver the report to the printers. Subsequently, there were extensions of a few months at a time. One can feel great sympathy for Barney in this situation. It was difficult to obtain capable staff for so short a period, and there was no time to plan a careful, thoughtful piece of work on this vast topic. Having it now billed as a "three year study" is therefore misleading.

Second, the method of GTS seems to have been roughly as follows: They set as an ideal a comprehensive multisectoral model along the lines of *The Limits to Growth* model, but using existing government models of various sectors appropriately tied together. They found, however, that it was very difficult to hook up these separate models, so they supplemented the contents and outputs of those sectoral models with additional data, outside contracts, expert judgments, and so on.

But the existing individual sectoral models were often inappropriate for the purposes at hand. Consider, for example, the future copper situation. The likeliest available model of the copper market (I cannot say which model was really used, because the GTS documentation has yet to be published) is one that explores the impacts of changes in the demand schedule due to changes in world income and population, and of changes in the supply schedule due to cost changes assuming technology is constant. When estimated with empirical data from year to year, the outcome will surely be that increased demand leads to higher prices, which will induce some increased supply but probably less copper per person than before. But this short-run model omits a key fact seen in the long run: As population and income have increased, the relative cost of copper has decreased rather than increased. And this is true because, with some time-lag, increased demand leads to improved technology, which then leads to lower prices. The GTS purports to be a long-run analysis, and therefore it should appropriately embody the long-run technology-increasing relationships. But it is most unlikely that any of the sectoral models employed do so. Hence, the elements GTS seeks to hitch together are not appropriate. Additionally, the overall "Government model" could not sensibly link together the various sectors, resulting in "inconsistency and missing links that are unavoidable." Naturally. As I see it, the result of the "linkage" is a useless hodge-podge.

With respect to the crucial income projection, though GTS refers to "The Government global model," there was *not* a "government model" that produced the crucial forecasts of future income. Anne Carter, the only academic economist on the seven-person group of "expert advisers" (who met for a total of two weekends) was under the impression that the basis of the GTS projection is a model built by Carter and Peter Petri. But Gerald Barney said that the projection came from the WAES model done by Carroll Wilson at M.I.T., which came to GTS via the World Bank. And Barney says that the documentation of the WAES model in their technical volume is "skimpy" and "unsatisfying," and he feels that there is "good reason for the reader to have difficulty understanding the basis for GTS' forecast." About these numbers upon which the whole study depends, Carter now says (following a report of my discussion with Barney): "I doubt that anyone knows where those income estimates come from."

Third, there is a lack of historical perspective. It is a reasonable rule of prediction in economics (if not everywhere) that experience is to be preferred to pure logic as a policy guide if plenty of experience is available and there is no obvious discontinuity. Yet biologists such as Ehrlich and Hardin, who are frequently quoted in the report, employ technological modes of analysis even when contradictory historical evidence is available. The most important aspect of the relevant historical experience is that humans use their imaginative and creative powers to change their situation when caught in a resource bind, and the final result is usually that we are left better off than before the problem arose.

Fourth, organizational self-interest may have been at work. It's reasonable that the Council on Environmental Quality is more likely to draw a big budget if Congress believes that there are big environmental problems.

Fifth, bad news makes headlines. Would the Global 2000 report have gotten a thousandth of the widespread publicity it received if it said: "More or less, and left to themselves without massive government interference, the world's people are slowly but steadily improving their lot in food and resource supplies, life expectancy, and a clean environment"?

Sixth, along with the First Great Law of Models (GIGO, garbage in, garbage out) should be added another law: PIPO, prejudice in, prejudice out. The list of staff and advisers indicates that this report comes to us from the very same Zero Population Growth people who brought us the *Population Bomb* and subsequent Ehrlich collaborations, plus *The Limits to Growth* (TLTG) bunch, the Worldwatch Institute, and population-control and environmental organizations. Indeed, no such group seems to be missing from the list.

There is an entire appendix devoted to tracing the intellectual passage from TLTG to GTS. This is despite the fact that TLTG has been as thoroughly discredited as any document can be, most compellingly in the repudiation by the sponsoring Club of Rome itself. Just four years after the huge foofaraw created by TLTG's publication and huge circulation—an incredible 4 million copies were sold—the Club of Rome, "reversed its position" and "came out for more growth." But this radical shift has gotten relatively little attention, though it was written up in such places as *Time* and *The New York Times*. The original message is the one which remains with most people.

The explanation of this reversal, as reported in *Time,* is a masterpiece of facesaving double-talk:

> The Club's founder, Italian industrialist Aurelio Peccei, says that *Limits* was intended to jolt people from the comfortable idea that present growth trends could continue indefinitely. That done, he says, the Club could then seek ways to close the widening gap between rich and poor nations—inequities that, if they continue, could all too easily lead to famine, pollution and war. The Club's startling shift, Peccei says, is thus not so much a turnabout as part of an evolving strategy.

In other words, the Club of Rome sponsored and disseminated untruths in an attempt to scare us. Having scared people with these untruths, the Club of Rome could then tell people the *real* truth.

Of course, it is possible that the Club of Rome did not really practice the deceitful strategy that it now says it did. Maybe they have now simply realized that the 1972 TLTG study was scientifically worthless. If so, the Club of Rome is *now* dissembling about what it *really* did, in order to save face. From the outside, of course, we have no way of knowing which of these ugly possibilities is the "truth."

Surely this is one of the more curious scientific episodes of recent years. Those who wrote TLTG have not recanted, to my knowledge, even though their sponsors have, and it continues to be cited as an authority, as seen in GTS. And the same Peccei is cited worshipfully in the first paragraph of each of the first three chapters on world models in Volume II of GTS.

The Facts

I said earlier that the facts, as I read them, point in quite the opposite direction from the conclusions of Global 2000 on every important aspect of their prediction for which I could find any data. That is strong talk, but I'll now back it up with data, starting in the order of the topics mentioned in the Global 2000 capsule summary cited earlier, and then moving on to some other areas.

We can all agree that historical trend data are the basic raw material for the projections. As GTS put it, "The process chosen for the Global 2000 Study was to develop trend projections using, to the fullest extent possible, the long-term global data and models routinely employed by the Federal

Agencies." The most striking aspect of the report, however, is the absence of these very trend data.

Item: "more polluted." Though the GTS projection refers to the world, the available data are mostly for the U.S. With respect to the main pollutions of the air, the available time-series are short, but they are all I have been able to find in the reports of the Council on Environmental Quality of elsewhere. Figure 1-1 shows that the U.S. situation has recently been improving rather than deteriorating.

With respect to water quality, the key measure is drinkability. Figure 1-2 shows that by this measure water quality in the U.S. has been getting better rather than worse.

About such charges as "Lake Erie has died," see Selection 43.

Great Britain had already made great improvements in its environment by the time that the U.S., in the 1970s, became fully aroused about environment degradation.

> British rivers . . . have been polluted for a century while in America they began to grow foul only a couple of decades ago. . . . The Thames has been without fish for a century. But by 1968 some 40 different varieties had come back to the river.
>
> Now to be seen [in London in 1968] are birds and plants long unsighted here. . . . The appearance of long-absent birds is measured by one claim that 138 species are currently identified in London, compared with less than half that number 10 years ago. . . . Gone are the killer smogs. . . . Londoners . . . are breathing air cleaner than it has been for a century . . . effects of air pollution on bronchial patients is diminishing . . . visibility is better, too . . . on an average winter day . . . about 4 miles, compared with 1.4 miles in 1958.

GTS says, "The life expectancy of a population is the most all-inclusive widely measured indication of a nation's environmental health" and I agree. The data show continued increase in U.S. life expectancy, and at an increasing rate—a gain of 2.6 years from 1970 to 1976, compared with a gain of only 0.8 in the entire decade of the 1960s. By this test, the environment certainly is healthier than ever before.

"The rate of increase of life expectancy has slowed," GTS says. Their own data show the opposite, however. They report life expectancies for the world population as follows: 1950/55—46.7; 1955/60—49.9; 1960/65—52.2; 1965/70—53.9; 1975—58.8. And these crude figures certainly understate the gains within particular countries, because the countries with lower life expectancies have a successively bigger weight in the calculation for the more recent years due to the fact of their increasing share of total world population.

Of course one can point to specific places where environmental conditions have fared worse rather than better, and to specific pollutions that have increased. A fair-minded assessment of the situation would not just pick and choose, but rather, would focus on these standard aggregate measures.

What trend data does the Global 2000 report rely upon for its frightening "projections" of the environment's pollution level? I could find none. There are frequent references from one chapter to another, but when arriving at the destination I often found no data, only reference to another reference elsewhere—a frustrating scavenger hunt with no prize for the participant. In the chapter on "analysis" which describes the method used, we read that "There is at present no adequate, formal and precise means of projecting world trends for renewable resources such as water, forestry, fisheries, soil, and the environment." GTS asked various government agencies to supply relevant analyses of the environmental situation, but what was received was "minimal or non-existent." In short, there is no factual basis given for the forecast of more pollution in the future, and the data we do have suggest a trend of less pollution in the U.S. and Great Britain.

Item: "less stable ecologically, and more vulnerable to disruption." These concepts are so diffuse that I have no idea how one would measure them directly, nor do the GTS authors give us any trend data on any relevant measures. Yet the assertions will be quoted for years as authoritative.

Item: "serious stresses involving . . . resources." There have always been "serious stresses" in the sense that people have to pay a price to get the resources they want. But the data on "stress," as measured by the relevant economic measures of scarcity—costs and prices—show that the long-run trend is toward less scarcity and lower prices rather than more scarcity and higher prices, hard as that may be to believe. The cost trends of almost every natural resource—whether measured in labor time required to produce the resource, in production costs, in the proportion of our incomes spent for resources, or even in the price relative to other consumer goods—have been downward over the course of recorded history. (See Part 1 of this book for more on this.)

This topic is of particular interest because I had the opportunity of discussing it at some length over the phone with Gerald Barney, GTS' director. The GTS projection is simply a 5 percent yearly increase in the real price of non-fuel minerals from now until the year 2000. The text notes that "the real price of most mineral commodities has been constant or declining for many years." But Barney believes that the Department of Interior's downward extrapolations from these trends are not sound because they omit various considerations that he considers important, notably "diminishing returns" and energy. What GTS here boils down to, therefore, is simply one man's judgment, in the face of all the long-run historical trends, and the one man is neither an economist nor a person who has studied this subject at length. Furthermore, the projection runs counter to the projection of the relevant government agency, even though Barney says that GTS should be thought of as "an image of the future as seen by government agencies," rather than as an independent study of the subject. Unfortunately, other government agencies in turn will offer GTS as the basis for *their* projections. (A study that is simply a compilation of others' "images" of the future is an information-and-belief system closed to fundamental inquiry from outside the government, and subject only to manipulation from the inside.)

Energy is a resource of particular interest right now. GTS says that "production costs will increase with energy prices," implying that prices will rise in the next four decades. But the long-run trends are toward lower energy prices. The facts about the cost of energy are much the same as the facts about other raw materials. The new strength of the OPEC cartel to control oil price obscures the cost of production, which in the Persian Gulf is perhaps a hundredth of the market price. It is reasonable to expect that eventually the price of oil will return nearer its economic cost of production, and the long-run downward trend in the price of oil will resume its course. (Selection 2 discusses this further.)

In short, the data show that energy has not been getting scarcer in basic economic terms, but, rather, has been getting more plentiful.

What about the GTS trend data on minerals and energy costs? Same story, no data. We are shown a diagram of energy consumption in the U.S., from 1850 to the present, and its upward course is frightening in this context, of course. (In another context it might be a sign of our increasing affluence and productivity.) But the data on the relevant economic magnitudes—costs and prices—are nowhere to be found in GTS, though the data for the graphs in this essay all come from *Historical Statistics of the United States,* a basic reference volume found in even the smallest library.

Other Topics of Concern

Here are some other projections of the Global 2000 report, and the relevant data that refute them:

Item: food. "Over the 30 years from 1970 to 2000 . . . a global per capita increase of less than 15 percent," claims GTS. But as we see in Table 2-2, over the period from 1950 to 1976 (less than 30 years), per capita food production rose by either 28 percent or 37 percent, depending on whether you use United Nations or U.S. Department of Agriculture figures. Why should one project a much smaller rate of increase (15 percent) for an even longer period?

It may be useful to inquire how the Global 2000 report arrived at a conclusion about growth in food supply so different from the past trend. We are told that this projection emerges from "a formal mathematical model made up of roughly 1000 equations." Anyone who has worked with computer models knows how the chance of an error leading to invalid or nonsense conclusions rises with the complexity of the model. Volume III, which is to describe the GTS models, has not yet been issued, and therefore one cannot ferret out the full story. This much we can discover, however. (1) Though the rate of increase of total grain production over the period 1951–55 to 1973–75 was calculated by the GTS at 2.7 percent yearly (the only trend calculation of the sort I could find in the 750 page report), they projected the rate of growth to fall to between 2.1 percent and 2.0 percent yearly by 1985–2000. No reason was given for this projected decline. (2) GTS says that "Two sets of population projections were used in the *Global 2000* study: Those made by the U.S. Bureau of the Census and those made by the Community and Family Study center (CFSC) of the University of Chicago." But apparently only the higher Census Bureau estimates were used in arriving at the "less than 15 percent" per capita increase; if the CFSC estimate were used, even with the total grain projection discussed above, the per capita increase over the 30 year period would be close to 30 percent rather than 15 percent—that is, 1 percent per year rather than half a percent per year—a very satisfactory rate of growth.

GTS says of food prices, "Real prices for food are expected to double." Compare that projection with the historical decline of food prices in Figure 6-2.

Item: trees. "Significant losses of world forests will continue over the next 20 years." I find no trend data on world forests in GTS. But the data on the U.S. tree stock show (astonishingly?) that more rather than fewer trees are growing now than in the past. (See Figures 41-1 and 41-2a, b, c). Despite these data—which were published by the GTS parent agency, the Council on Environmental Quality—GTS projects a decrease from 58 to 55 billion "cu m overbark" (whatever that means) from 1978 to 2000, and a reduction in "closed forests" from 470 to 464 million of hectares in the United States.

The source given for these estimates shown in Table 7 of Volume I is Table 13-29 in Volume II. The latter turns out to be identical to Table 7, and refers the reader to Table 8-9 in Volume II. Table 8-9 in turn is identical to Tables 7 and 13-29, and the source for it is said to be "calculation from preceding tables and deforestation rates cited in the footnote at the beginning of this chapter." It will not surprise you by now that nowhere in

Figure 41-1. Timber growth in the United States, 1955–1974.

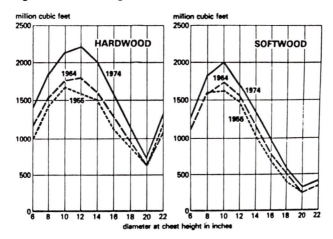

* Source: Redrawn from *Council on Environmental Quality, Ninth Annual Report*, 1978, p. 321.

the earlier tables could I find trend data that would serve as the basis for the projections given.

Item: fish. "The world harvest of fish is expected to rise little, if at all, by the year 2000." Here at last we find trend data from 1955 to 1975. But as I view the data—my series in Table 41-1 contain some data GTS does not show—it seems to me that it would be imprudent to bet against the fish catch increasing. Furthermore, any slowing in the marine fish catch could well have been the result of such man-made factors as the rise in prices for ship fuel, and the extension of national sovereignty further from the shores, rather than of the "over-exploitation of the sea" as the doomsayers have charged.

Item: population. GTS recommends that the U.S. should "cooperate with other nations in efforts to relieve poverty and hunger, stabilize population, and enhance economic and environmental production." But there are not now, and there never have been, any empirical data showing that population growth or size or density have a negative effect upon the standard of living, the level of pollution, or any other important measure of human welfare. This has emerged from historical time-series studies, and from cross-sectional studies of both more-developed and less-developed countries. And this non-finding is the more persuasive because it is despite the zealous efforts of large numbers of researchers who have sought to back their Malthusian logic with empirical proof. There is, therefore, no general reason other than personal intuition to conclude that population growth is necessarily for the worse—unless one simply believes

**Figure 41-2a. Growing Stock on Commercial Timberland in the United States
(all species)**

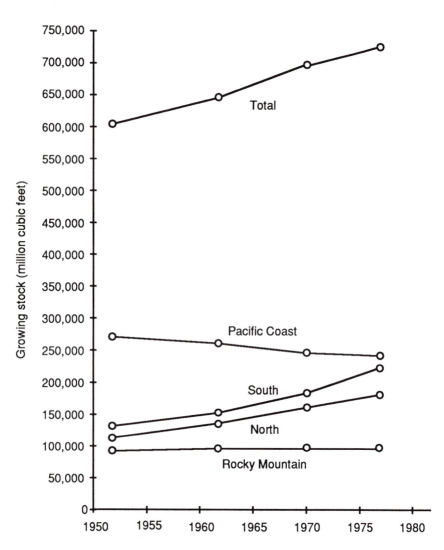

*Source: An Analysis of the Timber Situation in the United States
1952-2030,* U.S. Department of Agriculture, Forest Services, 1982.

Figure 41-2b. Softwood Growing Stock on Commercial Timberland in the United States.

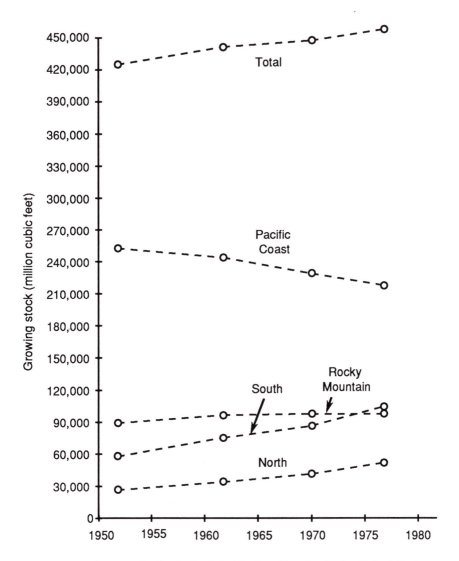

Source: An Analysis of the Timber Situation in the United States 1952-2030, U.S. Department of Agriculture, Forest Services, 1982.

**Figure 41-2c. Net Volume of Growing Stock on Commercial Timberland in
the United States
(hardwoods)**

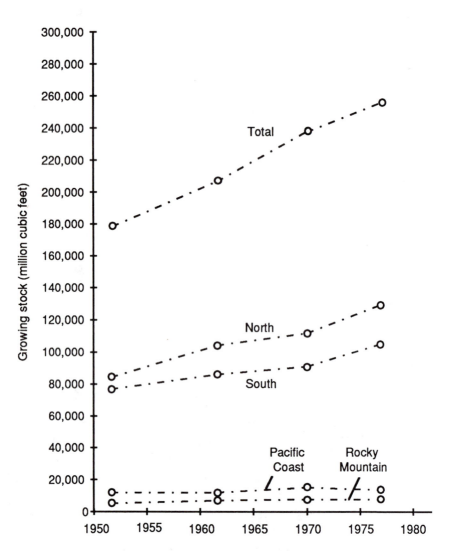

Source: An Analysis of the Timber Situation in the United States
1952-2030, U.S. Department of Agriculture, Forest Services, 1982.

that human beings are an evil in themselves, or that human life is too horrible to be lived.

Item: world land. "Arable land will increase only 4 percent by 2000." But why should that be so, given that arable land increased fully 16 percent in the 20 years from 1950 to 1970? The basis of the GTS estimate is simply "Global 2000 projections." One can, of course, make a convincing logical case for the fixity of land supply—but it is the same case that has been made over and over since at least Biblical times. Yet people have continued to increase the supply of arable land while making nonsense of the argument. Twenty and a hundred years hence, there probably will be the same confrontation between fixity theory and the facts of continuing expansion of agricultural land.

Item: acid rain. "Acid rain from increased combustion of fossil fuels (especially coal) threatens damage to lakes, soils, and crops." Maybe so. Here we encounter the sea-monster nature of pollution threats. As soon as one threatening arm is cut off and shown harmless, another rapidly takes its place. Since I started casually watching this scene in 1970, there have been mercury, fluorcarbons, DDT, the warming of the atmosphere, the cooling of the atmosphere, recombinant DNA research, saccharine, and a dozen others (including even garbage, which was said to overwhelm us soon). When the facts showed that these threats were either under control or manageable, new threats arose. Unfortunately, the number of potential threats is infinite.

Item: population density. Global 2000 says that in the future the world will be more crowded. There surely will be more people on earth in the year 2000 than there are now, barring a calamity. But a growing population does not imply that human living on the globe will be more "crowded" in any meaningful fashion. As the world's people have increasingly higher incomes, they purchase better housing and mobility. The homes of the world's people progressively have more floorspace, which means people dwell in less-crowded space with more privacy. The United States, for which data are readily available, illustrates the trends in developed countries, as discussed in Selection 1.

The world's people are getting better roads and more vehicles; therefore they can move around more freely, and have the benefits of a wider span of area. In the U.S., paved highways have increased from zero to over 3 million miles since the turn of the century. Natural park areas have been expanding (Figure 1-4a). And trips to parks have increased to an extraordinary degree (Figure 1-4b). These trends mean that people increasingly have much more space available and accessible to them.

Item: Regional water shortages will become more severe. In the previous decade or so, water experts have concluded that the "likelihood of the world running out of water is zero." The recent UN Report of the World Environment, for example, tells us not to focus upon the ratio between physical water supply and use, as Global 2000 does nevertheless, and emphasizes making appopriate social and economic as well as technological choices. From this flows "cautious hope from improved methods of management." That is, an appropriate structure of property rights, institutions, and pricing systems, together with some modicum of wisdom in choosing among the technological options open to us, can provide water for our growing needs at reasonable cost indefinitely.

Moreover, Global 2000's statements about the world's future water situation are completely inconsistent with—in fact, are completely opposed to—Global 2000's own analysis of what can reasonably be said about the world's water resources. It develops a sound analysis that finds that no reasonable or useful forecasts can be made about the world's water supply, but then proceeds to offer frightening forecasts totally inconsistent with its analysis. This inconsistency should be more than sufficient grounds to reject Global 2000's gloomy conclusions out of hand.

The Really Bad News

You may wonder: How can GTS get away with work so shoddy? The answer to the question, is, I think, another question. Who is there to stop them? In a democratic society, the staff of a government agency with access to a printing budget can publish whatever it chooses. There is no censor. Nor is there a "truth auditor" on the government payroll the way there are financial auditors to monitor money irregularities. As to outside checks, an individual outside the government must have the stomach to get into a long-odds fight against an opposition that is widely presumed to be in the right because it is "official." He or she must also be willing to invest the time and energy knowing that the probability of reaching a wide audience is exceedingly slim, especially if the government report says things that are already widely believed. The very best scholar is likely to judge that it is more important to get on with his or her own work rather than try to act as a one-person truth squad. Journalists seldom have the time and patience for deep digging into the scientific literature. So—*who is there to stop them?*

What damage comes from these unfounded predictions of a gloomy future? We cannot be sure, of course. I speculate, however, that the doomsaying in the past decade has sapped our national will. It may have led us to expect inexorable punishment for our supposed sins against nature, and for our exploitation of those persons viewed as living closer to a natural state in their poverty. The prophecy of such retribution may be self-fulfilling because we reduce our efforts to improve our situation, economic and political.

The saddest part of the Global 2000 Study is this vision I have of two staff members who happen to see this review. Alpha: "Nasty, isn't it?" Beta: "Sure, but bad reviews didn't hurt *Limits to Growth,* did they?" I'm afraid Beta is correct. The conclusions of GTS, the official government report with its "government model," will be cited as authoritative until the next GTS lookalike comes along, at which time the new authority will supplant the old without causing any changes at all. That's really bad news.

42

Introduction to *The Resourceful Earth*

A response and counterforce to The Global 2000 Report to the President *(see Selection 41) seemed desperately needed. Herman Kahn and I independently conceived of putting together a group of authoritative scientists who would address the issues raised in* Global 2000. *Officials at the Environmental Protection Agency also thought of producing a response. Somehow we all found each other, and Herman and I joined forces. Before we started, however, EPA was no longer associated with the venture, being replaced by Heritage Foundation and the freely given support of Burton Pines and Edwin Fuelner. And then Herman died too soon.*

The strategy was to find for each topic that scientists whose knowledge of the subject Herman and I agreed was first-rate, and who had previously written a magisterial review essay on or close to the topic in question. The latter requirement meant that producing the chapters we sought would not be a major undertaking for our authors, and therefore could be done quickly. It was to be a matter of updating and refocusing a previous essay, in most cases. This strategy worked well, and we were able to issue the volume in a hurry, in cooperation with the excellent and unusually speedy publishing processes overseen by René Olivieri and Christopher Kerr of Basil Blackwell.

The Resourceful Earth *chapters were produced without a penny's added cost to the public. The chapters were published exactly as written, with the authors having final authority over their chapters without bureaucratic tampering. This process contrasted with the staff-written and politically edited* Global 2000; *more details are given below about the process of financing, writing, and editing* Global 2000 *and* The Resourceful Earth.

From "Introduction" to *The Resourceful Earth,* edited by Julian L. Simon and Herman Kahn (New York: Basil Blackwell, 1984).

When the environmental movement learned of the cooperation of the Environmental Protection Agency with the editors—our views about Global 2000 *and our analyses of resources and environment already being on record—there began a campaign to prevent the project from being funded. The campaign included such public ventures as a leaked story in* The New York Times, *protest letters from congressmen to EPA, and a press release from Stanford University; the private politicking cannot be documented, but was widespread; and EPA never came through with funding.*

We initiated the project in May 1982 before it was certain that EPA would not fund it, because we found low-budget backup support from Heritage and because we were too impatient to wait for the EPA funding battle to come to an end. Along the way we offered to sell the product to any major government agency or responsible individual for just $1, but there were no takers. Our aim in making that offer was to obtain an "official" label for the volume. We adjudged that it was its "official" label that obtained such wide circulation for Global 2000.

The fact that The Resourceful Earth *received considerable attention early on was a pleasant surprise to us. But we had written that if a tenth or even a twentieth of the number of copies of* The Resourceful Earth *are sold as of* Global 2000, *one of us would eat a copy of this introduction—with an appropriate sauce, of course. Our digestions never were in danger of suffering that indignity.*

The original 1980 *Global 2000 Report to the President* (*Global 2000* hereafter) is frightening. It received extraordinarily wide circulation, and it has influenced crucial governmental policies. But it is dead wrong. Now *The Resourceful Earth*, a response to *Global 2000*, presents the relevant reliable trend evidence which mainly reassures rather than frightens.

Two paragraphs summarize the "Major Findings and Conclusions" of *Global 2000* on its page 1:

If present trends continue, the world in 2000 will be more crowded, more polluted, less stable ecologically, and more vulnerable to disruption than the world we live in now. Serious stresses involving population, resources, and environment are clearly visible ahead. Despite greater material output, the world's people will be poorer in many ways than they are today.

For hundreds of millions of the desperately poor, the outlook for food and other necessities of life will be no better. For many it will be worse. Barring revolutionary advances in technology, life for most people on earth will be more precarious in 2000 than it is now—unless the nations of the world act decisively to alter current trends.

To highlight our differences as vividly as possible, we restate the above summary with our substitutions in italics:

If present trends continue, the world in 2000 will be *less crowded* (though more populated), *less polluted, more stable ecologically,* and *less vulnerable to resource-supply disruption* than the world we live in now. Stresses involving population, resources, and environment *will be less in the future than now* . . . The world's people will be *richer* in most ways than they are today. . . . The outlook for food and other necessities of life will be *better* . . . life for most people on earth will be *less precarious* economically than it is now.

The high points of our findings are as follows:

1. Life expectancy has been rising rapidly throughout the world, a sign of demographic, scientific, and economic success. This fact—at least as dramatic and heartening as any other in human history—must be fundamental in any informed discussion of pollution and nutrition.
2. The birthrate in less developed countries has been falling substantially during the past two decades, from 2.2 percent yearly in 1964–5 to 1.75 percent in 1982–3, probably a result of modernization and of decreasing child mortality, and a sign of increased control by people over their family lives.
3. Many people are still hungry, but the food supply has been improving since at least World War II, as measured by grain prices, production per consumer, and the famine death rate.
4. Trends in world forests are not worrying, though in some places deforestation is troubling.
5. There is no statistical evidence for rapid loss of species in the next two decades. An increased rate of extinction cannot be ruled out if tropical deforestation is severe, but no evidence about linkage has yet been demonstrated.
6. The fish catch, after a pause, has resumed its long upward trend.
7. Land availability will not increasingly constrain world agriculture in coming decades.
8. In the U.S., the trend is toward higher-quality cropland, suffering less from erosion than in the past.
9. The widely published report of increasingly rapid urbanization of U.S. farmland was based on faulty data.
10. Water does not pose a problem of physical scarcity or disappearance, although the world and U.S. situations do call for better institutional management through more rational systems of property rights.
11. The climate does not show signs of unusual and threatening changes.

12. Mineral resources are becoming less scarce rather than more scarce, affront to common sense though that may be.
13. There is no persuasive reason to believe that the world oil price will rise in coming decades. The price may fall well below what it has been.
14. Compared to coal, nuclear power is no more expensive, and is probably much cheaper, under most circumstances. It is also much cheaper than oil.
15. Nuclear power gives every evidence of costing fewer lives per unit of energy produced than does coal or oil.
16. Solar energy sources (including wind and wave power) are too dilute to compete economically for much of humankind's energy needs, though for specialized uses and certain climates they can make a valuable contribution.
17. Threats of air and water pollution have been vastly overblown; these processes were not well analyzed in *Global 2000*.

We are confident that the nature of the physical world permits continued improvement in humankind's economic lot in the long run, indefinitely. Of course there are always newly arising local problems, shortages, and pollutions, due to climate or to increased population and income. Sometimes temporary large-scale problems arise. But the nature of the world's physical conditions and the resilience in a well-functioning economic and social system enable us to overcome such problems, and the solutions usually leave us better off than if the problem had never arisen; that is the great lesson to be learned from human history.

We are less optimistic, however, about the constraints currently imposed upon material progress by political and institutional forces, in conjunction with popularly held beliefs and attitudes about natural resources and the environment, such as those urged upon us by *Global 2000*. These contraints include the views that resource and environmental trends are toward deterioration rather than toward improvement, that there are physical limits that will increasingly act as a brake upon progress, and that nuclear energy is more dangerous than energy from other sources. These views lead to calls for subsidies and price controls, as well as government ownership and management of resource production, and government allocation of the resources that are produced. To a considerable extent the U.S. and the rest of the world already suffer from such policies (for example, on agriculture in Africa), and continuation and intensification could seriously damage resource production and choke economic progress. In particular, refusal to use nuclear power could hamper the U.S. in its economic competition with other nations, as well as cause unnecessary deaths in coal mining and other types of conventional energy production.

We wish that there were grounds to believe that a shift in thinking will take place on these matters, but we do not find basis for firm hope. So in this respect we are hardly optimistic.

We also wish to emphasize that though the global situation may be reasonably satisfactory or improving in some given respect, there are likely to be areas in which there are severe difficulties which may be on the increase. Such local problems may be due to local mismanagement, or they may be due to natural catastrophe which the larger community may not yet have been able to help mitigate. Such local problems should not be glossed over in any global assessment.

Background

Our positive statements about the recession of the physical constraints upon human progress are based primarily upon presently known progress, not taking into account possible or even likely advancements in technology. If we were to take into account such possibilities as the resources available to us in space and other such advances—even those possibilities which are already solidly worked out scientifically—our assessment would be much more "optimistic" than it is.

Why the Extraordinary Differences between *Global 2000* and *The Resourceful Earth?*

The stark differences between *Global 2000* and *The Resourceful Earth* cry out for explanation. There are several causes:

1. *The Resourceful Earth* relies heavily on trend data, which we present in abundance. *Global 2000* said that trend data are the proper basis for such an analysis, but nevertheless presented few such data. (It is ironic that we follow this recommendation of *Global 2000*, whereas the original did not follow its own advice.) Our projections of agriculture and natural resource availability exemplify the fundamental role of such trend data.
2. Even in the rare cases in which *Global 2000* did present trend series, it heavily weighted a few recent observations, rather than looking at the long-run trends. The fish catch may serve as an example. *Global 2000* presented a data series ending in 1975, and it extrapolated continued stagnation from the last few years' data leading up to 1975. Data for the years since 1975, which we show, indicate that in spite of the extraordinary rise and fall of the Peruvian anchovy fishery in the 1960s and 1970s, the long-run trend toward a larger catch has resumed, as we

would have expected based on the overall trend in the series, though the rate of increase may have been decreasing.

3. *Global 2000* drew far-reaching conclusions about many issues in the almost total absence of data. The rate of deforestation, and of species loss, are two examples. Reinspection of the skimpy data used to "demonstrate" species loss reveals that *Global 2000*'s extrapolation from those scraps of evidence is quite unsupported by the evidence. Our further investigation of deforestation time-series provides much firmer ground for our unworried assessments than the one-time survey data provided for *Global 2000*'s alarming projections.

4. *Global 2000* relied on inappropriate assumptions for its projections. For example, it projected that food prices would double, in large part because it assumed that energy prices would go up. This assumption about energy prices was unsound in several demonstrable ways. First, there was no sound reason simply to assume without evidence that energy prices would rise, especially in the face of the long-run trend of falling energy prices. Second, *Global 2000* focused on the price of energy rather than the price of fertilizer, the production of which accounts for much of the use of petroleum in agriculture. The price of fertilizer has been falling in the 1970s, due to technological improvements, even despite energy price rises. Perhaps most important, *Global 2000* implicitly assumed that private farmers do not respond to economic incentives to produce more food, which is as wrong as any assumption possibly could be.

5. There are glaring inconsistencies among *Global 2000*'s statements about particular matters in its various chapters. The very pessimistic assertions in the summary (Volume I) conflict sharply with statements in the working papers (Volume II).

The Forecasting Capacity of Government

The Resourceful Earth is not "the U.S. Government's projections," as *Global 2000* said about itself, or the projections of any other organization. Rather, *The Resourceful Earth* is a compendium of work by independent U.S. scientists who are employed outside the government, and who are considered authorities by their scientific peers. The work has not passed through any bureaucratic editing. Other authorities probably would disagree with some of our emphases and evaluations, but few (if any) would disagree with the trend facts adduced here.

The fact that the writers of *The Resourceful Earth* are outside government is crucial, in our view, because we believe that government agencies are not well-equipped to produce sound assessments of long-run future trends concerning resources. Too often the agency making the assessment has an axe to grind that derives from its perceived mission and which biases its forecasts. Furthermore, staff-produced government reports must pass through reviews at various stages up the chain of command, and the final conclusions of the staff report, therefore, are likely to emphasize conventional views and to reduce the range of opinion expressed. The resulting work cannot then be attributed to individuals, and no individuals need take full responsibility. In contrast, individuals take full responsibility in *The Resourceful Earth,* and our reputations hang on the quality of the work. Our aim here is not to denigrate the efforts of capable, hard-working, and dedicated civil servants, or to suggest that all (or even most) bureaucratic review is bad. Rather our aim is to point out that internally prepared assessments can and do suffer scientifically because of the organizational forces that prevail in government no matter what the administration. (If all this sounds a bit holier-than-thou, please forgive us. We admit we are proud of *The Resourceful Earth*'s independence as well as convinced of the importance of this fact.)

By its own admission, *Global 2000* did indeed present the public with views distorted by such bureaucratic procedures. Gerald Barney, director of *Global 2000,* has written, for example, that much "misunderstanding" was caused by the first four words on page 1 of Volume I in the "Major Findings and Conclusions" section, "If present trends continue." He notes that

> the statement "If present trends continue . . ." was that of an editor at CEQ, and although I objected to the statement as incorrect, it was not possible to have it corrected. (Barney, 1982, p. 9)

If bureaucratic editing can have that much effect, little in such an "official" report as *Global 2000* can be considered scientifically reliable.

Still another disability of internal "government" analyses is that they are often a hodge-podge of elements of unknown origin and nature. Barney says that *Global 2000* suffered from this disability, too. "The technological assumptions were left entirely to the professionals in the government's agencies" (Barney, 1982, p. 9), and were not necessarily the assumptions that the director or staff would have chosen. Independent outside studies of the sort that underlie *The Resourceful Earth* are less vulnerable to this danger. Again, the individual authors of *The Resourceful Earth* take full responsibility for the assumptions they make.

After completion of *Global 2000,* Barney made clear how troublesome these institutional circumstances are in carrying out a study such as that one:

> As they have evolved, the Government's agencies now have a hidden layer of decision makers—computer programmers and modelers. These decision makers

are, by and large, very skilled professionals, but they are often working in institutional circumstances which prevent them taking into account all the factors they know should be taken into account. Furthermore, the assumptions that they make have a profound influence on the range of policy options considered by senior government officials, and their assumptions are not well documented, are not understood by senior government officials, and are not available for peer review and comment. (Barney, 1982, p. 3)

The inability of government agencies to predict resource trends, and the ill effects of such "official" but badly made forecasts, would be amusing if not so sad. After a sharp price rise in the late 1970s, timber prices in 1983 fell about three-quarters, causing agony for lumber companies that contracted for government timber at the high prices.

Industry trade groups argue that the government owes the industry help because its policies led to the bidding disaster. In the late 1970s, [an industry spokesman] says, government economists predicted timber shortages and helped to fan the bidding. (*The Wall Street Journal*, 1 April 1983, p. 13)

The Department of Energy caused havoc for airplane manufacturers and airlines, for a host of other industries, and for foreign governments by its forecasts that the price of oil would continue to rise after 1979. And that was the forecast in *Global 2000*, in contrast to the editors of this volume and of the authors of the chapters on oil, who are all on record as predicting that the price would *not* continue to rise. The same story describes the recent histories of the other raw materials, too. (Being right does not endear one to others, or make one's opinions more sought, as a rule.) Does this history constitute the basis for increasing the role of government in these matters, or of decreasing it?

We suggest that it would be sensible to compare systematically the record of long-run government forecasts against the record of a reasonable sample of forecasts made outside the government, before making any decision in favor of further centralization. The only available data, those of Ascher (1978), suggest no advantage to government forecasts over private forecasts. To proceed without evidence of a governmental advantage in the activity would not seem responsible legislation.

We know of no body of scientific evidence assessing the effects of ill-founded pessimistic forecasts about resources and the environment upon public morale, innovation, and economic progress. We are agreed, however, that we adjudge the effects, past and future, to be severe and costly.

Political Fruits of *Global 2000*

Enter now the Global Tomorrow Coalition, an umbrella organization consisting (as of October 1982) of 49 environmentalist and population organizations with total membership of 5 million persons; it represents the Global 2000 movement that has evolved since the publication of *Global 2000*. In response to the circumstances mentioned in the quotation from Gerald Barney above, Barney and the Global Tomorrow Coalition are calling for more government computer modeling in the form of a "government global model," and for more centralized control of that modeling. "[I]ncreased coordination of models development and documentation (sic) is needed by the Executive Office of the President" (Barney, 1982, p. 3). Barney sees the matter as follows:

> Some of the problems of using computer-based models are illustrated by the difficulties encountered in using the government's models to conduct the *Global 2000* study. The *Global 2000* analysis was initiated with an eight-page memorandum listing all of the projections which would be needed for the study. This memorandum was circulated to the participating agencies along with an indication of which of the projections the agencies would be responsible for. The agencies were all visited and the most professional personnel, the best models, most current and complete data were located. The professionals were then asked to produce a first draft within six weeks.

> At the time the first drafts were due, a weekend-long retreat was held at the Belmont House in Maryland. The primary discovery at that meeting was that none of the professionals directly responsible for the long-term global analysis in each of the participating agencies had ever met. They were total strangers. The energy expert had never met the water expert. The food expert had never met the population expert, etc. As a result, our first priority was to make acquaintance and begin the process of seeing that the assumptions being used by the various departments were as internally consistent as we could make them.

> At that time we also began the analysis of the content of the models. We knew in advance that the Government does not have what is normally thought of as a "global model," i.e., a single model containing separate interacting sectors dealing with the population, resources, and environment. We discovered, however, the Government does have a "global model." In the Government's global model, the population sector is located in a computer at the Bureau of the Census. The energy sector is located in a different computer at the Department of Energy. The food sector is located in a different computer at the Department of Agriculture, etc.

> In analyzing these sectoral models, we discovered that they are in fact an interacting set of global sectoral models that collectively constitute the Government's global model. Each of the sectors needs information from the others. The energy sector for example, needs economic and demographic and water projections for input. The population projections require information on the social and economic conditions that influence fertility and mortality rates as inputs. The food model needs information on fertilizer and energy prices, on water availability, economic conditions, and demographic trends.

> In analyzing these models, we found that information was flowing from one sectoral model to another even though the persons responsible for the models

did not know each other. The medium of communication was the Government Printing Office. Studies were prepared with one sector of the Government's global model, sent off to the Government Printing Office, printed, purchased by another government agency, and the results entered into another sector of the Government's global model. In the process of conducting the *Global 2000* study, we introduced all the Government's professionals to each other, expediting interaction among the models by a factor of perhaps as much as a million simply by bypassing the normal mode of communication through the Government Printing Office. (Barney, 1982, pp. 16–18)

At the behest of the Global Tomorrow Coalition and its member organizations, legislation concerning "foresight capability" with respect to population and resource is now (August 1983) before the Congress. Integrating the various models used in government into a single grand "global model" is one of the objectives of these bills. Another aim is to establish an "Office of Research and Policy Analysis on Global Population, Resources, Energy and the Environment" (Willson memo, 17 September 1982, p. iii).

We do not share the belief that such integration of models will advance "global foresight capability." One of the outcomes of our preparation of *The Resourceful Earth* is that we believe even more strongly than ever that creating one big "government global model" by hooking up the various sectoral models used by various government agencies will *not* improve long-run predictions concerning the topics to which *Global 2000* is addressed. We have great respect for some computer models; almost all of the authors of *The Resourceful Earth* are heavy users of such models in our own work. But we are wary of the call for a governmental "global model" of the sort envisaged by the Global 2000 movement for these reasons:

1. Models that are developed for one purpose often are fatally flawed for other purposes; using them for such other purposes is likely to produce fallacious results. For example, a model intended to estimate the price and usage of oil in the U.S. in the short run of, say, the next month or year, will probably give worse results than no model at all for predicting price and usage in the long run of 5 or 10 years. Some of the key factors that operate in the long run—such as the substitution of other fuels in response to increased prices of oil—are not likely to be included in the short-run model.

2. We do not agree that data on all (or even on most, or some) of the various elements discussed in *Global 2000* are crucial inputs for predicting the other elements. For example, the future price of energy is not a key input for estimating the future price and quality of food; actions by governments concerning agricultural price controls and subsidies, and the amount of agricultural research done, among other forces, are likely to be

far more important in the long run of 20 and more years. Population growth may even not be a central variable if viewed in the conventional fashion of more people implying a higher price of food; in the long run the effect may be the opposite, as greater population density leads to better farm-to-market transportation, and to a host of institutional and technological developments, as has been the history of humanity until now. Ignoring most or all of the interdependencies among the sectors touched on by *Global 2000* may not be disastrous, as *Global 2000* suggests it is and necessarily will be. It may even be a prudent scientific strategy to ignore them. (This assertion may seem preposterous until you examine the track records of predictions about resources and environment made without extensive consideration of such interdependencies, and compare them with predictions of the global modelers who insist—at least in principle—on including such interdependencies in models.)

3. The strength of computer simulation models for prediction is dealing with the following type of problem: (a) each of the relevant intereacting forces is understood rather well, and (b) there is relatively little uncertainty about the underlying conditions, but (c) there are too many such forces for an analyst to be able to sort them out with paper and pencil alone. Properly programmed for the behavior of each of the forces, and their interactions and feedbacks, the great calculating power of the computer can work through the large number of necessary computations to arrive at a better answer than can an analyst without the aid of such computing power.

The analytic problems confonted by *Global 2000* have quite different characteristics, however, not only because the interaction of the individual elements is not well understood as yet—a drawback that has properly been emphasized by *Global 2000* and by its director after the completion of the Report—but even more because the key assumptions cannot be made with confidence. In the illustrative case of energy again, *Global 2000* believed it necessary to feed energy price forecasts into the agricultural and the resource models. But what forecast of energy prices should be used? That forecast must depend on such factors as whether OPEC will collapse, the state of future public opinion toward nuclear power from fission, and whether nuclear fission will become economical (which would affect the present price of oil even if fusion were not commercially available for decades). These are the kinds of considerations for which simple paper-and-pencil analyses are likely to prove best (perhaps with the help of the computer for parts of the analysis). The sort of "scenario" analysis offered in our chapter on the demand for oil exemplifies such analyses.

A major advantage of paper-and-pencil analyses is that they clearly reveal the extent of the uncertainties, and thereby reduce the likelihood of carrying faulty partial analyses from one part of an overall global assessment to another. The writers of *Global 2000* and the Global Tomorrow Coalition believe that more intensive and more integrated modeling is the answer; we believe that such reliance on complex modeling was responsible for the confusion caused in *Global 2000*'s agricultural analysis by the introduction into that analysis of the computer-generated forecast of energy prices.

Nobel prizewinner Gunnar Myrdal commented as follows on complex modeling, in the context of the Club of Rome's "Report," *The Limit to Growth*, of which *Global 2000* is a direct lineal descent both in its personnel and its approach to modeling:

> [T]he use of mathematical equations and a huge computer, which registers the alternatives of abstractly conceived policies by a "world simulation model," may impress the innocent public but has little, if any, scientific validity. That this "sort of model is actually a new tool for mankind" is unfortunately not true. It represents quasi-learnedness of a type that we have, for a long time, had too much of, not least in economics, when we try to deal with problems simply in "economic terms."

> In the end, those conclusions from the [*Limits to Growth*] Report's analysis that are at all sensible are not different and definitely not more certain than could have been reached without the elaborate apparatus by what Alfred Marshall called "hard simple thinking aware of the limitations of what we know." (Myrdal, 1975, pp. 204–5)

Great difficulties were caused for *Global 2000* by reliance upon the outputs of various computer models, which were inconsistent with each other and with judgments derived from other sources. This is starkly revealed in the section called "Closing the Loops," which deals with the environmental consequences of various projections of population and resources given elsewhere in *Global 2000*. As a reviewer noted:

> Whereas the report up to this point has emphasized the environmental impacts of the projections, now the direction of the analysis is reversed and the authors explore the effect of environmental considerations on the realism of the projections. This is a commendable undertaking for it reveals inconsistencies among the projections. But it is virtually a total repudiation of the projections made by the agencies and as modified by the *Global 2000* staff. Time and time again, the earlier projections are characterized as inadequate, incomplete, inconsistent, or inaccurate. Originally, the federal agencies' assistance had been sought because of their expertise, but here the study staff substitutes its judgments for those of the agencies.

> Why was such a curious and circuitous process followed? Once the projections were considered unreliable, why were they then published, only to be refuted? One is left to guess at the reasons, but whatever they may be, their effect is

confusing at best. At worst, the abrupt turnabout raises questions about the credibility of the entire project. (Clawson, 1981, p. 20)

4. Another perspective on the matter of "centralized foresight": a larger place for government activity in this field implies a smaller place for outside assessments—that is, fewer assessments such as we are now offering in *The Resourceful Earth*. More reliance upon a "government global computer model" implies less reliance on assessments built upon the entire armamentarium of scientific tools, including wide-ranging experience and historical perspective, such as is the approach of *The Resourceful Earth*. In considering the desirability of our approach compared with "centralized foresight" and a "government global model," it would seem prudent to compare track records. Many of the authors represented in *The Resourceful Earth* are on record with forecasts made more than a decade ago which ran exactly counter to the forecasts of the gloom-and-doom modelers in *The Limits to Growth* tradition, in the middle of which squarely stands *Global 2000*. And *The Resourceful Earth* authors were correct—especially on such topics as nutrition and famine; climate; pollution in the U.S.; prices and supplies of agricultural products, mineral resources, and oil. In contrast, the global modelers were dead wrong. Such a comparison does not build confidence or lend support for placing more rather than less reliance upon global modelers in *The Limits-to-Growth*-cum-*Global 2000* tradition. Comparison of predictive success would seem to recommend more reliance upon wide-ranging and independent outside studies such as we offer here, and less reliance upon global computer-simulation modeling in the view of *The Limits to Growth* and *Global 2000*.

5. Staff-performed government studies such as *Global 2000* have a built-in tendency toward self-perpetuating error in their chosen method of modeling by compilation of other government studies. (Barney said that *Global 2000* "should be thought of as an image of the future as seen by government agencies, rather than as an independent study of the subject." This is in stark contrast with *The Resourceful Earth*, which stands on its own, and can duck no responsibility for error by pinning the blame upon other studies which served as our base.) The self-perpetuating nature of the process may already be seen in the many government reports since *Global 2000* that base *their* conclusions upon *Global 2000* as a source of authoritative information.

6. Studies performed inside government are more subject to manipulation by political pressure groups than are studies by independent scholars. For example, governments usually do not like to say that a report which they urged upon the world was out-and-out wrong. Diplomats worry about

"credibility." Such a disavowal seems "unstatesmanlike," especially when a report is labeled "The U.S. government projection" as is *Global 2000*. Therefore, governments usually try to do an about-face without showing the movement—now you see it, now you don't.

7. Once a model is entrenched inside a government agency, it is likely to remain in use long after it is no longer credible, due to lack of channels for independent criticism. A frightening example of this tendency has recently surfaced right smack in the middle of the context of Club of Rome *Limits to Growth* models (as are also *Global 2000* and the Global 2000 movement's recommendation for further work). The Department of Defense—or more specifically, the Strategic Plans and Policy Branch of the Military Studies and Analysis Division of the Command and Control Technical Center (CCTC/C313)—uses as its "major analytic tool" what it calls the "World Integrated Model" ("WIM"), which is an outgrowth of the Mesarovic-Pestel model, which in turn was the Club of Rome's first successor to its *Limits to Growth* model. This DOD adaptation dates from 1974, and continues on its merry way regardless of the fact that the Mesarovic-Pestel and *Limits to Growth* models have been damned as foolishness or fraud by every serious economic critic; for example, Myrdal's assessment. No scientific support or even scientific publication—where criticism is possible—is cited for DOD's WIM model, and though its operators talk about comparing the output with actual data from 1975 to 1980, apparently no such comparison has been made. Its operators refer to it as "the finest global forecasting model available today" (Hamilton memo, p. 6). But the only basis given for belief in its usefulness is the following laudatory remarks from an "Executive Office of the President memorandum":

> Basically the Mesarovic-Pestel (WIM) is in a class to itself. There appear to be no detailed dynamic feedback models of similar quality that take a world perspective. The model incorporates a great deal of knowledge and has a strong systems perspective. (Hamilton memo, p. 5)

The WIM is run at great cost to the taxpayer; 2–3 person-years are required just to *update* the WIM model every 2 years; far more than the cost of the entire *The Resourceful Earth* enterprise. Worse, the WIM output is used for "strategic" purposes, on the assumption that there is a connection between impending violence, and the WIM model's forecasts about raw material and population forecasts.

In brief, WIM is a model using an economic framework and publicly available economic data, built and operated without roots in the community of professional economists and without publication for examination in the economic literature (none is cited in its list of references), and using a basic model (*Limits to Growth* type) universally condemned by economists who have looked into it. Yet so seductive is this kind of work that it continues to help shape the nation's fortunes.

In short, we must not be seduced by the magic that computer modeling promises but cannot deliver. Centralization of such modeling, as is called for by the Global Tomorrow Coalition, is particularly dangerous because it reduces the opportunity for independent checks upon erroneous programming and inappropriate assumptions. Difficult and unpleasant as it is for many people to accept, it is crucial to understand that governments are not repositories of wisdom, and can be as mistaken on crucial matters—including scientific issues—as the least-educated layman. Such understanding is especially important because of the Global Tomorrow Coalition's current push toward "centralized foresight."

Recommendations

The Resourceful Earth aims to provide sound and balanced assessments of key issues concerning resources and the environment, and thereby to correct false, gloomy impressions left by *Global 2000*. Policy recommendations are not our mission, and practically no recommendations are contained in the chapters. However, we do have a few views about possible policies which we mention briefly in passing. (We have already expressed our views about a policy of centralizing the government's "foresight capability.")

The recommendations that flow from *Global 2000,* and which are at the core of the Global 2000 movement and the Global Tomorrow Coalition, are contained in *Global Future: Time to Act* (called *Global Future* hereafter). In the words of that document:

> *The Global 2000 Report* to the President identified the problems; it did not attempt to find solutions. The President then directed agencies of the government to undertake the next step—to look at present government programs related to these long-term global issues, assess their effectiveness, and recommend improvements. One of us, Gus Speth, Chairman of the Council on Environmental Quality (CEQ), chaired this effort. [The other was Edmund Muskie, Secretary of State.]
>
> The report that follows, prepared by the Council on Environmental Quality and the Department of State, responds to the President's charge. (1981, pp. iii–iv)

Global Future contains approximately 100 recommendations which fall into three general categories: (1) mobilize interest in the general topic among foreign governments and within the U.S. public; (2) increase U.S. spending in Global 2000-related programs; (3) create governmental institutions that will centralize activities concerning resources and the environment and require various governmental agencies to heed the recommendations of these "global oversight" institutions. The specific recommended programs cover so many activities in the U.S. and abroad that we will not even try to characterize them. We wish to focus attention, however, on the last of the ten sets of recommendations, those which *Global Future* classifies as "Institutional Changes: Improving Our National Capacity to Respond." These recommendations are:

Recommendations (quoted from Global Future): The United States should:

Establish a government center as coordinator to insure adequate data collection and modeling capability as the basis for policy analysis on long-term global population, resource, and environmental issues.

Improve the quality of data collection and modeling for global issues and promote wider access to data and models.

Establish a Federal Coordinating Unit, preferably in the Executive Office of the President, to develop federal policy and coordinate ongoing federal programs concerning global population, resource, and environmental issues. Activities should include coordinating data and modeling efforts described above; issuing biennial reports; assessing global population, resource, and environment problems; and serving as a focal point for development of policy on long-term global issues.

Adopt action-forcing devices, such as budget review procedures, a Presidential message, creation of a blue-ribbon commission, establishing an office in each federal agency to deal with long-term global issues, or passage of legislation formalizing a mandate to federal agencies to address long-term global issues and creating a federal coordinating unit and hybrid public-private institute.

Create the Global Population, Resources, and Environment Analysis Institute, a hybrid public-private institution, to strengthen and supplement federal government efforts on long-term global analyses.

Improve the budget process to make technical expertise of U.S. agencies more readily available to other countries.

Assure environmental review of major U.S. government actions significantly affecting natural or ecological resources of global importance; designate tropical forests, croplands, and coastal wetland-estuarine and reef ecosystems as globally important resources.

Continue to raise global population, resource, and environment issues in appropriate international forums; work with and support appropriate international organizations and other countries in formulating solutions.

Enlist the business community in formulating responses to long-term global problems.

Increase public awareness of global population, resources, and environment issues. (1981, pp. li–liii)

A closely related recommendation made elsewhere in *Global Future*:

Develop a U.S. national population policy that includes attention to issues such as population stabilization; availability of family planning programs; just, consistent, and workable immigration laws; improved information needs; and institutions to ensure continued attention to domestic population issues. (1981, p. xxx)

The recommended government center deserves special attention. This is the full description:

Recommendation [of *Global Future*]: A single government center should act as coordinator for the federal government to insure availability of an adequate data and modeling capability to carry out policy analysis on long-term global population, resource, and environment issues. To be most effective, this center should be part of the Federal Coordinating Unit for policy, discussed below, or at least closely coordinated with it. The center should:

Identify long-range problems of global significance.

Promote the development of appropriate analytical tools and data required to assess long-term implications of global problems.

Coordinate and insure preparation, at timely intervals, of long-term projections of trends in global population, resources, and environment and carry out other studies related to these problems.

Prepare timely reports that assess the state of global modeling and data collection, evaluate these analytic activities in the federal government, and make recommendation for improvements.

Name lead agencies for each population, resource, and environment subject area to decide what data should be collected, by whom, and with what methodology.

Coordinate modeling activities of government agencies to insure linkage, feedback, and compatibility of data among various models.

Establish and support a nongovernmental center as part of the public-private Global Population, Resources, and Environment Analysis Institute, discussed below, to enhance global modeling and analysis. (1981, pp. 160–1)

We disagree with all of these recommendations by Global Future. Our reasons for disagreeing lie in one or more of these general propositions:

1. The public will be best served both in price and availability with respect to natural resources such as copper and oil, which are mainly produced by the private sector and whose environmental externalities can be dealt with by governmental rules in a reasonably routine fashion, if the

government takes no actions at all that affect production or distribution, except for building strategic stockpiles. (We do favor continued government funding of research in agriculture and some potential energy sources such as fusion.)

2. Scientific research and assessments of these topics should continue to be carried out independently in a variety of locations, rather than becoming more centralized than now. The government's policy tool affecting these activities is funding. We recommend against any funding for new government agencies of the sort envisioned by the Global 2000 movement by way of the Global Tomorrow Coalition or otherwise, unless that agency is able to win funding through competition in the normal research channels with peer-group review.

3. We believe that the government should *not* take steps to make the public more "aware" of issues concerning resources, environment, and population. We consider that the public has been badly served by having been scared by a very large volume of unfounded and/or exaggerated warnings about these matters. Many of these scientifically unsupported and injudicious warnings have derived from government agencies. The results have been disastrous from the standpoint of the allocation of social resources—for example, the contracts entered into by airlines for airplane manufacturers to build new fuel-saving airliners, contracts later cancelled by the airlines at high cost to all; the high price of natural gas resulting from long-term contracts to pay-or-take entered into on the assumption that energy prices would continue to rise; the federal regulations on average fuel mileage of automobiles sold by particular makers, leading to vast unnecessary expenditures for redesign, with consequent weakening of U.S. automobile firms; and federal grants to recycling centers that process waste at much higher social cost than ordinary waste disposal; we could fill a book with examples. The results of unfounded public fears about the future of resources and the environment probably have also caused declines in morale and the will to exert effort for continued improvements.

It is a matter of great public importance that we reverse these patterns of the 1960s and 1970s. The U.S. public must come to hear the truth that conditions have been getting better rather than worse, and that enthusiastic and vigorous efforts to do even better even faster will benefit the public as well as the individuals who act economically to bring about this social progress. In our view, the world is ready to turn its back on its pessimism, and is waiting to hear some good news. All the more reason to tell the true good news that there is to tell.

4. With respect to population growth in the U.S., whose "stabilization" is called for by the Global 2000 movement (as seen, for example, in the

recommendation by *Global Future*, p. 11, and in the bills before Congress urged by the Global 2000 movement), we make no recommendation other than that government should not attempt to influence individuals' family-size decisions in any fashion. Even if there were economic advantages to cessation of population growth in the U.S., too many wider issues and values are involved to justify such a far-reaching policy; human population is not simply an economic matter. We also do not consider it our place to discuss whether our government should attempt to stimulate fertility; we see no compelling economic reason for such a policy, and many sound reasons against discussion of the matter. Immigration is an extremely complex topic that is far beyond our purview—and beyond that of *Global 2000*, which implied, however, that immigration has been too great though *Global 2000* did not provide even the hint of a rationale for such a proposition.

Our viewpoint on population growth in the rest of the world is much the same as in the United States. Recommendations to other countries—and even more so, pressure upon them—to institute and carry out policies with respect to their population growth rates are not warranted by any facts about resources and population, and they constitute unjustifiable interference in the activities of other countries, because such policies must necessarily rest upon value judgments. Hence we consider that such recommendations by the Global 2000 movement are unfounded and unacceptable, ignorant and arrogant.

The cost of any policy recommendation should always be reckoned, even if the policy by itself might have positive effects. For example, the recommendation of the Global 2000 movement for government collection of more secondary "global" data seems unobjectionable, on its face. But there is no reason to presume that such collection or analysis of data would be done efficiently or cost-effectively. For example, the cost of *Global 2000* executed by the federal government was roughly 1 million dollars (Barney, 1982). The cost of *The Resourceful Earth*, carried out by independent scholars as an extension of the work they have been doing much of their professional lives, and in some cases which they have already largely completed or published in other contexts, is roughly $30,000, less than a thirtieth of *Global 2000*'s cost. Our contributors were paid out of private funds at the rate of $1000 per paper, truly only an "honorarium" for persons of this caliber and for work this serious; conference travel expenses took most of the rest. (Of course we believe that at *no* price would *Global 2000* have been a purchase of value.) This comparison, which we consider typical, does not build much confidence in the government's ability to spend taxpayers' money well for activities of this sort, and it testifies against internal staff-prepared reports on subjects that are essentially scientific.

As editors, it might be appropriate for us to boast in detail of the qualifications of our contributors. Instead of doing so, we suggest simply that you examine the lists of their writings and the writings themselves, check their professional histories in *Who's Who* and similar reference volumes, and compare those credentials with the credentials of the staff of persons who prepared *Global 2000,* listed in their introductory pages. Then think again about the costs of *Global 2000* and *The Resourceful Earth,* and what the public gets for its money with its expenditures for a staff-performed study such as *Global 2000.*

It does not follow that, because we are not proposing new things for governments to do about resources and the environment, we therefore think that nothing needs to be done. Much is being done spontaneously, by individuals, by non-governmental bodies, and by governments; and much more needs to be done. We believe, however, that it is a mistake to presume that the government usually handles these tasks better than, or even as well as, persons outside of government; sometimes government does better, sometimes worse. The case against government action is especially strong where there are relatively few difficult externalities, as is the case with the production of food, energy, and other natural resources.

Capsule Conclusion

The letter of transmittal of *Global 2000* to the President of the United States said:

> Our conclusions, summarized in the pages that follow, are disturbing. They indicate the potential for global problems of alarming proportions by the year 2000. Environmental, resource, and population stresses are intensifying and will increasingly determine the quality of human life on our planet. These stresses are already severe enough to deny many millions of people basic needs for food, shelter, health, and jobs, or any hope for betterment. At the same time, the earth's carrying capacity—the ability of biological systems to provide resources for human needs—is eroding. The trends reflected in the Global 2000 suggest strongly a progressive degradation and impoverishment of the earth's natural resource base.

We radically re-write the statement as follows:

> Our conclusions are reassuring, though not grounds for complacency. Global problems due to physical conditions (as distinguished from those caused by institutional and political conditions) are always possible, but are likely to be less pressing in the future than in the past. Environmental, resource, and

population stresses are diminishing, and with the passage of time will have less influence than now upon the quality of human life on our planet. These stresses have in the past always caused many people to suffer from lack of food, shelter, health, and jobs, but the trend is toward less rather than more of such suffering. Especially important and noteworthy is the dramatic trend toward longer and healthier life throughout all the world. Because of increases in knowledge, the earth's "carrying capacity" has been increasing throughout the decades and centuries and millenia to such an extent that the term "carrying capacity" has by now no useful meaning. These trends strongly suggest a progressive improvement and enrichment of the earth's natural resource base, and of mankind's lot on earth.

AFTER NOTE

Editors' Note on Economic Growth to the Year 2000 and Beyond

Underlying this volume's general point of view is the following implicit assumption about future economic growth in the world as a whole, and in the less-developed countries (LDCs) considered as a sector. We expect that in the long run—both before, and also subsequent to, the year 2000—economic growth will continue at a rate at least as fast as in the decades since World War II. The words "as fast as" are purposely vague with respect to absolute or percentage growth, because a similar rate of proportional growth in the long-run future, as in the past, would imply much faster (and ever-increasing) absolute growth that would soon have income at levels higher than ever seen before; the world's lack of economic experience with such high rates and income levels suggests we should be cautious about the possibility that such could be the case. Our intention is simply to imply that there is no reason to expect stagnation or a lower percentage rate of growth for the LDCs in the future compared to the past; this expectation is quite unlike the expectation stated by *Global 2000*.

Our main reason for making this assumption is that the history of mankind shows economic growth that generally has been proceeding at an increasing rather than a decreasing pace. This is true over the very long sweep of history as well as over the past century. And there is no persuasive structural reason—certainly not a shortage of raw materials, as we establish here—to expect that we are at a turning point now in that respect. Of course the world and the LDCs can find ways to do ourselves in, by such policies as pushing up the price of energy by foreswearing power from nuclear fission and from coal, or so structuring economic systems that incentives for individuals are reduced and the power of markets is choked off by government control. But we believe that if such disastrous policies are put in place, their effects will eventually teach nations to follow more productive policies—though perhaps only after economic growth has declined for a while.

Upon close inspection, the gloomy *Global 2000* projection of declining growth in per person income until the year 2000 is seen to arise directly and solely from the underlying assumption that the rate of increase in per person productivity will be declining. All the rest of their "modeling" depends entirely upon this key assumption. No justification is given for this key assumption, however. And the likely course of productivity change until the year 2000 is in sharp dispute by reasonable persons. A pessimist may cite the slowdown since 1973, which could be part of a cyclical downturn in the long upward trend. An optimist, on the other hand, may cite the fast world growth since 1950, and the observed rate of growth in the LDCs which is as high or higher than in the MDCs over that period (Morawetz, 1978); from the latter evidence an optimist may judge (as we do) that the recent downturn is not a reasonable basis for projecting a continued low rate of growth in coming decades. Additionally, international politics involving resource cartels such as OPEC, as well as domestic politics involving fiscal and monetary and welfare policies, can affect growth until 2000. And no one can build politics into an economic forecasting model with any confidence. So there obviously is much reason for lack of agreement about expectations for economic growth until the year 2000, and a confident forecast for that date itself would be foolish.

For the purposes of assessing and forecasting the state of *resources and environment* until the year 2000, however, it does not matter much whether the economic forecasts of even the extreme pessimists or the extreme optimists will prove to be the case; the availability of most resources and the cleanliness of the environment over only the next 17 years are not likely to be sensitive to such differences in income. Therefore we need not enter into detailed discussion of the matter; it would only obscure our main aim here. (It is not part of *The Resourceful Earth*'s mission to develop our own economic forecast, just as it was not part of *Global 2000*'s assignment.)

For the longer run, with some confidence we can say that future rates of economic growth no worse than those in the past will have many salutary effects upon the environment, as higher income permits countries and individuals to pay for cleaner, more attractive, and healthier living space. Similarly, higher income in the long run will probably lead to greater availability and lower prices of resources rather than greater scarcity and higher prices; such has been the entire course of human history, though in the short run increased income causes increased prices. Perhaps the largest and most threatening uncertainty connected with income growth concerns the climate, if there is continued fossil-fuel use rather than a shift to nuclear power; we assess that issue separately and at length later.

In short: for present purposes, detailed analysis and forecast of income growth until the year 2000 is unnecessary, and might misdirect the reader's attention from topics deserving that attention here. Therefore we shall not pursue the subject further.

43

An Interchange with Paul Ehrlich

An introduction to this interchange of articles and replies would be nugatory. I hope the reader will pay special attention to Ehrlich's use of evidence, his mode of argument, and his rhetoric. And note his extraordinary sentence in the third paragraph of his last response, in defense of using fallacious data—a denunciation of me as being nonscientific for proceeding in a fashion other than Ehrlich did and hence uncovering the error made by him and his colleagues.

Concerning Ehrlich's charge that I am guilty of the unredeemable sin of "alchemy," please see the introduction to my exchange with Garrett Hardin in the next selection, and Hardin's statements in the selection where he implicitly finds me innocent of the charge even as he is making the same charge himself.

Environmental Disruption or Environmental Improvement?—Julian L. Simon

The first sentence in Ehrlich's (1981) paper—"In my opinion, and that of virtually every ecologist I know, humanity is now faced with an unprecedented escalation of environmental disruption, a situation that threatens the persistence of civilization as we know it."—is a sweeping generalization, unsupported by data. And a wide variety of data contradict the assertion, as we shall see below. The evidence is at least as strong that the environment in the United States (and elsewhere in the world) is undergoing a repair process as it is that it is undergoing deterioration and disruption.

The first sentence, indeed the article as a whole, is vintage Ehrlich. After a dramatic broad statement without accompanying scientific justification, he asserts that a consensus of experts agree, labels anyone who

---

This work was supported in part by a grant from the Koret Foundation

disagrees a naif or an incompetent, and then draws far-reaching policy conclusions.

The first task of my paper is to examine the rhetoric used by Ehrlich, as an example of the practices of many writers who warn us of impending disaster from environmental and other catastrophes. The second task is to inquire why the fruits of these rhetorical methods are accepted and believed by so many people. I shall illustrate with examples from Ehrlich's present article, as well as from some of his other work, and incidentally give some relevant data which are not well known but which refute Ehrlich's first assertion, from which he has drawn inferences for public policy. I shall not take up Ehrlich's criticisms of economists, demographers and social scientists, both because I lack space and because the rapid-fire style in which the criticisms are made prevents me from getting a handle on the criticisms as a whole.

Some of the key elements I shall mention are these: disregard of historical trends about which we have facts; exaggerated statements justified by the putative public need to be warned of the seriousness of a threat; reduction of complex relationships to simple slogans; and employment of irrelevant theoretical ideas from other sciences. A charm of this particular paper is that in it Ehrlich charges social scientists with using some of these same misleading devices.

Disregard of Historical Facts

Ehrlich begins by saying that the environment's condition is getting worse, and at a rapid rate. Ehrlich does not define "environmental disruption" closely, but clearly he includes pollution (1981:14); "desertification" (1981:14); "loss of agricultural land to cities" by "paving over [and] plowing under" (1981: 14–15); "mining" (1981:15); and too much energy use (1981:14–15). Let us consider a few historical data on these matters; I have recently devoted a long paper to this topic (Selection 2), so I shall try to duplicate as little as possible here.

With respect to the main pollutions of the air, the available time series are short, but they are all I have been able to find in the reports of the Council on Environmental Quality or elsewhere. Figure 1-1 shows that the recent U.S. situation has been improving rather than deteriorating.

With respect to water quality, the key measure is drinkability. Figure 1-2 shows that by this measure, water quality in the United States has been getting better rather than worse.

The most global health index of pollution is life expectancy. The data show U.S. life expectancy continuing to rise, and at a faster rate—a gain of 2.6 years from 1970 to 1976, compared with a gain of only 0.8 in the entire decade of the 1960s (Metropolitan Life Insurance Company, 1977).

Of course one can point to specific places where environmental conditions have fared worse rather than better, and to specific pollutions that have increased. But a fair-minded assessment of the situation would not just "pick and choose," but would focus on these standard aggregate measures. One might also assert that the past tells us nothing about the future, because we are at a moment of discontinuity. But I know of no proof of such structural change, and without such proof such an assertion would be just that—an unproven assertion. More about this later.

About "loss of land" and "desertification": some arable land surely is deteriorating. But Ehrlich and current news stories imply a more general proposition: that the world's total supply of arable land is decreasing. Yet the truth is exactly the opposite: Kumar (1973) made a country-by-country survey of the changes in arable land from 1950 to 1960. His finding: there was 9 percent more total arable land in 1960 than in 1950 in the 87 countries (constituting 73 percent of the land area of the world) for which he could find data—a gain of almost 1 percent per year. And the more recent Food and Agriculture Organization data show a rise in "arable and permanent cropland" from 1403 to 1507 million hectares worldwide from 1961–65 to 1974, an annual increase of roughly 0.7 percent. In the developing countries the area increased by 1.1 percent annually over the decade 1960 to 1970 (FAO, 1975).

The increase in the quantity of land that is actually cultivated each year rose even faster—from 8.9 percent to 9.9 percent of the total area between 1950 and 1960. And the increase in effective crop area was greater yet, because of the increase in multiple cropping in Asia and elsewhere. In some places the extension of cultivation has reduced the quality of land, of course, but in other places the process has improved the quality of land.

About "mining," as Ehrlich calls it: the implied danger is that we are running out of mineral resources. But this is contradicted by the facts, paradoxical and hard to believe though they are. Economists agree that the only meaningful economic measure of scarcity is some variant of cost or price, despite Ehrlich's dismissal (1981:13) of Barnett and Morse (1963), who pioneered this line of work with respect to natural resources. And the historical trend of all measures of cost and price for mined resources is downward, as we can see in Figures 4-1 and 4-2 for the representative example of copper. This is despite the decreasing richness of ores, as seen in Table 43.1.

How does this mind-boggling process come about? Stimulated by impending price rises, innovators, working for profit or otherwise, seek out new lodes, develop new methods of extraction and invent substitute ways

Table 43-1. Results of Bet with Ehrlich et al.

	Copper	Chrome	Nickel
Sept. 22, '80	$200.00 ($1.02/lb)	$199.99 ($3.90/tn)	$200.01 ($3.06/lb)
Sept. 22, '81	$163.16	$217.94	$170.42
Sept. 20, '82	$136.87	$192.30	$125.94
Sept. 19, '83	$149.21	$192.30	$147.30
Sept. 14, '84	$126.41	$192.30	$139.39
Sept. 16, '85	$129.75	$192.30	$139.65
Sept. 15, '86	$126.56	$192.30	$110.46
Sept. 21, '87	$171.04	$192.30	$157.68
May 1988	$199.74	$161.53	$527.76
Sept. 26-30, '88	$246.00 ($1.25/lb)	$192.00 ($3.75/tn)	$335.00 ($5.13/lb)
(Fwd. 15 mos.)	$184.00 ($0.94/lb)	—	$217.00 (3.32/lb)

	Tin	Tungsten	Grand Total	Adjusted Total
Sept. 22, '80	$199.97 ($8.73/lb)	$191.00 ($13.50)	$991.07	
Sept. 22, '81	$177.55	$184.23	$913.30	
Sept. 20, '82	$145.86	$142.81	$743.78	
Sept. 19, '83	$146.66	$112.82	$748.28	
Sept. 14, '84	$142.25	$127.10	$727.45	
Sept. 16, '85	$136.52	$89.26	$687.48	
Sept. 15, '86	$79.50	$48.56	$557.36	
Sept. 21, '87	$96.44	$51.41	$668.88	
May 1988	$96.57	$91.40	$1,077.00 × .73 = $786	
Sept. 26-30, '88	$105.00 ($4.85/lb)	$44.00 ($3.00)	$922.00 × .73 = $673	
(Fwd. 15 mos.)	—	—	$742.00 × .73 = $542	

Note: In a recent year nickel had been as high as $10/lb.

Weights: copper, 196.56; chrome, 51.28; nickel, 65.32; tin, 22.91; tungsten, 2856.21

Source: Metals Week, various issues.

of filling the same needs. And it is crucial that this process is not fortuitous, not a "race" between technology and demand. Rather, it is a series of developments *induced* by changes in demand as a result of income and population growth.

But, one may ask, is this not a moment of discontinuity, of structural change? For example, the third-degree polynomial fitted to the price data for wheat in Figure 43-1 seems to imply an upward tendency for wheat prices. But all this proves is that one can find a mathematical technique suggesting discontinuities or reversals in trend if one desires to. My own judgment is that the long-term trends seen in the price of resources is downward. Of course this is only one person's judgment. We *can* say scientifically, however, that if in the past one had acted systematically on the belief that the long-run price trend was upward rather than downward, one would have lost money on the average.

Predictions

Ehrlich says (1981:18) that ecology "can really provide only three things of importance to decision makers. The first is specific predictions on

Figure 43-1. Price of wheat deflated by consumer price index.

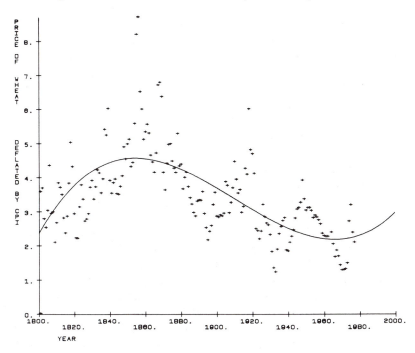

certain limited problems.'' Ehrlich proceeds on the next page to "predict with extreme accuracy the end result of continuing our assaults on Earth's systems: the collapse of civilization as we know it.'' There can hardly be a more complete prophesy of doom. He also predicts "catastrophic famines, plague and probably thermonuclear war.''

Let us examine a few of Ehrlich's past prophecies, to see how much trust to place in his present prophecies. In 1969 he wrote, in a "scenario" of the future: "The end of the ocean came late in the summer of 1979" (1969:1), and he went on to specify "the final gasp of the whaling industry in 1973''; "the end of the Peruvian anchovy industry in 1975" (p. 1); reduction of the fish catch to 30 million metric tons in 1977 (p. 1), contributing to "50 million people per year . . . dying of starvation" by 1977 (p. 1).

As of 1980, the sea is not "dead" by any measure I know of. For better or for worse, 27,000 whales were killed in 1976 despite decreasing world quotas (FAO, various years). And the fish catch was 73 million tons in 1977, the last year for which I have data, after rising rather steadily from 19 million tons in 1948; the fish catch for human consumption only has risen even more steadily (FAO, 1978). (See Table 41-1).

Ehrlich predicted worsening air pollution in dramatic detail; we have seen the fate of that prediction above. And he predicted "skyrocketing" food prices, a U.S. food shortage and "in the 1970s . . . hundreds of millions of people are going to starve to death" (1968: Prologue). Another of Ehrlich's scenarios had the 1999 U.S. population at 22.6 million, a 90 percent drop, and a leukemia rate "70 percent higher than the 1960 base rate." Famine is to kill 65 million Americans from 1980 to 1989 (1970). In fact, in real terms grain prices have been falling, as Figures 6-1 and 6-2 show, and consumption per capita has been increasing, as we see in Figure 1-1.

Ehrlich predicted that the U.S. "resource situation" would get "bad, and bound to get worse" (1969:4). In fact, the only extractive resource which did not follow the benign trends of copper and wheat shown in the figures was energy, and that exception clearly has been due to the politics of cartel power. And even so, the course of gasoline prices shown in Figure 43-2 has hardly shown the signs of disaster for the human race.

One might say that Ehrlich's predictions did not come to pass because of human efforts to avoid them. But such a response would obscure the fundamental mechanism at work; people are often willing and able to deal with worrisome, impending problems, and their efforts to do so frequently leave us better off than we were before the problem arose. A forecast that a driver will smash into a tree unless she rounds a bend in a road, which she routinely does, would hardly be a meaningful prediction. Ehrlich's

Figure 43-2. Real gasoline prices at the service station (1972 dollars).

real gasoline prices at
the service station (1972 dollars)

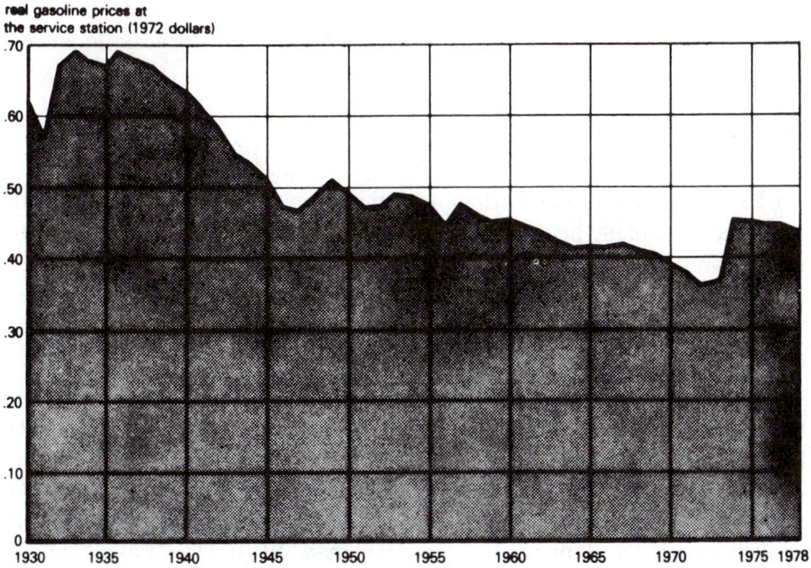

predictions must be taken as unconditional if they are to be meaningful, and in that form they have been empirically falsified across the board.

Faced with the demographic facts of the 1970s, Ehrlich and Ehrlich recently said, "we were all dead wrong" (1979:88). Their willingness to admit error is laudable. But this statement, too, is dead wrong. Barnett and Morse (1963) and many others were not wrong in *their* predictions. And perhaps it will enhance the credibility of my own criticism of Ehrlich as a forecaster if I recall that I have been steadily saying the same things I write here since around Earth Day, 1970 (Simon, 1973). My assertions then are compatible with the way the events of the last decade turned out.

One thing more about predictions: Ehrlich makes wild statements without being willing to take the consequences of being wrong. For example, he says, "If I were a gambler, I would take even money that England will not exist in the year 2000" (Ehrlich, 1970, quoted by Dixon, 1973). Well, why *won't* he bet on that fact if he believes it? I'd be happy to bet with him. In fact, I'll go further, and, as we say where I come from, I'll put my money where my mouth is. This is a public offer to stake $10,000, in separate transactions of $1000 or $100 each, on my belief that the cost of non-government-controlled raw materials (including grain and oil) will not rise in the long run. If you will pay me the current market price of $1000 or $100 worth of any standard mineral or other extractive product you name, and specify any date more than a year away, I will contract to pay you the then-current market price of the material. How about it, doomsayers and catastrophists? First come, first served.

Ehrlich's Style

I have said above that Ehrlich does not support his dire forecasts with hard data. Instead, he employs a variety of rhetorical devices, most of which can be found in his paper here. One such is the "all experts know" device. Such a phrase opened the talk which was the origin of this paper: "In my opinion, and that of virtually every ecologist I know, humanity is now faced with an unprecedented escalation of environmental disruption" is the way the speech draft that I received read. Such phrases are also found in *The Population Bomb*. "Everyone agrees that at least half of the people of the world are undernourished (have too little food) or malnourished (have serious imbalances in their diet)" (1968:36). It is most certainly not true that "everyone agrees" with that; for two scholarly debunkings of such views, see Bennett (1954) and Poleman (1979). Or, "Lake Erie has died . . . No one in his right mind would eat a Lake Erie fish today, if one could be found . . . Lake Michigan will soon follow it in extinction" (1968:62). Though the catch in Erie fell in the 1960s, it has recently increased, and in 1977, 10 *million* pounds of fish were caught there, leading to questions about who is not in whose "right mind." For the Great Lakes as a whole, the catch was at its lowest in recorded history in 1965 (56 million tons), but has since rebounded to 73 million tons in 1977, not far from the average since World War I (U.S. Bureau of the Census, 1976:555; 1979:741). By 1977 Lake Michigan had become "an angler's paradise . . . the finest fresh-water fishery in the world," a $350 million-a-year sport fishing industry (*The Wall Street Journal*, September 15, 1977:1). In 1980 *Newsweek* could report that Lake Erie's "blue waters are alive once more with fish . . . fishermen expect to haul in 17 million walleyes, whitefish and prized Lake Erie blue pike this year . . . conditions have never been better . . . most of the beaches have reopened" (September 8, 1980:12).

Another device used by Ehrlich is the "most citizens are unaware" ploy, as in his first paragraph here. This implicitly says "we (I) know better" than laymen. Related is the we-know-better-than-other-specialists approach which we also find in this paper, e.g., the criticism of the "refusal by demographers to accept conclusions . . . of the ecologists" (1981:11), though Ehrlich offers no evidence that the ecologist's conclusions are indeed more sound. He also says that social scientists "must become well informed on the ecological dimensions of the human predicament" (p.8). More knowledge is always helpful. But why ecology rather than archaeology or space engineering or social work, all of which can make sound arguments for their importance to social scientists?

Then there is plain name-calling and ridicule. "Náivete" is one of Ehrlich's favorite epithets, applied repeatedly in this paper to those with whom Ehrlich does not agree. And in fact, his criticism of other people's ideas often does not proceed much beyond such name-calling—for example, sentences such as "Growth mania is a fixation on growth for growth's sake . . . 'the creed of the cancer cell' " (1981:12), and his story (without documentation) about an economist who is said to have urged that cattle be fed exclusively on their own droppings (1981:13). And Ehrlich (1981:10) says that resource economists are not "familiar with the real world," implying that he himself is. (Ironically, in the course of that name-calling he himself errs about the nature of the "real world" of business by assuming that it is the whaling industry collectively which makes profit-maximizing calculations. In fact, it is whaling *firms* that make such calculations and business decisions; if it were otherwise, as Ehrlich assumes it is, the result might be closer to what he desires.)

Doomsayers often assert that society's grave danger is sufficient justification for exaggeration and unfair rhetoric, e.g., "We are faced with a crisis involving the future of our country, and indeed the world, the seriousness of which cannot be exaggerated" (Silverman, 1970). What this boils down to is total assurance of being right plus a conviction of "urgency" (1981:7) so strong that the normal rules of scientific evidence and discourse should be suspended. This view is not very flattering to science; it implicitly suggests that scientific procedures are only appropriate for unimportant issues. And it smacks of the "eleventh hour" thinking (1981:18) that usually is not open to new evidence, especially evidence that past predictions of the same sort have been falsified. But as Oliver Cromwell wrote to the Church of Scotland, "I beseech you, in the bowels of Christ, think it possible you may be mistaken" (*Bartlett's Familiar Quotations*, 14th ed., p. 328).

Why Is Ehrlich's Sort of Talk Accepted and Relied Upon?

This is a most difficult question. One partial explanation is that Ehrlich provides simplified answers, despite his emphasis in his article on the complexity of ecological and social systems. If memory serves, before tens of millions of television viewers Johnny Carson asked Ehrlich to explain the population problem and related issues and Ehrlich repeatedly responded, "It's very simple." This appears in his writings, too: "The facts of human population growth are simple" (1967, quoted by Chase, 1977:397).

The simplest assertion about population is the Malthusian proposition that, with a fixed supply of land and other capital, additional workers must necessarily mean less output per worker. This bit of economic theory is at the heart of Ehrlich's writing on population and resources. And it is such a seductively attractive idea that it seems to require no factual proof that it really applies—even though it does *not* fit the long run of human history during which additional persons have improved and adopted technology, and thereby increased output per worker. The facts about population and resources and the environment are much more complex than Malthus thought they were when he wrote the first edition of his *Essay* in 1798, and as Ehrlich himself urges us to believe in this paper.

Another likely reason why people accept Ehrlich's view is that he apparently offers scientifically warranted, value-free propositions, even though his own value judgments are implicit in his conclusions. For example, he has written: "I can't think of any reason for having more than one hundred fifty million people" in the United States (1972:49), and, "The greatest gift that the United Nations could ask for the world would be *no* births in 1979 (Ehrlich and Ehrlich, 1979:2). [This is the pseudoscientific framework within which such observations are offered: on the first-page puff of *The Population Bomb* it says (italics added): "Paul R. Ehrlich, a *qualified scientist,* clearly describes the dimensions of the crisis . . . and provides a realistic evaluation of the remaining options."] But Ehrlich's statements really depend upon the value judgment that some people's lives have no value to them and/or to Ehrlich. I believe that Ehrlich's own values are shown clearly in this well-known first paragraph of *The Population Bomb:*

> The streets seemed alive with people. People eating, people washing, people sleeping. People visiting, arguing, and screaming. People thrusting their hands through the taxi window, begging. People defecating and urinating. People clinging to buses. People herding animals. People, people, people, people (1968:5).

In his article, Ehrlich makes much of how values enter the work of others. But he does not mention—if indeed he "recognizes," a word he uses frequently—that his own assertions about population are based squarely upon his own values. And Ehrlich is ready to coerce us to accept his values. "We must have population control at home, hopefully through a system of incentives and penalties, but by compulsion if voluntary methods fail" (1968: Prologue).

Another reason why Ehrlich's sort of rhetoric works is that dire threats can shock us enough so that we do not apply the same critical faculties to them that we do with less emotional statements. If someone shouts at you "Rockslide! Jump back!," you are likely to jump first and inquire only later into the basis for the warning. (Furthermore, these fearful threats may morbidly fascinate us in such a manner that an enjoyment of them keeps us from evaluating them dispassionately. But this is only speculation on my part.)

Were there no price to pay for unfounded threats of doom, we could simply revel in them like horror movies. But life is not so benign. False threats can reduce credibility of true threats and cause loss of public trust in public communication. As Philip Handler, president of the National Academy of Sciences, testified to congressmen in the midst of the environmental panic of 1970: "The nations of the world may yet pay a dreadful price for the public behavior of scientists who depart from . . . fact to indulge . . . in hyperbole" (1971:30).

An Economist in Wonderland—Paul R. Ehrlich

Simon's criticism illustrates the types of errors some economists make when they deal with problems of population, resources, and environment. Issues associated with the data used are discussed.

I am not at all surprised that Professor Simon (1981) was unable to reply to my criticisms (1981) of economics or the other social sciences. I am, however, deeply grateful to him for providing the readers of *Social Science Quarterly* with so many additional examples of the sort of blunders Simon and other economists of his ilk commit when they attempt to deal with problems of population, resources, and environment.

1. Simon is wrong about air pollution. While the problem of *urban* air pollution has been somewhat alleviated in the United States (although not in many other parts of the world), the total area influenced by toxic air pollutants has been increasing. The best evidence for this increase has been the steady expansion throughout the 1960s and 1970s of the area receiving acid precipitation—one measure of the atmospheric burden of sulphates and nitrates. In part the cause is "the trend toward building taller stacks to relieve local pollution problems [that] has turned the local problems into regional ones" (Likens et al., 1979).

Direct toxic effects of air pollution on people, moreover, are only a small part of the problem. The acid rains are not merely an indicator of atmospheric contamination, but themselves threaten crucial ecosystem services over enormous areas (CEQ, 1979; Lewis and Grant, 1980; Brezonik et al., 1980). Perhaps the most serious "air pollution" problem of all is the injection of CO_2 into the atmosphere, with its potential for producing climatic changes that could greatly disrupt agriculture and cause massive famines (see, e.g., Schneider and Mesirow, 1976; Baes et al., 1976; MacDonald et al, 1979). Simon's Figure 1-1 does not speak at all to the crucial CO_2 problem.

Simon also does not understand the issues surrounding water quality, and his information is out of date. The most recent CEQ report (1979) does not indicate that water quality is improving. Previous apparent progress has been overridden by increased contamination with poisons and carcinogens that are more difficult to detect and remove, and by the discovery that extensive pollution of groundwater supplies has occurred. The recent report of the U.S. surgeon general predicts an *increasing* threat to public health until the flow of dangerous chemicals into the environment can be controlled (Joyce, 1980).

In the light of Simon's little sermon on "fair-minded assessment" and not "picking and choosing" (p. 32), one wonders why he failed to find out what was actually happening with sulphates and nitrates, ignored the CO_2 situation and completely neglected to mention the horrendous increase in toxic-waste pollution (CEQ, 1979; Raloff, 1980). The latter is now well known even to a substantial segment of the lay public, thanks to the Love Canal disaster and Michael Brown's (1980) excellent popular book on the subject. And finally, why did Simon only reproduce half of the figure on page 352 of the 1975 CEQ report? [because only it is relevant to human life. J.S.] What the omitted half shows is that, based on the more comprehensive water quality criteria for the protection of aquatic life, the situation was deteriorating between 1961 and 1967. By 1974 it had recovered only to the 1961 level, after I and others had sounded the warning and clean-up efforts had been started.

2. Simon's comment on life expectancy merely underlines my point (p. 31) that economists confuse "pollution" with the more serious problems of loss of ecosystem services. But if Simon wished to focus on the direct effects of pollution on life expectancy, he still did it wrong. The important question there is not what the index is doing, but what it would be doing if everything else were held constant and only levels of pollution varied. For instance, better medical care for infants and minority groups and higher survival rates during surgical operations may be causing increases in *overall* life expectancy in spite of higher death rates due to environmental pollutants. An additional complication Simon would have to consider is the long lag time between the induction of many cancers and the deaths they cause. As any epidemiologist could explain to Simon, the aggregated statistic tells little or nothing about trends in the direct impact of pollution

on health. And, I repeat, the direct health effects of pollution are a relatively minor part of the environmental problems faced by humanity.

3. Simon does not understand why there is concern about the amount of land under cultivation. He does not deny that considerable amounts are being lost to desertification and urbanization, but he does not construe this as a reason for checking population growth. His reason, given in a *Science* article (1980), is that new cropland can continue to be created by "draining swamps and irrigating deserts." He is apparently cheered by the record, although the works he cites clearly show that the rate of addition of new land did not remotely approach the pace of population growth. But, as usual, Simon misses the really important points. *The bringing of more land under cultivation constitutes an assault on the ecosystems that provide society with indispensable services* (Ehrlich, 1981:19). That arable land continues to be "created" is, contrary to Simon's view, a measure of the problem, not of the solution. In addition, relatively high quality arable land is being degraded, and most of the new arable land is marginal, less productive and subject to even more rapid degradation. Ecologists fear the consequences of having to replace ruined land by bringing more virgin land under cultivation. They, unlike Simon, are also conscious of other risks related to the cultivation of arid lands, such as the depletion of "fossil" water supplies.

4. Simon is wrong about mining. There is no danger whatever of humanity "running out" of nonfuel mineral resources, and I have not said there is. Those resources remain on the surface of the earth after mining and use. Humanity is not destroying them—it is dispersing them. What *will* run out, however, is the capacity of the environment to absorb the punishment associated with mining ever-lower grades of ore or reconcentrating what is already dispersed. Secondarily, the ability to do the job at an attractive cost will also "run out."

5. Simon is wrong about the economics of mineral resources. So were Barnett and Morse in 1963. Their thesis was utterly demolished by geologists long ago (Cloud, 1968; Lovering, 1968, 1969; Cook, 1976). The trough-like pattern long predicted for mineral resource prices has now shown up, as Cook (1976) points out, for all industrial metals except lead and aluminum. *This includes copper.* Those wishing to see the actual shape of the curve of copper prices against constant dollars are referred to Peterson and Maxwell's (1979) Figure 15.

I and my colleagues, John P. Holdren (University of California, Berkeley) and John Harte (Lawrence Berkeley Laboratory), jointly accept Simon's astonishing offer before other greedy people jump in. We have offered, in a formal contract, to pay him on September 29, 1990, the 1990 equivalent of 10,000 1980 dollars (corrected by the CPI) for the quantity that $2000 would buy of each of the following five metals on September 29, 1990: chromium, copper, nickel, tin and tungsten.

6. To understand Simon's baseless optimism about resource availability, one must go beyond his geological and ecological confusions and examine his apparent beliefs in large-scale alchemy and science fiction. He has written (1980) that "future quantities of a natural resource such as copper cannot be calculated even in principle" because, among other reasons, "*copper can be made from other metals*" (p. 1435, my emphasis). He goes on to say, in arguing against the idea that any resource is finite: "Even the total weight of the earth is not a theoretical limit to the amount of copper that might be available to earthlings in the future. Only the total weight of the universe . . . would be such a theoretical limit." One wonders if Simon could not at least find a junior high school science student to review his writings.

7. Simon clearly does not grasp the difference between a scenario (a device for helping one to think about the future) and a prediction. The whole purpose of scenarios that I have written is to show one possible result of letting current trends continue, in the hope of stimulating action to alter those trends. The 1969 scenario, for those interested in checking it, came frighteningly close to representing what actually happened in many instances. And I'd like to think that it and my other writings helped to generate the environmental regulations of the 1970s, which, among other things, reduced the flux of chlorinated hydrocarbons into the sea to well below the level that would have resulted from continuation of the trends of the late 1960s. Even so, the situation in the sea has deteriorated seriously since the scenario was written.

On this issue, as on others, Simon has been confounded by aggregate statistics he does not understand (for other instances that will amaze social scientists, see his *Science* article). The statistics he quotes include both marine and freshwater fisheries. The absolute size of marine fish catches has remained essentially constant since 1970. The most recent statistics (FAO, 1976 and 1978) show a total of 54.3 million metric tons of marine fishes extracted from the oceans in 1970 and 56.2 million metric tons in 1978. There is considerable slop in fisheries data (and they are under constant revision), but these numbers show an increase of 3.5 percent in eight years. The statistics Simon quotes, the aggregate of all fisheries catches—which include marine, freshwater and diadromous fishes; crustaceans; mollusks; whales; seals; aquatic plants; etc.—show a more positive trend than the marine fish statistics, an increase of about 6.3 percent in the same eight years. *Even using his more optimistic statistics, this means that per capita catches have plummeted—since in the same period the human population increased some 16 percent.* This is a point Simon curiously neglects to mention.

Furthermore, this rapid per capita decline is not the most ominous trend in human extraction of food from the sea. Present marine yields have only been maintained by moving to the exploitation of nontraditional species as the traditional ones have become fully exploited or overexploited. (Council on Environmental Quality and Department of State, 1980). For example, Alaska pollack and capelin, numbers 1 and 2 in the 1978 catch statistics, have shown increases since 1964 of more than 300 and 8000 percent respectively (FAO, 1978 and 1970). When additional species to exploit and overexploit run out, Simon doubtless believes new ones will be synthesized, possibly out of copper! For lack of space, I'll leave to the reader the simple task of determining why the "For Human Consumption" figures Simon quotes give no more cause for rejoicing.

My statement about who would eat fish from Lake Erie was true in 1968 when it was made, and commercial fishing in the lake was banned because of mercury contamination soon after I made it. Although herculean efforts have partially revived the lake, *The Wall Street Journal* recently reported (September 3, 1980) that its future still is in doubt. I would not knowingly eat a fish from it today. As the *Journal* relates, people who live near certain toxic hot spots in the lake would have to consult a 60–80-page book to determine whether a given fish was safe to eat.

Nothing in the fisheries statistics gives the slightest reason for optimism about maintaining humanity's vital flow of protein from the sea. The words of the *Global 2000 Report* (Council on Environmental Quality and Department of State, 1980:111–12) on this point are germane (my emphasis):

> Industrialization, which is heaviest in the Northern Hemisphere, is now introducing pollutants into oceans in quantities which are beginning to cause significant deleterious effects. . . . The important coastal zones are being changed at ever increasing rates to the detriment of natural resource productivity . . . pollution of oceans at increasing rates will likely have the effect of *reducing* overall yields of marine resources.

8. My statement about the whaling industry is correct and was easily understood by the economists who reviewed and heard my paper. Simon's quibble is especially amusing coming from an economist who confuses the cost and price of goods (1980:1435).

9. I think most of the rest of what Simon has to say will be transparent to *SSQ* readers. Those interested in my values might wish to consult *Ecoscience* (1977) which also integrates and thoroughly documents the positions I've taken. My values are further displayed in *The Race Bomb* (1977), *The Golden Door* (1979), and *"Variety Is the Key to Life"* (1980).

Two of my values are not explicitly mentioned in these works. One is that one should do everything possible to improve the lives not only of the present passengers on Spaceship Earth, but also of future generations of passengers. The second is that, when one takes advocacy positions, the work should be thoroughly reviewed by others so that the facts on which judgments are based are as sound as the state of the art permits. The latter is a value that Simon might consider adopting.

Finally, I accept that Simon and others do not like direct use of the English language. That is their privilege. I am convinced that the nice circumlocutions and euphemisms that characterize the "scholarly" literature are inappropriate both to today's desperate situation and to communicating with lay persons. Other scientists have drawn the same conclusion (Holdren et al., 1979). Therefore I will not hesitate to use words like "desperate," "dangerous," "grim" and "unprecedented" in describing today's human predicament. Nor will I eschew words like "wrong," "incompetent" or even "moronic" in describing the works or views of others when the shoe fits.

Afterword—J. L. Simon

Ehrlich's response mentions that he and two colleagues agreed to a bet I had offered, to wit, that the price of any raw material would indefinitely decline, adjusted by the consumer price level for inflation. Ehrlich et al. chose a date ten years from October 6, 1980, and they specified five metals—copper, chrome, nickel, tin and tungsten. The history of those prices since then is shown in Table 43-2. The operative column is the adjusted summation at the end, indicating that prices have indeed declined until now, and that if there were no further change, they would owe me the difference between that sum and $1000.

In addition, in the manner of normal commercial dealings, I wrote them on October 5, 1988:

Dear Professors Ehrlich, Harte, and Holdren:

This letter is to get on record about our arrangement of October 6, 1980.

If this were an ordinary commercial transaction in actively traded goods on the futures markets, I could as of this date buy futures for the date of the end of our arrangement at prices well below the original prices, without even taking into account the cost of living adjustment. Or, I could buy the physical commodities at this time, stockpile them even at very high storage prices, allow for the money tied up, and be way ahead of the game. The only reason that I actually don't do so, and therefore lock myself into a profit and "winning" right now, is the absence of markets for transactions of this size to buy now and to sell these commodities at the date of the completion of our futures contract.

Table 43-2. Copper Ore Grade History, 1900-1973

Year	Average grade of ore mined (percent copper)
1900	4.00
1910	1.88
1920	1.63
1930	1.43
1940	1.20
1950	0.89
1955	0.83
1960	0.73
1965	0.70
1970	0.60
1973	0.53

Note: This table shows how drastically the richness of copper ore has fallen over the years. Yet technology has improved sufficiently, and enough substitutes have been developed so that the relative price of copper has fallen over this period.

Source: Council on Environmental Quality Report, 1976, p.328. Originally from Sheldon P. Wimpten and Alvin W. Knoerr, "World Resources vs. Copper and Aluminum Demand to the Year 2000," paper presented at the Eighth World Mining Congress, Lima, Peru, November 3-8, 1974, U.S. Department of the Interior, Bureau of Mines, Copper, a preprint from Bulletin 667 (Washington D.C.: U.S. Government Printing Office, 1976)

I hope that this assessment makes clear that, from an economic point of view, it is already established that I could not lose the bet with you, and in the absence of a sudden rise I would be a heavy winner. The reason for locking myself into a profit as of now, of course, is that there is always the chance of some most unusual temporary price rise due to external conditions, such as happened in the 1970s, which might fortuitously cause me to lose, after having been in a winning position since the day of the wager.

I do not crow over these results even though, if the results had gone in the other direction, Ehrlich et al. would be crowing that they had vanquished my arguments and me. Eight or ten years are still a short span of time in historical context, and price movements have often run against the long term for at least this long. I have simply been lucky that this particular period coincided so nicely with my argument. Please understand my larger point: If this bet were to be repeated again and again throughout history, *on average* my side of the bet would be a big winner.

Paul Ehrlich Saying It Is So Doesn't Make It So—J. L. Simon.

In a recent *SSQ* symposium, Ehrlich (1981) published an article to which I replied, and to which he then responded. This in turn is my response.

The main issues I raised (Simon, 1981) were these: (1) Ehrlich tries to persuade with rhetorical devices rather than objective facts. (2) Ehrlich's assertions and recommendations rest upon his own values, but his assertions and recommendations are often worded to seem as if they are purely scientific and value-free. (3) His predictions of the last decade or so about increasing scarcities and a worsening environment in the United States have proven wrong almost without exception—a track record of poor predictive validity which should lead one to have little confidence in his present predictions.

Ehrlich's response provides more examples of these practices.

1. On rhetorical devices, Ehrlich (1981b:48) winds up with this: "Finally, I accept that Simon and others do not like direct use of the English language. . . . I will not hesitate to use words like 'desperate,' 'dangerous,' 'grim,' and 'unprecedented' in describing today's human predicament. Nor will I eschew words like 'wrong,' 'incompetent' or even 'moronic' in describing the works or views of others when the shoe fits."

The issue here is not direct English. The term "moronic" is not particularly direct. It *is* simply an ad hominem argument, an attack on a person rather than that person's idea. It asserts much, but it proves nothing. His saying it is so does not make it so.

The reader should not think that there is anything special or personal about Ehrlich applying his rhetorical devices to me. Rather, these devices are his stock in trade, the tools of his writing craft. For example, in a previous *SSQ* exchange with William Petersen, he and Anne Ehrlich (1977:331) wrote: "It is too bad that some social scientists don't see fit to have their work reviewed by ecologists or other natural scientists before they publish silly statements about the agricultural situation or 'pollution.' " Now in his response to me (1981b:46) he writes almost identically: "One wonders if Simon could not at least find a junior high school science student to review his writing." Peterson (1977:329) replied that such devices are "a gratuitous slap at *Social Science Quarterly,* whose typical contributor is far more competent in social analysis than biologists who presume to have conquered its complexities."

Just as he speaks poorly of his opponents, Ehrlich has words of praise for himself. With respect to water quality in the United States he says, "By 1974 it had recovered only to the 1961 level, after I and others had sounded the warning the clean-up efforts had been started" (Ehrlich, 1981b:45). About a 1969 article whose "scenario" for the future proved completely off the mark, he writes (1981b:47): "I'd like to think that it and my other writings helped to generate the environmental regulations of the 1970s, which, among other things, reduced the flux of chlorinated hydrocarbons into the sea to well below the level that would have resulted from continuation of the trends of the late 1960s."

Ehrlich is prideful that his writings have had positive effects in speeding environmental cleanup. Perhaps he is correct; I hope so. But what about the possible negative effects of his (and his colleagues') exaggerated cries of alarm and incorrect predictions upon the belief of the public in the honesty and the soundness of judgment of persons who bear the label "scientist"? And what about the effects on national will, and on morale generally, of unfounded assertions about physical limits upon our capacity to change the conditions of our lives? I suggest that Ehrlich try a more rounded cost-benefit analysis of his activities, taking into account not only the possible benefits but also the possible costs.

2. About the place of his values in his social assessments: Ehrlich did not reply to the issues I raised, but instead changed the subject to other "values" such as that "When one takes advocacy positions, the work should be thoroughly reviewed by others . . . " (1981b:48). Therefore, I simply repeat some key value statements of Ehrlich's so readers will know where he stands: "I can't think of any reason for having more than one hundred fifty million people" in the United States (1972:49). "The greatest gift that the United Nations could ask for the world would be of *no* births in 1979" (Ehrlich and Ehrlich, 1979:2). "We must have population control at home, hopefully through a system of incentives and penalties, but by compulsion if voluntary methods fail" (Ehrich, 1968:Prologue).

3. The substantive issue that Ehrlich addresses at greatest length in his response is the fish catch. This issue is representative of many others that test his predictive validity. To show that his 1969 prediction of a reduction in the fish catch had not panned out, I presented data for the "total" and "for human consumption" catches from 1938 through 1978, which show a trend that is still increasing, to my eye. Ehrlich (1981b:47) then replied: "The absolute size of marine fish catches has remained essentially con-

stant since 1970," and "On this issue, as on others, Simon has been confounded by aggregate statistics he does not understand" (1981b:47).

By good luck, John Wise sent me an analysis of recent trends, together with the very latest data. Table 43-1 shows his summary series. Column d presents the marine fish catch Ehrlich refers to. It rises from 57.2 to 65.2 million metric tons over the nine year period Ehrlich refers to as "constant"—a 14 percent increase, or roughly 1.56 percent per year. Can you imagine what Ehrlich would say to me if the roles were reversed?

Ehrlich wrote that "for other instances (of aggregate statistics he does not understand) see his *Science* article" (Selection 2). Ehrlich, along with colleagues John P. Holdren, Anne H. Ehrlich, and John Harte, challenged one of the aggregate statistics I presented there, the trend in electricity prices. I think my reply in Selection 2 will help the reader decide just who understands what (the figure mentioned in the reply showed the downward trend in real electricity prices since the 1920s).

Ehrlich and colleagues accepted my offer to bet that resource prices will come down in the future. Now that Ehrlich has demonstrated that under circumstances he thinks are attractive he *will* wager, will he now also bet with me about the matter that kicked off the matter in the first place? "If I were a gambler, I would take even money that England will not exist in the year 2000," he wrote (Ehrlich, 1970, quoted by Dixon, 1973). I suggest $1000 deflated by the Consumer Price Index as the stake once again.

That's Right—You Should Check It For Yourself—P. Ehrlich

Interested readers can determine independently whether Simon or Ehrlich is correct. They might want to start by comparing my entire statement about fisheries statistics (1981:47) and what Simon implies I said. The accuracy of my statements can be checked in the FAO statistics I cited. Readers might note that, even if the revised statistics quoted by Simon *are* correct (his calculation of the percent annual increase is not), they still show a *per-capita* decline, the point I emphasized. Further, Simon still ignores the crucial point on the shift in the fish species that make up the catch.

The electricity prices quoted by Simon (1981c) require close inspection. The one typographical error, when corrected, makes *stronger* the position taken by Holdren et al. (incorrectly cited by Simon as Ehrlich et al.). It shows that the bottoming of electricity costs occurred in 1970, even *earlier* than 1971 (as indicated by the typo), and the trend has been upward since.

In a typical case of obfuscation, Simon tries to focus attention on the typo, claiming that correcting it would have "changed their conclusion entirely." Inspection of the data shows this to be entirely false. Don't take my word for it; look at Simon's own numbers. Furthermore, I think *SSQ* readers will agree that Holdren et al. were not "imprudent." What scientist would phone the author of a standard source to make sure there were no typos in a series of numbers *showing a general trend with which every analyst in the field is completely familiar?*

Apparently Simon feels confident that people will not bother to check his statements, and his confidence may be justified. After all, in the past two years his errors have been rather more spectacular than failing to detect a typo. For example, he has managed *in print* to express the belief that the universe can be turned into copper (1980:1435–36) and that there is "no long-run physical limit" to the amount of food that can be produced on our planet (1981a:76). In another attempt to prove that natural resources are "really infinite" (1981b:42–50), he resurrected Zeno's paradox, confusing infinite quantity with infinite divisibility. He also demonstrated his confusion about the nature of resources (since he was under the delusion that resources are infinitely divisible—which, of course, they are not). Simon has even concluded (1981b:346) that the human population can grow "forever." And yet he is still taken seriously in some quarters.

The really interesting question is not whether Simon is right—no one with a modicum of knowledge about how the world works could believe that. It is, how does someone whose writings are dense with such elementary errors get so widely published and praised? Are Simon's conclusions so reassuring to some people that they will pay no attention to how those conclusions are reached? Is there a powerful conspiracy to promote one last gasp of the old "growth-at-any-cost" economic system? Is it possible that a whole array of editors and reviewers know nothing of physics and have to take off their shoes to count up to twenty?

Social scientists may be able to determine whether it is a waste of time for those familiar with thermodynamics, ecology, the mathematics of infinitites, and so on to try and counter the ideas of cornucopians, flatworlders, anti-evolutionists, and the like. Humanity could be entering a time of millenarian cults and fads which will swamp any attempts to treat the world's problems rationally. Recent cuts in federal funding of the social sciences may indicate the beginning of an era dominated by the Simonesque.

For the time being, however, I and my colleagues intend to swim against the tide. For those who wish to join in, access to recent sources on many of the issues can be found in the references in agricultural economist Lester R. Brown's recent book, *Building a Sustainable Society* (1981). That book also contains a very readable summary of much of the resource situation. Documentation on other key issues can be found in Ehrlich and

Ehrlich (1981), and the trend in energy prices is continuously presented in the *Monthly Energy Review* published by the U.S. Department of Energy.

Simon still seems to be under the illusion that disputes can best be settled not by analysis but by betting. This is patent nonsense, but the lure of easy money can be irresistible. Therefore, professors John Harte and John P. Holdren, of the Energy and Resources Group, University of California, Berkeley, and I attempted to take Simon (1981:39) up on his entire $10,000 raw materials wager. But the "standard commodity-market agreement" that Simon imagined he was offering us in his first version of the bet was nothing of the sort. After we had explained this to him, he agreed to a fair form of wager for which we drew up a legal contract. But he insisted on limiting the bet to changes in the real value of only $1000 worth of minerals. At that rate it was hardly worth our time. Let others tempted to respond to one of Simon's bombastic challenges learn from our experience! (*SSQ* has copies of the correspondence.)

I (1981:48) referred Simon to places where he could read about my values if he wished to. That I believe my statements to be value-free is a conclusion of Simon's that is directly contrary to my actual views, as social scientists who have co-authored publications with me would be glad to testify. One of my three annual lectures to all incoming graduate students in our department deals with the theory of systematics and emphasizes the values scientists inevitably bring to their work. I suspect Simon and I share many values. People, however, should not allow their values to blind them to the realities of a finite world. To do so diminishes the chances of reaching a humane future.

44

Is the Era of Limits Running Out?
A Conversation with Garrett Hardin and
Julian Simon

The choicest part of this discussion among Garrett Hardin, the Public
Opinion *staff, and me is the final set of paragraphs on Hardin's
rhetoric. It exemplifies the rhetoric used by many of the environmentalist leaders. Some other fine examples of such rhetoric, especially
ad hominem attacks, were seen in Paul Ehrlich's writing in Selection
43, as I noted in the second of my pieces in that same selection.*

*In this connection, the reader may find interesting and relevant the
comments of John Stuart Mill, quoted in the introduction to this
volume, about the relationship of the type of rhetoric to a viewpoint's
status as of the minority or the majority.*

Ben Wattenberg's title for this piece was a lovely stroke.

*I hope the reader notices that neither Hardin nor Ehrlich (either in
Selection 43 or 44)—nor anyone else, for that matter—challenges the
data that I present for either accuracy or breadth of coverage. The
critics' arguments are mainly abstractions about finiteness, diminishing returns, exponential growth, and the like. And they do not present
data that support these abstractions, choosing instead (or perhaps
not having any choice other than doing so) to argue purely on a
"theoretical" level, and a level that is practically impossible to
address empirically, such as that the "world" must "necessarily"
run out of energy "sometime."*

*Hardin taxes me with advocating alchemy, as did Ehrlich in Selec-
tion 43. This they consider the basest ignorance that a pretender to
knowledge may exhibit. (Elsewhere, Paul and Anne Ehrlich refer to
my statement that "Copper can be made from other metals" as*

Public Opinion, March 1982.

"[w]hat must be one of the most unscientific statements ever published", and characterize me as "An American specialist in mail-order marketing" (Earth, New York: Franklin Watts, 1988, p. 187).

But Hardin then proceeds to explain in this selection exactly how transmutation of copper can indeed be done; I suppose that Hardin (unlike Ehrlich) does not desire that others may think that he is unaware that this type of "alchemy" is possible with twentieth century knowledge. But in so doing Hardin implicitly indicts Ehrlich of being ignorant in this regard!

Hardin then goes on to argue that the proposition is foolish because the transmutation is expensive, given our present state of knowledge. But this immediately takes the issue out of the domain of ignorance of natural science ("alchemy"), and moves it to the domain of economic considerations ("cost"). And though a particular transmutation may be too expensive now to be practical, other transmutations are already cost effective, e.g., fission of uranium. It is to be expected that in the normal course of events, cost will decline as knowledge accumulates, and more such transmutations will become economically worthwhile. Hardin's argument supports what I have written, while refuting Ehrlich and himself.

(The idea of pricing other goods in their energy requirements, as Hardin suggests here, has been thoroughly discredited decades ago, but the elementary error surfaces again and again as it is reinvented by natural scientists who arrive innocent at economics.)

Ben Wattenberg: *Let me begin by referring to last year's Global 2000 report where the case was made that man as a species is at a perilous moment.*

"If present trends continue," the authors of Global 2000 stated, "the world in the year 2000 will be more crowded, more polluted, less stable ecologically, and more vulnerable to disruption than the world we live in now. Serious stresses involving population, resources and environment are clearly visible ahead. Despite greater material output, the world's people will be poorer in many ways than they are today. For hundreds of millions of the desperately poor, the outlook for food and other necessitites of life will be no better. For many it will be worse. Barring revolutionary advances in technology, life for most people on earth will be more precarious in 2000 than it is now."

That idea, if correct, has massive political and policy ramifications. Julian Simon, you vigorously criticized that idea. You have subsequently written a controversial book called The Ultimate Resource *which would make the opposite case—that we never had it so good. Rarely in these conversations do we get people who are at opposite ends of this spectrum, but, Dr. Hardin, I suspect we're pretty close to that here.*

I will begin by asking you, Julian, what is, in your judgment, the state of the species? And then, Dr. Hardin, you can respond.

Julian Simon: Ben, you began by saying that the Global 2000 has us at a perilous moment. But we've always been at a perilous moment. Today we're at a somewhat less perilous moment than we have been in the past. The future is likely to be decreasingly perilous because our powers to manage our environment have been increasing throughout human history.

Garrett Hardin: That assessment is so general I can't disagree. Our powers to manage our environment are indeed great, but the question is whether we will use these powers. What impediments are there in the way of acting intelligently? That's the nature of the problem.

I would also say this in defense of Global 2000. If you discover some things that aren't going very well, do you get those trends changed fastest by identifying them and crying them from the housetops or by telling people, "Don't worry; we've solved problems before so we'll solve this one"?

Those people who say "don't worry" do not contribute to solving the problem but rather to brushing it under the rug.

Wattenberg: *Would you accept Professor Simon's belief that as a species we are "better off than ever before"?*

Hardin: I wouldn't argue with it. But it's a silly point.

A lot depends on the level at which you're living. If you're in the upper 1 percent, you might have been better off 200 years earlier. If you're in the lower 25 percent, you're better off now than you would have been earlier. Both have been improved.

Karlyn Keene: *Can you identify some of the trends that you're talking about?*

Simon: Global 2000 and Dr. Hardin tell us that the food situation has been worsening and we can expect it to get even worse; that natural resources have been getting scarcer and we can expect them to get even more scarce (that is, the prices of raw materials can be expected to rise); that energy has been getting scarcer and can be expected to get even more scarce; that pollution has been getting worse in the United States and elsewhere and can be expected to get even worse. These are some of the trends.

I believe the data on long-run costs show that raw materials and energy have been getting less scarce rather than more scarce over the course of human history and over the 200 years of American history for which we have good data. There are ups and downs along the way, of course.

The data I see show increasing caloric consumption for the human species on average over the two-and-a-half decades for which we have fairly good data.

The pollution data from the Environmental Protection Agency and other government sources show that the air in the United States has been getting cleaner rather than dirtier, and that the water has been getting more drinkable rather than less drinkable.

I don't understand why Dr. Hardin and Global 2000 assert that these trends have been getting worse rather than better. I also don't understand why they project into the future that air and water in the United States will get worse when they have been getting better in the past.

Keene: *Are these data for the United States or are these worldwide?*

Simon: The data on resources are global. With resource prices, it doesn't matter whether you look at U.S. prices or whether you look at prices anyplace else in the world.

The pollution data refer to the United States. We don't have pollution data to speak of for any of the less developed countries. We have pollution data for England, and they show the same progression as the United States, but even more strongly and for a longer period of time.

Hardin: You've raised about twenty issues, and you've got them all wrong. We have to take them up one at a time. Let's take London. What happened?

The air pollution in the London area was getting worse until 1952, when they had a dreadful attack of smog. Hundreds of people died. This scared them, and they cleaned it up.

The point is this: The language you use is passive and suggests these things happened spontaneously.

Simon: We have made it get better.

Hardin: We have made it get better. That is the point. Using passive language like "It is getting better," is deceptive and encourages people who want to have an excuse to do nothing.

Wattenberg: *You are making the case that you are serving the same function as the smog albeit in a more benign fashion. You are going to scare people without killing them so they will respond wisely.*

Hardin: That's right. This is the point of human foresight. Circumstances such as the London smog will finally give you a warning. But if you can see ahead, if you can convince people that there will be trouble if certain trends continue, you can save a lot of pain. This is the point of Global 2000 and other reports like it.

Wattenberg: *In the course of doing that, is it proper to exaggerate?*

Hardin: It's never proper to exaggerate.
We are up against a difficult problem with respect to trends in the future. The figures aren't very reliable as Professor Simon will tell you.

Wattenberg: *Are you making the "better safe than sorry" argument?*

Hardin: Yes, this is because I'm a conservative. This is the original meaning of being a conservative.

Simon: You said I was wrong on twenty different points, but on the only point you've discussed, you said you agree with me, that, in fact, the air has been getting better . . .

Hardin: No. People have been making it better.

Simon: To say that it is not getting better because *people* have been making it get better is to use the English language in a way that is unrecognizable to anybody.

Hardin: No, we have both.

Simon: Both things are true. The air is getting better and people did make it so.

Hardin: The air in London in 1982 is better than the air in London in 1952.

Simon: Thank you.

* * *

Simon: I am also saying that the prices of raw materials have been falling. You're saying that this proposition is wrong. In what way is it wrong?

Hardin: The price of copper has been rising since the thirties. It's been falling for the last 200 years.

Wattenberg: *There are, apparently, a series of factual disagreements here. Let me see if I can capsulize them.*

Simon: The facts are fundamental.

Hardin: The facts are not fundamental. The theory is fundamental.

Wattenberg: *Let me see if I can characterize to both your satisfactions the factual disagreement. You are both saying that if you take a long-term trend, say, 200 years, prices of resources have gone down. However, Julian, you are saying this is a trend that is likely to continue.*

Simon: All I've said so far is this has been the trend.

Wattenberg: *The case you are making, Garrett, just so we understand it, is that if you plotted from A to Z, resource prices would be getting cheaper. But in recent years it started heading north. Take oil as one example. That curve is L-shaped.*

Hardin: A U-shape, down and then up. Julian says it goes down forever.

Wattenberg: *But it's not a full U. It doesn't go all the way up.*

Hardin: It depends on how far you want to pursue it.

Wattenberg: *Let us call it a fish hook curve.*

Hardin: Yes, a fish hook. The question is will it make a complete U.

Simon: At the American Association for the Advancement of Science meeting you said it makes sense to pay more attention to the more recent years.

Hardin: That's correct.

Simon: As a general matter, that's reasonable. But it also presents problems. For example, if we look at the most recent data, we see food prices have dropped 40 percent since last year. In response to that, you would say one year's too short a time frame, and ten years is just right. You can always find a period in any trend series where it goes one way rather than the other. You can seize on that and project in that direction. There is no logical way that we could ever say, on the basis of a given series, what the appropriate period was for forecasting. Using the longest run series to project what will happen rather than any shorter period provides better predictions.

Hardin: Let me explain it to you with an example. You have to understand the fundamentals. Take the case of copper.

Improvements in technology have been pushing the price of copper down. There have been improvements in technology continuously over 200 years up to the present. Presumably there'll be some in the future.

The exhaustion of the rich ores tends to push the price of copper up. When we first mined copper ore in this country, we mined 20 percent copper ores. Now we're mining 0.7 percent.

This is a very important point because the general theory that is made use of in thermodynamics shows that as you try to get anything from poorer and poorer ores using the same technology, it costs you more in terms of energy.

It takes energy to get the copper out of the ores, and, the poorer the ore, the more energy it takes. Fortunately for us, during most of our history the rate of improvement of technology has more than kept pace with the impoverishment of the ores.

But can one expect technology to improve forever? Will it keep up with the improverishment of the ores? Ultimately we'll be reduced to getting copper out of our junk heaps. After all, you can get copper out of any random sample of soil. But it costs fiendishly.

Wattenberg: *Doesn't that lead to recycling?*

Hardin: Yes, but the cost of recycling from a random sample of dirt is high.

Wattenberg: *To put it simply, you are making the case that we are running out of resources.*

Hardin: No. It is generally described as running out, but that's impossible because you never run out of an element like copper. You get down to the recycling stage, and finally recycle it from a random sample of dirt.

Wattenberg: *Copper will, therefore, get more and more expensive and consequently we will have less access to it and we will get poorer relatively.*

Hardin: No. We'll use more energy to get it.

Wattenberg: *If we use more energy, then it becomes more expensive because of energy costs.*

Hardin: The data since 1930 show that it has.

Simon: Earlier you said that the force of the improved technology was greater than the force of the diminishing richness of the ores—

Hardin: Up until 1930. Now, the curve is beginning to turn up.

Simon: But in the long run . . .

Hardin: If you want to take it from 6000 B.C. to 1930 it's down. From 1930 to the present it's up.

Simon: But at least we agree that whatever the forces are, whether it be technology or richness or the poverty of the ore, the overall effect has been a long-run decline in the cost of copper—

Hardin: This is useless. You're just building a straw man.

Simon: The most important price of copper is the price of copper relative to our time because our time is the most important thing to us. The price of copper as measured by its price relative to wages has gone down. That's the story of civilization right there.

Hardin: Energy is the important issue here.

Simon: Are you saying that price ought to be measured relative to other commodities rather than to the amount of time it takes to produce a good?

Hardin: Relative to other things.

Simon: Why?

Hardin: Relative to the price index, the price of copper has been rising. This is where you spend your money.

Wattenberg: *If we have not exhausted the copper, we've exhausted the argument for a moment.*

Let me just address a question to you, Dr. Hardin. You say that one should never exaggerate but that there is a range of scenarios and you feel safer describing the worse range rather than the better range. Have you found in the last ten years or so in the environmental movement a tendency to use worst-case scenarios? Isn't there a danger for the environmentalists of the boy who cried wolf? Today for example, one hears that everything causes cancer.

Has the environmental movement reached a point of diminishing returns in making worst-case scenarios?

Hardin: At the moment, it's at a low point, particularly because the Reagan administration is an anti-environmentalist administration. Jim Watt was put there for a purpose.

Wattenberg: *Is that anti-environmentalism reflecting a public climate of the sort I'm describing?*

Hardin: No. The Harris poll and some of the others have shown that the general public is still greatly concerned about environmental matters. The people who are in control of the shop are not the general public.

They are doing what they think is right. It does represent a reaction to environmentalism, part of which was earned by environmentalists.

There are many people speaking as environmentalists and some of them say some very foolish things. For example, many people speak as if it were possible to have absolutely safe foods, absolutely pure foods. This is not possible. It's a matter of relative risk, the cost of the risk versus the cost of doing something else.

The Delaney Amendment to the Pure Food, Drug, and Cosmetic Act mandated a zero tolerance level when it came to things that might cause cancer. This is absolutely intolerable scientifically. You cannot have zero concentration of anything.

The more contaminants you try to get out of a material—the purer you try to get it—the more it costs you. Just to give you an example, 95 percent alcohol sells for a certain price. One hundred percent alcohol sells for ten times that amount. Getting that last 5 percent out costs like hell. The same thing is true of every one of these pollutants or contaminants.

Wattenberg: *But environmentalists argue that we have to get the last bit of particulates out of the air.*

Hardin: I would not want to lump them that way. The Delaney Act was passed because congressmen are old men. They are afraid of cancer. Because they're scared, they wanted zero tolerance. They did not get any scientific advice.

Environmentalists who are scientists would never support a zero tolerance level for anything. There are a lot of environmentalists who have poor scientific training.

Keene: *Do you think people in society are less willing to take risks than they were ten or fifteen years ago?*

Hardin: What I do see and am sure of, is that the law has made it more difficult to take risks. Liability has been broadened and broadened so that it resembles the defensive medicine doctors practice.

In this aspect, I'm not sure that *people* are less willing to take risks. This curious complex we call the law has much to do with the level of risk taking. Lawyers want to make money. Juries want to give awards.

Wattenberg: *Haven't the environmentalists been making the case for a no-risk society or lower risk society?*

Hardin: They often have, indeed. In the past—going back quite a few years—a man could build a factory, put any sort of smoke into the air and get away with it, even though that undermined the health of the people living around the plant, and dirtied clothes and windows. Those were externalized costs.

Long before environmentalism we started writing laws on smoke stack effluents.

The basic environmental position is that the costs of every process should be internalized and not commonized or spread out over the whole public. The product produced by the factory has to go on the market at a higher price.

* * *

Simon: I want to go back to square one, which is what's happened in the past. The credibility of my point of view and of Dr. Hardin's rests on the correctness of our assessments of the trends in the past and of the data.

We as human beings have caused the price of copper to fall for the past 180 years, for the past 4500 years. The price has fallen.

Not only has the price of copper fallen relative to wages over time, the price of all metals has fallen. The prices of food, that is, the prices of wheat and grain, have fallen over these long periods. We have made them fall. Both statements are true. The quantity of food per person that people have eaten in the world for the past twenty-five years has risen.

We have made it rise. The air has gotten cleaner in London. We have made it cleaner.

Is it not a fact that the price of various raw materials, including food, is lower now than it has been in the past? You have written that the price has been going up. Let's get down to the business of which way the trend has gone because our credibility, yours and mine, hangs on this.

Hardin: We've been beating copper to death.

Simon: Try iron, aluminum, or zinc.

Hardin: Let's try something far more interesting and fundamental, namely food. Here we can begin with agreement that the amount of food available per person in the United States and in the world has risen in the last twenty-five years.

Wattenberg: *That statement is contrary to what many alarmists have been saying.*

Hardin: The amount of grain per capita around the world has increased slightly year by year for the last twenty-five years. But most of this increase has taken place in the rich countries, not in the poor countries. The per capita food allowance in rich countries is quite a bit better now than it was twenty-five years ago. In the poor countries, it is just marginally better. There still is a difference between the two.

Wattenberg: *But that's marginally better at a time of rising population.*

Hardin: Yes, in spite of the increase in the size of the population. What worries environmentalists is not the trends but the base—the soils from which the food comes. These improvements have taken place largely in corn because of valuable agricultural research. This has made the greatest difference because in the first place, 50 percent of the grains in international commerce come from the United States. Most of this is corn.

This has given a false impression of how good things are because 90 percent of the food that is eaten every place in the world is produced locally. The grains in international commerce are only 10 percent of the food.

The food in international commerce is the easiest to count. We're not really sure how much better the food situation is worldwide.

Wattenberg: *But it is better. Consumption as opposed to production.*

Hardin: Consumption is probably marginally better. Of course, there are fantastic differences between places.

Simon: How big is marginal?

Hardin: People may be eating 2 or 3 percent better than they did twenty-five years ago in the poor countries.

Simon: Two or 3 percent is incorrect. It's about 15 percent.

Hardin: The Food and Agricultural Organization tries to make these calculations. It doesn't do a very good job. Nobody else does either. We can reasonably estimate the food that goes to them in international commerce. It is much more difficult to estimate the food grown locally.

Simon: One of the important things about food is its price. Would you agree?

Hardin: For us, yes, but for a poor country it is not as important. Most of the food they grow locally does not enter the market at all.

Simon: The price of food has been falling over the long run by any measure you like. The price of food relative to wages in the United States has fallen very sharply.

Hardin: If you're a poor person in India, it doesn't make any difference.

Simon: The price of food relative to other products has been falling over the long run as well.

Hardin: Something must be rising.

Simon: That's correct.

Hardin: Julian, everything that you mention is rising relative to other things. Everything is falling relative to everything.

Simon: No, that's simply not right. The consumer price index includes all kinds of goods, including manufactured goods and other goods and services. The price of wheat and raw materials has been falling relative to this basket of goods.

So it's not that everything is falling relative to everything else, but raw materials are falling relative to manufacturer and produced goods and services. That's the relationship.

Let's be clear. It's not a matter of everything falling relative to everything else. Raw materials are falling relative to manufactured goods and services.

Hardin: Yes.

Simon: Okay. Fine. That's one of the things I said before and you said it was incorrect.

Hardin: Suppose you go on.

Simon: Okay. That's a lot right there.

Hardin: What is it that's rising now?

Simon: Services are rising; manufactured goods are rising relative to raw materials.

Hardin: Correct.

Simon: Now, this is particularly interesting because the people in the rich countries are saying, "My goodness, we've got to worry about the increasing scarcity of raw materials."

The people in the poor countries, however, have always worried and still worry about rising prices of manufactured goods.

Their perception is that their raw materials are getting less scarce and cheaper relative to other things. They are right on the facts whereas the people in the more developed countries and you in your writings in the past and Global 2000 have said the opposite. These facts are all important. That is why I keep coming back to them.

We can ask, what about the price in that place, what about the price in this place, but it is important that we not just try to qualify these facts out of existence. We must examine whether the statements about past trends that have been made in documents such as Global 2000 circulated to hundreds of millions of Americans and people in the rest of the world, are right or wrong.

Wattenberg: *Has the price of raw materials fallen relative to industrial goods?*

Hardin: Yes. You can also say industrial goods have risen in price relative to raw materials.

Simon: Yes, indeed.

Hardin: Perhaps that is the problem.

Simon: No. They have both fallen in price relative to our time which is as good a reference as anything.

*   *   *

Wattenberg: *Is the environmental movement elitist?*

Hardin: I refuse to discuss seriously the idea of elitism because I am a scientist. This is an elite group. All intellectuals are an elite group. This is the tar that people try to smear on people to keep them from thinking.

Wattenberg: *But science can be applied toward political ends. For example, zoning laws which restrict homebuilding in the suburbs in the name of environmental purity benefit the upper classes.*

Hardin: Environmentalists try to get the costs of production internalized, to reduce the smoke in the air, the air that is breathed by everyone. That is not an elitist point of view.

Wattenberg: *At the American Association for the Advancement of Science meeting, you made the case that the massive increase in the numbers of people using national parks was a sign of something gone wrong, not something gone right in our society. I thought that was being elitist.*

Hardin: Let's take another example. Take the Mona Lisa. We know the size of its. For curiosity, I once calculated what would happen if we gave everybody an equal share of the Mona Lisa. Each would would get about one-tenth of a millimeter square piece of it as a share. This would not be elitist, but it would be ridiculous. There's no Mona Lisa if you do that. Everybody can't look at the Mona Lisa. Just figure out how many thousands of people would have to go zipping by it every minute even to keep up with the birthrate—two hundred thousand more people each day just to keep up the birthrate. Everyone cannot enjoy the Mona Lisa.

Wattenberg: *One of the greatest achievements of civilization is the technology that enables all of us to see it.*

Hardin: In discussing the various technological improvements which have made it possible for more people to see the Mona Lisa, I find that you and I have different perceptions of reality.

I don't particularly like the example of the Mona Lisa. I'd rather take Van Gogh. If you compare Van Gogh paintings and prints of them, you realize that the print is not the reality. The camera has not captured it. You have to ration the real thing, because if everybody tries to see it, nobody does.

This is the point I wanted to make about the national parks. If everyone goes there, the very values you go there for—solitude and peacefulness—are destroyed. There's no way to build a four lane highway into the wilderness. We have a number of goods that involve scarce values.

The larger the population in toto, the smaller the fraction that can enjoy it. I view this with alarm because you're likely to get a revolt of the masses who say "To hell with it. If I can't enjoy it, let's build a dam over it because we need the water."

Simon: My own view of population size and growth in the United States is that in the long run, more people in the United States lead to a higher standard of living for all of us. More people imply more imaginative people to provide new knowledge and new ways of producing things.

They also provide increased demand for goods which leads to increased productivity. On balance, these effects tend to outweigh the negative effects of dilution of capital. This is why we can have larger numbers of people and at the same time, increasing incomes and larger homes to live in and, at the same time, more visits to national parks. More people do, at the same time, lead to new problems, and expected shortages. The result of these shortages and problems is that people see ways to profit from them, and they therefore get to work and develop solutions. The history of civilization seems to be that we wind up better off afterwards than if a problem had never arisen, better off than if the population had never grown to present us with that problem.

Garrett, you disagree with me about the centrality of the knowledge-producing capacity of additional people.

Wattenberg: *Julian, would you make your case globally as well?*

Simon: I make it for the entire more developed world. It is pretty clear that the less developed world has been the beneficiary of the knowledge that we in the more developed world have created.

Wattenberg: *Is it beneficial for population to continue to increase in the poor world?*

Simon: That's a very difficult question. That depends, among other things, on what their values are. "Beneficial" is not simply a scientific concept. It's a matter of the value of life to them. It also depends on their time horizons. It is very clear that an additional child is a burden immediately. Someone has to house the child, feed the child. It's only much later that the child can make a contribution. If your time horizon is short, then you simply say it's not worth it.

If you look at a longer term, you are likely to envisage benefits from additional children, a long way down the pike, and give them considerable weight in your present evaluation. Here Garrett and I agree. One of the best things ecologists have done for us is to urge us to take a long-range view.

Keene: *Our Agency for International Development policies have been directed toward birth control, toward the idea that fewer people are better in the less developed countries. Have our policies been correct?*

Simon: As I read our policy, and as I read AID discussions of our policy, it has not simply been to help people get the family size they want. It has been our policy to lean on these people to change their view of how many children they want. Furthermore, we have made certain kinds of aid contingent on complying with our views. Thus far in this administration there's been no basic change in AID's population policy.

Hardin: In keeping with your views on numbers, would you say we should reverse policy for India and urge them to have more children, to increase their birthrate so that they will have more people to solve their problems faster?

Simon: Not at all.

Hardin: Then you would encourage them to have fewer people?

Simon: No, I wouldn't encourage them at all.

Any decision about how many children a family should have, how many births a country should have, involves values.

I consider that it is neither my place nor the place of my country to recommend policies about these issues, because their lives, and their values must matter.

Wattenberg: *Do you feel so strongly about it that if you were asked, you would say, "You have no right to ask me?"*

Simon: They have a right to ask.

Wattenberg: *Would you give an opinion then?*

Simon: I would say, "Please tell me what your values are. Please tell me how much human life means to you. Tell me how important it is to you in human terms, how much you are willing to give up in the short run to have additional children," just as if a couple comes to you and says, "Ben, we just got married. How many children should we have?"

You begin by asking them some questions. And when they give you some answers about factual matters and their perceptions of their future, you can begin to synthesize their answers and give them your thoughts. But without gathering all this information about what their druthers are and what their views of the future are—how much they emphasize the future versus the present—you would be the worst kind of meddler to suggest such things to another person.

Hardin: You successfully evaded that so let's get on to another issue. When you say more people are better, this is viewing people as a commodity—if five is good, ten is twice as good and fifteen three times as good and so on. Although England has eleven times the population today it had in Shakespeare's day, there are not eleven Shakespeares in England. There may not even be one. The business of creativity is far more subtle than the commodity approach.

A man who is training research students does not take 2000 research students and train them all at once. Typically he has one to five. There are few successful people who have as many as twenty-five graduate students at the same time. With large numbers, you don't get more Shakespeares. You get fewer.

Wattenberg: *Belgium can't put up a space shuttle. They would not have enough engineers to do it.*

Hardin: Putting up a space shuttle is something else. That requires an immense infrastructure in manufacturing.

Simon: It requires a lot of engineers.

Hardin: They may have all the mathematicians they need to draw up the plans, but they can't build it. They give the plans to someone else. That's different.

Simon: When the populations of Rome and Greece were larger, there were more scientific discoveries than when they were smaller.

That's a better basis than an anecdotal reference to a single Shakespeare on which to argue. We have data to prove the point.

Similarly, at the AAAS meeting, I said we are growing more wood. You then said that we are running out of hardwoods. I then produced data which show we are growing more hardwood, too.

Hardin: I should have said cabinet grade hardwoods. Talk to any cabinet maker and get him to show you things that he made fifty years ago and things that he makes today. He cannot get the quality of cabinet woods that he could earlier.

Simon: You can take the argument to the point at which there are no facts that one can possibly adduce which will contradict what you are saying. You say hardwoods. I provide data for hardwoods. When I bring up data for hardwoods, you say you're not talking about hardwoods, but paneling.

Hardin: Hardwoods include oak, low grade oak to burn in the fireplace.

Simon: My definition of hardwoods is the definition the U.S. Department of Agriculture uses.

* * *

Garrett, you may be surprised to hear me say this but as far as I'm concerned, you are a more thoughtful and more imaginative advocate of environmental views and ideas than anybody else in the business. That's why I would like to know, given your capabilities, why you and people such as Paul Ehrlich resort to the kind of arguments you do—the ad hominem attacks, the editorializing? Even in our conversation today, you called something I said at the outset "silly." You use terms like "evaded." In your review of my book in the *New Republic,* you used terms like "car salesman," "budget evader," "jesuitical," "cancerous," "simple-minded," and "fast-change artist." Why do you use these tactics, and why do they seem to be concentrated on your side of the debate?

I'm not worried about the toughness of the argumentation. It's the lowness of it that affects me.

Hardin: That's a serious question and deserves a serious answer. Let's go back to your article in *Science* in June of 1980. That article, as you know, raised the blood pressure of the scientific community a good twenty points. Dozens of people asked me to do something about it. Let me take one point from it.

You said that when we run out of copper, we can make it from other metals. All of a sudden every scientist said, "My God, alchemy." We got rid of alchemy 300 years ago, and here's this idiot—I'm quoting other people—proposing to revive alchemy.

They blew up and they called you on it. Now, let me get to the facts before I get to your response. The facts are that it is possible to make copper from other metals. The most feasible method is to make it from the following. You start out with nickel-62; you irradiate it in a high energy machine. You get nickel-63. And then nickel-63 changes to copper-63. The half life of this reaction is 100 years. That's a little slow for the manufacturing process.

To put it another way, if you had 144 pounds of nickel-63 on January 1 you would get one pound of copper-63 by December 31. A pretty poor yield there.

But let's forget that. Let's just assume that this process takes place instantaneously. There are two ways to reckon the cost. One is money. The other is energy. I've done both. Given the present cost of electricity, and ignoring the lag time, the price of copper would be $2 billion a pound versus the present 80 cents a pound.

In terms of energy, think of it this way. The ordinary coal car has about 100 tons of coal in it. There are usually 100 cars in a train. To produce one pound of copper, you would have to have 150,000 trains of coal cars. It's a bad trade-off on energy and cost.

What was your defense? You said that in the past we thought other things couldn't be done. This is a Santa Claus defense. If we dream of Santa Claus, we will have Santa Claus.

But when something is so out of the realm of ordinary calculations, as your explanation was, you should have said you goofed. But you presented a very wordy defense saying that because some people thought electricity was not possible in the year 1820 and we have electricity today, therefore, anything we think is impossible now we will have in the future.

Simon: But is it not conceivable that we might have it in the future?

Hardin: We might have Santa Claus.

Wattenberg: *But somebody in 1819 said we would not have had electricity.*

Hardin: That's right. But this is where the prudent man rule comes in. The prudent man does not spend the money today he hopes to have tomorrow. Yours was a disgraceful defense. No scientist would have mounted this defense. I'm telling you frankly, Julian, why people are so intolerant of your low level of scientific inhibition.

Simon: I still question the ad hominem attacks. Why the attacks which say, (*a*) all economists do certain things; (*b*) you are an economist; and therefore (*c*) you are silly. Why?

You talk of yourself as a scientist. Of all the things which scientists pride themselves on, it is purging their language of editorializing. When the Royal Society of London set itself up in the seventeenth century, one of the main purposes was to purge scientific discourse of unscientific elements.

You repeatedly refer to yourself as a scientist, and yet you repeatedly use this kind of rhetorical device, which I believe is unscientific.

Hardin: I have tried to explain to you numerous times that you have to get beneath the figures. One acre listed in an Agriculture Department acreage table is not like another. Just because the figures add up, the issue isn't settled. This is the worst feature of economists. They deal only with figures and sometimes don't know what's behind them. You have to look behind the figures.

Afterword to Selection 44

Dr. Pangloss Meets Cassandra
Review of The Ultimate Resource *by Garrett Hardin in* The New Republic

If the reception of *The Limits to Growth* and *The Global 2000 Report* taught us nothing else it should have taught us that the Greeks were right. In the public relations game only optimism sells. Cassandra spoke the truth, but she was not believed. As Teiresias in Euripides's *The Phoenician Women* says: "A man's a fool to use the prophet's trade. For if he happens to bring bitter news he's hated by the man for whom he works."

In an engagingly frank introduction to *The Ultimate Resource* economist Julian L. Simon tells us that he used to be a Malthusian. At a particular well-remembered moment in 1969 he had a revelation that turned him into a born-again optimist. He is now making a very good thing out of his salvation, selling optimism by the bucketfuls to newspapers, magazines, and television.

The ultimate resource, Simon says, is people, and no limit can be set to what people may accomplish. What we usually call resources are mere phantasms. Simon's conclusions are highly palatable to budget evaders, car salesmen, realtors, advertisers, land speculators, and optimists in general; scientists find them appalling. According to Simon, natural resources are getting less scarce; pollution is decreasing; worldwide, food per person is increasing; the faster the population grows, the greater the prosperity; every additional person born into the population is a boon;

larger is better than smaller; the more immigrants we take in the better off our economy will be; diminishing returns is a meaningless concept; and there are no diseconomies of scale.

This is not optimism, this is euphoria. There has been nothing like it since the Marquis de Condorcet wrote his hymn to hope in 1793, *An Historical Picture of the Progress of the Human Mind,* while hiding from the French Revolution (which he had supported from the beginning). Condorcet made a grand survey of the history of humanity. The succession of stages—tribalism, pastoralism, agriculturalism, the Greek experience, the Dark Ages, the birth of science, etc.—he divided into ten epochs of which nine had been completed. Humanity was now moving into the tenth and last (Utopians apparently cannot free their dream worlds from the illusion of finality). Affiliating his persona to the panorama of time, Condorcet was, despite the bleakness of his prospects, intoxicated with the future of history. Speaking of himself as "the philosopher," i.e., the lover of wisdom, he concluded his book with this paean: "How admirably calculated is this picture of the human race [to console the philosopher] for the errors, the crimes, the injustice, with which the earth is polluted, and whose victim he often is!" We cannot but admire his courage in writing so optimistically of mankind when his personal situation was so hopeless. Shortly after finishing his book (which was published two years later), Condorcet left his refuge and immediately met the fate he foresaw—death at the hands of the Revolution.

That alarums should breed euphoria may seem strange, but on closer examination it makes sense. Nature has her own dialectic: when the future looks really hopeless you might as well be euphoric. Since no future is ever absolutely determined, psychological denial puts you in the best shape to seize whatever opportunities fortune may throw your way.

The parallel between Condorcet and Simon is more than superficial. The revolution that threatens Simon's peace is not political but intellectual. The simpleminded concept of progress (largely technological progress) that governed most policymaking during the past 200 years is now under severe attack, and the bitter news of real limits is more than the naive devotees of progress can bear. Denying reality, they embrace euphoria. Simon gives them an intellectual base for being born again as optimists.

Simon's first problem is to exorcize the terror of the finite, which he does by trend analysis and theory. Since the price of refined copper and wheat, in real dollars, has (ignoring short-term fluctuations) been on a downward trend for the past 200 years, it follows (he implies) that these commodities will forever become cheaper. But, as René Dubos has said, "Trend is not destiny." The last two centuries are only a moment in the life of the human species. What does the future hold?

The most important unknown in the future is the rate of development of new technology. Unfortunately there is no simple way to measure this rate. For a variety of reasons, the number of patents applied for and the number of scientific papers published per year do not give us the answer. For one thing, the "publish or perish" policy of universities encourages a cancerous growth of scientific papers. A measure of true progress has not been devised, but that does not stop Simon from pronouncing, "The pace of development of new technology in general is increasing." The Pope is not the only one who can speak *ex cathedra*.

That there might be theoretical limits to the supply of resources or the development of technology Simon denies on the most general grounds. The method he uses to establish the essential limitlessness of the world was exactly figured by Condorcet. In Simon's words:

> The length of a one inch line is finite in the sense that it is bounded at both ends. But the line within the end points contains an infinite number of points; these points cannot be counted, because they have no defined size. Therefore the number of points in that one inch segment is not finite. Similarly, the quantity of copper that will ever be available to us is not finite, because there is no method (even in principle) of making an appropriate count.

The translation of this statement is simple: anything that is infinitely divisible is infinite in quantity. So Simon says.

If this is the proper way to analyze resource problems Simon should, as a licensed economist, also tell people: "Don't worry about the small size of your bank account. You can always divide the dollars into cents, and if you still don't have enough divide the cents into mils. If that still isn't enough we can create a yet smaller unit so that you can have as many units as you want. You're rich!" Had Simon illustrated his argument with the appropriate economic example he would surely have seen his error.

Or would he? Possibly sensing the preposterousness of his position he falls back on two other arguments. As concerns our copper resources we must consider "the possibility of creating copper or its economic equivalent from other materials." Create copper from other materials? This is sheer alchemy, which science abandoned three centuries ago. True, nuclear physics furnishes a marginal—to use a favorite word of economists—defense of this possibility. With high energy radiation it is possible to produce a tiny amount of copper from other metals, but this yield is so slight that no one has ever bothered to calculate the cost. This is hardly the way to create what a responsible economist would call an infinite supply of copper.

As for the "economic equivalent" of copper, this raises the popular thesis of the "infinite substitutability of materials." It is true, of course, that as copper becomes higher in price we find that we can substitute aluminum for the copper. What happens as aluminum becomes scarcer? Presumably we could substitute some other metal—perhaps silver or gold. But each new substitute also exists in finite supply. There can hardly be an infinite number of substitutes, and in any case the mass of the earth (or of the solar system, or of the Milky Way, if you wish) is limited. The substitutability game is a game of musical chairs. Substituting one element after another for copper eventually brings us back to copper itself. We cannot transcend a finite supply.

Simon's other attack on the concept of finitude can only be called jesuitical. Discussing the petroleum situation he says: "The number of wells that will eventually produce oil, and in what quantities, is not known or measurable at present and probably never will be, and hence it is not meaningfully finite." One can only conclude from this that whatever is "not meaningfully finite"—whatever that may mean—is infinite. I am sure mathematicians will be delighted with this new insight into the meaning of the infinite.

Important though Simon considers his theoretical approach, he mostly relies on empirical facts to beat the reluctant reader into submission. "Information overload" is endemic in our time so every expositor has to choose only a fraction of the published material available. As one might expect, Simon chooses optimistic reports. For instance, he bases his rosy view of the future of petroleum resources on the pronouncements of Vincent McKelvey, a long-time director of the U.S. Geological Survey. McKelvey spoke from a prestigious platform, but it is astonishing that Simon does not realize how thoroughtly McKelvey's pronouncements have been discredited. For nearly a quarter of a century there was a running battle between McKelvey and his fellow geologist M. King Hubbert. In effect Hubbert said, "The end is nigh," while McKelvey said, "Don't worry—there's plenty for everyone." Like Cassandra, Hubbert was not believed. Then, as the 1973 oil crisis approached, other geologists reexamined the arguments of McKelvey and Hubbert and concluded that Hubbert was right, noting that his projections had been uncannily accurate for two decades. Director McKelvey had been talking through his hat—his political hat. For the past ten years everyone who follows energy closely has known that M. King Hubbert is right, but his name is not to be found in Simon's book. Neither is there any recounting of his analysis. This is a pity because Simon, who leans heavily on the most simpleminded trend analysis, could learn much by a careful study of the sophisticated, ingenious, and open-minded methods of analysis used by Hubbert. Leaving Hubbert and his work out of a book-long discussion of resources is like omitting the names and works of Adam Smith and John Maynard Keynes from a treatise on economics.

Simon is, he admits, a "cornucopist," a person who thinks there's always plenty more in nature's cup. In his idiosyncratic view agricultural productivity will increase forever. Is water scarce? Drill more holes in the ground. The fact that water secured in this way is mined water and hence subject to depletion (as are all mined substances) goes unmentioned by Simon. Anyway, if water becomes more expensive, we can resort to trickle irrigation. The fact that the benefits of this will soon be eaten up by the exponential growth of demand is never considered.

Discussing the stock of agricultural land under the pressure of population growth, Simon, like the fast change artist at a county fair, befuddles the reader with rapid rhetorical interchanges of "arable land," and "cultivated land," whereby he "proves" that the amount of agricultural land is increasing in the world. To Simon, as to a legion of economists, an acre is an acre, and a table of figures is the ultimate reality. Such economists are unable to see the difference between the rich glacial soil of Iowa corn land and worn-out tobacco land in Georgia. True, it is astonishing what a farmer can do with generous amounts of fertilizer and irrigation, but every corrective costs money (and energy). Agriculturalists are appalled when rich glacial till or fertile alluvial soil in an old flood plain is covered over by shopping malls, factory buildings, and highways. As M. Rupert Cutler, formerly Assistant Secretary for Agriculture, said: "Asphalt is the land's last crop." So it is in the rich countries; in poor countries the last crop is desert.

The Department of Agriculture estimates that the U.S. is losing a million acres of prime farmland each year to urban sprawl. Does this bother Simon? Not a bit! The paragraph in which he demolishes this bugaboo of the environmentalists is worth quoting in its entirety for it gives the flavor of the entire book.

> The idea that cities devour 'prime land' is a particularly clear example of the failure to grasp economic principles. Let's take the concrete (asphalt?) case of a new shopping mall on the outskirts of Champaign-Urbana, Illinois. The key economic idea is that the mall land has greater value to the economy as a shopping center than it does as a farm, wonderful though this Illinois land is for growing corn and soybeans. That's why the mall investors could pay the farmer enough to make it worthwhile for him or her to sell. A series of corn-y examples should bring out the point.

Note the sleight of hand by which the economist substitutes "prime land" for "prime farmland," thus preparing the reader to evaluate the land solely in terms of price on the open market. At a particular moment an acre may indeed be more "valuable" (more revenue-producing) as a part of a shopping mall than as a grower of crops. A purely economic decision focuses on the moment. In practice, economics makes no allowance for future shifts in relative values. In the future the price of corn *relative* to the price of such competing economic goods as the stuff stores sell may rise precipitously. It certainly will if population growth gets out of hand.

A change in relative prices calls for a change in the economist's definition of "prime" and "highest use." If economic calculations could allow for such quite likely future changes, then society could safely put the future in the hands of free-market economists. But the standard technique of "discounting" the future with a negative exponential functions lays waste to the real future. With the high rate of interest prevailing now, the future—as the economist anticipates it—virtually disappears. When money is earning 20 percent interest, land anticipated to be worth a million dollars as farmland a generation from now (30 years) would command only $1238 of today's money. What counts most is what income the land can bring in right now. High interest has the effect of virtually destroying the future—in the economist's calculations.

The professional inability of the economist to deal adequately with the future has an equally unfortunate corollary: economics is blind to the irrevocable. Thirty years from now a change in the relative prices of grains and commercial gewgaws may make land more valuable as farmland than as shopping malls; but the cost of clearing millions of tons of concrete, asphalt, glass, and chromium from what was once prime farmland can make the correction of the earlier error in judgment economically impossible. A society that listens only to economists ratchets its way to destruction.

Economic libertarians and doctrinaire free-market economists who concede no limits to the simpleminded method of discounting the future are today's providentialists. Pure economics will, in their view, create the best of all possible worlds. We need another Voltaire to write a new *Candide*.

Only political restraints (which are unacceptable to libertarians) can keep a laissez-faire system from destroying itself in a limited world. It is probably their inchoate realization of this truth that leads so many libertarians to deny the reality of limits. If limits can be set aside as some sort of unreality, then growth can continue forever without an increase in the price of money. Everyone can then forever prosper in a free market. The specter that haunts the minds of libertarians and cornucopists is the specter of material limits.

The exorcism of this specter has been greatly aided by a recurrent confusion between material and immaterial resources. Condorcet's book was an account of the progress of the human *mind;* he said that "nature has assigned no limit to the perfecting of the human faculties.'' This is perhaps true; for the sake of argument let us grant that it is. But where does "mind" fit into the scheme of things? Science deals with three kinds of reality: information, matter, and energy. The second and third are material and are bound by conservation laws. The first, information, is immaterial and is not constricted by conservation. Mind operates in the realm of information.

From Condorcet to Simon, compulsive optimists have shown the utmost ingenuity in confusing information with the material aspects of the world. A thesis proved in one realm is surreptitiously transferred to the other. Where nonconservation holds sway, limits may not be terribly important; but in the conservative world of matter and energy, limits are central to all disciplined thinking and planning. Economics professors love to tell their students that "there's no such thing as a free lunch" thus expressing an orientation that aligns economics with the natural sciences as a conservative discipline. But the usefulness of economics to commerce, which thrives on providential thinking, corrupts some economists into denying limits and abandoning conservative thinking. Pollyanna becomes the patron saint. Intoxicated with the progress of technology during the past two centuries, some economists now say there must be a free lunch somewhere.

The literary world has long realized that the putative subject of a work of fiction may not be the real subject. It is not so widely recognized, however, that economists and scientists, when they set forth what they conceive to be the policy implications of their disciplines, may also be trying to free themselves through psychoanalysis. Simon puts his confession at the beginning of his book, and he frankly uses the first person. The source of his anxiety is not external, as was Condorcet's, but internal. Simon's mind used to be caught in the Malthusian mode and he was "in the midst of a depression of unusual duration." He escaped this depression by freeing himself of the Malthusian belief that material limits are real. Now he wants to free others—and to find companions. "Some others hold a point of view similar to mine. But there are far too few of us to provide mutual support and comfort. So this is a plea for love, printer's ink, and research grants for our side."

Malthus, a devout and practicing Christian, would not begrudge Simon the love he seeks. But would Malthus—or should we—grant him his other requests? Observation shows that printer's ink and research grants (publicity and power) are bestowed in abundance on the Pollyannas of this world. Simon is being greedy when he asks for more than the plethora he has been receiving since he became a born-again optimist. Cassandra is the one who needs support. If the limits of the material world are real—if Cassandra is right—continued denial of those limits will be disastrous for our descendants.

45

Global Foresight Bills: The Danger of Centralized Data Sources

To those persons whose vision of the social world is not infused with the intuition of, and belief in, the workings of the Hidden Hand and "spontaneous order"—that is, those persons who do not share the ideas that have come to us from Mandeville, Hume, Smith, Menger, Mises, Hayek, and Friedman—it is literally inconceivable that government planning is not a valuable activity. And if government is to plan economic activity, it makes sense that government should set up facilities to forecast the future.

This selection directly attacks the latter assumption about the value of government forecasting. Then by implication the selection attacks the former assumption about the necessary value of government planning.

This viewpoint is greeted with incredulity by enthusiasts for "rational" government organization of economic life. It is seen by them as a sign of invincible primitive ignorance, as resistance to the power of science and intellect. The dominance of their planning viewpoint among policymakers, not just in socialist countries but also in "capitalist" countries, is of huge importance, I believe. (An interesting question is why a statist planning view has not been converted into action more completely in U.S. society. But that is a question for another day.)

More generally, an important element in scarcity fears is the lack of understanding by so many persons in our society of the nature of a spontaneously evolving economy, and especially of a market economy. Many—including many in the highest echelons of power and (regrettably) also many economists even though this is the central lesson of economics that has been taught us by the classics—do not

Heritage *Issue Bulletin*, Feb. 24, 1984.

understand how independent individuals, acting on their own behalf, interact without any central direction in ways that produce the goods and services that we need more effectively than could any centrally directed organization. Too many of us do not trust that this process will provide us wheat and natural gas and beautiful trout streams and housing for the poor, reliably and at low cost, despite the overwhelming evidence from economic history that government farms are inevitably a failure, and rent control always results in a decrease of available housing.

Sometimes people have trouble believing in spontaneously developing social structures because of their occupational training. For example, no matter how much a bunch of generals talk up free enterprise—as in Chile right now, for example—they usually fall back on telling people what to do from command center, rather than moving toward free private enterprise. Others believe that the poor and uneducated—that is, people without PhD's—are not sufficiently rational to make wise decisions about their procreative lives and about job and family, and need their educated betters—the philosopher princes (and princesses)—to guide their lives. Plato is the most famous spokesman for this way of thinking.

For those persons not accustomed to seeing the spontaneous evolution of cooperative human activity, a visit to a squatters' barrio in a Latin American city is enlightening. From the outside it seems to be an anomic collection of social misfits. Inside, discussion with the residents usually reveals highly organized committees to provide services to the neighborhood, and to bargain for improvements with the city's officials. And indeed, most of the residents are likely to be hardworking folks who have moved there to build their own homes so that they can live more cheaply than in rented apartments elsewhere in the city.

Introduction

Will major U.S. industries be damaged, as were the auto and air transportation industries in the 1970s, by inaccurate government energy forecasts? Will huge subsidy programs based on such forecasts, like the controversial Synfuels Corporation, be set up and later be seen as a waste? Will unnecessarily large stockpiles of raw materials such as tin be held by the federal government because of unsound forecasts of tin prices and requirements? Will flexibility-reducing and cost-increasing regulations be imposed on agricultural land? Will the public be thrown into despair about the world's future, as when great pessimism followed the doomsday forecasts about resources culminating in the *Global 2000 Report to the President?*

Perhaps so, if plans materialize for establishing a federal agency to centralize and manage what is called "global foresight capability." Several bills before Congress seek to do this. Among them are the Hatfield-Ottinger bill (S.1025/H.R.2491), the Gore-Gingrich bill (H.R.3070), and H.J.Res.248. Backing these bills are two private organizations—the Task Force on Foresight Capability and the Global Tomorrow Coalition—and the official Congressional Clearinghouse on the Future.

There is, of course, an appropriate role for the federal government in providing basic data, such as censuses of population and agriculture, that cannot and will not be produced independently. Such data are relatively safe from political manipulation and are crucial grist for private as well as public decisionmaking. But the U.S. needs a diversity of analyses of basic American and global trends by a variety of the best thinkers on these subjects. The proposed centralized activity would likely have the opposite result. The analyses probably would be made by run-of-the-mill staff persons. Diversity would be edited out of them so that consumers of the data (such as the President and Congress) would be unaware of the extent of the uncertainty. The results would be accessible to political influence, while independent voices would come to have less attention and less weight in decisionmaking. This is a disastrous outlook for the national economic health.

Forecasting Bills Before Congress

Legislation introduced by Representative Albert Gore (D-TN) and Representative Newt Gingrich (R-GA) calls broadly for the "assessment of critical trends and alternative futures," not specifying which trends are meant. It says "while the Government has available to it enormous information resources, there is a need to supplement existing capabilities to provide a systematic and comprehensive use of that information to guide policymakers concerning critical trends and alternative futures." The bill is offered as an amendment to the National Energy Conservation Policy Act. For this reason, as well as because of the groups backing the bill, it presumably would focus mainly on natural resources and the environment.

Gore-Gingrich calls for establishing an "Office of Critical Trends Analysis" in the executive office of the President. Its functions would be:

. . . identification and analysis, of critical trends and alternative futures for the ensuing 20-year period; a description of the relationship of such trends and alternative futures to the economic, technological, political, environmental, demographic, and social causes and consequences; an analysis of such trends and alternative futures with respect to present and future problem areas and potential future opportunities; an evaluation of the effects of existing and alternative government policies on such trends; and an identification of the information and a discussion of the analysis upon which conclusions in the report are based.

In addition to these functions, which ostensibly concern simply the provision of information, the Office would:

(1) analyze available information to identify present policies and policy options for the United States in a relation to critical trends and alternative futures: (2) review Federal laws, regulations, programs, and other activities of the Federal Government to determine their long-term effects; (3) prepare reports for the President as necessary and appropriate; (4) insure that the Federal departments, agencies, and establishments with responsibilities in the area of policy under consideration are provided an opportunity to comment on the potential effects of Government policies on critical trends and alternative futures; (5) consider the comments of such Federal departments, agencies, and establishments in performing its functions under this section; and (6) include the official comments of such Federal departments, agencies, and establishments in any reports provided to the President by the Office under the authority of this section.

The bill introduced by Senator Mark Hatfield (R-OR) is called the "Global Resources, Environment and Population Act of 1983" (S.1025); it focuses on population control. The purposes of this Act are:

(1) to provide for coordinated national planning for changes in national population characteristics; (2) to facilitate the attainment of a balance, both national and through cooperation with other nations, globally, between population characteristics, the use of natural resources, and environmental change; (3) to encourage national population stabilization and to encourage voluntary family planning in accordance with the World Population Plan of Action adopted in Bucharest in 1974 by the United States and 136 other nations . . .; (4) to assure that, in the interpretation and administration of Federal laws, regulations, and policies, and the planning and administration of the programs of the Federal Government, the goal of national population stabilization and projections on national and global trends in population characteristics will be considered; (5) to establish an interagency council to improve the capability of the Federal Government to provide the President, the agencies, and the Congress with accurate, timely and internally consistent projections of short-term and long-term national and global trends in population characteristics, the availability of natural resources, and environmental change; and (6) to assure coordination of the activities of all agencies which assess the effects of the national and global trends referred to in clause (5) on the national security and the economic well-being of the people of the United States, and on Federal, State, and local policies and programs relating to education, employment, housing, agriculture, com-

merce, energy, the environment, transportation, communications, and services to senior citizens.

The interagency council proposed by this bill would:

(1) (A) coordinate population research . . . and compile . . . trends, (B) analyze and interpret such information . . . and (C) . . . submit . . . studies . . . to promote the purposes of this Act . . .; (2) review the laws, regulations, programs, and activities of the Federal Government . . . make recommendations [for] achievement or implementation of the purposes and policies of this Act; (3) develop and recommend to the President and the Congress a national population policy, including a national policy on immigration, which will . . . promote national population stabilization in the United States; (4) conduct investigations relating to . . . the impact of the population characteristics on the availability of natural resources, the environment, and achievement of national population stabilization . . .; (5) develop and recommend to the President policies and programs which will encourage global population stabilization at a level which is consistent with the highest possible standard of living and does not deplete the natural resources of the world or degrade the global environment. . . .

The texts of these foresight bills (see also Selection 54) make very clear that research, analysis, planning, and policy advice are intended. They go far beyond what Representative Robert Edgar (D-PA), a leading advocate of a global foresight agency and Chairman of the Congressional Clearinghouse on the Future, says is only to be a "forum" for bringing together members of Congress in an atmosphere where they can take a long look into the future. Edgar talks of getting the President and others to "look over the wall" to see what lies beyond the immediate present. It sounds as if what he intends is exactly what the Congressional Clearinghouse on the Future already provides, apparently very effectively.

But creating a forum for discussion does not require a bill in Congress, an agency, and a fat budget. The resources and the interest already mobilized for the Clearinghouse and similar organizations are sufficient for such a forum. If there is to be an act of Congress, the results will be much more substantial than a mere lecture and debating society for the President and the Congress. The bills make this very clear.

It is the nature of a bureaucracy, moreover, to stretch to, and then beyond, the limits of its charter. Rather than limiting itself to organizing discussion, a "global foresight" agency is almost certain to venture into directive planning. This is likely to happen even if the agency is set up with the most honest intentions. For some foresight sponsors, however, directive planning may be the long-term goal. R. J. Smith of the Council for a Competitive Economy reports that at meetings of the Global Foresight Roundtable he has heard participants emphasize the importance of the environmental movement in pulling together for the establishment of a certain kind of an agency, because once in place it can be transformed into a more active and far-reaching activity than it is originally described to be. There is sufficient latitude in the Gore-Gingrich and Hatfield bills to allow such vast expansion of powers.

Double-Speak about "Planning"

The term "planning" occurs frequently in the Hatfield bill; the phrase "coordination of the activities of all agencies" also appears. The texts of the bills seem to indicate that, from the activities of the agency, there would flow to, and then perhaps through, the President and Congress instructions for conducting businesses—regulations about the use of raw materials, choice of mode of transportation, and kinds of labor to hire. In the Hatfield bill, the meddling in the lives of individuals is shown most clearly with respect to population size. It calls for "population stabilization." Senator Hatfield says that he is in favor of "voluntary" stabilization, but in the same sentence he talks about the government "encouraging" the "voluntary" stabilization. Whatever "voluntary" means here, it is not that people will simply be left alone to do what they think best about their families, in an atmosphere of complete independence, without any kind of government meddling. If such were to be the case, then there would be no role for the government and no place for Hatfield's bill. It would seem that "voluntary" and "encouraging" are contradictory terms, suggesting one goal, but in fact aiming at another.

The backers of these bills are candid about their careful use of language to avoid raising the hackles of those who oppose more government planning of business activity and personal lives. Russell W. Peterson, President of the Audubon Society and Chairman of the Global Tomorrow Coalition, told the House Energy and Commerce Committee's Subcommittee on Oversight and Investigations:

> I recognize that "planning," and even worse, "long range planning," have become buzz words. Government planning is equated in some quarters with Soviet 5 year plans and thus has about it an aura of communism, or at least, socialism. And that is very strange, because it is considered perfectly splendid, indeed a necessity, for business and industry to have long range planning. But applied to government, it somehow becomes unsavory. In recognition of this unfortunate connotation often given to planning, we have substituted the term "foresight capability.

Writes Donald Lesh, Global Tomorrow Coalition executive director, in its magazine:

Language can be a bridge, or a barrier. We all are well advised to think carefully about the effects of the words we use. . . . The experts are right in saying that "plan" is a four letter word for many people. . . . In some circles the very words "government planning" are enough to set off sirens and alarms. To many, those words are synonymous with Big Brother, socialism, communism, authoritarianism, totalitarianism . . . choose your "ism." That's why we spend time searching for descriptive circumlocutions. . . . Right now, the term for that process is "national foresight," and that's not bad—especially if you can't say "planning."

Most of the backers of these bills probably believe that greater government activity in collecting information on matters of resources, environment, and population is all that would occur. But other backers surely aim at increased government planning for land use, industrial policy, family size, resource production and use, environmental regulation, and the like.

A major flaw in the case made by foresight advocates is the analogy they draw between government and business planning. They disregard the very large differences between private and public planning. Businesses and individuals plan for their own activities and thereby control only themselves. Government agencies, on the other hand, plan for and control persons other than the voluntary members of the group being planned for (except in the widest sense). Businesses and individuals, moreover, bear the consequences of their own planning; a business loses its assets if it plans badly. In contrast, government agencies suffer no personal loss if they plan badly. And expectations are very different when plans are made by individuals who will benefit or pay the costs than they are when others receive the benefits or pay the costs. In their planning, individuals and businesses take advantage of the special knowledge available to them because of their closeness to their own situations. This is not the case with governmental agencies, which try to use knowledge about others, in the collection of which they have no special advantage.

Concerning the proposition that, if private planning is good, government planning must also be good, Nobel Laureate economist Friedrich A. Hayek wrote:

The dispute between the modern planners and their opponents is . . . *not* a dispute on whether we ought to choose intelligently between the various possible organizations of society; it is not a dispute on whether we ought to employ foresight and systematic thinking in planning our common affairs. It is a dispute about what is the best way of so doing. The question is whether for this purpose it is better that the holder of coercive power [the state] should confine himself in general to creating conditions under which the knowledge and initiative of individuals are given the best scope so that *they* can plan most successfully; or whether a rational utilization of our resources requires *central* direction and organization of all our activities according to some consciously constructed "blueprint." The socialists of all parties have appropriated the term "planning" for planning of the latter type, and it is now generally accepted in this sense. But though this is meant to suggest that this is the only rational way of handling our affairs, it does not, of course, prove this. It remains the point on which the planners and the liberals disagree.

Foresight Quality: Government vs. Nongovernment

Pennsylvania Congressman Robert Edgar speaks of the benefits of a governmental forecasting agency if its tasks were "done well." But there is no ground for presuming that such an agency would perform the tasks better than might be done by independent individuals or firms, either commissioned by the government to do such work or simply doing it in pursuit of their own scholarly and policy interests. The reasons:

1. Johns Hopkins political scientist William Ascher's study of forecasts by various persons inside and outside government does not show any advantage in accuracy for government forecasts. And unless the government forecasts were superior, it would seem that outside forecasts would be preferable for the following reasons:

(a) Government forecasts are likely to be much more expensive. For example, the Gore-Gingrich bill budgets $5,000,000 each year. Yet the government could commission outside studies by university scholars and professional organizations to cover all the topics desired for a small fraction of that sum, say $100,000.

(b) Government forecasts are likely to be treated with more respect than nongovernment forecasts even though they are not necessarily more reliable. For example, the publication of the *Global 2000 Report to the President* was greeted by full-page stories and banner headlines.

(c) A single government forecast is likely to be the mid-point or consensus of several separate forecasts, which obscures the variation that would be apparent if all the separate forecasts were shown. This variation is important information that ought not be lost.

The inability of government agencies to predict resource trends accurately, together with the credibility that attaches to "official" forecasts, has proved especially damaging in the past decade. For example, after a sharp price rise in the late 1970s, federal "experts" predicted timber shortages. Yet timber prices in 1983 "plunged to a quarter of their highs," causing agony for lumber companies that had contracted for government timber at the high prices—and a request for an industry bailout on the grounds that their troubles stemmed from government actions.

The Department of Energy caused havoc for airplane manufacturers, airlines, a host of other industries, and foreign governments by its forecasts that the price of oil would continue to rise after 1979. In contrast, many private sector experts predicted that the price would not continue to rise. The story is the same for other raw materials. Does such a history constitute the basis for increasing the role of government in these matters—or for decreasing it?

It seems sensible to compare systematically the record of long-run government forecasts with the record of a reasonable sample of nongovernment forecasts before making any decision in favor of further centralization. To enact legislation without evidence of a government advantage in the activity would not be responsible.

The validity of the *Global 2000 Report to the President* of 1980 is important evidence here. For one thing, it is repeatedly cited as the point of departure for the global foresight movement by sponsors of the bills and others. For another, it is a test case for government forecasting capacity because it was an expensive effort and is the flagship of the movement. Congressman Edgar told a Heritage Foundation seminar that *Global 2000* makes a powerful argument for continuation of similar efforts of data collection and analysis. Yet *Global 2000* is wrongheaded in its methods and results. Even the authors of *Global 2000* no longer seem willing to argue its validity on a factual basis.

2. As Clemson University economist and Heritage Foundation Senior Fellow Richard McKenzie puts it, "the Office of Critical Trends Assessment would not be, as presumed, staffed by eminent visionaries with talents dramatically elevated above those of many other Americans or government workers. Rather, it would likely be managed by political appointees and run-of-the-mill bureaucrats who have no greater grasp of the future than anyone else."

3. Forecasts from outside government are likely to be based on a wider variety of information than are those from inside the government, because forecasts emerging from a single setting—even by different individuals— are likely to draw upon the same information base. Forecasters in the same agency talk to each other and share data, and if they disagree sharply, they are likely to talk each other into less extreme positions. But forecasters who work independently for different organizations far removed from each other physically are more likely to dig up varying sources of information and not to blur the sharp edges.

4. Notes Robert Rockwell, an anthropologist with Softlab in Munich: For any given forecast topic, there are usually a fair number of persons outside of government who have specialized in the matter whose expertise based on their long and expensive investment into knowledge of the subject can be called upon relatively cheaply. But if the forecast is done inside government, the work must be performed by persons who have not spent

much of their professional lives on the topic. Because acquisition of such knowledge by government staff members is very time consuming and expensive, there will be neither time nor funds to make as great an investment as has been made already by the experts outside government who have already devoted much of their lives to the topic. In other words, government can commission forecasts much more cheaply, and gain information on a broader knowledge base, from outside experts than if the work is done internally.

Congressman Edgar asserts that "we need to have the best thinkers available" to the Congress and to the executive branch in order to foresee the long run as well as possible. But it is nearly certain that the best thinkers will be found outside government and Washington. To locate forecasting and foresight inside the government means that the work will probably not be done by the best thinkers.

(a) Example: The acid rain problem has been studied recently by a committee convened by the National Academy of Sciences, which is more an academic than a government activity. This does not guarantee that the conclusions are sound, or even that it is the best possible committee. But it is extraordinarily unlikely that any staff could be hired by a government agency that could equal the NAS committee in accumulated knowledge or professional stature.

(b): Example: The American Statistical Association organized a study by some of its top members of the dangers of cigarette smoking. It is inconceivable that the existing staff of any government agency, or any additional staff hired for the purpose, could compare to the ASA group.

The work done by the NAS and ASA committees was obtained by the government at a fraction of what it would have cost to have less-qualified people on the federal payroll do the work.

The Bias in Government Forecasts

Outside forecasts would be preferable even if they were no better than inside forecasts. But government forecasts also probably will be worse, in the sense that they are likely to be biased. Reasons:

1. Government produced reports must pass through reviews all the way up the chain of command. The final conclusions of a staff report therefore are likely to emphasize conventional views and to reduce the range of opinion expressed. The resulting work therefore cannot be attributed to individuals, and no individual need take full responsibility. In contrast, private individuals are fully accountable for their analyses. Their reputations rest on the quality of their work. This is not to denigrate the efforts of hardworking civil servants, but rather to suggest that internally prepared

assessments suffer because of the organization of government. This certainly was the case with *Global 2000*. Its director Gerald Barney has said that, although he regarded a key statement in *Global 2000* "as incorrect, it was not possible to have it corrected." Since bureaucratic editing can have that much effect, little in such a report should be considered scientifically reliable.

2. Internal government analyses are often a hodgepodge of elements of unknown origin and nature. Notes Barney:

> As they have evolved, the Government's agencies now have a hidden layer of decision makers—computer programmers and modelers. These decision makers are, by and large, very skilled professionals, but they are often working in institutional circumstances which prevent them taking into account all the factors they know should be taken into account. Furthermore, the assumptions that they make have a profound influence on the range of policy options considered by senior government officials, and their assumptions are not well documented, are not understood by senior government officials, and are not available for peer review and comment.

3. Government assessments will be biased in favor of advising government activity. As Softlab's Rockwell puts it:

> It is both predictable and appropriate that a government-sponsored commission would recommend that some new government initiative is needed. If you go to an architect, tell him your problems, your plans, and your dreams, he will recommend you build a building. Why else did you come to him? If you take your problems to a doctor, you get a prescription; if you go to a programmer, he'll say you need a computer. This is not even self-serving in the negative sense: You asked these guys what they can do for you, and they told you. The president says "what should government be doing?" and the answer comes "set up an office to handle it."

4. There is a tendency for governmental organizations to report bad news rather than good news because it seems to confirm the need for organizations to act as watchdogs and early-warning agencies and because it supports the need for government activity and funding.

5. Even the least cynical person knows that any report emanating from a government agency is subject to political warping. The director of the *Global 2000* report complained of this, as did Michael Brewer, research director of the National Agricultural Lands Study, one of the most important recent government environmental studies.

Many persons in and out of government—perhaps most notably former President Jimmy Carter—believe that there is vital need for government forecasts about future resource availability, the state of the global environment, and a host of other critical matters.

In the case of resources, if it were to be the government's responsibility to provide natural resources or ensure that they were provided, the government would need forecasts about future availability. But if it were to be the responsibility of the private sector to provide such resources, there would be no need for such forecasts, except for the very limited purpose of deciding how much to stockpile for military security. Private firms need forecasts on which to base decisions about investment activities. But they know the business of forecasting for their own purposes better than any government agency is likely to. There are, moreover, always a variety of conflicting forecasts. In an orderly market, the bullish forecasts balance out the bearish forecasts. A single government forecast is likely to do no more than unduly influence the welter of conflicting forecasts and inflict damage, as occurred with government energy forecasts in the 1970s—and as happened to Japan and other countries with respect to resource forecasts following 1973.

Conclusion

The crux of the problem seems to be that many persons in and out of the government do not (perhaps cannot) understand that natural resources and other materials are best provided by the spontaneous process that takes place as a result of billions of individual decisions all over the world. It requires no government planning; it would be hampered by it. To those unfamiliar with this market process, it seems chaotic. They thus call for governmental action to end "chaos" and assure "efficiency." They do not take notice that the market has in the past, and continues today, to provide such materials to the world. The call for government "foresight" reflects the belief that the market will not and cannot provide the needed flow of resources and other goods but that governments can.

Those opposing government forecasting and foresight are not against such information *per se*. They simply point out the lesson of history that the most reliable and useful information about resources usually is provided by private individuals, not the government. It is a difference in place and type of analyst, rather than a difference in interest in the results, that separates the two points of view.

The discussion about creating a central global foresight agency may be seen as part of an argument raging at least since the time of Plato. There are those, like Plato, who believe that a society can find and elevate to office true philosopher-kings, who are few in number but who can be relied upon to have deeper insight and greater wisdom than the rest of the people. On the other side are those who believe that usually such inherently superior persons do not exist (except "me," of course, when "me" is each of us), and even if they do exist, society is not likely to be able to identify them. This side of the argument believes that a process intended to find and place in office philosopher-kings is likely to put in place boob-kings, who will simply exploit the power handed them. Federal forecasting and foresight seem a certain prescription for elevating boob-information and data to an official position. This is something that the American people and economy can very well do without.

Part 7
PROGRESS, WORLD VIEWS, AND MODES OF THOUGHT

Introduction

Part 7 makes heavier reading than do other sections in this volume because it deals with the philosophical underpinnings of the earlier discussions of specific issues.

Differences among forecasts about resources, environment, and population derive in part from different "world views." And differences in world views in turn derive in part from differences in values.

Lest this be thought obvious, please remember how people were spooked—the excitement peaking on the astonishing 1970 Earth Day—by supposedly "scientific" assertions about the evil of population growth and the impending pinch of natural resources. Those who worried most did not recognize that such assertions are conditional upon values and paradigms that can be (and are) chosen at will. This blurb from *The Population Bomb,* the basic document of the environmentalist movement at that time, was noted earlier: "Paul Ehrlich, a qualified scientist, clearly describes the dimensions of the crisis. . . . over-population is now the dominant problem. . . . population control or race to oblivion?" (1968, cover). The purported value-free scientific objectivity of such statements caused widespread despair and led to vast misallocation of resources here and abroad.

Simon N. Patten opened his 1907 *The New Basis of Civilization* as follows:

> One summer day I took my note-book to a wooded hillside whence I could overlook a rich and beautiful valley. The well-tended farms, the strong stone houses, the busy men and animals moving peacefully over roads and fields, would inspire me, I was sure, with the opening theme of this book. As I seated myself under a chestnut tree a fellow-guest at the hotel came by, and glancing at my memoranda asked if I, like himself, was writing a lecture. He too had come to the woods, he said, to meditate and to be inspired by nature. But his thesis, enthusiastically unfolded, was the opposite to mine. It was a part of his faith as a Second Adventist that the world is becoming more unhappy and more wicked; and it is now so evil that the end of it approaches. . . . Where I marked the progress of humanity and thrilled with the hope that poverty will soon be banished from the world as it has been from this happy valley, he saw a

threatening scene of worldliness where prosperity lulled spiritual alarms to a dangerous moral peace. (1907/68, pp. 3–5.)

In addition to our world views and values influencing our selection and assessment of the facts, the reverse influence also operates; the facts that come within our ken influence the value judgments that we make. For example, philosophers have recently written much about resources and population in connection with such issues as the rights of present versus future generations; the rights of poor versus rich countries; policies toward immigration; and the necessity of limiting freedom. All those I have read base their analyses on the assumption that additional persons imply less natural resources per person. (A variety of these philosophical views are collected in Sikora and Barry, 1978, and reviewed by Bayles, 1980.) See also Parfit, 1982. If the philosophers had consulted Barnett and Morse's classic *Scarcity and Growth* (1963) or various work following in that tradition, and if they had placed credence in its trend lines showing natural resources becoming less rather than more scarce with the passage of time, their judgments and recommendations could hardly have been what they have been. The lesson about elegant philosophical meditation upon economic phenomena in splendid innocence of the relevant data could hardly be clearer.

Selection 46 explains the basis of my forecast that the long-term trends of raw-material prices are toward increasing availability rather than toward greater scarcity. Selection 47 argues that an evolutionary process has shaped humankind in such manner that people tend to create more than they use up or destroy, and hence there is a general trend toward increased resources and a higher standard of living. Selection 48 deals with the question of whether we can assume that discovery of new resources and other elements of economic advance will continue in the future, in contrast to judging that it is uncertain whether progress will continue or we will lapse into overpopulated misery and want. Selection 49 analyzes the relevance of the concept of entropy and the Second Law of Thermodynamics for the future of humanity; it concludes that the Second Law points in the wrong direction, toward a closed and limited world view, rather than toward an open world view that is consonant with a vision of eternal material progress. Selection 50 offers an explanation of why the thinking of ecologists and economists concerning resources has differed in the past, and suggests how the two modes of thinking may be harmonized. And lastly, Selection 51 discusses the abstract ideas that enter into people's doom-and-gloom thinking about resources and population growth.

46

Forecasting the Long-Term Trend of Raw Material Availability

Philosophers and practical decision makers have long struggled with this question: How may one best predict the future of some important dimension of the economy? This selection argues that in the absence of strong reason to believe that there has been a radical change in circumstances, the longest available run of historical data constitute the best basis for a forecast (in this case, of the future of resource availability), in conjunction with theory if there is persuasive theory available.

In the case of natural resources, there is indeed persuasive theory available—not the conventional Malthusian theory, but rather the theory of adjustment to impending shortage by response to economic opportunity. The key sequence runs as follows: (1) increased pressure of population and income growth upon resources, causing an increase in prices, (2) perception of the scarcity problem with its attendant opportunities, (3) search for new solutions to the problem, (4) discovery of solutions that leave us better off than if the original problem had never arisen. This theoretical framework, together with the longest skein of historical data available for each raw material, strongly suggests that the prices of all natural resources will continue declining forever.

The article discusses forecasting for raw materials. The elements of forecasting in general can be stated broadly as follows: (1) Get hold of as much data as you can, especially records of the past as far back as possible, paying attention to the quality of the data. (2) Combine the data with sound theory of the phenomenon in question, ensuring that the theory realistically describes the dynamics of the situation. That is, bring good judgment to bear. (3) Don't let yourself

International Journal of Forecasting, Vol. 1, 1985.

be heavily influenced by a few recent dramatic exceptions to long-term trends, or by claims that somebody's complex mathematical method supercedes the data and good theoretical judgment.

1. Introduction

Will raw materials be more scarce, or less scarce, in future decades than at present? The actual outcome will have important consequences for our economic lives. And our *expectations* about the outcome will probably have even greater consequences than the outcome itself. Yet there are large and violent disagreements between two points of view, the "doomsdayers" who expect us to "run out" and who therefore forecast higher prices, and the "cornucopians" who expect prices to be progressively lower as raw materials come to be more available rather than less available. My own forecast is simply stated: I am quite sure that prices of all natural resources will go down indefinitely.

The aim of this paper is to set forth what I believe should be the basis for such a forecast. The nature of this particular forecasting situation forces us to consider the very foundations of long-run economic forecasting, and indeed, of all forecasting.

My forecasting "method" may be summarized as follows:

1. Ask: Is there any convincing reason not to consider the percentage changes from year to year in the longest available data series on a resource's price to be a representative sample of the "universe" from which the past, present, and future of this resource are drawn? That is, is there some convincing reason not to generalize from the sample already drawn to samples that will be drawn in the future?

If the observations had been those of secular constancy in the past, rather than secular decline, the sample-universe logic would seem more straightforward. But the constancy of an amount of change, or of a percentage rate of change, is based on the same foundation; predictions about a spacecraft circling the earth, and a spacecraft traveling away from the earth toward the stars, are on much the same footing.

Many persons assert we are now at a "turning point in history" with regard to resources, which implies that the past is *not* a representative sample of the universe from which the next set of years to come will be drawn. If their reasoning is convincing to you, then my predictions will not be credited by you. (One of my arguments against such a turning point now is that such an assertion has been common in the past.)

2. If you do not reject the past as a sample of the universe from which the next set of observations will be drawn, then we next ask if there is a reasonable "theoretical" explanation for the observed trend. Such an

explanation is not necessary for one to believe that the trend will continue. Few of us could explain why a spacecraft circles the earth or travels away from it, and people prudently did not await an explanation for the transmission of cholera before acting on the information that there was a geographic pattern connected with certain wells in London. But a theoretical explanation increases belief that the observed trend is not just caused by chance.

The explanation that the trend of decreasing cost results from market feedbacks causing new discoveries, substitutes, etc., accompanied by externalities which leave us better than before shortages arose, is persuasive to me. Of course one never can be sure that a theoretical explanation is sound; the test is your general wisdom and judgment.

3. If the answer to (1) is "no" and to (2) is "yes"—or even if the answer to (2) is "no" but the data in (1) are so many and so consistent that your statistical sense tells you that they are overwhelming—then you will extrapolate the observed trend with a monotonic function that seems to fit the data relatively well. That is the nature of my forecasting method. As I read Barnett and Morse (1963), which is the source of my general point of view on the history and future of raw material availability, this also is the forecasting method implicitly used by them. And it is the forecasting method used by many—but certainly not all—other makers of forecasts throughout the ages.

The paper will proceed as follows. Section 2 discusses appropriate ways to measure economic scarcity of raw materials. Section 3 provides some long-run history of raw material scarcity. Section 4 sets forth the Malthusian theory, which is at the heart of pessimistic forecasts of raw material scarcity, and explains why I do not find that line of thinking persuasive; it offers another way of thinking instead. Section 5 offers a very general argument about why trends can help predict; this takes us down to the foundations of scientific knowledge about the world we live in. Section 6 discusses the appropriate weights to put on long-ago data versus more recent information, which is much the same as discussing whether the longest-run trend should be believed rather than more recent "reversals."

2. Measurement of Scarcity Trends

Economists generally view the expenditures in physical or money terms necessary to obtain a good, relative to some other quantity of expenditures, as the appropriate measure of scarcity. This is in contrast to measuring scarcity with an actual or hypothetical estimate of physical quantities that are thought to "exist," as technologists are wont to do.

Two measures of cost are of particular interest here: The price of the raw material relative to consumer goods, and the price relative to wages. Each measure needs a further few words.

The price relative to consumer goods is the most popular measure, perhaps largely because of its similarity to an inflation deflator. But the average cost of all consumer goods taken together—an index of consumer prices—has fallen over the years in more-developed countries, measured in terms of what an unskilled worker can buy; this is shown by the long-run increase in the standard of living. Therefore, if a raw material has remained at least level in price compared to the average of all (or of consumer) goods, its "real" cost has fallen. Therefore, even if raw material prices had not fallen as fast as consumer goods—as in fact they have—it would not be ground for alarm about resources exerting a braking effect on economic growth, or becoming an increasingly serious constraint.

The price of natural resources *relative to wages* is, in my view, the best measure of scarcity with respect to human welfare. This measure tells us how much of our most valuable resource, our own lives, that we must give up in order to obtain the resources. This bears considerable relationship to the measure of the labor input time per unit of output that Barnett and Morse used, but it is easier to obtain, and is more comprehensive.

We should note that it is not really the natural resource itself that is of interest to us, but rather the services that we get from the resource. Just as it is not a computer itself, but rather the computing services we get from it, and then the use of those computing services in the production of other goods, that affects us, it is not copper or land or oil that matters to us, but rather the services that they render in the creation of final products. Therefore the relevant measure of the available resource is the cost of the services that we get from the resource. The market price of new pieces of capital is an upper-bound estimate on this cost of services because of progressive increases in productivity of capital, e.g., the cost of computing services has fallen sharply over the years.

3. Trends in Resource Scarcity

Now that we have arrived at some operational measures of scarcity, let's look at the record, in accord with the first step in my forecasting method. The historical cost record of raw materials is easy to summarize. Following on Barnett and Morse (1963), I have written at length elsewhere [Simon (1981)] about this matter, so I'll be brief here: Scarcity has been decreasing rather than increasing in the long run for all raw materials except lumber and oil, and even they have shown recent signs of becoming less exceptional. Figures 1-1 and 1-2a and b show this effect for copper, which is representative of all the metals. And this trend of falling prices of copper has been going on a very long time. The price of copper in labor time in the year 1 A.D. was about 120 times as great as it is in the U.S. now. The price of iron was about 240 times as great then as now, and in 800 B.C. it was 360 times as great, while in 1800 B.C. it was 1620 times as great [calculated from data in Clark (1957, pp. 652ff) and Childe (1942/ 1964)]. Food is an especially important resource, and the evidence is especially strong that we are on a benign trend despite rising population (see Selection 7).

4. Malthusian and Other Theories

Now let us move to the second step in my forecasting method, the theory. First let us consider contrary theories, because they cast light on the credibility of the theory I offer. The question that we wish to address theoretically must be kept firmly in mind: Must the cost of one or more important raw materials rise in the long run? The doomsayers assert that there is theoretical reason to answer the question in the affirmative, that there is no escaping a rise in raw material cost in some very long run. Their reasoning is as follows: The reservoir of some raw material X is fixed, meaning that the reservoir cannot be increased just as the reservoir of authentic Mona Lisa paintings cannot be increased. (They have in mind, however, generic materials such as, say, copper and land and energy rather than one-of-a-kinds such as the Mona Lisa; about those one-of-a-kinds there is no dispute.) Next they assume that the demand for the use of the material will either (a) increase due to population growth or income growth or both, or (b) the reservoir will decline due to some of it being lost or otherwise unavailable, or (c) there will be both increased demand and decreased reservoir. If humankind first exploits the richest lodes and ores, successive mining operations will be successively more expensive. Implicitly, those writers are also assuming that eventually there will be either stationarity of technology or a growth in technology slower than the rate of decrease in richness of lode. Under those assumed conditions, cost must indeed increase.

Certainly costs do increase during some periods, as reflected in real price rises at some times in history. And it is reasonable to suppose that during those periods the doomsday conditions hold (though price rises may sometimes be due to non-physical causes such as the formation of OPEC).

If the Malthusian concept of diminishing returns is given content by specifying a period of the order of a human life expectation, give or take an expected length of life, that "theory" fails completely in its predictive record; as we have seen, the trends in scarcity have been downward throughout history despite forecasters having made dire predictions implicitly based on that concept since the beginning of recorded history and surely before.

If, instead of testing the Malthusian theory on the past, one looks to the future, but if one does not specify some observable (or even identifiable) time period during which prices will rise permanently to levels above what they are now, and, instead, one simply says increased scarcity will happen "sometime," then the Malthusian theory is meaningless scientifically, according to the standard canon of scientific meaning; a theory about "sometime" cannot be tested, not even in principle.

A very different theoretical viewpoint sees the process by which resources have become progressively more available as part of the broader story of the creation and adoption of new technology largely in response to increased demand and/or increased prices for the resources due to population growth. The relationship between technology and demand assuredly is not that which is suggested by the vulgar idea of a "race" between them. More people certainly imply increased demand in the short run, and therefore higher costs than otherwise in the short run. But the long run is not just a sequence of short runs in this case, and hence it is fallacious to draw any conclusions from this short-run analysis. In the longer run, technology's advance comes from people, and technological advance is the sole factor responsible for the long-run declines in material cost.

The process by which increased demand due to more people and higher income causes advances in resource technology is only a special case of the general relationship between demand and technical advance. Two famous natural-resource cases that illustrate the process were described in earlier selections: the shortage of ivory for billard balls in the nineteenth century (Selections 4 and 5) and the impending coal crisis in the mid-1800s (Selection 5).

In addition to a theoretical explanation of past trends, a forecast seems even more convincing if the future of the relevant variables is predicted as a function of an independent variable whose future magnitude is itself predicted with some confidence. Increases in natural resource availability have accompanied (and in my view, have been caused by) increases in population and total demand. It seems reasonable to forecast continued increases for population and total demand in the future. Hence, this constitutes additional basis for forecasting continued increases in natural resource availability.

So, I believe that the first two steps of my forecasting method examination of the experiential data, and analysis of theoretical arguments and, especially, inquiry into a theoretical mechanism that explains the observed data, lead solidly to the third-step conclusion that it is reasonable to forecast a continuation of the observed trend, continued decline in re-source prices and increase in availability.

I also said that even if there were no satisfactory theoretical mechanism to explain the observed data, it might well be reasonable to forecast a continuation of the trend observed in the data if the statistical evidence is sufficiently overwhelming. Critics who have not noticed the theoretical mechanism described above have sometimes said "All you are doing is extrapolating," and they often call this "mindless extrapolating," suggesting that extrapolating in the absence of theory has no scientific foundation. I disagree, and I wish next to argue that there is indeed a solid logical basis for doing so. This may be considered as a contribution to the debate about the scientific basis of induction which has raged ever since Hume.

5. Do Trends Predict? If So, Why?

The main reason that I forecast increasing availability of natural re-sources is that such has been the trend throughout human history. But this then raises the question: Why is it reasonable to assume that a trend—even a long-run trend—will continue?

There seems plenty of casual evidence that the best first-approximation forecast of a social or economic or psychological state of affairs tomorrow is that it will be just as it is today. But *why* should that be so? Furthermore, a useful adjustment to this first-approximation forecast often is that the *rate of change* between tomorrow and today will be the same as the rate of change from yesterday to today. But why? That is, why should past trends be useful in prediction? At first thought the answer may seem obvious. But a second thought makes one wonder if the matter is as simple as it seems on first thought.

A related matter: You may improve a forecast of variable y—say, the type of car a family will own tomorrow—if you (a) know a relevant factor x, such as the family's income today, and (b) predict the family's income tomorrow on the basis of today's income. But *why* should one variable x help you predict another variable y?

The best way to begin, in my judgment, is just as we do in much other scientific work, by making assumptions. (These assumptions need not be true in an ultimate sense; all we ask of them is that they help us achieve our goals.) The key assumption I wish to make is that the world is not completely random, not totally disordered, that is, not in a state of maximum entropy, as the natural scientists would put it. Lack of complete disorder is the sort of picture that would emerge, for example, if the world were shapeless and void and then one enormous shock was inflicted on it, distorting it in innumerable ways. The result would be non-homogeneous and a lessened entropy; there would be "form." But there would not be order of the fashion of an orderly garden arranged according to someone's design. Someone once commented to me that "God wrote a set of equations, and it is the scientist's job to discover them." My view—the view that Einstein made most famous—is the opposite: man/woman the scientist writes a set of equations that more-or-less fit the uneven forms of the universe.

The fact that the assumption of inhomogeneity works in forecasting is a powerful reason to make the assumption. But for those who like to go to what they call "first principles"—by which they often mean physical principles—there also seems to be cosmological evidence for this assumption, as a recent *Science* magazine review of the present state of astronomical thinking notes in its opening sentence "To begin with, there is structure: the universe is obviously and grossly inhomogeneous [Waldrop (1983, p. 1050)]. Physicists and mathematicians have recently begun to analyse various phenomena with a point of view similar to what I am suggesting here, with what is known as the theory of "chaos." (This seems an unusual choice of terminology. "Chaos" is defined as "constrained randomness" rather than the complete randomness that it seems to connote in common parlance. See *Newsweek,* July 18, 1983, p. 53.)

In a state of complete random disorder no prediction would turn out any better than any other prediction, except by chance. If all the materials of the world were scattered throughout the world in the same manner as random numbers are distributed in a random-number table, it would be just as impossible to make a better-than-chance prediction about any phenomenon as it is to predict the next random digit with better-than-chance accuracy. That is, no system of prediction of random numbers is better than any other. (If we could perceive a random world, it might seem like being in the middle of a well-mixed pile of sand of several colors.) But in fact many of our predictions clearly are much better than chance; they could not be so if the world was in a state of complete entropic disorder.

In passing, we might note that the assumption of non-disorder is much simpler and more "parsimonious" than is an assumption that the universe follows a set of built-in equations, or has the sort of designed order that a logical thinking mind would develop.

Another way of defining complete disorder is that a given material or social element would then have no more similarity to the element next to it than to a random element far away from it. That is, in a totally disordered world, adjacent elements are—by definition—"independent." But if we assume that the world is not totally disordered, we are implicitly assuming that at least some adjacent elements are not independent of each other, and bear some similarity to each other. This is the assumption made so frequently in mathematics when "continuity" is assumed. And *given this assumption, if one knows the properties of a given element and then predicts that the adjacent element has the same properties, one will be right more often than chance.* Furthermore, if the degree of similarity is the same among various adjacent elements, the higher the similarity between elements *A* and *B,* the better will be a prediction that *C* is like *A* (assuming *A, B,* and *C* are arranged in that order in a line). This is the process of "extrapolation," predicting the unknown case from the known case.

Let us consider a homely example. You observe that the owner of the third house on the block owns a big new car. If you predict that the next-door neighbor in the fourth house also has a big new car, you will be right more often than if you make that prediction for randomly chosen home-owners (on the assumption that the world, or rather the United States, is not in complete disorder). Furthermore, if you then observe that the fourth-house owner does have a big new car, a prediction that the fifth-house owner also has a new car is more likely to be correct than if only the fourth house and not the third house had a big new car. That is, the high degree of similarity between the third and fourth houses increases the chance of accuracy in a prediction that the fifth house would be like the fourth house.

The dimension on which one element is "next to" another need not be geographic. Frequently the relevant proximity is in time. The number of minutes of daylight tomorrow may be predicted on the basis of the number of minutes of daylight today and yesterday. A patient's mental state tomorrow may be predicted on the basis of her/his mental state today. And the speed it takes a rat to traverse a maze in trial 22 may be predicted on the basis of its elapsed time in trial 21.

To summarize this section, why is it reasonable to assume that a trend will continue? The short answer is that continuity of state and continuation of trend are a basic feature—perhaps the most basic feature—of the world we live in.

6. How Long Should the Base Period Be for a Long-Run Forecast?

If you find that there has indeed been a trend during the relevant past, then it is often reasonable to extend that trend as the basis of your prediction. But the pattern of the past is often not consistent, in which case you must decide which parts of the past to pay most attention to.

In my view, the most important element in making sound long-run predictions from trends is to examine the sweep of history as far back in the past as possible, to ensure that what one thinks is a trend is not just a blip in history.

The main reason for looking at a longer rather than a shorter period is because the longer period contains more information. But the relevance of the information from various periods in the past is, of course, a most difficult question. It is generally reasonable to weigh the recent past more heavily than the distant past, though never completely forgetting the distant past. The commonest source of error is extending an apparent trend during a short period of time—an uptrend in copper prices within the last three years, say—into a prediction for the long-run future—say, prices two decades from now. One of the many sad examples of fallacious short-trend extension was the conclusion by individuals and governments that the raw material scarcity that appeared in 1973–1974 would continue to get worse into the indefinite future. That conclusion was very costly in waste of social and personal resources. For excellent discussion of the accuracy of forecasts, see Ascher (1979) and Armstrong (1978).

7. Summary

To summarize: I forecast that prices of all natural resources will go down. My forecasting "method" is as follows:

1. Ask: Is there any convincing reason not to consider the percentage changes from year to year in the longest data series on a resource's costs to be a representative sample of the "universe" from which the past, present, and future are drawn? That is, is there some convincing reason not to generalize from the sample already drawn to samples that will be drawn in the future?
2. If you do not reject the past as a sample of the universe from which the next set of observations will be drawn, then we next ask if there is a reasonable 'theoretical' explanation for the observed trend. Such an explanation is not necessary for one to believe that the trend will continue. But a theoretical explanation increases belief that the observed trend is not just caused by chance.

    The explanation I accept for the trend of decreasing cost is a set of market feedbacks resulting in new discoveries, substitutes, etc., with externalities that leave us better than before shortages arose.
3. If the answer to (1) is 'no' and to (2) is 'yes'—or even if the answer to (2) is 'no' but the data in (1) are so many and so consistent that your statistical sense tells you that they are overwhelming—then it seems reasonable to extrapolate the observed trend with a monotonic function that seems to fit the data relatively well.

    The appropriate economic measurement of raw-material scarcity is cost or price. The very longest trends throughout humankind's history exhibit decreasing rather than increasing scarcity for all raw materials except saw-logs and oil, and there are persuasive reasons to think that they, too, will show decreasing scarcity in the future. Malthusian diminishing returns theory does not fit these observed facts and is not compelling intellectually; a theory of endogenous invention is more persuasive, in my view. An explanation of the persistence and predictive power of trends was offered, and it is argued that, *ceteris paribus*, longer trends are a preferable basis than are shorter trends where the two conflict, because the longer trends contain more information.

47

Are We at a Long-Run Turning Point Now?

The trends in health, the standard of living, and human opportunity, as well as the trends in availability of natural resources—in fact, just about all trends pertaining to human welfare—point in a benign direction. (See Selection 1 and Part 2.) It is logical, then, to ask whether all these individual trends are part of some larger trend.

This selection argues that an evolutionary process has shaped humankind in such a manner that people tend to create more than they use up or destroy, and hence there is a general trend toward increased resources and better living. This evolutionary process involves the development of rules, customs, institutions, and all the rest of what we call "culture" or "civilization." The selection principle is that those aspects of culture that conduce to the survival of a particular human group tend to be retained, in competition with other human groups and their cultural characteristics.

Even such doomsayers as Paul Ehrlich and Garrett Hardin now agree that man's history has been one of increasing availability of resources (as measured by falling prices), together with an improving standard of material living (as measured by life expectancy and the quantity of consumer goods). But, they say, this benign trend will not continue in the future. Rather, they make such statements as "the age of cheap energy is over" and "we have entered an age of scarcity following on the age of affluence." They even predict life expectancy will fall.

There is no way to prove with the force of deductive logic that we are *not* at a turning point in history now; it is indeed *possible* that, starting in our time, these very long-term trends will indeed reverse. But *is it likely* that this is so?

"Does Doom Loom?," *Reason*, April, 1984.

The doomsayers' arguments for the turning-point hypothesis are of two kinds, empirical and deductive. The empirical argument—whether the argument was made in 1970, 1975, or now (and probably the same argument was made in 1300, 1600, and many other times)—is that *the last few years* have shown increasing prices (relative to wages) in some raw materials. But when we look at the long-term trends, we see that frequent temporary price upturns are followed by resumption of the long downward trend. These historical series indicate that reliance on just a few years' data usually leads to disastrously wrong long-run predictions.

The doomsayers' theoretical, or deductive, argument begins with the supposed "finiteness" of all resources, especially energy, and a consequent reduction in the stock of resources as some are used up. In my book *The Ultimate Resource* (Princeton, 1981), I argue at length that the underlying concept of finitude is fatally flawed as a foundation for scientific reasoning and forecast. (See also Selection 4.)

Rejection of the doomsayers' arguments, however, still leaves us in limbo; for although the doomsayers have no solid reason to believe that we are now at a turning point, the historical series of falling prices is not conclusive proof that these benign trends will continue. Nonetheless, experience *is* a powerful guide to the future, and this has been the main argument of those who have argued that—absent strong theoretical reasons to the contrary—things will continue to get better.

Moreover, historical experience is buttressed by the observation that people respond to newly arisen or soon-expected problems by developing solutions that leave us better off than we began. Still, many long-run trends do reverse—the number of horses in the United States, for example. So it behooves us to seek a deeper understanding.

In my view, we can improve our understanding by going beyond the trends in particular resource prices and quantities per person to examine the larger trend of which these particular trends are a part. And the greatest and most important trend is the world becoming ever more livable for human beings. We see signs of this in increased life expectancies, our improved knowledge of nature, and the subduing of the elements with respect to our own safety and comfort.

But though this larger trend buttresses the particular resource trends, it still provides no *causal* explanation of the phenomenon we seek to understand. Evolutionary thinking, however, and (more specifically in economics) the sort of analysis suggested by Austrian School economist Friedrich Hayek, offers an explanation of the observed long-term trend. And that explanation in turn provides the basis for a grounded forecast of a continuation of the great long-term trend (of the world becoming ever more livable for people). Hayek suggests that, as there has been an evolutionary selection for survival among those societies that have existed in the past, humankind has evolved rules and patterns of living that are consistent with survival and growth rather than with decline and extinction.

Hayek assumes that these particular rules and living patterns have had something to do with the societies' chances for survival. For example, he reasons that patterns yielding higher fertility and more healthful and productive living have led to groups' natural increase and hence survival— and therefore, where conditions are not too different from those conditions that held in the past, inherited patterns constitute a machinery for continued survival and growth.

This is consistent with a biological view of humankind as having evolved a genetic pattern that (under historical conditions) points toward survival. But Hayek presupposes no such genetic evolution, in part because its time span is so great that we cannot understand it as well as we can understand the evolution of cultural rules. It may be illuminating, however, to view humankind's biological nature as part of the long evolutionary chain dating from the simplest plants and animals, a history of increasing complexity of construction and greater capacity to deal actively with the environment.

Let us apply Hayek's general analysis to natural resources. All sorts of natural resources have been a part of human history ever since the beginning. If humankind had not developed patterns of behavior and association that increased rather than decreased the amounts of resources available to us, we would not still be here. If, as humankind's numbers increased (or even as they remained nearly stationary), its behavior had led to diminished supplies of plants and animals, less flint for tools, and disappearing wood for fires and construction, I would not be here writing these pages, and you would not be reading them.

What then, *are* the key patterns of culture that maintained and increased human life? It is interesting and important that we try to learn what they are. Certainly the evolved cultural patterns include voluntary exchange among individuals, and markets that function to provide resources in increasing quantities; institutions that pass on knowledge, such as schools; libraries and legends and storytellers, all of which store knowledge; and monasteries and laboratories and research-and-development departments, which produce knowledge. Biological patterns that have evolved to aid survival include the hunger signals we get when we lack food and the attention that we focus on apparent regularities in nature when they appear before us. But ignorance of these cultural and biological patterns is not devastating for us, and such ignorance ought not be surprising, given the complexity of these patterns and the difficulty of any one person seeing much of any pattern.

The belief that our evolved history is, as I suggest, toward humans being creators rather than destroyers may be strengthened by some evidence that such evolution spontaneously occurs within most human groups, independent of one another, as a result of the conditions that humankind faces. For example, people build dwellings that shelter them from sun, rain, and snow. And the exchange mechanism evolves everywhere as a way of handling differences in people's abilities, in order to improve their capacities to construct and create new goods as well as to distribute existing goods. Chiefs of work gangs somehow assume their roles so that constructive tasks can be carried out efficiently. Communities reward creators of works in a variety of ways that they do not reward destroyers of the community works. (Warriors against other groups are not exceptions to this proposition. But perhaps it deserves mention as an exception that songs are written about such destroyers as the James Gang as well as about such creators as John Henry.) Probably everywhere mothers ooh and ah about their children's sand castles. And though I have no evidence—and feel no need to consult anthropologists on the matter—I'd bet that early tribes in dry climates gave greater honor to persons who found water than to those who polluted water sources, and greater honor to those who procured food than to those who showed considerable ability to consume food supplies.

The above illustrations are intended to show that human groups spontaneously evolve patterns of behavior—and of training people for that behavior—that, on the whole, lead people to create rather than destroy. And this supports the view that humans are, on net balance, builders rather than destroyers. The evidence is seen in the historical records and in the state of civilization and economy that our ancestors have bequeathed to us, one that contains more created works than the civilization and economy they were bequeathed.

In short, humankind has evolved into creators and problem-solvers to an extent that people's constructive behavior has outweighed their destructive behavior, as evidenced by our increasing life expectancy and richness of consumption. And in recent centuries and decades, this positive net balance has been increasing rather than decreasing.

This view of man, as (on balance) builder, conflicts with the view of man as destroyer that underlies the thought of many doomsayers. From those holding the latter view come such statements as, "The United States has 5 percent of the (world's) population, and uses 40 percent of (its) resources"—without reference to the *creation* of resources by the same U.S. population. (Also involved here is the misleading view of resources as physical quantities, rather than as the services that humankind derives from some combination of humankind's knowledge and physical conditions. According to that superficial view, *people* are not "resourceful" and do not convert physical conditions into resources, but resources somehow are waiting for the plucking, like cherries on a tree. Many writers have commented on the fact that naturally occurring materials, such as copper and oil and land, were not resources until humans discovered their uses, found out how to extract and process them, and thereby made their services available to us. Hence resources are, in the most meaningful sense, created, and when this happens their availability increases and continues to increase as long as our knowledge of how to obtain them increases faster than our use of them, which is the history of all "natural resources.")

If one notices only the destructive activities of humankind, without understanding that in order for us to have survived to this point, constructive behavior must have been the dominant part of our individual-cum-social nature—which is confirmed by the increasing positive net balance in our resources—then it is not surprising that one would arrive at the conclusion that resources will grow scarcer in the future.

Paradoxically, rules and customs that lead to population growth rather than to population stability or decline may be part of our inherited capacity to deal successfully with resource problems in the long run, though the added people may exacerbate the problems in the short run. Such rules and customs probably lead to long-run success of a society in two ways.

First, high fertility leads to increased chances of a group's survival, other things being equal. (This key idea comes from Hayek.) For example, though the Parsis of India have been, as individuals, very economically successful, as a people they seem doomed to the failure of disappearance in the long run, due to their marriage and fertility patterns.

Second, high fertility leads to resource problems, which then lead to solutions to the problems that usually leave humanity better off in the long run than if the problems had never arisen. In a more direct chain of events, rules and customs leading to high fertility yield an increased supply of human ingenuity, which responds productively to the increased demand for goods.

But even if one accepts that up until now humankind has evolved into a creator rather than a destroyer, it is certainly not unreasonable to wonder whether there have been changes in conditions, or "structural changes" in patterns of social behavior, that might point to a change in trend, just as structural changes might have contributed to the fate of the dinosaur and of some extinct human groups.

Changes in natural conditions, such as climate, are suggested by few writers, so we can pass them by. "Internal contradictions" in societies or economies may be more relevant. This concept represents the intuitive notion that, because of our large, fast-growing population and because of the way we produce goods and organize ourselves socially, our civilization is unwieldy and hence must collapse of its own weight—by, for example, nuclear destruction, or the failure of an all-important crop.

Many who are pessimistic about the outcome of the present course of civilization suggest that pollution is an "internal contradiction" that will do us in. Some political organizations and devices have evolved to deal with the matter, and we have both public and private cleanup and collection of various kinds of garbage, as well as laws that regulate pollution behavior. But the possible changes in pollutants and the recency of the onset of regulatory activities certainly leave room to wonder whether we have yet evolved reliable ways of dealing with pollution problems.

Intergenerational relationships with respect to resources are another frequently mentioned possible "internal contradiction"—one generation is feared to be exploiting a resource, leaving too little for the next generation. But the advent of futures markets—both for buying and selling the resources themselves and for buying and selling stock in resource-supplying firms—protects against this potential danger. And we have had enough experience by now to believe that this evolved mechanism is reliable and satisfactory for the purpose.

What I am suggesting, in sum, is that humankind has evolved culturally (and perhaps also genetically) in such a manner that our patterns of behavior—social rules and customs being a crucial part of these patterns—predispose us to deal successfully with resource scarcity. That is, over the centuries, these evolved patterns have given us greater rather than less command over resources.

This view of human history is consistent with both the observed long-term trend toward greater resource availability and the positive, growing net balance between our creative and our exploitative activities. It provides a causal foundation for the observed benign resource trends and thereby buttresses the simple extrapolation of past trends that produces a forecast of increasing rather than decreasing resource availability.

The market system, of course, is part of the evolution of resource-expanding behavior. But it is not the whole of it. The story of Robinson Crusoe (which has been badly twisted by economists, who make it a story of allocation when it is really a story of ingenuity and the use of the knowledge that Crusoe brought to the island with him) also illustrates this point—that is, that we have developed a body of knowledge and a set of cultural patterns that enable us to improve our resource situation rather than make it worse, even as we use resources and even in the absence of an exchange mechanism.

Thus, as time goes on, I think we can with confidence expect to observe greater rather than less availability of resources, whether they be arable land or oil or whatever, just as we observe this trend in the past. If I am correct, we now have systematic grounds to believe that we are not at a turning point in resource history caused by man's propensity to destroy rather than create. On the contrary, humankind is on balance a creator rather than a destroyer.

48

Knowledge in the Future

Those who worry about whether civilization can sustain its economic progress inevitably doubt that discovery of new resources and other elements of economic advance will continue in the future. They therefore conclude that we must lapse into overpopulated misery and want. Such concern is misplaced for two reasons. First, existing technology provides more than enough knowledge to provide for our material needs into any foreseeable future. Second, there is sound reason to expect discovery to continue at an unabated or increasing rate, forever.

At the root of much fear of population growth is the putative negative effect of more people upon the availability of natural resources. And indeed, in the long run it is only the physical environment that could conceivably lead to negative effects of more people. If there were no raw-material physical constraint, additional people could simply hive off into new colonies no poorer than the old colonies. (This assumes away the role of man-made physical capital. This is not unreasonable because, with a horizon as long as one or two decades, physical capital adjusts to other circumstances, as in Germany and Japan after World War II, though there certainly is temporary cost.)

At this point I might just as well bite the bullet, say it right out, and face your incredulity immediately: The rate of technical advance with respect to natural resources is unimportant today, because the world's natural resource problems have been resolved for all time with technology already developed. Very briefly, if energy is sufficiently cheap, all other raw materials can be made available at low prices, because energy allows extraordinary transformations of many kinds (Goeller and Weinberg,

1978). And nuclear fission with the breeder—and even more so, nuclear fusion if it becomes practical—provides an unlimited amount of energy at constant cost forever—or at least for billions of years beyond the horizon of any conceivable social decision.

Space for living and working is the only other resource requiring special attention here. And construction technology now provides such space for people in huge quantity, relative to that amount used up until now, by building multistory buildings, and by heating and cooling areas heretofore considered unusable for human habitation because of their extreme climates. If we wish to imagine a bit further, the sea and outer space can provide additional living space in vast quantity, and are not impractical from a cost point of view. An evaluation of future technical advance might tell us how fast the costs of space and energy will fall, but that rate is not crucial to any decision about population growth. For more details, see Simon (1981), Kahn (1979), or Barnett and Morse (1963).

Of course it was not always so. In past eras, natural resources were an effective constraint upon human progress. But it is no longer so, and we ought to proceed on the basis of this up-to-date fact.

If natural resources are not a vital need, let us then ask whether we do have needs for which technical advance may be important. Health and life come first to mind, of course. But if we accept the contention (see Fries and Crapo, 1981) that our bodies inevitably wear out around age 90 no matter how effectively individual diseases are prevented or controlled, then we are already most of the technological way we can go, and there is not much possibility of further advance. Of course biogenetics might engineer a different constitution for us by making us a different sort of species, but this is not obviously something that we would consider an advance, and it is too complex and controversial to concern ourselves with here.

We certainly would value advances that would help us live lives that are more serene, more exciting, and more enjoyable, in greater harmony with our fellows. We also would greatly value advances that would improve teaching and learning in such fashion that individuals could more fully take advantage of the talents with which they are born in order to make a greater contribution to others and to live more satisfying lives than otherwise. Science may be able to help. But such knowledge is likely to come from fields other than physical science. Once we enlarge the concept of technology to include such social and psychological knowledge, we move to a different sphere of discourse, one in which, for example, the concept of "breakthrough" must have a very different meaning than it has in the physical sciences.

The argument, then, boils down to this: The contributions to living that advances in productive technique might make in the future differ fundamentally from those that it has made in the past. We now possess knowledge about resource locations and processing that allows us to satisfy our physical needs and desires for food, drink, heat, light, clothing, longevity, transportation, and the recording and transmission of information and entertainment sufficiently well so that additional knowledge on these subjects will not revolutionize life on earth. It still remains to us to organize our institutions, economies, and societies in such fashion that the benefits of this knowledge are available to the vast majority rather than a minority of all people. And our desires for (among other things) leisure, wisdom, love, spirituality, sexuality, adventure, and personal beauty are quite unsatiated, and perhaps must always be so. But the sort of advances in productive knowledge that in the past brought us the possibility of satisfaction for our physical needs cannot sensibly be measured in a fashion comparable to future advances in other beneficial knowledge, given our present skills in measurement. Therefore, we should not concern ourselves about the rate of future advances in physical knowledge compared with the rates in the past.

Though I argue that the future of physical discovery will not be like its past, I do not believe that we are at a turning point now. The shift I describe has been going on for at least a century, perhaps much longer, depending on how you view it, and should continue indefinitely. No discontinuity is to be seen here.

This is not an argument for neglect of scientific and engineering research. I hope that we vigorously continue to increase our technology, and thereby reduce the cost and increase the distribution of the means of satisfaction of our physical needs as, for example, in agricultural research. Furthermore, science is a great human adventure, worthwhile for the observers as well as the participants; space exploration may serve as an example. And even if we do not "need" the technical advances that may occur in the future, we may well find that they are worth far more to us than we would be willing to pay for their fruits, in which case there is justification for social support of such activities; space exploration, with the economic benefits it already has begun to provide, may again serve as an example.

I am arguing instead that we need not worry about whether future technical advances will support the physical needs of a population of present size or much larger. We should not fear that the future rate of advances in technical knowledge will fail to continue the history of past advances at a rate fast enough to keep us from sinking into poverty; we already know more than enough to prevent that from happening. But this confidence does not imply general complacency. There is no shortage of needs for new knowledge in nonphysical spheres to give us all the challenge we need.

49

A Unifying Concept to Support the Vision of Eternal Progress

Physics has always impressed social scientists, who have endeavored to appropriate its concepts where they have thought it possible. One of the favorite adoptees has been the Second Law of Thermodynamics and the notion of entropy. This concept has lately been the subject of the amazingly ignorant book, Entropy, *by Jeremy Rifkin. But even economists of the skill and reputation of Nicholas Georgescu-Roegen and Paul Samuelson have paid respectful attention to the idea's application in economics.*

This selection suggests that the attention to physics and to entropy is quite misplaced in discussions of population growth and resources. It draws thought away from the unlimited possibilities for humankind, and instead leads one to believe that there are "limits" that constrain the expansion of our possibilities and aspirations. That is, the Second Law points in the wrong direction in such discussion—toward a closed and limited world view. A long quote by William James at the end of Selection 49 makes the central points quite nicely, and shows how the intellectual material for effective rebuttal to fear of population growth due to entropy has been available for a long time, even to the nonphysicist.

The mind-bending power of the laws of thermodynamics can be seen in an editorial by the editor of Science *(July 3, 1987). It is entitled "Inexorable Laws and the Ecosystem," and the first paragraph reads:*

> *It has been said that the three laws of thermodynamics can be paraphrased. First law: "Life is a zero sum game." Second law: "You can't win." Third law: "You can't get out of the game." The same appears to*

be true of the global environmental problem. We have only one atmosphere whose balance between carbon dioxide, oxygen, and ozone is critical to our survival. We have one earth and ocean whose fertility and purity are equally important. Increasing population and increasing industrialization pose threats to that environment, the consequences of which will fall on all, except for a few who plan to live out their lives huddled in rockets speeding toward Mars.''

He then goes on to say that "As the world population grows and as underdeveloped nations become more industrialized, the threat to the environment is going to increase, and very drastically. . . . the population explosion has to move to top priority.'' And he calls for "better global planning'' and "programs for effective population control'' to fight the "policies and priorities that are dooming our ecosystem.'' The rest of the editorial is replete with demonstrably false propositions such as "The suburban sprawl of the United States is continually overrunning the best farmlands of the country.'' Of course no evidence is given for any of the editorial's assertions.

With the second law out of the way, the path is clear for this selection to offer another vision—an open world view that enables us to realistically imagine eternal progress. And lest this vision seem contrary to elementary science, I turn for authoritative physicists' permission (of course!) to Freeman Dyson, who in his Gifford Lectures book, Infinite in All Directions, *said, "Boiled down to one sentence, my message is the unboundedness of life and the consequent unboundedness of human destiny'' (New York: Harper and Row, 1988, p. vii).*

The concept of the second law of thermodynamics underlies the environmentalist-ecologist (E-E) vision of the human condition as inexorably sliding toward the worse in the long run. (And let there be no doubt that they envision our eventual demise.) Ours is a closed universe, they assume, and within such a closed system entropy necessarily increases. Nothing can avail against this tendency toward decreasing order, increasing disorder, and a return to chaos—to the formless and shapeless void described in the first words of Genesis.

This E-E vision is emphasized in the frequent appearance of the term "finite" in the literature of the environmental-cum-population-control movement. The vision is well set forth by the noted mathematician Norbert Weiner, who at least viewed the grim future with an attitude of Whitmanesque nobility rather than of panic.

> In a very real sense we are shipwrecked passengers on a doomed planet. Yet even in a shipwreck, human decencies and human values do not necessarily vanish, and we must make the most of them. We shall go down, but let it be in a manner to which we may look forward as worthy of our dignity. (1950, p. 58)

This vision is embodied in the policy recommendations for our everyday political life offered by Nicholas Georgescu-Roegen (1971; 1979) with the approval of Paul Samuelson and Herman Daly (1973; 1977), who urge that we should budget our energy and other resources with an eye to optimum allocation over the next seven billion years or so until the system runs down. (So help me, they are serious.) One might think that this recommendation is too silly to take seriously. But to dismiss it as silly is to leave the field to a very large group of people—the Global Tomorrow Coalition advertises that its constituent organizations number more than 5,000,000 Americans—who build a very specific agenda upon this foundation, and who have enormous political clout in Washington.

The political agenda of the doomsayers implies greater central planning and governmental control. I do not know whether there is a direct link between an exogenous world view that requires more control (in turn the result of being persuaded that the second law of thermodynamics is the appropriate model for thinking about these matters) or whether doomsayers tend to be people who fear disorder and therefore concern themselves with constructing methods of controlling aspects of our social world so as to fight such disorder. Whichever, these persons consistently invoke both sorts of ideas. For exmaple, in the current debate about illegal immigration, those who are in favor of tighter laws and tougher sanctions frequently link such concepts as "chaos," "anarchy," and "loss of control of our borders." And there is a very large overlap between the anti-immigration movement (which focuses much of its attention on illegal immigration) and the environmental and population-control movement.[1]

We should note in passing that even if the E-E vision were to be accepted as valid, it would not necessarily imply that we should make efforts to reduce our consumption of raw materials and energy. The mere fact that the richness of the lodes from which we draw our resources declines with use does not imply that as demand rises the cost of production will increase in terms of labor time or wages, or even in terms of consumer goods. The historic fall in the cost of natural resources is documented extensively in the classic *Scarcity and Growth* by Harold Barnett and Chandler Morse (1963; see also Simon, 1981).

The E-E vision raises two questions: First, does the vision square with the empirical evidence, such as it is? And second, is there another concept that might underlie a very different vision?

All the available empirical evidence contradicts the idea that order is decreasing in the universe. Biologically—as is suggested by the very word "evolution"—the earth has changed from a smaller number of species of simple creatures toward a larger number of complex and ordered creatures, whereas the second law implies decreasing diversity. Geologically, the activities of human beings have resulted in a greater heaping up of particular materials in concentrated piles, e.g., the gold in Fort Knox and in gold jewelry compared to the gold in streams, or the steel in buildings and junk piles compared to the iron and other ores in mines. The history of human institutions describes ever more complex modes of organization, a more extensive body of law, richer languages, a more ramified corpus of knowledge, and a greater range of human movement throughout the universe. All this suggests more order rather than less with the passage of time.

The finitists assert that this empirical evidence is irrelevant because it describes only a temporary "local" increase in order, superimposed on the long-term decrease that they say *must* be taking place. And the basis for their *must* is their assumption about the operation of the second law. So we must next inquire into the validity of the application of the Second Law to the subject at hand, and into whether there might be another concept that might substitute for it.

The E-E's often assert that the "other side"—people like me—say what we say either because of our ignorance of physics and the second law, or because of willful and dishonest disregard of it.[2] Any other possibility seems unimaginable. But I urge that there *are* other possibilities.

We should first notice that the body of physics knowledge that the E-E's urge upon us is only a century old. And there is left to humanity a period 700,000,000 times that long to discover new principles before the sun runs out. Even now, the cosmologists are in controversy about whether the universe should be viewed as closed or as open and expanding, which apparently implies lack of agreement about the validity of the sort of view of entropy held by the E-E's.

(Those who view any given state of knowledge as unquestionable might keep in mind some of the amusing and not-so-amusing switches in scientific views that have occurred historically. We need only mention theories of the shape of the earth, medical doctrine about leeching, belief that the elements are inviolate and one metal cannot be transmuted into another, and the shift within just a few years of dentists switching from advising hard toothbrushes in an up-and-down motion to advising soft brushes in a horizontal motion—the latter recommendation probably as little backed by experimental proof of efficacy as the former.)

I do not, of course, offer a new cosmology that is logically alternative to that which the E-E's based upon the second law of thermodynamics. Rather, I note the controversies among physicists and astronomers over the curvature of space, whether space is expanding or contracting, and so on, and I suggest that within the bounds of those controversies lie many possibilities for physical principles that would clearly negate the relevance of the second law for the purposes at hand. And in the presence of lack of agreement in contemporary physical theory, a vision of the world in which humankind might dwell as long as the biological and social evolution of the species will call for natural resources should not seem foolish or naive or illogical.

Just one more word about the physical domain before leaving it: Einstein over and over again referred to the "order" in the universe. And though I could not find any statement by him that bears upon the *persistence* of such order, the *disappearance* of order in the future does not seem consistent with Einstein's vision of order. And perhaps this is (at least in part) why Einstein was so comfortable with the word "God," a word that seems anathema to so many other persons, even though Einstein explicitly rejected the concept of an anthropomorphic personal-deity that has a finger in human history, and even though he probably had reservations about religious institutions (as did William James who, like Einstein, felt comfortable with religious ideas and religious persons). Einstein's statement about God not playing dice with the universe also seems inconsistent with the vision of a random process that eventually leads to all dice-throwing processes eventually having the same outcome.

Which brings us to an alternative vision of the human world that can substitute for the vision of limits, growing disorder, and eventual demise. The concepts of openness and expansion, which are the opposite of closedness of system, limits to growth, and finiteness, seem to imply that progress is possible forever.[3] Or, at least there is no obvious physical reason why progress—in the sense of growth in human numbers, and increasing differentiation in human activities—cannot continue indefinitely. This by no means implies that progress *must* increase forever, and even less does it imply that it must continue to take place within any given span of time. Rather, this vision is consistent with a model of human history in which for each step backward we take about 1.0001 steps forward.

* * *

The shade of William James now appears in two connections. First, James was the great apostle of an open view of the world, of people, and of ideas. He urged upon us the benefits of pluralism in contrast to monism of thought, and he opposed rigid system building. I hope, then, that I do not violate the spirit of his thinking when I suggest the above single vision, which may even be thought as a system (I rather hope not) even though that vision is one of openness.

Second, James long ago provided a crushing critique of the use of the entropy law in connection with human affairs. It is worth re-reading now for its unusual clarity and not just for its prescience. (From his "Letter to American Teachers," originally printed for private circulation, but recently published, with a preface by Mr. Brooks Adams, under the title: "The Degradation of Democratic Dogma"; in *The Letters of William James,* vol. ii, pp. 344-347.)

BAD-NAUHEIM, June 17, 1910.

DEAR HENRY ADAMS,*—I have been so "slim" since seeing you, and the baths here have so weakened my brain, that I have been unable to do any reading except trash, and have only just got round to finishing your "letter," which I had but half-read when I was with you at Paris. To tell the truth, it doesn't impress me at all, save by its wit and erudition; and I ask you whether an old man soon about to meet his Maker can hope to save himself from the consequences of his life by pointing to the wit and learning he has shown in treating a tragic subject. No, sir, you can't do it, can't impress God in that way. So far as our scientific conceptions go, it may be admitted that your Creator (and mine) started the universe with a certain amount of "energy" latent in it, and decreed that everything that should happen thereafter should be a result of parts of that energy falling to lower levels; raising other parts higher, to be sure, in so doing, but never in equivalent amount, owing to the constant radiation of unrecoverable warmth incidental to the process. It is customary for gentlemen to pretend to believe one another, and until some one hits upon a newer revolutionary concept (which may be tomorrow) all physicists must play the game by holding religiously to the above doctrine. It involves of course the ultimate cessation of all perceptible happening, and the end of human history. With this general conception as *surrounding* everything you say in your "letter," no one can find any fault—in the present stage of scientific conventions and fashions. But I protest against your interpretation of some of the specifications of the great statistical drift downwards of the original high-level energy. If, instead of criticizing what you seem to me to say, I express my own interpretation dogmatically, and leave you to make the comparison, it will doubtless conduce to brevity and economize recrimination.

To begin with, the *amount* of cosmic energy it costs to buy a certain distribution of fact which humanly we regard as precious, seems to me to be an altogether secondary matter as regards the question of history and progress. Certain arrangements of matter *on the same energy-level* are, from the point of view of man's appreciation, superior, while others are inferior. Physically a dinosaur's brain may show as much intensity of energy-exchange as a man's, but it can do infinitely fewer things, because as a force of detent it can only

---

*From his "Letter to American Teachers," originally printed for private circulation, but recently published, with a preface by Mr. Brooks Adams, under the title "The Degradation of Democratic Dogma," in *Letters of William James,* vol. ii, pp. 344–347.

unlock the dinosaur's muscles, while the man's brain, by unlocking far feebler muscles, indirectly can by their means issue proclamations, write books, describe Chartres Cathedral, etc., and guide the energies of the shrinking sun into channels which never would have been entered otherwise—in short, *make* history. Therefore the man's brain and muscles are, from the point of view of the historian, the more important place of energy-exchange, small as this may be when measured in absolute physical units.

The "second law" is wholly irrelevant to "history"—save that it sets a terminus—for history is the course of things before that terminus, and all that the second law says is that, whatever the history, it must invest itself between that initial maximum and that terminal minimum of difference in energy-level. As the great irrigation-reservoir empties itself, the whole question for us is that of the distribution of its effects, of *which* rills to guide it into; and the size of the rills has nothing to do with their significance. Human cerebration is the most important rill we know of, and both the "capacity" and the "intensity" factor thereof may be treated as infinitesimal. Yet the filling of such rills would be cheaply bought by the waste of whole sums spent in getting a little of the down-flowing torrent to enter them. Just so of human institutions—their value has in strict theory nothing whatever to do with their energy-budget—being wholly a question of the form the energy flows through. Though the *ultimate* state of the universe may be its vital and psychical extinction, there is nothing in physics to interfere with the hypothesis that the penultimate state might be the millennium—in other words a state in which a minimum of difference of energy-level might have its exchanges so skillfully *canalisés* that a maximum of happy and virtuous consciousness would be the only result. In short, the last expiring pulsation of the universe's life might be, "I am so happy and perfect that I can stand it no longer." You don't believe this and I don't say I do. But I can find nothing in "Energetik" to conflict with its possibility. You seem to me not to discriminate, but to treat quantity and distribution of energy as if they formed one question.

There! that's pretty good for a brain after 18 Nauheim baths—so I won't write another line, nor ask you to reply to me. In case you can't help doing so, however, I will gratify you now by saying that I probably won't jaw back. It was pleasant at Paris to hear your identically unchanged and "undergraded" voice after so many years of loss of solar energy. Yours ever truly,

WM. JAMES.

[Post-card]
NAUHEIM, *June* 19, 1910.

P. S. Another illustration of my meaning: The clock of the universe is running down, and by so doing makes the hands move. The energy absorbed by the hands and the *mechanical* work they do is the same day after day, no matter how far the weights have descended from the position they were originally wound up to. The *history* which the hands perpetrate has nothing to do with the *quantity* of this work, but follows the *significance* of the figures which they cover on the dial. If they move from O to XII, there is "progress," if from XII to O, there is "decay," etc., etc.

W.J.

Notes

1. In this connection, I hope that it is not too invidious to quote a Mafioso, "Boss of Bosses" Joseph Bonanno. "Uncle Stefano also endowed me with a love for our Tradition. He spoke of it lovingly and zealously. He said Tradition was the bulwark against chaos" (1983, p. 28). The most fascinating part of this statement is its complete perversion of the term "tradition." True tradition leads to patterned behavior through individual belief and voluntary choice. The Mafia "Tradition" controls people in exactly the opposite fashion, using violence (and the threat of violence) to coerce people into actions that they will not do voluntarily.
2. Garrett Hardin expresses the point especially vividly: "I was appalled at your omission, misunderstanding, or denial of the second law of thermodynamics, conservation laws, the idea of limits. . . ." (letter, November 17, 1981).
3. Jeremy Campbell (1982) provides an excellent discussion of why an open view of the world is reasonable scientifically, and of the implications of openness.

50

Now (I Think) I Understand the Ecologists Better

Economists have long been derided by some people who call them-selves "ecologists." Among these, Paul Ehrlich is noteworthy. Here is a quote from him in a newspaper article that was introduced as follows: "Next to the possibility of war, the danger that concerns Dr. Ehrlich most is economic growth":

> *Economists think that the whole world is just a market system, and that free goods are infinitely supplied. They are a discipline built on transparent mistakes, from the point of view of a physicist or a biologist.*
>
> *Economists are probably the most dangerous single profession on earth, because they are listened to. They continue to whisper in the ears of politicians, all kinds of nonsense. Everybody feels that the economic system is what dominates human affairs, when actually the economic system is hopelessly embedded in the physical and environmental systems. Economists say it's jobs or the environment, when actually if you don't treat the environment right, there will be no jobs. (Steward McBride, "Doomsday Postponed",* The Christian Science Monitor, *Aug. 26, 1980, pp. B10 and B11)*

*In 1987, "World Bank president Barber Conable . . . announced a major reorganization of the bank that will include much more atten-tion to resource conservation and the environmental aspects of devel-opment projects. . . . Conable has named the environment as one of his top three concerns, the others being population growth and the status of women in developing countries" (*Science, *May 15, 1987, p. 769). This is despite the fact that the economists on the Bank's staff did not agree on the soundness of the proposed policies of the Bank— which is, after all, supposed to be an economic institution with*

The Futurist, September-October 1987.

economic justification. At an earlier Bank meeting referred to in the same article, it was noted that "Economists and environmentalists do not understand each others' languages . . . the economists at the meeting rejected the idea that resources could be finite. . . . The economists also rejected the idea that population growth necessarily has adverse consequences on economic growth in developing countries. . . ."

Robert Goodland, the Bank's ecologist, said that "the most important thing for the environmental movement is to revamp economic thinking." That aim certainly is not overly modest.

These ecologists advertise a set of larger and more penetrating concepts than the concepts used by economists. This selection tries to explain why the thinking of ecologists and economists concerning resources has differed in the past, and suggests how the viewpoints may be harmonized.

Ecologists and economists have been much at odds. Each side thinks it understands the other but that the other does not understand them. Recently I recognized that this economist, anyway, has not understood the ecologists in at least one important fashion. I have not grasped the grand vision of nature and humanity that underlies their thinking. Perhaps if I (on behalf of other non-ecologists) try to state that vision and say why I do not share it, the ensuing dialogue will be helpful.

When I say "ecologist" I have in mind those who are interested in, and usually also concerned about, the overall order of living things and their relationship to the environment. Persons interested in conserving or preserving some particular aspect of our environment, such as the Santa Barbara coastline or the quantity of farmland in Westchester County, are a very different type for the purposes of this discussion, and I shall not be talking to or about them here.

Perhaps I can best describe the ecologists' vision, as I understand it, with an analogy that may show my basic sympathy with them. I had planned to go to medical school after I got out of the Navy in 1956. One reason I chose not to study medicine was my preference that I and others not take medical drugs except when the need to do so is overwhelming. I feared that that preference would make me out of sync with the profession I would be studying and practicing. I'm not sure how much of this preference was due to worry about side-effects, and how much to some vague belief (whose logic I could not pin down) that it makes sense not to disturb the very complex system that is our body, if one can avoid doing so. Psychological experiments showing that rats and babies often can choose diets wisely had impressed me, as had Cannon's notion of "the wisdom of the body." I thought it likely that tampering with such a complex system that we understand so little was inherently dangerous. Medical practice nowadays is closer to that intuition of course, and most people agree that this change is a good thing.

The ecologists' conception of humans and nature is similar to my conception of the body, if I understand them correctly. "Concerned" ecologists believe that we ought not to make changes in the existing order unless there is pressing reason, and unless our knowledge of the likely consequences is extensive, because so many undesirable effects may be indirectly caused by a particular alteration. Rachel Carson in *Silent Spring* (1962, which I will here use as scripture for convenience) expresses this point of view well with respect to modern fertilizers and pesticides.

> The rapidity of change and the speed with which new situations are created follow the impetuous and heedless pace of man rather than the deliberate pace of nature. . . . Under primitive agricultural conditions the farmer had few insect problems. These arose with the intensification of agriculture—the devotion of immense acreages to a single crop. Such a system set the stage for explosive increases in specific insect populations. Single-crop farming does not take advantage of the principles by which nature works; it is agriculture as an engineer might conceive it to be. Nature has introduced great variety into the landscape, but man has displayed a passion for simplifying it. Thus he undoes the built-in checks and balances by which nature holds the species within bounds. (1962, pp. 17 and 20.)

Economist Ezra Mishan expresses similar concerns:

> The second reason for feeling less than sanguine about the contribution of technology in maintaining the existing growth rates is that we are moving into an area of increasing uncertainty. In order of diminishing tractability we can list four types of global risk, none of which existed before the industrial revolution. (1) Insofar as the chief effluents poured into the air, lakes, rivers, and coastal waters are known and their toxic effects understood, they can be effectively curbed in a number of ways, of which enforcing minimal standards of purity may well be the most economic. The success of this method depends upon the efficacy and frequency of monitoring, and on the severity of the penalties exacted for failing to comply. What economists do not sufficiently allow for, however, are the limits to our present knowledge. There cannot be many effluents whose full range of toxic effects are known to us. Moreover, in consequence of rapid chemical innovation, new gases and fluids are being produced whose effects on the ambient environment and on our health may not be discernible for many years, and possibly only after substantial and irreversible damage has been done.
>
> (2) To these risks that we run from pushing on in a state of semi-ignorance, we may add (*a*) those arising from the indiscriminate use of chemical pesticides

such as DDT, from the gradual dissipation of the protective ozone mantle by the gases emitted in supersonic flight, and from the accumulating deposits of synthetic material that resist absorption into the ecological cycle, and (b) those arising out of the growing assortment of chemical compounds appearing each year on the market, about whose ultimate biological and genetic effects, taken singly or in combination, we know next to nothing. Nor can we reasonably expect to detect the dangers in time. Luckily, the mutilative potential of the medically recommended sedative, Thalidomide, was discovered before it became a genetic calamity—and then, not by doctors or scientists, but by a private citizen working on a hunch. We may not be so lucky with a number of other common drugs on the market. If, after a number of years, the death or sickness of a small proportion of the human population can be traced to some new substance or to some new combination of substances, it will be likely that the disease is latent in a much larger proportion of the population. What is more, it may not be possible to find an adequate antidote in time, and even if one is found in time, its side effects may eventually prove to be more dangerous than the disease it is intended to cure. (1973, pp. 67–68)

The complexity in the system, and our imperfect knowledge of it, causes ecologists to worry (if I understand them correctly) that an alteration could knock the whole system out of whack, which will then induce a series of additional changes to compensate, which will then have even worse effects, and so on until the whole system comes apart or explodes. To illustrate, consider these quotes from *Silent Spring:*

Only within the moment of time represented by the present century has one species—man—acquired significant power to alter the nature of his world. . . .

To adjust to these chemicals would require time on the scale that is nature's; it would require not merely the years of a man's life but the life of generations. . . . The whole process of spraying seems caught up in an endless spiral. . . .

Future generations are unlikely to condone our lack of prudent concern for the integrity of the natural world that supports all life. (pp. 16, 17, 18, 22)

And this is Carson's head quote, from Albert Schweitzer: "Man has lost the capacity to foresee and to forestall. He will end by destroying the earth." (1962, p. vii)

In my view, however, this vision—together with the analogy of the human body and drugs—is not appropriate for understanding and dealing with the modern economic and environmental situation. Yes, it is possible to avoid large "unnatural" alterations in the way we treat our bodies, in comparison to the way people lived in earlier millennia. Though we cannot have a similar mental environment, we can sleep the same way, exercise in not dissimilar ways, and even eat much the same way, if we choose to do so; even the casual diet of a person who is not faddishly given to one kind of food or another probably does not depart fundamentally from the diet of our long-dead ancestors. But with respect to our macro-relation-ships to the environment, the situation is entirely different. We cannot say "Stop the world, I want to get off," or even "Stop the world, I want to stay on." There is no way we can avoid large "unnatural" human-made alterations, because our whole life-support system is composed of human-made artifacts. What happens, for example, to our heating, our cooking, our mobility if we turn off our electric motors, or stop digging in the earth? Even aside from the fact that stopping progress is not acceptable to most inhabitants of the world, we cannot even say, "Things seem more-or-less okay as they are now for middle-class people in the United States, so let's keep things pretty much as they are." We cannot just go on doing what we've been doing without change, because the existing system—like all existing systems—necessarily runs itself down unless we replenish and refurbish it. For example, a "soft path" to energy and growth is a nice idea, but it usually does not work because sunlight is too diffuse to be practical for most purposes.

In our commitment to creating decent sustenance and opportunities for participation in modern society for all, we are something like persons in the year 1900 who have committed themselves to getting to the moon. If we satisfy ourselves with simple Wright-brothers technology, we won't make it and can only get killed in a crash as reward. If we continue to improve the technology, we accept the chances of as-yet-unknown (and perhaps more disastrous) hazards than are possible with a primitive airplane. But with time and thought we are more likely to make the system increasingly safe, as has happened with air travel. It is now safer to go to the moon than it was then to fly 1000 yards with the Wrights. And with a little luck and a lot of human effort and ingenuity, in the future we may be able to provide physical and mental sustenance at a high level—and a better environment—to a large proportion of an even larger humanity. And it will probably happen sooner if we do not think of such advances as flying as "unnatural," that is, if we forego the view that "If God wanted us to fly, he'd have given us wings."

Another example of how our only feasible alternative is to keep forging ahead with new knowledge rather than trying to maintain a stable state or to get closer to the "natural" untouched-by-humans state: Would you oppose developing new antibiotics that kill microbes that foil existing antibiotics? Calling a moratorium on drug development will increase the death rate. Discarding all the newfangled "artificial" drugs will increase it even more. Of course the new drugs bring new problems, too, such as even more wily microbes. But which course points to a better future a century from now?

As Olson, Landsberg, and Fisher put it some years ago:

Just as economic growth brings serious risks, so it also yields resources which offer some degree of insurance against many risks. At the individual level, it is obvious that a sufficient accumulation of wealth lessens or eliminates the need for insurance; at the social level, too, additional wealth and productive capacity gives a society the power to solve some very costly problems which might have proved fatal to a poorer society. This is aptly illustrated by the "Southern corn leaf blight" of 1971, to which the growth-oriented "genetic engineering" or hybridization left the nation's corn crop extraordinarily susceptible. Alarming as this type of susceptibility is, it is also important to remember that the scientific advance and capital accumulation association with economic growth made it possible to produce a record crop only one year after the blight epidemic began. Thus it is not by any means certain—though it is possible—that a no-growth policy would reduce the risks of ecological catastrophe. (1973, p. 239)

How does population growth fit in? More people increase the demands upon the system, and therefore "disturb" it more. But more people also bring about greater understanding of the system and increased capacity to bend it to our will. This results from the increased demand for goods and services that more people cause, which leads to improved technology, and also from the greater potential for knowledge creation that more people represent (all else equal). The difference is between a world of 10,000 people many millennia ago, who inadvertently disturbed little and could not intentionally alter very much, and as we are many billions now, who disturb much but who can purposely alter even more.

51

Dump on Us, Baby, We Need It

The introduction to this selection explains how it came about. The underlying idea that humans create more than they destroy, on average, is developed in a more abstract fashion in Selection 47. At first hearing this idea strikes people as just plain ridiculous, as the following letter to the Chicago Tribune *says:*

> *Julian Simon's defense of the indefensible (pollution) was so stupid that I had to read it twice to make sure it wasn't a joke. . . .*
>
> *I'd suggest he go consult with a good ecologist, who may be able to cure him of his severe myopia.*
>
> *His twisted reasoning is an excellent example of the pollution of thought which he professes to be against.*

It was Martin Luther King Day, and the researcher from Cable News Network was in a terrific snit. Because of the holiday she couldn't find anyone to comment on a scary new pollution report that had just broken. The danger? Disposable diapers using up so much landfill that we will soon run out of farmland, causing food to become scarce.

Waste disposal is not my specialty, so I gave her the home phone numbers of some experts whom I know. But afterward I reflected on the entire problem of waste disposal.

Many "environmentalists" worry that the unintended by-products—the "externalities," in the economist's term—of humankind's economic activities are malign even if the direct effects of production and trade are beneficial. But a case can be made that even activities that are not intentionally constructive *more often than not* leave a positive legacy to subsequent generations. That is, even the unintended aspects of humans'

"Humanity Doesn't Waste the Benefits Found in Trash," *Chicago Tribune*, February 27, 1989, p. 11.

use of land and of other raw materials tend to be profitable for those who come afterward.

Going one step further, population growth that increases the volume of trash may increase our problems in the short run, but it bestows benefits on future generations. The pressure of new problems leads to the search for new solutions. The solutions constitute the knowledge that fuels the progress of civilization, and leaves us better off than if the original problem had never arisen. That is the history of the human race.

Would Robinson Crusoe have been better off if there had preceded him on the island a group of people who had produced and consumed, and left the trash in a dump that Crusoe could uncover? Sure he would. Consider how valuable that dump would have been to Crusoe. If his predecessors had had a low-technology society, the trash would have contained sharp stones and various animal parts that could be used for cutting, binding, carrying, and so on. If the preceding society had had high technology, the dump would have contained even more interesting and useful materials— metal utensils, electronics parts, and the like—which a knowledgeable person could have used to get help.

What is waste to one community at one time is usually a valuable resource to a later community that has greater knowledge about how to use the material. Consider the "borrow pits" by the sides of turnpikes, from which earth is taken for road-building. At first look the pits seem a despoliation of nature, a scar upon the land. But after the road is finished the borrow pits turn out to be useful for fishing lakes and reservoirs, and the land they occupy is likely to be more valuable than if the pits had never been dug.

Even a pumped-out oil well—that is, the empty hole—probably has more value to subsequent generations than a similar spot without a hole. The hole may be used as a storage place for oil or other fluids, or for some as-yet-unknown purposes. And the casing that is left in the dry well might be reclaimed profitably by future generations.

Humans' activities tend to increase the order and decrease the randomness of nature. One can see this from the air if one looks for the signs of human habitation. Where there are people (ants, too, of course) there will be straight lines and smooth curves; otherwise, the face of nature is not neat or ordered.

Production of material goods brings like elements together. This concentration can be exploited by subsequent generations. Reflect on lead batteries in a dump, or the war rubble from which Berliners built seven hills that are now lovely recreational spots. The only reason that used newspapers are worth so little now is that we have learned how to grow trees and manufacture paper so cheaply. When I was a kid, we collected and sold bundles of old papers to the paper mill at the edge of town. And then when the mill pond froze in the winter we exploited it as our hockey rink.

Many acts that we tend to think of as despoiling the land actually bestow increased wealth upon subsequent generations. Ask yourself which areas in the Midwest will seem more valuable to subsequent generations—the places where cities now are, or the places where farmlands are?

One sees evidence of this delayed benefit in the Middle East. For hundreds of years until recently, Turks and Arabs occupied structures originally built by the Romans 2000 years ago. The ancient buildings saved the latecomers the trouble of doing their own construction. Another example is the use of dressed stones in locations far away from where they were dressed. One finds the lintels of doorways from ancient Palestinian synagogues in contemporary homes in Syria.

Still more generally, humans have for tens of thousands of years created more than they have destroyed. That is, the composite of what they sought to produce and of the by-products has been on balance positive. This is evidenced by the increasing standard of material living generation after generation, the decreased scarcity of all natural resources as measured by their prices throughout history, and the most extraordinary achievement of all, longer life and better health. Other evidence is the found treasures of civilization that our ancestors bequeathed, each century's inheritance greater than the previous one. The core of the inheritance, of course, is the productive knowledge that one generation increments and passes on to the next generation.

If human beings destroyed more than they produced, on average, the species would have died out long ago. But in fact people produce more than they consume, and the new knowledge of how to overcome material problems is the most precious product of all. The more people there are on earth, the more new problems, but also the more minds to solve those problems and the greater the inheritance for future generations.

Do I have a solution to the used-diaper problem other than burning them for energy? Not at the moment. But there is every likelihood that, as with other wastes created in the past, human ingenuity will find a way to convert them to a valuable resource rather than a costly nuisance. The same is true of nuclear waste, of course. I just wish I could feel as hopeful about the pollution of human thought and intercourse that we all contribute to both in our private relationships and in our public utterances—of which this scare report about disposable diapers is an example. Now that's a problem more worth our attention than the disposition of disposable diapers.

52

Bunkrapt: The Abstractions that Lead to Scares about Resources and Population Growth

Some characteristics of unsound thinking about the nature of natural resources and their supply, and about the effect of additional people upon environment, resources, and the living standard, is discussed in my 1981 The Ultimate Resource, *and therefore will not be repeated here. The new material presented here was "introduced" in the Introduction to this volume, as were some of the reasons why people do not easily change their minds about these topics even when the empirical evidence completely contradicts the ideas that they hold.*

In an important sense, the heart of the economics of population and resources is the mode of thinking that is brought to bear upon the subject—what we might call the "meta-economics." The needed kind of thinking—focusing on the indirect, long-run, diffuse influences, rather than on the immediate and direct effects—does not excite the mind as do those two old Malthusian seducers, Turgotian diminishing returns (Malthus' assertion that food would grow only at an arithmetic rate) and exponential growth (the rate at which population would grow). A recent example of the charms of exponential growth comes from Pat Robertson, the preacher and then-presidential candidate:

> *At the center of Mr. Robertson's economic thinking lies a fascination with compound interest. In his newsletter, he said that "if 30 pieces of silver given to Judas Iscariot had been invested tax-free at 4 percent interest continually compounded until now, it would amount to a sum so vast that it could provide $300,000 to every man, woman and child in the world."* (The Wall Street Journal, *March 7, 1988, p. 46)*

Bunkrapture (sic sic sic; actually, it is more like despair than rapture) afflicts the most unlikely people. My excellent physician Dr. O. is fully aware of the extraordinary improvements that have occurred in health and in medical possibilities during the past half century. Yet he feels that the world is in trouble. When I ask him why he thinks so, he simply says that it is an impression that he gains from reading the newspapers.

My mother was born in 1900, and saw her only son saved from death at age 7 by the first new wonder drug. In her eighties she knew that her friends had mostly lived extraordinarily long lives. She recognized the convenience and comfort such modern inventions as the telephone, air conditioning, and airplanes have brought. Yet she insisted that life was worse in the 1980s than it was when she was younger. When I pressed her why she thought so, she said, "Look at all the terrible headlines in the newspapers."

How could these people of generally good judgment hold beliefs so contrary to the facts, on the basis of such flimsy and ephemeral evidence? The only answer that makes sense to me, as I wrote in the Introduction, is that none of us can carefully inspect the evidence for most of the beliefs that we hold, and we simply adopt the most easily available ideas out of convenience. And this is not a scandal; when a March 28, 1988, page in Newsweek *can be headed "More Bad News for the Planet" (p. 63) in a year and decade of almost unbroken good news for the planet and the human enterprise, who can blame casual readers from sharing that point of view? It is scandalous, however, when people insist on holding onto these ideas even when they are challenged on them and exposed to more reliable information, just because the beliefs have become so ingrained.*

It often seems that we seek ways to characterize the situation as frightening or worsening even when the signs point the other way. In the midst of a spate of excellent economic news and a better state of the economy than in many years, an April 4, 1988 Newsweek *column by Robert J. Samuelson (p. 51) was headed "Looking for Bad News? The better the economy does, the more we worry that its good behavior won't continue." And it ends by noting that economists are "expressing their doubts spotting a lot of potential problems, but their analyses aren't especially focused. They reflect a general anxiety about the future as much as a clear picture of what lies ahead. It's a bewildering game; everyone keeps getting good news and looking for the bad."*

Garrison Keilor vividly describes a common state of mind that he finds inimical to the spirit of the founding of the United States, and which he escapes by going outdoors. "Indoors all the news is second-hand, mostly bad, and even good people are drawn into a dreadful fascination with doom and demise; their faith in extinction gets stronger; they sit and tell stories that begin with The End." (Newsweek, *July 4, 1988, p. 33) A newspaper reporter writes about a New Jersey sixth-grade class: "Despite their youth, these children have few illusions about the times in which they live. 'We have freedom in this country, but it stinks,' says 11-year-old Sean Hooks. 'Drugs, alcohol, crime. There's no good news anymore.' "* (The Wall Street Journal, *September 26, 1988, p. 29) Wow! This state of mind is indeed "bunkrapture," and the bunk is dangerous.*

Lest one doubt that false bad news causes damage, we can now document each link in this chain: (1) A local or temporary problem is seized upon by newspapers and television as the harbingers of a long-term deteriorating trend, e.g., the extraordinary attention paid to energy in the 1970s (documented by Rothman, Lichter, and Lichter; S. Robert Lichter, "The Media 'Irrelevant'? It's Not True," Washington Post, *September 17, 1988, p. A-21), and the urbanization of farmland (not even a temporary problem but simply a false report; see Selections 8 to 11 and 53.) (2) The public evinces fear and considers the matter a national problem (Gallup polls concerning pollution and energy in the 1970s). (3) Costly and counterproductive government policies are put into place to deal with the "problem," e.g., price controls on gasoline that caused gas-station queues, and controls on oil and natural gas that caused billion-dollar scandals, and also the fuel-efficiency CAFE standards that have hobbled the U.S. auto industry.*

Long ago Thomas Hobbes knew that booklearning can sometimes unhinge people from common sense and lead them to believe foolish ideas. "But they that trusting only to the authority of books, follow the blind blindly, are like him that, trusting to the false rules of a master of fence, ventures presumptuously upon an adversary, that either kills or disgraces him." (Leviathan, p. 147)

This phenomenon may be seen in poll data which indicate that people with more education were more likely to be taken in with false news of energy and pollution crises. For example, in 1971 R. Simon polled Illinoisans and found that "Of those with a college education, 83 percent said they thought that world population was growing too fast, compared with 42 percent of those with a grade school education. Sixty-eight percent of the college respondents said they thought there was a food shortage in the world today, compared with 45 percent of the grade-school respondents." (Rita James Simon, "Pub-

lic Attitudes Toward Population and Pollution," The Public Opinion
Quarterly, *vol. 35, Spring, 1971, 93–99, p. 97)*

Why do we hear bad news about population and resources that is not
true? And, why do we hear that things are getting worse when they are
really getting better?

Individual self-interest is part of the explanation—the activities of the
media in trying to catch big audiences with scary stories, the preservation-
ists who prefer bucolic surroundings to resource development, and organizations such as the U.N.'s Food and Agricultural Organization (FAO) and
Fund for Population Activities (UNFPA) and the U.S. Council on Environmental Quality (CEQ), whose budgets depend upon people fearing resource scarcity and population growth.

Also influential is the marvelously evocative inflammatory rhetoric that
has been created to arouse fear—"population bomb," "empty pumps,"
"save the children," "end of the world as we know it," and "end of the
age of affluence," for example. (See *The Ultimate Resource,* Chapter 22,
for a long discussion of this rhetoric.)

Also at work is simple racism, especially with respect to population
growth in other parts of the world, and with respect to immigrants of
various shades and ethnicities entering the United States.

Important, too, is an attitude toward the factual truth that induces
people to exaggerate and even lie when convinced that the eleventh-hour
danger to the public justifies such dishonest practices. Joining the environmental movement is seen by many as a last chance to do good, in the way
that joining the Communist Party in the thirties seemed an opportunity for
social contribution by many generous-minded people. Once having joined
the movement, foul means are deemed acceptable by many if the end is
thought to be beneficial. Still another important element is the structure of
the human inferential mechanism. The beliefs we hold are affected, for
example, by the vividness of information—for example, television shots
of horrid scenes—all out of proportion to the importance of those pieces
of evidence. Beliefs are also affected by the volume of messages that we
are exposed to, in this case the two decades of stories on television and in
newspaper about the horrors of population growth. (See in this connection
the interesting book by Robert Nisbett and Lee Ross, *Human Inference,*
Prentice-Hall, 1980)

This selection leaves aside these important elements of the explanation,
however, and focuses only on the *ideas* that undergird the newspaper and
television stories, the intellectual infrastructure that gives these stories
credibility. The ideas to be discussed fall into two categories: misunder-

standings of the nature of resource creation and population economics, and misunderstandings of the nature of a modern complex social-economic system. The essay attempts to explain why so many people are enraptured with this kind of bunk—that is, bunkrapt.

Misunderstanding the Nature of Resource Creation and Population Size

The Seductiveness of the Malthusian Logic

Beneath the Malthusian notion of diminishing returns, we find an inter-related set of fundamental ideas that we may call, after Holton, a "thema." The thema underlying the thinking of today's conventional writers about resources and population is the concept of fixity or finiteness of resources in the relevant system of discourse. This idea is found in Malthus, of course. But the idea probably has always been a staple of human thinking, because so much of our situation must sensibly be regarded as fixed in the short run—the bottles of beer in the refrigerator, our paychecks, and the amount of energy that parents have to play basketball with their kids.

In contrast, the thema underlying my thinking about resources—also a fair-sized minority of others now, with such predecessors as William Petty, Friedrich Engels, Simon Kuznets, Friedrich Hayek, and the main devel-oper of the idea, Harold Barnett—is that the relevant system of discourse has a long enough horizon that it makes sense to treat the system operationally as not fixed, rather than finite. We view the resource system as being as unlimited as the number of thoughts a person might have, or the number of variations that might ultimately be produced by biological evolution. That is, a key difference between the thinking of those who worry about impending doom and those who see the prospects of a better life for more people in the future apparently is whether one thinks in closed-system or open-system terms. For example, those who worry that the second law of thermodynamics dooms us to eventual decline necessar-ily see our world as a closed system with respect to energy and entropy; those who view the relevant universe as unbounded view the second law of thermodynamics as irrelevant to this discussion. I am among those who view the relevant part of the physical and social universe as open for most purposes.

Which thema is better in the context of resources and population is not subject to scientific test. Yet the choice profoundly affects our thinking. I believe that here lies the root of the matter.

Academics are particularly susceptible to the notion of Malthusian diminishing returns, perhaps because academics are more likely than are laypeople to believe in abstract theories. (Academics properly spend much of their lives battling to persuade others that abstract theorizing has importance and is not just an "ivory tower" recreation.) In my experience, journalists and businesspeople are less likely to be taken with the simple Malthusian abstraction, perhaps because they have no professional stake in this idea (in contrast to many biologists and some economists) and perhaps because journalists are more attuned to reaching judgments and making decisions in light of the full richness of a situation—on their "intuition"—rather than upon the logical relationships in a simple model. (More generally, businesspeople and newspeople seem to be more open to new ideas than academics, perhaps because a continuous flow of creative change is more crucial in their occupations.) Another element is the dead hand of expertise. As Kuznets tells, "Experts are usually specialists skilled in, and hence bound to, traditional views; and they are, because of their knowledge of one field, likely to be cautious and unduly conservative" (in Rosenberg, 1972).

It is a puzzle why so many people—with biologists and physicists notable among them—seem so sure that there *must* be some constraint to prevent humanity from growing both ever richer and ever more populous, and why theirs is the thema of unexpandable limits. One possible explanation is that each of us tends to bring our professional modes of thought to bear on other situations even if those modes are not appropriate to the situation at hand. For example, biologists liken the human population to an animal population and then apply the animal-ecology notion of "carrying capacity," though that notion is quite inapplicable to natural resources in a human context.

Another attraction of the closed-system thema is that the closure of the system enables one to use interesting mathematics, especially the calculus and other optimization devices. From a purely physical point of view, a proposition about finiteness (or entropy) requires a bounded system. But where is the relevant boundary for our material world? Around the earth excluding the sun? Around the earth plus sun plus solar system? Around other suns? Around a "universe" which may or may not be finite or expanding in the astronomer's eye? No boundary, no finiteness.

Still another root of the closed-system thema is the bewitching medieval notion of "first cause" or "ultimate cause," the idea that nothing happens which is not the result of other forces. And pushing back the causal sequence in an infinite regress, it seems as if there must have been an original causal force. This suggests a complete, and therefore closed, system.

For some, the closed-system thema arises because of a natural abhorrence of the loose-endedness of an open system.

An interesting example of how this thema permeates our thinking: If you say that copper might be made of other metals, hearers say "alchemy." When you point out that nuclear bombardment transmutes metals, the hearers say "not practical," implying that it never *could* be practical. They may well be correct. But there is no *logically* binding impossibility theorem applicable here. One can only be sure that something is impossible or impractical if one can be sure that the state of knowledge will not change in the future, that is, that capacities are limited because knowledge is limited. But isn't this just what people said in the past about the possibility of finding smaller constituent parts within the "fundamental" electron, say? And about the possibility of obtaining the vast amounts of energy that we get from a small pile of stuff called uranium? Or for that matter, getting vast amounts of heat out of the black rocks that we call coal? The example of copper and "alchemy" is interesting for the infrathinking that it brings into the open.

The psychologies of open-system and closed-system thinking must be complex and deep-rooted. Perhaps closed-system thinking is related to focusing on the social equality of distribution of a fixed pie, rather than on expanding the amount of pie to the possible neglect of equity considerations; this focus often stems from the emotion of envy (Schoeck, 1969). But whatever the roots, most puzzling is why people who are themselves creative and imaginative should lack faith in others' capacities to respond to problems and shortages with limit-expanding ideas. How can people as powerfully creative as John Bardeen (the only two-time Nobel-winning physicist) and George Mitchell (the Texas oilman and developer) share this thema of limits with the nondoers—as they do?

Misunderstanding and Misapplication of the Slogan "There is no free lunch"

The slogan "There is no free lunch" seems to imply that we have to pay for everything we get. Here a good thought is going wrong by being applied to situations it was not designed for. This slogan was originally intended to suggest that the *government* cannot supply free lunches to *all of us*, that there is no magic trick by which we can increase our total national resources by passing laws and setting up bureaucracies; rather, we as taxpayers have to pay indirectly, sometime.

In other contexts, however, there *are* free (or below full cost) lunches all the time. None of us always pays the full cost of production for what we get. In the modern world each generation gets its lunch at a lower cost of labor than did earlier generations, because earlier generations responded to their economic problems with ingenuity and energy. Our ancestors bequeathed us the intellectual wherewithal to get our lunch, if not entirely free, at least much cheaper than if we had to start from scratch. Compare what we "pay" to what Europeans had to "pay" for lunch and the other meals a few hundred years ago. They paid most of every day's work, whereas we can buy the same amount of raw food with a small fraction of the work time it cost them. And there is no economic or physical force, and no concept in standard economic theory, that suggests that this progressive reduction in the cost of lunch cannot continue indefinitely. We eat our cheap lunch courtesy of the sweat of our ancestors' brows in mental as well as physical labor.

Lack of Historical Perspective, and Propensity to Compare the Present to an Idealized State Rather Than to the Actual Past

It is not surprising that most people do not keep in mind the lower real prices of resources in past years than now; to do so requires adjusting for inflation, and necessitates awareness of data all the way back to 1900 or 1800. Hence it is not surprising that views about impending resource scarcity are not informed by the contrary long-run trend of increasing availability.

It *should* surprise us, though, when mature experienced journalists in high positions, people such as James Reston and John Oakes of *The New York Times,* write about how bad things are now without reference to how things were in the past. In 1980 columnist Reston could write about "the civilized world that is now in such deep trouble," saying that "you can hardly pick up a paper these days without wondering what's wrong," and decrying our lack of leadership. Can this man have lived through the depression of the 1930s, Hitler, World War II, the Cold War, the Korean War, and the Vietnam War? And ex-senior editorial writer Oakes reproduces the pessimistic findings of the *Global 2000 Report* almost word for word, like a press-conference handout. How can he, too, have lived through such disastrous times in the past, when the environment was much more degraded and the materials more scarce, and continue to write as if the world is headed straight toward doom? Perhaps it is relevant here to mention surveys (that I cannot now document, unfortunately) showing that respondents judge people to have been happier in the past than in the present—but if given the choice would choose to live in the present rather than in the past. We compartmentalize our minds in interesting ways.

Lack of Distinction Between the Long Run and the Short Run

The distinction between long run and short run is crucial to making sense of the economics of population. In the developed world, additional people—babies or immigrants—are a burden in the short run. And focusing only on the short-run burden leads to a negative judgment about population growth. But in the long run, more people mean a higher standard of living for others. So the judgment about whether more people are good or bad economically depends on how one trades off the present versus the future. By most of my calculations, the discount rate would have to be quite high for additional people not to have a positive present value.

Furthermore, short-run costs are inevitable and obvious, whereas long-run benefits are hard to foresee. If your neighbor has another child, surely your school taxes will go up and there will be more noise in your neighborhood. And when the additional child first goes to work, per-worker income will be lower than otherwise, at least for awhile. It is, however, more difficult to foresee and to understand the possible long-run benefits. Because the increase in knowledge created by more people is nonmaterial it is easy to overlook. Writers about population growth mention a greater number of mouths coming into the world, and more pairs of hands, but never mention more brains arriving. This emphasis on physical consumption and production may be responsible for much unsound thinking and fear about population growth.

Disbelief in the Relationship Between Population and Knowledge Creation

To many, it is implausible that additional people cause more technical knowledge and advance in productivity, *ceteris paribus*. One source of misunderstanding is the common belief that new technical knowledge usually arises spontaneously, and without connection to social needs. But there is now ample evidence that increased output and investment in a given industry induce more inventions to be made and applied. This "demand-side effect," as economists call it, can be seen in systematic studies of learning-by-doing, where the time required to complete an airplane or ship decreases as more units are made. The effect can also be seen in systematic studies of comparative productivity in the industries in the United Kingdom and in Canada that are relatively large and relatively small compared to the same industries in the United States. And Bernal in *Science and Industry in the Nineteenth Century* (1953/1970) provides additional evidence—case studies of steel; electricity, light, and power; chemistry, bacteriology, and biochemistry; and the theory of heat and energy in the nineteenth century—showing that innovations respond to economic demand. In the case of electricity, for example, "The barrier, or rather the absence of stimulus to advance, was economic. Electricity developed quickly when it paid, not a moment before" (p. 131). And a large population size and density imply higher total demand, *ceteris paribus,* which is why Edison's first street lighting was in New York City rather than in Montana. It is also clear that countries with more people produce more knowledge, assuming income is the same, e.g., Sweden versus the United States. And Bernal shows how the power of final demand works indirectly, too. "Once electric distribution on a large scale was proved feasible and immensely profitable, then came a demand for large efficient power sources" (p. 129), leading to the development of turbines. And the development of light bulbs led to advances in creating vacuums, after the subject "had stagnated for about two hundred years. . . . Here was another clear case of the law of supply and demand in the development of science and technology" (p. 125).

On the "supply side" there is also much misunderstanding, especially the belief that the number of potential inventors does not matter. One source of this misunderstanding for some is the idea that one need only contrast innovation and creativity in tiny Athens in the Golden Age with monstrous Calcutta now, or Calcutta with Budapest of the 1930s, to see that more people do not imply more technical knowledge being produced. This argument leaves out the all-things-equal clause; Calcutta is poor. And, underlying this argument is the implied (but unwarranted) assumption that Calcutta is poor *because* it has so many people.

If we make more appropriate comparisons—comparing Greece to itself and Rome to itself during periods with different population sizes and growth rates, and industries of various sizes in different countries now— we find that a larger population is associated with *more* knowledge and productivity, because there are more potential inventors and adopters of new technology. Graphs that plot the numbers of great discoveries, and the population sizes in various centuries in Greece and Rome, bring out this conclusion very nicely (Simon, 1980 or 1981).

On the related question of whether material well-being can be improved through there being more ordinary persons—not geniuses—who contribute to our knowledge in their everyday work, the story of electricity and power production is again illuminating. Bernal describes the "stumbling progress of the first fifty years from 1831 to 1881 . . . the effort put into the development (1831–1881) . . . was small." The people who made the necessary technical developments "were not geniuses . . . and others no more gifted could have hit upon these ideas earlier if the field had attracted enough workers" (pp. 130–131). As said by Soichino Honda, the inventor and founder of the Japanese motorcycle and auto firm bearing his name, "Where 100 people think, there are 100 powers; if 1000 people think, there are 1000 powers" (*The Wall Street Journal,* February 1, 1982, p. 15).

*Confusion Between Trends and Levels. Between Whether Things Are
Getting Better or Getting Worse and Whether They Are Good Now*

A frequent and crucial error in the thinking of the doomsayers is neglect
of historical data. And often the doomsayers criticize their opponents for
extrapolating from the past on the assumption that the past usually bears
some resemblance to the future. For example, when I say that the history
of humankind is the history of people responding to existing and impending
problems with solutions that leave us better off than if the problem had
never arisen, others poke fun at the notion that experience of the past is a
sound basis for forecasting the future. These persons prefer that we form
our conclusions purely by analysis of the structural elements, physical and
otherwise, that they decide are the most important variables. This is
ironic, because to the extent that we have knowledge of these elements,
that knowledge is based upon experience—systematic and otherwise—of
the operation of those elements in history and in scientific experience. As
Macaulay, I believe, put it about 150 years ago, if we cannot learn from
history, what *can* we learn from? More generally, if we cannot base our
judgments about the future largely upon past experience, in conjunction
with reasonable theoretical explanations of that experience, then all of our
experience is without value. I doubt that many people really do wish to
reject experience as a teacher in this manner.

This is not to say that the future is simply an extension of the past; the
number of horses in the United States did not continue growing throughout
the twentieth century. Nor am I downplaying the role of theory, which is
a generalized and formalized structure that embodies our accumulated
experience in a particular field. What I *am* saying is that to assume,
without solid reasons to believe otherwise that the future will bear no
resemblance to the past in a particular context, is to invite serious error.

Many make an unwarranted double logical leap from the fact that things
are *not good* in *some* places to the fact that things are *getting* worse
everywhere. This leap is coupled with a lack of historical perspective—for
example, a sense of how much worse-off Mexico City and its inhabitants
were twenty or fifty years ago compared to today. And when the doomsayers cannot avoid admitting that at least some of the trends in the past have
not been toward things getting worse, but rather toward things getting
better, they often reply: But history is not a good guide in this connection
because we are now at a turning point in history.

The issue of whether we are now at a turning point needs some close
attention to dispatch it satisfactorily (see Simon, 1984). But all throughout

history people have felt that they are at a turning point, and it has not turned out to be so.

Belief That What Is in Print, and What Is Said "Officially," Must Be Right

Consider this statement from a recent letter:

[Y]ou said that the transformation of farmland to urban use is far less than society is led to believe. I find this very outraging because I think you made a very blind statement. You have given many people the idea that we're not really losing that much farmland than what the Government or Department of Agriculture or Farmers claim. I have enclosed a pamphlet [from the "official" National Agricultural Lands Study] which is proof to my claim.

Well, you might say, the writer doesn't sound very sophisticated. But the "official" label that gives statements the full authority of the federal government, and which the letter writer finds decisive, was prominent in most newspaper and television stories about the "vanishing farmland crisis" of the early 1980s. If reports of the National Agricultural Lands Study had not displayed a government label, they probably would never even have appeared in print, let alone been discussed in national publications, because their level of technical competence and scientific proof was so low. (Well, maybe that statement is too strong. *The Limits to Growth* was widely publicized even without an "official" label. But that book had the backing of the wealthy Club of Rome and a hired public relations agency; the details of that campaign were given in *Science*.)

Differences in Conceptions of Human Nature

The main interest of David Hume and Adam Smith was human nature, and they came to study economics as an outgrowth of that interest. Differences in conceptions of human nature are at the root of much disagreement about economic issues, and evidence about the validity of these different views is relevant to decisions about the economic issues themselves. (Unfortunately for the discipline, that explicit focus of attention has been lost entirely in the mathematics that constitutes so much of modern "sophisticated" and "rigorous" and "elegant" economics.)

For example, those who desire more government intervention in the production and consumption of natural resources, and those who argue for nonintervention of the government in resource markets, usually differ in their views of how individuals and private enterprisers behave in the face of economic opportunity; they also differ in their views of the performance of government personnel and agencies when entrusted with economic tasks. This thought struck me as I was jogging one morning near Asheville, North Carolina, and I found myself on "Old Toll Road" going up a secluded mountain. Long ago, private enterprisers must have built that road in hopes of making a profit from traffic across that difficult country. And the end result of their private desires was a benefit for the public that continues until today. Interventionists are likely to believe that if government does not provide such services, they will not be provided at all.

I am not suggesting that government should play no role in our economy. Space certainly would have been explored later without government action (or without competition between governments, perhaps), which might (or might not) have been an economic loss. But when opportunity is present, private enterprises undertake more ventures than doomsayers expect, more quickly, and at less cost to the public partly because individuals rather than taxpayers bear costs of the failing ventures.

Concerning the difference in views of public and private performance: At a meeting I attended of the potato-chips and snack food association (yes, you're right), I imagined a conversation with a potato-chip distributor about possible competition by a government agency. I guessed that the distributor's first reaction would be to laugh at the possibility that a government bureau could even nearly match her/his prices and quality without massive subsidies. But then she/he would reflect that if a government agency got into trouble because it could not compete, it could lower its prices to the competitive level, lose money, and then reach into the public pocket to make up the losses. That would be less funny, and not unrealistic.

Another difference in views of human nature concerns its changeability. Reformers, starting perhaps most vividly with William Godwin (to whom Malthus' *Essay on Population* was a response), invariably believe that human nature is quite malleable—for example, that self-interested behavior can be reduced by the proper social environment. This belief is very important in Marxism. It implies that one can design a social system that has particular properties, and then safely expect people to be molded to fit that system. In contrast, the classic Scottish writers—Adam Ferguson, Hume, Smith, and their friends—tended to see human nature as relatively immutable, which implies choosing a social and economic system that produces the best results given that fixed human nature.

Misunderstanding of the Necessary Nature of an Efficient Modern Social System with Many Participants, Goods, and Production Techniques[1]

Yearning for an Organization of Society which Reflects the Best Aspects of the Family Mode of Organization

In a family, members share goods out of love and altruism, and their decisions about individual and family activities (at least sometimes) are affected by care for one another. But this mode of social organization cannot work effectively when individuals cannot know the preferences of all others in the society, when their capacity for empathizing with another is diminished by lack of intimate relationship, where there is no accepted hierarchy (as there is between parents and children), and where the number of goods and possible transactions is very large.

Yet many persons find it abhorrent to turn over the distribution function to the impersonal market. And market distribution seems especially abhorrent when the goods seem to have (though they may well not have) quite inelastic supply and are especially important to physical survival—for example, food, land, and clean air and water.

Belief in the Need for Centralized Control of Important Activities

Hayek asserts that belief in centralized control of economic activity in society is a misplaced analogy to the way engineers plan a dam or bridge. He traces socialist theory back to the creation of the great engineering schools in France at the turn of the nineteenth century. Whether or not his account of intellectual history is correct, Hayek's analysis of the contemporary sources of the belief in the need for control is sound, I think.

Many people believe that without planning and controls, the system just cannot work well. For example, in a debate over whether Champaign County (Illinois) should permit rezoning of farmland for industry, people were heard to say, "I'm for growth, but for *controlled* growth, of course." If you ask people why growth must be controlled by a planner or an agency, they look at you blankly, as if you lack elementary intelligence.

Many seem to fear that anarchy is the necessary result of absence of centralized control. Hayek argues that this belief in the need for control is related to lack of understanding of how a large group of people, acting without any prearrangement, can develop an orderly structure of production and exchange based on individual desires and perceptions of other's desires and intentions. He also mentions the common failure to understand the difficulty of organizing an economy nearly as well by central planning, even with the aid of unlimited computing capacity and the most detailed imaginable information gathering, as with a market. These are subtle ideas, not easy to grasp, so it is not surprising that even well-educated laypeople often have not thought them through and do not understand them.

Support for a centrally-directed society also flows from the belief that *others* who are not so well-educated and intelligent cannot figure out how to conduct self-supporting lives that will also thereby contribute to economy and society. (An example is the belief that welfare support will be necessary for immigrants—who are often thought [wrongly] to come to the United States with little education and knowledge of English.) This belief is simply the arrogance of educated people.

Beckmann and others have connected this view with intellectuals' desire to be needed by the society, and their assumption that their trained intellects ought to achieve for them places of special importance and reward in the economy and society. As Beckmann says about a capitalistic society, "The highly skilled jetliner pilot and the lowly cleaner of sewage systems get a reward beyond dollars—the heady knowledge that they are voluntarily supported because they are genuinely needed. Such a reward is unknown to the professor of Turkish medieval poetry" (1978).[2] In Western civilization this is an old story going back at least to Plato. As Popper put it, Plato "charmed all intellectuals with his brilliance, flattering and thrilling them by his demand that the learned should rule" (1966, p. 199).

A related idea is disbelief that others—especially the uneducated and poor—can *create* resources by creating new ideas. Perhaps this disbelief is due in large part to lack of understanding of how human intervention underlies behind the resources that we take for granted, e.g., the fertile Midwestern prairie that was a useless malarial swamp before settlers drained it.

The extent to which demographic studies are founded on the assumption that individual couples' reproductive behavior should be influenced by their government is seen in the very title of the University of Michigan School of Public Health's "Graduate Programs in Population *Planning* and International Health" (italics added).

Belief that Externalities of Self-interested Actions Are Usually Bad

Environmentalists worry that the unintended by-products—the "externalities"—of humankind's economic activities (especially those that affect the environment) are malign even if the direct effects of production and trade are benign. But I believe that a case can be made (see Selection 52) that even activities which are not intentionally constructive usually leave a positive legacy to subsequent generations. That is, even the unintended aspects of humans' use of land and of other natural resources tend to be profitable for those who come afterward.

A related trait of mind focuses only upon the dangers of a projected line of activity, and urges us to "play it safe." This way of thinking is appropriate for safety engineers, but paralyses the social will and causes rejection of new technical possibilities when misapplied about natural resources and the environment. When discussing a social scheme, a talented game theorist and I kept disagreeing about whether particular systems would work or not. Finally we discovered that I focused upon the *aggregate* effects *on average,* whereas he focused upon *worst-case analysis*; the latter, he said, is characteristic of his trade. And worst-case analysis causes one to reject as not acceptable many possibilities that on average are desirable. Much of the thinking of the environmental movement seems to be worst-case analysis.

Another analogy in another context: Nathan Leopold, of the Loeb-Leopold murder case, wrote in his fascinating autobiography that it is extraordinarily difficult to persuade prison administrations to accept new ideas for running the prison because they know that a thousand pairs of eyes are looking for the slightest loophole in the new setup which can be exploited for escape or other troublemaking. But as Einstein said about nature, God may be tricky but he is not malignly trying to do us in. And our situation with respect to resources and the environment is not like that of a prison, and we need not think as do prison administrators or safety engineers.

Nuclear-power debates provide many instances of what we might call the safety engineer-Leopold syndrome. Opponents of nuclear power point to scenarios conceivably leading to, say, 50,000 deaths. Proponents of nuclear power point out that the risk of such a scenario occurring is miniscule, and the "expected number of deaths"—using "expected" in the statistical sense—is very small. The anti-nukes are not impressed by such a probabilistic argument, saying that the worst case has a meaning to us that cannot be treated as part of any set of averages. Nor are anti-nukes impressed by other examples of similarly large worst-case risks that we routinely accept, such as risks that electrical-power dams might break and kill hundreds of thousands of people, or airplanes falling from the sky into stadiums seating 70,000 people, risks that are probabilistically greater than those from nuclear energy.

There seems to be a value judgment at the bottom of the anti-nuclear argument, a value that cannot be rebutted logically any more than other values can be rebutted logically. But it is logically possible to point out neglected costs of such policies as foregoing nuclear power. It is appropriate for a safety engineer not to be concerned with the costs of avoiding a dangerous activity, because the cost/benefit calculation will be made at higher levels of management. But in discussion of such activities as nuclear power, it would seem that all discussants have an obligation to have a balanced view and not focus on just one side of the matter, because there is no arbiter in a court of public opinion who will take into account all sides of the matter, as higher levels of management are responsible for doing in an industrial setting. Also, it seems appropriate to point out in such discussions that if we routinely follow such a line of thinking, lives will be shorter and poorer, and fewer people will get a chance to enjoy life, because of the life-shortening effects of air pollution from coal, and the industrial accidents that kill so many people in coal-mining and petroleum operations.

The case of hydroponic vegetable growing may sharpen the point. Hydroponic agriculture is now profitable for a good many farmers around Washington, D.C., during the months when vegetables are not grown outdoors nearby (Davis, 1984). Hydroponic farming takes up only about one-twelfth as much land as does ordinary agriculture. Shortage of crop-land for growing food is one of the common arguments why population growth should slacken now and must eventually cease. But the mention of hydroponic farming usually evokes a long series of what-if objections. What if there will be a shortage of water? Of chemicals? Of sunlight? Of glass to build greenhouses? And so on and so on. It is impossible to rule out every imaginative scenario without detailed analysis. And of course there is always the logically unrebuttable objection: This cannot go on *forever;* we would even totally run out of room on earth for hydroponic farming. (Of course there is plenty of room *in space* for spaceships carrying hydroponic farms, a possibility for which the technology is already available without even waiting for further developments.) Each of these objections is offered as argument against change and growth, and in favor of proceeding as if hydroponic farming is not a real option. But to put weight on any of these objections rather clearly is poor thinking.

Two other aspects of a market-directed economy that often are not understood, and whose lack of understanding leads to the call for a directed society, and worry about resources in a market society: (*a*) the capacity of markets to deal with the future and (*b*) the capacity of correctly structured markets to deal with externalities. There is no space to say more about these matters here, however.

*   *   *

For lack of space I will not speculate here why we now hear more false bad news about resources and population growth than in some other decades. These scares seem to wax and wane. Other periods have heard *opposite* false ideas that fueled overoptimism about resources and popula-tion growth. It is as if there are two sets of incomplete ideas on the shelf, both of which are capable of bemusing people because of the elements of truth each contains. Which set of ideas will be taken off the shelf and made the marching order of the day depends upon a variety of other conditions. Once a set of ideas is taken off the shelf, however, it has the self-reinforcing power to retain its hold on people's minds for some time, probably until objective conditions falsify the exaggerated or wrongheaded predictions implied by that set of ideas, at which point it yields its place for a while to its opposite number.

Notes

1. This section is heavily influenced by Hayek's works. There also is a fair amount of common ground here with the recent literature on why people are attracted to socialism (e.g., Kristol, 1978; Beckmann, 1978), because resources and environment are part of the "economic problem" that socialism purports to "solve."
2. Consider this remark by a Chicago columnist about summer work cleaning up garbage from Lake Michigan beaches:

> I remember the mornings when the beach was particularly filthy—the fifth of July was always the worst—and halfway through the job, looking back and seeing only the bare golden sand where before there had been a half-ton of garbage.
>
> I learned that summer the palpable satisfaction of doing a job well, even if that job is picking up garbage. (Roger Simon, 1982, p. 7)

Part 8
PUBLICATION, FUNDING, AND THE POPULATION ESTABLISHMENT

Introduction

Like other communities of interest, the media and the individuals and groups that make up the environmental and population "establishment" do not delightedly rush to greet and embrace points of view that call their own into question. The essays in this section chronicle some of their responses. Selection 53 tells the story of the relationship of the newspapers and television to manufacturing, sustaining, and then not correcting the farm-land urbanization scam discussed in Selections 9, 10, and 11. Selection 54 describes the events surrounding the publication of an article of mine in *Science* in 1980 (Selection 2) that was an important opening for my work on this topic. Selection 55 reviews a 1986 report by the National Academy of Sciences that almost completely reversed its previous 1971 position on population—in the direction of the views expressed in this volume—but that left quite a different public impression through the press reports. Selection 56 describes some of the funding patterns and defensive activities of the population establishment.

53

Sometimes the Truth Will Out . . . but Even Then Barely

Let us examine the connection of the press and television to the vanishing farmlands scare, as an example of media treatment of the entire body of scares about resources, environment, and population. This issue has the advantage that it has been described at length in an independent magazine by an independent writer, so you have more to rely upon than my account.

For two decades now, newspaper and television stories have gotten at least one issue wrong almost every time out.

It is easy to document that the stories about natural resources, food, the environment, and population growth have pointed in the wrong direction—toward things getting worse rather than getting better. But the *reasons* for the inverted stories are harder to nail down. My candidate for the most important reason: Abysmal ignorance of the central concept of economics—the unbeatable efficiency of the "hidden hand" working through unplanned free markets.

Even when the good news is acknowledged, it is given a bad-news twist. Examples: "Low Energy Prices Viewed as Threat to Conservation" (*Washington Post,* March 27, 1988, p. A14), and "Good Crops a Bad Sign" (*Washington Post,* August 14, 1985, p. A2).

The Vanishing Farmlands Scam

Let's now consider in depth a case where the failure of the press and television is undeniable and inexcusable. Even the original purveyors of the false facts have 'fessed up and now agree that the widely reported scare was without foundation.

These were some typical headlines: "The Peril of Vanishing Farmlands" *(The New York Times)*, "Farmland Losses Could End U.S. Food Exports" *(Chicago Tribune)*, "Vanishing Farmlands: Selling Out the Soil" *(Saturday Review)*, and "As World Needs Food, U.S. Keeps Losing Soil to Land Developers" *(The Wall Street Journal)*.

The "crisis"? The urbanization-of-farmland rate supposedly had jumped by a multiple of three from the 1960s to the 1970s, from less than one million acres per year to three million acres per year. This assertion was wholly untrue, as we shall see.

Nor is there reason to regret "paving over." Hard though it is to believe, all of the following are true at once: Knowledge-based increase in food productivity provides us ever more food per person on less and less cropland. The price of unprocessed food continues to fall, as it has throughout human history. Farmland prices have been falling rather than rising since the 1970s. Meanwhile, the quantity of trees and the recreational area increase, and people abroad eat better than ever. Moreover, this logic-defying process by which all good things increase at once can go on without limit, so far as we can tell. For the details, I recommend to you *The Ultimate Resource* or Selections 2, 9, and 11.

The entire "crisis" was hokum. This was not a regrettable but understandable exaggeration of a real problem, but a nonproblem manufactured by the Department of Agriculture and some members of Congress out of whole cloth under the guise of concern about food production for the starving world. The crisis was created for the benefit of (*a*) the environmentalists, and (*b*) people who own homes that abut on areas that might be developed into housing developments, and whose vistas and ambience might thereby be affected. The connection between the farmland scare and prevention of housing construction has been documented for California by Bernard Frieden in *The Public Interest* (Spring 1979).

This scam was not only refuted at the time by almost all of the data, but it has since been acknowledged to have been wholly wrong by the USDA agency that manufactured the "crisis," the National Agricultural Lands Study (NALS). The story has an authentic public-servant hero, too, which should have appealed to any red-blooded journalist with even an anesthetized nose for a dramatic story. But for much more than a year no one was willing to write about the story even when it was documented and called to their attention.

When newspaper and television stories about "vanishing farmlands" first began to appear around 1979, I was living in Champaign-Urbana, Illinois, the heart of the Illinois farm belt. The front-page of the *News-*

Gazette carried the same 1970s scare stories about the world's food supply that deliciously agitated the intellectual trendsetters in Washington and New York. The farm page, however, printed exactly the opposite news—agricultural prices were falling and production was increasing all over the world. The Champaign-Urbana paper, and other papers in agricultural states, got the facts straight (at least on the farm page!) because those facts were directly relevant to the farmers in the area, who could see the trends when they went to market. Farmers were worrying about too much rather than too little food production when they made their planting decisions each year.

The issue caught my attention because my research had shown that population growth is a benefit in the long run rather than a barrier to world development. The apparently impending shortage of farmland was thrown at me as a counterargument, along with the related assertions that the world was in danger of running out of copper, oil, water, and you-name-it.

Even without research, there were good reasons to believe that the USDA-NALS vanishing-farmland assertions were wrong. First, huge changes usually do not occur rapidly in major sectors of our economy or in the economic side of society, and therefore the report of any sharp change is immediately suspect. Second, each and every one of the previous doomsday scares in connection with population growth had turned out to be a nonscare. Third, local Champaign-Urbana farmland-preservation enthusiasts—the environmental movement was particularly strong in the area because of the presence of university faculty and students, especially the biologists and political scientists—were campaigning to prevent pieces of the county's farmland from being converted to a shopping mall, an industrial complex, and even second farmhouses for farm families' grown children. The numbers that these persons were publicizing would have been laughable if they were not being used toward a serious purpose and in a politically effective manner. My research began with these numbers. (See Selection 10.) The people publicizing the local numbers—including the editorial writers of the local newspaper—had never bothered to check their data even though the data defied belief. One can only assume that the numbers were used so uncritically simply because they fitted preconceptions and values.

Then several scholars—including William Fischel of Dartmouth, Clifford Luttrell of the St. Louis Federal Reserve Bank, then-President Emery Castle of Resources for the Future, and John Fraser Hart of the University of Minnesota—began to dig into the U.S. data. We all found that the three-million-acres-a-year rate was most implausible in light of various sets of data from other sources, and given the nature of the surveys from which the NALS estimate was drawn.

Shortly, we began to get a great deal of help from H. Thomas Frey, a geographer who had been the keeper of the urbanization and other land-use data for the Economic Research Service of the USDA for many years. Tom could find no support for the scary new numbers in the standard set of sources from which he yearly distilled his estimates, and he had no reason to believe that the rate had increased from the rather constant rates over several previous decades. So he kept us alerted to useful pieces of information as they appeared.

This was the situation: Everyone agreed that in 1967 the total urban and built-up area in the United States (excluding highways, railroads, and airports) was on 31 to 35 million acres. It was also agreed that the rate of urbanization was slower in the 1960s than in the 1950s. Yet NALS said that over the ten years from 1967 to 1977, there was a 29 million acre increase in urban and built-up land.

That is, over the course of more than two centuries, in the process of reaching a population of about 200 million people, the United States built towns on 31 to 35 million acres. NALS asserted that suddenly in the course of another ten years, and with a population increase of only 18 million people, the urban and built-up areas increased by 29 million acres (almost none of it due to transportation)—a near-doubling.

To put it differently, the long-run trend in the decades up to 1970 was about one million acres of total land urbanized per year, and constant or slowing down. The Soil Conservation Service in conjunction with NALS asserted that the rate then jumped to between two and three million acres yearly from 1967 to 1975 or 1977 (depending on which version you read).

It is hard to understand how thoughtful journalists, let alone USDA researchers, could believe the NALS scenario. But believe it they did—or at least they promulgated the scenario widely. This credulity belies the picture of journalists as hardboiled skeptics.

Tom Frey also began to have a personal problem. He began this episode as an amiable organization man who went through channels, did everything by the book, and was accommodating whenever he could be. But the widely publicized estimate did not square with the facts as he knew them, and he so informed his superiors. They systematically bypassed and ignored his assessment at each level all the way to the Secretary of Agriculture, Bob Bergland.

As time passed, Frey became stronger and more outspoken even as the heat upon him intensified, and even though no one else in the USDA would speak up for his position. The pressure was always indirect, but its presence was sufficiently unmistakable that Frey worried about his future. He was forced into confrontation with Michael Brewer, research director of NALS. And his manuscripts were altered to the extent that he refused to put his name on them.

Still, the more pressure his superiors put on him, the more strongly Frey insisted that his estimates were correct. And he distributed his estimates to those he felt would make use of them. He hardened into an authentic hero. He was not a whistle-blower in the conventional sense because he never "went public" himself. But he did his job effectively and with courage, the sort of government servant that the public deserves but whose existence we sometimes doubt.

There were two bases given for the publicized three million-acre number; NALS shifted from one to the other when either was criticized: (1) A small-sample resurvey of part of the 1967 sample "inventory" of farms, done by the Soil Conservation Service. (A similar inventory had previously been done in 1958.) (2) The 1977 sample inventory. Seymour Sudman, an expert in research design, joined me in a technical analysis showing that there were so many flaws in both the 1975 resurvey and the 1977 survey that both should be considered totally unreliable. The flaws included an incredible boo-boo that put the right numbers in the wrong columns for big chunks of Florida.

(Though I talk about "bases" for the NALS estimate, this may be giving it too much dignity. The three-million-acre figure was presented in a booklet entitled "Where Have the Farmlands Gone"—of which 500,000 copies were sent out—*weeks before the NALS "study" even opened its doors* in the fall of 1979. Everything else that NALS did may be seen as an effort to defend its initial position. This would seem to have been a choice bit of business for the press to have exposed—but it never happened.)

Various government agencies were mobilized to rebut our criticisms. The *Journal of Soil and Water Conservation* wrote that

> [T]he new information [that Illinois farmland was increasing rather than decreasing] came out of a feud between the Illinois Department of Agriculture [then headed by John Block who became Secretary of Agriculture under Ronald Reagan] and Julian Simon. . . .
>
> Simon's assertions did not sit so well with Illinois agriculture officials. They decided to contact the Bureau of Census in Washington because they could not believe that land in farms had increased. The Bureau responded that the 1969 and 1974 censuses had underenumerated land in farms.

That is, the Census Bureau now said that the earlier acreages for Illinois were really higher than the published figures showed, and hence there could have been an actual decline even though the record showed an increase. The "[r]evised figures showed that between 1974 and 1978 Illinois' land in farms had declined by 425,000 acres. The earlier figures had shown a 639,000 acre increase."

NALS then got the Census bureau to produce a similar adjustment for the United States as a whole. "The result: The latest data show a national decline of 88 million acres in land in farms between 1969 and 1978—an annual rate of 9.8 million acres. . . .", wrote The *Journal of Soil and Water Conservation*.

Analysis of the adjustment showed it to be as full of holes as Swiss cheese. And eventually the Census of Agriculture revealed detailed data on the appropriate adjustment showing that land in Illinois farms and in cropland had, as we said, indeed increased from 1974 to 1978.

Ironically, John Block ran into trouble because of his belief that farmland was becoming more scarce. "Financing arrangements used by Agriculture Secretary John R. Block to prop up his multimillion-dollar farming empire, apparently shaken by falling land values . . . are raising questions on Capital Hill." His banker explained: "We thought we were going to have to feed the world." (*Washington Post,* June 3, 1984, p. A3).

Nowadays, Block is president of the National Wholesale Grocers' Association, which has a stake in cheaper food production. And on July 16, 1988, Block wrote in the *Washington Post* criticizing Lester Brown, who was and is one of the great enthusiasts of the NALS point of view: "In 1980, respected agricultural experts were predicting an impending food shortage and possible mass starvation . . . but the suggestion that the world [now] stands on the ragged edge of food shortages is preposterous. . . . I don't buy the suggestion that the world is running out of productive land." Yeah man.

Somewhere along the line the NALS principals fell out. In the press, NALS research director Michael Brewer accused NALS head man Robert Gray of inflating the key estimate for political purposes. By the time NALS closed down, Gray and Brewer were no longer speaking to each other because of this and related disagreements.

After several articles by us academics in technical journals and in *The Public Interest* and *The American Spectator,* the urbanization-of-farmland scare seemed to die down a bit, but not before the private American Farmland Trust was organized in 1980 from former employees of NALS. Annually it spends a couple of million dollars a year to "protect" the United States from the danger of vanishing farmland.

Following upon NALS publicity, in 1980 Congress provided a tax break to owners who will attach a "conservation easement" to their land that will keep the land out of development and in agriculture in perpetuity. And to ease the owners even more, some states have programs to recompense the owners the difference between the current market value and the value after the easement. That is, as usual the public purse is being tapped to further the purpose of the special interest group. And in 1981 the Farmland Protection Policy Act was enacted by Congress. Hundreds of state and local laws restricting farmland conversion also were passed. And the American Farmland Trust's 1985 Annual Report brags that in that year "Congress adopted . . . a Conservation Reserve. . . . Conceived and championed by AFT" as part of the 1985 Farm Bill. All this legislation was based on wrong information, and with no reasonable prospect of doing good for the nation, but with much prospect of causing harm to individuals and damage to the nation. So it goes in America.

Now fast forward to 1984. The Soil Conservation Service issued a paper by Linda Lee of Oklahoma State University, on leave with SCS, that completely reversed the earlier scare figures and confirmed the estimates by "our side." And the accompanying press release (April 10, 1984, kindly sent by Tom Frey) made it clear that the former estimates were now being retracted. "[T]he acreage classified as urban and built-up land was 46.6 million acres in 1982, compared to 64.7 million acres reported in 1977." Please read that again. It means that whereas in 1977 the SCS had declared that 64.7 million acres had been "lost" to built-upon land, just five years later SCS admitted that the actual total was 46.6 million acres. That is, the 1977 estimate was fully *fifty per cent too high,* a truly amazing error for something so easy to check on as the urbanized acreage of the United States.

With unusual candor, the USDA press release added, "The 1982 data, which correlate closely with data from the 1980 U.S. Census of Population, [the census was not available at the time of the argument described above, but later fully corroborated Frey's estimates based on prior data] are considered accurate because of the availability of better maps, more time for data collection, many more sample points, and better quality control." The press release continued: "The 1977 estimate thus appears to have been markedly overstated." You might say so.

It is good that the USDA chose to state the situation forthrightly even though it meant acknowledging a mind-boggling amount of egg on its face. But how could the USDA earlier on have been that ingenuous—or that disingenuous? And how could it hold onto those estimates for several years in the face of persuasive criticism from several quarters?

It is relevant that the press did nothing to uncover the scam. Even the press-release reversal and "confession" did not evoke coverage even though the original scare story was a front-page headliner for the *Chicago Tribune* and a cover story for news magazines.

After waiting some months for the coverage that never appeared, I decided to contact some newspapers, thinking they would find it an interesting story because of the self-admitted government scam and the authentic "little man" hero who stood up to the "bosses." My across-the-alley neighbor who worked for *The Wall Street Journal* liked the idea, but the writer to whom he passed the material decided after several months to do nothing. I then got in touch with a reporter from *The New York Times* who works on related topics, but he was not interested. Nor the *Washington Post*. Nor the *National Journal*. Nor some others that I have forgotten. In short, nothing.

In late 1985 I got in touch with Gregg Easterbrook of the *Atlantic Monthly*. Editor Bill Whitworth had excerpted three chapters from a 1981 book of mine, and therefore I figured the *Atlantic* might be interested and sympathetic. Both found the story appealing, and Easterbrook's piece "Vanishing Land Reappears" was in the February 1986 edition. It confirms many of the facts mentioned here, and describes the political infighting involving NALS.

Did the farmland crisis then vanish for lack of factual support? Fat chance. The false news continues to reverberate. One item that appeared in my mailbox was a July 1986 newsletter of Population-Environment Balance which says that "The National Agricultural Lands Study projects that at the current rate of conversion, Florida will lose all its prime agricultural land by the year 2000." And a July 14, 1987 AP story in *The New York Times* begins with "City sprawl, highways and other non-agricultural uses are taking American farmland at an annual rate that could involve acreage equal to the entire State of Missouri by the year 2030" (whatever that means). About half of the long article quotes Robert J. Gray of the American Farmland Trust. No other person outside of the Department of Agriculture was quoted. The Fall 1987 issue of the Newsletter of Californians for Population Stabilization says that "The President and the Republican administration admit to the very conservative estimate that 2.1 million acres of agra-land are paved over in the United States on a yearly basis. Experts in this field believe the true figure to be closer to 3 million acres per year." And the 1987 Annual Report of the American Farmland Trust says that "Between 1967 and 1982 alone, urban sprawl accounted for the loss of forty million acres of American farmland . . . farmland conversion shows no signs of slowing." That statement and the program that AFT rests on it would seem to well justify the word "scam."

Would anyone care to bet that this week some U.S. newspaper will not write again that 3 million acres are being paved over?

Free-lance journalist Julian Weiss gathered data for the Media Institute on how the print and electronic media handled the farmland-urbanization story. These were some of his findings:

1. " 'We cultivated a good relationship with papers around the country,' declares Mr. Gray [NALS director]." Indeed they did. The first move was to mail their booklet with the 3-million-acre figure to 1800 newspapers, three to each newspaper. "Some material in the Study's 'package' was 'used verbatim' he says."
2. Of the 80 journalists Weiss interviewed in February-May 1983, 72 (90 percent) still remembered NALS.
3. "63 (86 percent of those who remembered it) felt that NALS influenced their own coverage of farmland conversion."
4. "Even after dissidents from the Lands study [members of the staff who told Gray that the publicized estimates were wrong] offered convincing evidence of the distortions contained in the final report . . . the media . . . with few exceptions [did not report] these charges".

The Soil Erosion Caper

Soil erosion is a related and exactly-parallel story. In the early 1980s there was a huge foofarah about the terrible dangers of farmland being ruined. In a January 11, 1983, speech to the American Farm Bureau Federation the President of the United States said, "I think we are all aware of the need to do something about soil erosion." The headline on a June 4, 1984, *Newsweek* "My Turn" article typified how the issue was presented: "A Step Away from the Dust Bowl." (It may or may not be coincidence that the soil-erosion scare began just about the time that the paving-over scare seemed to peter out in the face of criticism.)

But the aggregate data on the condition of farmland and the rate of erosion do not support the concern about soil erosion. The data suggest that the condition of cropland has been improving rather than worsening. Theodore W. Schultz, the only agricultural economist to win a Nobel Prize, and Leo V. Mayer of the USDA, both wrote very forcefully that the danger warnings were false. Schultz cited not only research but also his own life-time recollections starting as a farm boy in the Dakotas in the 1930s. Even a Nobel laureate's efforts could not slow the public-relations juggernaut that successfully co-opted the news media and won the minds of the American public.

The USDA press release of April 10, 1984, contained a second quiet bombshell: "The average annual rate of soil erosion on cultivated cropland dropped from 5.1 tons per acre to 4.8 tons per acre." That is, erosion was *lessening rather than getting worse,* exactly the opposite of what NALS claimed. But newspapers and television either did not notice or did not credit these criticisms. Even after the USDA admitted that the newer data clearly show that the danger was not as claimed, nothing appeared in print (to my knowledge) to make the public aware of this new nondanger and of how the public was misled. (Ask a few of your acquaintances their impressions about farmland urbanization and cropland erosion.)

The Larger Picture

Environment reporters tend to automatically credit the reports of worsening trends by government agencies and environmentalist organizations in preference to those of us who point to improving trends in resources and environment. When shown the facts, these journalists usually say that even if cries of an environmental danger are somewhat overblown, they contain the germ of truth. I hope that the farmland cases sober them a bit.

Fears about running out of metals, grains, water, and energy cannot be so easily shown to rest on faulty or cooked data because they lack recantations by the sources of the wrong information. But subsequent events have completely falsified the well-publicized 1970s gloomy prophecies of Paul Ehrlich, Lester Brown, Garrett Hardin, and Daniel Yergin—prophecies accepted by the entire Global Tomorrow Coalition of more than fifty environmentalist and population-control organizations with five million members. There is little reason to think that these other issues are different in nature from the farmland-urbanization and soil-erosion issues.

In summary, the press and television have consistently purveyed a wrong-headed vision to the public of resource availability and the environmental condition. In so doing, they have aided and abetted government agencies and "environmentalist" organizations in scaring Americans about such nonproblems as the disappearance and erosion of farmland. Years after the original source retracted the alarming reports, the press and environmental groups continue to spread the false information.

I come not in anger but in pain. Journalists take pride in their objectivity. But in reporting on population growth, natural resources, and the environment, objectivity goes out the window. The price in economic loss, misguided policies, and damage to national morale has yet to be calculated. But the costs may be fearfully high.

What to Do About It?

Lamenting, criticizing, and complaining are best redeemed by suggestions for improvement. But I am not loaded with ideas for curing the problem at hand. Certainly I do not want to legally fetter the press in any way; I'm one of those who favors free speech with no "buts" at all.

Nor will I bother recommending better education for journalists, though of course I favor the best education all of us can get for what we do. It is a pipe dream to hope that journalism students will learn the crucial Mandeville-Hume-Smith-Menger-Hayek-Friedman idea of a spontaneously evolving efficient free market, because of the subtlety of the idea as well as because of the ideological opposition to the "invisible hand" from college teachers of political science who are influenced by Marx.

Watchdog organizations and publications are certainly worthwhile. But the mainstream press must ultimately publish the reports of its own failings or the watchdogs have no teeth.

Journalistic competition can help in the political sphere, where papers with one ideological ax to grind can hold the opposition's feet to the fire. But in the case at hand, there is no journalistic competition. All the papers and networks share the common desire for larger audiences that follow upon doomsday scares.

The ombudsman certainly is a valuable institution. But ombudsmen tend to share the common beliefs of their colleagues, as happened in the single case I tested. A *Washington Post* science reporter wrote a story that parroted the environmental movement's scary assertion that a considerable portion of the world's species are rapidly on the way to extinction. I had never before called a reporter to complain of a story, feeling that to do so was vaguely off bounds, but this time I decided to try. I told the reporter that his story was not supported by the scientific literature, which shows at most one proven case of extinction per year. The writer asked for my documentation, and I sent him a recent article in *The New Scientist,* a very reputable journal. Nothing happened. After several further inquiries, I brought the matter to the ombudsman. Several exchanges moved him not at all. His reason was that my "views" were already "well-known to the paper's readers."

As a journalist's mind turns to disclosure and a lawyer's mind turns to laws and sanctions, the economist's mind turns to prices and costs as regulators. But the costs imposed for libel are irrelevant here. And how many papers or stations will fire a person for inaccuracy that produced "a hell of a story?" What other market incentives might keep journalists in line in a case like the one at hand?

Journalists have said that "we" should create an organization that will battle to have "our" views heard. An advocacy view may indeed be necessary for legitimacy and media attention. But, it is not easy to create such an organization.

Once I asked Simon Kuznets—a Nobel prizewinner and the greatest economic-historical statistician of all time—if he had considered turning to the public with the views that he and I shared on population growth's effects. He replied, "If I did that I could not get my work done." Trying to create an advocacy organization is tough, made tougher in this case by a vicious circle. I have tried to build the Committee on Population and

Economy, and some well-known and impressive people are willing to lend their names in support. But activities require money for a staff. And every single request for foundation funding has been turned down—often on the grounds that the cause is obviously ridiculous, as proven by the fact that one reads and hears only the contrary in the papers and television!

Ladies and gentlemen, *you* tell *me* the best partial answers. You have been thinking about your industry and occupation for many aggregate lifetimes now, and you have imagined and discovered what can be figured out. What's the answer?

54

Adventures Getting Truth Published in the United States

The publication of Selection 2 in Science *was a turning point in my attempts to gain an audience for my ideas about population economics. It was a first domino whose fall caused many others also to fall. I am grateful to fate that the event did occur. But this does not cause me to feel benign toward the editor who put me through a small hell in the process. [Eventually he disavowed the piece, and said he wished he had not published it (Bethell, 1986, p. 39).]*

This selection is about the events during that publication process. The reader may be suitably impressed by the stature of Philip Abelson, as indicated by the AAAS-Philip Hauge Abelson Prize, which was created in 1985 "To Be Awarded to a Public Servant or Scientist" annually. That award was announced on the same page of Science *with an ad for Abelson's book* Enough of Pessimism *(an astonishing title in light of Abelson's editorials on resources, population, and the environment). The ad says that "Readers of* Enough of Pessimism *can share with Philip Abelson his remarkable affinity with science and his astute observations, which are consistently ahead of their time."*

Despite the "ideological" difficulties I have had (and still have) getting my technical work published (certainly there are many other elements also involved, too), I am ever aware of, and grateful for, not living in a country such as the Soviet Union where the means of publication are controlled centrally and where it is dangerous for individual editors to publish dissident work. There are enough book publishers and enough journals in the United States so that even the most unconventional work can eventually find some kind of outlet, though the process may be arduous and the audience small or isolated from the mainstream. Lucky we are that we do not have to resort to typewriter-and-carbon-paper samizdat to circulate unconventional research results and theories. Lucky we are.

   I am also grateful to those editors—it gives me pleasure to mention as shining examples book editors Sanford Thatcher at Princeton University Press, Rene Olivieri at Basil Blackwell, and Irving Louis Horowitz at Transactions Press, and there have been a fair number of journal editors, too—who have considered it their proper function to brave the prevailing winds and publish that which is not conventional, assuming it meets their standards of quality. And luckily our system allows such exceptional editors to exist and even prosper rather than purging them for their temerity.

Complaints about editorial decisions and publication policies are rife in academia. With experience one learns that many horror stories are just sour-grapes excuses. It is important, then, for you to know that the story I tell here ends with success; the article in question was published, and resulted in wide republication and other good things. It is this non-sour-grapes aspect that I hope will induce you to take seriously this ugly story; I would not tell it otherwise. And for each such case such as mine that by a miracle gets past the gate, there must be many unconventional but worthy writings still outside the fence literally crying to be printed and read; this is the problem that needs our attention and ingenuity.

   The story ends with the editor of the world's most important scientific journal, *Science,* rigging the system so as to keep me from defending myself and my ideas, in contravention of established rules of fair play in scholarly journals. The story begins in 1969–1970 when the first Earth Day's organizers broke the rules we had agreed upon, and thereby set me up for public denunciation of my dissenting views. (For some background on how I arrived at my current point of view, see the Introduction to this book.)

   Because of a talk I gave on campus at the University of Illinois saying that science alone does not show that population growth is a bad thing, I became the campus token opposition invited to meetings so people could hear the "other side." Soon questions people raised forced me to expand my views to cover the relationship of population growth to natural resource scarcity and to the state of the environment.

   Public interest in these topics peaked in 1970. To cap the first Earth Day a massive evening meeting was planned for the university auditorium (seating almost two thousand people) with the country's foremost family planning figure, Alan Guttmacher, as the main speaker. I was invited to be one of three panelists to comment on Guttmacher.

When I asked who else was to be on the panel, and how long each panelist would speak, I was told that one of the two others would be Paul Silverman, a biologist (and later a state university president) who was then very active in population-environment affairs on campus, in a style reminiscent of Paul Ehrlich. I declined the invitation because I had previously had an unpleasant experience speaking in a class of Silverman's, after having been invited by a student in that class. The organizers then asked if there were any conditions that would make me feel comfortable. I replied that I would be willing to participate if *(a)* all participants would agree to comment only upon Guttmacher and not upon each other, *(b)* I could speak after rather than before Silverman, and *(c)* the ten-minute time limit would be rigidly enforced. The organizers agreed.

After Guttmacher spoke and was warmly applauded by the packed auditorium, the chairman called on me—before Silverman. I had no choice, so I got up and said what was then and now my standard piece, which also was responsive to Guttmacher: There is no evidence of general deterioration in environmental conditions in the United States; resource scarcity is not increasing, as measured by long-run cost trends; no empirical study shows population growth to have a negative effect on economic growth; and without auxiliary value judgments science can render no judgments about whether there is or is not "overpopulation." Audience applause was polite but sparse.

Silverman then spoke, and there ensued the very situation I had sought to avoid. Silverman devoted his remarks almost entirely to me and my previous campus talk, and he made some rather unpleasant charges (here transcribed from a tape made by the campus radio station): He repeated several times that what I said "lacks scholarship." Then by quoting me out of context he attributed to me the view that "that there is no difference between murder, abortion, contraception, and abstinence from sex." And he went on: "Now, although this doctrine may have been inspired by Professor Simon's contact with the Bible, it is a doctrine that goes far beyond the Old or New Testaments. In fact it goes beyond any of the doctrines contained in Eastern or Western religions as I have come to know them. Indeed, a new religious doctrine has been enunciated in which murder and abstinence from sex are not distinguishable." Finally noting that I had previously written a book on *How To Start and Operate a Mail Order Business* (he hadn't mention three technical books on other subjects I had written until then) he continued:

I find it hard to relate to this new religious doctrine to the hard-nosed manager of advertising campaigns, as Professor Simon describes himself, unless, of course, he's convinced that the economics of a stable society threaten the mail-order business. Whatever the explanation, let us not be deflected by false prophets from the serious task which we must sustain for the rest of our lives. We have to educate, to research, and to promote concern about our environment and the size of our population. . . . We can realize a new quality of life, free from avarice which characterizes our current society. Thank you.

After speaking 21 minutes, Silverman received loud applause.

I then asked for the floor and the chairperson recognized me. During Silverman's talk I had been making notes frantically, but I realized that I could not rebut him effectively. I am not a poised spontaneous speaker, and in argument I tend to get rattled and fail to get my points across. I therefore decided to say only this: Because I had had previous experiences with Silverman's attacks on me, I had been willing to speak only if there was an agreement that Silverman would speak before me and would address himself only to Guttmacher, and not comment upon my views, and that he would speak only ten minutes. But the organizers and Silverman had broken our agreement. I then sat down.

For the first and last time in my life, an audience responded to me with strong, continued applause, much louder than the applause for Silverman. There seemed no way to interpret this other than as support for fair play in public discussion, even when emotions run high. Afterwards people told me that they didn't agree with a word I said but thought Silverman's remarks a shame. I was astonished then, and I am still surprised—though very grateful and proud that my fellow Americans could behave that way.

That year I expanded my talk, and sent it off to *Science*. The article was mostly analytical and anecdotal rather than statistical because of lack of data at that time. For example, I handled pollution with accounts of the improvements in London's air and the Thames' water, rather than the now-available EPA time-series data on air and water quality in the United States. And I included a section on the values implicit in the rhetoric of those who called for population control (a section that was also in the earliest draft of my 1980 *Science* article (Selection 2) but which was edited out, as will be discussed later).

The 1970 article received generally positive referees' reports; one referee said that such views needed to be heard. (Regrettably, my search has so far failed to yield up the old files with the original language.) But the piece was rejected because I referred to Ehrlich et al. as "coercionists"— a label which Ehrlich's and others' language substantiates.

The story now picks up after a hiatus of about seven years. I had by then finished the draft of a book intended for a nontechnical audience, based on my professional articles and my 1977 technical book on population growth, together with associated broader writing on resources and the environment, the latter an outgrowth of the 1970 events. I had never been able to get any of my 1970 article or writings following on it published except for a short piece in a reader by Edward Pohlmann, who had seen a privately circulated draft.

At the beginning of May, 1977, I sent Philip Abelson, editor of *Science,* a six-page draft beginning with the Sahel-Waldheim-*Newsweek* anecdote that begins my June 27, 1980, article (Selection 2) together with brief statistical rebuttals to conventional wisdom about resources, environment, population density, and values. The cover letter suggested that I would be happy to write a longer article if asked. In middle or late May, 1977, Abelson called and expressed interest. I then wrote a draft, and sent it off July 27.

The article received excellent referees' reports, and on October 11, 1978, I received a letter from Abelson that other contributors to *Science* told me is tantamount to acceptance. On November 10 I sent off a revision in response to the referees' comments. But publication was not until nineteen months later, during which time the manuscript was in my hands less than a month (from May 30 to June 20, 1979). The rest of that time the manuscript apparently was on the desk of Sylvia Eberhart, an associate editor.

About two months after receiving the postcard acknowledging receipt of the revision on November 17, I queried *Science* about the article's status, but received no response. A few weeks later I queried again, but received no response. On April 9, 1979, Eberhart called and opened the conversation with: "To start with, we want to publish the article." But I did not receive the manuscript until May 30, 1979. Eberhart sent a heavily edited typescript, cutting out many sections I believed both sound and important, including some that had been (word for word) in the original prospectus I had sent Abelson. On June 20, 1979, I returned the manuscript, approving much of her copy editing but indicating I wanted to keep many of the sections she had cut. I then heard nothing until a phone call from Eberhart on September 4, 1979, which ran almost an hour, of which a close transcription was made. She challenged the scientific, philosophical, and moral soundness of what I had written, and she accused me of lying to her about the manuscript having originally been written in response to Abelson's suggestion. She also encouraged me to withdraw the manuscript.

In short, on her own initiative, Eberhart deleted important sections of the article on the grounds that her knowledge of the subject matter was better than mine. When I would not go along with her cuts without asking for Abelson's own judgment, she attempted to block publication of the article, and did so for a long time starting in November, 1978.

On September 10 Abelson wrote me a letter which was difficult to interpret and which made publication uncertain again. For the first time in my experiences with perhaps a hundred articles and nine books, I decided to call an editor on the phone. My first conversation with Abelson occurred when I called him on September 17. I found it most difficult to ascertain exactly where I and the manuscript stood. Finally we agreed that I would send him clean copies of Eberhart's version and of the version I wanted. Then he would choose one and would send it to the printers. I sent off the drafts October 1.

I received no acknowledgment of receipt, queried November 2, received no answer, and called Abelson November 15. At first he seemed not to remember my name. Then afterwards he said with a laugh that "[we] want to censor the paper a bit." The call ended with his saying that the call would "initiate action" to get the paper into print. (Transcriptions of the two conversations with Abelson were made.) The next day I wrote him summarizing our conversation, but received no response. On December 11 I sent a handwritten note to Abelson, but still no response. I then asked a University of Illinois colleague on the *Science* editorial board to make an inquiry for me, which he did in the course of a routine conversation. About the piece Abelson said to him, "I guess we've got to crap or get off the pot."

On December 24, 1979, I received a formal letter confirming that the piece would be published, which also said that some figures would have to be deleted to save space. I then replied with some comments about which figures to delete. I received no response. On March 10 I called Eberhart, and was told that she had not touched the manuscript since the formal acceptance in December. But she said that it would go to the printer "in a matter of weeks." On April 2 I called Eberhart again, and was told the piece had not gone to the printer. She went over some of the history of the articles (inaccurately), and said I could still withdraw the article. She said she was no longer trying to stop the article's being printed, though she had done so earlier. As to the delay, she said she "had not been doing that consciously, but perhaps subconsciously." Apparently the article finally went to the printer sometime that month. On May 23 Eberhart called my home and spoke to my wife, who is thoroughly experienced in these matters because she served as head editor of her professional association's "flagship" journal, *American Sociological Review*. Ostensibly the call was about minor changes. But she also said that "we have never had a manuscript that has taken so long to process." And she added that "Dr. Simon can still withdraw his manuscript if he doesn't accept the version as it now stands—without the figures." The conversation lasted twenty minutes. The article appeared June 27, 1980.

At the last minute Eberhart deleted three of my best figures on grounds of space shortage, and then the article appeared with enough white space on the last page to encompass all three diagrams.

The article, together with its reprinting in the *Washington Post* and excerpting elsewhere, aroused much interest. And *Science* received more letters than it had received in recent years about any article, perhaps ever, according to Gilbert. And sharply critical letters were signed by persons as eminent in the scientific establishment as Nobel-winner Norman Borlaug and National Academy of Sciences president Philip Handler.

The most clearly unethical part is still to come, however. On October 6 I received the galley proofs of the set of letters on the article, constituting about 4200 words. The cover letter asked for a 1000 word reply within two weeks. Over the phone, Christine Gilbert, the letters editor, told me that the two-week deadline was not firm, but to reply as soon as possible. And when I said that it would be hard to write a suitable reply in that brief a space, she suggested I write down what I wanted to say, and then to try to reduce it to general statements. At my request, Gilbert also kindly sent me the letters that *Science* was not using. That set contained a good many positive letters, whereas the letters to be printed were all negative.

When I began to write, two things became clear: (1) More than 1000 words were required for any kind of comprehensive reply, and (2) the only two questions of fact about my data that the letters offered were both absolutely wrong, an assertion about electricity prices by Holdren et al., and one about air quality by Chang (see Selection 3). And I needed almost 1000 words plus some graphs to deal with those two factual matters. Of course those errors and my refutation of them would enhance my credibility and strengthen my original case by making the point again that those who see negative trends in resources and environment often purvey incorrect bad news.

I sent off a rough 3500 word reply, with several figures, on October 26, in hopes of winding up with space for 2000–2500 words. I then received a call from Gilbert saying that I must cut to 1000 words. I said that if I absolutely had to do that, I'd take the first 1000 words, which contained a few general remarks followed by the rebuttal of Holdren et al. and Chang, plus a sentence saying that the rest of my reply would be available upon request. But I said that I wanted to talk to Abelson about the space decision. She said that he had not yet seen the material, and "He said he wants me to handle it!" I did not want to put her in a squeeze, so I insisted on talking to him. She said that she would show him the material and get in touch with me.

The next day or so Gilbert called me and said that after Abelson had looked briefly at the material, he decided to "take it home to study it" and "he wants to make some phone calls." The next day she said that it would be the following week before they could reach a decision about what to do, because Abelson "saw that Holdren et al. and Chang were clearly wrong, and doesn't see the point of running wrong material in *Science.*" I told her that all this was creating considerable anxiety in me, and she told me not to worry. We agreed to talk the following Wednesday.

The following Wednesday Gilbert told me Abelson's decision, and said she could only pass it on to me without comment: (1) Take out the Chang letter, which was wrong. (2) Take out the abusive letter by Grant that I had used as a vehicle to discuss the rhetoric of the letters. (3) Take out a sentence in the letter of Matthews that I had written was possibly libelous, and which *Science*'s lawyers agreed was libelous. (4) They would send me a 1500 word edited reply on a take-it-or-leave-it basis; I would not be permitted to choose which 1000 or 1500 words would be in my reply. That is, if I didn't accept it, they would print the letters without reply by me. (5) They would print a disclaimer by me.

I then said that I wanted to speak to Abelson. He simply repeated to me what Gilbert had said. He said that I had "irritated many people." He said that Chang's letter was being pulled out because it is simply a "straw man" (an unusual use of the term, given that it was his staff that had chosen the letter). When I objected that this was not fair, because it violated the usual rules of scholarly interchange and hampered me from making my case, he said that I had been given a "special opportunity" when they printed my original article.

Luckily, the story does not end there. I had talked to my friend Stanley Friedman, an entomologist who believes strongly in free scientific dialogue and also believes that scientists just "can't" act any other way. (He only laughs when I ask him what he means by "can't.") Friedman told the story to his colleague Judith Willis, who shares Stanley's feelings about scientific communication. And Willis had been on the Council of the AAAS until that year.

Willis volunteered to phone Frederick Mosteller, president of AAAS, in order to introduce me to him as a reasonable person. But when she called, Mosteller told her that he has a "policy" not to interfere with the running of *Science* in any way; aggrieved authors are a major hassle for each AAAS president. He did not discourage her, however, from calling William Carey, Executive Officer and Publisher of the AAAS. Willis phoned Carey but he was out; she left a message saying she had called after speaking to Mosteller, and wanted to talk about an article by me.

Willis then received a phone call from Abelson. First there was some personal discussion about me. Among other things Abelson said that I was "drooling" to be able to answer Chang, the letter on pollution that he was taking out. (I acknowledge being a bit eager to be able to rebut Chang.

Who wouldn't? And why not?) Willis suggested that I be allowed to say what I wanted in my own way. Abelson said he would think about it. He then did so, called her back, and informed her (as Gilbert then informed me) that I could have 1500 words to say what I wanted, though the material would have to be in Washington within seven days (giving me a weekend to write it, have it typed, etc.). The Chang and Adams letters would stay out, however. And that's the way it ended.

The preceding material is factual. Here follow some observations and views of mine about this saga:

1. I consider it a miracle that the piece ever came out in *Science*. I still pinch myself—and probably will do so forever—to check that I'm not dreaming such a stroke of luck. Clearly it had been on a knife edge for many months, and Eberhart had shown herself capable of preventing publication for a long time, as well as having the desire to keep it out entirely. No other medium of scientific communication has anywhere near the circulation and legitimating power of *Science*. And few, if any, run articles of this general type. On such thin chances hang big parts of people's careers and lives, and—much more important—whether minority views of an important public issue gets a hearing. That's scary.

2. Why did Abelson first encourage the piece, then dither, and finally publish it? I don't know. Perhaps he was attracted at first to printing a controversial piece that would attack and show up as untrue some ideas that he thought needed attacking. Perhaps later on the entire matter promised to turn out to be more hassle than it was worth. I don't know.

3. As the reader might imagine, the long uncertainty about the final outcome with this article—itself part of a decade-long struggle to tell the story it tells—was excruciating. The distress was especially heightened by my belief that so much of what is being told the public on these important topics is pure hokum, and that national policies are affected thereby. And I was outraged because the article was held up for a very long time— longer than any in memory of a *Science* staffer I talked to—because of the personal prejudices of an associate editor mixed to some unknown degree with the ambivalence of the editor. (*Science*, it should be noted, is not a private publication subject only to the whims of its owner, but the official organ of a quasi-public nonprofit organization, the American Association for the Advancement of Science.)

4. About the pulling out of letters often referred to, and the customary ethics of scientific exchange: Customarily, one first writes an article, critics are then given an opportunity to take their strongest shot at it, and the author is then allowed to defend his or her position as best he or she can. If the editor interferes to the advantage of one side or the other, it shows partiality. And not to allow the author to choose to say what he or

she wishes in reply, but to offer a choice of having edited words put in your mouth or not replying at all, is a mockery of fair play and the search for scientific truth.

5. Abelson showed good sense in this decision not to "stonewall" about my reply, I believe, and I am delighted that it went that way. But this last episode is more a tribute to a few people's faith and hard work than a sign that the story will always have such a benign ending.

6. The question, then, is what kind of mechanism might increase the chance that the gatekeepers can't shut the gate on unconventional research? In the United States the problem is not one of conspiracy or of centralized authority. Rather, it is that in each academic discipline there are only one or a very few journals that will give wide distribution to, and confer legitimacy upon, a writer's views; if unconventional views are published elsewhere, the majority who hold the conventional view can simply overlook or ignore the unconventional view, whether it deserves to be ignored or not. And by definition most potential referees and editors hold the conventional view. Therefore the odds necessarily are against the unconventional view even if it does not run into sheer prejudice (as views such as mine about population and environment and resources do too often). Prejudice is not necessary for a view not to be heard; the belief that, because the view runs counter to that learned in graduate school it must be kooky, is enough to have it adjudged to be without merit.

One possible solution is a partial shift from a representative-and-supposedly-neutral system of refereeing to an advocate system. Ironically—but probably not accidentally—*Science* has such a system; it asks authors to supply the names of potential referees. It is alone among professional journals in my experience in this (though some university presses use such a system, too). It may well be the case that authors of unconventional but worthy views can find at least *some* respected persons who will agree with them and are willing to "sponsor" them. If so, there is some presumption that the views should be heard more widely. If my piece had been sent out to "representative" writers in the field, it would have been a miracle squared if it had made it through the refereeing process. (Say 2 percent of potential referees would like the paper very much. Having two referees like it would have a probability of .02 x .02 = .0004).

It might be that other professional journals could adopt such a system, perhaps as a complement to their current systems. Or perhaps it would be possible to set up a court of last resort for major journals, or within disciplines, that would hear appeals by respected persons in the field on behalf of papers. I know that if there were such a system in economics, I'd give it some business immediately. Perhaps the drawback is that too many claims would be made. But estimating the demand for such a service could be done most efficaciously by actually trying it.

Is there at least room for discussion and committee work on this problem?

Personal Postscript (as Written in 1980)

This document, as well as the original article and reply to the letters, reveals a certain combativeness (though I'm not combative in my personal life). I hope that this fact does not turn you away from the argument I'm trying to make. I also hope that you will see that a certain taste for combat can be useful socially. There are several economists who think much as I do on many of the matters I wrote about and who have much longer records of basic contributions in the field, but who have not made their views known to a wide audience (even of economists) because they lack taste for the fight, carry less of the outsider's anger, and have no stomach for the abusive reactions these views arouse. Qualities that are negative in some contexts can be positive in others.

Afterword

An update on *Science* and me: On December 9, 1987, the new editor, Daniel Koshland, called and invited me to write an article on the effect of immigration upon unemployment. I was delighted to accept his invitation because I had just finished a long book on the economic effects of immigration that includes two chapters on the unemployment effects, and I had also just finished a several-year empirical study (with Stephen Moore) of that same subject in a cross-section of U.S. cities over two decades. There was no more valuable invitation that I could receive at that time.

After a bit of thought while still on the phone, I told Koshland—I was somewhat surprised that he did not know it already—that I had had a "controversial" article in *Science* in 1980. He said that he welcomes controversy as long as the material is factually based. I then added that the people at the Washington office would undoubtedly tell him that it was not good to do business with me. He dismissed that statement, and told me that he would send me a formal letter of invitation.

Twenty-four hours later Koshland called and disinvited me. He said that he had spoken to the people at the Washington office and was worried about possible complications that would arise if I prepared the material and it was not good enough to publish. I replied that I had already written up much of the material that would be used, and he would therefore be able to make an advance evaluation that would obviate that complication.

He then promised to look at the material. He ended by saying that he appreciated my telling him of the previous events, and said that I "showed integrity." On that note the conversation ended.

I then sent him the material with a cover letter.

No reply came. Two or three times I sent him xeroxed copies of the letter with a hand-written note saying "Did you receive this letter?" Still no reply. Then in the week ending April 1, 1988, I called three or four times, leaving my name and phone number. He did not call back. On Friday, April 1 I called again and he answered the phone himself. When I told him who it was, he said that he was in a meeting but would call back in half an hour. He did call back, and promised that during the following week when he would be in Washington he would look at the material and call me for sure. He ended by saying "I have been very rude and I am sorry."

I have not heard from Koshland since then.

In May, 1988, I stumbled across a copy of Koshland's July 3, 1987, editorial headed "Inexorable Laws and the Ecosystem" that I had earlier clipped as an unusually choice sample of the genre. It calls for "effective population control" because we "are dooming our ecosystem" (see the introduction to Selection 49 for quotations). The zeal (unbacked by evidence) displayed in that editorial, and in the quotation of Koshland with respect to life and death in the Introduction to Selection 51, certainly is consistent with behaving toward me as if I am an enemy of the public. Whether his behavior squares with his frequent editorials about the need for honesty, integrity, and ethics in science is for the reader to judge.

55

The "Global 2000" Juggernaut

The origins, early activities, and funding sources of the Global To-morrow Coalition are described in this selection.

This snippet of recent data about one of the organizations included in the ambit of this selection may help indicate what a contrary viewpoint is up against. The National Wildlife Federation has (as of 1988) 4.5 million members, a yearly budget of $60 million, and pays its president $139,000 per year (Access to Energy, *April 1988, p. 3).*

Introduction

The first days in June will see a major public event by the Global Tomorrow Coalition, a large and well-publicized Washington conference with highly paid speakers such as ex-President Jimmy Carter. This is clearly an attempt to show the muscle of the environmental lobby. It is likely to be politically impressive and effective.

The Global Tomorrow Coalition is the spearhead of the recently evolved Global 2000 and environmental movement. Very large and with vast resources, experts say is the most powerful in Washington. This lobby helps determine how policymakers and the press view the options available for addressing some of the Nation's most pressing problems.

The Global 2000 Movement

The Global 2000 movement has deeply affected the national policies of the United States and other nations. This is clear from speeches by President Carter and other officials in his Administration and in various congressional hearings. For example, in his inaugural address Jimmy Carter said, referring to resources, that "even our great nation has its

Heritage Institution Analysis, May 13, 1983.

recognized limits." On the other hand, Ronald Reagan's election-eve address quoted from John Wayne on his deathbed: "Just give the American people a good cause, and there's nothing they can't lick." But the Reagan Administration has had great difficulty in translating this view into action because of the enormous bureaucratic momentum to implement the limits-to-growth philosophy.

As of October 1982, the Global Tomorrow Coalition reckoned some 5 million persons enrolled in its 49 participating member organizations. These groups run the alphabet of environmental and population organizations.[1]

The member organizations of the Coalition have on their boards of directors a *Who's Who* of influential figures in business, law, foundations, and especially the media. For example, the first six of the 42 persons on the Advisory Council of the Population Institute include: Lord Caradon, Arthur Ashe, Isaac Asimov, Joan Baez, George W. Ball, and Simone de Beauvoir. The Global 2000 movement includes the elite Year 2000 Committee consisting of: Co-chairmen Robert O. Anderson of the Atlantic Richfield Corporation and Russell Train of the World Wildlife Fund (U.S.); Walter Cronkite; ex-President of the World Bank Robert S. McNamara; former secretary of the Department of Health, Education, and Welfare (now Health and Human Services) Elliot Richardson; former secretary of State Cyrus Vance; Marian Heiskell of *The New York Times;* Robert Blake; Lester Brown; Adrian DeWind of the Natural Resources Defense Council; Hans Landsberg; Roger Revelle; S. Dillon Ripley, Head of the Smithsonian Institution; William Ruckelshaus; Henry Schacht of Cummins Engine; John Sewell; and George Zeidenstein, President of the Population Council.

The movement presently has a number of bills and resolutions before Congress. (See Selection 45 for some of the text.) *S. 1771,* the Global Resources, Environment, and Population Act, "declares as national policy the coordination of research on global trends and projections" and "government-wide compliance" and "coordination of federal efforts to base decision making on these analyses." It provides for using "all practiceable means, including financial and technical assistance . . . for the achievement of U.S. population stabilization."

H.R. 907 is much the same as *S. 1771,* but would set up an Office of Population Policy in the Executive Office of the President.

H. Con. Res. 276 and *S. Con. Res. 197* resolve that "the executive branch should begin to systematically coordinate and improve its projections of world population, resource, and environmental trends and their analysis, as outlined in the Global 2000 study." In addition, there is the "Year 2000 Committee Legislative Initiative," which calls for regular reports of the Executive Branch, the General Accounting Office, and the

Office of Technology Assessment. The influence of Global 2000 on these legislative initiatives is evident in a letter from Senator Mark Hatfield (R-Ore.) to Senator William Roth (R-Del.) calling for the creation of a Council on Global Resources to unify government planning in the areas of natural resources, environment, and population policy. This is potentially a dangerous centralization of power. "The main impetus for this legislation," wrote Hatfield, "was the publication of the *Global 2000 Report to the President.*" (See Selection 56 for some latter legislative initiatives.)

The member organizations of the Global Tomorrow Coalition have a large number of staff members in Washington, many of whom lobby the Congress and the executive branch. Consider, for example, the Natural Resources Defense Council: 23 attorneys (13 in Washington, D.C.), 3 "scientists," 15 "resource specialists," 6 "consultants," 7 persons in "development" (which probably means fundraising), 2 in "membership," 3 in accounting, 27 support staff, 2 "helpers," 6 "interns," and 6 "administrators." And it is just one of the 49 organizations in the Global Tomorrow Coalition. Altogether, there now are over 80 registered environmental lobbyists on Capitol Hill, compared to two or three in the late 1960s. And there are five environmental political action committees, one of which—The League of Conservation Voters—had a budget of almost $900,000 to back about 70 candidates in the 1982 elections.

States the Population Action Council, a division of the Population Institute, in a 1982 report:

> P.A.C.'s efforts to educate the freshman class of Senators and Representatives on the problem of overpopulation and the U.S. role in the solution to these problems will be greatly intensified during the next three to four post-election months. Our legislative division has already embarked on a campaign to alert congressional and senatorial candidates (excluding incumbents) about the work of the Population Action Council. Each candidate is receiving a packet including PAC information, an offer of a population briefing once they're elected, and population fact sheets. Our past experience shows that this type of campaign can be a smashing success: *94 percent of the 1980 freshman class were briefed within the first few months following their victories!* (Italics in original.)

The P.A.C. report then proceeds to mobilize its national network:

IMMEDIATE ACTION

CONTACT YOUR LOCAL CANDIDATES FOR THE U.S. HOUSE OF REP-RESENTATIVES AND THE U.S. SENATE AND ASK THEM THEIR STAND ON U.S. SUPPORT FOR INTERNATIONAL POPULATION ASSIS-TANCE.

CONTACT THE WASHINGTON P.A.C. OFFICE BY PHONE OR MAIL AND LET US KNOW OF ANY RESPONSES YOU RECEIVE.

The extent of the network is vast:

> The Institute's Population Action Council also provides over 18,000 policy leaders, local activists, and editors in the U.S. and abroad with POPLINE, a monthly world population news service. POPLINE interprets population developments, opportunities, and urgencies. In addition, nearly 2000 leaders and activists in 134 other countries have joined in with the P.A.C. program to stimulate their governments and ours to more vigorous population action.

And these efforts apparently have been successful. The Population Institute said in its report:

> In December, *Budget Director David Stockman proposed the elimination of every penny of population money* from the 1983 AID budget. This action would have meant the collapse of family planning programs in much of the developing world, exactly where the population explosion which threatens the future of all of us is taking place.
>
> The Population Institute's public policy division, the Population Action Council, responded instantly to the Stockman proposal by alerting powerful leaders in government and across the country, who appealed directly to the President and other high-level officials for restoration of the population budget. Thanks to P.A.C. initiatives, supported by others in the population community, the Administration reversed itself within 8 days.

By means of personnel interlocks, access to the mass media is assured for the Global Tomorrow Coalition. For example, John B. Oakes, who is on the NRDC Board of Trustees, is former senior editor and presently frequent columnist of *The New York Times;* his January 21, 1981, column was little more than a rewrite of Global 2000 press handouts.

Another example of Global Tomorrow Coalition activities is the propaganda campaign of the World Wildlife Fund (not a member of the U.S.-based Global Tomorrow Coalition, but of the same persuasion). Reported *The Wall Street Journal:*

> The World Wildlife Fund is run by savvy people recruited mainly from big business, advertising and public relations. . . .
>
> [T]elevision stations around the world will be asked to show a short documentary bearing the message "If we turn the world into a desert, man is doomed." That documentary reflects another of the World Wildlife Fund's connections to business: It was produced for the fund courtesy of the advertising firm of Ogilvy & Mather.
>
> Mr. Palmer, the WWF campaigns coordinator, says David Ogilvy of the ad agency became interested in the WWF five years ago and offered the worldwide services of his company; its London office alone is estimated to have spent $700,000 on WWF work so far. . . .

Prince Bernhard of the Netherlands was the president of the group for 15 years. His place has been taken by Britain's Prince Philip.

The reader's reaction may be: So what? The World Wildlife Fund probably is engaged in a laudable effort to fight real environmental threats. But the two main threats that WWF purports to fight are:

> "[W]e are losing one more animal, plant or insect species every 10 minutes," the World Wildlife Fund warns. "Approximately one million different species will be gone by the year 2000." It rates 25,000 plant and 1000 vertebrate species as threatened with extinction. . . .
>
> The fund says rain forests are vanishing at a rate of 49 acres a minute.

Both statistics are wholly wrong—unbelievably so. (See Selection 13.) The only scientific evidence on actual species loss cited in the environmental literature—including that by Norman Myers, the central figure in the matter—is one species per year at present, rather than one species every ten minutes. The WWF claim is off by a mere 5,256,000 percent. Recent authoritative surveys done at Resources for the Future by Sedjo, Clawson, Barnes, and Allen found that the rate of decrease of forests is nowhere near the figure that WWF cites. This is a reasonable sample of the evidential situation with the Global Tomorrow Coalition generally.

Various Global Tomorrow Coalition member organizations obtain large amounts of funding from, among other foundations, those shown in the Appendix to this Selection. The latest major foundation grant to a Global Tomorrow Coalition affiliate was $15 million by the MacArthur Foundation to Gus Speth, former head of the Council on Environmental Quality and one of the two main signatories of the Global 2000 Report. The member organizations also obtain funding from many corporations, as shown in the Appendix. And over the years, massive support—hundreds of millions of dollars—has gone to them directly and indirectly from the State Department's Agency for International Development, and also from the United Nations Fund for Population Activities, which itself is largely supported by the U.S. government.

On the other side, there is no organized opposition, no organization that lobbies the Congress against policies intended to produce "population stabilization" in the United States or abroad, or against measures whose object is the centralization of "foresight capability"—that is, giving a government agency funds with which to organize "research" and publicity about environmental issues and to require Congressional response. The right-to-life groups are the only organizations even philosophically in opposition. And they restrict themselves entirely to the abortion issue, thereby separating themselves from other individuals who might also oppose the initiatives of the Global 2000 movement.

Background

Where did the Global 2000 movement come from? The *Global 2000 Report to the President* focused on issues raised in such 1960s and 1970s environmental writings as Paul Ehrlich's *The Population Bomb,* which has been printed in millions of copies. Anne Ehrlich, in fact, was one of the seven key Global 2000 advisers. The Global 2000 intellectual approach was the same as that of *The Limits to Growth,* of which 4 million copies were published; that work was fathered by Jay Forrester, who was an adviser to Global 2000. *The Limits to Growth* was followed by several other books in the same spirit sponsored by the Club of Rome whose founder, Aurelio Peccei, has an extraordinarily large and honored place in the *Global 2000 Report.* In 1976, the Club of Rome repudiated the conclusions of *The Limits to Growth,* but this repudiation has gone almost unnoticed. *The Limits to Growth*-Club of Rome principals were all involved in the preparation of Global 2000.

Global 2000 was the subject of full-page stories in such national news media as *Time* and *Newsweek,* and it made front-page banner headlines across the country (for example, in Champaign-Urbana, Illinois, where I live) as an "official" government study forecasting global disaster. It has been printed in over a million copies and already has been translated into six languages. Other governments, such as West Germany, have initiated their own imitative studies with similar titles in the same spirit. In the U.S., there have been Year 2000 Committees set up by several states, all in touch with the Global 2000 movement.

The formation of the Global Tomorrow Coalition is told well in the following from its first newsletter.

The Global Tomorrow Coalition is the direct descendant of an informal, unstructured grouping of individuals who came together for the first time in early October 1980 in Washington. In a day-long meeting at the National Parks and Conservation Association, roughly 60 persons representing diverse nonprofit organizations, foundations, government agencies, church groups, and at least one labor union gathered to discuss the implications of *Global 2000* for their respective programs and activities, share current information, and find ways to be mutually supportive. At that meeting, there was a collective decision to continue to hold similar monthly meetings on global issues, and to call the informal and unincorporated group the Global 2000 Citizens Committee.

The Global 2000 Citizens Committee met on a regular basis through the fall of 1980 and into the winter and spring of 1981. Several organizations shared in the leadership during this period, particularly Zero Population Growth and the Natural Resources Defense Council. The immediate goals of the Citizens Committee were: (1) to encourage public responses to the invitation by CEQ Chairman Gus Speth to submit suggestions for the compilation of policy recommendations that eventually became *Global Future: Time to Act;* (2) to bring the *Global 2000 Report* to the attention of a wider audience, including public officials; and (3) to create a continuing "public-interest group constituency" for *Global 2000* to help keep the importance of the report in focus over the turbulent period of a change of administrations in the federal government.

New impetus for these efforts was provided in late January 1981 by the National Leadership Conference on Population, Resources, and Environment, convened by the National Audubon Society with cosponsorship by a total of 60 organizations. At this two-day conference, attended by over 275 individuals, a report was presented on the work of the Global 2000 Citizens Committee. The enthusiastic reception among the participants led to a consensus on creating a permanent structure to accommodate the shared interests and concerns of the many organizations involved.

Planning and arrangements culminated in late May at the inaugural meeting of the Board of Directors, when the Global Tomorrow Coalition officially came into being, welcoming into its ranks those who wished to continue the work they had begun under the auspices of the Global 2000 Citizens Committee. Having served its purpose well, the latter group ceased to exist. The two-person staff of the Global Tomorrow Coalition opened an office near Dupont Circle on July 1.

During the fall and winter of 1980–81, a separate but related organization was being born: The Year 2000 Committee. Unlike the Global Tomorrow Coalition, which is a consortium of organizations whose combined national memberships exceed five million Americans, The Year 2000 Committee is by design a small group of individuals, and intends to remain small. In most cases, its members will act in their own right rather than through the institutions of which they may be a part.

But the members of The Year 2000 Committee are persons of such prominence, recognition, and accomplishment that they share a remarkable capacity for access to decision-making levels in both government and the private sector. They intend to use that unique capacity over time to convey a simple message: that the complex, long-term issues posed by *Global 2000* and other studies demand concerted national attention and action; they are not limited to a given administration, political party, or partisan group. The specific means by which The Year 2000 Committee will choose to transmit that message are to be decided in a meeting on November 10.

Conclusion

In short, a large number of like-minded persons are producing a mass movement to achieve their goals for environmental and population policy, justifying the movement with frightening but fallacious research. There are no organizations or communications media dedicated to setting the record straight or to opposing the Global 2000 initiatives. These activities already have caused misallocation of natural resources in the United States, sapping of the national will, deterioration in public morale, and loss of confidence (with consequent reduction in risk investment) in the business community. How will this juggernaut, fueled by false information and special-interest values, be stopped short of disaster?

Note

1. Action for World Development. Alan Guttmacher Institute. American Farm Foundation. American Institute for Biological Sciences. American Society for the Prevention of Cruelty to Animals. Audubon Naturalist Society of Central Atlantic States. Bolton Institute for a Sustainable Future. Carrying Capacity. Center for Law & Social Policy. Concern, Inc. Conservation Foundation. Defenders of Wildlife. Environmental Coalition of North America. Environmental Defense Fund. Environment Fund. Environmental Policy Center. Environmental Policy Institute. Federation for American Immigration Reform. Friends of the Earth. Greater Caribbean Energy & Environment Foundation. International Institute for Environment & Development. Izaak Walton League. League of Women Voters. Monitor International. National Audubon Society. National Family Planning & Reproductive Health Association. National Wildlife Federation. Natural Resources Defense Council. Negative Population Growth. New York Zoological Society. Ohio Conservation Foundation. Overseas Development Council. Planned Parenthood of New York City. Population Crisis Committee. Population Communication. Population Institute. Population Resource Center. Population Services International. Rachel Carson Council. Renewable Natural Resources Foundation. Scenic Shoreline Preservation Conference. Sierra Club. Texas Committee on Natural Resources. Trust for Public Land. U.S. Association for the Club of Rome. U.S. Women's Health Coalition. Wilderness Society. Windstar Foundation. World Population Society. Zero Population Growth.

Appendix

Some Foundation Grants to Environmental Organizations, 1979–1981

FORD FOUNDATION

Grants to environmentalist organizations in 1979–81

Alaska Native Foundation	$ 20,000
Alan Guttmacher Institute	1,000,000
American Friends Service Committee	75,417
Aspen Institute	29,395
Center for Law and Social Policy	12,000
Conservation Foundation	25,000

Consumer Energy Council of America .... $ 76,546
Environmental Defense Fund   404,000
Hawaiian Coalition for Native Claims   25,000
Institute for Democratic Socialism   5,000
Massachusetts Audubon Society   10,000
Native American Rights Fund   600,000
Natural Resources Defense Council 1,740,000
New England Natural Resources Center   335,500
New York Lawyers for the Public Interest   16,000
Population Council 7,408,000
Sierra Club Legal Defense Fund   170,000
Survival International   60,000
Washington University Center for Biology of Natural Systems   79,443
Wisconsin Center for Public Policy   268,000
Youth Project   10,000
World Wildlife Fund   25,000

ATLANTIC RICHFIELD FOUNDATION

Grants to environmentalist organizations in 1979–80

Aspen Institute $1,436,000
California Conservation Project   15,000
Center for International Environmental Information   10,000
International Institute for Environmental Information   20,000
National Wildlife Federation   50,000
Sierra Club Federation   30,000
U.S. Association for the Club of Rome   5,000
Wilderness Society   15,000
World Wildlife Fund   10,000

ROCKEFELLER FOUNDATION

Grants to environmentalist organizations in 1979–81:

Aspen Institute .... $ 313,000
Conservation Foundation   15,000
International Institute of Applied Systems Analysis (Club of Rome) ...   108,000
John Muir Institute   24,310
Lindesfarne Association   35,000
Massachusetts Audubon Society   34,000
Natural Resources Defense Council   25,000
Population Council 3,015,000
Population Resource Center   200,000
World Watch Institute   35,000
Zero Population Growth Foundation   37,500

ROCKEFELLER BROTHERS FUND

Grants to environmentalist organizations in 1979–80:

American Friends Service Committee .... $ 25,000
Aspen Institute   60,000
Center for Law and Social Policy   115,000

Conservation Foundation   50,000
International Federation of Institutes of Advanced Studies (Club of   60,000
    Rome) ....
National Center for Policy Alternatives   140,000
Natural Resources Defense Council   50,000
New Alchemy Institute   120,000
Population Council 3,650,000
Survival International   25,000
Zen Center (San Francisco)   50,000
Northern Rockies Action Group   120,000

ROCKEFELLER FAMILY FUND

Grants to environmentalist organizations in 1979–81:

Community Nutrition Institute .... $ 25,000
Citizens for a Better Environment   40,000
Conservation Law Foundation of New England   120,000
Environmental Action Foundation   20,000
Environmental Defense Fund   55,000
Environmental Law Institute   10,000
Environmental Policy Institute   130,000
National Audubon Society   50,000
National Wildlife Federation   20,000
Natural Resources Defense Council   210,000
Public Lands Institute   10,000
Sierra Club Legal Defense Fund   110,000
Southwest Research and Information Center   15,000
Wilderness Society   60,000
World Wildlife Fund   20,000

Source: Environmental News Service—date not known.

56

Review of *Population Growth and Economic Development: Policy Questions*, a Report of the National Academy of Sciences in 1986

This 1986 NAS report turned sharply away from the alarmist NAS report of 1971 and—in the assessment of Allen Kelley, another reviewer in the same symposium—moved about 80 percent in the direction of the views of "our side." But the conclusion of the report, and even less the press release, do not reflect the body of the report. Instead, they represent what is called "damage control" or "spin reversal" in Washington argot. "Let me write the press release and I won't worry a bit about the content of the document itself," one prominent public relations person said recently.

My review of the NAS report in this selection focuses on that discrepancy between the actual report and the summaries of it, and speculates how it came about, in connection with funding organizations and political pressures. More generally, the selection discusses the danger that such "official" research may be affected by the politics of funding, and it documents some of the pressures placed upon the committee in the presentation of the report.

A section of my review was censored by the editor of Population and Development Review, *the journal that published the review. In retrospect, perhaps I overreacted in protesting the excision. I certainly have a tendency to be imprudent in not going along more genially rather than fighting tooth-and-nail for a principle when the matter is already in extremis, and when the other side is giving me an important opportunity; perhaps more opportunities would be open to me if I were different in that respect. But following my usual bent, here is the story:*

Population and Development Review, Vol. 12, No. 3, September 1986.

*To help document that foundations pressure population-research
grantees to arrive at the conclusions desired by the foundations, I
quoted some sections from the Mellon Foundation letter reproduced
in Selection 57. The rest of the discussion followed the lines of the
discussion in Parts 1 and 2 of Selection 55. The material relating to
Mellon was then cut out by editor Paul Demeny, over my strongest
possible objections to him and to George Zeidenstein, the president
of the Population Council, which publishes the journal. The core of
Demeny's letter (September 5, 1986) was:*

> *To reiterate our position on the excised material, it is the editorial policy
> of the journal—consistent with the tradition of scholarly journals—not to
> publish anything in the nature of a personal expose. This both because it
> is not deemed scholarship and because it is not fair play since the attacked
> party has not the opportunity to reply for some six to nine months. For us
> to relax this policy would risk its recurrence; it would change the character
> of the journal and amount to an abdication of our editorial responsibilities.*

*The reader can judge (see Selection 57) whether or not my use of the
quote is "fair play." I replied (in part):*

> *If your letter of [September 5, 1986] is to be taken at face value and you
> are concerned about a "personal expose"—incidentally, I "attack" (your
> word) no one, and am simply trying to expose corruption in the scientific
> establishment—you may run the Smith letter without letterhead or identi-
> fying signature, thereby removing any possible basis for your stated
> objection. I am willing to make this compromise to avoid your stated
> concern, though I believe that the piece would be less effective in that
> form. I consider this an honorable meeting of the minds, even though I
> think that your editorial practices in the past do not substantiate the
> description of your policy as you now state it with respect to "fair play"
> and so on. (September 9, 1986)*

The offer to delete the name of the writer of the letter, and thereby
to remove the supposed basis of editor Demeny's objection, was not
accepted.

The Population Council presently receives $490,000 per year from
the Mellon Foundation.

The editor of the journal in question was at that time (and perhaps
still is) a member of the AAAS committee that received the Mellon
letter.

(Here I wish to record my appreciation to Demeny for soliciting
and publishing my review at all. Though persons involved in it have
said that the NAS inquiry was undertaken in response to my work, I
was given no opportunity by the NAS to contribute to the work in any

form, either as a member of the committee or as the author of a background paper or as a commentator on it when presented. Nor was I asked to take part in other formal official discussions such as that held by the PAA. Editor Demeny provided my only opportunity, which I appreciate).

The NAS report is a thoughtful, diligent, and honest draft, mainly by Samuel Preston with chapters by Ronald Lee and Geoffrey Greene, and finally shaped by the Working Group on Population Growth and Economic Development as a whole. Its survey of the literature is wide ranging and accurate. It bravely wrests itself from many unsound propositions published widely in the past (including a 1971 report issued by the NAS). And it reaches several well-founded judgments that needed to be heard by the public at large as well as by demographers, of which the following are examples:

> The scarcity of exhaustible resources is at most a minor constraint on economic growth in the near to intermediate term. . . . On balance, then, we find that concern about the impact of rapid population growth on resource exhaustion has often been exaggerated. . . . (pp. 16, 17)

> The extent to which slower population growth would alleviate [agricultural] problems depends on the degree to which the problems lead to other solutions through institutional and technological adaptation. . . . Experience in several countries suggests that such induced innovations can offset much of the initially negative impact of population growth on labor productivity. . . . [I]f institutions do not adapt as rapidly as needed, slower population growth can retard the decline of labor productivity and the degradation of common resources. (pp. 33, 34)

> [T]here is no evidence to suggest that slower population growth would significantly decrease the savings rate, and some evidence actually suggests a positive effect. . . . Thus, while capital deepening does appear, at least in theory, to be a genuine positive consequence of reduced population growth, such growth by no means appears to be a decisive influence. (p. 46)

The differences between these judgments and the conventional wisdom of past decades are very great indeed.

Were it not for a small handful of sentences, I would simply point to the many good features of the report. But its central objective was to reach a conclusion, for purposes of policymaking, concerning the effect of population growth on economic development. The few sentences that state the report's overall conclusion are therefore crucial. I believe that the report reached an unsound conclusion that does not follow from the evidence it assessed (though it also does not directly contradict the evidence), to wit:

that economic development will be faster, especially in developing countries, if fertility is lower. In this conclusion, the report has provided the basis for the continuation of misguided and dangerous policies on the part of the United States and other countries, policies originally justified by Coale and Hoover in *Population Growth and Economic Development in Low-Income Countries* (1958), which I interpret the NAS report as repudiating (pp. 2, 4). I shall therefore devote this review entirely to an assessment of the conclusion, while hoping that this concentration does not detract from recognition of the virtues of the body of the report.

There is considerable variation in how important the effect of population growth is adjudged at various places in the document, among various commentators on it, and (of great import) between the report itself and the official press release about the report. But apparently there is nothing in the report that will force a change in U.S. policy toward population programs abroad. This may be seen in the comment in the report by Steven Sinding, then head of the US Agency for International Development's population program, who "said he felt enormous 'relief' at the committee's conclusions" (Holden, 1986, p. 1494), and in the remark by Nyle Brady, standing in for AID administrator Peter McPherson at the NAS presentation of the report: "Despite the various qualifications in the report, the overriding conclusion is that slower population growth would be beneficial to economic development for most developing countries" (Brady, 1986, p. 4). That is, AID now has a warrant to continue its activities as before. And William McGreevey of the World Bank, the agency that, along with AID, is the most important voice and source of support for "controlling" world population growth, writes: "[T]he differences between [the Bank's *World Development Report 1984*] and [the NAS report] reflect differences in the purposes of the documents rather than in the scientific or policy conclusions which they offer" (1986, p. 5). (It should be noted, however, that some other readers of the report do not agree with McGreevey. More generally, there is very great variation in how readers interpret the conclusions of the report, which may be an inevitable consequence of its creation by a committee. And as is often the case in such situations, some or much of the ambiguity may even have been intended as a way of papering over differences within the committee.)

The report's summational language—which will be the focus of my discussion—is: "On balance, we reach the qualitative conclusion that slower population growth would be beneficial to economic development for most developing countries. . . . Thus, there appears to be a legitimate role for population policy, providing its benefits exceed its costs" (pp. 90–91). But the report very self-consciously avoids making explicit how large it assesses the influence of population growth to be, as was made clear in the refusal by Preston, when he represented the Working Group on Population Growth and Economic Development at the National Academy of Sciences presentation of the report to the public, to accept *any* adjective as a characterization. And the phrase "On balance" makes clear that the Working Group found forces operating in both positive and negative directions, of various strengths under various circumstances, which represents a major break from the past monolithic characterization of additional people as a drag upon development across the board.

The statement of the conclusion in the headline of the NAS-NRC press release read: "Slower Population Growth Generally Benefits Developing Nations' Economies: Is One of Several Key Factors Cited." This seems to me quite different from the report's conclusion. The headline also seems to be subtly but importantly different from the first sentence in the press release: "Slower population growth helps improve the economic well-being of most developing countries, but is only one of several key factors in raising the standard of living in these nations. . . ." Yet there is nothing in the report itself that is clearly at variance with these press-release statements or that falsifies them.

I will attempt to explain both why the report reached the conclusion that it did and why the differences in the above versions of the conclusion arose. There are three parts to the explanation offered: (1) the relationship of the conclusion to the treatment of the time horizon; (2) the mode of scientific reasoning used in the analysis; and (3) the political-institutional-funding environment within which the study was done. I will end with some thoughts about the activities that the NAS report supports.

The Relationship of the Conclusion to the Time Horizon

Any book promising to teach a whole subject in one lesson, let alone one sentence, seems to promise the impossible. But Henry Hazlitt goes far toward this goal in his book *Economics in One Lesson* when he writes:

> The art of economics consists in looking not merely at the immediate but at the longer effects of any act or policy; it consists in tracing the consequences of that policy not merely for one group but for all groups. (1962, p. 17)

This lesson is particularly relevant to an analysis of the effects of population growth, wherein the very-long-run effects—the creation of new knowledge—clearly are the opposite of the very-short-run effects. In the very short run, a cohort of additional children is an economic burden to all involved; in the long run, the additional knowledge created by that cohort, in response to both the existing problems and the new problems caused by that cohort, is of value to people living then, at which time the costs of that cohort and the problems it caused will have ceased to matter. But the NAS report makes no distinction between short run and long run in its conclusion—though it certainly makes this all-important distinction at many other places in the report, for example, with respect to natural resources (Chapter 1) and technical change (Chapter 5). The reader of the conclusion therefore is given no reason to doubt that it is intended to imply that the economic level reached at *any* future time will be lower if population growth at present is higher. This fatal flaw of the Coale-Hoover study is here writ worse, because (unlike the NAS report) even a cursory look at Coale-Hoover reveals that its main focus was on the economic effects within the next three decades, though of course it gave no hint that the long-run effects might be the opposite of the short-run effects.

If there were no other reason to reject the conclusion of the NAS report—though this does not, I repeat, imply rejecting the main body of the report, which has many virtues—the lack of time specification would be reason enough to do so.

The Mode of Thinking and the Conclusion Reached

At least from the time of the Greeks, and as epitomized by Malthus, the standard mode of thinking about the economic effects of population growth has been deductive: A given quantity of resources divided among a larger number of workers leads to lower production per worker; and a given quantity of goods divided among a larger number of consumers leads to a lower standard of living. Occasionally, writers in the nineteenth century (important examples include Alexander Everett and Friedrich Engels) confronted this deductive logic with contrary empirical evidence, but the anecdotal nature of their contrary evidence did not prove persuasive.

It was only in 1967 that time-series and cross-national analyses by Kuznets and cross-national analysis by Easterlin (though preceded by a little-known article by Alfred Bonne) opposed the deductive reasoning with systematic empirical evidence. That evidence shook my belief in the simple Malthusian model. And I continue to believe that that evidence, taken together with the overall course of human civilization during which there has been a concurrent drop in mortality, rise in total population, and increase in standard of living, is more persuasive than the deductive reasoning even when bolstered by empirical evidence bearing upon some of the mechanisms involved in the population/economic development nexus.

The basic mode of analysis of the NAS report is, however, deductive in the traditional mode. The report states that "simple correlations between population growth and per capita income, although intriguing, ultimately provide little insight into the causal impact of a policy-driven decline in fertility. A scientific assessment of that impact requires that one identify the major mechanisms by which population growth is hypothesized to affect economic development; assess the evidence for each hypothesis; and, finally, synthesize the net effect of the simultaneous operation of these mechanisms" (p. 7). Another sort of deductive thinking is found in the assertion by Ronald Ridker (at a session of the April 1986 annual meeting of the Population Association of America devoted to the report) that first-hand experience with many African countries is sufficient to convince a reasonable observer that population growth is too fast there; such case analysis, without even the unsystematic scientific controls found in the long-run record of economic-demographic history, is inherently deductive in its logic despite its appeal to observation.

When writing as an individual, co-chairman of the NAS Working Group Ronald Lee criticized the World Bank's *World Development Report 1984* on exactly these grounds. In the context of remarking on the absence of reference to empirical data on the relationship between education and population growth, Lee says: ". . . and so we are forced back once again on the kind of a priori reasoning that has rendered many aspects of the 'population impedes development' case unconvincing" (1985, p. 129). Why does not "unconvincing" apply with equal vigor to the NAS report for the same reason? And this mode of thinking in the Bank's report, together with the absence of mention of the "dozens of [aggregate] cross-national studies (and some with a longitudinal dimension) of population growth rates and density in relation to growth rates of per capita income" (p. 128), led Lee to "question the underpinnings of these conclusions" (p. 128). Why, then, should one have any confidence in the similar conclusions of the NAS report?

In my view, it would have been particularly appropriate and useful had the NAS pursued the issue of the reliability of those aggregate-relationship empirical studies and the validity of their conclusions in light of the best statistical-econometric thinking. Such an examination is badly needed because on the rare occasion when these studies are mentioned, they are dismissed as either unpersuasive (as in the NAS report) or as completely without scientific value. (For example, Repetto [1985] recently called all aggregate-relationship empirical studies "meaningless," saying, "Everyone knows that statistical correlations between two variables don't tell which is influencing the other, or whether a third variable is influencing both.") A full-scale assessment badly needs to be done, and I hope to publish such a study on another occasion.[2] A few of the main points follow without amplification.

First, two-variable correlation studies certainly do not indicate the forces that influence economic development. But a two-variable zero correlation can be very strong evidence, especially when buttressed by multivariate studies with a variety of specifications, that one variable (population growth) does *not* cause the other (economic development).

Second, many of the studies of population and economic development have indeed gone beyond simple two-variable correlations.

Third, not only does a correlation not "prove" causation, as the popular saw has it, but no other scientific procedure—not even a lengthy series of experiments—can "prove" causation, either.

Fourth, simple correlations of the rate of economic growth and the rate of population growth are biased toward a more negative (less positive) correlation, because the appropriate measure of economic development is the rate of change of output per worker while the usual variable is per person; substituting the former for the latter pushes the correlation coefficient in a positive direction.

In his individual writing (though not in recent conversation) Ronald Lee seems to view the matter much as I do. He wrote:

Dozens of studies, starting with Kuznets', have found no association between the population growth rate and per-capita income growth rate, despite the obvious fact that at least since World War II, population growth rates have varied considerably. These studies control for other factors such as trade, aid, and investment to varying degrees. Two recent studies add historical depth to this analysis; even within countries (and thus looking *only* at disequilibrium) over periods as long as a century or as short as 25 years, there is no significant association [of the population growth rate and the rate of change of per capita income], for either DC's or LDC's; put differently, one can't reject the hypothesis that the regression coefficient . . . is unity. (1983, p. 54, references omitted)

After dismissing two studies showing contradictory results on the grounds that "data problems render these results suspect," Lee goes on to assess the econometric validity of this body of work:

This kind of finding may be welcomed as reassuring us that population growth is of little consequence for economic performance in LDC's, or it may be questioned as misleading. Indeed, Cassen and others suggest that the estimates are distorted by simultaneous equation bias, since, it is argued, more rapid economic growth leads to more rapid population growth, introducing a positive association. I am skeptical of this argument, since to a first approximation, it is the *level* of income, and not its rate of change which should affect it. (p. 54, italics in original, references omitted)

And he ends the article with: "In general, these cross-national studies [of all kinds, and not just the aggregate relationships] have not yet provided what we might hope for: a rough and stylized depiction of the consequences of rapid population growth; unless, indeed, the absence of significant results is itself the result" (p. 54).

I interpret the preceding quotations from Lee as putting much more weight on the econometric results than did the NAS report, and as being a vote for the point of view that I urge on this matter.

The Political, Institutional, and Financial Environment of the Study

Speculation that scientific writing is affected by considerations other than the search for truth is not only unpleasant but difficult to substantiate. Yet when important national policies, as well as the interests of sponsors—the U.S. Agency for International Development, the Rockefeller Foundation, and the Hewlett Foundation—are at stake, and when some persons having an effect upon the outcome have direct or indirect professional connections with the sponsors and with other organizations having a position in the debate (such as the World Bank), the issue cannot be ducked, even if the result is only to present a clean bill of health. If the public-choice school of economics has done nothing else, it has made us sharply aware of what Adam Smith also knew well, that it is folly to presume that persons acting on behalf of the public will totally divorce their actions from their personal interests: "We are not ready to suspect any person of being defective in selfishness" (quoted by Hirshleifer, 1985, p. 55). And in this connection, Theodore W. Schultz has warned us of dangers in our own line of work. (See headnote to Selection 57.)

Because of the evanescent nature of the process under discussion, it is difficult to find hard evidence that it exists. But can there be the slightest doubt that one must always be concerned about whether the conclusions of a piece of research on a topic such as population and development have been affected by the views of the funding sources? Here again I quote T. W. Schultz: "the distortions of economic research will not fade away by accommodating the patrons of research funds" (p. 121).

In the case at hand, I personally am satisfied that the original draft was wholly unaffected by any considerations other than the search for the plain truth about these complex matters. And I do not have any reason to believe that the final product differed from the original draft except insofar as it reflected the inevitable differences of views and compromises among members of the Working Group and of the Committee on Population. But not only the report, but also the choice of people to prepare it and its presentation and the press release, affect what the public receives and the influences upon national policies. Would it not seem imprudent to have people—no matter how unbiased and dedicated to the truth they may be—

serve on the Working Group, as well as members of the larger Committee on Population, whose very jobs in such organizations as the World Bank and the Population Council depend upon the proposition that the world faces a population "problem"? Here I think there are grounds for concern that the funding sources influenced the conclusion presented to the public.

Nonscientific considerations certainly affected the shape of the report through the choice of the membership of the committee. The National Research Council's news release stated that "The committee's study was requested by AID in 1983 following reports by some analyst that rapid population growth was an important long-term stimulus to economic development." In light of that fact, notice must be taken that no person who can be identified as one of those "analysts" was involved in the preparation of the report in any way. This squares with the fact that the participants were chosen explicitly as people "who were not known to have a strongly fixed position . . . not at one or another end of the continuum," in order "to avoid the group becoming a battleground" (conversation with Robert Lapham, original study staff director, 21 May 1986).

Additionally, the NAS-NRC staff's press release makes population growth seem more important than the Working Group saw it to be. The word "key" in the headline of the press release was placed there by the staff together with the Office of Public Affairs, without consultation with D. Gale Johnson, Samuel Preston, or Ronald Lee of the Working Group, though Preston characterizes that term as "not a fair adjective" (in conversation), and Johnson seemed surprised when I told him that "key" appeared in the headline. This wording may have been wholly a response to the natural desire to make the matter newsworthy. But such a change in wording also might seem responsive to such elements of the situation as the comment by Congressman Sander Levin (a principal in the population movement) at the rehearsal the night before the NAS-NRC presentation that the presentation was "not dramatic enough." And the press officer for the NAS-NRC suggested rehearsing Preston's presentation with him, to instruct him about how to deal with politically difficult topics such as abortion.

Where Does the NAS Conclusion Lead?

Which causes does the NAS report strengthen? We have seen that AID asserts that its activities have been supported by the report. And though the report frequently mentions the importance of markets, it is far from clear that it calls for true economic freedom (though the records of some of the members, e.g., Johnson, and the private conversations of others strongly assert that such freedom is crucial in economic development and is a vital good in itself). Consider this sentence in the press release from the National Research Council about the NAS report: "[T]he recent widespread famine in Ethiopia and other African nations and similar food shortages in China during 1959–61 can be attributed in part to 'very badly functioning markets combined with rapid population growth.' " That is very different from an assertion that those food shortages were caused by dictatorial governments which beggared farmers by appropriating their land and heavily taxing their output, together with denying them the right to move freely to wherever they wished to work and live—which almost all observers now seem to agree was the case. The press release sentence sounds like the "market failure" notion that is used to justify greater government interference in and control of the activity in question, rather than a call for a reduction in interference and control that would allow the market to function more effectively. And the sentence contradicts statements in the report that properly emphasize the ill effects of food subsidies and credit-market distortions, and even the property rights that are mentioned elsewhere in the press release. Even worse, it suggests that attention be paid to population growth in lieu of fighting tyranny and working for economic freedom.

Also, one reads in the report (p. 88) that "[T]he potential value of government intervention for market regulation . . . is widely acknowledged." This is exactly the language of the people who oppose free markets. Conversations with some members of the Working Group indicate that the group very much wished to strengthen the hand of those who espouse free markets and economic liberty, but this perhaps-inadvertent language also strengthens the hand of those who oppose economic freedom, with the overall outcome in doubt.

Here it needs to be said that the importance of markets rather than controls is no longer a matter of ideology or subject to dispute. By now there is sufficient evidence and analysis of the subject that one can state as a scientific fact that economic freedom is a crucial element of economic development—the sort of element that population growth was formerly believed to be.

The NAS report also—again, I would guess, against the wishes and intentions of many or most members of the Working Group—strengthens the hand of those who wish to go "beyond family planning," that is, to go beyond the simple provision of contraceptive information and devices.

> When a couple's childbearing decision imposes external costs on other families—in overexploitation of common resources, congestion of public services, or contribution to a socially undesirable distribution of income—a case may be

made for policies that go "beyond family planning." Such policies include persuasive campaigns to change family size norms and combinations of incentives and taxes related to family size. (p. 93)

The Working Group apparently believed that such externalities are unlikely to occur or, if they do occur, are unlikely to be important. But the language that makes provision for them allows the interpretation that the report looks favorably upon such activities. This may be the inevitable outcome of writing by committee, but the consequences might be tragic. It also may be an argument against commissioning official committee-created reports on such topics.

Conclusion

What is one to make of the text of the NAS report, and of its conclusion, which does not follow from the text, even if the two are not logically contradictory? Perhaps we should see the disjunction as the inevitable result of a committee process wherein bargains are made about which viewpoints are represented. Blame certainly cannot be held against the principal writer, or against any member of the committee. And loyalty to the group may decently prevent any member from dissenting from any single element in the report; as co-chair Johnson put it: "It is not quite the document I would have written, but unless one understands that will be the case and is willing to accept some compromises, one should not accept appointment to such committees." (letter of 3 April 1986).

My own inference from this experience is that reports on topics like this one should not be attempted by committees. The justification for such committees is that they bring together more knowledge and a greater variety of experience, with a better balance of judgment, than one writer can muster. But these virtues can be outweighed by the defects of committee work.

Even more important, such reports should not be prepared by committees sponsored by government organizations, the products of which emerge with a halo of conclusiveness and objectivity that is no more appropriate here than in the case of any private individual's writings about the same topic. Certainly, no confidence is evoked for this report when we remember that a previous NAS report (1971) on much the same subject arrived at a viewpoint that was implicitly rejected by the current publication. More bluntly, why should one put more trust in a new NAS report than in one or another private scholar's writings, when one would have gone wrong in trusting a previous report generated by the same process and appearing with the same official label, rather than in some private scholar's views expressed at that earlier time? This unfortunate experience with population economics is buttressed by our sorry experiences with official U.S. government assessments concerning natural resources, energy, and the environment published during the last decade or so, of which the *Global 2000 Report to the President* is only the best-known example.

It is a matter for regret that the report did not take more steps away from the conventional wisdom that population growth is an unmitigated destructive force. And it may be hoped that the distance this report has come since the previous one—Allen Kelley calls it "revisionist" in his comments in this same review symposium—may turn out to be of great importance in the long run. But admiration for the distance traveled, the diligence of the effort, and the soundness of many of its findings should not distract us from the all-important wrong conclusion that is communicated to the population community and to the public at large.

Notes

1. National Research Council, Working Group on Population Growth and Economic Development, Committee on Population. Washington, D.C.: National Academy Press, 1986. ix + 108 p. $10.00 (pbk.).
2. An earlier version of this review, containing a lengthier discussion of the topic, is available on request.

57

The Population Establishment, Corruption, and Reform

Since the middle 1950s there has evolved in the United States, with developing links to the United Nations and the World Bank and organizations in other countries, a closely interrelated population "establishment." This establishment has heavily influenced U.S. policy toward population growth and family reproductive behavior abroad as well as at home. Many of its activities are unacceptable by most standards of decency.

These activities take place through a nexus of overlapping boards of directors in which the same individuals are often on both the donor and recipient sides of money transactions, and influence each others' access to publication and other perquisites. The network is not described here because analysis of it has previously been published (Bachrach and Bergman, 1973; Demerath, 1976).

Some have said that professional demographers have not taken part in the population establishment's activities described here. But recently there have appeared several writings from officials of the mainstream professional institutions *which can be taken as authoritative evidence that demographers have been intimately inter-related with the nonprofessional activist institutions in these activities. Indeed, much of this writing expresses pride in these activities.*

As is inevitable, the demand by governments for research and for programs to advance population-control was met by a supply of such services by demographers. The Director of the Population Division of the United Nations, Jean-Claude Chasteland, wrote that concerning "Relations between demographers and politicians . . . a kind of modus vivendi—*or rather,* modus operandi—*has been gradually established, which is often a source of mutual enrichment." ("State of*

Population Research and Research Needs As Expressed At the International Conference on Population and Its Preparatory Meetings," Population Bulletin of the United Nations, Nos. 21/22 (New York: UN, 1988, p. 1 of 1–15)

Mary Kritz, an official of the Population Division of the Rockefeller Foundation notes that "It is not uncommon to find demographers serving as heads or members of population commissions in developing countries." She applauds the development of "national demographic capacity" for this and other purposes, saying that "if national demographers are not available, they cannot be brought into the policy process." (Indeed so.) ("Building Demographic Capacity for Population Policy in Developing Countries", PPA paper, 1988, p. 17)

A former Director of the Population Division, Milos Macura, tells some of the history of this relationship.

> *The Belgrade Conference [in 1965] was the first United Nations meeting of its scope at which fertility was discussed not only as an explanatory variable, but also as a policy [control] variable. . . . At the Belgrade Conference it was already obvious that most population specialists were in favour of some kind of population policy. . . . The International Planned Parenthood Federation . . . was firmly committed to the idea.*

> *By the end of the 1960s a feeling had developed that the next population conference . . . would have to be on policy issues rather than on scientific questions. . . .*

> *[In 1974] at Bucharest. . . . There were no scientific or technical topics on the agenda of the Conference. . . . The key issue at the Conference was the adoption of a population plan of action. . . .*

> *By 1984 [in Mexico City] it was possible for R. Salas to address the Conference in an open and direct manner. He suggested,* inter alia, *that an overriding objective of population policies should be the stabilization of the world population. . . . ("The Significance of the United Nations International Population Conferences",* Population Bulletin of the United Nations, Nos. 19/20 (New York: UN, 1987, pp. 20–22)

Still another former Director of the Population Division Leon Tabah, wrote:

> *It is common knowledge that politics took control of demography a long time ago, with unexpected reversals—today's Malthusians becoming tomorrow's anti-Malthusians, and vice versa. . . . [!]*

> *In an area as basic as population, scientists and technicians often have ties to the people with decision-making power. Under pressure from their Governments, leading scientists have often been seen defending points of*

view which they had been opposing shortly before. [!!!] ("Interrelationships Between Population and Development", Population Bulletin of the United Nations, *Nos. 19/20 (New York: UN, 1987, p. 98)*

It is most unusual to see such honest statements in print. The last one above is a straightforward accusation of scientific prostitution. And it refers not to isolated cases, but to the core of the profession.

It should be noted that the above statements, and others to come, are all by persons who headed the entity which they were describing, and who are sympathetic to the mainstream thrust of that trend, to wit, that population growth is detrimental to economic development and therefore must be controlled by governments. If someone on the other side of the issue had written those statements, they would be dismissed as partisan and paranoid.

Tabah goes on to assert that the sensibilities of "the Catholic segment of the American population . . . were partly responsible for the United States position at the Mexico City Conference" (p. 104). I am not comfortable with that statement, given that my scientific work entered into that policy statement, and that I am not Catholic. And I certainly would not suggest—nor would Tabah, I'm sure—that opposing positions were simply the result of a Protestant-Jewish-Muslim cabal, independent of their scientific merit.

Paul Demeny, former president of the Population Association of America and Vice-President and Director of the Center for Population Studies of the Population Council, long the preeminent institution in the field, recently wrote:

Population policy was . . . transmogrified . . . into a goal-oriented "industry" (p. 13) [to reduce population growth] . . . the new population industry . . . is a money-, labor-, and technology-intensive construct. (p. 15)

Social science provided the rationale for the creation of the population industry but, once established, the industry took command. Its needs for large-scale funding and the intrinsic logic of the underlying policy concept dictated that much of the resources supporting the population sector come, directly or indirectly, from government budgets. Soon this was true also of social science research that was considered relevant for the industry's concerns. The official population sector became the dominant patron of "social science research" on all matters related to industry interests. (p. 16)

Big money projects tended to drive out small-money research; industry-sponsored work outbid, eclipsed, and displaced work not so sponsored. (p. 16)

The particular uses to which industry resources allocated to social science research have been increasingly put, at least since the early 1970s, was powerfully shaped by strong convictions held by the funding agencies and by the population industry at large on what research priorities should be in the population field. With remarkable consistency, the industry insisted that social science research concentrate on and be maximally helpful in assisting and backing the day-to-day execution of the received population policy line. (p. 17)

Resource allocation for social science work as mandated by the large funding agencies puts highest priority emphasis on "program evaluation". . . . the industry considers it important to demonstrate that when fertility continues to be high, that condition is linked to various inadequacies and lacunae with the existing family planning program. Conversely, when fertility is declining or has declined, it is important to attribute the change to the effects of the family planning program. (p. 20)

. . . social science research directed to the developing countries in the field of population has now become almost exclusively harnessed to serve the narrowly conceived short-term interests of programs that embody the existing orthodoxy in international population policy. . . . the population industry . . . seeks, and with the power of the purse enforces, predictability, control, and subservience. Pushed to its extreme, this stance generates research that finds what the sponsor already knows to be revealed truth. (pp. 25–26) ("Social Science and Population Policy", The Population Council, May, 1988)

The professional organization of U.S. demographers, the Population Association of America, lobbies for more money to be spent in the ways described by Demeny. Typically, the head of its Public Affairs Committee, "For the Fiscal Year 1987 . . . Dr. Teitelbaum urged the Subcommittee [on Labor, Health, and Human Services and Education of the Senate Appropriations Committee] to continue its support for research at NICHD and to appropriate $503 million in funding for FY '88." (P. A. A Affairs, Summer, 1987, p. 2)

What we have, then, is co-optation on a vast scale of government and its taxing power by antinatalist activists with the cooperation of demographers. The movement is driven at bottom by—along with humanitarian sentiments—such emotions and values as the "rights" of other species and the environment, the importance of "pristine nature," racism, and fear for the human species found on ignorance of the basic processes of biological, cultural, and economic evolution—as well as the naked self-interest of the "scientists" involved. And almost all concerned are so convinced of the rightness of their activity that they never inquire into whether it constitutes dirty business.

There is a most interesting article or book yet to be written on the politicization of a science, using population studies as a case example.

Can the reader imagine what it takes to go up against such unanimity of views and such wealth of resources? Hence almost no one did make the attempt, and no one did so successfully. And hence, others are discouraged from doing so, and so it continues.

In its earlier years the population establishment mainly stood apart from other institutions. It then depended largely upon support from the various Rockefeller foundations, and from the Population Council, which had been founded by the Rockefellers. In the years since then, with the final impetus from the 1980 Global 2000 *Report to the President, the population-control groups have joined with such environmentalist groups as the Audubon Society, the World Wildlife Fund, and the Natural Resources Defense Council to form the umbrella organization Global Tomorrow Coalition. The latter coordinates legislative activities and lobbying, and focuses federal grant-seeking. (See Selection 55.)*

This selection documents some of the population establishment's unethical activities. It includes only matters for which there is hard evidence in print, and only those occurrences which came to the attention of a single worker in the field without special investigation.

The activities described include:

• Laundering of AID funds through international organizations so that the money could eventually return to domestic U.S. organizations. Some of this money is used to propagandize for, and to support, coercive population-control activities abroad and domestically.

• Heavy-handed pressure by foundation funders—an astonishing letter from the Mellon Foundation is shown—upon even such respected organizations as the American Association for the Advancement of Science to produce conclusions predetermined by the foundation.

• Acceptance of funds in compliance with the funder's demands by such organizations as AAAS.

• Misinterpretation of NAS-NRC study conclusions in the press release and the public-relations conference in the direction desired by AID, under pressure from pro-population-control congressmen and in the context of AID providing the bulk of the funding for the study. (See Selection 48.)

• Statement by the Center for Population Research of NIH in its Request for Proposals of the expected direction of research findings on the consequences of population growth. (NIH is, along with AID, the main source of funds for population research.)

• *Orchestration of a campaign of telegrams by the American Public Health Association (and involving the International Union for the Scientific Study of Population in the telegram text) to protest a cut in federal funds going to population activities abroad which heavily benefit U.S. institutions and individual researchers. APHA even promised the senders it would pay for the cost of the telegrams as an inducement to people to send the telegrams.*

• *NIH organizing its research support in such fashion that practically no research on the economic consequences of population growth is federally sponsored, in the presence of knowledge that prior research had not found the deleterious consequences that the population establishment warns about.*

• *Co-optation of the Population Association of America into joint action with the politically activist Population Resource Center, using money from membership dues and foundation grants indistinguishably.*

• *Use of taxpayer grants given to support true family-planning activities in the United States to pay for newspaper advertisements that lobby in favor of population-control activities abroad and in the United States (especially by Planned Parenthood).*

• *Use of millions of dollars of tax monies by the Population Information Program at Johns Hopkins University to develop "formal population education" programs for schools to "encourage them [students] eventually to have smaller families."*

• *Supporting directly, and through the United Nations Fund for Population Activities, programs of coercion abroad—for example, in China, Indonesia, and Africa—that would not be tolerated in the United States, and then misdescribing these activities as being purely voluntary.*

I have tried to avoid excess in the essay's argument, as a contribution to keeping discussion of these matters in the realm of reasonable discourse and away from extremist boundaries. To this end, motivations are not analyzed, the focus is upon events and not individuals, and no mention is made of any activity for which the evidence is only hearsay or cannot be documented publicly.

Several suggestions are made for reform of the system.

This essay was first "published," in an earlier and more personal form, by my standing in the main reception room at the 1987 meeting of the Population Association of America next to a sign inviting passersby to take a copy of it and of related essays (Selections 23 and 24). Don Quixote for sure, except that Quixote had a knightly sense of himself whereas I have a six-year-old's sense of dignity. My willingness to play the buffoon—and if the negative consequences are not too serious, to enjoy it if it evokes some laughs—surely is counterproductive, but (I think to myself) what the hell.

As a device to illustrate the vicissitudes that a person offering an alternative to the conventional wisdom faces in attempting to find publication outlets and research funds, and the pressures on person and career, in an earlier draft I adduced some of my own experiences because they are available to me and I could document them. But two friendly critics replied that despite such difficulties as existed, I have been able to get most of my books published, and have my views heard to the extent that many persons are aware of them. One suggested delicately, and the other told me bluntly, that I seemed to be complaining. Therefore I have emended that material, though I believe that doing so weakens my argument. Write me if you would like to see a wad of this stuff.

Introduction

It is not pleasant or easy to believe that one's community distorts knowledge and suppresses truth out of self-interest.[1] It is natural to presume—a presumption which explains much conservative and pro-establishment action—that the established institutions serve the public welfare, especially an institution motivated by such good intentions, and populated by so many decent people, as the "population establishment" in the United States. But to refrain from criticizing on this ground serves no good.

The corruption mentioned in the title of this essay refers to the nexus of connections among research funding, individuals' perquisites, individual and institutional decisions about research topics to pursue, choices of people to hire and invite, emphasis placed upon various findings in the research, and sometimes the research conclusions themselves. In his 1982 presidential address to the Population Association of America, John Kantner candidly discussed the place of money in the thinking of the profession. This was his colorful description of the prior years:

> Heady times those, and something in it for everyone—the activist, the scholar, the foundation officer, the globe circling consultant, the wait-listed government official. World conferences, a Population Year, commissions, select committees, new centers for research and training, a growing supply of experts, pronouncements by world leaders and, most of all, money—lots of it.

I agree with Kantner that much of that activity is no loss because it was wasteful.[2] But I do not agree with him when he says that reduction in research funding[3]—aside from reduction in frills—is bad. I judge that much of the research bought with the funding was scientifically worthless or worse. More about this later.

The Population Establishment

The make-up of the "population establishment" as of the early 1970s was analyzed by Peter Bachrach and Elihu Bergman in *Power and Choice* (1973). When read today, their description of the closely woven pattern of people, organizations, and money that developed from 1956 to 1970 seems eerily up to date. The evolution of this establishment's views into national policy for the United States is set forth well in *World Population Crisis* (1973) by Phyllis Piotrow, a committed member of that establishment. The joining together of population and environmental issues is the only recent development.

The banner of that joining together is the Global Tomorrow Coalition (see Selection 55), which includes more than 50 organizations ranging from the Audubon Society to Zero Population Growth, and represents over 5 million members. The environmentalist movement is said by journalists to be among the two or three strongest lobbies in Washington. Its officers interlock, past and present, with each other, the State Department, AID, the Council for Environmental Quality, and other relevant government agencies. The Coalition is also interrelated with the Year 2000 Committee, whose 18 members include George Zeidenstein of the Population Council, Robert McNamara, George Mitchell (the Texas oil and real-estate billionaire who supports the Woodlands Conferences), and Walter Cronkite. GTC's publication *Interaction* (p. 11, date lost) boasts of its "elite Year 2000 Committee [which] is by design a small group of individuals . . . persons of such prominence, recognition, and accomplishment that they share a remarkable capacity for access to decision-making levels in both government and the private sector."

The various individual organizations in the GTC work together to promote federal legislation (see examples in Selections 45 and 55).

Support is drawn from broader-based organizations as well. For example, the main-line organization of U.S. scientists, the American Association for the Advancement of Science (AAAS), itself runs an active program of "research" on population and related matters, which is discussed at length below, and its flagship journal *Science* frequently carries news articles about population and environmental issues.

The population establishment operates worldwide. Domestic and international groups take on assignments with U.S. taxpayer money that cannot (for reasons of legality or "delicacy") be handled directly by AID or U.S.

Planned Parenthood. An official of OECD wrote this about the Pathfinder
Fund:

> . . . the relationship that has developed between Pathfinder and AID works well
> and is to the advantage of both parties. AID, which has always made extensive
> use of intermediary nongovernmental bodies in all sectors of its development
> programme, finds that in the field of population assistance, Pathfinder, with its
> close and varied contacts in developing countries, offers possibilities for action
> that it would often be difficult for it to take itself, operating on a direct
> government-to-government basis. Thus it has been able to finance some modest
> population work in countries where government population policies are still
> ambivalent (Tanzania, Zaire), or are in the very early stages (Rwanda, N.
> Yemen), or even are overtly negative (Bolivia, Paraguay). Sometimes the AID
> grant may even enable Pathfinder to make a first contact in a country that has
> hitherto been opposed to any kind of family planning activity (Pathfinder is
> hoping to discuss possibilities in both Burma and Malawi, for example). In other
> cases, while there may be no problem about the government's sympathies, it
> may still be desirable to undertake some particularly controversial activity on a
> purely private basis. . . . Where Pathfinder finances an activity out of the AID
> grant, it is AID's criteria that must be applied. . . . However, when these
> constraints become particularly irksome, Pathfinder is always free to use its
> private source funds for activities that AID will not support. (Wolfson, 1983,
> p. 173)

The United Nations Fund for Population Activities (UNFPA), in conjunction with the Population Crisis Committee and spearheaded by Werner
Fornos, has since 1978 been mobilizing the opinion of "parliamentarians"
throughout the world. This is how Fornos describes the effort in UNFPA's
publication *Populi* (Vol. 11, No. 1, 1984):

> The growing awareness among legislators in developing and industrialized coun-
> tries that rampant population growth must be contained is a major stride that
> has been achieved since the World Population Conference was held in Bucharest
> 10 years ago.

> Indeed, if the world is to cope successfully with the immense challenge of
> slowing down excessive global population growth, it is self-evident that legisla-
> tors must play an integral role.

> United Nations Secretary-General Javier Perez de Cuellar maintains the parlia-
> mentarians, as communicators between governments and peoples, are in "a
> unique position" to help secure policies appropriate for their time and place and
> to ensure the success of these policies once adopted.

The aim of exerting influence to reduce population growth rates, rather
than simply helping people plan their families, is obvious in the above
quotation, and the quotation gives the lie to the UNFPA's (and especially
the late head of UNFPA Raphael Salas') careful and frequent statements

about individual rights, as do numerous statements in the UNFPA's official "Declarations."

Conspiracy is not suggested, but rather a consensus of belief that leads to a concert of action which can be the equivalent of joint planning even if there is no actual joint planning. This may be seen in two decades of official pronouncements and media stories.

Some Examples of "Establishment" Activities

Regrettably, I cannot present a broadly based systematic investigation of this topic. Collecting a wide sample of evidence would be difficult due to lack of support, unwillingness of persons to weaken organizations they consider valuable, my own distaste for asking questions about such matters, and the infrequency with which the most pervasive abuses are put on paper.[4] Therefore, I shall simply relate a few events that I can document with written evidence. It should be noted that my direct access to documentation is small because I have not held office in any of the organizations under discussion, or participated formally or informally in their politics or governance (or been invited to participate); also, I have few friends who have been participants. All the more amazing, then, that even this much material is available.

Mellon Foundation Letter to the AAAS

A committee of the American Association for the Advancement of Science (AAAS) sought funds to study the relationship of population, resources, and the environment. Among other potential funding sources, the committee turned to the Andrew W. Mellon Foundation and received a "feasibility grant." This is an excerpt from a letter to AAAS discussing further funding, signed by J. Kellum Smith, Jr., Vice President and Secretary of that foundation:

> Because the links among population, resources, and environment are so obvious and strong, I was very much in favor of the idea that the AAAS seek ways of thinking systematically about those links. . . . I hope the suggestion of an alternative title [to the original one] does not indicate diffidence, in your group, on the matter of facing up to the malign consequences of rapid population increase. Should such diffidence exist, I would suppose that it might cripple the program and that therefore the exercise might as well be halted forthwith. . . .
>
> . . . the first task of the program must be to elucidate the links. . . . Suggestions for improvement of the situation will come along later; and when they do, most obvious and important among them will presumable be methods of reducing the rate of population growth. Social and technological accommodations to high

fertility, though perhaps of ancillary utility, are unlikely to be primary solutions. . . .

I am disconcerted by the suggestion that there is a problem in handling "the widely divergent views of the Cornucopians and Malthusians." If by "the Cornucopians" is meant Julian Simon and his few allies, I should think a footnote would be sufficient to dispose of them. . . .

If there is nervousness on the point, it had better be faced up to forthwith. The issue of population increase is central to the proposed program . . . the crucial element in any responsible approach to the overall problem will be restraint of population increase. Although it may be unscientific to make the statement that boldly, I do so because I think that outcome so highly probable that if your group finds it unpalatable perhaps the exercise should be abandoned. (January 12, 1984)

This letter came into my hands only because my name was in it and a friend on the committee wanted me to see it. I cannot know how many other similar letters are not seen by me to be reported here. And Mellon is one of the key sources of funding for population work. The full text of the Mellon letter is available from me on request by anyone who wishes to see the quotes in context.

The AAAS Project and the Response to Mellon

As a result of that demand that the outcome of the inquiry be fixed in advance as a condition of the funding, one of the members of the AAAS committee protested against what was happening, and left the committee. Nevertheless, the AAAS took whatever actions were necessary to satisfy the Mellon Foundation. The grant was made, and the project is under way. On May 30, 1986, *Science* announced that "a new interdisciplinary program on population resources, and the environment, supported by foundations is moving ahead. We mean to give it the best we have. . . ." The same editorial by AAAS chief executive William D. Carey also asserted that "On the bright side, China emerges as a model for economic development," and presumably for population policy as well (p. 1073). (It may also be relevant that the then-president-elect of AAAS, Gerard Piel, who is the Chairman of the Board of *Scientific American,* which has published many articles on our subject, denounced in an editorial in *Science* the position of the United States in Mexico City in 1984—misstating it in the process, I might say—as

Population increase, our representatives declared, is not of itself a bad thing. . . . On the supply side, they argued, intervention by the state must not be allowed to inhibit the response of sufficiently motivated entrepreneurs.

This advice, not endorsed by the delegations of other market economies [but quite consistent with the NAS report of 1986, as I read it], carries the faults inherent in prescription from narrow ideology [whatever that is]." (October 26, 1984)

In an editorial the following month, the then-president of AAAS wrote about "the relation of growing populations to aspects of social and economic development. Concern over these issues is also reflected in the creation of a AAAS Committee on Population, Resources and the Environment" (David A. Hamburg, November 16, 1984). And AAAS has long been active as an advocate of population control. The Controller General, in the Report to the Congress on AID (probably 1986, p. 55) mentioned:

Under a $1.2 million contract the American Association for the Advancement of Science organized working groups of U.S. and developing country anthropologists and others to provide policymakers with information on consequences of rapid population growth and to help family planning program administrators identify and modify cultural factors associated with expansion and improvement of family planning delivery systems.

Can there be doubt that, in a case like this one, there is danger that the conclusions have been affected by the views of the funding sources?

Loss of Research Funds for Disputing the Conventional Wisdom

An example of how people and institutions pay a price for voicing views that run against those of the establishment is found in the experience of the University of Pennsylvania population center. Its head, Samuel Preston, was the principal author of the "revisionist" NRC-NAS report. Mellon grants went to several population study centers in 1986, but a grant was denied to the University of Pennsylvania, one of the most prestigious among the centers. Preston is head of that center.

Laundering of AID Funds to Support Domestic Activities

The lengths to which institutions and individuals are willing to go to obtain funding money is illustrated by the unethical (if not illegal) money-laundering[5] that takes place whereby AID funds are funneled back (sometimes directly, sometimes through the United Nations Fund for Population Activities) to U.S. population organizations (e.g., Worldwatch, Population Institute, Population Crisis Committee, Institute of Society, Ethics and Life Sciences, Population Council, Pathfinder Fund, AVS, Planned Parenthood, and so on) and used for domestic population-control propaganda.

These activities are documented in my 1981 book; no question has been raised about the factual validity of that evidence in the years since publication. Evidence of the persuasive and ideological (in contrast to research) activities of all those organizations may also be found in that book.

Additional documentation arrived the day this is being written, an advertisement for "Globescope 87," a conference to be held April 29–May 1, 1987, organized by The Global Tomorrow Coalition in conjunction with the United Nations Environmental Program (UNEP) and Cleveland State University. This conference is a domestic activity of the environmental movement; the roster of speakers includes representatives from the entire range of environmentalist and population organizations. The "donors" include UNEP, funneling back into this domestic propaganda program money that it receives from U.S. taxpayers. Another "donor" is Worldwatch Institute, which gets money from UNFPA, which in turn gets money from U.S. taxpayers; in this case the money makes three stops after leaving the taxpayer. Other "donors" include National Wildlife Federation, National Audubon Society, World Resources Institute, and Population Crisis Committee, some of which almost surely get U.S. taxpayer money at present, both directly and by way of the U.N., though I have not been able to check the present status.

It should be kept in mind that I have made no systematic investigation of these matters since 1979. It would be interesting to learn what an inquiry into these flows of money could uncover. But no one is employed in tracking down this scandalous mess.

Propagandizing the U.S. Public

The extent to which one point of view—that population growth is bad—is accepted by the relevant professions, and promulgated as scientific fact, may be seen in the report on "Population Education in the Schools," by the Population Information Program at Johns Hopkins (March–April, 1982), which is funded with millions of dollars from AID. It begins: "Formal population education is designed to teach children in school about population issues and, in many cases, to encourage them eventually to have smaller families." The "education" programs are shot through with assertions about population, environment, and resources that have no scientific support and are founded upon a particular set of values. Planned Parenthood is so much involved with changing public opinion that it spent $197,000 to pay for advertisements opposing a nominee to the Supreme Court in 1987 (*Washington Post,* March 27, 1988, p. A8).

Buying the Political Action of Demographers

This item is revealing because of its amazing pettiness. At the IUSSP conference in Florence in 1985, a form was circulated by the Chair and the Past Chair of the Population and Family Planning Section of the American Public Health Association, which "facilitated" (their word) members of IUSSP sending telexes to their U.S. senators and congresspeople in opposition to the Kemp amendment. (That amendment was intended to prevent federal funds from going to any organization that "supports or participates in the management of a program of coercive abortion.") The organizers "facilitated" by providing the language for the telex, and stating that "Your message, sent by telex, will be adapted by APHA to suit the Senate and House situations. . . . All you need do is put your *name, home address and zip code* on this sheet and place it in boxes being distributed for the purpose" (italics in original).

The circulated cover memo also said, "If you are willing for a telex to be sent in your name, *at no cost to you* . . ." (italics in the original). Several persons who accepted the offer and sent telexes denied to me that they were influenced by wanting to keep funds flowing to such organizations as IUSSP, which finance a large part of the travel to the conference. He who pays the piper does *not* call the tune among IUSSP demographers, I was told by them. But clearly the persons who drafted the request thought that the tiny cost of a telex could affect people's propensity to telex their congressional representatives. And if a handful of dollars for a telex—less than the cost of a cheap meal—is thought by the *organizers* to influence IUSSP members, is it unreasonable to think that thousands of dollars of travel money and/or grant funds might have influence, too?

The cover memo is available upon request if you wish to see the quotes in context.

Predetermination of Research Conclusions by NIH

Much of the research work done with the money mentioned by Kantner in an earlier quotation was purchased to bolster one particular conclusion arrived at in advance, a conclusion that the data do not support. In 1979 the NIH Center for Population Research promulgated a Request for Proposals (RFP) for projects on the consequences of population growth in MDC's, following upon (if memory serves) two conferences in preparation of the RFP. The RFP contained this statement in introducing the subject: "The proposition was derived from these conferences that a reduction in the rate of population growth is both inevitable and useful." Such an introduction—and please keep in mind that it referred to MDC's and not

LDC's—is not likely to lead to unbiased research, and must surely discourage application for, and approval of, studies that would show positive consequences. In effect, those who responded to the RFP were handed the direction of the conclusions before they began. They were told which sides of the bread the butter was on.

The bias of federal research support can be seen in the list of topics discussed by the Interagency Committee on Population Research (ICPR) listed in the annual *Inventory and Analysis of Federal Population Research* published by NIH. Four to six topics have been discussed each year since 1970. There has not been a single listing that suggests the support of disinterested economic research concerning the effects of population change. But there have been such listings as "Foreign Public Opinion on Issues Relating to Population Control" (1972, note "Control"); "The United States Role in Resolving the World Population Problem" (1975, note "Problem"); "Report on a Trip to Asia to Study Population Problems, Programs, and Policies" (1976); "Observations of Recent Visit to China: Implications for Population Research" (1977); "Population and Energy Issues" (1980, in response to the oil price rise in 1979); "Global 2000 Study: Overview and Population Aspects" (1980); and "Impact of Population Change on Urbanization and Agricultural Land" (1980).

Influencing the Products of the NAS-NRC Study

My 1986 review of the NAS-NRC study (Selection 56) documents how the conclusions and the press release were affected by funding at Congressional pressure.

Starving of Research on the Consequences of Population Growth

A major reason for the poor state of knowledge about the consequences of population growth is that remarkably little research has been funded on the entire topic of population growth's consequences (perhaps on the assumption that the consequences are obvious). In preparation for a conference on future directions for population research held by the Rockefeller Foundation in 1981 or 1982, I looked at the 1976 and 1980 issues of the NIH *Inventory and Analysis of Federal Population Research,* which happened to be at hand. The topic "Consequences of population change" received funding of $134,000 for 3 projects in 1976, out of $18 million total for 227 projects in social and behavioral science. In 1980 the figures were $221,000 for 3 projects out of $33 million for 231 projects—much less than 1 percent in each year. More was spent on the consequences of animal behavior than of human behavior. Furthermore, the studies listed under the heading "population change" do not seem intended to assess economic changes.

In 1986, there was exactly one study on "consequences of population change," accounting for $50,000 among a total of $43 million for the "social and behavioral sciences" (page 28), a total of $203 million overall (p. 25), and that was a study of "Aging and the Interaction of Demography and Hearing Loss." Economics was listed as having one study, for $342,000 (p. 30); I could not determine which study that was, but odds are that it concerned the determinants rather than the consequences of population change.

I do not wish to judge studies that I have not examined, but I do note that Senator Proxmire could have a ball with his Golden Fleece Award amid such research titles as—here is just one page's sample that I picked almost randomly—"Female Partner Satisfaction," "Sexual Adjustment of Alcoholic, Maritally Conflicted, and Normal Couples," "Psychological Impact of Pregnancy for Rural Adolescents," "Attachment Across Generations in Families of Adolescents," "Consequences of Pregnancy Loss to Urban Adolescents," "Arousal and Anxiety in Dysfunctional Men and Women," "Eastern Caribbean Fertility Transition," and "Genetic Counseling and Reproductive Decision Making" (p. 172). And that represents well over a million dollars of taxpayer money. (The preceding page 171 goes for about $7 million of similar topics.) I am confident that inspection of the document from which I have drawn these examples will reassure the reader that I have not selected examples that misrepresent the overall situation.

Vast amounts of government funding go to support studies that might help implement policy that follows from the conclusion that population growth is bad—that is, studies of the determinants of fertility. I do not suggest that all or even most of that work is without scientific value. I do suggest, however, that its scientific payout relative to its cost would not seem favorable compared to many other things the society might do with its research budget, unless one assumes that there is a very high value in reducing population growth throughout the world. Yet the PAA (Population Association of America), through the Population Resource Center (PRC), officially lobbies for more money to be given for research.

Also relevant is the pattern of institutional funding. Large sums go to population organizations and to environmental organizations that are explicitly or implicitly antinatal (Simon, 1981, p. 298). I know of not a single penny going to any organization that might recognize any positive aspects of population growth. More generally, reduction of population growth is urged by a very large set of organizations, many of them part of the Global Tomorrow Coalition. On the other side are—*no organizations at all.*

Is it any wonder that those who espouse lowering population growth claim that "all informed persons agree" with their belief? They are so sure of the rightness of their views that they even call for stopping inquiry and discussion of the issues: In the words of Sirageldin and PAA President Kantner: "This is not an area for frivolous approaches [they were referring to my work] or one where academics may contend confusedly with no great harm to anyone. It is an area where an effective mobilization of public will and commitment based on understanding of issues is essential" (1982, p. 173).

Imagine yourself a demographer considering research into the consequences of population growth, facing the institutional situation described above. How would you conduct your professional life? It should not be surprising that the economic studies of the consequences of population change that have shown *positive* effects—for example, the effects of population change and density on productivity, investment in irrigation, road networks, agricultural practices and the like—have largely been done by persons who are not members of the demographic establishment, and mostly without funding by the organizations that ordinarily support population research. The real surprise is that with the incentive structure being what it is, few if any studies funded by population organizations (or any other studies, for that matter) have found empirical evidence of *negative* effects of population growth on long-run social or economic performance. It also seems amazing that despite all the research and publicity about the conventional view, there is as much public interest about (in Kantner's term) "revisionist" thinking as there is, as well as the positive reception that Kantner deplores.

Given this situation, cuts in funding of research by NIH, AID, and other sources may not be a social evil.

Support for Coercive Population Programs

The population establishment claims to be "pro-choice" with respect to the individual rights of women and couples. But at the same time, these organizations and individuals speak in favor of reducing population growth, a goal that is inconsistent with the goal of simply helping people attain their individual preferences. This leads them to the "consciousness-raising" dodge: If people don't want to do what you want them to do, press on them until they change their minds and are ready to do what you want. The most casual reading of population establishment documents—even the most carefully written of them, the UNFPA statements—make clear that this is the explicit strategy. And of course this is how the Chinese family-planning program obtains what it calls "voluntary" one-child families. (See Selection 24.)

Indeed, in their desire to reduce births—let us leave their motivation aside as not being a desirable subject of inquiry here—the population establishment has embraced China's population program. We have seen this earlier in the quotations from William Carey and Gerard Piel of AAAS. The UNFPA gave its first award to China (along with India), and Theodore W. Schultz, who was on the committee as a Nobel prizewinner, promptly resigned in protest, saying that the selection process "was a travesty completely at variance with the good faith with which I accepted your invitation. (His shocking letter of resignation, dated July 18, 1983, is available upon request.)

The central policy issue for the population establishment at the moment (1988) is to restore the AID funds that were cut from UNFPA in order that the money would not go to China for abortions. The emphasis on this is seen in the legislative "initiative" quoted earlier, and also in a series of expensive newspaper advertisements by Planned Parenthood (e.g., *The Washington Post,* March 12, 1987, p. A17), referring to those who want to cut the funds as "irresponsible extremists" who are "standing in the way" of "Women in the developing world [who] want choice." (See Figure 57-1.)

As this is being written, there arrived the *Newsletter* of Californians for Population Stabilization (formerly California ZPG), inviting the reader to attend an "Awards Dinner in Honor of The People's Republic of China." The details—please note the omnipresent Werner Fornos—are as follow:

Guest Speaker	Werner Fornos, President Population Institute, Washington D.C.
Comments and Film	Lin Guozhang, Deputy Consul General People's Republic of China
Entertainment	Chorus music during social hour
Roving Microphone	Available for commentary by individuals and organizations during dinner
Ceremonial	To honor People's Republic of China for acknowledging overpopulation and encouraging family planning.
Educational	To raise general awareness of California's elected representatives and public of the need for population concern abroad and at home. Information packets available for all guests.

Figure 57-1.

THE RIGHT-WING COUP IN FAMILY PLANNING.

#*1 in a series*

For two decades, poverty-stricken Third World countries have turned to the United States for help with their vital family planning efforts.

The aid has only cost you about a dollar a year, but the impact has been tremendous. Rapid population growth has slowed in some countries. In others, even the poorest families have been given the means to plan their own futures.

Millions of children have been spared the ravages of hunger. Thousands of women are alive today who would have died in their ninth or tenth or sixteenth pregnancy.

Planned Parenthood is proud to have played a leading role in helping the people in more than fifty nations help themselves. Where there was only desperation, we have brought hope.

Incredibly, however, everything we have achieved is now in jeopardy. In hot pursuit of an ideological victory, a handful of extremists at the White House and the Agency for International Development (A.I.D.) aim to destroy America's international family planning program—and Planned Parenthood in particular.

Their motive? Unable to impose their fanatical anti-family planning agenda on the American people, they have decided to victimize people who can't fight back.

It looks like an easy win, to them. And the fact is, unless *we* fight back, hardship and suffering will come to those who rely on us for help.

The very survival of women and children is at stake in this battle. So are the long-term prospects for dozens of developing countries.

In the next few weeks, we are going to tell you the full story of this disaster—who is at fault, what it will cost, and what you can do about it.

In doing so, we expose ourselves to attack from extremists who have proven they will stop at nothing. If that is the price, we will pay it. Because of all the rights we fight to defend, the most fundamental is the right to speak.

To protest the Administration's attack on international family planning, write M. Peter McPherson, Administrator, A.I.D., Room 5942, 320 21st Street, N.W., Washington, D.C. 20523. Send copies to your Senators and Representative.

If the extremists win, the whole world loses. Help us fight back.

⊡ Planned Parenthood

Social	To introduce members of the private public-interest sector to elected representatives and to each other; to explore the possibility of united action; to impress upon the members of the public-interest sector the impact of population growth upon their individual concerns.
Cultural	To introduce to California's elected representatives and the public-interest sector the people, philosophies, problems, and concerns of the People's Republic of China in a relaxed atmosphere of food, drink and general good fellowship.

The above may seem like a satire, but I assure you that it is direct quotation.

PAA Involvement with Political-Activist PRC

Concerning the financial and personnel relationship between the Population Resource Center (PRC) and the Population Association of America (PAA): (1) The publicly stated basis for the connection lacks justification. And (2) the connection supports activities that are obviously inappropriate for a scientific organization. These two matters will be examined in order.

1. The PAA-PRC connection is said by the officials of the PAA to be good for the demographic profession. More specifically, it is said that the PRC acts as the PAA's "eyes and ears in Washington" to help get more money for demographic research. (Yes, money again.) That the PAA *ought* to lobby for more money is simply assumed to be an unquestioned good thing.[7] There is apparently no concern that (a) the research funds in question come from taxpayers, and (b) there may be other uses of the resources that may be of higher social value than the demographic research which might be foregone—even (!) the spending of the moneys for their personal use by the taxpayers who earn the money. Perhaps demographers believe that what they are doing is more important than what others do— a belief held by almost every other known group of human beings, of course, and therefore suspect because of the mutual inconsistency in those views. Or perhaps demographers simply believe that it is justification enough that the funds will do good for their own group, a view that is cynical even if it is common. Neither of these propositions is self-evident or is supported by evidence, and therefore the PAA's tie with PRC is unjustified.

2. The funds that go to PRC come from PAA members' dues, and are commingled with other PRC funds which go to further purposes that at least some members find partisan and objectionable. PRC is a politically oriented group working to advance the idea that population growth is a

danger and ought to be controlled. No one with even slight knowledge of the population movement can look at the Board of Directors—which includes names like Harriet Pilpel, Richard Benedick, Charles F. Westoff, and Congressman John E. Porter—without knowing that this is an organization dedicated to reducing the world birth rate. It is unfair to tax members to support activities that run against their professional knowledge and personal values.

In 1982, as part of a longer letter to the officers of PAA (from which I have extracted other paragraphs above) I complained as follows about the association of PAA and PRC, as mediated by the PAA Public Affairs Committee:

Particularly inappropriate is the matter of the PAA's Public Affairs Committee. This group of persons is designated by the PAA to give PAA's "official" view to Congress and bureaucrats about public policy related to demographic issues. Such a group inevitably creates the impression that its pronouncements are settled scientific doctrine. And it pronounces not only about strictly demographic variables, but also about issues concerning food, immigration, resources, and so on.

For example, the description of the activities of the Public Affairs Committee as of Fall 1982 includes this description of "The Project on Population and the Private Sector":

> designed to identify specific areas of mutual interest and concern both to private corporations and to organizations working in the field of population and international development. . . . Executives from U.S. corporations were brought together with senior leaders from the U.N. Fund for Population Activities, the U.S. Agency for International Development, the State Department, foundations, private population and development groups and the U.S. Congress. . . . Five major points of intersection between the interests of the corporate community and those of population and development organizations were identified by the participants in this Project:

> . . . *creation of a more favorable environment for investment, trade, and commerce in Third World countries over the medium and long term,* which will be assisted by reductions in adverse population pressures . . ." (*P.A.A. Affairs,* Fall 1982, p. 1, italics in original).

Not only is this out-and-out propaganda for one point of view—a point of view that, at a minimum, may now be said to be a matter for mainstream controversy [see the 1986 NAS report], but also suggests that the reason for U.S. involvement in world population control is for self-interest rather than for "humanitarian" motives—the Ravenholt scandal again [see Simon, 1981]. To assert that the PAA's involvement is solely in connection with purely "technical demographic" matters is simply throwing dust in the eyes of those who question the matter.

Furthermore, the PAA Public Affairs Committee does this in "collaboration" (*PAA Affairs,* Summer 1982, p. 2) with the Population Resource Center. The latter organization says that it "does not espouse a particular population program or philosophy to 'solve' population problems" (1981 *Annual Report,* p. 2). But it clearly evinces the belief that population growth in LDC's and elsewhere is a bad thing. (This shows through in its *Annual Report* and *Executive Summary,* and it is signaled clearly in the Population Resource Center's participating membership in the Global Tomorrow Coalition along with such organizations as Environmental Fund, FAIR, Negative Population Growth, Population Crisis Committee, Population Institute, U.S. Club of Rome, World Population Society, ZPG, and a host of environmental organizations.)

Since I first made the above complaint I have found that—contrary to the "nonespousal" quoted above from *PAA Affairs*—"The Public Affairs Committee has been working hard through its association with the Population Resource Center (Fall 1982, p. 1)" on the "Project" mentioned above. But curiously, this "project" was claimed by PRC as an apparent sole activity in its 1981 "Year-End Report." Such is the close association between PAA and PRC.

The nondissociation of the PAA from these political and ideological and propagandistic "briefings" is made crystal-clear by the following extract from *PAA Affairs:*

Public Affairs Committee
Michael Teitelbaum and Al Hermalin delivered the committee's report with the assistance of Anne Harrison Clark of the Population Resource Center. During 1981, the Population Resource Center, in collaboration with PAC, organized 24 briefings and policy discussions in 16 cities involving over 70 PAA members. The sessions involved the connections between population factors and a wide range of policy issues on the local, state, national and international levels. Representatives from private foundations, Congress, U.S. Government agencies, State and Local governments, international organizations and private corporations participated in these discussions. A brochure outlining these sessions is available from the Population Resource Center and summaries of the briefings are available from the Population Reference Bureau. Another busy year of briefings is anticipated and may well be highlighted by an invitation to provide a large briefing for the National Governor's Association. PAC and the past, present, and future presidents of PAA have sent a letter to all members of Congress to protest provisions of the "super Hyde" bill sponsored by Sen. Helms that would prohibit all research related to abortion.

PAC also has provided input to the debate concerning the Population Policy Bill and to the Immigration Reform and Control Act of 1982. PAC has provided advice concerning witnesses and issues to the agencies of Congress involved with these matters. PAC has also sponsored and will continue to sponsor meetings with key members of the federal administration to assure that the interests of the population research are well known to those conducting oversight of population data gathering and research support. (*PAA Affairs*, Summer, 1982, p. 2)

Hewlett Foundation funds are given for this PAA activity. This is said to absolve the PAA of responsibility for PRC. But if the funds for the activity come from elsewhere, why are they channeled through PAA?

The continuing organizational goals of PRC are made clear by the background of the president it installed in 1987.

Jane S. De Lung has been chosen to be the new President of the Population Resource Center. De Lung brings to the Center twenty years of experience in family planning, demographic research in the health and human service area, and public policy. Recently, De Lung started her own consulting firm through which she designed a $7.1 million demonstration project working with teen mothers on welfare. She also assisted in a demonstration project to increase minority male participation in family planning and reproductive health clinics. (*PAA Affairs*, Winter 1987, pp. 2–3)

Ad Hominem Attacks Upon Persons Perceived as Threats

The extent to which an establishment is prepared to go in defense of its beliefs and perogatives can be judged by the tactics that it uses. Standard for the population establishment are vilification, religion-baiting, and aspersions on the motives of those who disagree with them. These are some frequently used varieties of the ad hominem device: (1) Allege that the person making the charge is paranoid. (Even if true, so what?) (2) Say that the person making the charge is motivated by the sense of failure and the desire to get even because of the failure. (Again, even if true, so what?) (3) Dismiss the person making the charge as a pathological arguer who gets his or her kicks by saying the opposite of everyone else. (No notice is taken of the fact that science is only useful when its findings are counterintuitive and counterconventional. Under such circumstances it has high "information value," in the sense of information theory.) (4) Say that the person making the charge has another axe to grind. The press is particularly quick to speculate that one's motivation is either an "ideology" or a money payoff from a business organization.

It is simply unbelievable to many that a person may be mainly motivated by the feeling of a responsibility to determine the scientific truth and then bring it to people's attention, just for its own sake, in the belief that in the long run the human enterprise is best served by the truth. Dismissing this as a possible motivation is a sad commentary on the members of the profession who say it.

Colin Clark, a world-class economist who might well have won a Nobel prize if he had not spoken out about population growth, was for long the target of much abuse and belittling as a way of getting rid of his views. When discussing his work, Lincoln and Alice Day refer to him as "Colin Clark, an internationally known Roman Catholic apologist" (1964, p. 134). And Ehrlich, Ehrlich, and Holdren (1977, p. 807) embellish a bit more by calling him an "elderly Catholic economist." I feel confident that if the Days, the Ehrlichs, and all the other respected members of the population establishment were to discover comparable racial epithets made by someone in public life—even if the remarks were made privately (as with Earl Butz or Jesse Jackson), let alone in print—these good people would be up in arms to pillory the epithet-maker. But there is no campaign to pillory the Days, the Ehrlichs, and the Hardins.

Reluctantly, I shall resist the temptation to quote the choicer descriptions that I, too, have been granted over the years.

Suggestions for Changes

It is always more attractive, and usually more virtuous, to go beyond criticism and offer suggestions for changes to mitigate problems being criticized. In that spirit, I offer the following suggestions to the PAA, the only organization among those referred to here to which I belong. Furthermore, as a professional organization, it has special responsibilities not to further any political ideology. I also have a few brief suggestions for the professional journals in the field, and for the federal grant process.

1. The PAA should sever its connection with the PRC.
2. If some connection between PAA and PRC is to continue, it would seem reasonable to "balance" it with equal support for one or more organizations with an opposite interest. I believe that this is a vastly inferior suggestion to the first one, however, because I believe that *all* such partisan activity is inappropriate, and furthermore, it would be difficult to produce truly "separate but equal" treatment.
3. Whether *all* PAA "public affairs" activities should be terminated, and whether there should be a Public Affairs Committee, given the difficulty of constituting it to provide a fair and balanced view, are matters requiring serious discussion. Given the unsavory history, the Committee's activities should at least be halted until such an investigation is complete.
4. If there is to be a Public Affairs Committee, it not only should have balanced representation, but it should have no special formal or informal relationship to a special-interest lobbying organization such as Population Resource Center.

5. If a PAA president gives a partisan presidential address that will then be published in PAA's official journal, *Demography*, as with Kantner's, space for rebuttal should be made available.
6. The official journal *Demography* should find ways to publish work on the consequences of population change, along with work on the determinants and on mathematic demography. And it should ensure that all sides of the matter are represented. I believe that it will be possible to find papers which meet the highest "professional" standards if the conventional prejudices are not operating.

In the United States (unlike the U.S.S.R.) the difficulties for unconventional research do not stem from conspiracy or centralized authority, as discussed in Selection 54. The main difficulty is that (by definition) most potential referees and editors hold the conventional view. That a view runs counter to what was learned in graduate school is enough to have it adjudged as "kooky" and without merit. (I suggest a possible solution at the end of Section 54.)

References

Peter Bachrach, and Elihu Bergman, *Power and Choice: The Formulation of American Population Policy*, Lexington Books, Lexington, Mass., 1973.

Ansley Coale, and Edgar M. Hoover, *Population Growth and Economic Development in Low-Income Countries*, PUP, Princeton, 1958.

Lincoln H. Day, and Alice Day, *Too Many Americans*, Houghton Mifflin, New York, 1964.

Paul R. Ehrlich, Anne H. Ehrlich, and John P. Holdren, *Ecoscience: Population, Resources, Environment*, 2d ed., W. H. Freeman, San Francisco, 1977.

————, "Review of *The Resourceful Earth*," in *Bulletin of the Atomic Scientists*, February 1985, p. 44.

Alexander H. Everett, *New Ideas in Population 1826/1970*, A. M. Kelley, New York.

Werner Fornos, "A Time For Action," *Populi*, vol. 11, no. 1, 1984, pp. 32–35.

David A. Hamburg, "Population Growth and Development," *Science*, vol. 226, no. 4676, November 16, 1984.

Garrett Hardin, *The New Republic*, October 28, 1981, pp. 31–34.

Henry Hazlitt, *Economics in One Lesson*, 2d ed., Arlington House, New York, 1962.

Jack Hirshleifer, "The Expanding Domain of Economics," *The American Economic Review*, vol. 75, December 1985.

Constance Holden, "A Revisionist Look at Population and Growth," *Science*, vol. 231, March 28, 1986, pp. 1493–1494.

"Implications for U.S. Policy of the NAS Report on Population Growth and Economic Development: Policy Questions," Xerox, March 6, 1986.

Frederick S. Jaffe, cited in Simon, 1981, taken from Robin Elliott, Lynn C. Landman, Richard Lincoln, and Theodore Tsuruoka, "U.S. population growth and family planning: a review of the literature," 1970, in *Family Planning Perspectives,* vol. 2, repr. in Daniel Callahan, ed., *The American Population Debate,* Anchor Bks., New York, 1971, p. 206.

Dina Kaminskaya, *Final Judgment: My Life as a Soviet Defense Attorney,* Simon and Schuster, New York, 1982.

John F. Kantner, "Population Policy and Political Atavism," *Demography,* (forthcoming).

Allen C. Kelley, "The National Academy of Sciences Report on Population Growth and Economic Development," *Population and Development Review,* vol. 12, September, 198 pp. 569–577.

Ronald Lee, "Economic Consequences of Population Size, Structure and Growth," International Union for the Scientific Study of Population Newsletter no. 17, January–April 1983, pp. 43–59.

———, "Review of *World Development Report 1984,*" *Population and Development Review,* March 11, 1985, pp. 127–130.

William Paul McGreevey, "World Development Report 1984—Two Years Later," Xerox, April 1986.

National Research Council, Committee on Population, and Working Group on Population Growth and Economic Development, *Population Growth and Economic Development: Policy Questions,* National Academy Press, Washington, D.C., 1986.

Don Oldenburg, "Whistle Blower's Anguish," *The Washington Post,* March 31, 1987, p. C5.

Gerard Piel, "Let Them Eat Cake," *Science,* vol. 226, no. 4673, October 26, 1984.

Phyllis Piotrow, *World Population Crisis,* Praeger, New York, 1973.

Population and Family Planning Section American Public Health Association, Memo to "All US Citizens, Members and Attendees at the IUSSP Conference," undated.

Robert Repetto, "Why Doesn't Julian Simon Believe His Own Research?", Letter to the editor, *The Washington Post,* Nov. 2, 1985, p. A21.

Theodore W. Schultz, *Investing in People,* University of Chicago Press, Chicago, 1981.

Julian L. Simon, "The Concept of Causality in Economics," *Kyklos,* vol. 23, fasc. 2, 1970, pp. 226–254.

———, *The Economics of Population Growth,* PUP, Princeton, 1977.

———, *The Ultimate Resource,* PUP, Princeton, 1981.

———, "Disappearing Species, Deforestation, and Data", *New Scientist,* May 15, 1986, pp. 60–63.

——— and Paul Burstein, *Basic Research Methods in Social Science,* Random House, New York, 3d ed., 1985.

Ismail Sirageldin, and John F. Kantner, "Review," *Population and Development Review,* March 1982, pp. 169–173.

Margaret Wolfson, *Profiles in Population Assistance,* Development Centre of the Organization for Economic Co-operation and Development, 1983.

Forthcoming in Godfrey Roberts (ed.), *Population Policy*

Notes

Samuel Preston, Donald Warwick, and Susan Watkins gave me useful advice about this essay.

Before writing this article and aiming it for a "public" audience, I have raised many of these matters "internally" to the profession—in long letters with much of the documentation contained herein, to two presidents of the PAA, to the IUSSP, and to the president and chief executive and board of the AAAS. And there have been people within the "establishment" who have conscientiously given a public hearing to the views about population economics that I espouse, or have themselves fairly represented similar views, and on some occasions suffered for doing so. Among these persons are Richard Easterlin, Allen Kelley, Dudley Kirk, Ronald Lee, Larry Neal, William Peterson, Edmund Phelps, Samuel Preston, and Theodore W. Schultz. Scholars in this category but outside the establishment include Colin Clark, Thomas deGregori, Nicholas Eberstadt, Milton Friedman, Friedrich Hayek, Jacqueline Kasun, and Alan R. Waters. There are others in both categories whom I have unfortunately forgotten. I hope that none of these persons is embarrassed by being included in the list.

It surely is because of their professional knowledge of what is at heart an economic subject—the usable-resource effect of population growth—that almost all of the persons in the list are economists. It is more puzzling that many of the most zealous persons on the other side of the issue are biologists. The only explanation I can offer is that biologists assume the absence of the peculiarly human adjustment mechanisms which are the crux of the difference between human and animal systems.

1. An interesting example of the reluctance to believe otherwise is Dina Kaminskaya the attorney with the most experience in defending Soviet dissidents, and the person who had shown the most courage in doing so, She tells in her memoirs (1982) how difficult it was to believe that psychiatric treatment is used for repressive purposes in the U.S.S.R.

    For completeness, I note that the United States also is not perfect in this respect. Psychiatry has been misused for political purposes here, too. See Oldenburg (1987).

2. For example, after seeing how much money was obviously being spent for the meeting of the International Union for the Scientific Study of Population (IUSSP) in Helsinki in 1979, I consulted the Union's annual report. Extraordinary sums were being received from governments (at the same time that membership fees were going up by leaps and bounds) and then being disbursed mostly for travel and meetings, with the attendees seeming to be part of a well-orchestrated international old boy's club. Not being on the gravy train certainly makes it

easier to feel that the train should be stopped. But even some of those who are on that train are appalled by the waste.

3. Kantner refers to this as "an outbreak of criticism aimed at the foundation of population policy." This he considers as "add[ing] insult to [funding] injuries I have been reviewing" (p. 13). This is the "line of argument which, for convenience, we may refer to as 'revisionist.' " (I do not like the label, but will use it for convenience here.)

4. The reader will understand that because of the evanescent nature of the process under discussion, it is most difficult to find hard evidence. The business usually is conducted with "You know what I mean?" and a wink. And it is discussed after pledge of confidentiality; for example, staff members of the U.N. have told me privately that they knew that aspects of working papers for the Mexico City conference twisted the facts because that was what was wanted, but I cannot document the conversations or even attribute them.

Peter J. Donaldson, in studying "The Origins and Implementation of America's International Population Policy" (PAA paper, 1987), read through many files concerned with AID operations. He found that

> Much of interest and impact was not put in writing. In a typical example, one AID official wrote of a committee report on America's foreign assistance, "All concerned should realize that this report was prepared for the President, and therefore there are certain things in it that one must read between the lines." (General Advisory Committee, 9.,2, World Food Situation, 286-73-159)

6. By "money laundering" I mean transfers of funds that enable the funds to be used for purposes not intended, not acknowledged, or not legal by the original donors.

7. PAA president George Stolnitz wrote as follows:

> As to the Population Resource Center and its relations to the PAA, it is enough to relate that half of PAA's funding to the Center for Association purposes is to foster active "lobbying" support for precisely the non-policy advocacy objectives stated above. The other half of PAA's funding of the Center's work for us, financed by a Hewlett grant to PAA, is for educational briefings on factual population trends. Such briefings are conditioned by the precisely *specified* understanding between the Center and PAA that substantive-policy advocacy positions or other normative positions are to be avoided. So far as others and I can tell, such instructions have been scrupulously observed. (Letter of April 22, 1983)

58

Population Control and the High
Moral Ground

This selection erupted after years of frustration at observing the population-control and environmentalist organizations accuse those who disagree with them of being (among other negative characteristics) venal, devoid of public spirit, and shortsighted, while they say lovely things about themselves and their motives. I do not claim that all persons within that movement share all of the sentiments and views discussed in this piece. But the organizations work together, and they do not disavow these sentiments and views of the others. Hence it does not seem unfair to lump them together in this fashion. And common intellectual threads connect these views—notably the desire for more government intervention, and a relative lack of interest in individual freedom.

The most striking characteristic of the population movement—at least to me—is the willingness to decide upon life or death for others, based on their own values and their own assessments of the objective facts as well as the meaning of life to others. And this seems particularly salient among biologists. Many examples are given in The Ultimate Resource. *For a more recent example, Daniel Koshland, editor of* Science, *writes: "To feed starving populations is desirable, but if new crops help add a billion people to a crowded globe, is that necessarily good?" (June 5, 1987, quoted in* The Wall Street Journal, *July 28, 1987, p.32).*

The population-control "establishment"—the fifty or so organizations whose names run from Audubon Society to Zero Population Growth, and

557

include more than five-million members—claims the moral high ground for its point of view.

For example, Planned Parenthood recently ran an expensive series of advertisements in *The Washington Post* and *The New York Times,* as well as on Washington buses and in the subways, describing those who disagree with them as "fanatical" and as "extremists . . . driven by ideology, uninfluenced by facts or ethical considerations, let alone the actual needs of hundreds of millions of people." Their headline slogan is "If the extremists win, the whole world loses."

The population controllers work both sides of the street, too. The target of the first Planned Parenthood Campaign was people who opposed giving U.S. money to China's self-admittedly coercive population program. Then PP turned around and ran another full-page ad denouncing Robert Bork for a position that PP only *imputed* to him: "State-Controlled Pregnancy? It's not as far-fetched as it sounds. Carrying Bork's position to its logical end, states could ban or require any method of birth control, impose family quotas for population purposes, make abortion a crime, or sterilize anyone they choose." The hypocrisy of PP in the service of whatever it wants politically at the moment is breathtaking.

All others have let go unchallenged the moral claims of the population establishment. Not a word has been written in opposition to the Planned Parenthood ads, for example, except for a column by George Will that chides them for practicing the politics of paranoia.

The pro-population-control people believe they have compassion and decency on their side. They say they are motivated by selfless sympathy for all persons in the world. By contrast, they regard those who disagree with them—call us the "pro-population-freedom" people—as lacking compassion. And they accuse the "freedom" people of being motivated by "narrow" interests.

In truth, the shoe is on the other foot. To a greater or lesser extent, the population controllers are motivated by sectarian self-interest. To boot, their position is tinged with racism, if not in intent then at least in practice. The foreign governments that implement the U.S. population establishment's point of view—among others China, Indonesia, and India from time to time—engage in documented coercive practices that are unacceptable to most Americans.

One reason that the pro-freedom people have not disputed the moral claims of the population-control movement is because we believe that arguments about motivation are odious. A second reason is that there have been exactly zero organizations dedicated to the pro-population-freedom point of view in the United States.

The pro-controllers claim to help people get what they want by assisting couples avoid "unwanted" children. Actually, they attempt to foist off upon other people their own desires that fewer children be born into the world. They pressure couples to have fewer children than the couples desire because the pro-controllers believe that will speed economic development. And in their name, the U.S. government pressures foreign countries to pressure their citizens to reduce fertility below what couples would freely desire.

In contrast, the pro-freedomists are not against birth control. We are four-square in favor of helping people obtain the number of children that they want. We don't want to pressure people in either direction. The slogan that Planned Parenthood used at one time—"Children by choice, not chance"—expresses our belief exactly. So—just which side really is "pro-choice"?

The pro-controllers believe that governments improve the lives of the poor by "guiding" their family behavior. In practice, that means restricting poor peoples' choices by limiting couples to one child in China. In contrast, we have faith in the judgment of the poor, like the nonpoor, to make decisions that will be best for them and for their families.

Because the pro-controllers believe that breastfeeding would be better, they claim to improve the health of children by stopping the sale of infant formula to nursing mothers. In contrast, we are in favor of providing to mothers as much information about the characteristics of formula as possible, and then letting them decide what to do. Mothers are best able to judge the optimal combination of breast feeding and formula, given the demands of their own lives, we believe. Again, is it not we who are really pro-choice rather than the population establishment?

The population establishment claims to work for a better future of the human species. In that name, their movement has long favored eugenic practices. From Francis Galton to Margaret Sanger to William Shockley, they have invoked supposedly objective scientific findings to justify increased fertility for some groups and decreased fertility for others.

We say that those ideas can be used in favor of whichever group one belongs to. Remember the arguments used against the immigration of Slavs and Jews early in this century, and also the death camp experiments under Hitler? We consider it arrogant—biologically, psychologically, and sociologically—to think that one knows which "strain" of human beings will better serve humanity in the long run, or whether any reduction in the variety of humans will help the species. (Personally, I would guess that any *increase* in variety would be of benefit in the long run.)

Supposedly on behalf of the human species, the controllers urge reducing the number of human beings. This seems most peculiar to us. They say that more people means poorer survival chances for the species. We read the evidence and the theory as suggesting that a larger rather than a smaller number of human beings is favorable in the long run for our species just as for as other species. This research fits hand-in-glove with our value that people not be pressured to have fewer children.

Again claiming to be working for the human species, the pro-controllers are prepared to trade trees for people, and baboons for babies. In 1984, a California medical team replaced the defective heart of "Baby Fae" with the heart of a baboon. But Lucy Shelton, the "southern California coordinator" for the animal-rights group that demonstrated against the operation, said: "We oppose the killing of a perfectly healthy baboon." In contrast, we believe that human lives are more precious than the lives of trees and baboons, without qualification. (You ask: What about one human life versus a whole country's forests? Such unrealistic scenarios impede reasonable discussion.)

The pro-controllers say they want less human suffering. But they want themselves to be the judges of the suffering, and then make the choices about who will be allowed to live and who not. Sheldon of the animal-rights group continued, "We feel all they are doing is prolonging the suffering of the child." The pro-freedomists, on the other hand, say that the parents of the baby have the best right to judge. And we suspect that the anti-suffering argument is phony and is put forth simply to help save the life of the baboon.

According to the pro-controllers, low-income people in India suffer so much—presumably because they lack the autos, college educations, and jet vacations that the pro-controllers enjoy—that their lives are not worth living. With this assumption, the controllers justify birth-control programs to prevent those Indian lives from happening. In contrast, the pro-freedomists believe that the pro-controllers do not know enough about human nature (nor do we) to decide such matters for other people. Hence we say that, based on their own life experiences, Indian couples are the best judges whether the lives of their potential children are worth living. We feel our view is more respectful of persons, and therefore more moral, than is the pro-control view.

The pro-controllers redefine couples' wants in the interest of the population establishment's goal. They refer to a baby as "unwanted" if the woman says that before the baby was conceived she did not want it. The father's desire is excluded from this definition, as is the jointly decided desire of the couple. And a mother's change of heart after the baby is born does not count.

The pro-controllers want the government to prevent "unwanted children" by raising women's consciousness to ignore the wishes for children of her husband and the couple's parents. We think that individuals and privately funded organizations have every right to conduct such campaigns. But we do not want the government to judge whose hand is to be strengthened or whose consciousness is to be raised, partly because we worry about the possible misuse of such power in favor of whoever has it at the moment.

The pro-controllers say such government actions are necessary because of past male exploitation. We say that such arguments can be twisted in favor of any group. They accuse us of wanting to force couples to have "unwanted" babies. In fact, we advocate that governments not meddle in the decision-making of individual families in favor of either wife nor husband. Is the pro-control position moral and ours immoral? Or vice versa?

They claim "concern" for the poor peoples of the world. Their way to deal with the troubles of the poor is to reduce the number of these people—a very different prescription than making them less poor.

They are prepared to take away the power to procreate of poor women in Virginia and India, by sterilizing them against their wills. We believe that a system that allows more people in any category to live is better for that category of people—including the poor, as well as people of all colors.

The pro-controllers say that they are for reproductive freedom. We say that interfering with people's freedom to choose and have as many children as they like—for example, the fines in China for bearing more than one child, and the forced sterilizations of poor black women in Virginia, programs supported by the population establishment—is the worst sort of offense against reproductive freedom. Our approach to reproductive freedom is to respect everyone's right to have as many or as few children as they wish, and to assist them with knowledge of how to do so.

Many pro-controllers are so sure of the rightness of their causes that they lie (as the Club of Rome later confessed it lied in its *Limits to Growth* book), exaggerate (Planned Parenthood's claim to reduce crime and other social ills with population control) and cheat (the United Nations laundering population funds from AID on its way to U.S. organizations). The pro-controllers happily tap the U.S. taxpayers for hundreds of millions of dollars every year for population activities, much of which goes into the pockets of the U.S. population establishment groups and leaders. And they commonly use atrocious rhetoric to achieve their ends. For example, Roger Conner, head of Federation for American Immigration, claims that the U.S. exploits immigrants—legal as well as illegal—in a fashion akin to slavery. We believe that such tactics would not be justified by any ends, let alone by the ends the pro-controllers have in mind.

The pro-controllers say that aliens suffer so much from "exploitation" by employers that the United States should not allow guestworkers. We pro-freedomists believe that potential temporary immigrants are the best judge of whether their "suffering" is worse under such conditions of employment, or in their lives at home without temporarily migrating to work in the United States. And we wish to make illegals legal to avoid any abuses that may occur because of their unlegal status. Again we believe that our view respects persons better than does the pro-control view.

Barring individuals from moving across national boundaries is justified by the pro-controllers in the name of the abstract principle of national sovereignty. Pro-freedomists see national sovereignty as quite compatible with people freely moving from country to country as they wish, and as they have been able to in other times and places, regulated as little as possible and only for specific reasons. As with many of the differences between pro-freedomists and pro-controllers, we are on the side of liberty, whereas they want to restrict people to the options the pro-controllers themselves think acceptable.

The pro-controllers denounce slavery and exploitation. But they approve of denying individuals the opportunity to move from the countryside to cities in China and elsewhere, arguing that the cities are too crowded. We pro-freedomists consider this control a new form of feudalism. And our desire to let people move as they like is supported by economic research which concludes that in the end a policy of free movement will have the best economic effects for both city and country.

The pro-controllers claim to be selfless and generous. But they justify reducing immigration "to help the working people" of the United States. And they support population control in foreign countries—the long-time director of the Office of Population of the Agency for International Development, physician Reimert Ravenholt, was especially vocal on this point— to assist our foreign trade. The proposition is economic nonsense, but the motive clearly is the purely selfish economic welfare of U.S. citizens.

By contrast, the pro-freedomists favor allowing more immigrants to come if they wish. And we hope that people abroad will have the children that they desire. Whose program is more generous and selfless?

The pro-controllers habitually compare existing imperfect alternatives that they do not like against more attractive but unattainable scenarios. For example, they compare a U.S. guestworker program against rapid economic development in Mexico, which would keep potential migrants at home. This sort of arguments rules out the alternative—immigration—that people choose but which the pro-controllers do not like. But rapid economic development in Mexico is not within our power. We think it more honest to compare only the reasonably attainable alternatives so as not to compel people to accept worse alternatives than the alternatives that they prefer.

The pro-controllers claim to be for "all the people," whereas they say the pro-freedomists are for "narrow" ideology and groups. But the Simpson-Mazzoli immigration law they supported is sufficiently compatible with anti-Hispanic racism so that even the main sponsor—Senator Alan Simpson—said the motivation of some supporters was racist.

The 1960s program of opening birth-control clinics in the United States was demonstrably linked to racism. Statistical analyses by sociologists Kammeyer, Yetman, and McClendon, and by me, show that the primary variable explaining which states opened clinics earliest was not low-income need, but rather the proportion of the population that is black—as is obvious even without the statistical analysis. Have the Deep-South states of Alabama, Georgia, South Carolina, Mississippi—who led the way establishing the clinics—generally been known for undertaking "progressive" social measures ahead of the rest of the states? I mention this event not because we pro-freedomists oppose the clinics but rather to spotlight which side has which motivations.

All of these comparisons make clear that the pro-controllers have contempt for the intellectual and spiritual capacities of poor people. In contrast, we respect the capacities of poor people in all countries to conduct their lives as wisely as possible given the conditions they face.

The pro-controllers urge building nature preserves, and caring for the environment, on behalf of future generations. But their population policy goes exactly the other way. It aims to take account of the welfare only of those who are alive right now, ignoring the benefits that additional people now will create for future generations. With respect to these long-run benefits, they constantly quote Keynes' silly pronouncement that "In the long run we are all dead." Such a generationally selfish population policy does not at all square with their ecological views that we ought to bequeath a better world to those who follow after us.

In contrast, we think that our taking into account the welfare of future generations in both ecology and population growth is not only consistent but also is appropriately generous.

The pro-controllers worry about our use of resources on grounds that coming generations will be victimized by our generation. In fact, greater use of natural resources generally leads to larger supplies of resources for future generations due to the new discoveries that are induced. Furthermore, for centuries each generation has tended to be richer than the one that went before, contrary to the laments of our newly arrived yuppies. Why then should a less-wealthy current generation subsidize more wealthy generations to come?

Even more fundamental is the contradiction between the truly pro-life concern voiced by pro-control organizations about nuclear war and pollution, and their advocacy of population control, which is purely anti-life. Of course the pro-freedomists also are against war and pollution—who isn't?—but we are also in favor of increasing life.

The aim of all these comparisons is not to make the pro-controllers seem to be baddies, or to cloak the pro-freedomists in virtue. What we need is less discussion of general motives, and more discussions of individual programs. Let's judge governmental population activities on their merits, not on the basis of who speaks for or against them, or on the basis of claims of high morality on the part of advocates.

Books by the Same Author

Population Economics

The Effects of Income on Fertility (1974)
The Economics of Population Growth (1977)
The Ultimate Resource (1981)
Theory of Population and Economic Growth (1986)
The Economic Consequences of Immigration (1989)
Essays on The Effects of Population Growth in LDC's (forthcoming)

Other

Patterns of Use of Books in Large Research Libraries (with Herman H. Fussler, 1969)
Basic Research Methods in Social Science (1969; third edition with Paul Burstein, 1985)
How to Start and Operate a Mail-Order Business (1965; fourth edition, 1986)
Issues in the Economics of Advertising (1970)
The Management of Advertising (1971)
Applied Managerial Economics (1975)
Effort, Opportunity, and Wealth (1987)
Good Mood: The New Psychology of Overcoming Depression (1989)

Edited Books

Research in Population Economics: Vol. I (1978); Vol. II (1980) (with Julie daVanzo); Vols. III (1981) and IV (1982) (with Peter Lindert)
The Resourceful Earth (with Herman Kahn, 1984)

Index